Operations Management for Business Excellence

All businesses strive for excellence in today's technology-based environment in which customers want solutions at the touch of a button. This highly regarded textbook provides in-depth coverage of the principles of operations and supply chain management and explains how to design, implement, and maintain processes for sustainable competitive advantage. This text offers a unique combination of theory and practice with a strategic, results-driven approach.

Now in its fourth edition, *Operations Management for Business Excellence* has been updated to reflect major advances and future trends in supply chain management. A new chapter on advanced supply chain concepts covers novel logistics technology, information systems, customer proximity, sustainability, and the use of multiple sales channels. As a platform for discussion, the exploration of future trends includes self-driving vehicles, automation and robotics, and omnichannel retailing. Features include:

- A host of international case studies and examples to demonstrate how theory translates to practice, including Airbus, Hewlett Packard, Puma, and Toyota.
- A consistent structure to aid learning and retention: Each chapter begins with a detailed set of learning objectives and finishes with a chapter summary, a set of discussion questions, and a list of key terms.

Fully comprehensive with an emphasis on the practical, this textbook should be core reading for advanced undergraduate and postgraduate students of operations management and supply chain management. It would also appeal to executives who desire an understanding of how to achieve and maintain 'excellence' in business. Online resources include lecture slides, a glossary, test questions, downloadable figures, and a bonus chapter on project management.

David Gardiner has a lifetime of practical experience as a business consultant in operation management while employed by IBM and Gardiner Consulting Group. He was a contract lecturer at the University of Auckland Business School, New Zealand, for 25 years and currently teaches under contract at Massey University, New Zealand.

Hendrik Reefke lectures across a variety of topics in supply chain management and is deputy director for the MSc in Logistics and Supply Chain Management at Cranfield University, School of Management, UK. His research has been published in internationally leading academic journals, refereed conferences, and books.

Operations Management for Business Excellence

Building Sustainable Supply Chains

Fourth edition

David Gardiner and Hendrik Reefke

Routledge
Taylor & Francis Group

LONDON AND NEW YORK

Fourth edition published 2020
by Routledge
2 Park Square, Milton Park, Abingdon, Oxon, OX14 4RN

and by Routledge
52 Vanderbilt Avenue, New York, NY 10017

Routledge is an imprint of the Taylor & Francis Group, an informa business

© 2020 David Gardiner and Hendrik Reefke

First edition published by Pearson Education 2006
Second edition published by Pearson Education 2010
Third edition published by Pearson Education 2013

British Library Cataloguing-in-Publication Data
A catalogue record for this book is available from the British Library

Library of Congress Cataloging-in-Publication Data
A catalog record for this book has been requested

ISBN: 978-0-367-13597-3 (hbk)
ISBN: 978-0-367-13598-0 (pbk)
ISBN: 978-0-367-13599-7 (ebk)

Typeset in Sabon
by Apex CoVantage, LLC

Visit the companion website: www.routledge.com/cw/gardiner

Publisher Credits

Contents

List of figures   xviii
List of tables   xxi
Author biographies   xxiii
Contributor biographies   xxv
Preface   xxix
Introducing Dr Hendrik Reefke   xxx
Acknowledgements   xxxi

1   Operations and strategy   1

Perspective: Airlines – need to stay competitive 1
Introduction 4
History of operations management 4
  Industrial Revolution 4
  Scientific management 5
  Human relations movement 5
  Operations research 5
  Just-in-time and lean production systems 5
  Recent developments 5
Operations management 6
  The customer 8
  Transformation process 10
  Products and services 13
  Service package 15
  Servitisation 16
  Customer experience paradigm in operations 17
Strategy 18
  Strategy defined 18
  What is strategy? 19
  Strategic capability 22
  Core competence 23
  Corporate strategy 24

Strategic decisions in functional areas 25
Operations strategy 26
Competitive capability 28
Structural decisions in operations 32
Infrastructural decisions in operations 34
Integration decisions in operations 35
Chapter summary 36
Discussion questions 37
Key terms 37
Notes 38
Additional reading on operations and strategy 39

2   **Demand management and forecasting in operations**   40

Perspective: Forecasting – constrained or unconstrained 40
Introduction 42
Demand management 42
Forecast management 44
Forecasting horizons 46
Strategic role of forecasting 49
Forecast deviation 52
Measuring forecast deviation 53
Forecast value added 58
Quantitative forecasting 60
Quantitative forecasting methods 63
Decomposition of a time series 67
Performance measurement aka forecast accuracy 70
Qualitative forecasting 73
Other approaches to forecasting 74
Dependent and independent demand 75
Chapter summary 75
Discussion questions 76
Key terms 76
Notes 77
Additional reading on demand management and forecasting
   in operations 77

3   **Capacity and revenue management**   78

Perspective: Electricity – how much is enough? 78
Introduction 80
Capacity management in operations 81
Strategic capacity 81
Strategic capacity planning 83

Strategic capacity planning process 84
Strategies for balancing supply with demand 87
Production planning approaches 89
Production planning model 92
Facilities and capacity 100
Capacity flexibility 101
Revenue management – also known as yield management 103
Revenue management overview 103
Revenue management process 106
Complications and extensions of revenue management 111
Service capacity 113
Queues and waiting lines 113
Chapter summary 114
Discussion questions 114
Key terms 114
Notes 115
Additional reading on capacity and revenue management 115

4   **Process design and strategy**   **116**

Perspective: Digital ubiquity – embracing digital technology 116
Introduction 118
Customers and relationships 118
Customer-centricity 118
Classifying customers by type or attitude 119
Strategic importance of process 122
Process thinking 122
Value adding and cost adding 124
Strategic decisions for process 128
Process flow structures 131
Process variability 134
Perfect process 136
Strategic service vision 136
Characteristics of service operations 137
Service encounter 138
Service-profit chain 139
Linkages in the service-profit chain 139
Service-profit chain in perspective 144
Chapter summary 145
Discussion questions 146
Key terms 146
Notes 146
Additional reading on process design and strategy 147

5   **Applying lean thinking to operations**   148

Perspective: Chelsea Sugar – lean thinking 148
Introduction 150
Lean thinking 150
   Introduction to lean 150
   History of lean 151
   Understanding and implementing lean thinking 153
   Five principles of lean 154
   The Toyota Way 155
   14 Principles of the Toyota Way 156
   Value and waste 157
   Value stream mapping 162
   Continuous improvement 163
   Plan-do-check-adjust cycle (PDCA cycle) 164
   Lean production and scheduling 165
   Lean enterprise 167
   Basic seven tools of quality 168
   Lean leadership 175
   Lean services 176
Statistical process control 177
Chapter summary 185
   Discussion questions 186
   Key terms 186
   Notes 187
   Additional reading on applying lean thinking to operations 187

6   **Achieving balanced results and measuring performance**   189

Perspective: Nokia – how do we measure performance? 189
Introduction 190
Developing balanced results 191
   Business performance scope 191
Hoshin kanri process 197
   Without a hoshin-style process 197
   With a hoshin-style process 197
   Regular hoshin reviews 198
Balanced scorecard 199
   Performance measures from four perspectives 199
   Linking strategy with operations 203
   Closed-loop management system 204
Driving performance metrics 205
   Performance metrics are changing 205
   Benchmarking 207
   Measurement determines behaviour 208

Chapter summary 210
   Discussion questions 211
   Key terms 211
   Notes 211
   Additional reading on achieving balanced results and measuring
     performance 212

7 Quality management and product design   213

Perspective – customer requirements in product design 213
Introduction 216
Design for the customer 216
   Voice of the customer 216
   Customer requirements 217
   Kano model 217
   Quality function deployment 220
   House of quality 221
Total quality management 223
   What is quality? 223
   Service definition of quality 225
   Traditional costs of quality 228
   Quality management frameworks 230
Process capability and six sigma quality 232
   Process cause and variation 232
   Process capability measurements 235
   Six sigma quality 244
   Define-measure-analyse-improve-control 245
   Lean six sigma 246
Strategic product design 246
   Structured product development 247
   Product development portfolios 248
   Robust design 249
   Design for operations 250
Chapter summary 251
   Discussion questions 251
   Key terms 251
   Notes 252
   Additional reading on quality management and product design 253

8 Inventory and resource planning   254

*Perspective: Fonterra – too much milk then and not enough
   milk now 254*
Introduction 257
Inventory and inventory management 258

Inventory purpose 259
Why hold inventory? 260
New approaches and considerations 262
Generic inventory management model 264
Inventory management systems 266
Fixed reorder quantity model 267
Economic order quantity model 267
Fixed reorder cycle model 270
Newsvendor problem 271
Material requirements planning (MRP) 276
Demand driven material requirements planning (DDMRP) 279
Other planning and scheduling systems 282
Resource planning 284
Sales and operations planning 284
Scheduling 288
Process industries 288
Theory of constraints 290
Performance measurement 291
Logical thinking process 292
Logistics including drum-buffer-rope scheduling 294
Scheduling using theory of constraints 296
Operating guidelines 297
Chapter summary 298
Discussion questions 298
Key terms 299
Notes 300
Additional reading on inventory and resource planning 301

9   Collaborative supply chains   302

Perspective: Weta Group – the creative art of motion pictures 302
Introduction 304
Supply chain management 305
Supply chain overview 305
Supply chain management from a strategic view 308
Bullwhip effect – demand amplification 309
Collaborative supply chains 313
Characteristics of a collaborative supply chain 314
Advantages of collaboration 315
Competitive advantage 318
Service chain management 319
Primary value components of service chain management 320
Strategic view of supply chains 321
Strategic role of inventory in supply chains 325

Demand chain management 326
  Effective and responsive data exchange 327
  Exchange of process and design information 327
  Pull-based supply methodology 327
  Rhythmic planning cycles 328
  Efficient consumer response 328
Purchasing 330
  Supplier selection 331
  Multiple suppliers 331
  Replenishment 333
  Supply chain system metrics 335
Chapter summary 336
  Discussion questions 336
  Key terms 337
  Notes 337
  Additional reading on collaborative supply chains 338

10 **Advanced supply chain concepts: Technology and sustainability**   339

Perspective: Warehouse of the future 339
Introduction 342
Autonomous vehicles 342
  Categories and benefits of autonomous vehicles 343
  Autonomous vehicles in logistics 344
Robotics and automation 348
  Technical basics of robotic systems 349
  Stakeholders and risks of robotics and automation 349
Omnichannel logistics 354
  Reverse logistics and returns management 355
  Retail returns network design 358
Sustainable supply chain management 361
  Sustainability stakeholders 362
  Sustainable supply chain operations 363
Chapter summary 365
  Discussion questions 366
  Key terms 367
  Notes 367
  Additional reading on advanced supply chain concepts 368

Case study summaries   369

  Case 1: Three crises for Toyota 369
  Case 2: Tube Forgings of America, Inc. 369
  Case 3: Jarden Fresh Preserving 369
  Case 4: Airbus and the A380 369
  Case 5: PUMA Sportlifestyle 369

Case 6: Ottoman Co. 369
Case 7: SteelCom 370
Case 8: Tait Communications 370
Case 9: Nat-pak and Tastie-food 370
Case 10: Waikato District Health Board 370
Case 11: Implementing circular economy at HP 370
Case 12: Fischer fixing systems 370
Case 13: Bridging design prototypes 370

Case 1 Three crises for Toyota 371

JEFFREY K. LIKER

The Great Recession 371
The recall crisis 372
The great East Japan earthquake and tsunami 374
Discussion questions 375
Notes 376

Case 2 Tube Forgings of America, Inc.: Surviving and thriving during the downturn 377

CAROL A. PTAK AND CHAD SMITH

Company overview 377
Early days 377
The task ahead 378
Challenges to the system 378
Solution 378
Dynamic buffer calculations 380
Commentary 380
Summary 381
Discussion questions 381
Notes 381

Case 3 Jarden Fresh Preserving 382

THOMAS F. WALLACE

Author's comments 382
Management of market risk 382
Why sales and operations planning (S&OP) became a priority 383
Fresh Preserving S&OP design 383
Modelling supply flexibility 384
Bridging demand to supply 384
Scenario planning and mitigation 385
Results 386
The moral of the story 386

Discussion questions 386
Notes 387

Case 4 Airbus and the A380   388
LINCOLN C. WOOD AND LINH N. K. DUONG

Discussion questions 392
Notes 392

**Case 5 PUMA Sportlifestyle: Journey towards sustainable supply chain
management**   393
HENDRIK REEFKE

Company overview 393
Criticism and controversies 393
Sustainable supply chain management 394
PUMA's sustainable supply chain 395
Discussion questions 396
Notes 397

Case 6 Ottoman Co.   398
LALEH HAERIAN ARDEKANI

Business model 398
Process design 398
Challenges and current problems 399
Solutions for facing challenges ahead 399
Discussion questions 400

Case 7 SteelCom   402
LINCOLN C. WOOD

Company and products 402
Inventory management 403
Discussion questions 404

Case 8 Tait Communications   405
DAVID GARDINER

Discussion questions 407
Notes 408

Case 9 Nat-pak and Tastie-food   409
ANSON K. T. LI

Introduction 409
Nat-pak 409

Tastie-food 411
Discussion questions 412

**Case 10 Waikato District Health Board: Consumables supply for
elective surgery**   413
CRYSTAL BEAVIS

Introduction 413
   The rebuilding programme 414
   The need to gain control of the consumables inventory system 414
Map of the original process 415
Process improvements 416
*Map of the new 'BOM' process for supplying consumables for
   elective surgery 418*
Evaluation 418
   Process weaknesses 418
   Process strengths 419
   How the new process helped enhance and strengthen the value
      chain in other ways 420
Discussion questions 421
Note 421
References 421

Case 11 Implementing circular economy at HP   422
CARL KÜHL AND HENDRIK REEFKE

Company overview 422
HP and circular economy 422
Implementing CE at HP 423
Discussion questions 424
Notes 425

**Case 12 Fischer fixing systems: Moving forward with the workforce –
change communication at the Global Distribution Centre**   426
KLAUS MÖLLER, JULIAN GABEL, AND FRANK BERTAGNOLLI

Introduction 426
The fischer group of companies 427
Logistics processing via the Global Distribution Centre 427
Further investment in automation for productivity growth 428
Employee communication 429
Challenges in the change management 430
Decision making 431
Note 431
Additional readings 432

Case 13 Bridging design prototypes 433

GLORIA GOMEZ, MAIGEN WILKI THYGESEN, ANDREAS MELSON,
MATHIAS HALKJÆR PETERSEN, CASPER HARLEV, ENIKÖ ROZSNYÓI,
AND THOMAS A. RUBAEK

Understanding user needs for feature design 433
*Case A: Evaluating digital games for dementia with the bridging
    design prototype principles 434*
MAIGEN WILKI THYGESEN AND ANDREAS MELSON

Case B: Bridging design prototype of a plant sensor 436
MATHIAS HALKJÆR PETERSEN AND CASPER HARLEV

*Case C: Bridging design prototype of a user research framework for
    a robotics start-up 438*
ENIKÖ ROZSNYÓI AND THOMAS A. RUBAEK

Discussion questions 440
Notes 440
References of student cases 440

Index 441

Figures

1.1	Major functional responsibilities of the organisation	7
1.2	The customer is the next process	9
1.3	Transformation process showing inputs, value-adding transformation, and outputs	10
1.4	Drivers of strategic capability	23
2.1	Apple® product volumes for ten years (2009–2018)	41
2.2	Strategic nature of forecasting customer demand	46
2.3	Forecasting horizons	47
2.4	Operations and supply chain management view of forecasting to plan, schedule, and control operations	50
2.5	Forecast value added process	60
2.6	Components of demand – cyclical, trend, random, and seasonal – shown separately	62
2.7	Components of demand – composite picture including total demand	63
2.8	Seasonalised forecast for years 1, 2, and 3 for worked example 2.5	72
3.1	Capacity management hierarchy	82
3.2	Capacity planning sequence	85
3.3	Balancing capacity and supply with demand: Attempting to maintain perfect balance	88
3.4	Production planning model	93
3.5	Inputs to production planning	93
3.6	Graph of production plan data for worked example 3.1 Plan 1: Level production method	95
3.7	Graph of production plan data for worked example 3.1 Plan 2: Chase production method	97
3.8	Graph of production plan data for worked example 3.1 Plan 3: Mixed production strategy	98
3.9	Raising the booking limit	108
3.10	Revenue management process	108
3.11	Revenue management process to balance demand with supply in fixed-capacity situations	110
4.1	A hierarchical organisation chart showing a functional focus	119
4.2	A customer-centric organisation totally focused on the customer	120
4.3	Process adds value to the customer	128

4.4	Product focus and process focus	129
4.5	Product-process matrix	133
4.6	Extension of the basic transformation process with variables	135
5.1	Simplistic value stream mapping example	163
5.2	Plan-do-check-adjust cycle	165
5.3	Plan-do-check-adjust cycle with blocks preventing a return to previous behaviour	166
5.4	Cause-and-effect diagram example	169
5.5	Check sheet example	170
5.6	Flowchart example	171
5.7	Histogram example	172
5.8	Pareto chart example drawn from a check sheet	173
5.9	Scatter chart example	174
5.10	Control chart examples	175
5.11	Establishing control limits based on ± 3 standard deviations from the process mean	178
5.12	$\bar{x}$ chart for worked example 5.1	183
5.13	R chart for worked example 5.1	184
5.14	Chart interpretation	185
6.1	Capacity requirements and demand forecasting performance measurement report	193
6.2	Balanced scorecard – Performance measures from four perspectives	200
6.3	Schematic of benchmark process with sample benchmarks	208
7.1	Kano model diagram	218
7.2	House of quality	221
7.3	Total cost of quality made up of external failure, internal failure, appraisal, and prevention	229
7.4	Total costs of quality should approach zero as an ideal	230
7.5	Process variation satisfies the customer when variation is within tolerance range	233
7.6	Standard Normal distribution	234
7.7	Process operating with process specifications equal to design specifications	235
7.8	Process operating with process specifications equal to half the design specifications	236
7.9	Process operating with a process drift of 1.5σ	237
7.10	Process capability ratio, C_p, with the numerator equal to the range and the denominator equal to 6σ	238
7.11	Process capability index, C_{pk}, with the numerator the distance from process mean to closest limit and the denominator 3σ	239
7.12	Illustration for worked example 7.1	240
7.13	Illustration for worked example 7.2	241
7.14	Illustration for worked example 7.3	241
7.15	Illustration for worked example 7.4	242
7.16	Illustration for worked example 7.5	243
7.17	Illustration for worked example 7.6	244
7.18	Strategic design drivers by decade	247

8.1	Fonterra's annual milk production (Southern Hemisphere) peaks in September and October	256
8.2	Generic inventory management model	264
8.3	Fixed reorder quantity model	267
8.4	Fixed reorder cycle model	270
8.5	Area under the Normal curve	274
8.6	Elements leading to DDMRP	279
8.7	Components of DDMRP	280
8.8	Buffer zones with inventory as an asset or a liability	281
8.9	Drum-buffer-rope using a time buffer	295
8.10	Drum-buffer-rope using a constraint buffer	295
8.11	Drum-buffer-rope using a constraint and a time buffer	296
9.1	Supply chain management involving manufacturers, distributors, and retailers	306
9.2	Supply chain management for service providers	307
9.3	Echelons of supply chain management	307
9.4	Bullwhip effect showing demand information flow and supply flow	310
9.5	Collaborative supply chain in action	314
9.6	The aim of collaboration is to achieve better benefits-to-price ratio than the competition	317
9.7	Value creation cycle using supply chain collaboration	319
10.1	Stakeholders of robotics and automation in logistics	349
10.2	Comparing the carbon footprint of a human worker and an industrial robot	352
10.3	The strategic and the operational returns management processes	357
10.4	Centralised and decentralised returns network designs	360
10.5	Model for returns management in omnichannel businesses	361
10.6	Sustainability stakeholders	362
10.7	Characteristics of transportation modes	363

Figure cases

2.1	Production volumes for 2005–2012	379
2.2	Sales growth 2002–2012 using 2002 as the base	380
3.1	The Jarden model for risk mitigation and opportunity enhancement	385
10.1	Process map of the original process at Waikato DHB	417
10.2	Process map of the improved process at Waikato DHB as of October 2014	419

Tables

1.1	Examples of the transformation process in production industries	11
1.2	Examples of the transformation process in service industries	12
1.3	Comparison between products and services	14
2.1	Characteristics of long-range, medium-range, and short-range demand forecasting	49
2.2	Demand, forecast, algebraic deviation, and absolute deviation data for worked examples 2.1 and 2.2	55
2.3	Demand and forecast data showing absolute deviation and absolute variation in worked example 2.3	57
2.4	Six months of sales data for worked example 2.4	64
2.5	Six months of sales data and calculation results for worked example 2.4	65
2.6	Forecast calculation results for worked example 2.4	65
2.7	Microsoft Excel® summary output report for worked example 2.4	66
2.8	Demand data for worked example 2.5	68
2.9	Deseasonalised demand data and the extended fields for worked example 2.5	69
2.10	Microsoft Excel® summary output report for worked example 2.5	71
2.11	Seasonalised forecast for years 1, 2, and 3 for worked example 2.5	72
3.1	Demand data for worked example 3.1	94
3.2	Production plan data for worked example 3.1 Plan 1: Level production method	95
3.3	Costs for Plan 1: Level production method	95
3.4	Production plan data for worked example 3.1 Plan 2: Chase production method	96
3.5	Costs for Plan 2: Chase production method	97
3.6	Production plan data for worked example 3.1 Plan 3: Mixed strategy	97
3.7	Costs for Plan 3: Mixed strategy	98
3.8	Forecast demand data and planning data for worked example 3.2	99
3.9	Solution data for quantities for worked example 3.2	99
3.10	Solution data for costs for worked example 3.2	100
4.1	Major classifications and types of processes	127
5.1	Factors for determining the ± 3 sigma control limits for $\bar{x}$ charts and R charts	180

5.2	Data table for worked example 5.1	182
10.1	Omnichannel and multichannel characteristics	355

Table cases

5.1	PUMA's environmental profit and loss account 2010	395
6.1	Product routing showing resource requirement and type by workstation	401
6.2	Workforce type, skill level, and number of workers available	401

Author biographies

David Gardiner is a contract lecturer in operations management and supply chain management. For 28 years, he lectured postgraduate and undergraduate students on subjects including operations strategy, forecasting and demand management, capacity planning and revenue management, sales and operations planning, process and product design, process improvement, service design, constraint-based scheduling, inventory systems, enterprise resource planning, six sigma quality, total quality management, lean thinking, and project management.

He currently holds a teaching contract with Massey University (New Zealand) where he delivers the operations management and logistics course, a core component of the Master of Business Administration (MBA) programme. Previously, he lectured on the MBA and Post Graduate Diploma in Business at the Graduate School of Management at the University of Auckland Business School (for 25 years), in the Master of Engineering Management programme at the University of Canterbury (for three years), in the MBA at Waikato University (three years), and the MBA at University of Canterbury (one year).

He is a director of Gardiner Consulting Group, a management consulting company specialising in operations management and supply chain management and based in Wakefield, New Zealand.

He developed his practical experience in distribution and manufacturing systems during an illustrious career as a manufacturing industry business consultant for IBM. In this senior role, he designed and implemented many distribution and manufacturing solutions for companies throughout New Zealand, Australia, and South-East Asia.

Formal qualifications include a Bachelor of Science degree from the University of Canterbury, and a post-graduate Diploma in Business and Industrial Administration from the University of Auckland. The Association for Supply Chain Management (ASCM) recognises David as Certified at the Fellow level in Production and Inventory Management (CPIM-F).

Dr Hendrik Reefke is a lecturer in supply chain management and deputy course director for the full-time MSc in Logistics and Supply Chain Management at Cranfield University, School of Management in the UK. Before joining Cranfield University, Hendrik held positions at the University of Auckland and was part of the New Zealand Centre for Supply Chain Management. In addition, Hendrik has held visiting academic positions in Germany. Prior to these academic roles he gained practical experience in project management and in the automotive sector. He lectures on a variety of courses in logistics, procurement, and supply chain management, warehousing, operations management, and humanitarian logistics.

Hendrik is an active researcher, focusing primarily on sustainable supply chain management, service supply chains, performance measurement, warehousing and automation, and humanitarian logistics. He embraces a variety of methodological research approaches, including simulation, process design, modelling, surveys, group-decision techniques, case studies, and conceptual theory building. His refereed articles have been published in a variety of journals in the field including, among others, *Decision Support Systems*, *Omega – The International Journal of Management Science*, *Journal of Cleaner Production*, and *Service Industries Journal*.

Hendrik holds an award-winning PhD from the University of Auckland as well as a Master of Commerce and Bachelor of Commerce (Honours) in operations and supply chain management. He furthermore has a degree in business administration and engineering from Germany.

Contributor biographies

Case 1

Jeffrey K. Liker, PhD, is professor of industrial and operations engineering at the University of Michigan. He is the author of the international bestseller, *The Toyota Way: 14 Management Principles From the World's Greatest Manufacturer*[1], and numerous other books about Toyota, including *Toyota Under Fire* [2], which provides more detail about the crises described here.

Case 2

Carol A. Ptak is a partner with the Demand Driven Institute, and was most recently at Pacific Lutheran University as Visiting Professor and Distinguished Executive in Residence. Previously, she was vice president and global industry executive for manufacturing and distribution industries at PeopleSoft where she developed the concept of demand driven manufacturing. She is the co-author of *Orlicky's Material Requirements Planning* (3rd ed.).[3]

Chad Smith is a partner with the Demand Driven Institute and is the co-author of *Orlicky's Material Requirements Planning* (3rd ed.). He is also co-founder and managing partner of Constraints Management Group, a services company specialising in demand driven manufacturing and supply chain management systems for mid-range and large manufacturers.

Case 3

Tom Wallace is an author and teacher specialising in sales and operations planning, and is a Distinguished Fellow of the Ohio State University's Center for Operational Excellence. He has taught well over 10,000 business people in Australia, Belgium, Canada, China, France, Great Britain, Mexico, New Zealand, and the United States. Tom has written 12 books, including *Sales and Operations Planning: The How-to Handbook* (3rd ed),[1] *Sales and Operations Planning: The Executive Guide*,[2] and *Sales and Operations Planning: The Self-audit Workbook*.[3] His books have been translated into Chinese, French, Italian, Mongolian, Portuguese (Brazil), Russian, and Thai.

Case 4

Dr Lincoln C. Wood is a senior lecturer in operations and supply chain management in the Department of Management, the University of Otago (Dunedin, New Zealand), and an Adjunct Research Fellow at the School of Management, Curtin University (Perth, Australia).

Dr Linh N. K. Duong is a lecturer in supply chain and operations management in the National Centre of Food Manufacturing, the University of Lincoln (United Kingdom).

Case 5

Dr Hendrik Reefke is a lecturer in supply chain management at Cranfield School of Management, Cranfield University (United Kingdom). Hendrik is an active researcher, focusing primarily on sustainable supply chain management, service supply chains, and performance measurement and warehousing. He is a co-author of *Operations Management for Business Excellence: Building Sustainable Supply Chains 4e.*

Case 6

Dr Laleh Haerian Ardekani completed her PhD in the Operations Management Department in University of Auckland Business School in 2011. She titled her PhD thesis, 'New insights on the multistage insertion formulation of the traveling salesman problem: Polytopes, algorithms, and experiments'. Laleh is currently a business systems analyst at Mackenzie Investments in Toronto, Canada.

Case 7

Dr Lincoln C. Wood is a senior lecturer in operations and supply chain management in the Department of Management, the University of Otago (Dunedin, New Zealand) and an Adjunct Research Fellow at the School of Management, Curtin University (Perth, Australia).

Case 8

David Gardiner has a lifetime of practical experience as a business consultant in operations management and supply chain management. He was a contract lecturer at the University of Auckland Business School (New Zealand) for 25 years and teaches under contract at Massey University (New Zealand). He is a co-author of *Operations Management for Business Excellence: Building Sustainable Supply Chains 4e.*

Case 9

Anson K. T. Li, PhD, is a lecturer in operations management and supply chain management at the University of Auckland Business School (New Zealand).

Case 10

Crystal Beavis, MA (Hons), PGDip (MgtSt), APR is an award-winning marketing and communications professional with more than 25 years' experience in developing strategic communications programmes for organisations across a range of sectors in New Zealand including research, education, health, and local government. She moved into this field of work after an early career as a business journalist for the *New Zealand Herald* and *National Business Review*. Crystal has a special interest in health and currently serves as an elected board member of the Waikato District Health Board, which is the subject of this case study.

Case 11

Carl Kühl is a PhD researcher at the Centre for Logistics, Procurement, and Supply Chain Management at Cranfield School of Management, Cranfield University (United Kingdom). His research interests focus around circular economy and servitisation. He is a Marie Skłodowska Curie Fellow and part of Circ€uit, the Circular European Economy Innovative Training Network. It is an action funded by the European Commission under the Horizon 2020 Marie Skłodowska Curie Action 2016.

Dr Hendrik Reefke is a lecturer in supply chain management at Cranfield School of Management, Cranfield University (United Kingdom). Hendrik is an active researcher, focusing primarily on sustainable supply chain management, service supply chains, and performance measurement and reporting. He is a co-author of *Operations Management for Business Excellence: Building Sustainable Supply Chains 4e*.

Case 12

Dr.-Ing. Klaus Möller is professor for distribution logistics at the Business School at Pforzheim University (Germany).

Dr.-Ing. Frank Bertagnolli is professor for lean production and resource efficiency at the Business School at Pforzheim University (Germany).

Julian Gabel received a BSc in business administration – purchasing and logistics and an MSc in information systems at the Business School at Pforzheim University (Germany).

Case 13

Dr Gloria Gomez is co-founder, design strategist, and researcher at OceanBrowser Ltd and an honorary senior lecturer at the University of Sydney (Australia). Dr Gomez undertakes applied design research in educational product development with bridging design prototypes (BDP). She currently supervises postgraduate students in the areas of visual design, inclusive design, social design, and online medical education. In Colombia, Denmark, New Zealand, and the United States, she has lectured and supervised graduate students of engineering and design backgrounds on projects using human-centred design methods, including the BDP approach.

Maigen Wilki Thygesen is a packaging and graphic designer at Smurfit Kappa Global Experience Center with head offices in Amsterdam.

Andreas Melson is a partner at Applikator and interested in user interfaces for people with cognitive disabilities.

Mathias Halkjær Petersen, MSc product development and innovation, is an innate number-cruncher obsessed with intangible conundrums in innovation, design, and management.

Casper Harlev, BSc product development and innovation, is co-founder and CEO at Sensohive, which sells IoT sensors for food and construction applications globally.

Enikő Rozsnyói, MSc product development and innovation, is currently a product manager for digital products and experienced in new product development projects.

Thomas A. Rubaek is vice-president of product development at Blue Ocean Robotics.

Notes

1 Liker, J. K. (2004). *The Toyota Way: 14 Management principles from the world's greatest manufacturer*. New York, NY: McGraw-Hill.
2 Liker, J. K. (2011). *Toyota under fire*. New York, NY: McGraw-Hill.
3 Ptak, C. A., & Smith, C. J. (2011). *Orlicky's material requirements planning* (3rd ed.). New York, NY: McGraw-Hill.

Preface

Dramatic changes in technology, communications, and customer expectations dictate that firms keep ahead of their competitors and find improved methods to optimise the balance between demand and supply without incurring disproportional cost increases. This perpetuates my inspiration for this edition.

I invited my good friend and colleague, Hendrik Reefke, to join me for this edition, and he provides his excellent knowledge of operations, sustainability, and supply chain management with passion and vitality.

The second edition heralded the inclusion of a 'perspective' at the start of each chapter. While not a full case study in an academic sense, these provide an insight into the chapter topics and a basis for discussion, either before covering the material, or afterwards. These perspectives are an excellent way to introduce the topics especially to readers with little or no operations (or even business) experience. With that in mind, we have updated and revised all perspectives.

The third edition appended nine case studies to provide the basis for detailed discussion after studying and understanding the topics. The contributors have updated these and we have added four additional case studies. We sincerely thank the authors for their contributions.

In this edition I introduce a chapter on advanced supply chain concepts and discuss autonomous vehicles, robotics and automation, omnichannel retailing, and sustainability. Reflecting on my career and noting the dramatic changes in technology that I have experienced, I can only marvel at what lies in store. My advice is to embrace change with enthusiasm because it just will not disappear.

I thank all the students who attended my classes at the University of Auckland, University of Canterbury, Waikato University, and Massey University (all New Zealand) over the past 28 years. They challenged my thinking on the subject areas and encouraged me to improve my teaching methods. I sincerely thank you all.

I acknowledge and appreciate the assistance from executives within the organisations in the perspectives and the case studies. They ensured more balanced results.

Finally, and most importantly, to my wife, Phillippa and the rest of our family, your continued love and support is truly appreciated.

David Gardiner
Wakefield, NZ
September 2019

Introducing Dr Hendrik Reefke

The previous editions of this book have served me exceptionally well throughout my academic career with regard to structuring lectures, explaining concepts to students, and encouraging discussions about business challenges. I have always enjoyed the approachable nature of the book and its focus on a selection of key issues in operations and supply chain management.

For the third edition, David Gardiner kindly invited me to contribute a case study on sustainable supply chain management. The case studies as well as the perspectives are a highly valuable addition to the book. Not only are they instrumental in introducing the readers to the chapters, but they also illustrate the multifaceted nature of the various topics. I would like to thank all authors and especially the authors of the new cases for their valuable contributions. I know that all cases will be highly appreciated by our readers.

With his wealth of experience in academia, consulting, and industry, David has always been a mentor to me. This started from supporting him in his postgraduate courses at the University of Auckland, to seeking his advice when I started teaching my own courses, to collaborating on this new edition of this book. This will always be David's book and I hope that my contributions will continue to keep it just as relevant as it has always been. I would like to express my sincere gratitude for inviting me to join him on this journey. I learned a lot from him in the process.

This book has always been focused on the readers and their requirements. This includes fellow university instructors but most importantly learners at all stages of professional development. I would like to thank everyone who has attended my classes over the years, most importantly at the University of Auckland in New Zealand, at Cranfield University in the United Kingdom, and at Pforzheim University in Germany. Their diverse backgrounds, ambitions, and opinions have taught me invaluable lessons.

Finally, thanks to my family and friends. Academia and especially writing can be time intensive and I truly appreciate your continued support.

Hendrik Reefke
Cranfield University, School of Management
September 2019.

Acknowledgements

We are delighted that the nine original case study authors contributed to this revised edition:

- Jeffrey K. Liker shares his knowledge of Toyota and that company's understanding and interpretation of lean thinking.
- Carol A. Ptak and Chad Smith provide an insight into demand driven material requirements planning.
- Tom Wallace championed the sales and operations planning campaign for many years.
- Lincoln C. Wood and Linh Duong revised the A380 case study and Lincoln revised the SteelCom case.
- Laleh Haerian describes how a company prepares a response when a large competitor comes to town.
- Anson K. T. Li describes the supply chain strategies of two quite different organisations.

We welcome the new contributors:

- Crystal Beavis is an elected board member of the Waikato District Health Board, which is the subject of her case study.
- Carl Kühl, a PhD researcher at the Cranfield School of Management, writes on the circular economy.
- Dr.-Ing. Klaus Möller, the professor for distribution logistics at the Business School at Pforzheim University, Dr.-Ing. Frank Bertagnolli, the professor for lean production and resource efficiency at the Business School at Pforzheim University, and Julian Gabel, from the Business School at Pforzheim University, revised their case study on fischer fixing systems.
- Dr Gloria Gomez, co-founder, design strategist, and researcher at OceanBrowser Ltd, invited three of her students in Finland to share their research in building prototypes. The three students each teamed with an executive from their respective case company to share their research. Thank you to Maigen Wilki Thygesen, Andreas Melson, Mathias Halkjær Petersen, Casper Harlev, Enikő Rozsnyói, and Thomas A. Rubaek.

Finally, we acknowledge the following:

- Roger Gray, Group General Manager Airports, Air New Zealand, for reviewing the perspective in Chapter 1.
- Tony Grant, Production Manager, Chelsea Sugar, for reviewing the perspective in Chapter 5.
- Liana McPherson, Communications Manager, Weta Workshops for reviewing the perspective in Chapter 9.
- Chris Patient, Manager Hardware Engineering, Tait Communications, and Bryn Somerville, Head of Communications, Tait Communications for inputs and ideas for Case 8.
- Fonterra Communications, Fonterra Co-operative Group for reviewing the perspective in Chapter 8.

Operations and strategy

Learning objectives

At the end of this chapter, you should be able to:

- Trace the history of operations management.
- Define operations management.
- Define the customer and recognise their basic requirements.
- Describe the transformation process.
- Distinguish between products and services.
- Discuss the service package and the concept of servitisation.
- Explain the role of operations management within the context of the whole organisation and the customer experience paradigm.
- Explain strategy and strategic capability.
- Explain the concepts of core competence and competitive advantage.
- Explain operations strategy and the linkage with business strategy.
- Explain competitive capability.
- Distinguish between structural, infrastructural, and integration decisions in operations.

Perspective: Airlines – need to stay competitive

The airline industry is truly global and an intensely competitive service industry with annual (2018) revenue of $834 billion. The International Air Transport Association (IATA) represents 290 airlines from 120 countries and carries 82% of the world's air traffic.[1]

IATA measures passenger growth in revenue-passenger-kilometres (RPK) which counts the revenue received, multiplied by the number of passengers carried, multiplied by the number of kilometres travelled. Total passengers carried was 4.358 billion in 2018 and passenger growth (RPK) has exceeded 5.3% year-on-year for each of the past nine years with over 8% in 2017 and over 7% in 2018. IATA measures freight in freight-tonnes-kilometres (FTK), and the increase in this measure exceeded 9% in 2017 and exceeded 4% in 2018, with over 60 million tonnes of freight carried in 2017 and 2018. These are outstanding operating performance increases for any industry.

Total operating profit exceeded $56.3 billion for each of the four years, 2015–2018, representing an operating profit margin greater than 6.8% for that period. The corresponding net profit margin for the same period exceeded 4.1%. These are outstanding financial margin performances for any industry of comparable size.[2]

The airline industry uses aircraft technology and innovation dominated by Airbus (Europe) and Boeing (United States). Airline companies depend on other organisations for their performance and their outcomes – airport companies, air traffic controllers, government aviation regulators, security checking agencies, food outlets, ground transport, and parking operators. Most of the decisions for these dependencies lie outside the direct control of each airline. Additionally, airlines depend on supply chain management for their choice of aircraft, maintenance services, fuel supplies, food supplies, and information technology solutions. Decisions for these dependencies lie within the direct control of airline management.

With the preceding data, it is relatively easy to calculate the average performance for an airline. That means, of course, that half the airline performance data is better than average and the other half is worse than average. It is doubtful that any company would strive to be the worst. So, what does an airline company have to do to be the best? They must develop and execute a strategy to remain profitable and offer service products that satisfy the requirements of most of their customers so that customers build loyalty and keep coming back for more.

Successful airlines are realising the power of data analytics as customers have almost total freedom in searching the Internet and using web-based applications to find the best airlines, the best service, the best schedules, the best airport lounges, and the airline with the most innovation. Customers make choices that provide the best total experience.

AirlineRatings.com analyses and publishes world airline reviews for full-service airlines, regional airlines, and low-cost airlines. Their full-service carrier product criteria include product rating, safety issues, aircraft age, investment grade rating, innovation, customer feedback, operating profit, environmental issues, industrial issues, premium economy, and flat beds in business class. The industry uses their findings extensively in promoting and benchmarking services.[3]

Air New Zealand received the accolade 'Airline of the Year' for the five years from 2013 to 2017.[4] Air New Zealand challenged their business models and improved their business processes just to stay alive and remain competitive. Their strategy has been to satisfy customers by providing them exactly what they want, to be the first to introduce new ideas, to give customers no reason to consider the competition, and to challenge competitors to match the offerings if they wish.

Perhaps the most significant process improvement in recent years was the revision of the check-in process using the axiom of 'no queues' as a driving force. All airlines know that the traditional airport queue is a stressful process for passengers. Relaxation is impossible, since passengers cannot anticipate the length of the queue and do not know how much time to allow before reaching the front to complete the check-in process before their flight closes. Traditional queues zigzag across the foyer and passengers must continually pick up and move their luggage a few more metres.

At a time when competitors were introducing check-in processes up to 12 months in advance of the flight, Air New Zealand redesigned their processes to allow check-in as close as possible to departure.

When passengers for domestic flights arrive at the airport with no printed flight documentation, they go to a self-check-in kiosk, identify themselves, and generate a copy of the boarding pass. Passengers with the Air New Zealand app installed on their smartphone can bypass the printing of the boarding pass and use the app when boarding the plane – no hassle. Passengers with luggage to check in proceed on arrival at the airport to a self-check-in kiosk and identify themselves using the Air New Zealand app, a credit card, or a frequent flyer card, typing their name on the screen, or showing the barcode on the computer-generated document sent to the passenger when making the booking. That covers most possibilities, if not all. Moreover, the frequent flyer card does not have to be an Air New Zealand one – it could belong to another airline – no problem. The passenger takes the tagged luggage to a drop-off bay and places the luggage on a conveyor belt. What a great example of automation making the service experience a little bit enjoyable.

When travelling with no checked-in luggage, a passenger on a domestic flight can check in online and go directly to the boarding lounge. When boarding the domestic aircraft, passengers can use the Air New Zealand app on their smartphone as documentation – again, no hassle.

Passengers use the self-check kiosks for international flights as well, but not exclusively. When used, the kiosk scans passports, matches that data to the booking reference, prints a boarding pass, and prints luggage tags for all the checked bags. The passenger takes the tagged luggage to a drop-off bay and places the luggage on a conveyor belt.

On international flights between Australia and New Zealand (in both directions), passengers with the Air New Zealand app on their smartphone do not require a boarding pass; the app is enough documentation for boarding the aircraft.[5]

When unaccompanied minors check in at the airport, they can elect to have a small wristband attached to their wrists. When activated, this wristband sends messages to up to five contact addresses so parents and guardians at the drop-off location as well as at the pick-up destination know when the child departs, when they arrive at the destination, and when they are picked up safely.

As soon as a passenger with the Air New Zealand app on their phone enters the frequent flyer lounge, the app asks the passenger whether they want their usual coffee ordered and sends a subsequent text message saying the coffee is ready. This is not a big deal, but it does make the frequent flyer feel special.

These process improvements have revolutionised the airport and travel experience. Air New Zealand claims the redesigned check-in process was a world first and significantly streamlined the airport experience, setting them apart from their competitors. The total service package looks different from competitors, feels faster to customers, and is providing benefits to high-value customers.

Innovative process design and process improvement can have a strategic effect on the success of the business as it competes fiercely with other businesses. Air New Zealand identified who their customers were and what was important to them and redesigned the customer experience to differentiate service offerings and to support the brand. Their customers keep coming back, increasing their spending, and talking about their customer experience with friends, family, and business associates.

Now, we want you to imagine that you are the chief executive officer of a very successful airline and you are about to sign an order for additional aircraft. Each aircraft may cost a few hundred million dollars, has a delivery lead time of three, four, five, or six years, and has an expected fleet life of 15–20 years. Now, how many aircraft will you buy, what size will they be, when will they be delivered, what routes will they serve, what loading factors will apply, what maintenance requirements will exist, what are the staffing and training requirements, what is the pay-back period, will this be a profitable acquisition, and has finance been arranged to pay for them? Executive management will prepare the answers to these questions for you, but they will need a well-defined and well-communicated strategy.

Introduction

It would be virtually impossible to present a book on any function within an organisation, let alone operations management, without mentioning strategy. Strategy is at the heart of any business, whether it is a manufacturer, service provider, government department, or not-for-profit organisation. If the organisation exists, it must have a purpose. If it has a purpose, it must have a strategy, which outlines how it plans to achieve that purpose.

The chapter starts with a brief trace through the modern history of operations management. We then define several terminologies and concepts, including operations management, customer, transformation process, product, service, strategy, core competence, value, and the service package.

Business strategy defines and links the functional strategies for new product development, operations, marketing, and finance. This provides the basis for developing these functional strategies and prepares each function for achieving the goals and vision of the organisation.

Operations management and supply chain management play a strategically important role in the ultimate performance of the organisation. We discuss strategic capability, core competence, and competitive capability with specific reference to competing on cost, quality, delivery, flexibility, and service. These quantifiable dimensions have an enormous impact on an organisation's performance.

Chapter 1, therefore, lays the foundation and sets the scene.

History of operations management

Industrial Revolution

The Industrial Revolution towards the end of the eighteenth century signalled the change from cottage industries to factory production. Before the industrial revolution, residents conducted all production processes in their homes. Food preparation and processing were domestic activities. Farmers and transport operators fabricated vehicles such as trailers, carriages, and other horse-drawn vehicles in a home environment.

In 1769, Thomas Newcomen developed a rather crude steam engine and James Watt modified it by introducing a condenser that remained cool while the cylinder was hot. Watt's engine soon became the dominant design for all modern steam engines and helped bring about the Industrial Revolution.

In the period from 1773 to 1785, several significant industrial developments occurred in the textile mills in the United Kingdom. These included the flying shuttle, the 'spinning jenny', the water frame, the mule spinner, and the power loom. All improved production processes.

In the early 1800s, Eli Whitney developed the concept of using a design on which to base high-volume production. He used patterns and templates to allow unskilled workers to perform tasks previously undertaken by highly skilled artisans and introduced the concept of interchangeable parts.

Scientific management

Charles Babbage (1791–1871) was an English mathematician who invented an automated calculating machine that eventually led to the development of computers. He is the 'father of computing'.

Frederick W. Taylor developed what he called his four principles of management – research, standardisation, control, and cooperation. His systems included cost accounting, unit time study, inventory control, production control, planning, output scheduling, functional operation, standardised procedures, a mnemonic system of classification, and means for maintaining quality production. Taylor discovered that basic scientific laws govern work and that every person is different. It was the managers' job to exploit these differences. He introduced wage-incentive plans and separate responsibilities for workers and managers.

Human relations movement

At the Hawthorne plant of Western Electric in the 1920s, Elton Mayo conducted several experiments, the most notable being the illumination experiment. He studied the effects of group incentives on productivity, social psychology, and worker performance.

Operations research

Operations researchers and management scientists developed mathematical models to solve operations problems such as personnel and production scheduling, vehicle routing, facility location, capacity planning, facility design, queuing, inventory planning, and statistical quality control.

Just-in-time and lean production systems

The Toyota Motor Company developed just-in-time and lean production systems just after World War II and focused on total quality management, lean production, continuous improvement of products and processes, the elimination of all waste, flexible manufacturing systems, and computer-aided design/computer-aided manufacturing.

Recent developments

More recently the use of electronic systems such as the Internet, the World Wide Web, electronic commerce, business-to-business linkages, business-to-customer linkages, and artificial intelligence have generated significant change in the management of supply chains, especially global supply chains. Additionally, people now recognise the importance of service operations management.

The recent ubiquity of digital technology is transforming the very essence of business. If we envisage operations as empowering individuals to make decisions to deliver services more effectively, then we take the next step forward and expect digital technology to transform the very nature by which organisations define and deliver that decision-making power. Progressively, the design and delivery of software services dictates the operating environment.[6]

Operations management

Operations management

Operations management is the effective management of all the activities for creating, implementing, and improving processes that transform resource inputs, such as raw materials, technologies, and labour, into output goods and services that meet the customers' needs.

Operations management is the effective management of the direct resources required to produce the goods and services provided by an organisation. The primary focus is providing the product or service to satisfy the customers' needs. The process does not have to be efficient, but it does have to be effective. The distinction between these two words is important. Historically, operations managers have endeavoured to produce products efficiently using large batches, long production runs, and holding vast quantities of products in warehouses. Unfortunately, this does not work in current environments that demand the required volume and desired variety immediately. Online retailing is a brilliant example of modern-day operations management and supply chain management.

Many young people looking at career opportunities desire occupations that provide excitement and immediate gratification. They view operations management and supply chain management as boring, lacking imagination, and providing no excitement. True, when the operations function is performing as per schedule, it is easy to perceive the day-to-day activities as being boring and monotonous. Professional skill ensures that long-term as well as short-term planning, scheduling, and controlling steps perform properly.

Excitement erupts when the organisation launches innovation, when ideas become reality, when improved processes become recognised market leaders, when competitors acknowledge superior performance, when new markets open as achievable opportunities, and all of this translates into enhanced financial performance. The earlier perspective illustrates examples of exciting innovation involving operations management to the delight of all personnel and stakeholders and most customers and suppliers.

The transformation process transforms inputs and resources into outputs. It can either be production (goods producing) or service (service providing). Examples of transformations include manufacturing, distributing, transporting, retailing, farming, mining, refining, providing healthcare, educating, entertaining, providing tourist facilities, cooking, providing accommodation, construction, repairing, and assembling.

The general objective of operations management is to produce a specified product or service on schedule at minimal cost. Most organisations have additional performance measurements, including volume of output, costs, utilisation, quality, product reliability, delivery in full, on time, and in specification (DIFOTIS), return on investment, product flexibility, and volume flexibility.

Operations has always encouraged decision making based on data such as historical demand data to aid forecasting, inventory usage data to calculate optimum inventory levels, process data to ensure statistical quality control, and tolerance data to design superior products. The recent ubiquity of digital technology and the rise in business analytics is transforming what grants an organisation the power to create value for customers, capture value for shareholders, and to share value with the environment.

Figure 1.1 shows the major functional responsibilities of the organisation as demand management, finance management, new product design management, and operations management. Demand management covers generally the function of sales and marketing and is primarily concerned with understanding customer needs and satisfying them. Finance management covers generally all aspects of cash flows in and out of the organisation and investments. New product design management covers generally the design and improvement of products and services.

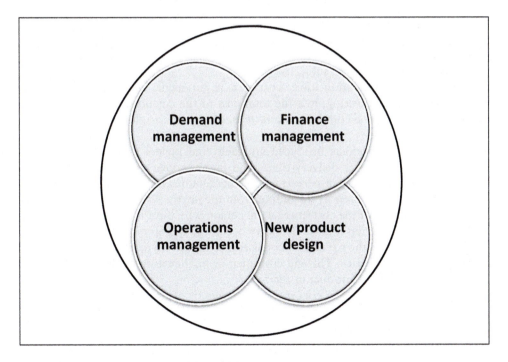

Figure 1.1 Major functional responsibilities of the organisation

The customer

Customer

The customer is the next process; the customer is where the work goes next. This view can lead to internal and external customers, but the implementation of the concept of satisfying the customer must consider the customer as the next process.

The customer's point of view is paramount when considering the objectives of operations management and supply chain management. The customer is the next process; the customer is where the work goes next. Customers can be internal to the organisation as well as external.

Communications and technology are transforming the relationships between customers and suppliers. The challenge for the organisation is to capture the attention of the customer, entice the customer to pay for the products and services, and make a profit.

Customers determine the quality of the required output. So quality, in this sense, is to understand exactly what the customers want, when they want it, how they want it, and why they want it, and then deliver that to them. End customers, who receive service or consume products, may not have input at the early stages of production, so the internal customers assume responsibility for product design and process design.

Customers do change their minds. This does not mean they are indecisive. Over time, they change their behaviours, preferences, styles, ideas, desires, wants, needs, and relationships. Therefore, the supplier needs flexible processes to understand these changes and to have the capability to deliver required products.

The merging of products and services makes it harder to measure customer satisfaction. Customers demand higher levels of service, and suppliers must truly understand the customer objectively and subjectively.

Customers always mention lower cost as a requirement. However, it is not just the price that needs lowering; it is the total cost to the customer. Some firms, especially in information and communications technology, refer to this as the total cost of ownership.

Customers want products produced and delivered in less time. This requires a shorter cycle time, shorter delivery times, and faster service response. However, the real measure is consistency of performance. This requires less variability; the output from one session is the same as the output from the next.

Most people think of the customer as the person who buys the product or service. The payment for products and services may occur at any point in the supply chain or at the end. Essentially, the payment recognises a change of ownership for a product or the completion of a service. The end customer, or final customer or consumer, is the person who pays for the product or service.

However, to appreciate the concepts and drivers of operations management fully, consider the customer as the next process and that is where the work goes next.

In a production environment, a factory takes delivery of raw materials. As the material moves through the factory, it travels from one process to the next. At each process, the operator expects higher levels of quality, a higher degree of flexibility, higher levels of service, lower costs, shorter lead times, and less variability. Eventually the factory produces the product and sends it to a distributor, who also expects higher levels of quality, a higher degree of flexibility, higher levels of service, lower costs, shorter lead times, and less variability. On the material path through the factory, there were no changes of ownership and no exchanges of money. Each process is the customer of the preceding process, and each process is the supplier of the following process.

In a service environment, such as a hospital, all the employees work together. No money is changing hands. The admission staff, surgical teams, nursing staff, kitchen staff, orderlies, pharmacists, radiologists, maintenance staff, and administration staff perform various aspects of the required job. A patient moves from admissions to a ward, from the ward to the operating theatre for an operation, from the operating theatre to recovery, and from recovery back to the ward before going home. There is a customer-supplier relationship at each step expecting higher levels of quality, more flexibility and service, lower costs, shorter lead times, and less variability. Figure 1.2 illustrates the customer-supplier relationships at each step.

The demands and requirements of the customer are summarised by the concepts of lean consumption,[7] which requires the supplier to:

- Solve the customer's problem completely by ensuring that everything works the first time.
- Do not waste the customer's time.
- Provide exactly what the customer wants.
- Provide value where the customer wants it.
- Provide value when the customer wants it.
- Continually aggregate the solutions to reduce the customer's time and hassle.

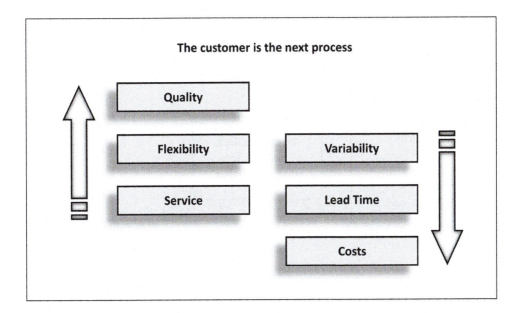

Figure 1.2 The customer is the next process

Transformation process

Transformation process

Transformation is the process of converting inputs into outputs. Inputs include materials, customers, labour, energy, components, ideas, machines, or requirements. Outputs include finished products, satisfied customers, unsatisfied customers, components, subassemblies, developed ideas, or developed concepts.

The transformation process lies at the foundation of operations management. The entire function of operations management is to find value-adding processes that take inputs and transform them into outputs. The transformation process should maximise the value added and reduce the costs to the customer by making the product more readily available, by delivering a faster service, by providing customers with additional relevant information, and/or by customising the product to the customer's specific needs. Ideally, this transformation performs so well that the customer is fully satisfied. If not, then the organisation should redesign and improve the transformation process so that the customer is fully satisfied.

Figure 1.3 illustrates the transformation process with inputs such as workers, managers, equipment, facilities, materials, services, land, and energy and with the outputs being products and services with the overall objective of maximising customer value.

Web-based applications, digital technology, and the connectivity of devices and products are transforming the transformation process itself. Modern businesses are searching for ways to capture data at every decision point and to analyse that data to create additional value. Uber has totally transformed transportation services by digitising every aspect of searching for the availability of a ride, ordering a ride, tracking

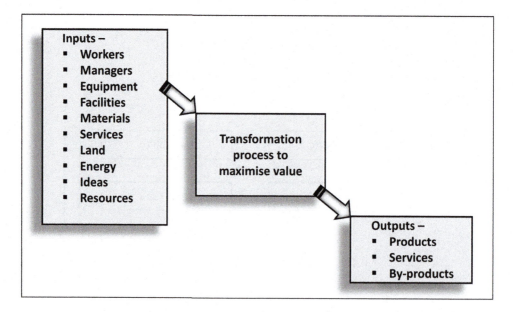

Figure 1.3 Transformation process showing inputs, value-adding transformation, and outputs

the vehicle arrival, handling the payment system, providing customer service, analysing driver performance, and maintaining historical reporting data.

Tables 1.1 and 1.2 provide examples of transformation processes for various industries in production and services. The inputs use nouns; the transformations use verbs; and the outputs use nouns. This simple definition using grammar helps to visualise the process.

The inputs include any starting position for a product or service. A furniture manufacturer has raw material inputs, including wood, fabric, fasteners, glue, packaging materials, instructions, and care leaflets. The manufacturer uses labour, machine inputs, energy, and management expertise and the transformation will take place in a

Table 1.1 Examples of the transformation process in production industries

Organisation	Inputs	Transformation process	Outputs
Electrical appliances	Raw materials	Fabricating	Finished goods such as stereos, television sets, radios, digital devices, household appliances delivered to warehouses and retail outlets
	Components	Assembling	
	Printed circuit boards	Inserting components in PCB	
	Insertion machines	Packaging	
	People skills	Distributing	
Bakery	Flour	Mixing ingredients	Bakery items such as buns, bread, muffins, biscuits delivered to warehouses and retail outlets
	Sugar	Baking	
	Flavourings	Packaging	
	Packaging	Distributing	
	Energy		
	People skills		
Clothing	Fabrics	Laying fabric	Range of garments such as pants, shirts, dresses, coats delivered to retail outlets
	Threads	Cutting fabric	
	Findings (buttons, clips, and clasps)	Sewing garments	
	Energy	Packaging	
	People skills	Warehousing	
		Distributing	
Packaging	Paper	Preparing artwork	Packaging items such as cases, cartons, boxes, packets to meet customer specifications warehoused and delivered to production facilities
	Plastic	Printing	
	Glue	Guillotining	
	Inks	Slitting	
	Energy	Distributing	
	People skills		
Dairy products	Milk	Pasteurising	Dairy products such as milk, cream, yoghurt, flavoured drinks delivered to supermarkets
	Flavourings	Separating	
	Containers	Mixing	
	Packaging	Packaging	
	People skills	Distributing	

Table 1.2 Examples of the transformation process in service industries

Organisation	Inputs	Transformation process	Outputs
Air transport	Airport infrastructure	Reserving seats	Passengers with reservations for travel
	Reservation system	Scheduling flights	Passengers safely on board aircraft
	Aircraft	Scheduling crews	Passengers fed and watered during flight
	Flight crews	Checking-in passengers	Passengers and luggage safely delivered to destination
	Cabin crews	Maintaining aircraft and equipment	Freight carried and delivered
	Ground staff	Cleaning and provisioning aircraft	
	Fuel	Preparing meals	
	Food		
Computing centre	Computing equipment	Updating records	Information processed quickly and accurately for internal and/or external customers
	Stationery	Maintaining security	
	Energy	Printing	
	People skills	Enveloping	
		Distributing	
Restaurant	Kitchen and table equipment	Setting tables	Guests enjoying ambience
	Food	Taking orders	Guests fed and watered
	Energy	Preparing and cooking food	An enjoyable experience
	People	Waiting at tables	
	Wine and drinks	Washing cutlery and dishes	
		General cleaning	
Hospital	Medical supplies	Operating	Well patients
	Drugs	Nursing	Long-term patients
	Doctors	Dispensing drugs and medicines	New babies
	Nurses	Preparing meals	Trained staff
	Other staff	Keeping records	Dead people (unfortunately)
	Food		
Banking and finance	Bank buildings	Processing deposits and cheques	Money safe and available when required
	Computers	Investing money	Safe and profitable investments
	Tellers	Providing loans and mortgages	Money well spent
	Automatic teller machines (ATM)		

factory building located on some land. The quality, availability, and cost of these inputs will have a defining influence on the actual output of the transformation process.

People who are interfacing with customers are the major input for service industries.

A fundamental concept requires all transformation processes to add value and not cost. Discussion on this concept continues in Chapter 4.

Products and services

In the past, it was quite easy to differentiate between a manufacturing company and a service organisation. Manufacturing companies start with raw materials and after several processes produce products that customers buy. Service industries provide a service. That distinction is very simplistic, however.

Today, manufacturing intertwines with services to such an extent that it is difficult to find a manufacturing company that does not provide some elements of service and, likewise, it is difficult to find a service organisation that does not make something.

To help in the understanding of the relationships between these two quite different sectors, this book refers to manufacturing as production. In this way, services use production without the connotations sometimes associated with manufacturing.

Product

A product is any good or service produced for sale, exchange, or internal use.

Service

A service is an activity or a series of activities to produce an intangible perishable experience, usually involving the customer as a participant. Examples include repair, trade, commercial and infrastructural services such as transport, retail, communications, finance, and real estate and personal services such as health, education, research, recreation, arts, restaurants, hotels, barber, beauty, and laundry.

Products are things and consumers can touch them, see them, kick them, and/or destroy them. With products, quantitative measurements assess production quality. It is easy to see if the product meets specifications. Some products such as cars, electrical appliances, and drugs have very stringent testing to ensure satisfactory production processes occur for each batch of products.

The customer of a product becomes involved after production. A factory manufactures a home appliance, sends it to a distributor, who sends it to a retailer, who sells it to a customer before the customer starts to use or consume it. This has implications concerning the consumer input into the product. The consumer has very little input during production. They may interact with the retail salesperson, but the production team does not hear their specific voice.

The supply chain can store products for subsequent use. This allows the producer to make in advance of requirements and to supply a different quantity from the demand quantity. This affects demand forecasting, capacity management, and production scheduling. Production activities and customer usage activities occur at different times.

Services are intangible. Often, especially with pure services, the output is an idea, as in advertising, designing, and promoting. Some services, such as insurance, banking,

Table 1.3 Comparison between products and services

Products	Services
Tangible products and things	Intangible ideas and concepts
Customer involved after product made	Customer participates in production process
Operate as closed systems separate from consumer	Operate as open systems involving consumer
Can be stored for subsequent use	Cannot be stored
Created then consumed	Created and consumed
Production process not important to customer	Production process is important to customer
Oriented towards things	Oriented towards people
Defects can be found and remedied	Defective service needs recovery and repair

and investing, refer to their outputs as products, but customers cannot physically touch them. When you insure your house and contents against fire and theft, what do you have to show for it? You might have a piece of paper and you should have peace of mind. The product is intangible and this makes it harder to assess product quality. You might attend a concert, which entertains you thoroughly, and you enjoy the experience. However, another person might attend the same concert and not enjoy the experience. Was the concert a good service or not? Who knows? Quality is determined after the fact. Table 1.3 compares products and services.

The service industry, in the broadest sense, includes all organisations except primary producers (farming, mining, and forestry) and secondary producers (manufacturing). This definition of 'service industry' includes tertiary production (services such as restaurants, hotels, barber, beauty, laundry, and repair), quaternary services (trade and commercial services such as transport, retail, communications, finance, and real estate), and quinary services (personal services such as health, education, research, recreation, and arts).

The customer for a service product is usually involved during production and delivery of the service. In fact, the customer is in most cases an active participant. Patients enter a medical centre and request attention. They are physically present and the doctor performs the medical examination on them personally. The doctor prescribes any required medication just for them. This customer presence has a significant bearing on the quality of output, as the customer can make comments and request changes during service delivery. The service provider can change the delivery process and keep the customer satisfied.

Service providers cannot store service outputs (usually) and this requires a close match between the rates of supply and the rates of demand. Services need to cope with peaks in demand for transport, accommodation, medical services, communications, ticketing, banking, and call centres. Everyone, it seems, wants to travel during peak periods; everyone, it seems, wants to eat at the same time; everyone, it seems, is sick and requires immediate attention at the same time. This adds pressure on service providers to introduce innovative ideas to smooth out the peaks and lows. Especially with fixed-capacity services, such as airlines and hotels, the service is perishable. An empty airline seat on a plane that has just taken off cannot generate any income – the airline has lost that opportunity forever. Likewise, an empty hotel room for a night generates no income.

Products and service are similar in many ways. They:

- Use customer satisfaction as a key measure of effectiveness.
- Have common measures of satisfaction (for example, speed and quality).
- Require demand forecasting.
- Require product and process design.
- Depend on location and arrangement of resources.
- Involve purchase of materials, supplies, and services.
- Have customers demanding high and/or low volumes.
- Can be standard or customised.
- Are subject to automation.
- Need an operations strategy consistent with business strategy.

As seen from this list, products and services are very similar. All organisations can benefit from improving their processes. It does not really matter whether an organisation sees itself as a manufacturer or as a service provider. Customers are often on the 'shop floor' while consuming services. They may not use that term, but instead refer to the front office, the dining room, the operating theatre, the stadium, or the passenger cabin.

Throughout this book, the distinction occurs between products and services where they are significantly different and the classification needs explanation. This distinction is becoming harder to define and is not particularly useful. If you buy a software package in a store, you have bought a product. However, if you download it over the Internet, you have obtained a service. Operations and process management is important for all organisations. Project management is an example where the outcome is a product but the process is a service. This book refers to products and the reader should interpret this to include services. After all, service providers deliver service products and, as examples, banks and insurance companies refer to their offerings as products (banking products and insurance products).

Service package

Service package

The service package defines a bundle of goods and services provided in an environment. The customer experiences all the features that form the basis of their perception of the service. The bundle comprises the supporting facility, facilitating goods, information provided by the supplier or the customer, explicit services, and implicit services.[8]

Service managers often have difficulty identifying their product and this is partly a result of the intangible nature of services. The presence of the customer in the process creates a concern for the total service experience.

The service package defines a bundle of goods and services provided in an environment. The customer experiences all the features that form the basis of their perception of the service. The bundle comprises:

- **Supporting facility**, which is the physical resources that must be in place before the service can take place, such as a hospital, airport, hotel, golf course, or gymnasium.
- **Facilitating goods**, which is the material purchased by the supplier or provided by the customer, such as medical supplies, aviation fuel, hotel fittings and furniture, golf clubs, or fitness equipment.
- **Information provided by the supplier or the customer**, such as patient medical records, location of customer (to dispatch a taxi), available seats on an aircraft, or customer preferences.
- **Explicit services** including the benefits readily observed by the senses, such as the absence of pain, attitude of a waiter, exhaustion coupled with a sense of achievement after a session at a gymnasium, or the response time by an emergency service.
- **Implicit services** including vaguely sensed psychological benefits, such as the status of a university degree, security provided by a well-lit parking lot, stress relief after a session at a gymnasium, or the privacy of a personal loan office.

Servitisation

Servitisation

Servitisation is the process of transforming from a product-centric business model to a service-centric approach. Usually the firm is a manufacturer that changes from simply producing a product to including service in the total product offering.

As mentioned above, manufacturing intertwines with services to such an extent that it is difficult to find a manufacturing company that does not provide some elements of service and, likewise, it is difficult to find a service organisation that does not make something. Pure manufacturers may add service offerings to their product line to increase revenue and ensure that the customer is using and maintaining the product properly.

Tim Baines and Howard Lightfoot classify these offerings as base, intermediate, and advanced services.[9] At the base level, the manufacturer supports the product core offering by adding a range of services aimed at improving the functionality of the product. The service itself is not new; the added service is most likely a conventional offering from a service provider. Base services include maintenance, training, and after-sales service. With base services, the manufacturer adds the service offering.

With intermediate services, the manufacturer develops or acquires the services to improve the customer's processes and activities. It is common for firms to experience diminishing demand for their traditional products so they search for ways to reinvent themselves. Examples include IBM, an organisation that has moved away from manufacturing computers and has developed new business in general consulting and supply chain management.

Advanced services companies have integrated products and services and sometimes the firm takes a unique competitive position, building on its technological strength and competences to provide a new and unique offering.

Rolls-Royce, a global power systems company offers a complete engine and accessory replacement service on a fixed-cost-per-flying-hour basis. This means that an airline with Rolls-Royce engines onboard pays for the actual time the engines are earning revenue for the airline. This is not new for Rolls-Royce – they have had a variant of this service since 1962. The difference now is the advanced analytics that enables them to proactively plan maintenance and repair activity to minimise disruption.[10]

Caterpillar, a global company providing earth-moving equipment for basic infrastructure projects, wants its customers to produce more output with fewer resources by using intelligent data and analytics such as engine performance and maintenance requirements, fleet monitoring, and connected safety systems.[11]

MAN Truck and Bus UK aims to reduce the total cost of ownership for their customers by more than 50%. Their figures suggest that the initial acquisition cost represents about 11% of total cost of ownership while fuel, repairs, and maintenance represent just over 40% of all costs incurred over the life of the vehicle. They achieve this reduction by monitoring vehicle performance, scheduling maintenance, providing fix-price service, and constantly tuning the vehicle for optimal fuel consumption.[12]

Customer experience paradigm in operations

The service package encapsulates the traditional view on service strategy. Satisfaction is not the only outcome that customers desire; more customers want to be emotionally involved with the service delivery. Organisations that recognise this emotional involvement and modify their service to allow this, find their customers keep coming back, spending more, and bringing their friends along as well. Chris Voss, Aleda Roth, and Richard Chase introduced the concept of services as destinations as an emerging business model for classifying experiential service strategies.[13] Experience-centric describes a service for which the customer experience is at the core of the service offering. The customer has emotional connections engendered through engaging and compelling activities delivered in memorable and meaningful ways.

The perceived value of the service now includes experience factors that may start at the initial point of interaction. As an example, consider going online and trying to secure an airline reservation during a super promotion with the airline offering a limited number of seats for $1. Potential customers queue in anticipation and have webpages pre-activated so that as soon as the airline makes the availability announcement, the customers are ready to pounce. If they are successful, they brag about it to their friends. If they are unsuccessful, they simply try again and tell their friends how close they were to securing a cheap fare.

Each experience aims at the next encounter, and we measure success in terms of customer purchasing patterns, loyalty, and engagement behaviours that generate the unique nature of the experience, the knowledge, the novel aspects, the memories, and the sheer entertainment that provokes customer emotions, sensations, imagination, feelings, and perceptions. Social networking plays a significant role in creating loyal communities and fans. The customers' enthusiasm promotes the brand by word-of-mouth.

Static to dynamic

Customers treat some service venues as one-off events. Organisations redesign services to encourage multiple visits and to make each visit different. This has implications for the operations strategy. The strategy now must change from static to dynamic to make each repeat experience different – new colours, new recipes, or new offerings – or generate a progressive difference based on previous experience or acquired skill level.

Short to extended

Experiences are typically short-lived. They may be a few minutes or a few hours. The experience-centric strategy extends the experience by encouraging customers to arrive early and attracting a wider range of customers. Sports venues that involve the fans as part of the game and encourage the purchase of branded product allow the customer to relive the experience every time they display (wear) the branded product. Sports venues are thus becoming sports destinations.

Narrow focus to multiple experiences

The traditional operations view of services attempts to avoid operational complexity and to remain clearly focused on a narrow market segment. The experience-centric view provides a wide variety of experiences throughout the duration of the service encounter. Organisations can achieve this by expanding the concept of focus to include service focus and market focus. With a service focus, the number of markets served is large and the range of services is narrow, while with a market focus, the range of services is wide, but the number of markets served is few.[14]

To be successful in this environment, a firm may need to achieve either service focus or market focus by splitting into smaller businesses or operational units.

Experiential content to added experiences

Some services, such as mail order catalogues, have no experiential content. Firms that offer these services are trying to add experience by changing the format or the medium. Instead of using a printed catalogue, they may lure and retain their customers using an online webpage that includes games and other activities to make their customers feel that they are part of the total offering.

Strategy

Strategy defined

Strategy

Strategy identifies how an organisation will function in its environment. It specifies how to satisfy customers, how to grow the organisation, how to compete in its environment, how to manage the organisation, how to develop capabilities within the organisation, and how to achieve financial objectives. Strategy prescribes the long-term direction for the organisation.

Strategic plan

A strategic plan is a statement of an organisation's explicit mission, goals, and objectives, and the specific actions required to achieve those goals and objectives.

Strategic planning

Strategic planning is the process of determining the strategic plan.

What is strategy?

Strategy is one of the most fascinating topics in business. Senior executives spend many hours, days, weeks, and even months developing strategic plans and blueprints for the future. They are defining the basis of business competition.

Strategy has its origins in the military, where generals would manoeuvre troops and weapons into position before battle commenced hoping to outflank the enemy and secure a victory. A quick review of synonyms for 'manoeuvre' suggests the following verbs – contrive, plot, scheme, plan – and the following nouns – plan, trick, plot, scheme, tactic, move, exercise, movement, and operation.

In the military sense, the starting point is to ensure you have the right resources ready for action at the right places with the overall objective of winning the battle and, eventually, the war. Military strategy is a means to a political end.

Michael Porter, in the 1980s, advocated a framework for diagnosing the structure of industry,[15] and he based this on the competitive forces he claimed erode long-term industry average profitability. The five forces model explains the sustainability of profits against bargaining power and against direct and indirect competition. In general, an organisation following Porter would devise an effective strategy to take advantage of the identified opportunities by employing its strengths and avoiding threats by correcting or compensating for weaknesses.

Porter advocated strategy formation as an analytical process by selecting a strategy based on a clearly defined position in the market. He supported this by analysis rather than prescription. Academics used his models as the foundation of competitive strategy and empirical testing. However, what the organisation plans to do to achieve its long-term objective is missing.

Henry Mintzberg, in the early 1990s, provided the following five strategy definitions,[16] which help us to understand strategy better:

- Strategy is a **plan** or a consciously intended course of action, or a guideline to approach a business situation. This assumes businesses make strategies in advance and develop them consciously and purposefully – the intended plan.
- A strategy can be a **ploy**, or a specific manoeuvre, intended to outwit a competitor.
- Strategy is a **pattern**, or a consistency of behaviour, whether intended or not. Patterns represent realised strategy and divide into deliberate and emergent strategies. Deliberate strategies appear where previous intentions existed, while emergent strategies develop in the absence of intentions, or despite them.
- Strategy is a **position**. Strategy becomes the mediating force, or match, between an organisation and the environment – the link between the internal and external context.

- Strategy is a **perspective** shared by members of an organisation, through their intentions and/or by their actions; it is an ingrained way of perceiving the world.

If strategies can be intended (whether as general plans or specific ploys), then they can be realised. Defining strategy as a plan is not enough; we also need a definition encompassing the resulting behaviour. The definitions of strategy as plan and pattern can be quite independent of one another – plans may go unrealised, while patterns may appear without preconception. Mintzberg implies that the execution does not necessarily follow a deliberately chosen and logical path and that the outcome is uncertain.

Michael Treacy and Fred Wiersema restrict the basis of strategy formation. In their *Harvard Business Review* article, they assert that companies achieve leadership positions by narrowing, not broadening, their business focus. They present three value disciplines serving as the basis for strategy: Product leadership, operational excellence, and customer intimacy.[17]

- **Product leadership** disciplines produce a continuous stream of state-of-the-art products and services with the objective of quick commercialisation of new concepts and ideas. This requires research and development activities that are market-focused and agile.
- **Operational excellence** focuses on the production and delivery of products and services with an objective of leading the industry in terms of price and convenience. This implies excellent marketing, production, and distribution processes.
- **Customer intimacy** concentrates on designing and modifying products and services to satisfy a narrow definition of the customer with the objective of long-term customer loyalty and long-term customer profitability. This suggests processes stay close to the customer and build long-term relationships.

Organisations that succeed through product leadership invest heavily in product-related innovations; those that succeed through operational excellence do so by minimising their production costs. When the strategic emphasis is on customer intimacy, the organisation often builds close relationships with other companies who can provide distinctive services coupled to their products. When manufacturing companies compete on customer intimacy, they endeavour to offer a portfolio of integrated products and services with the product-centric services providing the major differentiating factors in the marketplace. This describes the servitisation of manufacturing as discussed earlier.

Mintzberg also described strategy as a pattern of actions.[18] Often it is very difficult for an organisation to define their strategy, but the actions an organisation takes or the behaviour it exhibits demonstrates their strategy in action. A realised strategy is a pattern in a stream of decisions, but we do not study decisions. The perspective referencing Air New Zealand, at the start of this chapter, illustrates a realised strategy. What we see is the result of the actions taken. The opposite is an unrealised strategy in which decisions do not precede the corresponding actions.

When an organisation looks at a competitor and endeavours to ascertain the competitor's strategy, they evaluate observed actions. In this case, the strategy is an intended strategy. A deliberate strategy is about control. Organisations demonstrate this by dictating to their employees exactly how they should operate with the assumption that whoever devised the strategy in the first place had the best ideas. This may not necessarily be the case, however. Mintzberg advocates an emerging strategy, which is about learning.

The ultimate purpose of any organisation is to exist and to provide value to its stakeholders. If the organisation wants to provide additional value, it must outperform its competitors. The organisation requires decisions to determine the structural and infrastructural activities of the organisation. Broadly speaking, an organisation develops an overall strategy and then formulates functional strategies in finance, marketing, new product and service development, and operations to achieve the objective. When considering your competitors, you need to know who is in front of you, and why, and who is behind you, and why. When you observe the competitor in front, you should know why they are in front. Are they better than you are? Are they faster? Have they trained harder? Do they have better physical and mental attributes? What allows them to be in front of you? Why are you behind them?

In addition, when you look back and observe the competitor behind, you should know why they are behind. Are they not as good as you are? Are they slower? Have they not trained as much? Do they not have the same physical and mental attributes? What allows them to be behind you and you to be in front?

An organisation does not have to be in front, but it does need to know where it is relative to its competitors and the reasons why it is in that position. It needs to know what it has to do to hold its place, what it must do to improve its position, and which organisation is biting at its ankles and trying to relegate it into the pack.

Gerry Johnson, Kevan Scholes, Richard Whittington, Duncan Angwin, and Patrick Regnér look at the long-term direction of the organisation as it tries to achieve some advantage, and they present a view of strategy that encapsulates these thoughts. They define strategy as the long-term direction of an organisation.[19] This simple definition boils down to the interpretation of long-term and direction. Long-term includes the deliberate actions and logical steps that develop from a well-constructed plan and recognises that incremental changes and emerging patterns evolve during execution. Direction implies change and allows the organisation to emphasise differences and competitive responses when challenged and to cooperate with other organisations should circumstances allow.

The scope of an organisation's activities and the concept of strategic fit trying to match resources and activities are important. The organisation should stretch its available resources, and this may require major resource changes. Values and expectations affect all decisions, not just operational ones.

Multinational organisations and conglomerates find strategic decisions complex. There is so much change in the world, and it is extremely difficult, for large organisations especially, to formulate a strategy that can add value and be successful in all areas at the same time.

Organisations make strategy decisions in situations of uncertainty. Technology will probably be the biggest driver of future change for business, but it is also the source of the most uncertainty since people do not know exactly what will happen and when. They can speculate, but they do not know the exact outcomes.

Most organisations are aware of the need to use a team approach in which the various functions work together to achieve joint outcomes. This requires functional integration. When functions operate in functional silos and endeavour to secure success for their function, often at the expense of the overall performance, then the organisation fails to add value.

Modern organisations do not operate in isolation. Indeed, they need access to good suppliers and they need a list of good customers. In this changing environment, they may have to manage and change relationships and networks outside the organisation.

Strategic capability

When organisations fully understand their business and social environment, they can position themselves relative to that environment. If they want to be competitive in that environment, they need to ensure they have the resources and the capability to be successful. This is the 'strategic fit' of the organisation. It describes how well the organisation fits into the environment. This positioning statement accepts the business conditions as a fact and endeavours to provide adequate resources to compete effectively in that given market.

While this approach is necessary for survival, it is also a very conservative approach, since the organisation knows the current business conditions and it just requires the organisation to match the need with adequate resources.

Business leaders must adapt, react, and gain the commitment of all stakeholders to ensure business excellence and the continual success of the business. The organisation should change to keep up with market changes. This requires a recognition that the market has changed and the ability to execute the required changes inside the organisation, otherwise the business backtracks and may not survive.

Often, though, an organisation may have a vision for the future requiring a radically different set of resources and processes than those used in the current market. This is particularly so for new and different entities such as:

- Airbnb (creating a sharing economy that utilises empty spaces).
- Google (technology to make information readily available).
- Dell EMC (providing information technology infrastructure).
- International Humanitarian City (facilitating first response to global crises).
- Ted (education – using the power of ideas to change attitudes).
- Trader Joe's (grocery retailing with great food and great prices).
- Uber (changing transportation with on-demand drivers and dynamic pricing).
- Virgin Atlantic (one size does not fit all airline in-flight service).
- Warby Parker (trendy eyewear with lower price points).
- Zara (customer at the heart of their fashion clothing business model).

These organisations stretch their resources to change the rules of engagement. Johnson et al. define the strategic capability as providing products or services that customers value, or might value, in the future. The available resources are the full set of resources available to the organisation. These split into inadequate, threshold, or unique resources as illustrated in Figure 1.4.

Organisations that do not maintain the pace have inadequate resources. Their customers are demanding something different and they are not able to deliver. It could be that the resources are just getting old or do not have the technological capability their

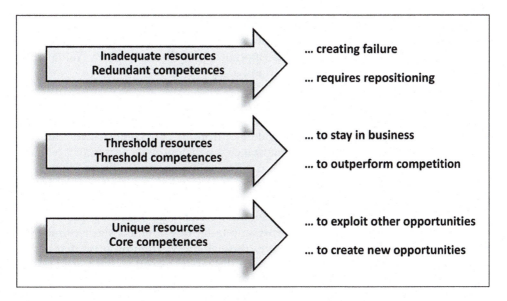

Figure 1.4 Drivers of strategic capability, adapted from Johnson, G., Scholes, K., & Whittington, R. (2008). Exploring corporate strategy (8th ed.). Harlow, England: Pearson Education, p. 95.

customers demand. Clearly, these resources need repositioning so they can deliver value to customers, or the business fails.

Organisations need threshold resources to exist in a market. They support the minimum level customers will accept and allow the organisation to stay in business. These resources are not static and require change to keep up with a changing environment.

Unique resources critically underpin competitive advantage and sustain the ability to provide value. They are better than their competitors' resources and are difficult to imitate. They allow the organisation to exploit other opportunities and create new opportunities.

Core competence

Core competence

Core competence is a skill that enables an organisation to provide the greatest level of value to its customers in a way that is difficult for competitors to emulate and provides for future growth. The skills of the workers in the organisation embody the core competencies. They develop through collective learning, communication, and commitment to work across the levels and functions in the organisation and with the customers and suppliers.

Competitive advantage

Competitive advantage is the advantage an organisation has over its rivals in attracting customers and defending against competitors. Sources of advantage may include factors such as technology, human skills, and brand name.

Value

Value is the amount customers are willing to pay for what an organisation provides. It represents a relationship between the benefits received and the price paid. Benefits can be informational and emotional as well as economic. Value is the quality received relative to expectations.

C. K. Prahalad and Gary Hamel developed the concept of core competence. A competence is the skill and ability to deploy resources effectively throughout an organisation. An organisation's competitiveness derives from its core competencies and core products. Companies identify core competencies, which provide potential access to a wide variety of markets and contribute to the customer benefits of the product. They advocated that a firm would compete successfully if it had resources available that were not available to the competition.[20]

Competitiveness comes when a business can develop and deliver a product or service and satisfy customers at a lower cost, at a faster rate, and in a shorter time than its competitors. Core competence develops through process improvement that has an organisation-wide focus. Organisations using this model recognise that some product functionality makes them excellent.

Once an organisation recognises a core competence, it focuses all functional activities to promote and enhance it. The core competence is an area of specialised expertise and underpins the value in a product or service. It results from harmonising complex streams of technology and activities.

An organisation enjoys success when customers recognise better products, better service, more innovation, a larger range from which to choose, more flexibility, and/or a more reliable delivery. Under these circumstances, a customer places value on solving the customer's problems and the supplier using resources to solve these problems. Thus, organisations should view these problems through the eyes of the customer.

Often it is difficult to isolate specific things that make a difference but the organisation is still successful. In this case, it may be a bundle of skills and technologies underpinning the ability to meet critical success factors.

The differentiating competence, or bundle of competencies, must be robust and should be difficult for competitors to imitate. It is difficult to copy when it is a complex harmonisation of individual technologies and production skills. Businesses reorganise and learn from alliances and focus on internal development. Above all, core competence provides opportunities for the business, not limitations.

Value is the amount customers are willing to pay for what an organisation provides. It represents a relationship between the benefits received and the price paid. Benefits can be informational and emotional as well as economic. Value is, therefore, the quality received relative to expectations.

Corporate strategy

The strategy document often contains broad statements and sometimes uses words and phrases having more than one meaning such as higher quality, better service, faster response, and shorter lead times. Thus, the language of strategy can create confusion and misunderstanding.

Early in the process of developing the corporate strategy, the organisation states the strategic mission, which is a statement of the future business scope, including customer needs, customer groups, processes, technologies, and core competencies.

Organisations often develop functional strategies independently and piece them together with some overriding theme. Many organisations require each function to provide a strategic statement but fail to integrate them as part of its overall strategy formulation. This means that corporate strategies stop at the interface between functions. This also applies to multinationals and conglomerates that are unable, or unwilling, to incorporate individual company statements into the overall corporate strategy.

Of all the functions in a firm, especially a manufacturing firm, the linkage between marketing and production requires clarity. This link is often not evident when reviewing books on strategic marketing and corporate strategy, implying it is not necessary.

As an example of this lack of linkage and clarity, consider a supplier signing a major sales order. The various functions in the firm view this sales order in different ways. Sales management and accounting management view the order in dollar terms and each dollar is the same. The sales representative may have spent the commission even before the ink is dry on the contracts. The company accountants may analyse the bank accounts and see this money flowing through their systems to pay the bills and generate huge profits. Production might view an order in terms of volume, product mix, and production resources. Some functions see the money and other functions see the quantity. The gap between these two views causes problems.

Executives put forward strategic proposals that do not require an essential interface, allowing their companies to make major decisions and committing the organisation for many years. The consequences of these actions are enormous. This type of approach narrows the opportunities and increases the risk. Moreover, the associated risk is not part of the process; it does not allow the type of strategic advantage coming directly from embracing key functional initiatives and developing a commonly agreed and understood corporate plan.

The result for many companies is an erosion of the profit margins and the disappearance of the base on which to build a sound and prosperous business in the future. Frequent strategy checks are necessary to evaluate the fit between the business and production capability to provide the necessary order-winning criteria of its various products. The absence of these essential insights leaves an organisation vulnerable and exposed. In times of increased world competition, this happens suddenly and can be fatal. In many cases, averting the end is the only option left. Switching from an operational to a strategic mode turns the organisation around. This requires a corporate review of the marketing and production perspectives and the financial implications of the proposals involved.

Strategic decisions in functional areas

At the corporate level, a company requires clear understanding of the markets in which it decides to participate now and in the future. Then the company can develop functional strategies (marketing, finance, new product development, operations, supply chain, and so on). Overall agreement and understanding are essential.

Marketing defines service levels, distribution methods, promotion policies, advertising practices, brand awareness, pricing algorithms, channel structures, product positioning, image requirements, product functions and features, and sponsorship policies.

Finance and accounting define advantage, cost of capital, levels of working capital, accounts receivable processes, accounts payable processes, financial control methods, lines of credit, currency hedging methods and timings, and relationships with banking institutions.

New product and service development defines technology platforms, research direction, concurrent engineering methods, time to market, criteria for selection, and methods of production development and introduction.

Operations management and supply chain management define the quality processes, products to produce, processes to use, location, physical layout, work systems, purchasing, outsourcing, out-partnering, vertical integration, scheduling systems, inventory philosophies, and process improvement initiatives.

Operations strategy

Operations strategy

Operations strategy is the total pattern of decisions that shape the long-term capabilities of an operation and their contribution to overall strategy. It should be consistent with overall business strategy.

All functions of an organisation have very important roles to play, and the outcomes are going to be more satisfactory for all the players when these functions work together. This book is about operations management, so it seems appropriate to give an operations-based perspective on strategy.

The following quotation from Robert Hayes and David Upton starts the ball rolling:

> The battle is won not in the boardroom but in the laboratories, on factory floors, at service counters, and in computer rooms . . . Companies that fail to exploit fully the strategic power of operations will be both hampered in their own attacks and vulnerable to those competitors that do exploit its power.[21]

Then this quotation from Nigel Slack and Mike Lewishelps position operations strategy:

> Operations strategy is the total pattern of decisions that shape the long-term capabilities of any type of operation and their contribution to overall strategy though the reconciliation of market requirements with operations resources.[22]

Strategy development is the easy part. The difficult part is the implementation, and this needs people. People interact with customers and suppliers, and the success, or otherwise, of the organisation depends on how these interactions take place.

First, we need the linkage between functions to be supportive. Organisations hire, train, educate, and empower employees to perform processes. The performance of these processes is a direct result of whom the organisation hires, how the organisation trains and educates them, and how the new employees accept empowerment. People are often the weakest link that needs support. Strategy may be set at board level, but it needs implementation at the coalface. The implication of this realisation has a huge impact on operations and supply chain management.

Business processes must align with business strategy. Process improvement initiatives need to concentrate on competencies, capabilities, problem solving, creativity, customer requirements, and communication. Typical examples quoted to support these arguments include:

BMW

We have a unique customer understanding through our ongoing, direct dialogue with our customers. We anticipate customer needs and desires. And we bring these to life – quickly and precisely – in innovative and emotional offerings and experiences. We leverage innovative technologies, digitalisation, and sustainability to deliver unique customer experiences.[23]

Inditex (parent company for Zara)

We want to create value through beautiful, ethical, quality products with a complete cycle of life. We act precisely and responsibly in every stage of the fashion process from design and sourcing, to manufacturing and quality control, logistics, and sales. At the centre of our business model is the customer.[24]

City of London, Mayor's transport strategy

Creating streets and street networks that encourage walking, cycling, and public transport use will reduce car dependency and the health problems it creates. A shift from private car to public transport could dramatically reduce the number of vehicles on London's streets.[25]

McDonald's Corporation

We know that serving more customers more often is the most meaningful way to grow the business and create value for all our stakeholders. That is why we focus on giving customers what they really want – hot, delicious food served quickly – with an overall experience and value for their money that meets their rising expectations.[26]

Ritz-Carlton Hotels

The Ritz-Carlton Hotel is a place where the genuine care and comfort of our guests is our highest mission. We pledge to provide the finest personal service and facilities for our guests who will always enjoy a warm, relaxed, yet refined ambience. The Ritz-Carlton experience enlivens the senses, instils well-being, and fulfils even the unexpressed wishes and needs of our guests.[27]

Southwest Airlines

They began with one simple notion: If you get your passengers to their destinations when they want to get there, on time, at the lowest possible fares, and make darn sure they have a good time doing it, people will fly your airline. And, you know what? They were right.[28]

Toyota

Our aim is to make the vehicles ordered by customers in the quickest and most efficient way, to deliver the vehicles as quickly as possible.[29]

An organisation requires an appreciation of the part the operations function plays, how that appreciation fits into the corporate strategy, and the unique capabilities the operations function can provide to support and influence overall strategic goals. The operations function should give the organisation its competitive advantage, such as low cost, flexibility, or high quality. The scope of decisions should be long term, and the organisation should make suitable investments in capital resources and in the workforce.

Operations strategy development in a service organisation is like the process followed in production. The positioning of a service strategy depends largely on intangible service characteristics rather than tangible product characteristics. This is a key distinction between service and production strategies.

Operations strategy, whether it is for production or service organisations, requires a customer-driven perspective. Process design and improvement activities are oriented to satisfying the customer. This, in turn, means understanding exactly what the customer wants and developing processes to deliver that.

A customer-driven operations strategy reflects a clear understanding of the long-term goals of the organisation and a cross-functional effort between marketing and operations to follow the needs of the marketplace and translate those needs into desirable capabilities, or competitive capabilities. Operating advantages relate to each of the organisation's processes and a business gains an advantage by outperforming competitors in one or more of these capabilities. An organisation gains competitive advantage from core competencies, by understanding the business processes, and by developing competitive capability.

Competitive capability

To develop an effective operations strategy, an organisation requires long-term decisions on how best to determine and develop a competitive capability consistent with the overall vision, mission, and strategy of the organisation. The strategic decisions on capacity, processes, facility, location, technology, and timing should represent a balance between readiness, policy, and the procedures of the organisation. Competitive capability adds a dimension to the product, making it an order winner.

There are five major groups of competitive capability:

- Cost.
- Quality.
- Delivery.
- Flexibility.
- Service.

These quantifiable dimensions have an enormous impact on an organisation's performance. The organisation should define these five groups and any other dimensions of competitive capability into the operations strategy in concise and measurable terms. Additionally, the organisation should integrate the operations strategy with other functional strategies such as marketing, research and development, finance, human resources, and information and communications technology.

Participants in all value chain activities must understand the goals and purpose of the operations strategy, since success for an organisation lies in the careful identification of those critical issues along with well-defined strategies for each activity.

Competing on cost

Most managers treat cost as a primary priority. Hardly a day goes by without business news media reporting that a given firm is on a 'cost-cutting exercise' or a firm has reduced prices to gain more market share. The usual emphasis is to just lower prices – and this inevitably lowers profit margins as well. A better approach from an operations viewpoint requires firms to redesign and improve processes to eliminate the cost-adding elements. This allows the business to lower the price while retaining profit margins.

Lowering prices can increase demand for products and services, but it also reduces profit margins if the business cannot produce the product or service at lower costs.

A company may gain competitive advantage by becoming a low-cost producer of goods and services. It must produce the product at a lesser cost or the company must accept lower profit margins. Generally, commodity goods compete on price and fall into this category. Mass-production technologies provide economies of scale, which in turn drive costs down. Supermarkets stock house-brand commodity goods, and customers, who are not brand conscious, buy these products since they are usually lower priced than branded ones.

Organisations may gain cost advantage by adopting lean thinking concepts and reducing the cost of non-value-adding activities in the value chain. When competing on cost, firms address labour at all levels, materials, supply chains, inventory investment, and overall costs and improve their systems by eliminating all steps not adding value to the customer. This may require more investment in automation, a streamlining of procedures, additional training, and employee development and usually results in a narrower range of products or services.

A 'no frills' airline competes on cost by reducing fares for the base service – travel with no checked bags, no free food, and just music entertainment. A customer obtains a very cheap fare if the travel portion is all they want. If, however, the customer wants more, they can pay extra for checked bags, lounge access, food and drinks, and video on demand.

Supply chains achieve cost advantage in raw material sourcing, warehousing, and distribution by:

- Procuring material direct from the manufacturer/supplier.
- Having a delivery schedule that can use budget or regular transport to reduce inventory and freight costs.
- Having long-term arrangements with suppliers to gain the most competitive price.

- Delivering raw material to the point of consumption.
- Sharing information about planned order requirements with suppliers.

Competing on quality

Organisations can achieve product differentiation by developing expertise in product quality and process quality. The aim is to provide superior performance products that meet the specifications and are reliable. Businesses differentiate their products when they are durable, safe, and serviceable. Added features supplement basic functions. As an example, having a multiple tuner in a digital television set to enable viewers to watch several channels simultaneously may be desirable for some, but is not a necessity.

Quality performance design means that the product or service has better performance, superior features, more reliability, more durability, and more serviceability. It satisfies customer requirements in all aspects.

Consistent quality occurs when every product conforms to the design specifications every time. While this may sound like an internal requirement, it is in fact an external requirement since the customer expects to receive the product as designed, presented, advertised, or promoted. Anything less would result in dissatisfaction.

Car companies such as Toyota and BMW compete on quality, since the concept of quality features at the top of their priority lists. Note that both companies will argue that they compete on other issues and not solely on quality.

Competing on delivery

There are three aspects to consider when competing on delivery – fast delivery time, on-time delivery, and development speed.

Fast delivery time means shortening the time from initiating an order to receiving the product or service. To achieve this, an organisation examines all process steps to remove the time-wasting elements such as waiting in a queue.

On-time delivery means delivering the product or service at the first customer-requested delivery time and measuring how often delivery promises happen. Organisations may think they are meeting delivery promises by shipping goods out the door on or before the delivery promise date and time. However, customers do not see it this way. They want the product or service and they measure on-time delivery based on the actual delivery of the product to their location and ready for use. Amazon provides an excellent example of fast delivery and on-time delivery by providing an estimated delivery date at time of order, confirming delivery date at time of dispatch, allowing the customer to track delivery progress online, and (in most cases) delivering as promised.

Development speed relates to the time interval that elapses from initial idea to product reality. Organisations enjoy first-mover advantages that include higher pricing, higher market share, productivity improvements, and reduced risks by developing and producing products ahead of the competition, Time-based competition has a goal of eliminating waste from all activities in the value chain. George Stalk, Jr. and Thomas Hout claimed that time is the equivalent of money, productivity, quality, and even innovation. In their path-breaking book,[30] the authors argued that the ways leading companies manage time in production, in new product development, and in sales and distribution represents a powerful source of competitive advantage. Time reduction methods include overlapping product development activities, improving communication channels, simplifying complex processes, reducing set-up times, and smoothing production flows.

Competing on flexibility

Flexibility allows an organisation to change volumes or products quickly to suit customer requirements. There are two aspects of flexibility – product customisation and volume flexibility.

Product customisation requires an organisation to modify products or services to match exactly what the customer wants and when they want them. This is more than a make-to-order environment. It relates to the ability of the firm to listen to the customer, deliver exactly what the customer wants, and having the processes in place to achieve it.

Volume flexibility allows an organisation to supply any quantity of product. This means the rate of production is variable and the firm can increase, or decrease, the volume without disruption.

Organisations achieve competitive advantage by developing flexibility in processes to meet the unique and changing needs of customers. They achieve flexibility by:

- Producing a wide variety of products.
- Accommodating specific customer needs.
- Having the ability to produce whatever quantity the customer needs.

Subway® Restaurants[31] (sandwiches) has built flexibility into their products and processes, and they meet specific customer needs without disruption.

When a customer orders a Dell computer, the actual computer may not physically exist. Dell Inc. has the manufacturing capability (flexibility) to assemble exactly what the customer orders and ship it to them within a few days. The company enhances this flexibility by pricing the configuration in favour of the components it can deliver easily. If a component (memory, hard drive, or screen) is in short supply, Dell offers that component at a higher price and encourages customers to choose another component at a lower price, and the alternative may be at a higher specification, which is even better.

Competing on service

Competing on service encompasses some of the other capabilities already discussed. Cost elements can be minimised by designing processes with value-adding steps. Organisations incorporate quality elements in service by fully understanding customer requirements. Training and process design improve delivery. Focusing on the specific needs of customers develops flexibility. Ritz-Carlton Hotels and Virgin Atlantic provide excellent examples of competing on service.

Competing on cost, quality, delivery, flexibility, and service

The preceding sections discussed each of these competitive capabilities separately. Most of them overlap and it is often difficult to identify a capability and to quantify precisely the effect it is having on performance.

Production involves process design, process technology, plant layout, deployment of human resources, and planning and control systems. To achieve a distinctive advantage an organisation should:

- Choose repeatable and reliable process design and technology.
- Choose value-adding plant layout, not cost-adding.
- Allow outside parties (subcontractors) to perform outsource activities if they can do that cheaper and better.
- Design and develop processes and controls that are difficult for competitors to imitate.
- Have the correct product-process match.
- Develop flexibility in production so that varying customer demands, in terms of flexible product mix and volume, is achievable without incurring higher costs, additional time, or disrupting normal working activities.
- Reduce set-up time by incorporating process flexibility.
- Develop process flexibility to speed up the introduction of new products.
- Ensure processes are capable and in control.
- Develop vertical integration of activities that add value to the customer.

McDonald's restaurants gain cost advantages by having long-term agreements with their food suppliers and all franchise outlets make consolidated orders. They achieve quality capabilities by conforming to specification and meeting customers' needs. They have very fast delivery processes and their 'made for you' technology provides volume and product flexibility. Integrity is the foundation of McDonald's success. People around the world trust the brand, and McDonald's earn that trust by respecting their customers and employees and delivering outstanding quality, service, cleanliness, and value.[32]

Structural decisions in operations

Structural decisions

The categories of structural decisions include capacity, facilities, process technology, vertical integration, and supplier relations.

Capacity

Capacity decisions determine how much the organisation can produce and in what time. An organisation should predetermine how many products or how much service it must produce, and then make sure it has enough capacity to deliver those quantities. It can obtain capacity prior to the need, just when required, or after the need. There is no correct time to increase capacity, as this depends on several factors, such as the incremental cost of increasing capacity, the competitive advantage that the extra capacity will provide to the organisation, and the capacity available to competitors in the same industry. Increasing capacity after the need requires the least risk and allows for full utilisation of existing facilities. Basing capacity on predicted growth involves significant risk, especially if the expected demand does not materialise. However, it can provide significant market opportunities and production capability.

Facilities

Organisations require at least one facility in which to operate. Decisions on location and products relate to the number, size, location, and specific nature of facilities. Location, for example, is important for service organisations that do not produce a tangible product. Fuel stations, motels, and fast-food restaurants cannot operate successfully unless they are near customers. Manufacturers, whose products are very bulky or heavy, must consider location and transport.

Many smaller facilities can provide better customer service in both the service and production sectors by reducing customer lead times. Facilities need to be large enough to justify their operating costs, but enlarging a facility does not necessarily guarantee a lower cost per unit. Facility decisions are key determinants of an organisation's ability to compete on cost and delivery.

Process technology

Process technology decisions determine which methods produce the products and services required to meet demand. The decision-makers consider the appropriate way to produce the product or service, given the cost, quality, delivery patterns, degree of flexibility, and response time necessary to accomplish strategic objectives. The decision-makers evaluate the use of technologies in manufacturing such as robotics, computer-assisted design/computer-assisted manufacturing, and flexible manufacturing systems. In services, they consider the use of automation and reducing customer contact. Variables such as volume, lot size requirements, degree of interaction with the customer, and the amount of customisation/standardisation influence the choice of process technology. Process technology decisions seek to bring about improvements in the competitive capabilities of cost, quality, and flexibility. They have a significant influence on costs since different technologies have different costs.

Vertical integration and supplier relations

Vertical integration decisions deal with the portion of the product or service an organisation will produce itself compared with the portion it will purchase and the extent to which it will market, distribute, and sell the product. Vertical integration of suppliers can be forward or backward, and it affects the supply base significantly. Key decisions within this category include the selection of the total number of suppliers, the number of suppliers for each purchased item, and the types of supplier relationships developed. The primary impact of vertical integration on competitive capabilities is the effect it has on cost and quality. Vertical integration decisions influence cost because of the influence suppliers' prices have on material costs. Many organisations use backward integration to gain more control over their raw material and purchased item quality.

Infrastructural decisions in operations

Infrastructural decisions

The categories of infrastructural decisions include quality, production planning and inventory control, new product and service development, performance measurement and reward, human resources, and organisation systems.

Quality

Quality systems have a significant effect on cost and delivery lead time. Processes designed and improved with quality as the driver help to reduce the cost of production and the time it takes. It may cost an organisation to improve the process capability, but this is usually more than offset by the reduction in scrap, rework, and other ongoing costs. Better understanding of the process capability improves flexibility.

Production planning and inventory control

Production planning decisions relate to product, timing, and method, as well as quantity. These affect cost, quality, delivery, and flexibility. Inventory location and stock levels affect quality, flexibility, and lead times. They can also affect costs, especially when inventory is in the wrong places and in the wrong quantities. Outsourcing decisions affect costs and flexibility. Outsourcing allows a firm to use another firm's capacity and skill but it usually comes with different levels of cost, quality, flexibility, and lead time.

New product and service development

New product and service development decisions affect the cost of bringing a new product or service to market and design decisions affect ongoing production costs. These design decisions also have a long-term effect on flexibility. New product and service development decisions have a positive effect on quality, since quality improvement is one of the main drivers for introducing new products and services.

Performance measurement and reward

Performance measurement and reward decisions have a significant effect on cost since most reward systems are monetary. Incentives and bonuses may affect quality of output and the timing of output.

Human resources

Human resources influence the selection, training, education, retention, and rewarding of employees who maintain customers and enhance customer experiences. The choices have a significant effect on cost, quality, and the customer experience, while the skill level and experience of the workforce influences quality, time, and flexibility. Salaries and wages paid to employees have a direct effect on cost especially for service organisations. A stable workforce improves conformance to quality simply because new staff members receive training for the production or service line with full knowledge of all the processes involved.

Organisation systems

The structure of the organisation influences flexibility and timing. An organisation may not make decisions quickly enough to be competitive, and reporting line methods may inhibit flexibility. The organisational culture may affect line and staff relationships, thus adding to cost, quality, and flexibility priorities.

Integration decisions in operations

Integration decisions

Structural decisions need to integrate with infrastructural decisions. The categories of integration decisions include communication, alignment, and linkage systems.

Communication

Business functions such as operations, human resources, and marketing must communicate among themselves so they are all aware of changes in schedules, supplier deliveries, customer requirements, customer preferences, and agreements made by one function that may affect another. One function may agree to a process concession and, without any communication advising the change, other functions may wait for the original arrangement to eventuate. The chairperson needs to communicate a planned delay in the start of a meeting to all attendees, or a salesperson needs to communicate a pricing adjustment to all affected parties when a customer accepts a slightly different product specification.

Alignment

Alignment refers to the degree of integration relative to the depth of the customer experience. As the depth of the customer experience increases (and this could be as a result of marketing and/or the actions of staff at the point of delivery), the need develops for significant effort to be given to collaboration and coordination across business functions such as operations, human resources, and marketing and to partners involved in designing and delivering experiences.

Linkage

Service delivery systems that enhance the customer experience require strong linkages between the classical traditional operations decisions, such as capacity planning, scheduling, quality, technology choice, the allocation of staff members, and the point of delivery of the customer experience. At the point of delivery of the customer experience, employees make spontaneous decisions that cannot reconcile against a traditional planning system. The timeframe is too short; it is all happening now.

The Ritz-Carlton Hotel Company use their employee empowerment processes to deliver an experience that enlivens the senses, instils well-being, and fulfils even the unexpressed wishes and needs of their guests.[33]

Chapter summary

The history of operations management started with the transition from cottage industries to factory production. Now, the operations function is a vital part of all organisations, and most organisations are striving to improve the way the operations function delivers goods and services.

The transformation process is fundamental to operations management. Organisations develop strategies to support the business strategy by closely examining the inputs, transformations, and outputs of the operations function.

We distinguished between products and services in case we need to make the distinction, but bear in mind that, for the most part, operations managers treat them the same. Products are things and consumers can touch them, see them, kick them, and/or destroy them. Factories make products and quantitative methods measure the quality of the production. It is easy to check product output against product specification. Services are intangible. Often, especially with pure services, the output is an idea, as in advertising, designing, and promoting. Some services, such as insurance, banking, and investments, will refer to their outputs as products but the customer cannot physically touch them.

Some companies integrate products and services and sometimes the firm takes a unique competitive position building on its technological strength and competences to provide a new and unique offering.

We explained the role of operations management within the context of the whole organisation and introduced the concept of the customer experience paradigm. Increasingly, customers want to be emotionally involved with the service delivery and experience the service offering. Satisfaction is not the only outcome that customers desire.

Developing and implementing an operations strategy starts with understanding customer needs, the corporate strategy, and the competition. Then an organisation can determine how to position operations; that is, how to match a firm's distinctive competence and its primary task.

The output of this positioning process is the general identification of those tasks that the operations function must do well. Competitive capability is the specific formalisation of these requirements. Of these, an organisation may choose to compete on cost, quality, delivery, flexibility, and/or service.

A sound operations strategy can help an organisation achieve its mission. It provides guidelines to all employees on how best to make decisions in a value-adding activity that produces a product or service. The idea is not which element of operations strategy to choose – it is translating this strategy into well-defined decisions that the organisation can pursue. Value-adding activities can offer competitive advantages. It is up to each organisation to identify its competitive capability and core competencies in a value activity to achieve its mission.

Operations strategy can have a strong impact on the cost, quality, delivery, flexibility, and service relating to the products and services of an organisation.

Discussion questions

1 What does 'operations management' mean?
2 How does the transformation process relate to value?
3 Explain the relationship between value and profits.
4 What are the reasons for formulating and implementing an operations strategy?
5 How would you determine whether an organisation had an operations strategy or not? What specific questions would you ask and what information would you gather?
6 Identify a company (or an organisation) with which you are familiar:

   • What are the company's resource strengths and weaknesses? Note: Resource strength represents a competitive asset and is a big determinant of its competitiveness and ability to succeed in the marketplace.
   • Describe the key value activities for the organisation. Note: A key value activity in this sense may be supply chain management, research and development, production, distribution, sales and marketing, or customer service.
   • Which activities does it do well? For each of the key value activities, indicate whether it is a competence (something an organisation has learned to perform well), a core competence (a competitively important activity that a company performs better than other internal activities), or a distinctive competence (a competitively valuable activity that an organisation performs better than its rivals).

7 Find an example of an operation in your local community that has been successful in simultaneously improving quality, reducing throughput time, improving on-time deliveries, and reducing costs. How has this operation been able to achieve these seemingly conflicting results?
8 Explain the motivation for a manufacturer to adopt an advanced servitisation strategy.
9 How would a manufacturer servitise successfully? How would it go about the transformation process, and where would it start?
10 Which (if any) decision type – infrastructural, structural, or integration – is most important? Explain.
11 Choose a product such as a television set or a telephone and research a historical timeline to demonstrate the product enhancements. Explain how innovation and customer needs helped develop the features available in current products.
12 How does the Internet change competitive capability?
13 How would you define the customer perceived value?
14 Discuss the effects scientific management has made to the current business environment.

Key terms

competitive advantage, 23
core competence, 23
customer, 8
infrastructural decisions, 34

integration decisions, 35
operations management, 6
operations strategy, 26
product, 13

service, 13
service package, 15
servitisation, 16
strategic plan, 19
strategic planning, 19

strategy, 18
structural decisions, 32
transformation process, 10
value, 24

Notes

1 International Air Transport Association. (2018). *IATA: Our members*. Retrieved from https://www.iata.org/about/members/Pages/index.aspx

2 International Air Transport Association. (2018). *IATA Pressroom facts and figures*. Retrieved from www.iata.org/pressroom/facts_figures/fact_sheets/Documents/fact-sheet-industry-facts.pdf

3 AirlineRatings.com. (2018). *AirlineRatings.com product rating criteria*. Retrieved from https://airlineratings.com/full-service-carrier-product-rating-criteria/

4 AirlineRatings.com. (2018). *AirlineRatings.com awards*. Retrieved from https://airlineratings.com/awards/

5 Roger Gray, Group General Manager Airports, Air New Zealand (personal communication, November 6, 2018).

6 Iansiti, M., & Lakhani, K. R. (2014). Digital ubiquity: How connections, sensors, and data are revolutionizing business. *Harvard Business Review*, 92(11), 90–99.

7 Womack, J. P., & Jones, D. T. (2005, March–April). Lean consumption. *Harvard Business Review*, 83(3), 58–68.

8 Fitzsimmons, J. A., Fitzsimmons, M. J., & Bordoloi, S. (2018). *Service management: Operations, strategy, and information technology* (9th ed.). New York, NY: McGraw-Hill Irwin, p. 18.

9 Baines, T., & Lightfoot, H. (2013). *Made to serve: How manufacturers can compete through servitization and product service systems*. Chichester, England: Wiley, p. 64.

10 Rolls-Royce media press release. (2012, October 12). *Rolls-Royce celebrates 50th anniversary of power-by-the-hour* [Press release]. Retrieved from https://www.rolls-royce.com/media/press-releases-archive/yr-2012/121030-the-hour.aspx

11 Caterpillar articles and customer stories (n.d.). Retrieved from www.cat.com/en_US/articles/customer-stories/

12 MAN Trucks UK Service Contract (n.d.). Retrieved from https://truck.man.eu/uk/en/services/repair-and-maintenance/man-servicecontracts/tco-services/TCO-services.html

13 Voss, C., Roth, A. V., & Chase, R. B. (2008, May–June). Experience, service operations strategy, and services as destinations: Foundations and exploratory investigation. *Production and Operations Management*, 17(3), 248.

14 Johnston, R., Clark, G., & Shulver, M. (2012). *Service operations management: Improving service delivery* (4th ed.). Harlow, England: Pearson Education, p. 40.

15 Porter, M. E. (1979, March–April). How competitive forces shape strategy. *Harvard Business Review*, 57(2), 137–145.

16 Mintzberg, H. (1992). Five Ps for strategy. In H. Mintzberg & J. B. Quinn (Eds.), *The strategy process* (2nd ed.). Englewood Cliffs, NJ: Prentice Hall, pp. 12–19.

17 Treacy, M., & Wiersema, F. (1993, January–February). Customer intimacy and other value disciplines. *Harvard Business Review*, 71(1), 84–93.

18 Mintzberg, H. (2007). *Tracking strategies: Toward a general theory*. Oxford, England: Oxford University Press, p. 6.

19 Johnson, G., Whittington, R., Scholes, K., Angwin, D., & Regnér, P. (2017). *Exploring corporate strategy* (11th ed.). Harlow, England: Pearson Education, p. 4.

20 Prahalad, C. K., & Hamel, G. (1990, May–June). The core competence of the corporation. *Harvard Business Review*, 68(3), 79–91.

21 Hayes, R. H., & Upton, D. M. (1998, Summer). Operations-based strategy. *California Management Review*, 40(4), 8–25.

22 Slack, N., & Lewis, M. (2017). *Operations strategy* (5th ed.). Harlow, England: Pearson Education, p. 24.
23 BMW Group. (n.d.). *BMW Group: Our strategy*. Retrieved from https://bmwgroup.com/en/company/strategie.html
24 Inditex. (n.d.). *How we do business: Our model*. Retrieved from https://inditex.com/en/how-we-do-business/our-model
25 City of London. (2018). *City of London, Mayor's transport strategy 2018*. Retrieved from https://london.gov.uk/what-we-do/transport/our-vision-transport/mayors-transport-strategy-2018
26 McDonald's Corporation. (n.d.). *McDonald's our growth strategy*. Retrieved from https://corporate.mcdonalds.com/corpmcd/about-us/our-growth-strategy.html
27 The Ritz-Carlton Hotel Company. (n.d.). *Gold Standards: Corporate philosophy and awards*. Retrieved from http://corporate.ritzcarlton.com/en/About/GoldStandards.htm Note: We discuss Ritz-Carlton Hotels further in Chapter 7.
28 Southwest Airlines. (n.d.). *We weren't just airborne yesterday: About SWA: History*. Retrieved from www.swamedia.com/channels/Our-History/pages/our-history-sort-by
29 Toyota Motor Corporation. (n.d.). *Toyota production system*. Retrieved from http://www2.toyota. co.jp/en/vision/production_system
30 Stalk, G., & Hout, T. M. (1990). *Competing against time: How time-based competition is reshaping global markets*. New York, NY: The Free Press.
31 Subway is a registered trademark of Doctor's Associates Inc.
32 McDonald's Corporation. (n.d.). *McDonald's food suppliers and food sources: About our food*. Retrieved from https://mcdonalds.com/us/en-us/about-our-food/meet-our-suppliers.html
33 The Ritz-Carlton Hotel Company. (n.d.). Gold Standards. *Op cit.*

Additional reading on operations and strategy

Beckman, S. L., & Rosenfield, D. B. (2008). *Operations strategy: Competing in the 21st century*. Boston, MA: McGraw-Hill/Irwin.
Fitzsimmons, J. A., Fitzsimmons, M. J., & Bordoloi, S. (2018). *Service management: Operations, strategy, and information technology* (9th ed.). New York, NY: McGraw-Hill Irwin.
Hill, A., & Hill, T. (2009). *Manufacturing operations strategy* (3rd ed.). Basingstoke, England: Palgrave Macmillan.
Johnson, G., Whittington, R., Scholes, K., Angwin, D., & Regnér, P. (2018). *Exploring corporate strategy* (11th ed.). Harlow, England: Pearson Education.
Johnston, R., Clark, G., & Shulver, M. (2012). *Service operations management: Improving service delivery* (4th ed.). Harlow, England: Pearson Education.
Kaplan, R. S., & Norton, D. P. (2009). *The execution premium: Linking strategy to operations for competitive advantage*. Boston, MA: Harvard Business Press.
Mintzberg, H. (2007). *Tracking strategies: Toward a general theory*. Oxford, England: Oxford University Press.
Pittman, P. H., & Atwater, J. B. (2016). *APICS dictionary* (15th ed.). Chicago, IL: APICS.
Prahalad, C. K., & Hamel, G. (1990, May–June). The core competence of the corporation. *Harvard Business Review, 68* (3), 79–93.
Slack, N., Brandon-Jones, A., Johnston, R., & Betts, A. (2015). *Operations and process management: Principles and practice for strategic impact* (4th ed.). Harlow, England: Pearson Education.
Slack, N., & Lewis, M. (2017). *Operations strategy* (5th ed.). Harlow, England: Pearson Education.
Womack, J., & Jones, D. T. (2005, March–April). Lean consumption. *Harvard Business Review, 83*(3), 58–68.

Chapter 2

Demand management and forecasting in operations

Learning objectives

At the end of the chapter you should be able to:

- Explain the nature of demand.
- Discuss demand management and the forecasting process.
- Understand and discuss the strategic role of forecasting.
- Explain how to use forecasting horizons.
- Explain and calculate forecast deviation – difference between the actual demand and forecast value.
- Discuss forecast value added.
- Distinguish between qualitative and quantitative forecasting.
- Identify the components of demand – trend, seasonal, cyclical, and random.
- Calculate a seasonal index.
- Calculate a regression equation to develop long-term trends.
- Evaluate forecasting performance measurement.
- Distinguish between dependent and independent demand.
- Discuss other approaches to forecasting.

Perspective: Forecasting – constrained or unconstrained

Forecasting is one of the most interesting and contentious topics in operations management. It is interesting because academics and practitioners have written numerous articles and books on the topic and that means that there is an abundance of opinions as to how one should forecast future demand for products and services. It is contentious because organisations cannot agree on whether forecasting is necessary or it is a complete waste of time.

Apple® provides an example of unconstrained demand. They are a company with a history of producing innovative products that at times have generated demand greater than the company's ability to supply immediately.[1]

To put forecasting into perspective, let us examine the sales performance for the major product categories for Apple Inc. over a ten-year period as in Figure 2.1.[2]

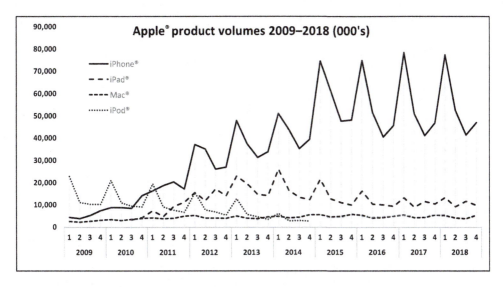

Figure 2.1 Apple® product volumes for ten years (2009–2018)

The first point to clarify is that this graph represents sales data; it does not necessarily represent demand. Our task is to ascertain the product volumes for the next three years (at least) so that we can guarantee supply of components, provide enough manufacturing capability, arrange distribution facilities, implement marketing programmes, facilitate sales capability, and cultivate after-sales support. The basis for the planning for these functional capabilities is projected demand; the basis for the execution is actual sales. Therein lies the difference and how do we cope with that?

The Apple product data illustrates the demise of the iPod® and that makes sense when we acknowledge the iPod® capability incorporated in newer models of the iPhone® and the iPad®. The Mac® desktops and laptop sales are relatively flat during the whole period under review. The iPad® sales show strong growth for five years with seasonal peaks corresponding to new product announcements. The iPhone® demonstrates phenomenal growth over the entire period with noticeable peaks at the end of each calendar year with each peak following major product model releases.[3]

Without knowing all the details and without knowing what demand data Apple used for their market planning, it should be obvious that the sales results reflect a direct consequence of business decisions made within the company. There is enough data to suggest that a structured analogy approach would allow the organisation to assess the likely range of each new product demand both statistically and visually. The concept of using a range of data allows the organisation to manage accordingly; this is much better than employing elaborate sales and supply plans based on point forecasts that are likely to be wrong. The organisation can assess alternative demand scenarios and mitigate risk.

There are numerous software products available claiming to improve forecasting accuracy. In this chapter, we introduce some quantitative techniques to understand the data and to provide a basis for spending decisions related to marketing, supply, capacity, distribution, support, finance, and maintenance. We caution readers to approach forecasts vigilantly and to plan for a range of outcomes rather than placing too much confidence in the accuracy of their figures.

Modern software has the capability to analyse historical data and provide visualisation with remarkable speed and clarity; use it to illustrate the variability, the risks, and the uncertainties in product behaviour.

This is unconstrained demand forecasting at work!

Which all leads to the question, 'Is forecasting a waste of time?'

Introduction

The emphasis in this chapter is on demand management and demand forecasting. Operations and supply chain management personnel use forecasts to make decisions about process selection, capacity planning, facility layout, production planning, scheduling, and inventory. A perfect forecast is a practical impossibility and the way to live with forecast inaccuracy is to have flexible production and delivery systems. An effective forecasting process allows the organisation to plan for all eventualities, to assess the likelihood of meeting the forecast values, and to evaluate the risk to the organisation of not meeting them.

Forecasting is essential in operations and supply chain management.

The purpose of demand forecasting is to determine the level of future spending. It costs money to buy capacity, to occupy a facility, to buy raw materials and components, to train and educate employees, and to deliver products and services to customers.

Knowing the exact nature of future customer requirements allows us to supply that need comfortably. However, we very rarely know exactly what the customer wants and we try to compensate for that by second-guessing. This dilemma disappears somewhat when we change the supply pattern such that we are always able to supply with enough quantities within the customer tolerance time. With this scenario, the emphasis changes from predicting the future to supplying the need.

The actual sales amount obtained for any product or service is the result of a combination of factors, including market share, actions by the organisation itself, actions by competitors, actions by suppliers and distributors, and actions by government agencies, to name a few. The supply function determines demand satisfaction and the resulting sales are a direct result of the ability to supply.

Demand management

Demand

Demand is a need for a product or service. At the finished goods level demand may not equate to sales. Demand is what the customer wants, while sales represent the ability to deliver.

Demand management

Demand management is the function of recognising all demand for goods and services to support the marketplace. Proper demand management matches supply with demand over time.

Demand is the need for a product or service. When customers have a need for a product or service, they approach their supplier and demand enough quantity to satisfy their need. Organisations exist to satisfy demand. Production firms make tangible products for consumption by customers, and service firms deliver services for customers to experience. In some circumstances, organisations may wish to satisfy all demand; in other cases, they may find they do not have enough capacity to satisfy all demand; and in other cases, they may elect, for whatever reason, not to supply the full quantity demanded.

All organisations should understand the nature of demand and position themselves to satisfy all or some of that demand. Demand occurs at all stages in a supply chain and at all stages in a service chain. Manufacturers demand raw materials, component assemblers demand fabricated and component parts, wholesalers/distributors/retailers demand finished products, retail customers demand finished products, and all stages along the supply chain demand services. Demand is different from sales. Demand is what the customer wants while sales represents what the supplier can deliver. We should measure demand on a daily usage basis.

It is a strategic decision for organisations to decide how much demand they want to supply. Most organisations need to prepare in some way for future demand. When a production firm manufactures products and stores them in a warehouse, they are anticipating future demand. When a service organisation occupies a facility and employs staff members, they are anticipating and preparing for future demand.

An organisation can accept the demand for its products or services as a given factor without any attempt to change demand, or it can be proactive in changing the demand for its products by changing the price, applying managerial pressure on the sales force, altering incentives and commissions, advocating promotional campaigns, and using other methods to change customer behaviour.

Demand management strategies can influence the timing, quantity, and nature of demand to take advantage of excess or insufficient capacity and/or resources. Demand management coordinates the decision making associated with demand and the decision making associated with supply for the benefit of the entire organisation. Marketing, for example, should fully consider the ability to supply in the customer-required timeframes when implementing promotional activities.

Demand management can dynamically calculate an available-to-promise date so customer service representatives can promise delivery on a customer-required date rather than quote a blanket lead time. They calculate the promised delivery date based on current stock availability (or service capability), future stock receipts (or service availability), how much of the current and future stock (or service capability) has already been promised to other customers, and the expected time to process and deliver the customer order.

Forecast management

Forecast

A forecast is an estimate of future demand. Analysts develop forecasts using quantitative methods, qualitative methods, or a combination of both.

Forecasting

Forecasting is the business process that attempts to predict demand for products and services so enough capacity and resources are available to meet the need.

Effective demand management requires forecasting since future demand is uncertain and several factors can work to influence demand. Most organisations, whether they are primarily concerned with delivering a manufactured product or a service to customers, need some form of forecasting to have any success with demand management. Most organisations benefit from forecasting, as the information it provides helps the organisation prepare for the changes in demand that forecasting attempts to ascertain. Forecasting assists an organisation to match supply with demand. The decisive moment occurs when demand happens and on receipt of an actual customer order. This moment tests all the previous demand planning, and the supply chain passes that test if it can deliver on schedule.

Even though demand forecasting can provide planning benefits to the demand management function, forecasting is not the magic bullet that solves all demand management problems. Forecasting provides a prediction of expected future demand, and these predictions are heavily reliant on the quality of the data gathered, the type of forecasting model employed, the timeliness of the information, the planning horizon, the assumptions made, and the many other variables that can affect demand.

Historical demand forms the basis of quantitative forecasting techniques that assume that what has happened in the past will happen in the future. Changes to demand patterns can be very sudden and very dramatic, however. Likewise, information value may vary depending upon the allocation of product families or groups, segmentation of the target market, degree of forward ordering and on-demand ordering, and the ability of salespeople to convert prospect opportunities into real business opportunities. Organisations design processes to gather relevant data and to analyse and manipulate it into valuable information.

Frequent price changes weaken the effect of using the selling price as an indicator of changing demand. The price of retail petrol alters with regular monotony (usually trending upwards) almost to the point that the pricing forms distinct patterns. Before long weekends and holiday periods it seems that prices increase, and towards the end of the weekend or holiday period it seems that prices fall. Analysis should determine whether any change in demand is a result of the weekend or holiday period, or because of price changes.

Marketing functions target promotions at specific markets or customer segments and devise very sophisticated methods to induce customers to buy. Extended credit of up to 60 months, for example, on large household items brings forward the true demand. Instead of being a future demand, promotions such as these create a current demand. The value of any data gathered during such promotions must consider the focused promotion; the information might not apply to the entire market.

Product life cycles, especially for electronic products, are shortening, and a life cycle of three months is quite common. This does not mean the product lasts for three months; rather it means that production occurs during a three-month period before the next product supersedes it. This limits the availability and value of historic item sales data. When consolidated into product groups, it may begin to provide additional relevant value. Point-of-sale data and loyalty cards provide an increasingly detailed picture of market trends and individual behaviours.

Nearly every organisation relies on some form of forecast. Manufacturers use a future demand forecast to reserve enough raw materials and production capacity to make the required products. Service groups want to establish capacity and personnel requirements so they can satisfy customer demand.

Slightly different terminologies help to explain the nature of demand forecasting. Estimating future requirements would apply when the future is very subjective and rather uncertain. Predicting the future is an art, as well as a science. It does not really matter how specific organisations arrive at their forecast. What does matter, however, is exactly what the organisation does with the forecast. These predictions are useful for organisations before making decisions that may give them a competitive advantage in the marketplace.

Knowing demand is increasing or decreasing may not help if that is all you know. However, it does help to know the rate of change, especially when the organisation needs to change capacity to satisfy changing demand. A firm of professionals (consultants, accountants, lawyers) may be experiencing steady business growth and may need to plan for an additional partner to join the firm. This addition does not happen easily or quickly, so the firm needs to forecast the start of their recruitment search.

The real measure, or purpose, of forecasts in the long, medium, and short term is to determine the level of spending. It costs money to buy capacity, to occupy facilities, to obtain production capability, to purchase raw materials and components, to train and educate employees, to produce products and services, and to deliver products and services to customers. Figure 2.2 illustrates the forecasting model.

Long-term forecasts assist capacity planning, the sizing of required facilities, and determining their locations. Medium-term forecasting assists the sales and operations planning process, revenue management, and resource planning. Short-term forecasts assist the detailed planning and scheduling of equipment, personnel, materials, and inventory.

How well, or how poorly, the organisation can satisfy demand depends on how much money the organisation spends and when they spend it. If the organisation spends the right amount, it will satisfy demand at minimum cost. If the organisation spends too much, it may find it has some under-utilised resources. If the organisation spends too little, it may be unable to satisfy demand and may miss the opportunity for sales.

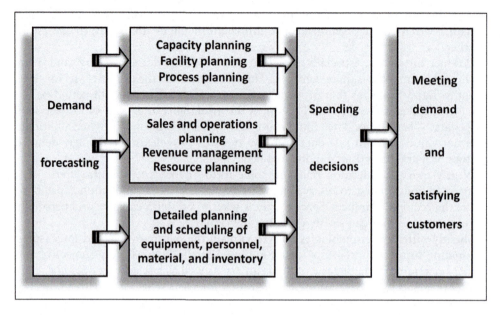

Figure 2.2 Strategic nature of forecasting customer demand

Forecasting horizons

Demand forecasting operates within three horizons – short range, medium range, and long range. As shown in Figure 2.3, the progression from long range to short range increases the level of detail required. Each horizon requires different planning decisions and possesses a different application and purpose for the firm.

Long-range forecasting

Long-range forecasting generally covers the period required to replace major resources. These forecasts are strategic in nature; they cover applications such as facility and capacity planning, technology and design planning, research and development, and process planning. This period is usually enough to acquire more strategic capacity and other resources. Therefore, for example, it covers the time to build and equip a new facility and to introduce a new product from concept to product launch.

Forecasting accumulates data into groups of similar products and indicates trends and resource imbalances. Therefore, a steel producer might forecast tonnes of output per year, an airline might forecast the number of passengers and tonnes of freight per route per month, and an electricity producer might forecast megawatt hours of electricity per month.

Long-range forecasting brackets the data into months, quarters, or even years. When planning the electricity requirements for a significant region you might examine closely the peak seasons for the next 10 or 20 years. Daily requirements are not

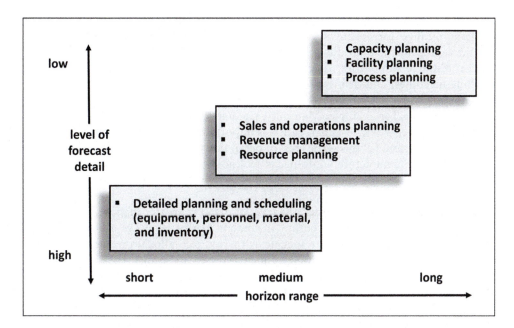

Figure 2.3 Forecasting horizons

important when planning 10 or 20 years ahead, but possible daily peak loads would be important. Long-range forecasting analysts do not consider the actual day the daily peak load will occur, but the year in which demand reaches the new peak level is important.

Long-range forecasting highlights changes to the trend line since this change has a significant bearing on resource availability and resource planning. The timing of the change is important and we call this the turning point – the point where the trend line changes direction, gradient, or slope.

The forecasts at this level of aggregation need to be in the 'ballpark'. In other words, accuracy is not relevant provided it is relatively close and clearly provides the trend data and required resource requirements.

Data with a relatively stable pattern forms the basis for most forecasts and analysts can develop a reasonably useful forecast based on that data. However, especially with long-range forecasting, the data may not be available or may be insufficient. In these cases, qualitative forecasting, as discussed later in this chapter, is a better option.

Medium-range forecasting

Medium-range forecasting uses sales and operations plans and can range from six months to a year or more depending on the organisation. With some labour-intensive service organisations, it may start at about three months. When capacity increments are difficult or expensive to obtain, the medium-term forecast may extend for several years. Applications include sales planning, analysing operations and supply chain plans, budgeting, revenue management, and staffing plans.

Medium-range forecasting models use some aggregation. Ideally, organisations should aggregate their products into between 6 and 12 groups based on transformation resource similarities. A white-goods manufacturer might place refrigerators, washing machines, and dishwashers into separate groups when separate production lines make each group of products. A hospital might group all patients into the type of care they receive, for example: Maternity, paediatric, psychiatric, elective surgery, or accident and emergency. The aggregation is important because (1) it is easier to gather the information, and (2) this is the level of detail that is relevant for that future period. A white-goods manufacturer only needs to know the total numbers of appliances planned for a timeframe that is 18 months to two years into the future. Short-range forecasts consider the mix of specific models.

With medium-range forecasting, the level of detail is greater than with long-range forecasting and the required accuracy is greater. At this level, we are dealing with more details and starting to get specific with resource allocation and scheduling. Revenue management, for example, endeavours to maximise the revenue from fixed-capacity resources. Hotels, airlines, and rental car companies use revenue management techniques since all these firms operate with limited fixed capacity. In the medium term, hotels and airlines cannot easily add capacity. Rental car companies may have some ability to add capacity in the medium term. Given these known and relatively fixed-capacity limits, these firms use a variety of tools to manage their anticipated revenues. A hotel may have some forward bookings for some guests, but largely plans on forecast numbers. They know the number of physical rooms they have available at their property and can match available capacity with actual and forecast reservations. Specific room allocation can come later. We discuss revenue management in Chapter 3.

The turning points, or significant changes in trend, assume only moderate importance at this level largely because an organisation planning in this period usually does not have the capability of adding additional capacity to meet any significant changes in demand. If planning works properly, the long-term plans highlight the anticipated change in demand. Medium-range demand planning needs to consider peak periods such as holidays, special events, and changes in shift capacity. Table 2.1 illustrates the various applications and data requirements for long-range, medium-range, and short-range forecasting.

Short-range forecasting

Short-range forecasting can range from the current to about six months, but can extend beyond. It usually involves detailed planning and scheduling for purchasing, job scheduling, and staffing rosters, as well as production allocations. Planners and operators working with short-range data do not notice any turning points since they endeavour to resolve only short-term demand and capacity issues. These are current and require immediate resolution. The planning process disaggregates product quantities so it can deal with specific combinations of products and services such as naming personnel for individual items at specific times on given days. The firm requires these very detailed allocations to make the firm's tactical decisions.

Table 2.1 Characteristics of long-range, medium-range, and short-range demand forecasting

Characteristic/range	Long range	Medium range	Short range
Applications	Business planning (type of hospital facilities)	Aggregate planning of sales and production	Short-term customer demand (peak periods)
	Capacity planning (size of call centre)	Revenue management for existing fixed capacity	Production schedules to meet demand fluctuations
	Capital investment planning (airliner purchase)	Volume demand by market segment (travel)	Employee schedules (shift rosters)
	Location feasibility (factory or restaurant location)	Seasonal levels of employment and inventory	
Detail	Broad, general	Some detail	Very detailed
Aggregation	High aggregation into product families	Some aggregation	Disaggregated by product, model, or style
Time frame	By month or quarter	By month	By week or day
Accuracy	'Ballpark'	Reasonable	High
Turning points	Important	Moderately important	Less important

Strategic role of forecasting

Forecasting demand for some products is more difficult than forecasting the demand for others. New products do not have established demand patterns; intangible forces, such as perceived desirability, influence fashion items, while commodity products sell on a regular basis. This, however, does not make forecasting any less worthwhile.

The major issue with evaluating demand, or even trying to evaluate demand, is that we never really know exactly what the customer really wants, and we rarely know if they receive that. However, if we make things more readily available within customer tolerance time (at any point along the supply chain) then does it matter? Demand driven techniques (discussed further in Chapter 8) emphasise strategic decoupling points based on factors like customer tolerance time. We ensure that these decoupling points never run out of stock. This approach dramatically changes the strategic view on forecasting; it shifts the emphasis from trying to guess what the customer wants to ensure that you have enough quantities always available at strategic points (decoupling points). When things are readily available, customers can buy what they want, and this provides a better picture of what the market is demanding given all the available choices. This information feeds back into the sensing and adapting aspects of demand driven systems.

Establishing the demand forecast for individual products that form a subset of a group of products is more difficult and less accurate than forecasting for the whole group. Aggregating or amalgamating several products together allows vicissitudes to balance out within the group. An aggregate forecast of a group of similar products is generally more accurate than individual forecasts of the individual products that make up that group.

Manufacturing firms forecast finished goods while they calculate the components of the finished goods. Finished goods exhibit independent demand while their components have dependent demand. They forecast independent demand and calculate dependent demand.

Forecasting is effective in helping with the demand management of an organisation, but forecasting is not a single tool to apply to all aspects of all operations to predict future demand. Many forecasting methods are applicable to the forecasting process. J. Scott Armstrong, in his book *Standards and Practices for Forecasting*, lists 139 principles for forecasting.[4] It is unnecessary to apply all the available forecasting tools, but each organisation will have some characteristics that are applicable to a forecasting method.

After the organisation agrees on the demand forecast, the forecast information transfers to the operations functions for planning, scheduling, and controlling activities. Figure 2.4 shows the operations and supply chain management view of forecasting to plan, schedule, and control operations.

One thing certain about forecasting is that it will be wrong. It may deviate from actual performance by only a small margin, but it will be different. This is enough to put some firms off the concept of forecasting. They wonder why they should put valuable resources into an activity that is always wrong.

The most recent data on demand and supply becomes the major input into the demand forecast for resources within the operations and supply chain functions. It

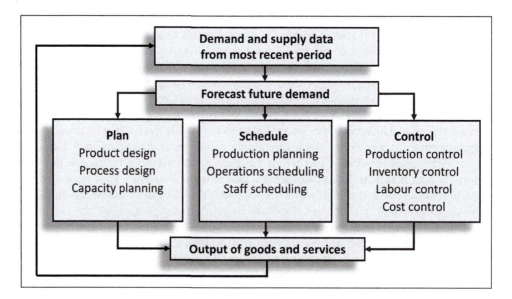

Figure 2.4 Operations and supply chain management view of forecasting to plan, schedule, and control operations

bases its ability to supply future demand partially on demonstrated capacity during the most recent period.

Planning activities correspond to long-range and medium-range forecasts and usually involve product design, process design, and resource capacity plans. These are relatively high-level activities designed to ensure supply is adequate to meet demand. Scheduling includes the allocation of specific jobs to specific machines at specific times, the allocation of specific employees to rosters, and the assignment of required tasks. Controlling activities ensure the planned activities complete satisfactorily and customers receive required products at required times. In other words, customers are happy.

Operations and supply chain functions compare the output of goods and services in this period with the planned output for this period and draw conclusions on performance measurements. The ability to supply, or not supply, a given demand pattern in this period may influence the forecast for demand and supply in the next period. Thus, it is a continuous cycle of assessing demand, ensuring supply resources are available, and checking that available supply can meet demand.

In a strategic sense, the organisation should understand the dynamics of the demand patterns and be prepared for whatever happens. Forecasting benefits times of uncertainty. Sudden demand changes occur because of external factors such as natural disasters, terrorist activities, weather patterns, major events, and accidents. Gradual changes may occur because of social, demographic, political, legal, and environmental change.

Organisations can expect some of these changes while the rest are unexpected. One could argue that organisations should expect the unexpected, and it is the magnitude and timing of the occurrence that is in doubt. Firms should prepare for whatever happens to their demand patterns. This does not mean that they should be able to react satisfactorily to all changes in demand. They may elect as a matter of policy not to service demand. They may have in their planning a statement suggesting that, should demand exceed a certain value, they will choose to reject it and not attempt to satisfy it. Organisations do not have to satisfy all demand. They might handle some deviation from expected demand but only up to a limit, beyond which the excess is unsatisfied.

In Chapters 3 and 8, we discuss the concept of forecasting a range of values (rather than one specific value) under the topic sales and operations planning. Organisations plan for an upper limit and a lower limit of values thus creating a range of expected values. Then they should plan for a variety of scenarios ranging from the upper limit to the lower limit. As future timeframes come closer to the current timeframe, the organisation may be able to narrow the range and inject more certainty into their calculations. Whatever the outcome, at least the organisation has considered expected responses to future demand.

Organisations spend money to prepare themselves for future demand. This spending may be on permanent fixtures, such as buildings and equipment, or it may be in hiring and training personnel, and it depends on a forecast of future requirements. Firms should consider the consequences of the forecast being too optimistic or too pessimistic. What would happen if the business did not achieve the forecast figures? Alternatively, what would happen if the business exceeded the forecast figures? What are the choices for action?

Several factors influence demand, such as changes in technology, competitor initiatives, or pricing levels. Forecasting helps firms to focus attention on the factors influencing demand and establish a relationship between those factors and actual demand.

Forecast deviation

Forecast deviation

Forecast deviation is the difference between actual and forecast demand.

Bias

Bias is a consistent deviation from the mean. It is the sum of the algebraic differences between actual demand and forecast demand divided by the sum of demand values.

Random variation

Random variation is a fluctuation in data caused by uncertain or random occurrences.

Organisations use the output of forecasting for spending decisions. It must be obvious that if the actual demand differs from the forecast values then spending will not be at the optimum level. A forecast deviation would suggest the firm is about to spend too much and have excess products and capacity available, or not spend enough and be unable to satisfy demand for its products and services.

Most organisations plan their supply chains assuming forecasts will happen. They start with this assumption and express regret, or blame market conditions, when they end up with product shortages or surpluses. Instead, they should start with a range representing the likely upper and lower bounds. Then, they should evaluate the demand and supply risk of those limits.

While it is not necessary (or even practical in all cases) for the forecast to be 100% accurate, the forecasting process would benefit if the organisation understood the reasons for the variation and if a learning process took place. This allows the forecasting process to improve and, in turn, allows the organisation to aim for the optimum spending of resources.

The following attributes cause forecast deviation:

- The forecasting model or method employed may not be suitable for the monitored demand.
- The data in the forecasting process may arrive too late to be of significant value.
- The data captured does not reflect true demand and/or it is being confused with sales data.
- The forecasting model uses inappropriate data. This attribute occurs when employees source the data for themselves and consolidate this data.
- The forecast uses past data that may not hold for future data points.

There are two types of forecast deviation – bias and random.

Bias deviations occur when making a consistent mistake, such as always too high or always too low. The causes of bias are:

- Failing to include the right variables.
- Using the wrong relationships among the variables.
- Employing the wrong trend line.
- Mistakenly shifting seasonal demand from where it normally occurs.
- Not recognising the existence of a trend.

There is no explanation for random deviations or 'noise'; they just happen.

Measuring forecast deviation

Mean absolute deviation (MAD)

The mean absolute deviation (MAD) is the mean of the absolute deviation between actual demand value and forecast value and is a measure of forecast accuracy.

Mean absolute percentage deviation (MAPD)

The mean absolute percentage deviation (MAPD) is the mean of the absolute deviation between actual demand value and forecast value divided by the mean of the demand values expressed as a percentage. This is like mean absolute deviation (MAD) but considers the significance by dividing by mean demand.

Mean absolute percentage variation (MAPV)

The mean absolute percentage variation (MAPV) is the mean of the absolute deviation between actual demand value and mean demand value divided by the mean demand expressed as a percentage. It is a measure of demand variation.

Various calculations measure forecast deviation. Most examine the difference between the actual demand and the forecast value. Some measures look at the algebraic difference, which offsets high forecast values against low forecast values. With algebraic calculations, it is possible to have wildly fluctuating forecast values and still conclude the forecast model is good. Other measures look at the absolute difference, which monitors the magnitude of the over or under forecast. It does not matter whether the forecast value is over or under – the measurement just examines the relative distance of the actual demand from the forecast value.

Both the algebraic deviation and the absolute deviation have little relevance when comparing forecast models unless the significance of the deviation relates to the actual observation quantity. A deviation of 50 when forecasting demand in hundreds is significantly different from a deviation of 50 when forecasting demand in millions.

Mean absolute deviation (MAD)

The mean absolute deviation (MAD) measures the absolute dispersion of the deviation. The formula for mean absolute deviation (MAD) is:

$$MAD = \frac{\sum |D - F|}{n} \qquad (2.1)$$

where D = the demand value for each period
F = the forecast value for each period
n = the number of period or observations

The mean absolute deviation is the mean of the sum of the absolute differences between the actual demand values and the forecast values. An absolute value does not have any sign. If the difference is negative, it is just a number; similarly, if it is positive, it is still just a number. The mean absolute deviation measures the average distance of demand values from forecast values.

Worked example 2.1

Use the data in Table 2.2 to calculate MAD for the period January to October.
Calculate the absolute deviation between demand values and forecast values for each month. Add them up and find the mean (average) value. This is the mean absolute deviation (MAD). Using equation (2.1):

$$MAD = \frac{\sum |D - F|}{n}$$
$$= \frac{450}{10}$$
$$= 45$$

Thus, the actual demand is, on average, 45 units from the forecast value.

Bias

Bias indicates whether a method of forecasting tends to favour a higher or lower value. The formula for bias is:

$$bias = \frac{\sum (D - F) \times 100}{\sum D} \qquad (2.2)$$

where D = the demand value for each period
F = the forecast value for each period

Bias is the sum of the algebraic differences between the actual demand values and the forecast values divided by the sum of the demand values. Thus, the pluses may

Table 2.2 Demand, forecast, algebraic deviation, and absolute deviation data for worked examples 2.1 and 2.2

Month	Demand	Forecast	Deviation	Absolute deviation
	D	F	(D – F)	|D – F|
Jan	500	550	−50	50
Feb	550	600	−50	50
Mar	420	490	−70	70
Apr	500	530	−30	30
May	610	530	80	80
Jun	600	550	50	50
Jul	680	610	70	70
Aug	670	670	0	0
Sep	720	690	30	30
Oct	750	730	20	20
Sum	6000	5950	50	450
Ave	600	595	5	45

offset the minuses. It is a useful measure especially when expressed as a percentage of actual demand.

Worked example 2.2

Use the data in Table 2.2 to calculate bias.

Bias calculates the algebraic difference between demand value and forecast value for each period. To make sure the algebraic sign is correct, ensure you subtract forecast from demand. This is easy to remember because D comes before F in the alphabet. The calculation is the sum of the algebraic differences divided by the sum of the demand values and expressed as a percentage. Using equation (2.2):

$$\text{bias} = \frac{\sum(D - F) \times 100}{\sum D}$$
$$= \frac{(6000 - 5950) \times 100}{6000}$$
$$= 0.833\%$$

Thus, the forecasting model has a bias in favour of demand of 0.833%.

Mean absolute percentage deviation (MAPD)

Mean absolute percentage deviation (MAPD) is the mean of the absolute deviation between actual demand value and forecast value divided by the mean of the demand values expressed as a percentage. This is like mean absolute deviation (MAD) but considers the significance by dividing by mean demand. The formula for mean absolute percentage deviation (MAPD) is:

$$MAPD = \frac{\sum|D-F| \times 100}{\sum D} \tag{2.3}$$

where D = the demand value for each period
$\quad\ F$ = the forecast value for each period

The MAPD describes a mean value, but the formula does not divide by the number of observations. This is simply because n, the number of observations, is the divisor for both numerator and denominator and cancels itself out. The formula could be the mean absolute deviation divided by the mean demand.

Mean absolute percentage variation (MAPV)

Mean absolute percentage variation (MAPV) is the average of the absolute deviation between actual demand value and mean demand value divided by the mean demand expressed as a percentage. The formula for mean absolute percentage variation (MAPV) is:

$$MAPV = \frac{\sum\left|D - \dfrac{\sum D}{n}\right| \times 100}{\sum D} \tag{2.4}$$

where D = the demand value for each period
$\quad\ n$ = the number of periods or observations

The MAPV describes a mean value, but the formula in total does not divide by n, the number of observations. This is simply because n, the number of observations, is the divisor for both numerator and denominator and cancels itself out. MAPV measures the variability in the demand.

Mean absolute percentage deviation (MAPV), on its own, is not strictly a forecasting measure. The usefulness of MAPV comes when comparing the forecast deviation with the volatility of the actual demand. A dynamic demand pattern is considerably more difficult to forecast than a stable (commodity) demand pattern.

Worked example 2.3

Use the data in Table 2.3 to calculate MAPD and MAPV for the period January to October.

MAPD is the mean of the absolute deviation between actual demand value and forecast value divided by the mean of the demand values expressed as a percentage. In this formula description, both numerator and denominator calculate average values

Table 2.3 Demand and forecast data showing absolute deviation and absolute variation in worked example 2.3

Month	Demand	Forecast	Absolute deviation	Average demand	Absolute variance
	D	F	$\lvert D - F \rvert$	$\dfrac{\sum D}{n}$	$\left\lvert D - \dfrac{\sum D}{n} \right\rvert$
Jan	500	550	50	600	100
Feb	550	600	50	600	50
Mar	420	490	70	600	180
Apr	500	530	30	600	100
May	610	530	80	600	10
Jun	600	550	50	600	0
Jul	680	610	70	600	80
Aug	670	670	0	600	70
Sep	720	690	30	600	120
Oct	750	730	20	600	150
Sum	6000	5950	450		860
Average	600	595	45		86

using the number of observations. In the formula, the number of observations, n, cancels each other out. Using equation (2.3):

$$MAPD = \frac{\sum \lvert D - F \rvert \times 100}{\sum D}$$
$$= \frac{450 \times 100}{6000}$$
$$= 7.5\%$$

Mean absolute percentage variation (MAPV) is the average of the absolute deviation between actual demand value and mean demand value divided by the mean demand expressed as a percentage. Using equation (2.4):

$$MAPV = \frac{\sum \left\lvert D - \dfrac{\sum D}{n} \right\rvert \times 100}{\sum D}$$
$$= \frac{860 \times 100}{6000}$$
$$= 14.33\%$$

Thus, the mean absolute percentage deviation (MAPD) is 7.5% of the mean demand and the variability of demand (MAPV) is 14.33%.

Forecast value added

Forecast value added (FVA)

The forecast value added (FVA) is the change in forecast accuracy due to an activity in the forecasting process. FVA compares the forecast accuracy after a process activity with the probable accuracy obtained without performing that activity. If the forecasting performance improves, the activity is adding value to the forecasting process. If the forecasting performance does not improve, the activity is not adding value to the forecasting process. FVA retains activities adding value and discards activities not adding value. When this measure applies to each step and to everyone in a forecasting process, it becomes possible to identify the non-value-adding activities and improve the overall process.

Most firms measure the performance of a forecasting system using some form of accuracy measurement. They seek to find the accuracy of the forecast calculations. Some firms use expensive forecasting software packages to manipulate historical data to derive their forecasts and then to analyse how well they are going. They typically use measures such as mean absolute percentage deviation (MAPD), mean absolute deviation (MAD), and bias.

MAPD is not a good measure when compared across different product ranges and different markets. It only tells the percentage variation. One would expect MAPD to be very low, say less than four percent, if in an established market, customers order products in regular patterns, and those products demonstrate stable, predictable demand. However, in a developing market, where the firm is endeavouring to become established and is experiencing high volatility of demand and that demand is in some way dependent on daily weather patterns, one would expect the MAPD to be high, say 40%. Now, when comparing the two forecasting systems, one might conclude that the model with the lower MAPD is better. However, is it the better one? It could be four percent represents a significant improvement opportunity, and 40% is exceptionally good given the circumstances.

MAPD is fine when used with various models across one demand stream. It is not appropriate when used across different demand streams. MAPD (in isolation) does not consider volatility of demand and does not give any indication of what the deviation should have been. Forecasting is about understanding variation.[5]

Mean absolute percentage deviation (MAPD), mean absolute deviation (MAD), and bias do not tell what the forecast should have been. They report past performance but do not attempt to assist the forecasting process to perform a better job.

Mean absolute percentage variation (MAPV) is not suitable as a forecasting model on its own. Its main purpose is to evaluate forecast deviations and to help understand the variability of actual demand.

The forecasting process should be attempting to improve itself. In other words, the process of arriving at a forecast requires constant evaluation and possible improvement. Given the existing hierarchy and the prevailing politics, most firms have individuals who can manipulate the forecast to suit their own needs without much ownership or responsibility for the result.

Some examples are:

- Sales representatives may underestimate sales potential since they want to protect their commission base.
- Marketing executives may overestimate the potential for new products and new markets since they are endeavouring to protect their position in the firm.
- Financial executives may downplay the expense required in mounting new campaigns and may play a conservative role in forecasting.
- Executive management may have revenue targets to meet and these revenue targets become the forecast.
- Managers, measured on their ability to achieve budget, ensure the forecast at least meets budget but does not exceed it.
- Production management may favour long runs of products they know they can supply and discourage production of products they have difficulty delivering.

To overcome these obvious bias steps in the forecasting process, organisations need some measures to tell them which parts of the process add value to the result.

Forecast value added (FVA) allows firms to evaluate the process and continually improve it. Dr Larry Lapide suggested it in an article entitled 'Forecasting is about understanding variations', published in the *Journal of Business Forecasting*.[6] Michael Gilliland has further advanced the concept.[7]

The forecasting process should start with demand history, which is usually quite difficult to obtain since most organisations have sales history but not demand history. The difference appears in the detail of quantities, products, and timings. Customers demand products in certain quantities and at certain times, and the organisation supplies quantities of products at certain times. Demand may not equal supply, but the firm measures supply; supply represents the firm's ability to deliver.

Causal data may have a known effect on demand, and it supplements and provides leading indicators for forecasts. Activities such as school holidays, sporting events, and religious festivals, which do not appear on the same dates each year, may affect demand periods for some products and services.

Various functions and individuals in the organisation representing sales, marketing, product development, finance, production, and anyone else who can make a meaningful contribution to the forecast output receive the quantitative forecast and prepare qualitative inputs to the forecasting process. Additionally, executive management would almost certainly want to have some inputs.

This is where the forecast value added analysis becomes effective. The organisation notes all inputs supplied by these functions and individuals and develops a consensus forecast.

Power, influence, hierarchy, knowledge, lack of knowledge, history, experience, and politics all play their part in developing the consensus forecast. Often, in power politics, the chief executive has the strongest voice, since few employees reporting below the chief executive stand up and argue strongly against the chief executive. Yet, it could conceivably be that the inputs from the chief executive are making the forecast worse.

Forecast value added compares the consensus forecast with the actual observations when they are available. Ideally, the consensus forecast should mirror the actual

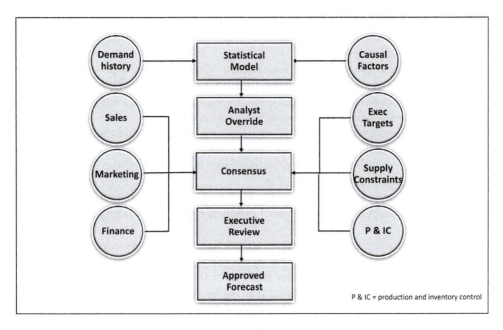

Figure 2.5 Forecast value added process, adapted from Gilliland, M. (2015). *Forecast value added analysis: Step by step.* Cary, NC: SAS Institute Inc.

observations. If it does not, and this is the usually expected outcome, then forecast value added examines each of the inputs to the consensus process to see the effect each input had in modifying the statistical forecast. In other words, forecast value added notes each modification to the quantitative forecast and analyses it to see if it added value to the forecast, or made it worse.

As shown in Figure 2.5, the forecasting process uses forecast value added to find all aspects of the consensus. The process promotes positive aspects and demotes negative aspects, resulting in a continuously improving process of forecasting.

If, for example, the marketing function can exert pressure and contribute positively to the consensus, then marketing will assume a stronger position in the next consensus round. If a function, or an individual, contributed to the consensus and made it worse, their inputs assume a weaker position in the future. Future consensus rounds may ignore their inputs altogether.

Quantitative forecasting

Quantitative forecasting

Quantitative forecasting assumes that the history of past data about the item can predict the future in some way. Quantitative techniques include time series models such as simple moving average, weighted moving average, exponential smoothing, decomposition of a time series, and regression analysis.

Trend component

Trend is a component of demand showing an increase or decrease of demand over time.

Seasonal component

Seasonal is a component of demand describing the variation that occurs because of the time of year, month, or week. A seasonal component generally repeats itself at least once a year, whereas a cyclical component usually takes longer than one year.

Cyclical component

Cyclical is a component of demand that occurs in a cycle greater than one year. Examples of cycles include economic, political, and/or business cycles.

Random component

Random is a component with no predictable pattern. For example, demand data may vary around a forecast value without any cause and with no specific pattern forming.

The observed demand for a product has four components – trend, seasonal, cyclical, and random.

Organisations usually identify the trend component as part of total demand. Firms might observe, for example, that sales have increased five percent this year compared to last year. Thus, the demand is increasing at about five percent per year. Trends do not have to be always positive and can be decreasing.

A common observation is the seasonal component. For example, firms report using 'seasonally-adjusted figures' to try to compare sales in January and July. In temperate regions the four calendar-based seasons – summer, autumn, winter, and spring – are the most widely recognised seasons. Tropical regions have two or three seasons – rainy/wet/monsoon, dry, and in some areas a cool or mild season. Sometimes loosely defined special seasons exist, such as a hurricane season, a tornado season, or a bush-fire season.

However, seasonal influences can occur monthly. Examples include the end-of-month practice of bringing revenue forward and/or delaying expense to enhance financial reporting, or holding back orders waiting for the start of the new month to take advantage of trading terms. The pattern observed is a lull at the end of the month and a surge at the start of the month. Seasons occur weekly in restaurant, hotel, and entertainment industries when they experience increased patronage towards the end of a week and during weekends.

Cyclical elements take more than 12 months to complete a full cycle. Political cycles taking three, four, or five years to complete are cyclical.

Removing the known factors (trend, seasonal, cyclical) from total demand leaves the remainder, which is unexplained and attributed to natural chance randomness.

Figure 2.6 illustrates the components of demand with each component shown separately.

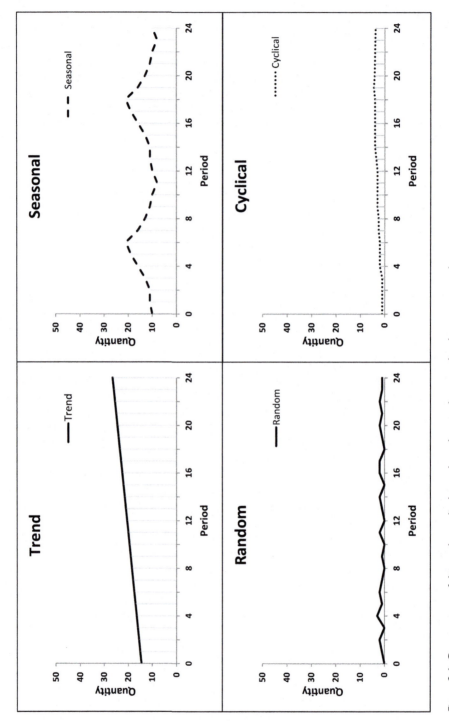

Figure 2.6 Components of demand – cyclical, trend, random, and seasonal – shown separately

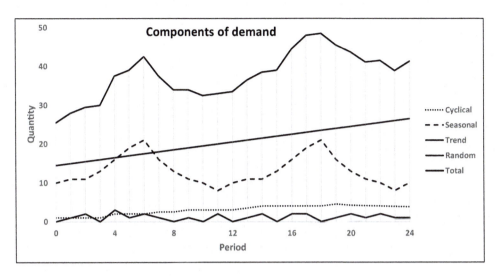

Figure 2.7 Components of demand – composite picture including total demand

Figure 2.7 illustrates the components of demand as a composite and the sum of the components equals total demand. Organisations observe and record total demand.

Quantitative forecasting methods

Quantitative forecasting assumes the history of past data can predict the future in some way, and advanced techniques include decomposition of a time series and regression analysis. If an organisation knows that repetition of the demand patterns will not occur, it should change the historical data in the forecasting calculations. An example of this non-repetition of demand would result from the inability of a supplier to deliver raw materials, which subsequently causes no sales of finished products. In this example, demand is occurring but the sales are not, and most firms record sales. Other examples include changes in legislation and known changes in the environment.

Firms often struggle with this concept of changing the actual data to reach a better forecast. They argue that the past data is history, and history is the basis of the forecast. It does not matter what data the firm uses to develop the forecast. What does matter is that the firm improves the forecasting process and derives a better result.

Regression analysis

Regression analysis

Regression analysis is a statistical technique for determining the best mathematical expression describing the functional relationship between one response and one or more independent variables.

Regression analysis enables us to determine the relationship between a variable of interest, called a dependent variable, and one or more independent variables. The equation describes a straight line, or linear function, and takes the form $\hat{y} = a + bx$.

$\hat{y}$ is the best estimate of $y = a + bx$

$$b = \frac{n\sum(xy) - (\sum x \sum y)}{n\sum x^2 - (\sum x)^2}$$

$$a = \frac{\sum y}{n} - b\frac{\sum x}{n}$$

(2.5)

where y = the dependent variable
       x = the independent variable
       a = a constant where the equation line cuts the y-axis
       b = a constant giving the gradient, or slope, of the equation line

Simple linear regression provides a mathematical way of estimating a and b. Analysts call the values of a and b the alpha and the beta. Simple linear regression defines the trend line by determining the values of a and b from the past data such that the sum of squares of the vertical differences between actual values (y) and values obtained from the line ($\hat{y}$) is a minimum.

In demand forecasting, linear regression derives a trend line by fitting a straight line through the time series demand data, with time on the x-axis and demand on the y-axis.

Worked example 2.4

Given the six months sales data in Table 2.4, develop a trend line using least squares regression analysis. Use the trend line to forecast the next three months.

The supplied data shows demand for six months. The x-axis is for the independent variable and is the monthly demand. The months on the x-axis are numbered 1 through 6. The y-axis is for the dependent variable and this is the observed demand. To calculate a, b, and the trend line, we need the values for xy and x^2 as shown in Table 2.5.

Table 2.4 Six months of sales data for worked example 2.4

Month	Demand
January	115
February	123
March	132
April	130
May	140
June	150

Table 2.5 Six months of sales data and calculation results for worked example 2.4

Month	Demand	x	y	xy	x^2
January	115	1	115	115	1
February	123	2	123	246	4
March	132	3	132	396	9
April	130	4	130	520	16
May	140	5	140	700	25
June	150	6	150	900	36
Sum		21	790	2877	91
Average		3.5	131.67		

Table 2.6 Forecast calculation results for worked example 2.4

Month	x	intercept	6.4x	$\hat{y}=109.27+6.4x$	Forecast
July	7	109.27	44.8	154.07	154
August	8	109.27	51.2	160.47	160
September	9	109.27	57.6	166.87	167

In this example, $n = 6$, $\sum(xy) = 2877$, $\sum x = 21$, $\sum y = 790$, $\sum x^2 = 91$. Using equation (2.5):

$\hat{y}$ is the best estimate of $y = a + bx$

$$b = \frac{n\sum(xy) - (\sum x \sum y)}{n\sum x^2 - (\sum x)^2}$$

$$= \frac{6 \times 2877 - 21 \times 790}{6 \times 91 - 21^2}$$

$$= 6.4$$

$$a = \frac{\sum y}{n} - b\frac{\sum x}{n}$$

$$= 131.67 - 6.4 \times 3.5$$

$$= 109.27$$

therefore $\hat{y} = 109.27 + 6.4x$

Substituting $x=7$, $x=8$, and $x=9$ into the trend line equation provides the forecast values as shown in Table 2.6.

We can automate the calculation using Microsoft Excel®. The software requires the data analysis add-in and we initiate the calculation using the 'Data' menu, followed by 'Data Analysis', and then 'Regression'. For the 'Input Y Range' select the column of y-values and for the 'Input X Range' select the column of x-values. The output report contains more data than is immediately required and we highlight the pertinent values in Table 2.7.

Table 2.7 Microsoft Excel® summary output report for worked example 2.4

SUMMARY OUTPUT

Regression Statistics

Multiple R	0.970312388
R Square	0.94150613
Adjusted R Square	0.926882662
Standard Error	3.336665002
Observations	6

ANOVA

	df	SS	MS	F	Significance F
Regression	1	716.8	716.8	64.38323353	0.001308949
Residual	4	44.53333333	11.13333333		
Total	5	761.3333333			

	Coefficients	Standard Error	t Stat	P-value	Lower 95%	Upper 95%	Lower 95.0%	Upper 95.0%
Intercept	109.26667	3.10627	35.17621	0.00000	100.64229	117.89104	100.64229	117.89104
X Variable 1	6.4	0.79762	8.02392	0.00131	4.18546	8.61454	4.18546	8.61454

Decomposition of a time series

Decomposition

Decomposition is a method of forecasting where the time series data splits into components of demand (trend, seasonal, and cyclical). Trend measures the general upwards or downwards direction, seasonal indicates the effect of different seasons, and cyclical shows the effect of a longer repeating non-seasonal period cycle. Forecasting projects each separate component into the future, and the sum of the projections becomes the new forecast.

Seasonal index

Seasonal index is a number used to adjust data to seasonal demand.

All the components of demand may be present when one observes actual demand. Actual demand, therefore, is a composite of all the components. Decomposition of a time series allows for the identification and separation of its components. Any forecasting methodology, qualitative or quantitative, projects these components into the future and adds them together to form the composite forecast. This method isolates some of the variables existing in the composite picture and allows the use of linear regression as a forecasting methodology on the trend component.

The model followed in this chapter identifies and separates the time series data into seasonal and trend components. When using an additive seasonal variation, the seasonal amount is a constant and does not depend on trend. In multiplicative seasonal variation, the calculation multiplies the trend amount by the seasonal index. The calculation to develop the deseasonalised time-series demand data divides the seasonal index into the observed demand data. This is the demand that would have occurred had there been no season.

To calculate the seasonal index for each season, divide the average of all the demands for that season by the average demand for all seasons. The formula to calculate the seasonal index is:

$$\text{seasonal index for a given season} = \frac{\text{average demand for the given season}}{\text{average demand for all seasons}} \quad (2.6)$$

To calculate the deseasonalised demand, divide the observed demand for the given season by the seasonal index for the given season. The formula for deseasonalised demand is:

$$\frac{\text{deseasonalised demand}}{\text{for a given season}} = \frac{\text{observed demand for the given season}}{\text{seasonal index for the given season}} \quad (2.7)$$

Worked example 2.5

Using the observed demand data for two years shown in Table 2.8, perform a regression analysis on deseasonalised demand to forecast demand for the winter season in year three.

Table 2.8 Demand data for worked example 2.5

Year	Season	Observed demand
1	autumn	205
	winter	140
	spring	375
	summer	570
2	autumn	475
	winter	270
	spring	685
	summer	960
Sum of demand		**3680**
Average demand		**460**

Start by calculating the seasonal indices for autumn, winter, spring, and summer.

The seasonal average demand for autumn is $(205 + 475) / 2 = 340$.
The seasonal average demand for winter is $(140 + 270) / 2 = 205$.
The seasonal average demand for spring is $(375 + 685) / 2 = 530$.
The seasonal average demand for summer is $(570 + 960) / 2 = 765$.
The average demand for all seasons is $3680 / 8 = 460$.

Using equation (2.6):

$$\text{seasonal index for a given season} = \frac{\text{average demand for the given season}}{\text{average demand for all seasons}}$$

$$
\begin{aligned}
\text{seasonal index for autumn} &= \frac{\text{average demand for autumn}}{\text{average demand for all seasons}} \\
&= \frac{340}{460} \\
&= 0.7391
\end{aligned}
$$

$$
\begin{aligned}
\text{seasonal index for winter} &= \frac{205}{460} \\
&= 0.445
\end{aligned}
$$

$$
\begin{aligned}
\text{seasonal index for spring} &= \frac{530}{460} \\
&= 1.1522
\end{aligned}
$$

$$
\begin{aligned}
\text{seasonal index for summer} &= \frac{765}{460} \\
&= 1.6630
\end{aligned}
$$

Table 2.9 Deseasonalised demand data and the extended fields for worked example 2.5

Year	Season	Observed demand	x	Seasonal index	Deseasonalised demand y	xy	x^2
1	autumn	205	1	0.7391	277.3644	277.3644	1
	winter	140	2	0.4457	314.1126	628.2252	4
	spring	375	3	1.1522	325.4643	976.3929	9
	summer	570	4	1.6630	342.7541	1371.0164	16
2	autumn	475	5	0.7391	642.6735	3213.3675	25
	winter	270	6	0.4457	605.7886	3634.7316	36
	spring	685	7	1.1522	594.5148	4161.6036	49
	summer	960	8	1.6630	577.2700	4618.1600	64
		3680	36	8	3679.9423	18880.8616	204

Calculate the deseasonalised demand for each season by dividing the observed demand by the seasonal index for that season as shown in Table 2.9. Then calculate the extended fields for xy and x^2 as shown in Table 2.9.

Now calculate b, a, and the best estimate of $\hat{y} = a + bx$.

Using equation (2.5):

In this example $n = 8$, $\sum(xy) = 18880.8616$, $\sum x = 36$, $\sum y = 3679.9423$, $\sum x^2 = 204$.

$\hat{y}$ is the best estimate of $y = a + bx$

$$b = \frac{n\sum(xy) - (\sum x \sum y)}{n\sum x^2 - (\sum x)^2}$$

$$= \frac{8 \times 18880.8616 - 36 \times 3679.9423}{8 \times 204 - 36 \times 36}$$

$$= 55.2648$$

$$a = \frac{\sum y}{n} - b\frac{\sum x}{n}$$

$$= 460 - 55.2648 \times 4.5$$

$$= 211.3084$$

therefore the trend line equation $\hat{y} = 211.3084 + 55.2648x$

Thus, the trend line for deseasonalised data is $\hat{y} = a + bx = 211.3084 + 55.2648x$.

Now substitute $x = 10$ corresponding to winter in the third year to get the deseasonalised value for that period.

when $x = 10$, the deseasonalised value for winter in the third year is

$$\hat{y} = 211.3084 + 55.2648x$$

$$= 211.3084 + 55.2648 \times 10$$

$$= 763.956$$

We can automate the calculation using Microsoft Excel®. The software requires the data analysis add-in and we initiate the calculation using the 'Data' menu, followed by 'Data Analysis', and then 'Regression'. For the 'Input Y Range', select the column of y-values and, for the 'Input X Range', select the column of x-values. The output report contains more data than is immediately required, and we highlight the pertinent values in Table 2.10. The Microsoft Excel® values differ slightly from our calculated values due to rounding; the difference is immaterial.

The deseasonalised forecast for winter in the third year is 763.956.

Now multiply the deseasonalised forecast (for winter in the third year) by the seasonal index (for winter in the third year) to calculate the seasonalised forecast for winter in the third year ($x = 10$).

Using equation (2.7):

$$\text{deseasonalised demand for a given season} = \frac{\text{observed demand for the given season}}{\text{seasonal index for the given season}}$$

$$763.956 \times 0.4457 = 340.4952$$
$$= 340 (0 \text{ dp})$$

Table 2.11 illustrates the seasonalised forecast for years 1, 2, and 3 for worked example 2.5. The question only wanted the value for winter in the third year but Table 2.11 shows all periods.

Figure 2.8 illustrates the seasonalised forecast for years 1, 2, and 3 for worked example 2.5.

Performance measurement aka forecast accuracy

Many organisations spend vast resources on attempting to improve the accuracy of their forecasts. This sounds great in theory but it requires a constructive understanding of the whole process. Using elaborate and overly complex processes often complicates the output. Earlier we discussed forecast value added which evaluates the inputs from each participant and measures the effect of each input – either positive or negative. Many firms place too much reliance on their historical data and they choose a forecasting model that matches (fits) history. This is not the objective; the objective is to forecast the future and not just to find a model that matches historical data. Other firms expect unreasonable forecast accuracy. Forecasting the outcome of a coin toss, for example, should not exceed 50%. Any more is inappropriate in the long term. Probably the main influence on forecast accuracy (or inaccuracy) is the introduction of volatility into business processes. End of month, end of quarter, and end of year sales promotions distort true demand and introduce demand volatility. Customers know that these promotions might happen so they hold back, or bring forward, the ordering processes to capitalise on the lucrative gains on offer.

Measuring medium-range and long-range forecast accuracy at the item level is pointless and unnecessary. The period required for medium-range and long-range forecasting usually exceeds the lead time on individual items. Forecast accuracy at the group (or family) level does have merit, however. The measurement system should track the forecast for each group of products and services from the long range to the medium

Table 2.10 Microsoft Excel® summary output report for worked example 2.5

SUMMARY OUTPUT

Regression Statistics

Multiple R	0.861203267
R Square	0.741671067
Adjusted R Square	0.698616245
Standard Error	86.29356541
Observations	8

ANOVA

	Df	SS	MS	F	Significance F
Regression	1	128276.2823	128276.2823	17.22620211	0.006008098
Residual	6	44679.47659	7446.579431		
Total	7	172955.7589			

	Coefficients	Standard Error	t Stat	P-value	Lower 95%	Upper 95%	Lower 95.0%	Upper 95.0%
Intercept	**211.30123**	67.23940	3.14252	0.02000	46.77233	375.83012	46.77233	375.83012
X Variable 1	**55.26479**	13.31539	4.15045	0.00601	22.68322	87.84637	22.68322	87.84637

Table 2.11 Seasonalised forecast for years 1, 2, and 3 for worked example 2.5

Year	Season	Observed demand	x	Deseasonalised trend line y	Seasonal index	Seasonalised forecast
year 1	autumn	205	1	266.566	0.7391	197
	winter	140	2	321.831	0.4457	143
	spring	375	3	377.096	1.1522	434
	summer	570	4	432.360	1.6630	719
year 2	autumn	475	5	487.625	0.7391	360
	winter	270	6	542.890	0.4457	242
	spring	685	7	598.155	1.1522	689
	summer	960	8	653.420	1.6630	1087
year 3	autumn		9	708.684	0.7391	524
	winter		**10**	**763.949**	**0.4457**	**340**
	spring		11	819.214	1.1522	944
	summer		12	874.479	1.6630	1454

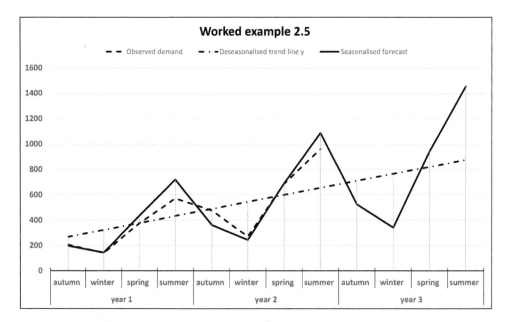

Figure 2.8 Seasonalised forecast for years 1, 2, and 3 for worked example 2.5

range with each alteration noted. At the transition period from medium range to short range, the organisation orders the specific configurations of each item and notes the group forecast. From the transition period, right through to product and service delivery, the forecast quantities may change. However, as the period approaches the current period, it becomes more difficult and expensive to deliver the change. The measurement system compares the quantity supplied with the transition quantity at the group level for accuracy and allows a tolerance percentage for each group.

Mean absolute percentage deviation (MAPD) and mean absolute percentage variation (MAPV) were two forecast deviation calculations discussed earlier. The forecast accuracy cannot get better when MAPD is less than MAPV.

Qualitative forecasting

Qualitative forecasting

Qualitative forecasting is subjective or judgmental. It uses judgements about the causal factors that underlie the sales of products and services and estimates the likelihood of those causal factors being present in the future. Examples include executive committee consensus, Delphi method, survey of sales force, survey of customers, historical analogy, and market research.

Delphi method

The Delphi method is a qualitative forecasting method that uses a group of experts to arrive at a consensus about the future.

Business managers sometimes use qualitative methods based on opinions, experience, and even best guesses. These methods apply when historical data is not available (such as launching a new product in a new market) or when the available data is not appropriate. Consider, for example, predicting the outcome of a sporting event at a neutral venue, when the organisers have limited comparative team data, the two teams have not met previously, and both teams have some injured players. There are just too many options to consider, but this does not stop sports fans from both sides being passionate about their view of the outcome.

Delphi method attempts to arrive at a consensus view of an issue or problem by sending questionnaires to a group of experts on the topic. The chosen problem would usually be something that would be hard to define and could generate widely differing views. The answers are usually based on value judgements rather than factual assessment. As an example, a Delphi method analysis is applicable when evaluating the effects that information and communications technology would have on business performance over the next 20 years.

The Delphi method is dialectic since it starts with a thesis, by stating an opinion or a view on a problem, then it develops a conflicting opinion or an antithesis and finally arrives at a consensus view called a synthesis. The participants are not aware of the other panel members, and each member makes their own response to each question without any contact with the others. Thus, each member is anonymous to everyone except the moderator who creates the questions, distributes them, and processes the questionnaires when returned.

After the first round of questions, the moderator collates the answers. On topics where a convergence is developing, the moderator will report to the members and may tend to close that thread of the discussion. When the participants express a divergence of opinion, the moderator prepares a report of the findings and adds additional questions in an endeavour to develop consensus. The moderator sends this report and additional questions to the panel for further feedback. The moderator repeats the process three or four times. The strength of this method is the anonymity and the feedback mechanisms.

When people gather in person to discuss any topic, it is quite common for the group to follow the leader, to follow the views of a persuasive individual, or to suppress ideas. Delphi method allows the free interchange of ideas without the peer pressure experienced when participants are all present in the same room.

Executive committee consensus is a result of executives agreeing on a possible outcome.

Survey of sales force, or grassroots analysis, is a consensus of employees who have the closest contact with customers.

A survey of customers establishes what customers are likely to order, and this translates into likely demand.

Historical analogy describes when a similar event occurs and assumes that the future will produce similar results. When colour television sets were about to supersede black-and-white television sets, the sales of black-and-white sets slowed for several months and suddenly disappeared from retail stores. Astute traders observed the same behaviour when high-definition digital products were about to supersede analogue colour sets. The behaviour was analogous to the earlier black-and-white supersession. The analogy extends to quantum-dot light emitting diode (QLED) television sets.

Research companies use market research for new products and for changing market perceptions. Most people are familiar with market research methods.

Other approaches to forecasting[8]

Modern technology allows firms to improve their internal and external processes, to change behaviours and subsequently arrive at a better forecast of future demand. Most forecasting systems accept the customer demand as given when it is quite feasible for firms to be proactive and influence demand.

Four very effective alternative approaches to forecasting are:

- Customer collaboration.
- Supply chain engineering.
- Demand smoothing.
- Proactive collaboration.

Customer collaboration allows suppliers and customers to work together and share information relating to demand. If a customer plans to increase demand for a short period by promoting and advertising a product, then it would make sense to have enough supply arrangements in place before the demand increases.

Supply chain engineering uses standard operations management techniques to improve the effectiveness of the supply chain. Techniques such as building flexibility into processes, shortening set-up times, minimising lead time, minimising or eliminating safety stock, using pull replenishment systems, and postponement tend to reduce the reliance on forecasts by shortening the forecast horizon.

Demand smoothing is a proactive approach that recognises the volatility of inherent demand caused by normal consumption of the product or service and the artificial volatility created by the organisation's own policies and procedures. End-of-period push, sales contests, trade promotions, channel-stuffing, bulk discounts, trading terms favouring start-of-month orders, and pricing changes all contribute to a pattern of demand variability beyond the normal variability of consumption. This is artificial and is all within the managerial control of the organisation.

The coefficient of demand variation (CDV) measures the inherent volatility of demand. The coefficient of demand variation is the standard deviation of demand divided by the mean demand. The value calculated for both supplier and customer should be the same. If they are not the same, then artificial volatility exists.

Proactive collaboration is like customer collaboration but operates proactively. Businesses work together to smooth demand and make demand patterns predictable. This results in an effective supply chain that should lower total supply chain costs. Communication and collaboration often lead to innovation and rapid process improvement.

Dependent and independent demand

Dependent demand

Dependent demand is the demand for all lower-level items calculated from the product structure of the end item. Manufacturers should calculate dependent demand and not forecast it.

Independent demand

Independent demand is the demand for an item that is unrelated to the demand for other items.

Demand forecasting processes apply to independent demand items and groups of independent demand items. Most products and services exhibit independent demand as these sell independently of all other sales.

Dependent demand relates to the component items of a product where the quantity of component items has a relatively fixed relationship to the quantities of the parent item. For example, the meat and vegetables of a restaurant meal, the purchased and fabricated items of a refrigerator, and the quantity of steel in a building are all dependent demand items. To calculate dependent demand, multiply the quantity per parent by the number of parent items demanded.

Chapter summary

Demand occurs at all stages in a supply chain and at all stages in a service chain. Manufacturers demand raw materials, component assemblers demand fabricated and component parts, wholesalers/distributors/retailers demand finished products, retail customers demand finished products, and all stages along the supply chain demand services.

It is a strategic decision for organisations to decide how much demand they want to be able to supply. Most organisations prepare in some way for future demand. When a production firm manufactures products and stores them in a warehouse, they are anticipating future demand to occur. A service organisation anticipates future demand when it occupies a facility and employs and trains staff members.

Demand forecasting operates within three horizons – short range, medium range, and long range. Organisations use demand management strategies, in some instances, to influence the timing, quantity, and nature of demand to take advantage of excess capacity, an oversupply, or undersupply, or to change the timing of demand.

Quantitative forecasting uses historical demand and assumes that what has happened in the past will happen in the future. Qualitative forecasting is more subjective.

Forecast value added is the change in forecast accuracy due to an activity in the forecasting process. Organisations compare the forecast accuracy after a process activity to the expected accuracy without performing that activity. If the forecasting performance improves, then that activity is adding value to the forecasting process. If the forecasting performance does not improve, then that activity is not adding value to the forecasting process. By applying this measure to each step and to everyone in a forecasting process, it becomes possible to identify the non-value-adding activities and improve the overall process.

Decomposition occurs when the time series data splits into components of demand (trend, seasonal, and cyclical). Trend measures the general upwards or downwards direction, seasonal indicates the effect of different seasons, and cyclical shows the effect of a longer repeating non-seasonal period cycle. The calculations project each separate component into the future, and the sum of the projections becomes the new forecast.

Qualitative techniques, such as Delphi, are usually based on value judgements rather than factual assessment.

Power, influence, hierarchy, knowledge, lack of knowledge, history, experience, lack of experience, market awareness, advertising and promotion, pricing, and politics all play their part in developing the demand forecast.

Discussion questions

1 Describe the strategic importance of forecasting.
2 Explain the difference between qualitative and quantitative forecasting.
3 Describe the use of MAPD and MAPV.
4 Forecasting is about understanding variations. Explain.
5 What is the difference between seasonal variation and cyclical variation?
6 How does an organisation respond and cope with seasonal variation of demand?
7 Explain how to calculate the seasonal index.
8 How do airlines, hotels, and rental car companies influence demand?
9 Explain how a planner would apply forecasts to capacity management.

Key terms

bias, 52
cyclical component, 61
decomposition, 67
Delphi method, 73
demand, 42

demand management, 43
dependent demand, 75
forecast, 44
forecast deviation, 52
forecast value added, 58

forecasting, 44
independent demand, 75
MAD. *See* mean absolute deviation
MAPD. *See* mean absolute percentage deviation
MAPV. *See* mean absolute percentage variation
mean absolute deviation, 53
mean absolute percentage deviation, 53
mean absolute percentage variation, 53
qualitative forecasting, 73
quantitative forecasting, 60
random component, 61
random variation, 52
regression analysis, 63
seasonal component, 61
seasonal index, 67
trend component, 61

Notes

1 Apple, iPhone, iPad, iPod, and Mac are trademarks of Apple Inc. registered in the United States and other countries.
2 Apple Inc. (2009–2018). *Apple reports results from 2009 to 2018* [Press releases]. Retrieved from https://apple.com/newsroom/archive/
3 iPhone 4, 5, 6, 7, 8, 9, and X were all announced in the third quarter of the year of their release.
4 Armstrong, J. S. (2001). *Principles of forecasting: A handbook for researchers and practitioners*. Boston, MA: Kluwer Academic.
5 Gilliland, M. V. (2004). New metrics of forecasting performance. *APICS 2004 International Conference Proceedings*. Alexandria, VA: APICS, p. A-04.
6 Lapide, L. (1998–1999, Winter). Forecasting is about understanding variations. *Journal of Business Forecasting*, 29–30.
7 Gilliland, M. (2010). *The business forecasting deal: Exposing myths, eliminating bad practices, providing practical solutions*. Hoboken, NJ: Wiley, pp. 81–108.
8 Gilliland, M. V. (2002). Is forecasting a waste of time? *Supply Chain Management Review*, 6(4), 16–23.

Additional reading on demand management and forecasting in operations

Armstrong, J. S. (2001). *Principles of forecasting: A handbook for researchers and practitioners*. Boston, MA: Kluwer Academic.
Gilliland, M. (2010). *The business forecasting deal: Exposing myths, eliminating bad practices, providing practical solutions*. Hoboken, NJ: Wiley.
Gilliland, M. (2015). *Forecast value added analysis: Step by step*. Cary, NC: SAS Institute Inc.
Gilliland, M., Sglavo, U., & Tashman, L. (2015). *Business forecasting: Practical problems and solutions*. Hoboken, NJ: Wiley.
Hanke, J. E., & Wichem, D. W. (2009). *Business forecasting* (9th ed.). Upper Saddle River, NJ: Pearson Prentice Hall.
Lapide, L. (1998–1999, Winter). Forecasting is about understanding variations. *Journal of Business Forecasting*, 29–30.
Pittman, P. H., & Atwater, J. B. (2016). *APICS dictionary* (15th ed.). Chicago, IL: APICS.
Savage, S. L. (2009). *The flaw of averages: Why we underestimate risk in the face of uncertainty*. Hoboken, NJ: Wiley.

Chapter 3

Capacity and revenue management

Learning objectives

At the end of this chapter, you should be able to:

- Discuss the strategic importance of capacity.
- Discuss the strategic capacity planning process.
- Explain the executive sales and operations planning process.
- Discuss strategies for balancing supply with demand.
- Discuss the level production method and chase production method.
- Discuss the demand management process by influencing demand.
- Calculate basic production plans using the production planning model.
- Discuss capacity flexibility.
- Evaluate the application of revenue management – also known as yield management.
- Discuss service capacity, queues, and waiting lines.

Perspective: Electricity – how much is enough?

In this chapter, we will define capacity as the capability to produce output over a period. Capacity required represents the process capability needed to make a given product mix or deliver a given service mix – assuming technology, product specification, and so on. Organisations measure the capacity available and the capacity required in the short, medium, and long term. For this perspective, we will forego examining the capacity requirements of an individual organisation, and instead, discuss the capacity requirements for an entire industry – the energy sector.

The energy sector has a central role to play when meeting every nation's most basic social and economic needs, with energy security being vitally important. It underpins every form of economic activity, powering industries, vehicles, workplaces, and homes. Most countries experience steadily increasing demand and thus, the secure supply of affordable, reliable, and environmentally sustainable energy is clearly essential for future economic growth and prosperity. Therefore, what are the consequences for consumers of not enough electricity? What are the consequences for suppliers of having too much? Essentially, the industry needs to understand the dynamics of a developing demand pattern and correlate this with an evolving supply pattern. Generally, the industry participants cannot easily – meaning cheaply – satisfy any significant imbalance between supply and demand in the short term.

The growth in total energy consumption varies by country, with India and China leading the way. India is experiencing an almost insatiable demand for energy as the process of urbanisation continues unabated. In other countries, the growth in total energy consumption is less than the rate of economic growth. We can attribute this to greater efficiency, technological improvement, the rapid growth of service industries that are less energy intensive, and a more moderate growth of the energy-intensive manufacturing sectors.

The demand-driven switch to electric vehicles is changing the dynamics for the total demand for electricity. The International Monetary Fund in a working paper on the transition from oil in 2040 quotes various sources that predict that electric cars will occupy 25–30% of all vehicles by 2030 and about 50% by 2040.[1] Try to quantify that additional demand by calculating the actual total electricity required and the timing for that requirement. The quantity is easy to calculate, but the challenge is to know the timing of each future prediction.

Producers generate electricity from a variety of sources including coal, gas, nuclear, solar, water, wind, and biomass. Coal is the most abundant fossil fuel available and producers use coal for large-scale continuous electricity production. Some countries are still building new coal-fuelled electricity generating plants, but the writing is on the wall for long-term, industry-dominated, coal-fuelled generation. The challenge to reduce greenhouse gas emissions is having a negative effect on the use of coal as a source for electricity. Improvements continue in combustion techniques to increase the thermal efficiency of power generating plants. This equates to more electricity for less fuel – thus less carbon emissions.

Natural gas as an electrical fuel source is increasing, and distributed generation is enhancing its use. Rather than having a large-scale generation plant, this practice allows smaller generating plants close to residential and industrial sites. Technology is assisting in the transportation of natural gas as a liquid. Many countries use nuclear power as a base generating source. Japan re-evaluated their planned use of nuclear power following the Fukushima accident in October 2011. The cost of running nuclear power plants and the environmental dangers that they present indicate that, in the long term, this option will be too expensive. The lower costs of natural gas and renewable energies place competitive downward pressure on nuclear power.

Solar power is increasing steadily as the cost of photovoltaic panels and battery storage decreases. In the United States, Germany, and Australia, decentralised rooftop panels generate most of their solar power as demonstrated by the Apple headquarters complex in Cupertino, CA. This site generates 17 megawatts of power.[2] The vast majority of solar power in India and China comes from expansive parks such as the Pavagada solar park, which should produce 2,000 megawatts of electricity, enough to power 700,000 households.[3] Hydropower generation is one of the cheapest renewable sources. Wind generation has the potential to complement hydro, but wind, on its own, is unreliable and requires flexible, fast-starting thermal peaking plants as supplements. Some countries have geothermal power production.

All this generating capacity requires connection to a robust transmission grid. Progressively, renewable energy sources are replacing the least efficient thermal generating units. The supply chain for electricity is quite straightforward once the infrastructure is in place. Generation begins in power stations, which are usually located near fuel sources such as coalmines, water reservoirs, natural gas pipelines, and windy landscapes.

However, most electricity customers reside in the cities and towns a long distance from the sources of electricity. The supply chain requires transmission from generators to customers. High-voltage transmission lines carry electricity from the generators to distribution networks in metropolitan areas. As supply gets closer to customers, transmission changes to lower-voltage distribution networks. Retailers buy wholesale electricity and package it with transmission and distribution services for sale to residential, commercial, and industrial customers.

Assume your role is to plan the electricity supply requirements for your country of residence. This requires planning to extend at least for 10 or 20 years. You should consider the current source and potential future sources of electricity and a steadily increasing base demand. What affect will electric vehicles place on your demand figures? What demand figures will you use and how will you guarantee reliable supply for the duration of your plan?

Introduction

The previous chapter developed a forecast of future demand and this forecast had a value or a range of expected values. In a strategic sense, the organisation should understand the dynamics of demand patterns and prepare for whatever happens by acquiring adequate buildings and equipment, and/or hiring and training enough personnel.

The electricity generation and supply industries have a requirement to manage short-range, medium-range, and long-range capacity. What are the consequences for consumers of not enough electricity? What are the consequences for suppliers of too much electricity?

Several factors influence demand such as changes in technology, competitor initiatives, and pricing levels. Forecasting helps to focus attention on the factors influencing demand and to establish relationships between those factors and the actual demand.

This chapter discusses the planning of capacity and the management of capacity, when there is a mismatch between available capacity and customer demand. The aim is to allow organisations to balance demand requirements with capacity availability. The chapter starts by examining capacity hierarchies, which are like the demand hierarchies of the previous chapter. It then proposes three methods to arrive at a satisfactory response to the demand forecast – level production method, chase production method, and demand management process. The executive sales and operations planning process allows organisations to plan at the aggregate level. Several worked examples illustrate the process of planning capacity.

The chapter introduces revenue management – also known as yield management – as a valuable process for maximising the revenue achieved for service organisations with relatively fixed capacity, such as airline, rental car, and hotel companies.

The chapter closes by discussing service capacity, queues, and waiting lines.

Capacity management in operations

Strategic capacity

Capacity

Capacity is the capability to produce output over a period. Capacity required represents the process capability needed to make a given product mix or deliver a given service mix – assuming technology, product specification, and so on. Organisations measure the capacity available and the capacity required in the short, medium, and long term.

Capacity management

Capacity management is the function of coping with mismatches between demand and the ability to supply.

Capacity planning

Capacity planning is the process of determining the amount of capacity required to meet market demand for products and services.

Capacity is the capability to produce output over a period. When customers have a need for a product or service, they approach their supplier and demand enough quantities to satisfy their requirements. Capacity management is the function of coping with the mismatches between demand and the ability to supply that demand. This does not necessarily mean that demand and supply must be equal. An organisation may choose to neglect some demand because it may not have the resources required and may not be able to acquire them. Likewise, capacity may exceed demand but the organisation retains existing capacity because it is easier and cheaper to hold on to that capability hoping – or knowing – the organisation will use it later.

In the previous chapter, the demand forecasting process generated forecasts of future demand in the long, medium, and short range. Capacity management copes with the mismatches of demand and supply over similar periods.

Long-range capacity management generally covers the period required to replace or divest major resources. For most organisations this is 18 months and beyond. Capacity planning ensures enough resources are available to meet long-range demand.

Medium-range capacity management works very closely with aggregate sales and operations plans. The time horizon can range from a few months to 18 months depending on the organisation. Capacity increments – or decrements – must be in place to meet that demand.

Short-range capacity management copes with the mismatches on a day-to-day basis. In the past, organisations planned capacity requirements in detail at this level. The business systems in place today do not require the level of detailed capacity planning necessary 20 or 30 years ago. Modern methods of lean thinking and flexibility reduce the need for detailed reports, provided organisations have performed long-range and medium-range capacity planning.

Thus, it is a continuous cycle of assessing demand, ensuring supply resources are available, and checking actual supply is responsive to demand.

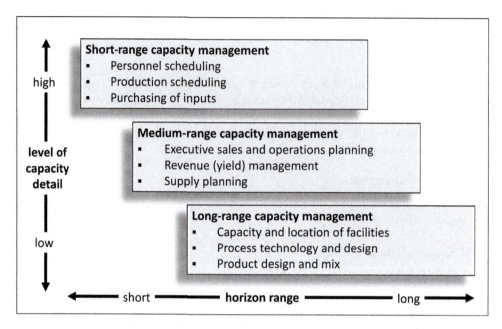

Figure 3.1 Capacity management hierarchy

Figure 3.1 illustrates the capacity management hierarchy and the types of business applications involved. Capacity planning is one of the most important and valuable business processes that an organisation can perform. With knowledge of required capacity, the organisation can make decisions on how to manage available capacity. When capacity management performs well, an organisation can capitalise on every opportunity presented; when done poorly, an organisation misses opportunities or fails to realise opportunities.

The term 'capacity planning' was traditionally associated with production industries where production scheduling calculated the capacity requirements of open manufacturing orders and attempted to schedule jobs through a factory at minimum cost and with minimum lead time. These were very detailed calculations and proved more trouble than they were worth, since the figures used for lead times, queues, set-up times, and run speeds were largely unreliable.

More recently, the term 'capacity planning' has been readily associated with planning the capacity of information and communications technology. Organisations in these industries need to have enough resources available to meet current and future demand.

Forecast demand and available capacity are not completely predictable. While there are elements of predictability in demand and capacity, the summation includes variation and unpredictability. Organisations realise the significance and benefits of capacity management when they appreciate the fluctuations of demand and capacity.

Organisations may convince themselves that capacity calculations are accurate, but the reality of set-up time variations, production rate variables, unavailability of resources at planned times, unexpected machine breakdowns, and transport disruptions, all contribute to the variations of output governing capacity decisions.

Capacity management must cope with the variations in demand and capacity. The previous chapter explored how forecasting is about understanding variation. The same applies to capacity. An organisation requires an understanding of what causes demand and capacity variation, which elements are predictable, and which are unpredictable.

Strategic capacity planning

The objective of strategic capacity planning is to specify the overall capacity level of resources – facilities, equipment, and labour – that best supports the company's long-range competitive strategy for production. If capacity is inadequate, an organisation may lose customers through slow service or by allowing competitors to enter the market. If capacity is excessive, an organisation may have to reduce prices to stimulate demand or else under-utilise its workforce, carry excess inventory, or seek additional, less-profitable products to stay in business.

Production and service organisations usually occupy one or more facilities at one or more locations. Organisations must resolve the following strategic decisions:

- Where should each facility be located?
- How large, or small, should each facility be?
- What process technology does each location require?
- Will the physical size of the facility be enough in the short term, medium term, and long term?
- What is the timing for capacity increments?
- What happens if the available capacity is too much?
- What happens if the available capacity is insufficient?

All these questions have a major bearing on the success, or otherwise, of organisations. If they can get it right, they find themselves in an enviable position of being able to capitalise on every opportunity coming their way – assuming they want to – and thus maximise revenues and profits. If they get it wrong, they may find themselves searching for additional capacity at a premium price or having excess capacity they are unable to sell.

To appreciate long-range capacity plans, organisations require a sound understanding of the forecasting process used to determine the long-range demand. If the organisation prepares forecasts in financial terms only, without any indication of the demand on capacity, the forecasts require translation into capacity units to allow for capacity management. In the ideal situation, the measurement units for demand and capacity are the same; at least there should be a linkage between them. A better understanding of both demand and supply enhances the management process.

Organisations have two contrasting choices when it comes to determining capacity. First, they can invest time and money into the forecasting process to make the forecast better knowing they require a valid forecast before planning capacity. The result, inevitably, is for capacity to be too much – a costly approach – or too little – thereby losing revenue and not satisfying customers. Secondly, the organisation acknowledges that demand will always be indeterminate, and they should invest time and money into making the production process as flexible as possible to cope with whatever demand eventuates.

Organisations prefer the first approach when they have difficulty reacting to unexpected demand in the short term. The second approach works well when the organisation develops flexible production processes or has customers who are prepared to wait for their demand to be satisfied.

Some organisations, such as an emergency department of a hospital, employ both choices. They do not have the ability to change short-term capacity easily, but they must be flexible enough to satisfy any possible demand.

Strategic capacity planning process

Executive sales and operations planning

Executive sales and operations planning is the executive portion of the sales and operations planning set of processes. It is a decision-making activity involving the leader of the organisation, their staff, and several middle managers and specialists. Its mission is to balance supply and demand at the aggregate level, to align operational planning with financial planning, and to link strategic planning with day-to-day sales and operational activities.

Sales and operations planning

Sales and operations planning is a process to develop tactical plans that provide management the ability to direct its businesses strategically to achieve competitive advantage on a continuous basis by integrating customer-focused marketing plans for new and existing products with the management of the supply chain. The process brings together all the plans for the business – sales, marketing, development, manufacturing, sourcing, and financial – into one integrated set of plans. Performed at least once a month, management review it at an aggregate (product family) level. The process must reconcile all supply, demand, and new-product plans at both the detail and aggregate levels and tie to the business plan. It is the definitive statement of the organisation's plan for the near to intermediate term, covering enough horizon to plan for resources and to support the annual business-planning process. Used properly it enables the organisation to view the business holistically and provide a window into the future.

Production plan

The production plan is the agreed plan coming from the sales and operations planning process, specifically the overall level of production output that the organisation plans to produce, usually stated as a monthly rate for each product family (group of products).

The business plan sets the scene for strategic capacity planning. This typically covers the general direction the organisation wants to take in the medium to long term. Topics considered at this level include market directions, customer preferences, export opportunities, input threats, technological advances, new products and services, competitive actions, production capability, and financial capacity.

The performance objectives the organisation wants, the perishability or storage capability of the inputs and outputs, and the degree of variability in demand and supply influence the level of capacity. The performance objectives may require the organisation to have a high service level. If production lead times are long, the organisation needs to invest in warehouse capacity. If production lead times are short, the organisation needs to invest in production capacity and flexibility.

The organisation requires high capacity levels when supply inputs, or demand outputs, are perishable and not suitable for storage. Fresh fruit and vegetables, grapes for wine production, and fresh-cut flowers require harvesting at the optimum time; the processing facilities must handle each day's supply on any given day. Waiting for a few days until capacity is available may deteriorate the quality of the harvest.

As shown in Figure 3.2, demand forecasting develops the aggregate demand forecast. The forecast at the aggregate level – not the detailed product level – passes through several filters determined by the business strategy, the operations strategy, and the capacity policies established by the organisation.

Hotels and airlines usually have some excess capacity since available capacity usually exceeds the average demand for services. Effective capacity reduces when there is variability in demand or supply. When supply is erratic and input volumes range from high to low, the production process may be idle at times and fully loaded at others. Likewise, when demand is erratic and output volumes range from high to low, the production process may be idle at times and fully loaded at others.

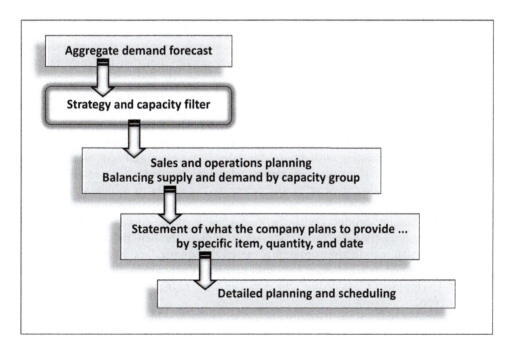

Figure 3.2 Capacity planning sequence

Organisations usually express long-range forecasts in dollar terms, and this requires translation into units of production at an aggregate level. The production units provide a measurement of the capacity requirements. It may be difficult to comprehend how much capacity $1 million, say, represents. It is much easier to say 1000 hours of production per week, or 500 surgical patients per month. The aggregation defines customer-focused marketing plans for new and existing products and the production capability of the supply chain.

Sales and operations planning seeks to find the combination of sales, production, labour requirements, inventory levels (production), and customer backlog (services) that minimises total production-related costs over the planning period. A sales and operations plan may be a formal report in one company and an informal directive in another.

An Australian company, for example, might decide as a strategic decision to concentrate on the Sydney and Melbourne metropolitan markets. The process filters out demands for products and services arriving from outside those regions (say from New Zealand), since the company deems these demands as 'non-strategic'. It is not appropriate to say this is right or wrong. It is a strategic decision to concentrate available resources in defined areas. Any dilution of resources to service other regions might limit service levels and future capabilities.

Operations filters might, for example, limit certain sizes, or certain colours, or specifications outside the range of capability, given the current and planned configuration within the organisation. Capacity policy decisions could also limit demand requests, which, for example, are more than current capacity limits.

The set of aggregate demand forecast data that gets past the filter becomes one of the inputs to sales and operations planning. The filtering process may be formal or informal and could be taking place without the organisation's knowledge. As an example, consider a business using online facilities to search for potential suppliers. They discover an organisation offering the services they require, but they notice comments limiting distribution capabilities, dimensional capability, or some other characteristic that suggests the organisation could not cope with a new demand. The business does not contact the organisation and the service supplier loses that opportunity forever.

The executive sales and operations planning process attempts to balance supply and demand at the aggregate level. It aligns operational planning with financial planning and links strategic planning with day-to-day sales and operational activities.

The sales and operations planning process develops tactical plans providing management with the ability to strategically direct its businesses to achieve competitive advantage on a continuous basis by integrating customer-focused marketing plans for new and existing products with the management of the supply chain. The process brings together the sales plan, the marketing plan, the new product and service development plan, production capability, material sourcing, and financial data. The process, performed at least once a month, reconciles all supply, demand, and new product development plans at both the detail and the aggregate levels and ties to the business plan.

Organisations balance the capacity choices to arrive at what is achievable in terms of capacity after presentation of the preliminary demand numbers. This may require agreement that existing resources can produce the planned demand, or it may require modification of demand to create the rate of sales consistent with existing capacity.

If there is a shortfall in available capacity, organisations may increase capacity, obtain temporary resources, outsource production capacity, or simply not deliver the forecast demand. If there is excess capacity, organisations may decide to sell the excess or close some resources.

Timing is critical. The usual timeframe for strategic capacity planning is in the region of 6 to 18 months, which is enough time for organisations to adjust the supply and demand patterns. Supply management develops supply and production plans consistent with the agreed capacity plan. Demand management attempts to modify demand consistent with the available resources.

When demand and supply agree on the aggregate numbers, the agreement is 'signed in blood'. This assumes that the agreed plan will happen. Signatories do not have the option of making excuses. They cannot make any excuses. By signing the agreement, each signatory agrees that they will take all possible actions to deliver the plan.

Strategies for balancing supply with demand

Production planning

Production planning is a process to develop tactical plans based on setting the overall level of production output to best satisfy the current planned levels of sales, while meeting general business objectives of profitability, productivity, competitive customer lead times, and so on, as expressed in the overall business plan. The business compares sales with production capabilities and develops an operations strategy that includes a sales plan, a production plan, budgets, pro forma financial statements, and supporting plans for materials and workforce requirements. One of the primary objectives is to establish a production rate that will achieve management's objective of satisfying demand by maintaining, raising, or lowering inventories or backlogs, while usually attempting to maintain a stable workforce. This plan affects most functions of the organisation and requires inputs from marketing, sales, production, finance, new product development, service, and distribution.

Supply

Supply is the actual, or planned, replenishment quantity created in response to a demand for a product or a component in anticipation of such demand.

Figure 3.3 illustrates the delicate balancing act required by most organisations. The aggregate demand is the quantity of products required with customer delivery dates. Capacity and supply represent the ability of the organisation to deliver those requirements on time. When balancing these two forces, the beam sits level on the fulcrum. When one or the other gets slightly out of balance, the beam tilts in favour of the force with greater quantities or more demanding delivery dates. The illustration has the rider 'attempting to maintain perfect balance', when really a perfect balance is virtually impossible to maintain for most organisations.

It is difficult to say which should come first – capacity or demand. An organisation that can look forward and visualise a demand pattern based on history, or their perception of what is about to happen, is in a strong position to determine the required

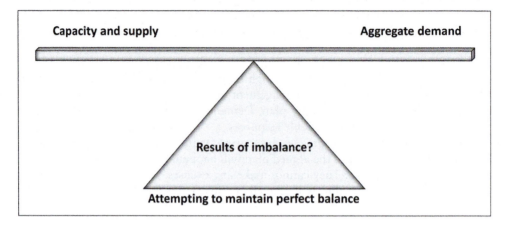

Figure 3.3 Balancing capacity and supply with demand: Attempting to maintain perfect balance

capacity or supply. This can be determined based on the quantity and the timing required. The supply pattern should be able to match the demand pattern. Organisations starting with a given capability to supply, or controlling a supply position, must search for demand opportunities to match the supply pattern.

The planning process at the aggregate level considers families or groups of products. Typically, an organisation has between 6 and 12 families or groups of products. This number is significant. A number less than six suggests the organisation is approaching a full consolidation of the total plans for the organisation; this would suit a business-planning exercise. A number greater than 12 makes the evaluation of the aggregate plans a very lengthy exercise. Assume the organisation allocates 30 minutes to discuss each family or group at a senior executive meeting. If the organisation has, say, 20 groups, then the meeting would last 10 hours, and this may lose the whole purpose of the meeting.

The organisation establishes current planned sales levels. These are different from the current planned demand levels. Demand is what the customers need, but the sales level shows what the organisation plans to achieve by way of actual sales. In an ideal world, the demand level matches the sales level, and all customers are satisfied completely. In the real world, there is usually a mismatch between demand and sales.

Executives match sales with the output production level to meet general business objectives of profitability, productivity, and competitive customer lead times consistent with the business plan. They evaluate the sales and production capabilities, and they develop a sales plan, production plan, financial budget statements, and supporting plans for materials and workforce requirements.

One of the primary objectives is to establish a production rate that will achieve management's objective of satisfying demand by maintaining, raising, or lowering inventories or customer backlogs, while, usually, attempting to minimise disruptions to labour requirements. This plan affects most functions of the organisation and requires inputs from marketing, sales, production, finance, new product and service development, service, and distribution.

For the most part, the production planner must live with the sales forecast and utilise a pure strategy or a combination of strategies. The capacity or supply planning options available include:

- Hiring additional staff members and making staff redundant.
- Working variable weeks or overtime.
- Varying the level of inventory.
- Varying the number of orders in the backlog.
- Varying the length of the queue of customers.
- Using subcontractors to supply additional capacity.
- Outsourcing parts of the organisation to free up resources.
- Adding or removing temporary capacity.
- Adding or removing permanent capacity.

These are reactive measures, and the controllability of these factors depends on union agreements, employment contracts, employment legislation, short-term constraints on physical capacity levels, customer requirements and preferences, and the amount of money invested in inventories.

In some organisations, pricing, advertising, and other proactive measures affects product demand.

Production planning approaches

Production planning approaches

The organisation takes production planning approaches to develop the production output to meet customer demand by setting production, inventory, and backlog levels. The main methods used are chase production method, level production method, and demand management process.

Chase production method

The chase production method varies production to meet demand. The plan adds and removes production resources as required to maintain a stable inventory level or a stable backlog (queue). This suits organisations that experience significant changes in demand and can add and remove resources easily and effectively.

Level production method

The level production method maintains resources at a constant level resulting in a relatively level production rate. This suits organisations with scarce or expensive resources or when building up stock levels in anticipation of seasonal demand.

Demand management process

The demand management process attempts to modify demand to meet available capacity. Used in conjunction with either a level production method or a chase production method, it employs methods such as pricing to promote off-peak demand, restricted service at peak times, advertising, promotion, reservations, and appointments.

The three main approaches for determining how to use capacity to balance demand are the level production method, the chase production method, and the demand management process.

Level production method

The lean-thinking approach to production planning is to follow a level production schedule, which focuses on holding production and available workforce constant for a period. When there is a difference between the constant rate of production and the varying rate of demand, inventory levels rise or fall, the number of orders in the backlog increases or decreases, or the length of the customer queue changes.

Operations managers often prefer this method since production rates are usually dependable, quality of outputs tend to be consistently high, and operating costs tend to be low. The emphasis is on production efficiency, and service goals are secondary. Staff levels remain constant, and supply lines deliver at a steady rate.

The disadvantage is that inventory levels do change, and this may require substantial warehousing arrangements to handle periods of low demand. Service organisations may require a process for handling lengthy customer queues.

As a summary, the level production method:

- Maintains scarce or expensive resources at a constant level.
- Meets resource utilisation goals.
- Produces a relatively level production rate.
- Makes production efficiency goals paramount.
- Makes service goals secondary.
- Minimises the need to employ, train, and terminate employees.
- Minimises overtime.
- Makes resource planning less complicated.
- Allows supply lines to operate at a steady rate.

Electronics manufacturers and home appliance assembly plants that produce high volumes of common products are examples of businesses that use level production methods.

A production organisation that is deliberately building up inventory in anticipation of future demand would usually use a level production method. Chocolate manufacturers start producing Easter eggs and other chocolate novelties in May or June of each year to prepare for the Easter season in March or April of the following year. The demand for specialty chocolate in this period is so high that most chocolate factories do not have the production capacity to cope, so they start early.

Packaging companies often start building up packaging supplies well before the commencement of the season requiring the packaging. Examples include seasonal produce such as apples, pears, kiwifruit, and some vegetables where the seasonal demand of the product is higher than the packaging production capability at the time. Therefore, the companies manufacture the packaging prior to receiving orders to improve their ability to meet demand when it happens.

Chase production method

The chase production method allows the production capacity to vary each period to match the forecast aggregate demand in that period exactly. Workforce levels vary by employing workers and terminating their employment as and when the needs arise. Overtime and temporary staff fill short periods of high demand. Often, subcontractors add additional capacity during peak periods. This method requires almost no finished goods inventory and eliminates the cost of holding inventory. Customer queues, if present, are constant. However, labour and material costs are much higher because of the disruptions caused by frequently scaling the workforce up and down and adjusting the volume of materials supplies. Essentially, the available capacity matches the demand.

As a summary, chase production method:

- Matches capacity with demand.
- Varies production rate, which necessitates volume flexibility.
- Needs supply lines with in-built flexibility.
- Maintains service availability and levels.
- May have idle resources at times since resource utilisation is not an issue.
- Employs staff members on flexible contracts.
- Uses overtime and temporary staff to fill short-term needs.
- Uses subcontractors to take load during peak periods.
- Presents a challenge to control costs.

Chase production method examples occur in most agricultural and horticultural seasonal harvesting activities where the production requirement occurs for a very short time during the year. It would be an ineffective use of resources to have staff members permanently on the payroll just for the seasonal activity.

Retail outlets experience high demand during November and December as customers purchase goods for end-of-year gifts. The outlets may employ temporary staff on fixed-term contracts and use subcontractors for deliveries. This means the retailer can match the service demand with supply and deliver items with their normal lead time rather than stockpiling items or delivering them much later.

Demand management process

Some organisations can modify demand to suit their available capacity. One obvious way is to adjust prices. A business increasing the price would normally expect demand to fall; likewise, a business decreasing the price would normally expect demand to rise. A business forecasting lower demand might elect, as a strategy, to lower the prices to increase demand. Likewise, a business forecasting demand that is higher than what they can reasonably handle with given capacity might increase prices to reduce demand. Pricing can be an effective tool to promote off-peak demand.

Telephone companies, airlines, hotels, and rental car companies change the prices of their services to promote off-peak demand. The objective attempts to level the supply. An organisation that experiences demand highs and lows could smooth out the highs and fill in the lows by varying prices.

Another way is to use advertising and promotion to change demand. In the opposite way to pricing, an organisation can increase demand by increasing the level of advertising and promotion. It can lower demand by decreasing the level of advertising and promotion.

Restaurants may offer a restricted service at peak periods. This is not a negative offering on their part; rather they usually promote the restriction as a positive. They may offer, for example, a special low-priced breakfast menu until 10:30 a.m. each day, allowing the restaurant to focus production activities on a narrow range of choices rather than the full range. The customer benefits by having a cheaper breakfast option prepared in a very short lead time. Other restaurants may display a 'specials' board, which sounds like it is offering something extra and 'special' when in fact it just means the chefs have sufficient quantities of those food items and can prepare them quickly and easily.

In summary, the demand management process:

- Attempts to modify demand by using advertising and promotion.
- Works in conjunction with the level and/or chase production method.
- Uses pricing to promote off-peak demand.
- May offer a restricted service at peak times.
- Designs specialist service channels such as medical practice hours for immunisations.
- Uses reservation systems and appointment books to level demand.

Production planning model

The production planning model balances the mismatches between demand and capacity by recognising that demand is variable and capacity is adjustable. The model considers the forecast demand, the available capacity, the required capacity, cost of production, cost of regular and overtime labour, cost of hiring and training new staff, cost of making employees redundant or laying them off, cost of holding inventory, cost of backlogging, cost of managing the queue, and subcontracting costs.

As shown in Figure 3.4, the development of a production plan uses the demand, the capacity, and the costs associated with production as inputs. The generated output shows the required production rate, the level of inventory, the length of the customer queue, the staffing levels required, and the rate of subcontracting required. The following represent a sample of questions to ask:

- Should we use inventories to absorb changes in demand?
- Should we vary the size of the workforce?
- Should we use part-timers, casuals, overtime, or idle time?
- Should we use subcontractors?
- Should we change prices to influence demand?

The production planning process attempts to find the optimal combination of:

- Demand pattern and product mix.
- Available staff levels.
- Number of workers needed for production.

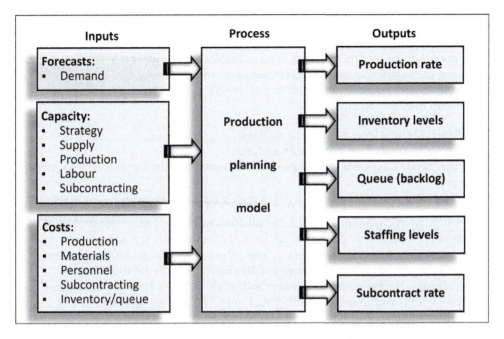

Figure 3.4 Production planning model

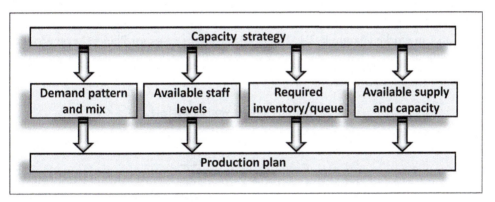

Figure 3.5 Inputs to production planning

- Inventory on hand at the start of the plan.
- Unused inventory carried from one period to the next.
- Queue or backlog.
- Number of units completed per unit of time.
- Customers waiting from one period to the next.
- Subcontracting requirements.

Figure 3.5 illustrates the production planning process.

Worked example 3.1

The data in Table 3.1 represents the forecast demand for 12 months commencing January. There are 25 employees on the current staff. The cost of hiring additional staff is $600 per employee, and the cost of making an employee redundant is $300. For planning purposes, each employee can make 200 units a month. A storage facility charges $1 per unit for inventory on hand at the end of each month to cover the cost of warehousing.

Develop three production plans:

- Plan 1: Using a level production method.
- Plan 2: Using a chase production method.
- Plan 3: Producing 4800 for the first six months and 5200 for the remaining six months.

Plan 1: Develop a production plan using a level production method

Start this plan by calculating the level production rate. The annual demand is 60,000, and there are 12 monthly periods so the level production rate is 5000 units per month. In January, the beginning inventory is zero, the production is 5000 and demand is 4400, therefore, the ending inventory is 600 units (0 + 5000 – 4400 = 600).

In February, the beginning inventory (following on from January) is 600, the production is 5000 and demand is 3200, therefore, the ending inventory is 2400 units (600 + 500 – 3200 = 2400).

In March, the beginning inventory (following on from February) is 2400, the production is 5000 and demand is 4000, therefore, the ending inventory is 3400 units (2400 + 5000 – 4000 = 3400).

Continue like this for the rest of the year, and end up with data as shown in Table 3.2.

Figure 3.6 shows the level production rate, the demand, and the resulting inventory for Plan 1 in worked example 3.1. Table 3.3 shows the costs for Plan 1: Level production method.

Table 3.1 Demand data for worked example 3.1

Month	Demand forecast
Jan	4400
Feb	3200
Mar	4000
Apr	5400
May	6600
Jun	5000
Jul	4000
Aug	3000
Sep	4800
Oct	6400
Nov	7000
Dec	6200
	60000

Table 3.2 Production plan data for worked example 3.1 Plan 1: Level production method

Month	Beginning inventory on hand	Production	Demand forecast	Ending inventory on hand	Number of employees	New staff	Redundant staff
Jan	0	5000	4400	600	25		
Feb	600	5000	3200	2400	25		
Mar	2400	5000	4000	3400	25		
Apr	3400	5000	5400	3000	25		
May	3000	5000	6600	1400	25		
Jun	1400	5000	5000	1400	25		
Jul	1400	5000	4000	2400	25		
Aug	2400	5000	3000	4400	25		
Sep	4400	5000	4800	4600	25		
Oct	4600	5000	6400	3200	25		
Nov	3200	5000	7000	1200	25		
Dec	1200	5000	6200	0	25		
		60000	60000	28000			

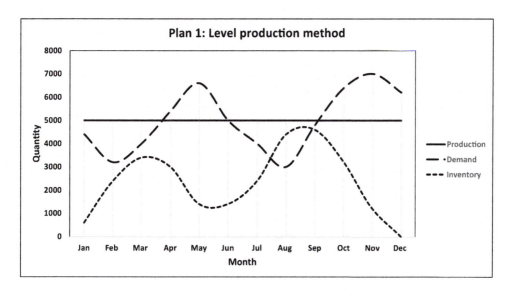

Figure 3.6 Graph of production plan data for worked example 3.1 Plan 1: Level production method

Table 3.3 Costs for Plan 1: Level production method

Inventory storage cost	(28,000 × $1)	$28,000
Cost of employing new staff		$0
Cost of staff redundancy		$0
Total costs		**$28,000**

Plan 2: Develop a production plan using a chase production method

In this plan, the production rate varies to match the demand pattern, and the organ-isation increases or decreases the number of employees to match the production rate.

In January, the demand forecast is 4400, so production is set to match that rate. Beginning inventory on hand is zero, production matches demand forecast, so the ending inventory on hand is zero. To produce 4400, we need 22 staff members (200 units per employee per month), so three employees become redundant. Their employ-ment contract should specify the temporary nature of their employment.

In February, the demand forecast is 3200, so production is set to match that rate. Beginning inventory on hand is zero, production matches demand forecast, so the end-ing inventory on hand is zero. To produce 3200, we need 16 staff members (200 units per employee per month), making a further six employees redundant.

In March, the demand forecast is 4000, so production is set to match that rate. Beginning inventory on hand is zero, production matches demand forecast, so the ending inventory on hand is zero. To produce 4000, we need 20 staff members (200 units per employee per month), requiring four additional employees.

Continue like this for the rest of the year, and end up with data as shown in Table 3.4.

Figure 3.7 shows the varying production rate, the demand, and the resulting inven-tory (equals zero for the whole plan) for Plan 2 in worked example 3.1. Table 3.5 shows the costs for Plan 2.

Plan 3: Develop a production plan producing 4800 per month
for first six months and 5200 per month for remainder

The calculations for this strategy follow the same pattern as Plans 1 and 2 except the production rate is set at 4800 for the first six months, and then increases to 5200 for the rest of the year. This represents a starting position in trying to optimise the plan. The number of employees increases and decreases to match the production rate. Table 3.6 shows the results of the calculations for Plan 3.

Table 3.4 Production plan data for worked example 3.1 Plan 2: Chase production method

Month	Beginning inventory on hand	Production	Demand forecast	Ending inventory on hand	Number of employees	New staff	Redundant staff
Jan	0	4450	4400	30	22		3
Feb	30	3250	3200	30	16		6
Mar	30	4050	4000	30	20	4	
Apr	30	5450	5400	30	27	7	
May	30	6650	6600	30	33	6	
Jun	30	5050	5000	30	25		8
Jul	30	4050	4000	30	20		5
Aug	30	3050	3000	30	15		5
Sep	30	4850	4800	30	24	9	
Oct	30	6450	6400	30	32	8	
Nov	30	7050	7000	30	35	3	
Dec	30	6250	6200	30	31		4
		60600	60000	360		37	31

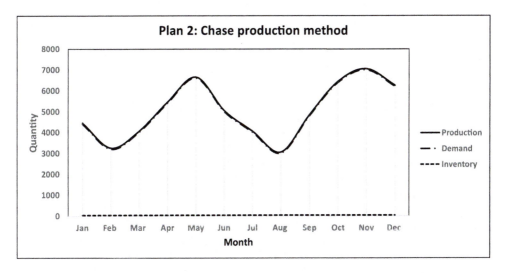

Figure 3.7 Graph of production plan data for worked example 3.1 Plan 2: Chase production method

Table 3.5 Costs for Plan 2: Chase production method

Inventory storage cost		$0
Cost of employing new staff	(37 × $600)	$22,200
Cost of staff redundancy	(31 × $300)	$9,300
Total costs		**$31,500**

Table 3.6 Production plan data for worked example 3.1 Plan 3: Mixed strategy

Month	Beginning inventory on hand	Production	Demand forecast	Ending inventory on hand	Number of employees	New employees	Redundant employees
Jan	0	4800	4400	400	24		1
Feb	400	4800	3200	2000	24		
Mar	2000	4800	4000	2800	24		
Apr	2800	4800	5400	2200	24		
May	2200	4800	6600	400	24		
Jun	400	4800	5000	200	24		
Jul	200	5200	4000	1400	26	2	
Aug	1400	5200	3000	3600	26		
Sep	3600	5200	4800	4000	26		
Oct	4000	5200	6400	2800	26		
Nov	2800	5200	7000	1000	26		
Dec	1000	5200	6200	0	26		
		60000	**60000**	**20800**		**2**	**1**

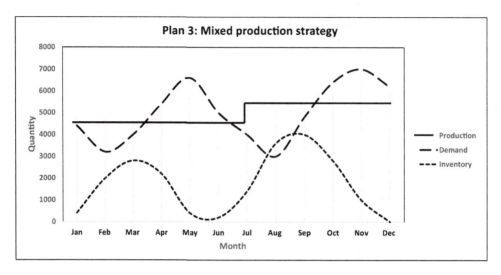

Figure 3.8 Graph of production plan data for worked example 3.1 Plan 3: Mixed production strategy

Table 3.7 Costs for Plan 3: Mixed strategy

Inventory storage cost	(20,800 × $1)	$20,800
Cost of employing new staff	(2 × $600)	$1,200
Cost of staff redundancy	(1 × $300)	$300
Total costs		**$22,300**

Figure 3.8 shows the varying production rate, the demand, and the resulting inventory for Plan 3 in worked example 3.1. Table 3.7 shows the costs of Plan 3.

Worked example 3.2

The data in Table 3.8 represents the forecast demand for four months commencing in February and additional planning data. In this example, there are a constant 20 days per month. When performed with real data one should enter the number of days per month as a variable to correspond to the actual days per month. There are 125 employees at the start of February. Reduce staff numbers for March and maintain the same workforce during April and May. The maximum overtime is 5000 hours per month.

Using this data develop an operations plan producing exactly to demand during February and March. Develop the plan to minimise cost.

There are four units produced per labour hour; therefore, to calculate monthly production hours divide the monthly forecast by this number. The holding costs represent the cost of storing inventory that is unsold at the end of the month. When a supplier does not supply the ordered quantity in full, the portion not supplied incurs backorder costs representing the additional costs of handling the order more than once.

Table 3.9 shows the production planning quantities. Staff numbers drop in March because of the forecast reduction, and the new level of staff numbers stays constant

Table 3.8 Forecast demand data and planning data for worked example 3.2

Month	Forecast
February	80,000
March	64,000
April	100,000
May	40,000
Planning data	
Units/Labour hour	4
Hours per day	8
Days per month	20
Hiring costs	$500
Redundancy costs	$800
Ordinary time per hour	$20
Overtime cost per hour	$25
Holding costs/unit/mth	$10
Back order costs/unit	$20

Table 3.9 Solution data for quantities for worked example 3.2

Month	Forecast	Beginning inventory	Production quantity required	Production hours required	Production hours available
February	80,000	0	80,000	20,000	20,000
March	64,000	0	64,000	16,000	16,000
April	100,000	0	100,000	25,000	16,000
May	40,000	−16,000	56,000	14,000	16,000

Month	Employees	Ending inventory	Planned production quantity		Overtime hours planned
February	125	0	80,000		0
March	100	0	64,000		0
April	100	−16,000	84,000		5,000
May	100	8,000	64,000		0

during April and May. The organisation authorises 5,000 hours of overtime during April, but this is not enough to prevent the shortfall in production, so they backorder 16,000 units.

Table 3.10 shows the costing data for worked example 3.2 adding up to $1,905,000. In practice, the management team would examine this output to see if it is acceptable in every facet. Cost is important, but so are the change in staff numbers, the working of overtime, the inability to supply the forecast demand, and the storage costs in May. The management team implements the modified plan when it is acceptable.

Table 3.10 Solution data for costs for worked example 3.2

Month	Redundancy cost	Backorder cost	Ordinary cost	Overtime cost	Inventory storage cost	Total cost
February			$400,000	$0		**400,000**
March	$20,000		$320,000	$0		**340,000**
April		$320,000	$320,000	$125,000		**765,000**
May			$320,000	$0	$80,000	**400,000**
	$20,000	**$320,000**	**$1,360,000**	**$125,000**	**$80,000**	**$1,905,000**

Facilities and capacity

Design capacity

The design capacity is the amount an organisation would like to produce under normal circumstances and represents the system-designed quantity.

Best operating level

The best operating level is the volume of output at which the average unit cost is at a minimum and represents the process-designed quantity.

Economy of scale

Economy of scale refers to the drop in the average cost for each unit of output as a plant gets larger and each succeeding unit absorbs part of the fixed costs. Economy of scale is important in capacity decisions.

Economy of scope

Economy of scope occurs when one versatile plant produces many different products at a lower cost than making each product in different plants at a higher cost.

Diseconomy of scale

Diseconomy of scale refers to the situation when the reduction in average unit cost is no longer possible through further increases in facility size because co-ordination of material flows and personnel becomes too expensive. This requires new sources of capacity.

Having enough capacity available is a strategic decision for any organisation. Manufacturers can store inventory. Service organisations do not have that option and must assess the required capacity in advance of requirements.

Design capacity is the production rate the facility can produce over the long term. In manufacturing, it is the size of the plant, the number of machines, the production rate of the machines, and the number of trained personnel. As the production rate increases, the capital cost and fixed operating cost of running the facility can be amortised over a greater volume of production; this lowers the unit cost of output. Eventually, however, the facility reaches a point where the unit cost of production starts to increase with every increase in the production rate. This is the result of over-loading the facility, having restricted material movements, and not having enough room to allow physical flows.

Economy of scale occurs as the average cost per unit decreases; diseconomy of scale occurs as the average cost per unit increases. The best operating level occurs at the transition from decreasing unit cost to increasing unit cost. Static efficiencies create economies of scale. The scale of the operation affects the unit cost of production through three economies:[4]

- Economies of volume, obtained through better allocation of the fixed cost.
- Economies of capacity, achieved through the indivisibility of resources.
- Economies of technology, achieved through investment in more efficient process technology.

Finding the right capacity in service industries has more cost implications simply because of the inability to store output. Under-utilised resources, including staff, do not generate as much incoming revenue and become expensive costs to the organisation. Over-utilised resources increase costs and impacts on flexibility and lead time.

Capacity flexibility

Effective capacity

Effective capacity is the output rate managers expect for a given activity or process. It is synonymous with rated capacity.

Demonstrated capacity

Demonstrated capacity is the proven capacity calculated from actual performance data.

Maximum demonstrated capacity

Maximum demonstrated capacity is the highest amount of actual output produced after optimising the resource. It is the most one could expect to produce in a short period, but represents an unsustainable rate over the long term. At the maximum level, utilisation of resources may be inefficient (such as increased energy costs, overtime, and higher maintenance costs).

Capacity buying

Buying capacity is a purchasing practice whereby a company commits to a supplier for a given amount of its capacity. The customer subsequently provides schedules for individual products or services. This usually happens when experiencing long lead times and the customer does not know actual production requirements until well inside the established lead time.

Learning curve

The learning curve, or experience curve, is a curve reflecting the rate of improvement in time per piece as production numbers increase. The learning curve is particularly useful in capacity planning when phasing in new products. The basis of the learning curve calculation is that workers can produce the product more quickly once they have experience in making it.

Capacity flexibility essentially means having the capability to deliver what the customer wants within a shorter lead time than competitors can offer. Organisations achieve this flexibility through flexible plants, processes, and workers and through strategies using the capacity of other organisations. Organisations increase their capacities as they learn better ways of producing products, delivering products, and using fewer resources to produce the same quantity of output. This is dynamic efficiency.

Set-up time is one of the determinants of capacity flexibility; managers often neglect to consider this aspect. Set up occurs at the start of a production run and is a function of the number of production runs executed. A machine is set up and the run-size quantity produced. The machine is then set up for the next product. Organisations often look at the production rate to determine capacity. Capacity, though, needs to consider set-up time as a non-productive period as well as the processing speed to determine capacity of a machine.

Two similar real-life examples come to mind, and when telling these stories, the listeners are often incredulous. For obvious reasons we have withheld the company names.

Set-up example 1

A company saw a processing machine at a trade fair in Europe. The processing machine was churning out product at such a rate that the demonstrators were continuously clearing away the output. The company ordered and installed this machine at the company premises as the primary production resource alongside several slower machines.

A typical job on the old machine takes 15 minutes for set up and run time. The new machine produces all the output of a typical job in five minutes; however, it requires 20 minutes to set up and ready for production. Therefore, the older, slower machines finish and wait while the new faster machine has not even started production.

Set-up example 2

Another company researched processing machines for over 12 months. They observed a machine operating in the United States that could produce at three times the output rate of their current machine. The company management were aware of the need to evaluate the set-up process but received assurances that, in the United States plant, set up was not a problem. The company ordered and installed one machine to replace the existing unit at a cost of $20 million.

In the United States, the set-up process was not a problem because a typical processing run would operate for six weeks before being set up for another product. The set-up time was eight hours, or one shift every six weeks.

In the new location, the production requirement quantities were considerably less, and the new machine had to produce six different products per week. That is, six set-up times per week, with each set-up time lasting eight hours. That is 48 hours per week just setting up and readying for production.

To be fair, a recent review of the set-up process managed to reduce each set-up time down to five hours.

A production facility works best when it reduces its flexibility and focuses on a limited set of production objectives. An organisation should not expect to excel in every aspect of production performance – cost, quality, flexibility, new product introductions, reliability, short lead times, and low investment.

Revenue management – also known as yield management

Revenue management overview

Revenue management or yield management

Revenue management is the application of discriminatory pricing to various market segments so relatively fixed capacity satisfies customer requirements and simultaneously maximises revenue.

The objective of revenue management – also known as yield management – is to increase revenues for organisations that operate with relatively fixed capacity. The subject comes under a variety of terms including yield management, pricing and revenue optimisation, and demand chain management.

The airline industry was the first to apply the concept of revenue management during the late 1970s, but since then several industries including hotels, rental cars, retail, advertising, electricity generation and transmission, tour operators, passenger transport, and freight carrying have applied the principles. Even restaurants are learning how to use revenue management to their advantage.

The airline industry is well versed in the application of revenue management, with airlines even going as far as offering free flights on selected routes.[5] Close to the day of the flight, airlines may offer discounted fares on lightly loaded sectors, and these bookings often require full payment, may be non-transferrable to another person, and are usually non-refundable. In some cases, they are changeable, but with the payment of a change penalty fee and by paying any applicable fare adjustment. Peak-hour flights are unlikely to have many fares at lower rates, since the airlines have little trouble selling tickets for peak-hour flights at higher prices.

Hotels practise revenue management by offering lower rates for weekends and during an off-season. They must be aware of both predictable, seasonal factors and unpredictable, individual customer demand by using a systematic approach with a combination of knowledge, experience, understanding, and forecasting. They combine predictability and uncertainty.

Restaurants typically focus on optimising the average meal receipt, or the number of customers in the restaurant. A focus on the average meal receipt encourages high-paying customers to linger over their meals and possibly occupy the table for longer periods leaving other customers waiting. A focus on the number of customers tends to encourage the sale of discounted meals such as two meals for the price of one. Sometimes this could be a profitable strategy, but it tends to focus on volume rather than dollar value. Restaurants should shift from a product-orientation to a demand-orientation.

Revenue management is most effective when the following exist:

- It is difficult to alter capacity in the short term (seats in an aircraft, rooms in a hotel).
- It is possible to segment demand by market, and each segment has varying needs, behaviour, and willingness to pay.
- Demand is highly variable (seasonal fluctuations) and uncertain.
- Customers can purchase the product in advance.
- Inventory is perishable (hotel room by night, airline seat by flight).
- It is possible to forecast demand with relatively high accuracy.
- Marginal capacity change costs are high, and marginal selling costs are low.
- Price is not an indicator of quality.
- Producers are profit-oriented and have freedom of action.

Difficult to alter capacity

There is no need to manage yield when capacity is flexible. An organisation can set a price the market would bear and meet market demand with enough capacity every time (using a chase production method). However, with fixed capacity, such as an airline seat or a hotel room, it is not practical to add or remove capacity units at will, and yet demand fluctuates widely.

Possible to segment demand by market

Airlines segment their market into general classifications of business class, full economy fares, and discount fares. Business travellers are time-sensitive, and they are likely to book late and require maximum flexibility. For that flexibility, they are prepared to pay a higher-priced fare.

The discount fares are of interest to leisure travellers who are price-sensitive, and they are likely to book early and accept restrictions on their ticket. The restrictions limit the ability to alter the booking later. A 'use it or lose it' policy may require the customer to make the booking a month or so in advance, to have maximum or minimum periods of stay, and may include a Saturday night to make it less attractive for business travellers.

The approach is to sell a calculated number of seats on each flight at a discounted rate until enough revenue covers the basic costs for the flight. The price-sensitive traveller takes advantage of these discounts but they may have to pay in advance and accept restrictions on changing flights later. This generates a base yield for the airline. Their forecasting systems predict how many seats they will sell at premium rates, so they hold back a number of these higher-priced seats for booking at the last moment.

Each segment of the market has its own demand curve, and the organisation has detailed historical figures to describe each segment. When all customers value a product identically and exhibit similar purchasing patterns, then there is little opportunity to exploit variations in willingness to pay, variations in product preferences, and variations in purchase behaviour. Revenue management success increases as the heterogeneous nature of the customer increases. More heterogeneity in customers creates more opportunity to exploit the differences to maximise revenues. Revenue-management pricing decisions are more successful when the price-sensitive segment is more price-elastic, and the time-sensitive segment is more price-inelastic.

Demand is highly variable

Demand for rental cars, conference facilities, hotel rooms, party equipment, and holiday services are all affected by highly fluctuating demand. Revenue management is a tool to smooth the demand pattern. In periods of low demand (winter at a seaside resort for the tourism industry), demand needs stimulation. In periods of high demand (summer at a seaside resort in the tourism industry), revenues need to be maximised.

Customers can purchase the product in advance

Customers choose to buy at different times, either well in advance, or at the last minute. Suppliers take advantage of this buyer behaviour, and they have an opportunity to influence that behaviour. They can sell at a discounted rate to those who wish to purchase in advance, but why would an organisation want to sell at the same price to customers who make a booking at the last minute? These last-minute bookings may be for customers who are desperate and must have the service at any price. When the same price applies regardless of booking time, the only driver encouraging customers to buy earlier would be a fear of unavailability of supply. With revenue-management pricing practices, customers buy early both to obtain availability and to obtain a cheaper price.

Inventory is perishable

Manufacturers can store products for subsequent sale. While it benefits a manufacturer to know the exact nature of demand, they can operate effectively when they store products for later use. Tangible products sitting in a warehouse are, in fact, stored capacity.

Intangible products, such as an airfare, are units of lost revenue if not sold by the time of departure. If a customer does not purchase an airfare by the time the flight departs, the airline loses that revenue forever. Similarly, the hotelier loses the revenue from an empty hotel room forever.

Possible to forecast demand with relatively high accuracy

The organisation will dynamically adjust pricing and will hold back on some capacity hoping to sell it at the last minute at a premium. The organisation needs to know how much to hold back. If it holds back too much, it may forego revenue. If it holds back too few, it may miss the high-revenue-generating last-minute sales.

Without a forecast, an organisation may be rudderless by setting prices too high that no one will accept, or too low and missing revenue-maximising opportunities.

High marginal capacity change costs

The cost of adding an additional aircraft with additional seats to the fleet is high. The cost of adding an additional hotel room requires the construction of a new hotel, and this is relatively expensive. The investment decision is significant, and the lead time for delivery is long. Companies in these industries cannot reasonably add and subtract available capacity because of the high marginal costs.

Low marginal sales costs

The cost of adding one more passenger to the passenger list is relatively low. The airline must handle the reservation, handle the check-in, carry the luggage, and make sure the passenger arrives at their destination. When compared to the cost of an aircraft, these transaction costs are low. Likewise, the cost of having an additional guest stay at a hotel room is relatively low. The only costs are cleaning in the morning and collecting the money.

Price is not an indicator of quality

Price is not a status symbol and should not be an indicator of quality. Using airline pricing as an example, most customers realise if they pay a high price for their seat, they will not get a higher quality flight when compared to a discount purchaser who purchases the same class of seat. The difference is in the timing of the purchase, not the delivery of the service.

Producers are profit-oriented

The assumption for revenue management is that the supplier of the service is profit-oriented. A hotel can charge different rates for each room and can hold back some rooms in anticipation of receiving higher revenue later. This approach is not feasible in an accident and emergency ward of a public hospital.

Revenue management process

The revenue management process starts by determining how far in advance the system will look ahead; airlines typically use 300 days.

Airlines segment their market based on purchasing behaviour, not just current or past classifications. They have a clear segmentation between leisure and business travellers. Hotels have short-term, long-term, leisure, business, and conference guests. Rental cars have similar segments to hotels. The duration of an airline flight is a distinguishing characteristic. When a passenger reserves a seat on a plane, the airline knows when that service will start and finish. This is not the case for hotels and rental cars; each hotel room or rental car hire is for a varying length of time. Additionally, having agreed to a hotel room or rental car hire, the customer may seek a reduction or an extension of time.

The supplier predicts customer demand based on forecast demand and capacity at each product/price level and attempts to optimise the price by mathematically determining capacity availability and price that maximises expected profit.

Revenue management uses graphical representation with curves generated for various conditions such as high season, middle season, and low season.

Thus, revenue management allocates the right capacity to the right customer at the right time and maximises revenue or yield at the same time. It builds on historical patterns, known current trends, and likely future happenings. It relies on being able to predict the expected behaviour of specific market segments within the overall market demand. Successful implementation of revenue management requires the business to be capable of continually monitoring and forecasting changes in demand patterns.

Two terminologies used to define the process are the booking limit and the protection level:

Booking limit

The booking limit is the maximum number of units available at each discounted rate.

Protection level

The protection level is the number of units not sold at the discount rate and held back in the hope of selling at a higher rate later.

A booking limit establishes the maximum number of seats or rooms available at the lowest discount rate. Therefore, for the leisure passenger or hotel guest, this is the number of fully discounted fares or cheap rooms available. After reaching this number, the supplier will offer only higher rates. In a two-rate system, when there are no more discounted products available, the remaining seats and rooms are available at full rate. When suppliers offer several classes of rates, they establish a booking limit for each class.

The protection level is the number of selling units (airline seats and hotel rooms) held back with the hope of selling them at the full rate. The supplier has already reached base revenue, and, even though the supplier has customers who want to use the service and are willing to pay the discount rate, the supplier determines that the discount rate is no longer available because they do not want to disappoint business and regular customers who arrive at the last minute. Therefore, the supplier has an opportunity to extract more revenue from the flight, or the night, by holding back in anticipation.

Figure 3.9 illustrates likely outcomes following an adjustment in the booking limit. The revenue manager can take a discounted rate now or hold back and hope for a full rate later. Organisations practising revenue management may have a team watching booking patterns and progress on an hourly basis. It is very dynamic.

Figure 3.10 illustrates the dynamic nature of revenue management. Some organisations monitor market behaviour very aggressively and the cogs move quickly.

Suppliers monitor bookings against availability and determine the acceptable range of variance from the historical average. The variance can be greater when the date of service is further away, since the supplier has time to address the reservation fill rate.

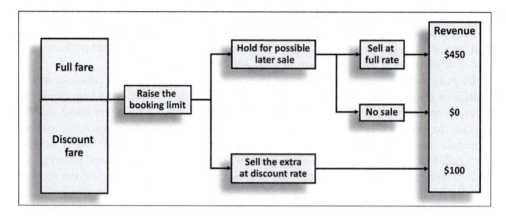

Figure 3.9 Raising the booking limit

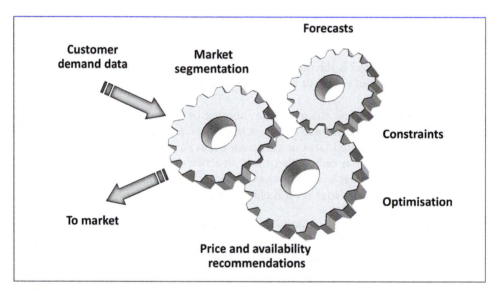

Figure 3.10 Revenue management process

They also communicate prices to customers through intermediaries such as websites and third parties. Suppliers dynamically recalibrate and continually monitor performance and update market response. It is a continuous process to keep surveillance on the response to the pricing levels and competitor reactions and to make further adjustments.

Several options are available to organisations as they attempt to maximise the revenue from their fixed capacity. The base requirement is to manage demand dynamically with the fixed capacity resource. The management of demand attempts to influence buyer behaviour to fit in with available capacity. Options to influence demand include:

- **Partition demand.** Segment the market based on purchasing behaviour – not just current or past classifications. This means identifying future patterns of buying behaviour. The most common examples are the partitions between business and leisure travel and accommodation.
- **Offer off-peak incentives.** When pricing off-peak services at a lower rate than peak services, customers will deliberately delay their demand for the service until the price incentive takes effect. Telephone services might offer lower rates after 7 p.m., for example, airline companies may offer lower fares during their off-season to certain destinations, or hotels may offer discount rates on weekends.
- **Promote off-peak demand.** This is like the off-peak incentives option, but relates to promotion activities and advertisements promoting off-peak demand almost to the exclusion of promoting peak activities.
- **Develop reservation systems.** Reservation systems and appointment systems regulate the demand. Customers know they must make a reservation, or an appointment, so this encourages them to book early to avoid disappointment. When formal systems surround the reservation and appointment systems, customers cannot demand services exceeding the predetermined capacity limit imposed by the reservation and booking system. This controls demand to the capacity limit.

Several options are available to manage the fixed supply capacity, but that usually means the physical facility has a fixed capacity. The options mentioned here relate mostly to human resources.

- **Share capacity with another supplier.** Capacity sharing occurs with airline companies when they fly one aircraft on a route, and it carries two or more airline flight numbers. For example, Qatar Airlines flies daily from London Heathrow to Hamad International Airport in Doha on QA006[6] with a codeshare BA7006 by British Airways.[7] The return trip flies from Hamad International Airport to London Heathrow on QA003 with a codeshare labelled BA7003 by British Airways.
- **Increase customer participation.** Customers may increase participation at any time or just in peak or off-peak periods. Online banking and automatic teller machines allow customers to conduct banking business without the need for bank personnel to be present while the transaction is occurring. This allows the fixed capacity of the banking system to be available for longer periods without needing additional staff. Restaurants may offer a buffet self-service meal during weekends when they may have trouble, or higher costs, with employing staff. This allows the fixed capacity of the restaurant to open for longer periods.
- **Cross-train employees.** By training staff members to perform a multitude of tasks, the organisation can accept any demand and know it has the capability of meeting that demand with available resources. If demand shifts to one area of their business, they can direct trained staff to meet that demand. If cross-training were not in place, they might not be able to offer the full range of services.
- **Employ part-time staff.** This allows the organisation to increase or decrease staff numbers almost at will to meet demand.
- **Create adjustable capacity.** This occurs when organisations do not normally use all available capacity, and they only open the additional capacity in peak periods and close it in quiet times. Tourist destinations often operate in this manner,

with some hotels closing completely for the off-season. Restaurants may operate with an extra dining room available when required. Some organisations may have subcontractors already lined up to satisfy extra demand that exceeds what the organisation can handle by itself.

Figure 3.11 illustrates some of the options for balancing supply with demand in the revenue management process.

Benefits of revenue management

Established airlines can behave very aggressively at the cheap end of the market and protect the high end. This makes it extremely difficult for new entrants to compete without the support of the high-end market. An extremely poignant quotation attributed to Donald Burr, former CEO of People Express, when he summarised the reasons behind the company's 1996 bankruptcy:

> We were a vibrant, profitable company from 1981 to 1985, and then we tipped right over into losing $50 million a month. We were still the same company. What changed was American [Airline]'s ability to do widespread revenue management in every one of our markets. We had been profitable from the day we started until American [Airlines] came at us with Ultimate Super Savers. That was the end of our run because they were able to under-price us at will and surreptitiously.
>
> We did a lot of things right, but we did not get our hands around revenue management issues and automation.[8]

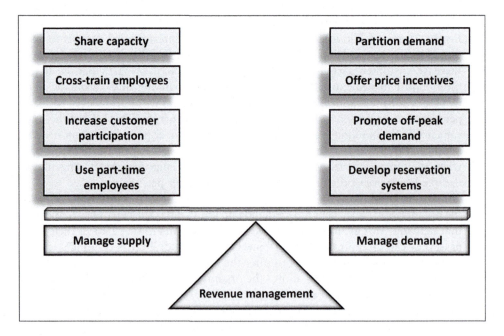

Figure 3.11 Revenue management process to balance demand with supply in fixed-capacity situations

Competing with low-cost operators

Maximising revenue based on fixed capacity is the obvious benefit of revenue management. Another advantage is the ability to compete with low-cost operators. With fixed prices, the supplier can discount with specials and communicate those specials to potential consumers. However, by managing revenue on a daily or a weekly basis, the supplier can reduce prices to compete with low-cost operators at any time. The supplier does not need to advise customers when changing the booking limit or the protection level. When customers use the Internet for making their reservations all they see is the lowest price on offer. They do not see the number of seats or rooms available at that rate. Thus, the supplier can dynamically change the number offered at each rate without the customer knowing. The same goes for competitors and pricing regulators.

An airline with high business-class traffic can offer heavily discounted fares and still be profitable. If the airline increases capacity on a route, it can manage that increase easily by offering more discounted seats until the capacity fills up; there is no need to publish the changes. The range of established fares remains the same; the only difference is the number on offer.

Complications and extensions of revenue management

Variability in available capacity

Hotels, airlines, and rental car companies all experience variability in the available capacity. Airlines can reschedule a different size of aircraft onto a flight if the number of reservations is significantly different from the plan. When this happens, the airline has follow-on scheduling issues of aircraft and crews. Rental car companies can reposition their fleet in anticipation of future demand. In New Zealand, for example, rental car companies have a constant requirement to shift vehicles north as significant numbers of tourists arrive in Auckland (in the north of the North Island), drive their rental vehicles south, and fly out of a southern city without returning to Auckland.

Hotels, airlines, and rental car companies can offer an upgrade to a larger room, business-class seat, or a larger vehicle when they experience an imbalance of demand and supply.

Group reservations

The complication caused by group booking applies more to hotels but could extend to airlines. A group organiser, or a conference planner, approaches a supplier with a request for, say, 300 customers. This number exceeds the booking limit. If the supplier refuses this request, they run the risk of missing the entire revenue from the 300 customers who may go elsewhere.

Demand forecasting

The demand forecast should reflect what is likely to happen rather than based on history. Organisations using revenue management tend to incorporate recent history, seasonality, special events, and known future-demand patterns.

Dynamic decisions

By keeping a close watch on the booking behaviour, revenue management analysts can dynamically adjust booking limits and protection levels.

Variation in capacity purchase

Business people are not the only one who purchases business-class hotel rooms or business-class fares on aircraft. There is nothing stopping leisure travellers from doing that. Likewise, business people can purchase heavily discounted products normally intended for leisure travellers. The airline loses this variation and mobility of capacity unless it identifies the purchaser.

Not all customers are alike

Guests in a hotel can stay for any number of nights. Many hotels offer different rates for every night. Therefore, a guest may have one rate for the first night and a different rate for every other night of the same stay. Other hotels offer packages that include, for example, a weekend. They group several nights together with some nights attracting higher rates than others do and accumulate them all in the package.

Business travel customers may demand a seat on a flight. If the supplier can satisfy requirements for this sector, the businessperson may book other sectors. Denying them the opportunity of buying one sector (because of price or availability) may preclude the follow-on revenue from the other sectors.

Inter-company conflicting objectives

Revenue management is a very analytical tool, and this could cause conflicts inside the supplier company. For example, a sales manager may want to increase total sales at whatever cost, but the revenue analyst may reject the booking in favour of holding out for higher-yielding bookings from another market segment not served by this sales manager.

Fleet management may wish to sell seats in one direction (one-way flights) while marketing may want to offer packaged return flights based on demand.

Competition

Competitive forces may constrain perfect revenue-management activities. Reactive pricing is not an option. Instead, a supplier should adjust booking levels and protection limits.

Information technology

Revenue management can manage the process manually by rule of thumb. However, the nature of the decision making required suggests that investment in information technology and artificial intelligence would result in increased speed of decision making and accuracy – revenue management requires both to succeed, not just survive.

Strategic buyer behaviour

Revenue management often assumes that a customer will purchase the product or leave without buying anything. However, customers with some knowledge of how the system operates may play games and wait for a better price in the future. This means they may enter the system and make the buy/no buy decision on several occasions. Customers exposed to last-minute deals still expect them to be available, and this influences their behaviour.

Service capacity

Service capacity is more time-dependent and location-dependent than manufacturing capacity. It is subject to more volatile demand fluctuations and utilisation directly impacts service quality. The production system cannot store services for later use, and the capacity must be available to produce a service when required. For example, an airline cannot transfer empty airline seats from an off-peak flight to a peak flight.

Service capacity must be located near the customer or at least be available to the customer before the service delivery. Hotel rooms provide an excellent example of this concept. Having empty hotel rooms in one city does not help a shortage of hotel rooms in another.

Inventory cannot smooth demand. Customers interact with the production system and can vary the processing time required for each delivery. Customer behaviour influences demand. Services experience off-peak and peak demand as well as in-season and off-season demands.

Planning capacity levels for services must consider the day-to-day relationship between service utilisation and service quality. The best operating point is near 70% of the maximum. That is enough to keep servers busy, but allows time to serve customers individually and keep enough capacity in reserve so as not to create too many managerial headaches.

Low rates are appropriate when both the degree of uncertainty and the stakes are high. This situation applies to accident and emergency services and fire services. Sporting events and concerts with sell-out crowds use the maximum capacity.

Queues and waiting lines

Queues are a natural consequence of service delivery. In many ways, a queue in a services environment is equivalent to buffer inventory in manufacturing. In production industries, the inventory acts as a buffer to allow the rate of inputs to be different from the rate of outputs. As an example, the production rate of finished goods into a warehouse can operate at a different pace from the rate of demand provided enough stock is available to meet that variation.

In services, the queue acts as the buffer between the arrival rate of customers and the supply-and-delivery rate of the actual service.

Chapter summary

Capacity is the capability to produce output per period. Capacity required represents the process capability needed to make a given product mix or deliver a given service mix – assuming technology, product specification, etc. Organisations measure the capacity available and the capacity required in the short, medium, and long term.

The objective of strategic capacity planning is to specify the overall capacity level of resources – facilities, equipment, and labour – that best supports the company's long-range competitive strategy for production. If capacity is inadequate, a company may lose customers through slow service or by allowing competitors to enter the market. If capacity is excessive, a company may have to reduce its prices to stimulate demand or else under-utilise its workforce, carry excess inventory, or seek additional, less-profitable products to stay in business. Having enough capacity available is a strategic decision for any organisation.

The three main production strategies for determining capacity utilisation to balance demand are level production method, chase production method, and demand management process.

Revenue management – also known as yield management – is a valuable process for maximising the revenue achieved for service organisations with relatively fixed capacity, such as airline, rental car, and hotel companies.

The production system cannot store services for later use, and the capacity must be available to produce a service when required. Service capacity should be located near the customer.

Discussion questions

1 What does the term 'capacity' mean?
2 How does capacity differ from capability?
3 Why is capacity management strategically important?
4 The management of capacity for services is more difficult than for manufacturing. Why?
5 Describe the capacity considerations for a hospital, and identify how this is different from a manufacturing unit.
6 What are the possible consequences of the demand rate being different from the design capacity rate?
7 Describe three ways an organisation can make short-term capacity adjustments when demand exceeds capacity.
8 Describe three ways an organisation can influence customers to shift demand from periods without adequate capacity to periods with excess capacity.
9 What industries use revenue management, and why?

Key terms

best operating level, 100
booking limit, 107
capacity, 81
capacity buying, 101

capacity management, 81
capacity planning, 81
chase production method, 89
demand management process, 89

demonstrated capacity, 101
design capacity, 100
diseconomy of scale, 100
economy of scale, 100
economy of scope, 100
effective capacity, 101
executive sales and operations
    planning, 84
learning curve, 102
level production method, 89

maximum demonstrated capacity, 101
production plan, 84
production planning, 87
production planning approaches, 89
protection level, 107
revenue management, 103
sales and operations planning, 84
supply, 87
yield management. *See* revenue
    management

Notes

1 Cherif, R., Hasanov, F., & Pande, A. (2017). Riding the energy transition: Oil beyond 2040. *International Monetary Fund*. Retrieved from www.imf.org/en/Publications/WP/Issues/2017/05/22/Riding-the-Energy-Transition-Oil-Beyond-2040-44932
2 Apple. (2018, April 9). *Apple now globally powered by 100 percent renewable energy* [Press release]. Retrieved from www.apple.com/newsroom/2018/04/apple-now-globally-powered-by-100-percent-renewable-energy/
3 Bengali, S. (2018, March 19). The biggest solar parks in the world are now being built in India. *Los Angeles Times*. Retrieved from www.latimes.com/world/asia/la-fg-india-solar-20180319-story.html
4 Raturi, A. S., & Evans, J. R. (2005). *Principles of operations management*. Mason, OH: Thomson South Western, p. 147.
5 Air New Zealand offered 3000 domestic flights to and from Christchurch for free on 2nd, 3rd, and 4th of November 2012. This was in response to a competitor that advertised tickets 'as low as $1'. Retrieved November 2, 2012, from http://grabaseat.co.nz/
6 Qatar Airways. (n.d.). *Choose a flight*. Retrieved July 27, 2018, fromhttps://booking.qatarairways.com/nsp/views/index.xhtml
7 British Airways. (n.d.). *Choose your flights*. Retrieved July 27, 2018, from www.britishairways.com/travel/fx/public/en_us?eId=111011&timestamp=0727070833
8 Talluri, K. T., & van Ryzin, G. J. (2005). *Theory and practice of revenue management* (International series in operations research and management science). New York, NY: Springer Science and Business Media, p. 9.

Additional reading on capacity and revenue management

Netessine, S., & Shumsky, R. (2002). Introduction to the theory and practice of yield management. *INFORMS Transactions on Education*, 3(1), 34–44. doi:10.1287/ited.3.1.34
Pittman, P. H., & Atwater, J. B. (2016). *APICS dictionary* (15th ed.). Chicago, IL: APICS.
Shy, O. (2008). *How to price: A guide to pricing techniques and yield management*. Cambridge, UK: Cambridge University Press.
Talluri, K. T., & van Ryzin, G. J. (2005). *Theory and practice of revenue management* (International series in operations research and management science). New York, NY: Springer Science and Business Media.
Wallace, T. F. (2008). *Sales and operations planning: The how-to handbook*. Cincinnati, OH: T. F. Wallace & Company.
Wallace, T. F. (2011). *Sales and operations planning: Beyond the basics*. Cincinnati, OH: T. F. Wallace & Company.
Wallace, T. F., & Stahl, R. A. (2006). *Sales and operations planning: The executive guide*. Cincinnati, OH: T. F. Wallace & Company.

Chapter 4

Process design and strategy

Learning objectives

At the end of this chapter, you should be able to:

- Identify customers and relationships.
- Classify customers by type or attitude.
- Discuss customer-centricity.
- Discuss the strategic importance of process.
- Discuss process thinking.
- Discuss value-adding and cost-adding processes.
- Discuss the strategic decisions for processes – process focus or product focus.
- Discuss process flow structures.
- Discuss the characteristics of project, job, and batch environments.
- Discuss the characteristics of repetitive and continuous processes.
- Discuss the product-process matrix – process structures and their relationship to output volume and variety.
- Explain process variability and the variables that could be present in a process.
- Describe the perfect process.
- Describe the strategic service vision.
- Discuss the characteristics of service operations.
- Discuss the service encounter.
- Describe the service-profit chain.

Perspective: Digital ubiquity – embracing digital technology

This chapter discusses process design, so, as a perspective, we put to rest the perennial fear that automation and technological advances will eliminate vast numbers of jobs and make human labour redundant. Henry Ford's moving assembly line provided the opportunity to mass-produce automobiles making many equestrian occupations redundant. Early automobile production still required human labour, albeit with different skills compared to the equestrian jobs it replaced. However, more recently, manufacturing robotics and autonomous material handling devices eliminated the need for repetitive human labour.

The fear now is that computers and machines will learn non-routine and cognitive tasks as evidenced by self-driving vehicles. This periodic fear pervades middle-class workers and education providers worldwide. Automation provides an unsettling effect on employment that brings disruption to the skill sets required for future jobs.

Manufacturing cannot claim this fear alone. The automated teller machine introduced over 50 years ago[1] was destined to eliminate bank tellers. This simply has not happened in such a dramatic form as eliminating the job. David Autor, when discussing 'Why are there so many jobs?' maintains that the number of bank tellers in the United States rose slightly during the 30-year period, 1980–2010.[2] The role performed by bank tellers changed from one almost entirely transaction-based, with tellers counting money deposits and dispensing money withdrawals, to a more varied and effective relationship encounter with customers. The cost of running a bank branch decreased but the effectiveness of the bank employees increased.

Erik Brynjolfsson and Andrew McAfee in their book, *The Second Machine Age*, offer an unsettling picture of the likely effects of automation on employment. They see a rapidly increasing digitisation bringing economic rather than environmental disruption. With computers getting more powerful, companies have less need for some kinds of workers and this technological progress will leave some people behind. The authors demonstrate that there has never been a better time to be a worker with special skills or the right education. These people can use technology to create and capture value. At the same time, there has never been a worse time to be a worker with only 'ordinary' skills and abilities because computers, robots, and other digital technologies are acquiring these skills and abilities at an extraordinary rate.[3]

Automation substitutes for labour by completing a task faster or for less cost. However, many forget that automation also complements labour by raising output in a way that leads to more demand for human workers to do the accompanying tasks that do not have automation. Essentially, workers become the supervisors of automation.

In their *Harvard Business Review* article, Marco Iansiti and Karim R. Lakhani discuss, with a raft of examples, how we are approaching digital ubiquity and how we should embrace future digital technology.[4] They suggest we should examine the cumbersome processes in our businesses and our industries and search for ways to digitise the process components. As an example, they mention how Uber transformed transportation services including reservations, tracking, billing, customer service, driver performance, and ratings.

They want us to connect our existing assets across companies in a manner like Nest, a manufacturer of digital thermostats, connects with public utilities to share data and optimise overall energy usage. Instead of driving the obsolescence out of established companies, we should look at how we can enhance their value and save some value for ourselves.

They provide numerous anecdotes about how General Electric strives for new modes of value creation and analyses data in innovative ways to enable old and new customers to add value. Use software to extend the boundaries of what you do. Digital transformation allows us to use existing capabilities and customer relationships as foundations for new opportunities.

Business analytics and artificial intelligence transform data into insight to allow better decisions. This means we can forecast planning scenarios more accurately, help quantify risk, and yield better choices through analysis and optimisation. Eventually this leads to data-driven decision making, greater productivity, and higher market value, as well as increased output and profitability.

Daniel Akst, writing in the *Wilson Quarterly*,[5] purports that like trade, automation makes us better off collectively by making some of us worse off. Therefore, we should focus attention on those disadvantaged by automation even if the wounds are 'only' economic. In other words, the issue is not technological, but distributional – which is to say, political. While there is cause for concern, there is no other way but forward.

Introduction

So far, we have formulated the strategy, developed a forecast of future demand, and ensured there is enough capacity. Now the concentration is on process technology and the physical layout of the process.

This chapter discusses process design, which considers the needs of the customer and the requirement to be consistent with the capacity of the available resources. The relationship between customers and suppliers is a function of the process design.

Technology in service design should be easy to use and provide features that enhance customer value. Automated service design is pointless if customers will not use it, or if they use it and do not think the service is worth it.

Good process design principles focus on customer expectations, and their perception of value is relevant to product- and service-related industries. Process designers can foster this by understanding what the customer wants and providing this in a responsive easy-to-use, yet flexible manner. These facets of process design are critical in fostering loyalty and ultimately profitability.

This chapter discusses various types of processes, which usually relate to volume and customisation. It contrasts the difference between producing a commodity product, like electricity, and a one-off product, such as a vehicle repair. It presents the concepts of value streams and process structures.

Public-service processes often operate with legislated powers of enforcement and may not possess the profit motivation of commercial business processes. In a sense, they are legal monopolies and may not see the need for process effectiveness and customer satisfaction.

Public-health services have a clear perception of customer satisfaction, but financial budget restrictions often bind decisions. Superior process design and subsequent process improvement enhances performance, service delivery, and capability.

The chapter concludes with the service-profit chain to increase profits through extremely satisfied employees. Process design aims at satisfying customers.

Customers and relationships

Customer-centricity

Many organisations treat all their customers the same and develop processes to make sure the treatment each customer receives is the same regardless of circumstances. Unfortunately, this fails to recognise that customers are different. Customer-centricity

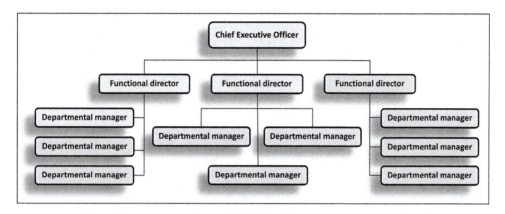

Figure 4.1 A hierarchical organisation chart showing a functional focus

recognises that some customers are more valuable to the organisation; some customers deserve treatment that is more special.

The traditional organisation arrangement is hierarchical with the chief executive officer at the top, a layer of senior managers reporting to the chief executive officer, possibly another layer of managers, and finally some process workers who make things and provide services. To fill these positions, a hierarchical chart is prepared, as in Figure 4.1, with each box representing selected individuals.

With the hierarchical focus, it is obvious everyone's attention is towards the chief executive officer. Each manager reporting to a manager is trying to look good in the eyes of the manager and protect their own position. Managers agree on performance objectives for subordinate managers to help achieve their own objectives. It is all about control and power. Whoever has the most control and power rises to the top. How quickly an individual can climb the ladder and secure a top position is the measurement of success.

This arrangement highlights product-centricity; the measurement systems are product-based. The managers use language related to the products the customers are buying and using. Yes, managers refer to customers and say that customers are important, but what they really mean is that customers are contributing to the success of the organisation, which translates to the career success of management.

This style of management encourages short-term decision making and stifles innovation. Recognition of creative ideas that might make a dramatic difference to the organisation takes too long, or the management style blocks the ideas on their way to the top. Managers base remuneration and promotion on functional performance measures such as achieving sales and profit targets and keeping within a cost budget. These measures have nothing to do with satisfying customers and growing the business through total customer satisfaction.

Classifying customers by type or attitude

Customer-focused organisations have an excellent understanding and appreciation of their customers. They know why customers need products and services, they know why they buy products and services, they know why they keep coming back, they

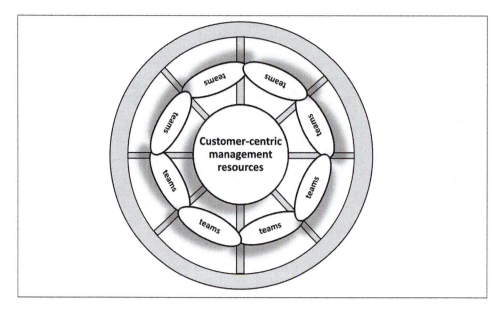

Figure 4.2 A customer-centric organisation totally focused on the customer

know what they will need in the future, they know why they have future needs, and they know why they recommend products and services to others. They listen for ideas through vision, innovation, and external networks; they listen to the customer.

The organisation must clearly define and communicate the value proposition and actively engage customers in the product- and service-design processes implemented to deliver the strategy. Modern communication and technology allow firms to lower the cost of providing information and facilitate customer choice. This has a downside when customers search for product information and pricing from several organisations before committing to just one organisation, with the decision invariably based on price and availability.

Every person in the organisation who is remotely associated with delivering a product or a service needs an understanding of customer behaviour. This means understanding the reasons why customers behave in certain ways and what motivates them to be a customer, since this may affect the production of the product and the delivery of the service. Figure 4.2 illustrates a customer-centric organisation where cross-functional teams work together to focus on the customer and deliver more value.

The orientation of this book emphasises the customer. Process design concentrates on the customer, and process improvement tries to satisfy the customer more than before. Johnston, Clark, and Shulver classify customers by their type, or attitude, as follows:[6]

- The **ally** arrives in a positive frame of mind, willing to help and provide feedback to facilitate a better service. The happiness of the ally rubs off onto other customers who believe the service must be good.
- The **hostage** is 'locked in' contractually. A hostage requires the service but has no choice, or has a potential financial penalty if they go elsewhere. Customers

buying new cars contract the franchise dealers to service the vehicles. The dealers may very well charge premium rates because they have a contracted customer. As soon as the service level slips, the hostage shows signs of anger and threatens to go elsewhere.

- The **anarchist** simply dislikes rules and systems. An anarchist objects when told to do something, or gets upset when filling in forms, which do not appear to have any rhyme or reason. An anarchist can cause a scene and may seem unreasonable. The danger lies in allowing anarchists to get their own way, as other customers see this as unfair.
- A **patient** is like the hostage and may turn into the anarchist. This type of customer already belongs to the organisation and feels they have little chance of escape. For example, they may be a hospital patient who cannot transfer to another institution, or a student who has enrolled in a course and has already paid the fees. In that sense, they are a hostage and may start pushing the limits and challenging the rules, which is like the anarchist.
- The **tolerant** customer may be passive and maybe ignored. The tolerant customer sits quietly and waits for service. They may not jump up and down and demand the immediate service that another customer might demand. They just sit quietly and wait. It is a mistake for service supply staff to ignore tolerant customers, as they may reach their limit, get up, go, and never come back.
- The **intolerant** often causes stress and problems. The intolerant customer does not sit quietly and wait. Instead, they make their presence and requirements known. They may not be very clear or even coherent in describing what they want, but they make sure supply service staff handles their problem. They typically are very vocal and could easily become a terrorist if not handled properly.
- The **victim** seems to attract bad luck. The victim is the recipient of a product or service when something goes wrong. The process fails and for some reason the victim just happens to be the customer. It is hard to predict exactly how a victim will react. They may be tolerant or intolerant, and blow the incident out of proportion.
- The **terrorist** mounts a damaging attack when you least expect it. The terrorist is a real danger, as they strike without warning and make sure they inflict as much damage as possible. They announce their displeasure knowing other customers are listening.
- The **incompetent** appears confused by procedures. Often incompetent customers are first-time customers and simply do not know what to do. They may stumble around looking for answers and may be doing irreparable damage as they go. Service supply staff should be very aware of the incompetent, otherwise this type of customer becomes high-maintenance in the future.
- The **champion** is supportive and helpful and has a positive word-of-mouth. The champion is more than an ally. They go out of their way to be helpful, co-operative, and friendly. Every organisation needs champions.

Most organisations aim for a steady stream of customers and should ensure that customers return for enduring business. Organisations recognise customer retention as a marketing ploy by using loyalty cards, frequent flyer programmes, loyalty status (platinum, gold, and silver status), credit card incentives, loyalty discounts, and rebate systems aimed at customer loyalty and retention.

Loyal customers generate long-term revenue streams and create high lifetime values. They tend to buy more than new customers and tend to increase spending over time. They may be willing to pay a premium for products and services. Retaining customers is usually significantly cheaper than attracting new ones. They provide new opportunities, especially when they act as advocates for the supplier.

Some organisations do not want loyal customers. One would hope hospital staff would not want a discharged patient to return with the same symptoms and for the same reason. In this case, the patient establishes loyalty during the hospital stay, and the customer types described above would apply. Additionally, satisfied customers tell other potential patients the service received satisfied their requirements and this is a good place for treatment. In a private hospital system (profit-oriented and fee-paying), a satisfied patient generates future business by spreading the word.

Schools and universities have satisfied customers who progress through the system and eventually leave or graduate. The reputation of the learning institution builds up over time by the ongoing success of the school leavers and the university graduates. The reputation becomes the satisfaction measure.

A corrections service managing a prison for offenders would not want loyal customers if the customers were the inmates. The discussion in this case centres on defining the customer, and most would accept that the customer is the taxpayer, the law-abiding citizen, and the community at large. The process is to punish and correct behaviour, and the inmate, not the customer, is the input to the process. In this example, the relationship between customer and supplier is quite strange; the customer (law-abiding citizen) is not involved with the process and usually has no contact with the supplier. The same applies to the police force and the armed services. Customers (the community-at-large) want these services to be there, but they do not want any contact with the supplier; they know the service is performing satisfactorily when they do not see the supplier and there is no need to call for help.

Strategic importance of process

Process thinking

Process

A process is a planned series of actions or operations that advances a material or procedure from one stage of completion to another.

Process thinking

Process thinking is a structured approach that considers an organisation and its various activities and functions as a system of interrelated processes, all designed, controlled, and continuously improved.

Process thinking creates an entirely different mindset whereby the organisation arranges processes totally focused on the customer, and this makes it easy for the customer to do business with the organisation. In this diagram, the customer is the central target with teamed resources all working together and aimed at the target. Customer-centric management resources have a clear definition of the customer, but the resources used are fluid and keep changing as customer requirements change.

Employers introduce job enlargement, enrichment, and rotation to change the tasks performed by individuals and to change their involvement with processes. Enlargement allocates a larger number of tasks to individuals to make the process more complete and fulfilling; enrichment increases the number of tasks in a job and may involve more decision making or greater autonomy; while rotation moves individuals between tasks to create more variety in the activities.

Michael Hammer changed the radical views that characterised his business process re-engineering approach of the 1990s in favour of a process view. In *The Agenda*, he describes, in a very easy-going personable manner, why process should be the focus for organisations. The key points from this text are:[7]

- Run your business for the convenience of your customers, not yours. He introduced the term ETDBW, which stands for 'easy to do business with'. Customers do not complain about the products and services they receive. They usually complain about how they find products, how they order products, how they communicate with the supplier, how they receive products, and how they pay for products. These are the real problems, but they receive very little attention from traditional management.
- Give your customers what they really want. In other words, deliver more benefits by designing processes to understand the customer needs and developing production processes flexible enough to deliver exactly what the customer wants, when they want it, and how they want it.
- Put processes first. Process thinking is not about overhead allocation and cost accounting; it is not about confusion and delay. It is a discipline that designs outstanding performance rather than relying on luck. Customers and shareholders are happy on a sustained basis.
- Create order where chaos reigns. Encourage new ideas with process and product innovation. However, these ideas require a process to facilitate their development into products and services that delight customers. Without a process, the innovation wallows in the mud and takes forever to reach reality.
- Measure it as if you mean it. Traditional company measurement systems look at history and tell you (approximately) what has happened. The missing link is telling you what to do in the future to make things better. That is where process thinking develops a structure to improve performance across the whole organisation. Hammer suggests that organisations make measuring a function of managing, not a part of accounting.
- Manage without structure. Do not infer from this that being disorganised is the way to go. Management styles are flexible, adaptable, and cooperative.
- Focus on the final or end customer to obtain an appreciation of real customer needs.
- Knock down the outer wall. Collaborate with customers and suppliers wherever possible.
- Extend your enterprise – virtually, not vertically. The Internet provides opportunities to break down existing barriers acting as a big wall of overhead and inefficiency between organisations. Breaking the barriers allows organisations to redesign processes together so they integrate and not just interface.
- Make it happen.
- Prepare for a future you cannot predict. Institutionalise a capacity for change.

Process thinking facilitates a better understanding of how individual and group efforts affect other individuals and groups. Discover barriers inhibiting cooperation and performance, as this provides a means of analysing and improving processes.[8]

Value adding and cost adding

Value

Value is the amount customers are willing to pay for what an organisation provides. It represents a relationship between the benefits received and the price paid. Benefits can be informational and emotional as well as economic. Value is the quality received relative to expectations.

Value adding

Value adding is a positive contribution that a process makes to the final usefulness or value of a product. The customer measures value in this sense.

Cost adding

Cost adding is a negative contribution that a process makes to the final usefulness or value of a product. The customer measures value in this sense – a cost-adding process does not add value; it just adds cost.

Primary process

A primary process is a process that performs the main value-added activities of an organisation.

Secondary process

A secondary process is a process, such as recruitment, that creates value for the internal customer.

When consumers take delivery of products or services, they are evaluating the result of numerous processes. If the products are manufactured items, the processes involved start with design innovation and progress through raw materials, work in process, and finished goods towards a distribution system that delivers the products. All these steps require processes.

Services have material, technology, and labour inputs, and processes manage all of these. When you examine these steps closely, it is virtually impossible to escape the concept of process. Processes are vitally important for the successful operation of all organisations.

A process is either value adding or cost adding. These are mutually exclusive; if it is not one, it is the other. Value is the relationship of the benefits received to the price paid. The concepts of exciting innovation and emotional benefits appear. One can think of value as the quality received compared to expectations. As a firm attempts to improve processes, it should examine the created value. Process improvement aims to eliminate cost-adding processes and progressively improve the value created in value-adding processes. When organisations begin cost-saving exercises, they should target cost-adding processes.

All customers want value, but value is not easy to define. There is no quantitative measure for value because it includes tangibles and intangibles. Putting it simply, value is a ratio between the benefits received by the customer and the price paid. Some people see value as the ratio between the quality received and customer expectations.

The price includes monetary considerations as well as all the other things required to obtain the benefits. These include attributes such as time, convenience, hassle, anxiety, and other emotions.

Customers base expectation on experience. If customers do not know any better, they will accept any level of quality. As soon as they experience a higher level of quality, their expectation rises accordingly. This adds to the price. Now the supplier must increase the benefits received to keep the ratio constant. Alternatively, they may have to lower the monetary price to keep the ratio constant.

Three core processes are important in the creation of customer value. First, it is necessary to design the new product development process to create solutions that customers need and want. In other words, there is no point designing a product or service if customers will not use it, or if they use it and find they do not think it is worth it. Secondly, supply chain management must organise the acquisition of physical and informational inputs and convert them effectively into customer solutions to avoid dissatisfaction. Finally, a customer management process must exist to create customer knowledge, shape a customer's perceptions of the organisation's service and image, and build relationships through positive customer experiences.[9]

Value is a perception, and customers defect when they perceive a competitor has more value than the current supplier provides. The current supplier, in this case, is not lowering standards or failing to deliver; the difference is that a competitor has raised the expectation.

Expectation does not have to increase. A supplier does not have to supply more products or more service; they may supply less. Discount airlines offer significantly less in-flight service than a full-service airline. Discount and bargain basement stores offer less than full-service, full-display stores. They compensate for their reduced offering by lowering the monetary price. The customer considers the ratio of benefits to price and realises the benefit has reduced and the price has reduced. The customer must now decide which value is better. It comes down to expectation.

A supplier with a higher ratio of benefits to price will experience a competitive advantage in the short term until competitors catch up. Competitive activity endeavours to close the gap.

Process design considers all these attributes of value. It does not stand still. It is an ever-moving target. Customers pay a premium for agility, flexibility, responsiveness, and understanding. Because they pay the premium, they can be demanding and want more for less. In other words, they want more value.

The drivers of process design aim solely at adding value to the customer. A process should establish exactly what the customer values and the design should contribute the most value. Customer value determines the type of supply chain and services required to retain customer loyalty.

Process design requires an appreciation of the nature of the process and an awareness of how the process adds customer value. All organisations are full of processes;

every function executes with a process. In fact, all work is a process. A process creates value and can deliver only what the process design allows – no more. Therefore, the primary focus is on the process that creates value (the value stream).

We talk about customer focused, but, really, we should talk about customer centred, whereby the customer is at the very centre of all processes. The needs, wants, and expectations of the customer are paramount, and this affects process design.

Organisational processes describe all the activities that transform inputs into outputs, the methods for conducting business, the ways of acting and interacting, the decision-making styles, the communication styles, and the patterns of learning. They also include how performance changes and improves over time.

Managerial processes start with strategy development and establish the vision, the mission, the core competence, and the direction of the organisation over the medium to long term. Process describes the methods for negotiating and obtaining necessary support and resources. Staff require motivating, and a process describes the motivation methods. Managerial processes define performance measurement and the steps for achievement.

Value-adding or primary processes create value for the external customer. When you think of a process, it is more likely to be a value-adding, primary process that comes to mind. The value-adding, primary processes interact with the customer; the output is visible to the customer. Thus, the customer can gauge the performance of the process and make a judgement on whether it is adding value. These processes cover consumption from intent to completion, new product and service development from concept to product launch, order fulfilment from receipt of order to product delivery, and maintenance and service from product launch through the entire life cycle of the product.

Supporting or secondary processes create value for the internal customer. These processes may be very important for the smooth running of the organisation, but the external customer usually will not place any value on them. They cover internal processes such as:

- Selecting and hiring new employees.
- Terminating the employment of existing employees.
- Checking the credit rating of new customers.
- Collecting outstanding accounts receivable within due date.
- Closing off the books at the end of a period without disrupting the normal operation of the organisation.
- Researching and developing new products and services.
- Developing prototypes of new products and services.
- Identifying new suppliers and sources of supply.
- Implementing policy.

Supporting, secondary processes do not add value to the external customer and this places these processes firmly into perspective. They must exist, but they are not the purpose of the organisation. All processes link activities that perform production or service tasks that advance some material or a procedure from one stage of completion to the next. Ideally, each activity adds value to the customer. This is the value equation. Table 4.1 highlights the major classifications and types of processes.

Table 4.1 Major classifications and types of processes

Classification	Type of processes	Examples
Organisational process	Functional	Transform inputs to outputs
	Procedural	Methods of conducting business
		Ways of acting and interacting
		Styles for decision-making, communicating, learning
	Change and improvement	Ways of changing and improving performance over time
Managerial process	Strategy development	Establish organisational direction and goals
	Negotiating	Obtain needed support and resources
	Motivating	Personal development leadership
	Monitoring and control	Performance achievement and measurement
Value-adding or primary process	Create value for the external customer	
	Consumption	From intent to completion
	Product development	From concept to launch
	Fulfilment	From order to delivery
	Maintenance and service	From delivery through the life cycle of a product
Supporting or secondary processes	Create value for the internal customer	Hiring new employees
		Checking customer credit
		Collecting accounts receivables
		Closing the books
		Building product prototypes
		Identifying new suppliers
		Implementing policy

The process itself is composed of inputs, outputs, and process variables. Process design, construction, operation, and maintenance determine performance. The next chapter examines process variables and the process to improve performance.

As shown in Figure 4.3, the process delivers specific value measured in terms of cost, quality, delivery, flexibility, and service. These are the five major groups of competitive capability as discussed in Chapter 1. Each of these competitive capabilities is important to the customer – some more than others. Cost is always important. However, too often organisations place too much emphasis on cost at the expense of the other four capabilities. Organisations should study each process to see what value it provides to the customer. Ask the customer to state exactly what they expect

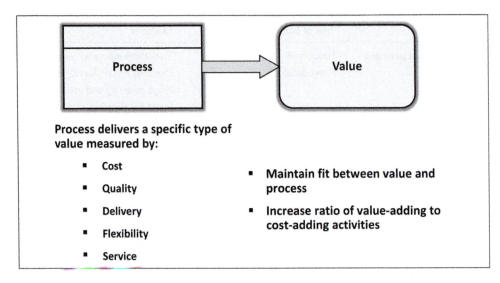

Figure 4.3 Process adds value to the customer

from the process. Quality, delivery, flexibility, and service should all add value. The examination of process starts by looking at every step in the process and determining whether it adds cost or value. The essential issue is to maintain the fit between value and process, making sure every step is in fact adding value. If it is not adding value, it is adding cost, and the process becomes a candidate for elimination.

The transformation process, as discussed in Chapter 1, is a generic form of the process. Typical inputs include resources, workers, managers, equipment, facilities, materials, services, land, energy, and ideas. Typical outputs include products, services, and by-products. Variables exist in inputs and outputs as well as in the actual transformation process itself. We discuss process variables and variation in Chapter 5.

Strategic decisions for process

Process focused

Process focused is a type of production organisation in which the production process delineates both plant and staff responsibilities.

Product focused

Product focused is a type of production organisation in which product, product line, or market segment delineates both plant and staff responsibilities.

Cellular production

Cellular production links the advantages of process focused with the advantages of product focused. The design provides effective flow with the high productivity associated with assembly lines and the flexibility of the job shop. The organisation can produce similar and diverse products without slowing the process.

The layout decision determines the placement of process technology, workstations, machines, operators, queues, and stockholding points within a productive facility. The overall objective is to arrange these to ensure a smooth workflow (in a factory) or a traffic pattern (in a service organisation).

Inputs to this layout decision include the specification of the objectives of the system in terms of output and flexibility, a forecast of product or service demand, processing requirements in terms of the number of operations and the amount of flow between departments and work centres, and space availability within the facility itself.

The basic layouts have either a process or a product focus. Figure 4.4 is a variant on the product-process matrix and emphasises the process focus found in project, job shop processes, and batch processes, and the product focus found in repetitive and continuous processes.

Process focused

When a supplier produces products or delivers services in small lots, often to customer specification, the supplier is (usually) process focused. When they arrange facilities around a process, it has a process focus. Products and service delivery follows highly irregular start-stop, jumbled-flow routes with sidetracking and backtracking.

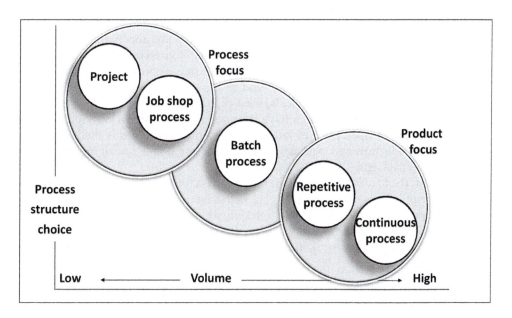

Figure 4.4 Product focus and process focus, adapted from Hayes, R. H., & Wheelwright, S. C. (1984). *Restoring our competitive edge: Competing through manufacturing.* New York, NY: Wiley, p. 209.

Flexibility is the key advantage of these systems; they can produce small batches of a wide variety of products. Additionally, they usually require less initial investment since they typically use general-purpose equipment and mobile material-handling equipment, which is usually less expensive. They, however, require greater employee skill, more employee training, more supervision, more technically trained supervision, and more complex production planning and control. Low-volume, high-variety processes are also known as intermittent processes.

Process-focused production systems include hospitals, universities, local and central government agencies, general medical practices, event planning, financial services and planning, insurance services, disaster relief, automobile repairing, shipbuilding and repair, inspection services, and architectural building design and construction.

Product focused

High-volume, low-variety processes are product focused. A product-focused producer arranges production technology around the products, which go through production along direct linear paths without backtracking, sidetracking, or stopping. The production route is 'continuous' or 'highly repetitive'. With product focus, product lines have dedicated production technology, and they use duplicate equipment to avoid backtracking resulting in a logical, straight-line flow.

Assembly lines are a special case of product focus. The most common assembly line is a moving conveyor that passes a series of workstations in a uniform time interval called the cycle time (the time between successive units coming off the end of the line). At each workstation, human workers, machines, or robots add components or complete assembly operations to build the product. The work performed at each workstation consists of many bits of work (termed tasks, elements, or work units).

Product-focused production systems using an assembly-line approach include automobile assembly, specialist medical facilities, factory house construction, fast-food restaurants, whiteware, and electronics. Examples using a continuous flow are electricity generation, telecommunications, food processing, brewing, chemical production, petroleum refining, petrochemicals, plastics, paper, and cement industries.

Process industry companies often have continuous operations in early production stages and repetitive operations in later stages. Examples using this dual approach include beer production and packaging, dairy processing and packaging, and food processing and packaging.

Historically, the focus of assembly lines has been on full utilisation of labour. Newer views of assembly lines take a broader perspective by incorporating greater flexibility in products produced on the line, more variability in workstations (such as the size of the workstation and the number of workers employed), improved reliability (through routine preventive maintenance), and high-quality output (through improved tooling and training).

Cellular production process

A cellular production process incorporates the best features of process focused and product focused. A cell, forming part of an assembly line, is a group of machines, which together perform a process. A product travels along an assembly line and branches into the cell for a specific process. The main advantages are that the cell is set up to perform a given task and does not need set-up for each job coming through. Additionally, if a product does not need the cell process performed (such as adding a special option), then the product can miss the cell altogether and speed up production throughput.

Process flow structures

Project

A project is a temporary endeavour undertaken to create a unique product, service, or result.[10]

Job shop process

A job shop process is a process for creating a large variety of products or services each in relatively small volumes.

Batch process

A batch process is a process producing varying quantities and following similar flow patterns with some repetition. This process structure lies between job shop and assembly-line repetitive processing. Examples include a suburban bakery that produces regular daily batches of bread and bread products. They use roughly the same process for each batch and just change the recipe.

Repetitive process

A repetitive process is the repeated production of the same discrete product or families of products or service. The method of production minimises set-ups, inventory, and production lead times by using production lines, assembly lines, or cells.

Continuous process

A continuous process is a production system that organises productive equipment and sequences the steps required to produce the product. The term denotes that material flow is continuous during the production process.

Project, job shop process, batch process, repetitive process, and continuous process classify process flow structures.

Project process

Project processes deal with discrete, usually highly customised products and usually require a lot of time and resources to complete. Construction projects, infrastructure projects, movie production, and large-event management are project examples. Most projects are unique, and that characteristic makes their definition and requirements vague. In many cases, problems evolve as the project develops, and the problem requires solution before the project can continue. As an example, a construction company knows in advance that a building foundation may require extra drilling and piling, but the company does not appreciate the full extent of the requirement until the drilling and piling has commenced.

Job shop process

The job shop process irregularly produces single items or small lots in a facility characterised by flexible machines and skilled workers.

Job shops place their competitive success on several strengths. They compete with large-scale producers like batch or repetitive processes, stressing their capabilities to fabricate large varieties of products. These higher-volume processes could produce a given output more cheaply, but only at order quantities large enough to provide economies of scale. Smaller job shops compete with larger ones by offering lower costs and quicker delivery times. Larger job shops compete with smaller ones by offering better, more productive equipment or better order-entry systems.

Job shops accumulate physical resources to achieve and maintain process flexibility because varied workflows do not allow them to keep equipment that can perform only limited types of work. Standard general-purpose machines provide flexibility.

Batch process

When a business manufactures a product routinely in moderate volumes, an operations manager may see an opportunity to eliminate some of the variability of a job shop by grouping orders into larger quantities and running them in larger batches. This creates a process system known as batch production. When competing against a job shop, the batch producer is up against the job shop's flexibility and ability to respond quickly. Normally they base their success on cost advantages. When competing against high-volume repetitive systems, they stress flexibility and often cost.

Repetitive process

A repetitive process arranges machines and special-purpose equipment in a rigid sequence to perform repetitive tasks for large orders. It has the capability to produce standardised products cheaper than any other process. In a cost-competitive environment for products that do not vary much, this provides a key competitive strength. Flexibility is difficult to achieve, and to overcome any weakness a repetitive system can introduce mixed-model scheduling, cellular manufacturing, and standardised product designs. Assembly lines use repetitive processes.

Continuous process

A continuous process produces highly standardised products with little or no variation, such as electricity, petroleum, liquids, gases, and minerals. Continuous flow production usually has just one input (such as oil, milk, timber, and iron ore) and processes these inputs into one or more output flows.

The concept of continuous flows originates with Oliver Evans, who modified his Delaware flourmill in 1784. Starting with a grain feed at one end and using a system of conveyor belts, chutes and milling devices, the factory produced flour at the other end.[11]

Product-process matrix

Product-process matrix

The product-process matrix maps product attributes against the major process structures to help an organisation define its production strategy.

Volume and variety are two important characteristics to consider when designing a process. Volume relates to the quantity produced or delivered per period. High-volume requirements require high volume production or delivery, while low-volume requirements need a production environment conducive to low volumes.

Variety and the need for repeatability are related. A product requiring customisation or produced in low volumes, would suit a production environment that can accommodate the range of sizes, fittings, materials, or customer requests. This product tends to be complex in nature since each unit of production is likely to be different from the next unit of production.

On the other hand, a commodity product such as electricity, sugar, flour, and petroleum, by its very nature, requires a continuous flow type of process. The product is relatively simple; this does not mean the production processes are trivial – far from it. The simplicity describes one unit of production as the same as the next unit of production.

Robert H. Hayes and Steven C. Wheelwright suggested the relationship between the process and the product structure in 1984 when they developed the product-process matrix[12] as illustrated in Figure 4.5.

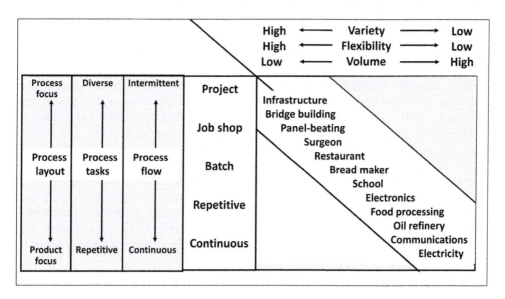

Figure 4.5 Product-process matrix, adapted from Hayes, R. H., & Wheelwright, S. C. (1984). *Restoring our competitive edge: Competing through manufacturing.* New York, NY: Wiley, p. 209.

The central vertical axis shows the process structures of project, job shop, batch, repetitive and continuous, while the horizontal axis shows the product structures based on variety, flexibility, and volume. The natural diagonal represents the most appropriate process structure for any volume-variety-flexibility position. Organisations should operate somewhere on that line. A high-volume commodity producer should be using a continuous process, while a construction company building a bridge should be using a project process. A selection of organisations and products appear on the diagonal line to illustrate the most likely process structure position after considering volume, variety, and flexibility.

The product-process matrix shows that as the volume increases and the product line narrows, standardised equipment and faster material flows become feasible. The choice of process technology forms the basis for the type of specific equipment that follows. Key factors to consider include the initial investment, desired rate or output, quality, labour requirements, flexibility, set-up and operating requirements, maintenance, obsolescence, work-in-process inventory, and system-wide impacts.

It is possible to operate in a relationship that is not on the diagonal line. To be in the top-right sector, an organisation would produce high-volume output using low-volume technology. For most organisations, this would be extremely expensive and not an effective use of resources. To be operating in the bottom-left of the matrix, an organisation produces low volumes and a high variety using an assembly line or continuous processes. This is an ideal position called mass customisation. The initial investment in technology is high, but the flexibility and customisation benefits that are achievable signal a competitive advantage.

Process variability

With every process, the inputs are variable, the actual transformation deals with controllable and uncontrollable variables, and the outputs are variable. Process inputs, including raw materials, human resources, ideas, skills, energy, and previous process outputs, can vary in quantity and specification. Some of the variation may be slight and not affect the result, but it is still a variable. Process design should allow for this variation of inputs. It is a compliment to the process when it handles variation with ease.

Uncontrollable transformation variation includes factors such as temperature, humidity, shift, and operators assigned to the process. Production might schedule the process at a different time and thus have different operators performing the required tasks. After making the resource assignment, the date, time, shift, team, and human resources are uncontrollable. We often call this variation 'noise'.

Controlled process variables include temperature, humidity, production rate, and process time. Note that temperature and humidity appear in the uncontrollable list as well as the controllable list. If the process operator performs this process outdoors, the temperature and humidity are uncontrollable. However, by bringing the same process indoors, those variables become controllable. The natural follow-on suggests that if temperature and humidity are significant in terms of the result, the process operator should make these variables controllable.

Output variables include yield, waste, capacity, downtime, and production rate.

Figure 4.6 illustrates an extension of the basic transformation process as discussed in Chapter 1. Inputs and outputs contain variables and the transformation process is variable.

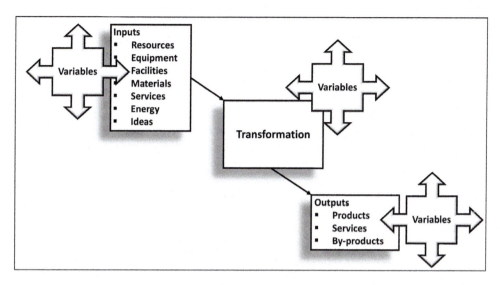

Figure 4.6 Extension of the basic transformation process with variables

As an example of a process with variables, consider a customer placing an order. The following process variables are possible:

- Variable inputs include the method of order receipt (Internet, email, fax, postal service, telephone, sales representative, and customer-service representative), the completeness of the order, and the accuracy of the order.
- Controlled process variables include the amount of training given to the person receiving the order, the amount of inventory on hand, the shipping methods available, and the delivery date promised.
- Uncontrolled process variables include the attitude of the person taking the order, the day of the week, the season of the year, the date of receipt required by the customer, the shift, and the service team.
- Variable outputs include the correctness of the order, the delivery time, and the package quality.

Average performances form the basis of most processes. In fact, business leaders base most business decisions on averages. For one example, assume that the expected sales budget for the year is $6 million. Therefore, the average expected sales budget is $500,000 per month. For another example, assume that a production run on average takes 30 minutes per 1000. Therefore, a production run of 10,000 will take five hours.

When Sam Savage proposed the flaw of averages, he said that decisions based on averages are wrong on average. Whenever anyone uses an average to represent an uncertain quantity, it ends up distorting the result since it ignores the impact of the inevitable variation.[13]

Processes mitigate variation by avoiding complexity, having fewer sources of variability, and by finding ways to control process variables. Given that variables exist, we must develop ways to detect variability, plan around it, and adjust to the sources of variability.

Perfect process

James Womack described the perfect process as one creating exactly the right value for the customer.[14] He acknowledged that value is hard to define for primary processes (supporting the external customer) and even harder to define for secondary processes (supporting the internal customer). Each process must be valuable, capable, available, adequate, and flexible.

A **valuable** process adds value to the customer and the customer recognises it as value adding and not cost adding. The customer notices a valuable process when the system does not perform it.

The **capable** qualifier comes from process capability and six sigma capability as discussed in Chapter 7. A capable process executes the same way with the same satisfactory result every time it runs.

Being **available** is a derivative of total productive maintenance and suggests the process is ready to execute every time it is necessary. This implies that production machines are available for use and not waiting for parts or maintenance.

The theory of constraints defines **adequate** processes as discussed in Chapter 8. An adequate process has enough capacity to perform when required without waiting.

Flexible processes are lean and based on the principles of the Toyota Production System as discussed in Chapter 5. Each step in a flexible process occurs only at the command of the next downstream step within the time available.

Additionally, the system connects the steps of a perfect process by flow (so that each step leads immediately to the next), pull (so that the customers' needs initiate the steps), and levelling (so that the process transmits true demand only).

Strategic service vision

James and Mona Fitzsimmons describe the strategic service vision[15] and apply this to services. However, the overall concept of the strategic service vision applies equally to production. The strategic service vision has four main sections:

- Delivery system.
- Operating strategy.
- Concept.
- Target market segments.

Delivery system

The delivery system describes structural elements (such as the facility location, design, and aesthetics), as well as the number of sites, proximity to suppliers and customers, capacity of the facility, number of employees, management of average and peak demand, degree of automation, and the interface with suppliers and customers.

At this stage, it is perhaps too late to avoid the customer defection. However, the information gathered from this exit interview helps in understanding customer wants and needs and how best the organisation can fulfil them. This helps the organisation to work out whether its strategies to make the business more profitable are working.

Banks increasingly indulge in price wars to get home-lending business. One customer who takes a mortgage earns profit for the bank for the next 30 years or so. Hence, any defection in this product is bad news. Quality of service keeps loyal customers, and loyal customers may not bother to compare other home loan rates in the market. Customers who take out a home loan often buy a second property. A loyal customer will go straight to their existing provider for the additional business. This is a lot less effort for the bank than generating business from new customers. Over the long term, loyal customers generate more profits.

Loyal customers source new business for the organisation by way of referrals. Highly satisfied customers generate positive advertising for a company by word of mouth and encourage acquaintances to use the same supplier. Banks are cautious of customers with only one product as these are the most likely to defect to the competition. Banks therefore encourage customers to buy more bank products to stimulate loyalty and, in the end, generate profits for the bank.

Customer satisfaction drives customer loyalty

The most important aspect of customer service is customer satisfaction. A very satisfied customer is the most loyal. Such customers are apostles, who not only give the organisation repeat business but also encourage the uninitiated to try the service, thus generating new business. Many organisations strive to be the number one in the industry on customer satisfaction.

Organisations use various methods to quantify customer satisfaction. However, although customer satisfaction is very important, some of the measurements used to quantify satisfaction are weak. Many organisations use internal surveys to collect customer satisfaction data, and in many cases the data gathered may suggest that customer satisfaction is very high. Yet, declining sales and profits tell another story. The reason for this is simply that the organisation manipulates the data to paint a rosier picture than what is happening. Sometimes the questionnaire handed out in the surveys has very few choices for the customers to be able to tell the organisation their true level of satisfaction. Organisations should substantiate internal surveys using other methods, such as mystery shopping and direct observations, to achieve improved, quality data on customer satisfaction.

Listening posts give information straight from the customer and they generate ideas to improve the levels of service. It is very important for service providers to allow customers full liberty to explain their experiences.

Service delivery value drives customer satisfaction

The customer gives the best definition of value. Customers recognise value in terms of service or a tangible product that they receive relative to the total costs incurred by them. The total costs include the price and any other cost incurred by the customer to acquire a product or service. Value depends on the way the supplier delivers the product or service to the customer and how that compares with the customer's initial expectations. Successful organisations aim to exceed those expectations to get highly satisfied customers. A major requirement to exceed a customer's expectations is to understand the customer and give freedom to the frontline staff to tailor the product or service to their individual needs.

The actual service received by the customer is the result of the interaction between the service provider, the customer, and the process that delivered the result. Service designers aim to improve the quality of the service provided by understanding the gap between the perception of the actual service and the service the customer expected. Many companies diligently collect data on customer expectation so they can further improve their standards.

The concept of 'doing things right the first time' is popular. This not only gives a good impression to the customer, but also saves a lot of time, effort, and cost in rectifying a mistake.

Employee retention drives service value

Employee retention can never be 100% as employees make career moves and organisations maintain a certain level of turnover. Customers may get agitated if they deal with a new person for each contact with their supplier. When an employee leaves, the employer incurs the cost of recruiting and training a replacement. There is a bigger cost in terms of loss of productivity, though, because the new employee is less experienced with the organisation's processes. In many business sectors, an employee who leaves one organisation takes valuable customers with them to the employee's new organisation. The loss generated with that defection is very difficult to replace with new business.

Retaining staff is crucial when unemployment rates are low and many companies struggle to hire good people. Salaries, compensation, benefits, and plush workplaces contribute to retaining employees. However, employee empowerment works best. Many successful organisations encourage employees to generate their own ideas on how to achieve results. This gives them freedom with a very high level of accountability. People who have a say in the way the business runs invest more of themselves into the organisation's culture and work harder to make their ideas a success.

Employees are highly motivated when they have clear career paths. Call centres often experience high staff turnover, and call-centre employers recognise the potential of promising employees and give them the opportunity to work in other departments. The chosen candidates take their skills as call centre representatives to these departments and enhance the back-room operations with great customer service. Customers seek stability, and the employees who believe in their own brand and the company they work for are the best representatives to give that to their clients.

Employee satisfaction drives retention

Most industries experience intense competition. Service examples include airlines and banking, while production examples include motor vehicles and electronic products. On the surface, there is not much of a difference between products. Banks can copy banking innovation products within a few weeks so they all end up with the same product, albeit under slightly different names. When banks enter a price war, which seems to happen quite frequently, any bank can beat the competitor's rate to steal the deal. The only difference that can win over customers to a brand is customer service.

Employees need to believe in the brand to develop the skill to win customers with service. They need to feel they are an important part of the organisation for them, in turn, to make customers feel good. Management leadership style drives a lot of this motivation and that contributes to how the employees feel about themselves in their workplace.

A workplace that is conducive to overall employee satisfaction generates respect for other employees. This feeling of employee satisfaction transfers directly to customers, and motivated employees work much harder to satisfy their customers.

Employee satisfaction directly drives employee loyalty. Employees who care about the culture and image of their company will not only strive to improve the quality of their work, but also stay longer with the company. If employees believe in their own brand, they are more likely to provide good service and enable customers to make the choice when buying their products. The best impression on the consumer is at the emotional level.

Internal quality drives employee satisfaction

Factors contributing to the internal quality of an organisation are:

- Workplace design.
- Job design.
- Employee selection and development.
- Employee rewards and recognition.
- Tools available to complete their job and serve customers.

All the above factors contribute to build a work environment that influences employee satisfaction. They also create an environment that is conducive to a positive work attitude that drives the employee satisfaction level higher. Workplace design, for example, can add to employee comfort levels that enhance their work capabilities.

It is very important the employees learn to recognise their internal customers, as their work may have a large impact on the work of other departments.

Employee selection and development makes a significant impact on the success of the organisation. When the employment market is tight, it is essential to not only attract the right kind of talent to a company but also develop and retain it. Some organisations measure the attitude of a prospective employee towards the job they have applied for by putting them through a questionnaire. This enables human-resource management to understand the suitability of the applicant to the job, the strengths of the applicant, as well as the areas needing development. They use this data to prepare a curriculum of training for the employee.

Employee rewards and recognition takes a new meaning if they cover customer feedback on the service they receive.

Service-profit chain in perspective

The service-profit chain has an underlying assumption that the business treats and values both employees and customers equally for their contribution to the success of a business. This philosophy is a fundamental shift from the scientific management[19] approach, where managers consider employees solely for their ability to contribute to the production line, or financially-driven thinking, which considers profits in isolation from employees' needs. Instead, in addition to valuing both customers and employees equally, the workplace design meets both parties' needs.[20]

Heskett et al. describe the service-profit chain as several factors that interact and directly influence whether a business is a success or a failure. Specifically, the service-profit chain suggests that employees will be less productive unless the business values them, recognises them, trains them, informs them, supports them, and gives them job satisfaction. Consequently, lost productivity will negatively affect customer service, sales, and profitability.

Employers acknowledge employees as the most valuable resource to both service and production industries. Unless employers provide the right work environment, high-performing, yet dissatisfied, employees are the first to leave a company. This has a negative impact on the ability of a business to provide a consistent, productive, and quality product or service. Consequently, this sets in play a negative, self-perpetuating spiral that reduces productivity, compromises the ability to attract employees with the right attitude, and constrains the establishment of a positive work culture. The service-profit chain recognises that the costs of poor employee retention are multifaceted, including increased training, loss of business knowledge, and reduced competitive advantage.

The service-profit chain proposes customers place more value on good service than on a good product. Consequently, customers who do not receive good service do not return to the business, and this reduces profits. This highlights the premise that maintaining a loyal customer base provides long-term business opportunities, which are more profitable than constantly recruiting a new customer base.

As well as describing several interrelated factors, the service-profit chain proposes a direct reciprocal relationship between employees and customers, referred to as the 'satisfaction mirror'. This increases sales but also provides valuable information, enabling an organisation to meet customer needs better. A loyal customer base forms when customer needs are satisfied, and this not only provides regular revenue, but the familiarity with a service increases the likelihood that the customer will feel comfortable if they need to complain. This feedback provides a business with the opportunity to respond rapidly to correct errors, which in turn improves customer satisfaction. Higher customer satisfaction equates directly with higher employee satisfaction. Higher employee satisfaction leads to employee loyalty that results in a more skilled and productive workforce. The overall premise of the satisfaction mirror is that satisfied customers directly correlate with satisfied employees, who increase the quality of service, productivity, sales, profitability, and subsequent competitiveness of a business.[21]

The service-profit chain draws on three theories compiled within an easy-to-understand model. First, it incorporates human resources theories by empowering employees, involving them in decision making, training them in the right job skills, and providing them with career advancement. Second, it utilises theories of quality improvement, whereby the needs of customers are paramount with data captured and analysed to improve service provision. Finally, the service-profit chain includes theories of operations management by considering the value of design, technology, and processes to support efficiency, effectiveness, productivity, competitiveness, and consistency.

Organisations' websites deliver many services, and many customers no longer interact face-to-face with service providers. In this instance, the website becomes the service delivery system, and this is critical for each organisation's value-creation strategy. The business processes embedded in the technology in an online environment have a greater impact on customers' perceived service value than any human interaction. Poor online service process design and process failure encounters dissatisfy customers.

Chapter summary

Customer-focused organisations have an excellent understanding and appreciation of their customers. They know why their customers need products and services, they know why they buy products and services, they know why they keep coming back, and they know why they recommend the products and services to others.

Value is the amount customers are willing to pay for what an organisation provides; it represents a relationship between the benefits received and the price paid. Value is the quality received relative to expectations. The organisation needs to clearly define and communicate the value proposition.

Process design requires an appreciation of how the process adds value to the organisation. All organisations are full of processes. Processes execute every activity.

A process is either value adding or cost adding. Value adding is a positive contribution that a process makes to the final usefulness or value of a product. Cost adding is a negative contribution that a process makes to the final usefulness or value of a product. Customers measure value. The objective is to eliminate all cost-adding processes and improve all value-adding processes.

Process focus is a type of production organisation in which the dominant orientation is to a technology or a material and whose production process tends to be complex.

Product focus is a type of production organisation in which the product, product line, or market segment delineate plant and staff responsibilities.

The process structures are project, job shop process, batch process, repetitive process, and continuous process. The product-process matrix maps product attributes against the major process structures to help a business define its production strategy.

The service-profit chain establishes a relationship between profits for the business, customer loyalty, and employee satisfaction. These links propose that customer loyalty drives profitability and growth, customer satisfaction drives customer loyalty, service value drives customer satisfaction, employee retention and productivity drives service value, employee satisfaction drives retention and productivity, and internal quality drives employee satisfaction.

Discussion questions

1 Describe the strategic importance of process design.
2 Discuss the concept of process value.
3 Distinguish between project, job shop, batch, repetitive, and continuous processes.
4 Distinguish between cost-adding and value-adding processes.
5 Discuss the impact of technology on process design.
6 Describe the service-profit chain.
7 Discuss the linkage between process and value.
8 The perfect process creates exactly the right value for the customer. Discuss.

Key terms

batch process, 131
cellular production, 128
continuous process, 131
cost adding, 124
job shop process, 131
primary process, 124
process, 122
process focused, 128
process thinking, 122

product focused, 128
product-process matrix, 133
project, 131
repetitive process, 131
secondary process, 124
service-profit chain, 139
value, 124
value adding, 124

Notes

1 The first automated teller machine (ATM) was opened on June 27, 1967 at a branch of Barclays bank in Enfield, north London. Retrieved from www.telegraph.co.uk/personal-banking/current-accounts/story-behind-worlds-first-cashpoint/
2 Autor, D. H. (2015). Why are there still so many jobs? The history and future of workplace automation. *Journal of Economic Perspectives*, 29(3), 3–30. Retrieved from https://economics.mit.edu/files/11563, p. 6.
3 Brynjolfsson, E., & McAfee, A. (2014). *The second machine age: Work, progress, and prosperity in a time of brilliant technologies*. New York, NY: W. W. Norton & Company, p. 11.
4 Iansiti, M., & Lakhani, K. R. (2014). Digital ubiquity: How connections, sensors, and data are revolutionizing business. *Harvard Business Review*, 92(11), 90–99.
5 Akst, D. (2014). What can we learn from past anxiety over automation? *Wilson Quarterly, Summer 2014*. Retrieved from https://wilsonquarterly.com/quarterly/summer-2014-where-have-all-the-jobs-gone/theres-much-learn-from-past-anxiety-over-automation/
6 Johnston, R., Clark, G., & Shulver, M. (2012). *Service operations management: Improving service delivery* (4th ed.). Harlow, England: Pearson, p. 76.
7 Hammer, M. (2001). *The agenda: What every business must do to dominate the decade*. New York, NY: Crown Business.
8 Raturi, A. S., & Evans, J. R. (2005). *Principles of operations management*. Mason, OH: Thomson and South-Western, p. 99.
9 Ramaswami, S. N., Srivastava, R. K., & Bhargava, M. (2009). Market-based capabilities and financial performance of firms: Insights into marketing's contribution to firm value. *Journal of the Academy of Marketing Science*, 37(2), 97–116.
10 Project Management Institute. (2017). *A guide to the project management body of knowledge* (6th ed.). Newtown Square, PA: Project Management Institute, p. 5.
11 Armytage, W. H. G. (2018). *Oliver Evans*. Retrieved from www.britannica.com/biography/Oliver-Evans

12 Hayes, R. H., & Wheelwright, S. C. (1984). *Restoring our competitive edge: Competing through manufacturing*. New York, NY: Wiley, p. 209.
13 First published Savage, S. (2000, October 8). The flaw of averages. *San Jose Mercury News* and subsequently. Savage, S. (2002, November–December). The flaw of averages. *Harvard Business Review, 80*(11), 21–22, and now Savage, S. (2009). *The flaw of averages: Why we underestimate risk in the face of uncertainty*. Hoboken, NJ: John Wiley & Sons.
14 Womack, J. P. (2005). Frontiers of lean thinking: Where we are and where we are going. *Industry Week Webcast*. Retrieved from http://leaninstituut.nl/publications/industryweek_webcast_slides.pdf
15 Fitzsimmons, J. A., & Fitzsimmons, M. J. (2008). *Service management: Operations, strategy, and information technology* (6th ed.). New York, NY: McGraw, p. 36; and this is somewhat based on Heskett, J. L., Sasser, W. E., & Leonard A Schlesinger, L. A. (1997). *The service-profit chain*. New York, NY: Free Press, p. 9.
16 Porter, M. E. (1985). *Competitive advantage*. New York, NY: Free Press, pp. 11–15.
17 Heskett, J. L., Jones, T. O., Lovemen, G. W., Sasser, W. E., & Schlesinger, L. A. (1994, March–April). Putting the service-profit chain to work. *Harvard Business Review, 72*(2), 164–174.
18 Heskett, J. L., Jones, T. O., Lovemen, G. W., Sasser, W. E., & Schlesinger, L. A. (2008, July–August). Putting the service-profit chain to work. *Harvard Business Review, 86*(7/8), 118–129.
19 Frederick W. Taylor discovered that basic scientific laws govern work, and that every person is different and that these differences can be exploited. He introduced wage incentive plans and separate responsibilities for workers and managers.
20 Schlesinger, L. A., & Heskett, J. L. (1991). Breaking the cycle of failure in services. *MIT Sloan Management Review, 32*(3), 17–28.
21 Heskett, J. L., Sasser, W. E., & Schlesinger, L. A. (2003). *The value profit chain*. New York, NY: The Free Press.

Additional reading on process design and strategy

Fitzsimmons, J. A., Fitzsimmons, M. J., & Bordoloi, S. (2018). *Service management: Operations, strategy, and information technology* (9th ed.). New York, NY: McGraw-Hill Irwin.

Hammer, M. (2001). *The agenda: What every business must do to dominate the decade*. New York, NY: Crown Business.

Heskett, J. L., Jones, T. O., Lovemen, G. W., Sasser, W. E., & Schlesinger, L. A. (2008, July–August). Putting the service-profit chain to work. *Harvard Business Review, 86*(7/8), 118–129.

Johnston, R., Clark, G., & Shulver, M. (2012). *Service operations management: Improving service delivery* (4th ed.). Harlow, England: Pearson.

Pittman, P. H., & Atwater, J. B. (2016). *APICS dictionary* (15th ed.). Chicago, IL: APICS.

Ramaswami, S. N., Srivastava, R. K., & Bhargava, M. (2009). Market-based capabilities and financial performance of firms: Insights into marketing's contribution to firm value. *Journal of the Academy of Marketing Science, 37*(2), 97–116.

Simchi-Levi, D., Kaminsky, P., & Simchi-Levi, E. (2008). *Designing and managing the supply chain: Concepts, strategies, and case studies* (3rd ed.). Boston, MA: McGraw-Hill/Irwin.

Snee, R. D., & Hoerl, R. W. (2003). *Leading six sigma: A step-by-step guide*. Upper Saddle River, NJ: Prentice Hall.

Chapter 5

Applying lean thinking to operations

Learning objectives

At the end of this chapter, you should be able to:

- Discuss lean thinking.
- Discuss the Toyota Way and the principles of lean.
- Distinguish between value and waste.
- Describe the seven wastes.
- Describe value stream mapping and the tools of value stream mapping.
- Discuss continuous improvement.
- Describe the PDCA cycle as a way of thinking and learning.
- Describe the basic seven tools of quality – Ishikawa.
- Discuss lean implementation and the need for strong leadership.
- Discuss statistical process control.
- Develop mean and range charts, and explain why we require both charts to determine whether a process is in control.
- Relate lean thinking to service organisations.

Perspective: Chelsea Sugar – lean thinking[1]

When Chelsea Sugar improved and streamlined the operations and processes of their business, they received immediate and obvious benefits – the ability to compete on speed of delivery and reduced costs. Additionally, and perhaps unusually, the retailer benefited, the consumer benefited, and even the transport company that lost the delivery contract benefited.

Chelsea Sugar supplies a full range of sugar products to the Asia Pacific region from its Birkenhead (in the Auckland metropolitan area) sugar refinery, which they have occupied since 1884. It used to operate an off-site facility, Premier Packers, located in Glenfield about nine kilometres from the main sugar refinery. Premier Packers milled and packed icing sugar and packed soft brown sugar because the main sugar refinery primarily handled bulk sugar and could not easily handle the small runs of these specialty sugars.

Just over ten years ago, management successfully applied lean thinking concepts when they decided to relocate the Premier Packers facility from the off-site location (at Glenfield) back to the main sugar refinery (at Birkenhead). They accepted a lean-thinking proposal to reduce the inherent waste and safety issues at the facility. There was significant production waste attributed to operating the two facilities – the main sugar refinery and the packing facility – even though the packing facility used four separate packing lines, packed about 3600 tonnes of retail sugar per year, and was a significant contributor to the overall business.

The supply chain was at least five days long with the value-adding time being less than one day. Any out-of-stocks at the distribution centre could take up to two days to replenish. They transported the white granulated sugar, used to mill icing sugar, in bulk road tankers, and they packed the soft brown sugar, which is sticky, not free flowing, and not suitable for bulk transport, into 25-kilogram bags and transported them on pallets. At Premier Packers, they hand-loaded the bags into the form fill and seal packing machine from a mezzanine floor that had a restricted working height, which increased the risk of injury. Premier Packers stored finished products and manually palletised them before transporting them back to Birkenhead for distribution. The remote site had a significant dust explosion risk and it did not have a food hygiene-controlled area.

(Note: The wastes identified below – *viz.* transport, motion, inventory, processing, and defect – form part of the seven wastes as discussed in this chapter.)

Because of the relocation, the company reduced transport waste by eliminating the need to truck 3600 tonnes of sugar from the main sugar refinery to the packing facility and 3600 tonnes of finished product from the packing facility back to the main sugar refinery each year. The relocation eliminated significant freight charges and transport movements.

Motion waste was minimised. Non-value-adding activities such as loading the packing machines, carting finished product away, and manually collating smaller retail bags into larger baler bags required ten employees.

They reduced inventory waste by up to 75% through not requiring the 25-kilogram intermediary bags and a reduction in batch sizes and safety stocks.

They eliminated processing waste of about 156 work shifts per year to pack and palletise the 25-kilogram bags, the labour required to physically load the packaging hoppers, and 172 work hours per year operating the bulk loading facility prior to transport.

Installing automated filling, packing, and stacking at the main sugar refinery reduced defect waste.

While it was not a key consideration at the time, it is now obvious the elimination in transport to and from the off-site facility had a beneficial effect on the environment; this should provide an advantage in future export market negotiations and competitiveness as the benchmarking of carbon emissions becomes increasingly prevalent.

Surprisingly, the outcome pleased the contract transport company since they were able to release dedicated vehicles, reassign under-utilised drivers, and did not have to service the short (less profitable) runs. The contract was profitable, but the transport company could make better use of resources elsewhere.

Continuous improvement is an incremental approach to achieving and sustaining improved operations over time, whereas a breakthrough, or stepped, improvement results in major changes to existing processes and usually involves larger investments.

The application of lean thinking to an existing process at Chelsea Sugar achieved the elimination of waste through process redesign (stepped and incremental) to remove non-value-adding tasks. Ultimately, this increased the company's ability to compete on speed of delivery and reduced their costs. The time to replenish an out-of-stock order from two days to less than two hours was a dramatic improvement in operational performance.

Thus, the application of lean thinking can result in significantly improved operations. In retrospect, the relocation was obvious and illustrates the common situation of process workers being so involved with an existing process that they are slow to visualise an improvement and often lack the resources to implement change.

At the time, CSR owned Chelsea Sugar; it is now 75% owned by Wilmar International and 25% owned by McKay Sugar Limited.

Introduction

Customers change, customer requirements change, technologies change, and processes change. The emphasis on this chapter is ensuring that processes improve to match the changing demands placed on them. Textbooks often discuss process improvement and lean thinking as synonyms, and they consider improvement as continuous. The Chelsea Sugar example, in the perspective above, uses a step-change of location to implement dramatic improvement.

This leads into thinking of production and throughput processes as flowing, which is the basis behind lean thinking. We present value stream mapping as a means of identifying inherent waste in processes and plan-do-check-adjust (PDCA) to facilitate continuous improvement.

We discuss statistical process control as a process for monitoring a process to maintain the output as expected.

Lean thinking

Introduction to lean

Lean thinking

Lean thinking is a strategic initiative that continuously seeks the ideal way to maximise customer value while minimising waste.

A lean thinking organisation truly understands customer value and continuously improves processes to create more value with fewer resources. Lean thinking allows an organisation to define customer requirements and customer value; it allows the organisation to identify the waste created by structural, infrastructural, and integration elements in all business operations. Lean thinking streamlines processes, that do not effectively deliver value, to deliver exactly what the customer wants and with fewer resources. It is holistic in its approach and practical in its implementation.

The implementation of lean thinking supports a strategic initiative in which the organisation attempts to differentiate itself from its competitors so that customers receive more value than if they went elsewhere. When we think of strategy, we often envisage an executive direction driven from the top down with the expectation that employees will follow diligently. This is tantamount to failure in lean implementation because, inevitably, executive management bases decisions on incomplete and erroneous information about the organisation's capabilities.

Recognising that lean thinking improves processes by adding more value from a customer perspective, it makes sense that the employees who perform the work and fully understand what they are doing can, with problem-solving training and education, transform themselves into a learning organisation capable of producing better products and services, with shorter lead times and considerably less cost.

The fundamental idea behind lean thinking is to produce products and services:[2]

- Exactly as customers want them.
- At the place customers want them.
- At the rate customers want them.
- With perfect quality.
- With minimum lead times.
- Without wasting resources.
- Thereby, reducing the customer's time and hassle.

The emphasis in lean thinking is to examine and optimise the entire system rather than concentrating on isolated facets. Organisations often optimise individual parts with the hope of optimising the entire system. They may install a faster machine, automate the warehouse, or outsource process steps and look good from a localised departmental view, but each of these changes may lead to a disaster from a lean-thinking viewpoint. The systems approach may be difficult for managers to implement, especially if they developed their careers while embroiled in a vertical silo style of management. When process improvement is localised, it is very easy to wait for problems to emerge and fix them. This gives the feeling of efficiency because each modification makes the process more efficient, but it just sub-optimises the whole system. Customers do not want efficiency; they want results; they want effectiveness.

At room temperature, water is a liquid with hydrogen and oxygen as its constituents. One does not gain an understanding of the properties of water by studying hydrogen and oxygen separately. Water is a system – just as lean thinking is a system.

Lean thinking strives for the ideal way of performing processes. Even when the process is approaching perfection there is still the possibility of doing it better, and lean encourages that approach.

Organisations using lean thinking create or modify processes to make products and services requiring less space, time, capital, and human effort. They produce the resulting products and services at less cost and with fewer defects when compared with traditional business systems. They reduce resources by eliminating waste along the entire value stream. Organisations can respond to changing customer desires with higher variety, higher quality, lower cost, and faster throughput times. The whole process becomes simpler and better.

History of lean

Jidoka

Jidoka allows a machine to stop safely when it detects a defect and when normal processing finishes.

Just-in-time (JIT)

Just-in-time (JIT) is a philosophy of manufacturing based on the planned elimination of all waste and on continuous improvement of productivity. The primary elements of just-in-time are to have the required resources when needed, to improve quality to zero defects, to reduce lead times by reducing set-up times, queue lengths, and lot sizes, to revise the operations incrementally, and to accomplish these activities at minimum cost.

The birthplace of lean, as we know it today, is Toyota. Sakichi Toyoda founded the company as Toyoda Automatic Loom Works Limited in 1926. Five years later Toyoda sold the patents for an automatic loom and used the money to finance Kiichiro Toyoda's (son of the founder) travel to Europe and the United States to research gasoline-powered automobiles. They produced the first production truck in 1935, built the first car in 1936, and, a year later, established Toyota Motor Company. They used the name 'Toyota' to simplify spelling and pronunciation in Japanese and to give it a more auspicious meaning in Japanese.[3]

Kiichiro Toyoda had experience with a flow production method using a chain conveyor in the assembly line of a textile plant with a monthly production capacity of 300 units, so he introduced this method into the body production line at one of the Toyota plants in 1938. He believed that machines, facilities, and people created the ideal conditions for making things when they worked together to add value without generating any waste.

After World War II, Eiji Toyoda became managing director. He was determined to use the mass-production methods used in the United States, but realised he could not justify the large batch sizes. The equipment available to him was general purpose, flexible, and designed for small runs.

Taiichi Ohno joined the automotive business in 1946 as a mechanical engineer and brought a no-nonsense approach to production. He concluded that Western production methods made large batches resulting in large inventories requiring a large amount of capital and large warehouse storage. He also realised the Western approach could not produce the diversity of product options that customers wanted. He endeavoured to make small batch sizes work by aggressively eliminating waste and cost from production processes. The automatic loom stopped when the thread broke, so Ohno introduced the concept of stopping production when something was wrong.

Ohno developed the Toyota Production System (TPS) based on *jidoka* and just-in-time. *Jidoka* allows an operator to monitor several machines with the clear knowledge that when one machine finishes the order quantity, it will automatically and safely stop. Additionally, if for some reason the machine produces defective output, the machine automatically detects the defect and safely stops. When the machine stops, it notifies the operator via an *andon*, or problem display board. Productivity increases since only good output continues along the production sequence and the quantity produced does not include any extras. Toyota describes this as 'automation with a human touch'.[4]

Ohno observed supermarket replenishment in the United States and developed his '*kanban* supermarket' allowing him to produce the required product when needed and in the quantity needed. The concept of just-in-time extended so that Ohno used only the required resources when needed. The quality improved and lead times shortened by reducing set-up times, queue lengths, and lot sizes, and all of this happened incrementally at minimum cost.

At a Toyota plant, production control issues a production instruction to the beginning of the production line as soon as possible after receipt of an order. The assembly line has small amounts of all possible parts so any configuration is possible. As the assembly line uses components, the component-producing process replaces them at the rate of consumption. Similarly, the component-supply process replaces its components at the rate of usage.

From 1950 onwards, Ohno found ways to improve his manufacturing methods allowing small-lot production of automobiles with the features that customers demanded. Thus, it became a learning organisation, providing customers with whatever they wanted. As volumes increased, the concepts used in small-lot production evolved into mass production. These concepts were continuously improved. Toyota refers to TPS as the Thinking Production System because it encourages people to think and solve problems.

Some writers attribute the birth of lean to Henry Ford when he introduced the moving assembly line. This certainly had the concepts of flow manufacturing and Ford introduced elimination of waste and simplicity in production methods. Toyota executives learned from the Ford systems and made numerous study trips to Ford Motor Company and General Motors. Toyota, perhaps out of necessity, pioneered the batch size of one while using high-volume production methods. They also used the simplicity of the *kanban* card for component replenishment. The aspects that distinguish Toyota are the continuous improvement and the learning incorporated into corporate culture. Thus, an impartial view attributes lean as a hybrid system using ideas from the United States and Japan. The progress made with the Toyota Production System was largely unnoticed in the United States until the early 1970s.

Understanding and implementing lean thinking

Lean implementation demands a clear and succinct understanding of how the concepts support the overall strategic vision for the organisation. Executives have struggled in the past with grasping the real meaning of lean thinking. As an example, some executives view lean thinking as a methodology to reduce costs and they embrace the opportunity to make employees redundant when processes improve.

Lean thinking example 1

A manufacturing company (unnamed) successfully implemented lean thinking. The process improvements allowed the firm to eliminate the entire third shift (operating from 11:00 p.m. until 7:00 a.m.). Finance and human-resource management saw this as an opportunity to save employee costs immediately. Production management successfully argued to retain all employees and they became 'floaters' for the remaining day shifts. As such, the employees filled in when regular staff were absent and assisted whenever problems developed. Normal attrition eventually allowed the firm to reduce employee costs. What happens to employee morale when redundancy is the reward for improvement ideas?

To provide an understanding of the essence of lean thinking, we present the five principles of lean, as developed by James Womack and Daniel Jones, followed by a discussion on the Toyota Way, which takes lean to the next level by extending beyond the factory environment to include the entire organisation. Finally, we discuss Jeffrey K. Liker's 14 Principles of the Toyota Way. He developed his principles to describe the culture behind the Toyota Production System.

Five principles of lean

The five principles of lean as developed by James Womack and Daniel Jones are:[5]

- Identify customers and specify the value desired by the customer. The lean supplier clearly defines value from the end customer's perspective and targets all the non-value-adding activities (or waste) for removal. This principle is easy to say but not so easy to achieve. Manufacturers often give customers products that suit the manufacturers. This preference to satisfy supplier requirements may result from the availability (or non-availability) of inputs and may result from constraints generated from existing facilities. These manufacturers have production resources that only produce given sizes, or given quantities, and they present this to customers as an extensive range, but the missing product (size and quantity) is what the customer really wants. Restaurants with inflexible menus and airlines with flight schedules that suit airline crew scheduling are examples of the need to identify the customer and the value desired by the customer.
- Identify the value stream for each product providing value, and challenge all the wasted steps (generally nine out of ten) currently necessary to provide it. For a manufactured product, the value stream encompasses the raw material supplier, the product manufacturer, the product assembler, and the distribution network. For a service, the value stream consists of suppliers, support personnel and technology, the service producer, and the distribution channel. This step identifies the inherent waste existing in delivering products and services to customers and aims to eliminate that waste. The focus should be on the product, or the end customer, and not on the machine, department, or process step. Customers measure the entire supply chain by the value stream they experience, since supply chains compete for customers and the supply chain is only as strong as its weakest link.
- Make the product flow continuously through the remaining, value-added steps. Eliminating the inherent waste ensures the product or service 'flows' to the customer without any interruption or waiting. Think in terms of batch sizes of one, which generates one-piece flow or one-document flow. By allowing batch sizes to increase to convenient sizes, or withholding production until convenient for production, just creates delays and inconvenience for the customer. This interrupts the flow.
- Introduce pull between all steps where continuous flow is possible. This helps to understand customer demand and to create processes to respond to this demand by producing only what the customer wants when the customer wants it. Pull means responding to short-term demand and not overproducing in anticipation of demand. Supply lines need to anticipate some demand and start the production

process generically, but the customer determines the final configuration. Supply chains sharing end-consumer demand reduce the risk associated with creating demand forecasts at each echelon (supply chain tier). Forecast uncertainty reduces with each extension of pull. Close to product delivery, pull means responding to short-term demand caused by customer requests such as opening extra checkouts at a supermarket.

- Manage toward perfection so the number of steps and the amount of time and information needed to serve the customer continually falls. Aiming for perfection encourages the total elimination of waste by making all activities along a value stream create value. This means delivering exactly what the customer wants, exactly when, at a fair price, and with minimum waste. The pursuit of lean is a never-ending process.

The Toyota Way

Fujio Cho, then President of Toyota, launched the Toyota Way in 2001. This takes lean to the next level by extending beyond the factory environment to include the entire organisation. Toyota has been practising lean for over 50 years, but they are still learning and trying to do better. Case 1 (at the end of this book) is a case study describing three crises for Toyota written by Jeffrey K. Liker. The case study does not mention the elimination of waste – for many years the backbone of just-in-time and lean thinking. Rather, it examines how Toyota management looked at the three crises and responded. In retrospect, they could have done better, so in that sense it was a learning experience.

Fujio Cho based the Toyota Way on five core values that all Toyota employees use in their everyday work. The five core values split themselves between continuous improvement and respect for people. Continuous improvement in the Toyota Way suggests that current success is not the final achievement. Toyota is never satisfied with where they are and will always improve their business by presenting their best ideas and efforts. Toyota people are keen to create better alternatives, question their accomplishments, and investigate future definitions of success.

The three building blocks shaping Toyota's commitment to continuous improvement are:

- Challenge to maintain a long-term vision and strive to meet them with courage and creativity.
- Use *kaizen* to improve business operations continuously, always striving for innovation and evolution. This recognises that no process is perfect and there is always room for improvement.
- Use *genchi genbutsu*, or go to the source, to find the facts to make correct decisions, build consensus, and achieve goals. The best way to understand a problem is to go and see it yourself. This provides a better perspective than having someone summarise the issues.

Respect for people refers to their own staff as well as the communities and stakeholder groups surrounding them. Toyota management respects their people and believes that individual efforts and good teamwork create their business success.

The two building blocks shaping Toyota's respect for people are:

- **Show respect** by making every effort to understand each other, accept responsibility, and build mutual trust.
- **Build teamwork** by sharing the development opportunities and maximise individual and team performance.

14 Principles of the Toyota Way

Jeffrey K. Liker developed his 14 Principles of the Toyota Way, based on the five principles from Womack and Jones, to describe the culture behind the Toyota Production System. He structures the 14 principles into four categories:[6]

- Base all management decisions on a long-term philosophy – philosophy.
- The right process produces the right results – process.
- Add value to the organisation by developing people and partners – people.
- Continuously solve problems to create organisational learning – problems.

Philosophy (principle 1)

Base all managerial decisions on a long-term philosophy, even if this sacrifices short-term financial goals. With a long-term philosophy established, align every function towards this common philosophical goal. Then generate value for customers, society, and the economy. This philosophy forms the basis of the remaining principles.

Process (principles 2–8)

This category creates a continuous process flow, uses pull signals to prevent overproduction, levels production schedules, builds a culture of stopping production to solve problems, standardises work processes, uses visual controls, and uses reliable and tested technology. This second category contains most of the five lean principles developed by Womack and Jones.

People (principles 9–11)

This category emphasises the importance of the employees, partners, and suppliers of an organisation. Employees are the greatest asset of the organisation. Investing in employee development translates into investing in the future of the organisation. Develop exceptional people and teams to follow the organisation's long-term philosophy. It is important for the organisation to have a common goal and to align all human development towards this goal. An organisation needs to grow leaders who understand and live the organisation's philosophy and can teach that philosophy to others. The organisation should recognise partners and suppliers as a natural extension of the organisation and treat them with respect.

Problem solving (principles 12–14)

The fourth category deals with the creation of a learning organisation through continuous solving of the root causes of problems. This involves going to the source of each problem and seeing the problem personally rather than theorising on what other people, or the computer screen, might say. When people know the root cause, they can decide how to solve the problem. People make decisions by trying to achieve consensus with all participants. This approach may be time-consuming, but it helps to implement solutions quickly after the consensus. The final principle aims at creating a learning organisation. This requires stable and standardised processes to be able to apply continuous improvement tools and process. Using frequent reflection meetings to identify lessons learned supports the goal to become a continuous learning organisation. Today, organisations use the seven types of waste to support continuous improvement.

Value and waste

Value

Value is the amount customers are willing to pay for what an organisation provides. It represents a relationship between the benefits received and the price paid. Benefits can be informational and emotional as well as economic. Value is the quality received relative to expectations.

Value adding

Value adding is positive contribution that a process makes to the final usefulness or value of a product. The customer measures value in this sense.

Non-value adding

Non-value adding is an activity that does not add value to a product.

Waste

Waste is any activity that does not add value to the product or service as valued by the customer.

Seven wastes

The seven wastes are overproduction (excess or too early), waiting (queuing), transporting (unnecessary movements), unnecessary inventory (stock that is sitting is accumulating cost without necessarily providing value), unnecessary motion (activities that do not add value), overprocessing (poor process design), and making defects (scrap or rework).

The previous chapter introduced the concepts of value and value adding. The early literature on lean thinking described the philosophy as the elimination of waste. It is incorrect to think of lean solely as the elimination of waste. Today, it is more about creating value, finding better ways of adding more value, and continuously learning and improving.

However, a difficulty arises when we come to define value and waste. A value-adding process contributes to the final usefulness, or value, of a product. Customers measure this value. Waste is any activity that does not add value to the product or service as valued by the customer. Therefore, a waste-adding process is making a negative contribution to the final usefulness, or value, of a product. Customers also measure this value; customers measure both value and waste.

Suppliers may view activities as waste, but customers may view them as value, and *vice versa*. A supplier may see inventory as waste, but if it is able to reduce the delivery lead time the customer may view it as value. Waste reduction is different from cost reduction. Further, we need to examine what effect waste reduction has on the entire system. It is possible for waste reduction to have no effect on cost.

Lean thinking operates with pull control and flow. Products and services move to the next stage when the downstream customer demands (pulls) them. There is no point in producing a product or service when there is no customer; this is a waste of resources. The principle simply says, 'replace what is used'.

Demand for the product or service must be relatively repetitive and delivery lead times must be relatively short. It also means component materials must be available in enough quantities so the supplier can produce any product, or deliver any service, on demand when a customer generates a visual signal.

Taiichi Ohno, who developed the Toyota Production System, composed the original seven categories of waste, which are:

- Overproduction – excess quantity or too early.
- Waiting – queues or delays.
- Transporting – unnecessary movement.
- Unnecessary inventory – items adding cost and not value.
- Unnecessary motion – activities that do not add value.
- Overprocessing – poor process design.
- Defects – scrap or rework.

Waste of overproduction – excess quantity or too early

Overproduction is producing a quantity greater than required. It occurs for several reasons. The worst is when management believes the cost of set-up can be amortised over a longer production run to lower the unit production cost. Managers base this belief on an estimated cost of set-up, which, for most organisations, is an arbitrary number with little science attached. When production thinking incorporates economic order quantities, it balances the cost of set-up with the cost of storage, and the run size is the quantity that minimises the sum of ordering cost and storage cost. Again, management usually establishes these figures arbitrarily and does not include, or consider, the quantity that the customer wants. They do not consider the cost of a stockout, or the inability to supply.

Overproduction is the waste of resources, including materials, energy, and time, used to produce unwanted output. There may be demand in the future, but at the time of production, nobody wants it. The organisation uses valuable resources to make unwanted output and does not make the wanted output. Overproduction discourages a smooth flow of goods and services. 'Too much, too early' translates easily into 'too little, too late' when the only difference is time.

Overproduction tends to increase lead times because the current batch must finish before transferring to the next process. That transit delay accumulates and increases the lead time. It is easy for process workers to overproduce because it is the safe option. They have made the required quantity, so there is no chance of a shortage, and a few more makes it certain. Production bonuses encourage workers to overproduce since the additional quantity produced increases their pay.

Lean thinking example 2

A metal components factory (unnamed) was manufacturing brass fittings. Night-shift operators would often finish their production schedule by about 5:00 a.m. If supervised, they would have ceased production and performed set-up duties ready for the day shift starting at 7:00 a.m. However, without supervision, they regularly kept producing until 7:00 a.m. and walked out, leaving the day shift to set up the next production run. The night shift benefited by receiving a production bonus on the total quantity produced (even though it exceeded immediate requirements), and the day shift lost a couple of hours of production while they performed the changeover.

Lean thinking example 3

A consultant questioned the managers of a furniture factory (also unnamed) as to why they were making furniture to add to the same products already available in large quantities in their finished goods store. They replied that the products in the finished goods store were the only ones selling. Their customers wanted products not in the finished goods store but the company could not supply these because there were none available and their storage area was empty. The weekly sales figures reflected sales of items in store, and the company did not record lost sales and out-of-stock items. The company based their production on actual sales, not orders.

The waste of overproduction also includes early production and delivery. It extends to underproduction, which is producing less than what the customer wants. In this case, an extra production run is authorised to make up the shortfall, and this may entail extra packaging and delivery costs.

Waste of waiting – queues or delays

The waste of waiting occurs whenever production interrupts the flow. Job shop processes are intermittent because they start-stop-start-stop. Lean thinking endeavours to eliminate the stoppages and make sure materials and production flow from initial process to final process. Waste occurs any time a product is waiting for the next step. Waiting for the arrival of resources or transport, the delivery of input material, the completion of maintenance on a production machine, and staff to turn up for work are all examples of the waste of waiting.

Waste occurs whenever a queue forms in services. Driving across town in peak hour usually necessitates stopping at numerous intersections waiting for the traffic lights to change. People accept this as normal and expected, but it is waste. It is possible to travel across town in peak hour without having to stop for the traffic lights to change. A driver may break the established traffic rules and run the red light (this works) or put flashing red and blue lights on the roof of the car and let the siren sound (this works as well). It is possible.

Waste occurs when we wait for technology to catch up. For example, if you telephone a call centre, you may wait for the answering system to start, wait for the advertising messages to be read, wait for the inquiry options to be read, wait for the connection to be made, wait for the inquiry options to be repeated, wait for the operator to call up the account details, wait for the computer technology to provide the required information, wait for the operator to enter the new details, wait for the operator to confirm the changes, and then you hang up. Usually, the hanging up is the fastest part of the process.

Waste of transporting – unnecessary movement

The waste of transporting is any unnecessary movement of materials or products. Inwards goods delivered to the wrong part of the building and getting materials handling to transfer them to the correct place is a waste of transport. Products sent in bulk to a remote location, then called back to the main centre to meet a customer need represents waste of transport.

Transporting waste includes the use of an unnecessary transport method given all the circumstances. As an example, an organisation might use air transport to cover a short distance when road transport would work just as well. Air transport requires road transport to deliver to and from the airport. Road transport on its own can go direct from supplier to customer without additional handling (provided road systems are available).

Transporting waste also includes the use of an inappropriate transport method such as a vehicle twice the size, or twice as expensive to operate, as a smaller more suitable vehicle. Customers do not like paying transport operators to follow indirect delivery routes. They may even be reluctant to pay for goods that follow direct delivery routes. Transporting costs are often unavoidable. However, a customer may choose a different supplier or a different distributor that offers reduced delivery charges and times, especially when the customer can create value by switching.

Waste of unnecessary inventory – items adding cost and not value

Inventory waste is the storage of items not needed. Inventory requires storage in a warehouse at a cost that would not occur if the inventory did not exist. Inventory tends to increase lead times, hide problems, and increases storage space requirements. Cost accountants may calculate unnecessary inventory costs based on the money tied up in inventory, but the true cost of unnecessary inventory includes many other factors.

Waste of unnecessary motion – activities that do not add value

Waste of motion is the use of activities that do not add value, such as placing heavy items on the floor rather than at waist height. Provided an operator can physically lift items, it is better to place them on a table rather than bending to place them on the floor and then, subsequently, bending to pick them up. Workplace layout and ergonomics play an important part in reducing waste of unnecessary motion. Using height-adjusted workbenches and allowing workers to stand and move (rather than sit on a stationary chair) increases output quality and reduces health and safety concerns.

Waste of overprocessing – poor process design

The waste of overprocessing is any processing step that does not add value; it usually arises from poor process design. Examples include heating ingredients to a temperature, allowing them to cool, and then having to heat them again when the rest of the process is ready. This is poor coordination of processing steps. Another example is packing products into small containers and then having to open several containers for the next processing step. An organisation could improve this process by storing the intermediate output in bulk. Another example is boiling too much water in a kettle (jug) to make a cup of tea. With earlier kettle designs, the user covered the exposed heating element with water, or the element overheated and burnt. Modern kettle designs have heating elements completely covered by the base of the kettle and have sensing mechanisms to switch off if the kettle contains insufficient water. The inherent waste in this example includes the time and energy to heat the excess water and the possible discarding of the unused water prior to the next time.

This waste also includes having large machines doing the work of smaller machines. Organisations purchase larger machines because they can produce outputs at a lower unit cost. However, smaller machines may provide better scheduling and maintenance options and allow the production of a variety of outputs simultaneously. All this adds value.

Waste of defects – scrap or rework

Producing defects, scrap, and rework is waste. Scrap is an output dumped at the end of processing because it does not meet customer specification. Why make the product in the first place? It may be quicker to just throw money away, or flush it down the toilet. Rework occurs when the process corrects a defective product by passing it through the processing step again. Painting that requires repainting is an example. When this waste occurs, the supplier makes the item twice, but the customer only pays once.

Eliminating waste in services

The elimination of waste also applies in services albeit in different forms which include:

- Bureaucracy and duplication – filling in multiple forms and repeating data.
- Unclear communication – creating a confusing customer experience through unclear instructions and industry jargon.
- Incorrect inventory – allowing products to be out-of-stock or expired.
- Errors – sending the wrong product to a customer, or possibly nothing at all.
- Lost opportunities – not recognising opportunities to 'go the extra mile'.

Value stream mapping

Value stream

Value stream is the process of creating, producing, and delivering a product or a service to the market. For a manufactured product, the value stream encompasses the raw material supplier, the manufacturing of the product, the assembly of the product, and the distribution network. For a service, the value stream consists of suppliers, support personnel and technology, the service 'producer', and the distribution channel. A single organisation or a network of organisations controls value streams.

Value stream mapping

Value stream mapping is an easy, fast, and goal-oriented method. Analysts draw the current state of the value stream directly on the shop floor with paper and pencil. They design a future-state model for each current-state map of the value stream, pointing out the direction of the continuous improvement process.

Takt time

Takt time sets the pace of production to match the rate the customer demands output. It is available production time divided by the rate of customer demand.

Value stream mapping is a visualisation exercise to provide a vision of the future state. It is an essential means to see value streams and continuously improve them. The exercise starts with the future-state map and works backwards to the current-state map; the analysis looks at the requirement to attain the future state. The future state encompasses the ideal customer and employee experience; it should be the perfect process. With the perfect process as the ideal, ask if each step is valuable, capable, available, adequate, and flexible. Examine the value stream map to ensure value flows smoothly from one step to the next at the pull of the customer, and interpret the map in terms of business purpose.

There are value stream mapping software products available, and they produce beautifully drawn maps. One can frame these and attach them to a wall. However, that misses the point completely. Good maps are action statements and highlight where the organisation can target improvement steps.

The first step in the mapping process is to define the purpose and scope of the exercise clearly. Clarify the aim, specify the period, and state the beginning and end of the value stream under examination. Then calculate *takt* time, which is the required production rate to match the rate of demand. This represents the demanded capacity and becomes the production drumbeat. Calculate *takt* time by dividing the total operating time by the required quantity. Be aware that *takt* time can vary along a value stream and can vary over time (over a year, for example). Many design tasks and new product development tasks have loose definitions and, as such, do not require *takt* time, or it is irrelevant.

Figure 5.1 illustrates a very simplistic example of a value stream map. Examine the process steps and issues relevant to the customer and ask whether the customer would pay extra for including each step.

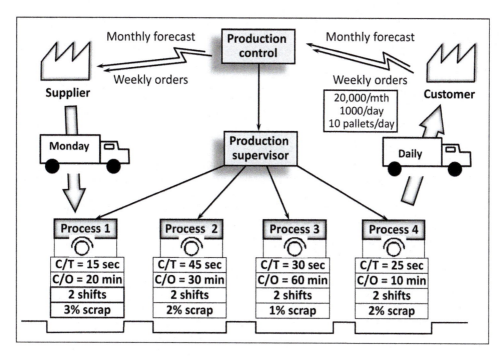

Figure 5.1 Simplistic value stream mapping example

Continuous improvement

Continuous improvement

Continuous improvement is an incremental (small and gradual) approach to achieving and sustaining improved processes over time, rather than breakthrough (large and rapid) improvements in processes.

Process improvement

Process improvement is the activity associated with identifying and eliminating causes of poor quality, process variation, and non-value-adding activities.

Kaizen

Kaizen is a philosophy promoting gradual and orderly continuous improvement.

Plan-do-check-adjust (PDCA)

Plan-do-check-adjust is a four-step process for quality improvement. In the first step (plan), we develop a plan to effect improvement. In the second step (do), we carry out the plan, preferably on a small scale. In the third step (check), we observe the effects of the plan. In the last step (adjust), we modify the process and make improvements as needed. We study the results to determine what we learned and what we can predict.

Process improvement is all about adding more value for the customer. However, how does the customer measure this value? The customer wants the product or service from a supplier because they perceive there is more value in that product or service from that supplier than any other product or service from any other supplier. The supplier believes they are delivering value at a time when customer perception is changing. Operations should be aware of changing perceptions on the part of the customer and treat the management of quality as a dynamic process.

Kaizen is a philosophy for continuous improvement. Its aim is to eliminate waste and make life an enjoyable experience. Continuous in this sense means never-ending. Improvement suggests finding better ways of performing tasks, making products, and delivering services. These changes occur incrementally, or gradually.

Kaizen is quite different from process re-engineering which talks about quantum leaps, dramatic improvement, and radical redesign. *Kaizen* philosophy looks at a process, a system, a product, or a service, takes it apart, and asks why. By resolving that question, the process (system, product, or service) operates in a better way.

Kaizen operates with three principles:

- It uses process and results, not just results.
- It incorporates universal process thinking by examining the big picture.
- It is non-judgemental and non-blaming.

Continuous improvement seeks a never-ending process of improvement of technology, machinery, materials, labour utilisation, production methods, ideas, and results through the application of suggestions and ideas of team members. Under continuous improvement, management continuously challenges and incrementally upgrades the performance level of the organisation. Continuous improvement requires a complete understanding of the process before attempting to improve it, and the easiest way to gain that understanding is to ask simple questions such as:

- What is the process doing?
- When does the process work?
- Who does the work?
- Where does the process take place?
- How long does it take?
- What steps does the process perform?

Then, like a four-year-old child, ask 'why?' and repeat the question five times.

Plan-do-check-adjust cycle (PDCA cycle)

The plan-do-check-adjust cycle is a very simple process for implementing change, but most organisations do not clearly understand it. PDCA is a cycle, and it is supposed to be rotating continuously. Figure 5.2 illustrates the PDCA cycle.

The first step is planning to determine the process goals and targets and the methods of reaching those goals. It is difficult to plan and set targets if there is no knowledge of what adjustments the organisation has already tried. So, establish a plan for future change after a process has been working and some history has accumulated.

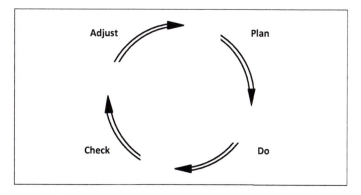

Figure 5.2 Plan-do-check-adjust cycle

Planning follows do, check, and adjust. It is critical to identify the gap between current performance and a target value and to identify the root cause of the difference. The temptation is to rush through planning and start doing. However, the more time and effort put into planning, the easier the implementation becomes.

The organisation implements the improvement during the second stage. This step is easy if the organisation performed the planning step well. The outcome was unknown in advance so it becomes a trial solution; the doing is provisional.

The third step checks the effect of the implementation. Did it work as planned? If not, why not? What can the organisation learn from this experiment to apply next time? It is a time to observe, reflect, and learn. If the organisation performed the earlier stages properly, then this step is positive. The checking and adjusting allows the organisation to compare the expected outcome with the actual outcome and to make further adjustments.

The fourth step takes appropriate action and standardises the process. Part of the fourth step is to ensure the old process does not return. The organisation presumably implements an improvement because it provides a better result so any return to the previous method would signal a worse result, and the organisation should not allow this to happen.

As shown in Figure 5.3, the organisation places a procedural block to prevent a return to previous behaviour. This may come in the form of training, redesign of documents, installation of new machinery, or some other method that completely replaces the original.

Lean production and scheduling

Lean production

Lean production is a philosophy of production providing high levels of quality, productivity, and customer response. Developed by the Toyota Motor Corporation, it focuses on the elimination of all waste, including defects requiring rework, unnecessary processing steps, unnecessary movement of materials or

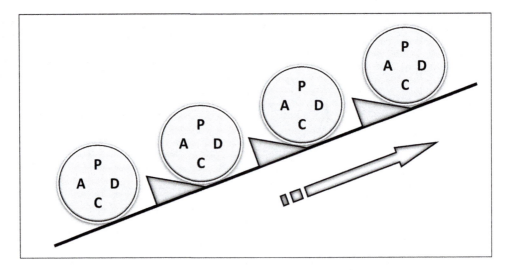

Figure 5.3 Plan-do-check-adjust cycle with blocks preventing a return to previous behaviour

people, waiting time, excess inventory, and overproduction. Lean producers employ teams of multi-skilled workers at all levels of the organisation and use highly flexible, increasingly automated machines to produce volumes of products in potentially enormous variety. It contains a set of principles and practices to reduce cost through the relentless removal of waste and through the simplification of all processes.

Heijunka

Heijunka is an approach to level production throughout the supply chain to match the planned rate of end-product sales.

Mixed-model production

Mixed-model production makes several different products in varying lot sizes so production matches the same mix of products sold each day. The mixed-model schedule governs the making and delivery of component parts, including those supplied by outside suppliers. The goal is to build every model every day according to the daily demand.

Kanban

Kanban is a flag or a piece of paper containing all relevant information for an order – part number, description, process area used, time of delivery, quantity available, quantity delivered, production quantity, and so on. The system writes the type and number of units required by a process on *kanban* cards, which starts the withdrawal and production of items through the production process.

Pull system

A pull system produces items as demanded or to replace those taken for use.

Production schedulers establish the schedule for several days or weeks into the future. The production volumes for every product are determined for a given period, such as one month. The schedulers calculate the period production rate by dividing the production schedule by the number of available working periods. This process is product levelling, or *heijunka*. They accomplish a stabilised production schedule, or uniform plant loading, by setting a firm monthly plan. Every day, the facility produces some quantity of everything, thus ensuring there is always a total mix available to respond to variations in demand.

Lean production develops the schedule at only one point in the overall value stream, and this point assumes the role of pacemaker. The pacemaker process pulls products from upstream processes and allows them to flow continuously to the customer through subsequent processes. The planned volume and mix at the pacemaker process typically correspond to the master schedule. The scheduled daily production mix is determined by product levelling.

The pacemaker process requires the calculation of pacemaker schedules using the *takt* time for all the items that pass through it. Services achieve uniform loads by using reservation systems, complementary services, and incentives for off-peak usage.

The concept of product levelling is to operate with the smallest valid interval and improve the process so the interval is even smaller. The ideal interval is one day so that the system can make every product, every day, on demand. Thus, the organisation can process small orders just like large orders. The advantages of product levelling include:

- A reduction in lead time across the value stream.
- An increase in flexibility and responsiveness.
- A reduction in work-in-process inventory.
- A reduction in space requirements.
- A marked improvement in quality.

Lean enterprise

The value stream defines the lean enterprise. The objectives of the lean enterprise are to specify value to the ultimate customer correctly and to analyse and focus the value stream so it does everything, from product development and production to sales and service. The lean enterprise removes steps that do not create value, and the customer pulls products in a continuous flow through steps that do add value. Activities in a lean environment include:

- Developing strategies for dealing with highly variable demand.
- Focusing on reducing variability and reducing the impact of variability on production.
- Levelling the schedule for both volume and mix.
- Creating a flow of products supporting the drumbeat of expected customer deliveries.
- Monitoring customer order patterns and validating daily production.

- Producing customer orders, whenever possible, at the exact day's mix using load-levelling techniques.
- Driving improvement activities so all processes can produce smaller quantities at shorter intervals.
- Creating a true mixed-model schedule, as well as more repetitive demand, for components pulled from upstream processes.[7]

Basic seven tools of quality

Basic seven tools of quality

The basic seven tools of quality are a set of tools that help organisations understand their processes to improve them. The tools are cause-and-effect diagram, check sheet, flowchart, histogram, Pareto chart, scatter chart, and control chart.

Kaoru Ishikawa developed the basic seven tools of quality; he maintained that these tools resolve most quality-related problems. The issue with problem solving is to identify the real problem. By understanding the real problem, the solution is easy. Many people implement change without understanding the cause of the issue they are trying to correct, resulting in unresolved problems. This wastes valuable time and effort by applying a change that appeared to be a solution.

The basic seven tools of quality are:

- Cause-and-effect diagram – helping to identify the causes of the problem.
- Check sheet – facilitating the user's interpretation of the results.
- Flowchart – drawn to understand processes better.
- Histogram – showing overall variation.
- Pareto chart – separating the significant few from the trivial many.
- Scatter diagram – showing factor relationships.
- Control chart – showing which variations to control and how.

Cause-and-effect diagram

Cause-and-effect diagram

Cause-and-effect diagram – also known as a fishbone diagram (because the completed diagram looks like a skeleton of a fish) and an Ishikawa diagram (because Kaoru Ishikawa first developed them) – is a tool for analysing process dispersion. A basic diagram places the effect at one end with the main causes and sub-causes leading backwards along the spine.

The cause-and-effect diagram, or Ishikawa's fishbone diagram, is a simple graphical diagram identifying as many causes for an effect as possible and sorting them into categories. To construct the diagram, place the problem at the right-hand side and the potential causes of the problem along the spine of the diagram, hence the fishbone analogy. Break each of these 'bones' down into more detailed causes by adding more bones to the diagram. Teams use brainstorming techniques to identify probable causes by asking who, what, when, where, why, and how. They evaluate each potential cause

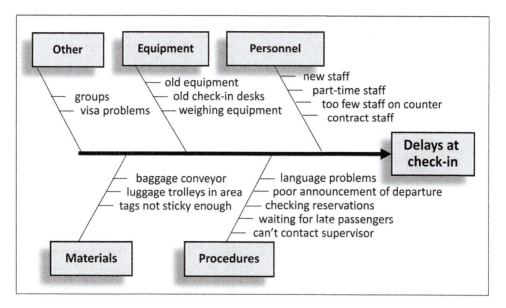

Figure 5.4 Cause-and-effect diagram example

and collect more data to narrow the potential cause before implementing any corrective action. They use the diagram to identify the underlying symptoms of a problem, or 'effect', as a means of finding the root cause.

Figure 5.4 illustrates an example of a cause-and-effect diagram drawn to understand the causes of a problem identified by delays at check-in procedures at an airport. In this example, an airline has had numerous complaints about slow check-in procedures. They place the effect, 'delays at check-in', at the right-hand side of the diagram. A team of people connected to the process conduct a brainstorming session and identify possible causes. The causes identified are personnel, equipment, materials, procedures, and other causes. These become the bones along the spine, which they break down into more detail on possible causes.

The team would then hypothesise the most important, or likely, cause and collect more data. Although all the above contribute to slow check-in, the team might decide that personnel are the most important cause of slow check-in. The major corrective action might take the form of more personnel at check-in times and comprehensive training for new and existing personnel. This would immediately speed up check-in through knowledgeable staff. They can implement other improvements in order of importance.

Check sheet

Check sheet

Check sheet is a simple data-recording device. The check is a tick, or a count, that tallies the number of occurrences observed.

Type of Call	Mon	Tue	Wed	Thu	Fri	Total
Account enquiry	卌	卌 III	卌 卌	卌 IIII	卌 II	39
Overdraft inquiry	III	IIII	卌 I	III	IIII	20
Open an account	卌 II	卌 IIII	卌 III	卌 II	卌 II	38
Close an account	I	III	III	IIII	III	14
Set up bill payment	IIII	卌 II	卌 IIII	卌	IIII	29
Cancel bill payment	II	III	卌 I	卌	III	19
Investment advice	II	III	III	IIII	卌	17
Branch location	卌	卌 I	卌 IIII	卌 III	IIII	32
Change of address	II	III	III	II	II	12
Total	**31**	**46**	**57**	**47**	**39**	**220**

Figure 5.5 Check sheet example

A check sheet is a historical record of data collected. Each check is an occurrence, so the sheet can easily count the number of times an occurrence occurs and where, or how, it occurs. The results are clearly visible on the check sheet as shown in Figure 5.5. However, it generally requires further processing. Improvement teams identify areas for improvement, either directly from the check sheet, or by feeding the data into one of the other basic seven tools.

The check sheet is suitable when one person, or one location, can collect and observe data constantly, when a production process collects data, and when a process collects data depending on the frequency, location, problem, or causes of defects. It facilitates the user's interpretation of the data recorded and counted for all the targeted reasons and types. It is a generic tool and can be adapted for a variety of purposes to improve processes.

Flowchart

Flowchart

Flowchart is a visual representation of the flow of a process. Flowcharts help identify non-value-added steps, the key parts of the process, and the interfaces between other processes.

A flowchart is a visual presentation of the flow of activities in a process. It creates a graphical representation of the steps involved in a process and pieces together the actual process as it occurs. By drawing each activity (connected by arrows to show the sequence), it is possible to ensure each step adds value, is necessary, and adds to streamlining the process. Visually seeing the process helps identify inefficiencies and potential improvements. It identifies where processes fail and where to make improvements.

Draw the flowchart before collecting process data. Aspects of the flowchart may highlight areas of interest such as queue formations, storage points, transport requirements, inspection stages, and repetition of process steps. Other basic tools quantify the problem.

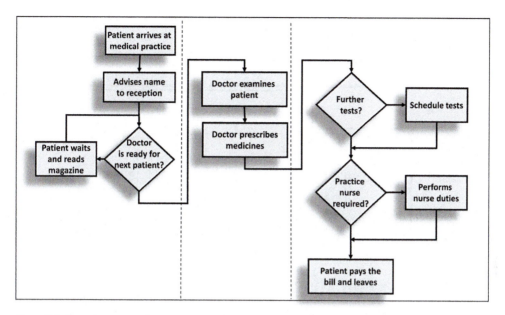

Figure 5.6 Flowchart example

Vertical and/or horizontal lines often separate functional activities or activities involving the customer and producer. Figure 5.6 is an example of a flowchart for a patient attending a general medical practice. The section in the middle involves the medical professional, the section on the left shows the activities occurring before the examination, and the section on the right illustrates activities after the examination.

Histogram

Histogram

Histogram is a frequency distribution chart of a range of items along the x-axis and the number of times the items occur on the y-axis.

A histogram is a frequency distribution chart used to illustrate patterns that may be difficult to detect in a simple table of numbers. It is ideal when data is numerical, when the analyst wants to see the shape of the distribution, when analysing the process to see if it meets customer requirements, and when analysing the changes occurring in the process from time to time.

Figure 5.7 is an example of a histogram drawn from raw data. The data in the upper box is raw and has little meaning by itself. By grouping raw data by frequency, as shown in the box on the left-hand side, the histogram develops meaning as information. The histogram drawn with vertical bars represents frequency of occurrence.

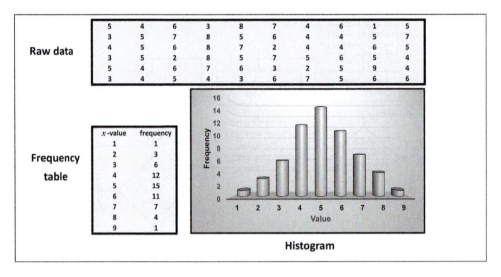

Figure 5.7 Histogram example

Pareto chart

Pareto chart

A Pareto chart is a graphical tool for ranking causes from most significant to least significant. The Pareto chart is the result of a Pareto analysis.

Pareto analysis

Pareto analysis developed in the 1890s when Vifredo Pareto found that in all economies small numbers of people control large portions of the wealth. This observation has evolved into the concept of 20% of any entity represents the very important, and the remaining 80% are less important. In process improvement, it allows an organisation to concentrate on the activities providing the most business benefits.

The Pareto chart is a graphical tool for ranking causes in hierarchical order from most significant to least significant. The format is a bar graph. The lengths of the bar represent the frequency of an occurrence such as cost, time, length, and reason. The graph has the longest bars (most frequent occurrences) on the left and shortest bars on the right. This way the graph highlights the situations of most significance. Called the 80–20 rule since about 80% of the problems originate from 20% of the possible sources, it separates the significant few from the trivial many. It makes it easier to identify where to gain the greatest possible improvement.

Pareto analysis is useful when identifying problem causes, when analysing the frequency of a problem, when there are many problems and the analyst would like to focus on the most significant one, when analysing broad causes by looking at the specific components, and when comparing one cause with others.

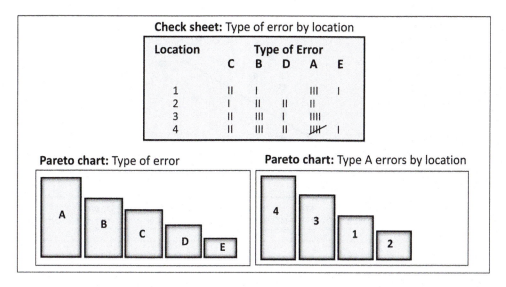

Check sheet: Type of error by location

Location	Type of Error				
	C	B	D	A	E
1	II	I		III	I
2	I	II	II	II	
3	II	III	I	IIII	
4	II	III	II	ƗƗƗ	I

Pareto chart: Type of error

Pareto chart: Type A errors by location

Figure 5.8 Pareto chart example drawn from a check sheet

Figure 5.8 is an example of a Pareto chart drawn from a check sheet. The check sheet at the top is counting the type of error by location. The letters C, B, D, A, and E do not have any meaning apart from identifying the type of error. The Pareto chart on the left shows the type of error ranked from the most common to the least common. The Pareto chart on the right shows the location of the type A errors. This clearly shows the most significant improvement would occur after concentrating improvement efforts on type A errors at location 4.

Scatter chart

Scatter chart

A scatter chart is a graphical technique to analyse the relationship between two variables.

A scatter chart is a graphical technique to show how two variables are related. The chart shows the two sets of data, with the *y*-axis for one variable and the *x*-axis for the other. The chart illustrates the relationship but does not indicate if the relationship between the two sets of data exists or only appears to exist.

The scatter chart is used when the process has numerical pairs of variables (such as height and weight), when each numerical variable has multiple values, when trying to resolve the relationship between two variables, such as identifying the root causes of the problem, and when testing the relationship of variables before constructing control charts.

Figure 5.9 is an example of a scatter chart. In this example, team management measured the height and weight of each player in the sports team to establish whether

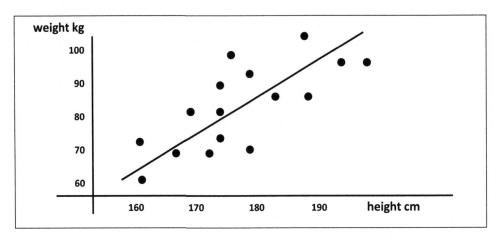

Figure 5.9 Scatter chart example

height and weight have any correlation. As height increases so does the weight, and this shows there is a positive relationship between height and weight.

Control chart

Control chart

A control chart is a graphic comparison of process performance data with pre-calculated control limits. The primary purpose of control charts is to detect assignable causes of variation in a process.

A control chart has upper and lower control limits calculated from data collected when the analyst believes the process is in control. The analyst takes measurements from subsequent samples and plots them to determine whether the process is still in control. Any trend within the limits, or any samples outside the limits, shows the probable existence of assignable causes. Control charts are useful when controlling the ongoing process and correcting the cause of process variation as and when it occurs, when determining whether the process is stable and analysing the pattern of process variation, when predicting the expected outcome of the process, and to analyse any additional improvements required to the process.

Figure 5.10 shows examples of control charts. The chart on the left relates to a process not centred on target values and not in control. A process operator entering the values into this chart should take immediate action to correct the problem. The process is unpredictable, erratic, and not in control. The middle chart shows the process has stabilised and centred. The control limits are closer together (compared to the left-hand chart) and a valid assumption suggests the process is now more predictable and performing better. The control chart on the right illustrates the result of further process improvements. The control limits are closer together (compared to the middle chart).

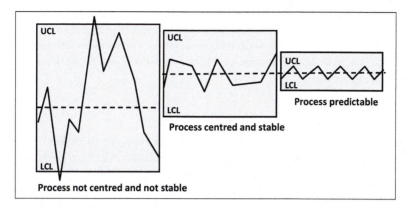

Figure 5.10 Control chart examples

Control limits are not specification or tolerance limits. We calculate control limits from process data when we believe the process to be in control and, in contrast, the customer dictates the specification or tolerance limits. We discuss control charts in more detail later in this chapter in the section on statistical process control.

Lean leadership

Lean implementation fails without buy-in from senior executives. The concepts of lean appear to be so basic and simple that senior management often view implementation with the same simplicity and assign middle management to supervise it. Nothing can be further from the truth. The concepts are basic because that is part of its purpose, which is to simplify and standardise processes. Complex processes are prone to misinterpretation and errors. Implementation requires senior management buy-in because it requires significant change. This change starts with work organisation, facility layout, employee responsibilities, rewards, and incentives. Changing frontline manager tasks are essential for lean to work. Without the drive from the top, many employees will not see the need and may at best just provide a half-hearted approach. The best we can ask for is active participation from the top.

Jeffrey K. Liker has studied the Toyota Way for several years. He believes the lean leadership style within Toyota is the reason behind Toyota's success with lean. To be successful with lean, organisations should follow the Toyota style or adopt something similar. The Toyota leadership style differs from traditional Western leadership in business decision making, problem solving, leadership style, and personal motives.[8]

Business decision making and problem solving

Toyota leaders have a 'True North' vision,[9] which is a clear view of the goals for which they are striving and work to perfect processes. Traditional management view a good process as one that is error-free, whereas Toyota view a good process as one that expects and reveals problems, without blame. Toyota leaders have a deep understanding of processes; they take time to plan and prepare people and processes for the long term. Before acting, they deeply understand problems and the root causes. They believe that the right process and well-defined targets will lead to the right result. In contrast, traditional management, to be successful, attempts to achieve short-term goals, which are primarily financial resulting, inevitably, with short-term decisions aimed at cutting costs.

Leadership style and personal motives

The Toyota management model assumes that a clear vision of success motivates many people to solve problems. They teach how to participate in setting goals and how to work effectively in teams. Managers are humble, they learn deeply and broadly, and then they take on increasing responsibility for the development of themselves and others. Metrics do not coerce desired behaviour, but provide individuals and teams with the tools to measure their own performance. The continuous use of plan-do-check-adjust becomes the desired behaviour, and leaders provide accountability and support for that behaviour.

Lean services

The concepts of lean production developed from the Toyota Production System, and so it is easy to assume that lean thinking benefits manufacturers and not service organisations.

However, the concepts of lean thinking apply directly to service environments, and many services already think lean, although they may not realise the terminology. Some of these concepts include:

- Consistently high-quality and defect-free services that deliver to the customer exactly what the customer wants, when the customer wants it, first time, and every time.
- Uniform facility loads using reservation systems, appointments, and differential pricing.
- Standardised work methods for consistency and repeatability of performance.
- Close ties with suppliers who provide frequent deliveries and short lead times.
- Demand-pull scheduling.
- Customised services using a flexible workforce.
- Automation to provide continuous services, such as online banking and automatic teller machines.

The prerequisite of relatively repetitive demand is difficult for most businesses to achieve. Service organisations use reservations and appointment books to level the demand. Production organisations use finished goods, supermarkets, and load-levelling mechanisms.

Traditional production environments and the production of low-volume, intermittent-usage products use order-release mechanisms. When lean thinking applies to high-volume products and services with relatively continual usage, the best way to communicate requirements is using demand-pull methods. Pull signals indicate the need to replenish the finished goods inventory or deliver a service replenishment inventory.

Statistical process control

Statistical process control

Statistical process control (SPC) is a methodology for monitoring a process to identify special causes of variation and signal the need to take corrective action when it is appropriate.

Statistical quality control

Statistical quality control (SQC) is the application of statistical techniques to control quality. It includes acceptance sampling and statistical process control.

$\bar{x}$ chart

The $\bar{x}$ chart is a control chart for variable data measured along a continuous scale.

R chart

R chart is a control chart using the range of sample observations to evaluate the stability of the variability within a process.

Control limit

A control limit is a statistically calculated line on a control chart. It may be the upper or lower control limit. When process samples lie between these two limits, the process may be in control.

Statistical process control involves testing a random sample of output from a process, while the process is running, to determine whether the process is producing within a pre-calculated range. The analyst calculates the control limits when they believe the process is in control. Tested output exceeding that range signals an investigation of the cause. The function of control charts is to indicate the possible presence of assignable cause variation.

If the process is not in control, or is heading in that direction, the analyst should adjust the process to bring it back in control. The analyst maintains statistical process control by measuring either attributes or variables.

Sampling by attributes recognises an item as good or bad, pass or fail, binary one or zero. For example, when testing light bulbs, a pass means it lights up, and a fail occurs if it does not.

Sampling by variables measures the amount of deviation from other units or from the design specification. For example, when testing light bulbs, the interest may be in the number of hours the bulb will shine, the brightness of the light, or the colour temperature of the light.

Process controls monitor quality while the process is producing the product or service. The most common charts for variable data measured along a continuous scale are $\bar{x}$ charts and R charts. Examples of variables data are length, distance, time, weight, pressure, temperature, and noise levels. The $\bar{x}$ symbol is the mean of sample measurements. The $\bar{x}$ chart is a plot of the means (averages) of sample measurements taken from a process. The range is the difference between the highest and the lowest numbers in the sample. An R chart is the plot of the ranges of sample measurements taken from a process. Process workers usually maintain the charts by hand. Standard deviation is a better measure of variability if a computer is maintaining the charts. Statistical analysis of past data for a given level of confidence determines the upper and lower control limits.

Figure 5.11 shows a distribution of sample means forming a frequency distribution diagram (histogram) rotated through 90 degrees.

The $\bar{x}$ chart tells us whether changes have occurred in the central tendency of the process. This might be due to such factors as tool wear, a gradual increase in temperature, a different method used on the second shift, or new and stronger materials.

The R chart values indicate when a gain or loss in uniformity has occurred. Such a change might be due to worn bearings, a loose tool part, an erratic flow of lubricants to a machine, or to sloppiness on the part of a machine operator. The two types of charts go together when monitoring variables.

A quality control supervisor draws control limits on a blank chart, and the operator records samples to monitor the process to ensure that the variation observed is within the natural variation of the process. The process is in statistical control when this occurs.

A process operating in statistical control has natural and expected variation coming from essentially uncontrollable sources; we call this natural variation. The process has no variation produced by specific, traceable, and assignable causes. Variation is at a minimum, given the process technology applied, and the variation represents merely random statistical variation, or variation without a cause.

Purists might argue that they can assign a cause to all variation. Therefore, when they observe natural variation, they treat it as assignable and make corrections to the process. The basic challenge in process control is to separate the assignable variation from the natural variation. This would follow a careful study of the process dynamics.

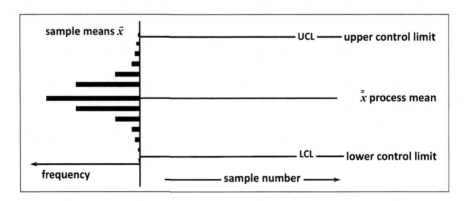

Figure 5.11 Establishing control limits based on ±3 standard deviations from the process mean

Analysts measure variables data along a continuous scale. Production examples of variables include weight (of a chocolate bar or a packet of cereal), colour (of paint or cosmetics), hardness (of a metal surface), viscosity (of oil or a smoothie drink), and temperature (of a room or a chemical process). Service examples of variables include arrival time (of an airline), errors (in financial statements), teaching evaluation, absenteeism, and cleanliness (of a hotel room).

Who enjoys a good cup of coffee these days?

Baristas worldwide try to fine-tune the extraction process to produce the perfect espresso. While discussing variation it is interesting to realise that baristas are manipulating four process variables – the coarseness of the grind, the temperature and pressure of the espresso machine, the extraction time, and the ratio of coffee to water. At this stage, we are just discussing espresso and have not even ventured into discussing milk for lattes, cappuccinos, and flat whites. Before the barista starts, we have variables for sourcing coffee beans (country and region of origin), variables for variety of coffee (arabica or robusta), variables for roasting beans (light, medium, or dark), and variables for the freshness of the roasted beans. However, let us just keep the discussion centred on variables of the coffee extraction process. We have variables for the grinding method and variables for the freshness of the ground coffee beans. Course coffee grinds make the coffee weak; fine grinds make it bitter and harder for the machine to force the water through the grinds. High temperature and pressure allow a shorter extraction time; low temperature and pressure does not easily extract the volatile oils that provide the flavour. The optimum extraction time provides the right amount of oils; a long extraction time makes the coffee bitter. Finally, we need good quality water – the addition of water dilutes the taste. *Ristretto* is a shorter pull than espresso; the grinds are the same, the temperature and pressure of the machine is the same, but the extraction time is less, providing a slightly sweeter drink with more intense flavours and without any bitterness. At the other end of the scale, the *lungo* has a lower coffee-to-water ratio and a slightly burnt, bitter taste. The crema, the tan-white foam on the surface of the espresso, is slightly thinner with the *ristretto* and diluted with the *lungo*. Now, what cup will we use to serve the coffee – a demitasse cup (70ml), a flat white cup (150ml), a tulip cup (170ml), a cappuccino cup (190ml), or a latte cup (280ml)? Enjoy!

Process control charts suggest trends. If a trend suggests a process is progressively getting worse, then it would be beneficial to investigate the process. If a trend suggests a process is improving, it may still require investigation to explain what is happening to make the improvement.

Establishing control charts and limits

Analysts establish process control charts when they believe the process to be in control and the output is predictable. This does not necessarily mean that the output is within the customer-defined specification, but it is predictable. Ideally, of course, it should be within the customer-defined specification, but the purpose of the control chart is to allow a process operator to monitor process output while the process is running and to make corrective action should the process start to deviate from expectations.

Decide on a measure of system performance, and collect representative historical data. This measure may be, for example, the weight of a packet of frozen peas, the length of time a customer waits in a queue, the volume of electricity generated by a power plant in a given period, or the length of a precision steel cut.

The measurements to establish the control limits occur when analysts believe the process is in control and the frequency distribution forms a Normal distribution. Using the properties of the Normal distribution the centre line equals the process mean $\bar{\bar{x}}$ (process average called x double bar), and analysts calculate the upper and lower control limits to correspond with ±3 standard deviations from the process mean. The ±3 standard deviations are the usual basis for calculating control limits. However, some organisations use ±2 standard deviations as warning lines.

The control limits calculation uses standard deviations, but, because of its simplicity, the most common method is to use the factors found in Table 5.1. Hartley's constant, d_2, a factor for estimating sample standard deviations, forms the basis of the table. Thus, the use of this table eliminates the need to calculate standard deviations. Instead, it uses the average of sample ranges $\left(\bar{R}\right)$ to calculate the ±3 standard deviation control limits.

The formula for calculating the average of sample means is:

$$\text{Average of the sample means} = \bar{\bar{x}} = \frac{\sum \bar{x}}{k} \tag{5.1}$$

where $\bar{x}$ = the mean of each sample
k = number of samples

Table 5.1 Factors for determining the ±3 sigma control limits for $\bar{x}$ charts and R charts

Sample size n	Hartley's constant d_2	Factor for $\bar{x}$ chart A_2	Factor for R chart D_3	Factor for R chart D_4
2	1.128	1.880	0	3.267
3	1.693	1.023	0	2.575
4	2.059	0.729	0	2.282
5	2.326	0.577	0	2.115
6	2.534	0.483	0	2.004
7	2.704	0.419	0.076	1.924
8	2.847	0.373	0.136	1.864
9	2.970	0.337	0.184	1.816
10	3.078	0.308	0.223	1.777

The formula for calculating the average of ranges is:

$$\text{Average of the ranges} = \bar{R} = \frac{\sum R}{k} \tag{5.2}$$

where R = the sample range
k = number of samples

Decide on sample size and calculate ± 3 standard deviation control limits (by convention).

Then take at least 30 samples. The number 30 is a derivative of the standard deviation formula, which changes when the number of samples exceeds 25 or 30. The sample size is the number of observations in each sample, and an ideal sample size is in the range of three to ten.

For each sample, calculate the mean (average) and the range (difference between the highest and the lowest values). Then, for all samples, calculate the average of the sample means and the average of the ranges.

Using the factor values in Table 5.1, calculate the upper and lower control limits for the $\bar{x}$ chart and the R-chart using the following formulas:

$$\text{Upper control limit for } \bar{x} \text{ chart} = UCL_{\bar{x}} = \bar{\bar{x}} + A_2\bar{R} \tag{5.3}$$

$$\text{Lower control limit for } \bar{x} \text{ chart} = UCL_{\bar{x}} = \bar{\bar{x}} - A_2\bar{R} \tag{5.4}$$

$$\text{Upper control limit for } R\text{ chart} = UCL_R = D_4\bar{R} \tag{5.5}$$

$$\text{Lower control limit for } R\text{ chart} = LCL_R = D_3\bar{R} \tag{5.6}$$

With the control limits calculated, plot the $\bar{x}$ chart on a graph with sample mean versus time, and plot the R chart on a graph with sample range versus time. Plot sample means collected at random on the $\bar{x}$ chart. Plot sample ranges collected at random on the R chart.

Worked example 5.1

The data in Table 5.2 represents 30 samples taken from a process thought to be in control. The process is packing cornflakes into packets with a net weight of 300 grams. Table 5.2 shows four observations for each sample. Therefore, using Table 5.1, we use the values in the row with $n = 4$ to use in the calculations. Table 5.2 provides the average of each sample and the range of each sample. Calculate the upper and lower control limits for the $\bar{x}$ chart and the R chart.

$$\text{Given} : n = 4, A_2 = 0.729, D_3 = 0, D_4 = 2.282, \bar{\bar{x}} = 302.25, \bar{R} = 6.87$$

Table 5.2 Data table for worked example 5.1

Sample	Weight (in grams)				Sample average	Range
1	307	302	303	305	304.25	5
2	305	305	303	308	305.25	5
3	298	305	302	300	301.25	7
4	300	304	302	305	302.75	5
5	298	305	300	299	300.50	7
6	300	295	305	302	300.50	10
7	309	306	301	301	304.25	8
8	300	299	305	295	299.75	10
9	305	304	298	299	301.50	7
10	298	308	305	300	302.75	10
11	296	300	304	299	299.75	8
12	302	302	303	307	303.50	5
13	303	300	305	305	303.25	5
14	305	299	296	304	301.00	9
15	298	304	305	305	303.00	7
16	305	299	301	299	301.00	6
17	306	308	306	299	304.75	9
18	309	300	300	299	302.00	10
19	298	302	302	300	300.50	4
20	299	302	304	302	301.75	5
21	300	305	307	304	304.00	7
22	301	304	308	302	303.75	7
23	305	299	299	304	301.75	6
24	296	305	300	305	301.50	9
25	306	302	306	301	303.75	5
26	306	300	305	302	303.25	6
27	299	304	304	300	301.75	5
28	301	299	299	306	301.25	7
29	305	306	300	305	304.00	6
30	297	303	298	299	299.25	6
				Process average	**302.25**	**6.87**

Using equation (5.3):

$$\text{Upper control limit for } \bar{x} \text{ chart} = UCL_{\bar{x}} = \bar{\bar{x}} + A_2\bar{R}$$
$$= 302.25 + (0.729 \times 6.87)$$
$$= 307.26$$

Using equation (5.4):

Lower control limit for $\bar{x}$ chart $= UCL_{\bar{x}} = \bar{\bar{x}} - A_2\bar{R}$
$$= 302.25 - (0.729 \times 6.87)$$
$$= 297.24$$

Using equation (5.5):

Upper control limit for R chart $= UCL_R = D_4\bar{R}$
$$= 2.282 \times 6.87$$
$$= 15.68$$

Using equation (5.6):

Lower control limit for R chart $= LCL_R = D_3\bar{R}$
$$= 0$$

Therefore, the control limits for the $\bar{x}$ chart are 307.26 grams and 297.24 grams, and the control limits for the R chart are 15.68 grams and 0 grams. Figures 5.12 and 5.13 show these limits superimposed and subsequent measurements plotted.

Figure 5.12 shows the sample means of the data used to calculate the limits. There are no trends or suspicious-looking readings, so a valid assumption suggests that the process is in control and these control limits will help to monitor the ongoing process.

Figure 5.13 shows the sample ranges of the data used to calculate the control limits. Again, there are no trends or suspicious-looking readings, so a valid assumption suggests that the process is in control and these control limits will help to monitor the ongoing process.

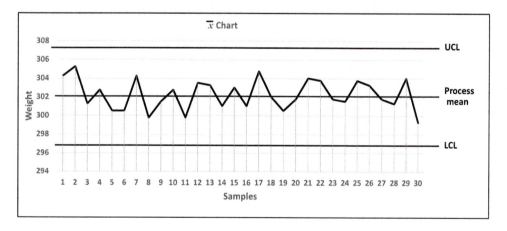

Figure 5.12 $\bar{x}$ chart for worked example 5.1

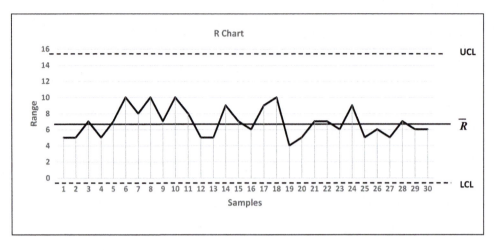

Figure 5.13 R chart for worked example 5.1

It may seem reasonable that there should be no variation in sample observations when packing cornflakes into a 300-gram bag. A desirable outcome requires the sample range to fall from the current 6.87 grams and approach zero. Process control requires a reason for the improvement for the process to remain in control. Chart interpretation is looking for any process variation that has an assignable cause. A process operator proposing a valid reason for any assignable cause validates the chart's purpose. If process improvement is the cause of the change in process variation, then the analyst should recalculate the control limits.

Interpreting control charts

Control limits represent the range between which all samples should fall if the process is in statistical control. If any samples fall outside the control limits, or if any unusual patterns appear, then some assignable or special cause has probably affected the process. It is not normal. When a sample lies outside the control limits, or several samples lie on one side of the centre line to indicate a shift in the process, the analyst should study the process to find the cause.

Figure 5.14 shows four examples of control charts. At the top left, the samples are fluctuating around the process mean, and the variation is natural. Therefore, the process is in control. In the top right, one reading pops up outside the lower control limit; this needs investigation. It does not necessarily mean the process is not in control; rather, something caused the stray reading; find out what it is and fix it. In the bottom left, there is a run above the centre line. All the readings are within the calculated control limits but this is not normal variation; again, this needs investigation. The bottom right shows a downward trend. All the readings are within the calculated control limits but this is not normal variation; again, this needs investigation.

If all the plotted values fall within control limits, it would indicate that the process is in control. Plotted values falling outside the control limits, or a run of seven values

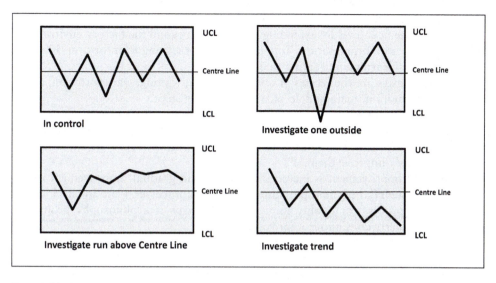

Figure 5.14 Chart interpretation

lying on one side of the mean, indicates a requirement to check the process and take possible corrective action.

Processes with wide variation often mask changes in process behaviour. When a narrow band represents process variation, it is easy to notice changes in process behaviour, and this makes process intervention decisions much easier.

Processes improve by progressively reducing process variability by identifying and eliminating assignable causes of variation. This requires better understanding of how processes operate and implies a requirement to learn about each process and gain knowledge about how each process will perform under different circumstances in the future. As processes improve, they gain a greater capability to deliver outputs at higher levels of performance.

Statistical process control has traditionally used control limits calculated using three standard deviations from the process mean. In Chapter 7, we discuss the concepts of six sigma quality. This is an extension of statistical process control with customer-defined limits (not statistically calculated), and it emphasises the negative effects that process variation delivers to customers. Analysts make every effort to ensure that processes operate with customer-defined limits that are at least six standard deviations (six sigma) from the process mean.

Chapter summary

Lean thinking is a philosophy of applying lean concepts to all business operations. The demands and requirements of the customer are summarised by the concepts of lean consumption.

This chapter started with a discussion on the history of lean and the principles of lean. Fujio Cho, then-President of Toyota, launched the Toyota Way in 2001. This takes lean to the next level by extending the practice beyond the factory environment to include the entire organisation. Toyota has been practising lean for over 50 years, but they are still learning and trying to do better.

The seven wastes are the wastes of overproduction, waiting, transportation, carrying inventory, motion, making defects, and processing steps.

Value stream mapping provides an integrated description of how a product passes through all stages of production. In this context, integrated means that we consider both material and information flows. It is an essential means to see the value streams and continuously improve them.

Continuous improvement is incremental (small and gradual) improvement rather than breakthrough (large and rapid) improvements in processes. Plan-do-check-adjust is a four-step process for quality improvement. *Kaizen* is a philosophy promoting gradual and orderly continuous improvement.

The basic seven tools of quality are flowcharts showing the flow of the process, check sheets showing the frequency of occurrence, histograms showing overall variation, Pareto analysis separating the significant few from the trivial many, cause-and-effect diagrams helping identify the causes of the problem, scatter charts showing factor relationships, and control charts showing which variations to control and how.

Statistical process control involves testing a random sample of output from a process while the process is running, to determine whether the process is producing within a pre-calculated range. Analysts calculate the limits of this range when they believe the process to be in control. Tested output exceeding that range signals an investigation of the cause. The function of control charts is to indicate the possible presence of assignable cause variation.

The concepts of lean production have developed from the Toyota Production System, so it is easy to assume that lean thinking benefits manufacturing companies and not service organisations. However, we can apply the concepts of lean thinking directly to service environments, and many services are already thinking lean although they may not recognise the terminology.

Discussion questions

1   Discuss the strategic value of lean thinking.
2   Describe the seven wastes and provide examples.
3   Explain how to use value stream mapping.
4   Discuss the Toyota Way.
5   Discuss lean thinking applied to services.
6   Explain the use of $\bar{x}$ charts and R-charts.
7   Discuss the basic seven tools of quality.

Key terms

basic seven tools of quality, 168
cause-and-effect diagram, 168
check sheet, 169

continuous improvement, 163
control chart, 174
control limit, 177

fishbone diagram. *See* cause-and-effect diagram

flowchart, 170

heijunka, 166

histogram, 171

Ishikawa diagram. *See* cause-and-effect diagram

jidoka, 151

just-in-time (JIT), 152

kaizen, 163

kanban, 166

lean production, 165

lean thinking, 150

mixed-model production, 166

non-value adding, 157

Pareto analysis, 172

Pareto chart, 172

PDCA. *See* plan-do-check-adjust

plan-do-check-adjust, 163

process improvement, 163

pull system, 167

R chart, 177

scatter chart, 173

seven tools of quality. *See* basic seven tools of quality

seven wastes, 157

statistical process control, 177

statistical quality control, 177

takt time, 162

value, 157

value adding, 157

value stream, 162

value stream mapping, 162

waste, 157

$\bar{x}$ chart, 177

Notes

1 Perspective written with inputs from Tony Grant, Production Manager, Chelsea Sugar.
2 Womack, J. P., & Jones, D. T. (2005, March–April). Lean consumption. *Harvard Business Review, 83*(3), 58–68.
3 Toyota Motor Corporation. (n.d.). *History of Toyota*. Retrieved from www.toyota-global.com/company/history_of_toyota/
4 Toyota Motor Corporation. (n.d.). *Toyota production system*. Retrieved from www.toyota-global.com/company/vision_philosophy/toyota_production_system/origin_of_the_toyota_production_system.html
5 Womack, J. P., & Jones, D. T. (2003). *Lean thinking: Banish waste and create wealth in your corporation* (2nd ed.). New York, NY: Simon & Schuster, pp. 16–27.
6 Liker, J. K. (2004). *The Toyota Way: 14 Management principles from the world's greatest manufacturer*. New York, NY: McGraw-Hill, pp. 35–41.
7 Gray, C., & Wallace, T. (2003, October). Master it (lean production scheduling). *APICS the Performance Advantage, 13*(9), 44–48.
8 Liker, J. K., & Convis, G. (2012). *The Toyota Way to lean leadership: Achieving and sustaining excellence through leadership development*. New York, NY: McGraw-Hill, pp. 227–252.
9 True North is based on the values of the Toyota Way, which provide a stable vision of where the company should be headed, and it is not negotiable.

Additional reading on applying lean thinking to operations

Bicheno, J., & Holweg, M. (2016). *The lean toolbox: A handbook for lean transformation* (5th ed.). Buckingham, England: PICSIE Books.

Gray, C., & Wallace, T. (2003, October). Master it (lean production scheduling). *APICS the Performance Advantage, 13*(9), 44–48.

John, J. A., Whitaker, D., & Johnson, D. G. (2005). *Statistical thinking in business* (2nd ed.). Boca Raton, FL.: Chapman & Hall.

Juran, J. M., & De Feo, J. A. (2017). *Juran's quality handbook: The complete guide to performance excellence* (7th ed.). New York, NY: McGraw Hill Education.

Liker, J. K. (2004). *The Toyota Way: 14 Management principles from the world's greatest manufacturer*. New York, NY and London: McGraw-Hill.

Liker, J. K. (2011). *Toyota under fire*. New York, NY: McGraw-Hill.

Liker, J. K., & Convis, G. (2012). *The Toyota Way to lean leadership: Achieving and sustaining excellence through leadership development*. New York, NY: McGraw-Hill.

Pittman, P. H., & Atwater, J. B. (2016). *APICS dictionary* (15th ed.). Chicago, IL: APICS.

Protzman, C., Whiton, F., & Protzman, D. (2019). *Implementing lean: Twice the output with half the input*. New York, NY: Routledge and Productivity Press.

Womack, J. P., & Jones, D. T. (2003). *Lean thinking: Banish waste and create wealth in your corporation* (2nd ed.). New York, NY: Simon & Schuster.

Womack, J. P., & Jones, D. T. (2005, March–April). Lean consumption. *Harvard Business Review*, 83(3), 58–68.

Chapter 6

Achieving balanced results and measuring performance

Learning objectives

At the end of this chapter, you should be able to:

- Describe measurements for business excellence.
- Describe the *hoshin kanri* process for setting goals and using measurement systems.
- Describe the balanced scorecard approach to performance measurement.
- Describe how the closed-loop management system links strategy and operations.
- Describe the driving forces of performance and benchmarking.

Perspective: Nokia – how do we measure performance?

Nokia represents an excellent example of a company that transformed itself several times, developed new technologies, and adapted to shifts in market conditions. The company started as a single paper mill operation, 180 kilometres north of Helsinki, in Finland, in 1865. It exported paper products for over a century, with its largest customer base in Russia. Over time, the company diversified into rubber boots, chemicals, cables, electronics, and telecommunications infrastructure equipment. This diversified success developed with its geographical presence from a Finnish-focused company until the 1980s, to a significant European company in the early 1990s, and onto a truly global company from the mid-1990s onward.[1]

For the first decade of this century, Nokia dominated the mobile phone market with innovative and smart inventions that expanded the customer experience. Nokia owned 40% of the world mobile phone market share in 2008. Their products introduced built-in cameras, enabled the ability to send and receive emails and faxes, and communicated with the internet. Customers referred to their phones by using just the product number (3310, 5110, 7650, and 8210 for example);[2] customers assumed the brand name was Nokia. Such was Nokia's dominance.

However, Nokia did not appreciate, or foresee, the value of the touchscreen. So, when Apple introduced the iPhone®[3] in 2007 that signalled the downfall of Nokia. In just a few years, the Nokia brand disappeared from the mobile phone market, and many people believed the company had vanished. However, to demonstrate resilience, flexibility, and versatility, Nokia shifted from being in the limelight to become a major force in communications technology.

Nokia is still heavily involved in communications technology. In 2017, they applied for over 1300 patents. All the big players in the mobile phone market (Samsung, Apple, and Huawei) have Nokia patents. At the World Economic Forum annual meeting, in Davos Switzerland, in January 2019, Rajeev Suri, President and Chief Executive Officer of Nokia Corporation, presented the Nokia view on 5G communications. He described how Nokia is developing technology to deliver 5G that possesses characteristics that make it truly transformative. 5G has virtually no delay when carrying out remote orders, speeds around ten times faster than previous networks, connection capability enabling up to one million linked devices per square kilometre, and all coupled with unparalleled reliability.[4] Boundless wireless connectivity and the rich intelligence from the unrestricted flow of data will enable companies to make, move, and run more leanly and agilely than ever before, thus having a dramatic effect on supply chains and logistics.[5] It is hard to imagine what that technology is capable of and where it will take us in the future.

He described Nokia's own 'conscious factory' in Oulu, Finland, where 99% of the factory is automated. The factory changes temperature and humidity automatically to keep machines in prime condition. Autonomous vehicles deliver parts, and employees can move everything around, apart from the walls, floor, and ceiling. Ubiquitous connectivity underpins robots, workers' tools, and the network. This factory has leveraged connectivity to become one of the most flexible, versatile, and productive factories in the world.

So, the bottom line is, 'How do we measure Nokia's performance?' From humble beginnings as a local paper mill, to dominating the mobile phone market, and now a prominent player developing communications technology to transform the very world that we live in. Financial success should not be the only measurement – if, in fact, success is the goal. Nokia has survived – surely, that is a good achievement. For a company that has changed our lives in the past and is destined to make dramatic changes in the future, we need other measurements. What do we measure? What do we measure against? What is the benchmark? What timeframe should we consider? Do we stop when we have achieved some predetermined goal, or do we just keep going?

Many companies measure themselves against their own strategic goals. However, this is not the complete picture since we can change strategic goals on a whim. How do we measure? What data do we consider?

Introduction

'Are we there yet?'
'How well are we going?'
'What's our sales (achievement)?'
'Have we reached budget?'
'Have we exceeded budget already?'
'What'll happen to the share price if we don't achieve what we advised the markets we would achieve?'
'What's the profit increase over last year?'
'Not another cost blow-out!'

'Why is this project late?'
'Do we ever meet customer delivery dates?'
'When will the new product be available for customer testing?'
'But I've promised delivery today!'
'How many customer complaints have we received this week?'
'What's our yield percentage?'
'What's our customer satisfaction rating now?'

This chapter is about performance measurement and management. The chapter topics of this book form the discussion topics to review the scope of business performance. The review describes each topic together with a brief discussion on how to measure that topic.

Stakeholders and the press demand information to enable the construction of rankings in public-sector service organisations. Hospitals, schools, local councils, and charities are among the organisations scrutinised on a regular basis against a set of performance measures. With this comes the problem of misunderstanding or misinterpretation.

It is relatively easily to understand traditional accounting measurements of profit and return on investment. They represent one approach to performance measurement based on quantifiable financial measurements. The approach today requires a proliferation of measurements, and these include quantitative as well as qualitative dimensions.

We could have introduced the *hoshin kanri* process in Chapter 1 (strategy) since *hoshin kanri* establishes the vision for the organisation and defines the key result areas for achievement. We could have introduced it in Chapter 4 (process design) since *hoshin kanri* provides a framework for achieving the vision. We could have introduced it in Chapter 5 (lean thinking) since *hoshin kanri* focuses on key processes and introduces new methods. However, we introduce it in this chapter because *hoshin kanri* requires regular review, measurement, and realignment.

We discuss the balanced scorecard approach, which provides a balanced view of both financial and operational performance measures.

Other books on operations management often cover performance measurement as an afterthought, or not even at all. However, why wait until the end? This chapter is a checkpoint to make sure we are on target.

Developing balanced results

Business performance scope

Performance measure

Performance measure is the actual value measured for a criterion; the performance criterion is the characteristic to measure.

To enable business leaders to make effective and timely decisions, an organisation needs to develop the key set of results required to monitor progress against the vision, mission, and strategy of the organisation.

Operations management plays a strategic role in every organisation, and the ultimate performance test is survival. If the organisation intends to remain a viable entity and survive, then, using survival as the measure, it is successful. Executives worry about the survival target, saying that 'to just survive' is an underachievement and most organisations should be able to do better. Look at it the other way. If the organisation does not survive . . . that is untenable. At the very worst, survival is the minimum positive achievement.

The operations function has an excellent opportunity for changing overall performance of the organisation. In fact, the foundation theme of operations is process improvement and product improvement in an environment of increasing customer expectations and requirements. Therefore, to have any chance of success, an organisation needs to raise the performance level at least as fast as customer requirements rise.

Performance measurement provides some advice on progress and may highlight areas of concern requiring more attention or more resource. The following sections discuss potential areas and topics.

Strategy

Strategy sets a vision for the direction of the organisation and the philosophy underlying the vision statement. It uses broad statements that set the direction for the organisation to take. It specifies how to satisfy customers, how to grow the business, how to compete in its environment, how to manage the organisation, how to develop capabilities within the business, and how to achieve financial objectives. High-performance organisations achieve these objectives.

Strategy may have long-term connotations, but underlying the strategy are the tactical plans and targets. These are usually shorter term than the strategy, and state specific achievements and periods. Tactical measurements are usually easier to achieve than strategic ones, as they tend to be quantitative in nature.

When the achievement of strategy objectives and tactical targets become the basis of executive measurement, there is a temptation to make the goals easy. They should be achievable but possess an element of stretch.

Demand management and forecasting

Most organisations use some form of forecast accuracy to measure the performance of their forecasting system. They typically use measures such as mean absolute percentage deviation (MAPD), mean absolute deviation (MAD), and bias. These measures do not tell what the forecast should have been; they report past performance, but do not attempt to assist the forecasting process to perform better.

Forecast value added (FVA) is the change in forecast accuracy due to an activity in the forecasting process. Forecast value added compares the forecast performance following a process activity with the performance achieved without performing that activity. If the forecasting performance improves, the activity is adding value to the forecasting process. If the forecasting performance does not improve, the activity is not adding value to the forecasting process. When this measure applies to each step and everyone in a forecasting process, it becomes possible to identify the non-value-adding activities and improve the overall process.

Capacity management

Organisations can measure capacity management at the aggregate level to improve performance. Most organisations have a future period restricting decision-making activities. This period may be two, three, four, five, or even six months. It is too late to make wholesale demand and capacity changes inside that period because of previously made commitments.

For example, an organisation may have outstanding orders for imported raw material that is in transit. Alternatively, it may have a building, or process technology, in construction. Changes inside these commitment dates can still be authorised, but the consequences may incur additional cost.

Capacity performance measurement links with demand performance measurement and the calculation for both occurs at the aggregate level. Using aggregate figures, the measurement system maintains a record of the capacity requirements and demand forecasts as illustrated schematically in Figure 6.1. In this diagram, in January, the system enters the capacity requirements and demand forecasts for February onwards. During February, the system enters the actual figures for February, and the capacity requirements and demand forecasts for March onwards. During March, the system enters the actual figures for March, and the capacity requirements and demand forecasts for April onwards. During April, the system enters the actual figures for April, and the capacity requirements and demand forecasts for May onwards . . . and so on for every month.

In July, for example, the organisation knows the actual figures for June, and the system compares these with the five figures above the June actual value. In the column

	Feb	Mar	Apr	May	Jun	Jul	Aug	Sep	Oct	Nov	Dec
January	xxx	xxx	xxx	xxx	xxx	xxx	xxx	xxx	xxx	xxx	xxx
February	Actual	xxx	xxx	xxx	xxx	xxx	xxx	xxx	xxx	xxx	xxx
March		Actual	xxx	xxx	xxx	xxx	xxx	xxx	xxx	xxx	xxx
April			Actual	xxx	xxx	xxx	xxx	xxx	xxx	xxx	xxx
May				Actual	xxx	xxx	xxx	xxx	xxx	xxx	xxx
June					Actual	xxx	xxx	xxx	xxx	xxx	xxx
July											
August											
September											
October											
November											
December											

Figure 6.1 Capacity requirements and demand forecasting performance measurement report

above the June actual, the performance report is showing the forecast figures for June as determined in January, February, March, April, and May. A careful analysis of these figures illustrates the changing dynamics of capacity requirements and demand over that period.

Utilisation should never be a performance measure unless demand exceeds available capacity in the long term. Production output should satisfy customer demand. When capacity exceeds demand and utilisation is the capacity performance measure, then excess unsold production is waste.

Process design

Real measures on process design relate to how well the process can cope with the variability of customer demand. This translates into shorter lead times and increased flexibility.

Value is the amount customers are willing to pay for what an organisation provides. It represents a relationship between the benefits received and the price paid. Benefits can be informational and emotional as well as economic. Value is the quality received relative to expectations.

A value-adding process contributes positively to the final usefulness or value of a product. A cost-adding process contributes negatively to the final usefulness or value of a product. A cost-adding process does not add value; it just adds cost. Customers measure this value. A process is either value adding or cost adding; they are mutually exclusive. If it is not one, then it is the other. The objective is to eliminate all cost-adding processes and improve all value-adding processes.

Process improvement

James Womack described the perfect process as one creating exactly the right value for the customer.[6] He acknowledged value is hard to define for external processes and even harder to define for support processes. Each step in the process must be valuable, capable, available, adequate, and flexible.

Michael Hammer believes organisations should think process all the time. He introduced the term ETDBW, which stands for 'easy to do business with'. Organisations should run their businesses for the convenience of their customers.[7]

Deliver more value-add by designing processes to understand the customer needs, and develop production processes flexible enough to deliver exactly what the customer wants, when they want it, and how they want it. Process thinking is not about overhead allocation and cost accounting. It is not about confusion and delay. It is a discipline that designs outstanding performance rather than relying on luck. Process innovation and product innovation encourages new ideas, but these ideas require a process to facilitate their development into products and services that delight the customers. Without a process, innovation wallows in the mud and takes forever to reach reality.

Traditional company measurement systems look at history and tell (approximately) what has happened. The missing link is telling management what to do to make things better. That is where process thinking develops a structure to improve performance across the whole organisation. By focusing on the final, or end, customer, an organisation obtains an appreciation of real customer needs encouraging collaboration with customers and suppliers wherever possible.

Lean thinking

Lean thinking measures how well:

- Organisations develop strategies to deal with highly variable demand and reducing variability.
- Managers provide individuals and teams with the tools to measure their own performance.
- Plan-do-check-adjust is the desired behaviour and leaders provide accountability and support for that behaviour.
- The organisation levels the schedule for both volume and mix.
- Production flows through the facility.
- The organisation monitors customer order patterns to coincide with daily production volumes.
- Process improvement activities produce smaller quantities at shorter intervals.
- Upstream processes pull mixed-model schedules and repetitive demand components.
- Supply and demand are balanced.
- The production and supply schedules are stable while demonstrating flexibility.

Often the metrics for lean thinking aim at technical issues or process issues of little or no value to the customer. Even some of the lean metrics above have little or no value to the customer. The real metric for lean thinking should be a measure of the value added, and the customer determines that value. Is the customer willing to pay? Is the customer willing to pay a premium?

The next metric relates to the waste inherent in the process. Few customers are happy paying for waste, and lean thinking is all about eliminating waste. Then include a measure on how well the production processes flow, without queues forming and with minimum levels of inventory, and ultimately ending up with perfect processes. The aim of lean thinking is the perfect process.

Organisations record inventory as an asset in current accounting systems, so any attempts to reduce inventory is unfavourable on the balance sheet. Similarly, overproduction is favourable in the accounting system since it absorbs overhead. A reduction in lead time may cause a reduction in orders as customers adjust, and this temporary negative effect requires acknowledgement before it happens. Having the right measurements is important.

Product design

Performance wants and excitement characteristics of new products and services provide an excellent opportunity for an organisation to gain competitive advantage. Knowledge about each market segment and changing customer requirements helps to hit customer targets. Quality function deployment is epistemic and allows invisible customer requirements to be visible.

Some companies set targets for new products and services introduced in the previous few years, and these targets may represent at least 50% of corporate sales. Innovation audits measure the effectiveness and sustainability of new product and service activities.

Quality

Total quality management is a management philosophy that achieves an aim of long-term success through customer satisfaction and by meeting stakeholder needs and expectations effectively, without compromising ethical values. It is a way of thinking about goals, about organisations, about processes, and about people to ensure the organisation does the right things right first time and every time. This thought process changes attitudes and behaviours – it achieves better results.

Excellence is creating sustainable customer value and achieving results that delight the organisation's stakeholders. It requires visionary and inspirational leadership, coupled with constancy of purpose. Using processes and facts and allowing employees to maximise their contribution through their development and involvement is the way to manage organisations.

Calculate the theoretical process capability, C_p, for all new products and processes and set high targets (exceeding 2.0). The actual process capability, C_{pk}, should be close to the theoretical process capability, C_p.

Inventory and resources

Base inventory measurements focus on increasing customer satisfaction, stock availability, service levels, forecast accuracy, supply chain confidence, honest and true communication, increasing flexibility, and throughput as customers demand products and suppliers deliver replenishments. Measuring stock turn ensures that products are not sitting for extended periods waiting for a customer.

Base inventory measurements on:

- Decreasing demand uncertainty.
- Decreasing the number of customer complaints because customers have the required products in the required quantities and the products meet the expected quality standards.
- Decreasing conflicts as organisations satisfy all demands and do not need to trade off one customer demand against another.
- Decreasing delivery quantities, safety stock, lead time uncertainty, lead times, and obsolescence as inventory flows through the system.

Balance the flow through the facility rather than capacity. Processes are subject to disruption, such as machine breakdown, operator absence, accidents, and defects. Variables can accumulate and lead to increased delays. Concentrate on developing a flow of material rather than trying to keep every process busy.

Supply chain management

A supply chain works well with a fair reward distribution throughout the chain. Organisations should not endeavour to optimise their position; rather, they should encourage other participants in the supply chain to improve everyone's performance and benefits. In other words, each business should strive to do what is best for the supply chain rather than what they believe is best for them. Clearly understood performance measures show how well each business is supporting the value chain and not just their individual enterprise. The objective of this metric is to promote alignment of the business's goals with the supply chain.

The supply chain should show high stock turns throughout the entire chain and not just at specific points, such as the retail level. There should be low product obsolescence because of the ability to manage product life cycles and consumer demand and to exchange data quickly. Organisations should exhibit a rapid product introduction and time to market and exhibit a high degree of trust as they reveal aspects of their operations that are confidential.

The participants of the supply chain should align objectives, since any misalignment leads to non-optimal financial performance. A collaborative supply chain demonstrates a propensity towards elimination of waste. This means a desire to deliver value to the customer; this requires continuous elimination of waste in all processes.

Hoshin kanri process

Hoshin kanri process

Hoshin kanri is a systematic process that looks at the organisation and defines long-range business objectives. The methodology provides for a breakthrough objective focus to determine the most effective actions and the development of plans to support those actions. It implements formal review processes to measure performance and provide a framework for learning.

Without a hoshin-style process

When an organisation operates without a hoshin-style planning and review system, there is likely to be no clear vision. Managers may think they know operational requirements and diligently try to achieve their goals, but these goals might not align with those of other executives in the same organisation. The goals themselves are often set arbitrarily without due focus on what the organisation is trying to achieve. Processes lack ownership, and one function may pass work to another function assuming they know what to do and how to do it. Most of the non-financial measurements are qualitative, rather than quantitative, and very few tangible measurements exist apart from those related to volume of work and those related to time constraints. Competitor performance is, for the most part, unknown, or simply brushed aside with a comment such as, 'They're no good and we're better'. This ignorance often leads to arrogance and complacency at all levels in the organisation. Opinions form the basis of decisions rather than facts. A punitive review process and a blame culture exist. When something goes wrong, the first attempt at correcting the problem is to find someone to blame, rather than trying to learn from the experience.

With a hoshin-style process

Any organisation wanting to exceed their customers' expectations and stay competitive needs a long-range strategic plan that is forward-looking, visionary, and achievable. The best way to obtain the desired outcome is to ensure that all employees fully understand the long-range goals and follow a coordinated plan to make that vision a reality. Additionally, the organisation requires a set of fundamental process measures that require monitoring to ensure the continuous improvement of the organisation's key business processes. Essentially, everyone is heading in the same direction with the same sense of control. This is the basic premise behind *hoshin kanri* planning.

Breakthrough activities aim at achieving significant performance improvements or making significant changes in the way the organisation operates. Usually, a hoshin-style process identifies critical business issues the organisation will face in the next five to ten years and implements plans to address these. In its broadest sense, these business issues may relate to profitability, growth, market share, and quality problems, or maybe the need for a new product or service. It is essential to identify critical business issues facing the organisation and to select an objective and a goal to overcome each one.

The process develops supporting strategies and establishes specific goals for each one. These require a regular review and monitoring of progress.

The fundamental business activities must keep going, and for most organisations, this is where they exert most of the effort. The organisation must perform, on a day-to-day basis, before any new breakthrough activities can realistically take place. So now, the attention turns to the major business processes and the implementation steps to improve these activities continuously. Process performance measures require constant monitoring and improvement using the seven basic tools of quality and the plan-do-check-adjust cycle, as discussed in Chapter 5. The organisation places process performance measurements, reflecting the improvement of individual process activities, inside key processes to ensure that the organisation performs value-adding steps at the correct time, the required rate, and with the required level of quality.

Regular hoshin reviews

Organisations implement formal review processes on a monthly and annual basis and may use balanced scorecard reporting (as discussed below) to develop the process performance measurement. The balanced scorecard approach might identify initiatives required, and the planning system itself might need revision.

The organisation uses a hoshin review table for each strategy, using the plan-do-check-adjust cycle to measure the progress against the target that was set at the beginning of the year (plan). They write actual results alongside each strategy (do), and note any difference between the target and the actual (check). They document the impact, or effect, of any difference (adjust). They conduct this analysis for the successful objectives and for those that were not successful, or not completed.

For each objective successfully completed, they perform an analysis to determine what went right and to determine if the supporting strategies and performance measures were appropriate. They note any exceptional results, with details on how they obtained them. This is a learning step and is vital to knowing how to do better and to transfer that knowledge to the organisation.

The organisation documents the reason for any difference in performance, or results for each objective that was not successful. Again, the aim here is to learn from the non-performance, and they do not treat it as a blame-apportioning exercise. When the organisation learns what went wrong and how it could have done better, it is positioning itself for improved performance in the future. In this sense, it is adaptive and self-healing.

As one management level completes the planning table, it passes down the hierarchy to the next level within the organisation, so the lower level can add their inputs and interpret the planning document as it affects them. This is the cascading attribute of the *hoshin kanri* process and is a vital step in empowering the organisation. It is all part of the buy-in at every level and a locking-in of the plan resulting in total ownership of the plan.

The *hoshin kanri* process encourages an organisation to learn from the solved problems and the business successes. It helps the organisation reflect on where it is heading, the best way to get there, and to do that while in full control.

Balanced scorecard

Performance measures from four perspectives

Balanced scorecard

The balanced scorecard is a set of performance measures designed to reflect strategy and uniquely communicate a vision to the organisation. Usually the scorecard includes a customer perspective, a financial perspective, internal business processes, and innovation and learning.

Robert S. Kaplan and David P. Norton developed the balanced scorecard in 1992.[8] They introduced it when most performance measurements were finance-based and aimed only at controlling the business from a financial perspective.

Traditional performance measurement compares results to a set of predetermined targets that the organisation had aimed to achieve. This may be, for example, to achieve a given sales target or keep within a given cost budget. The organisation was successful by achieving these targets. By relying on traditional financial measures, however, management does not receive the necessary feedback to stimulate continuous improvement and innovation.

The balanced scorecard approach aims at cross-functional integration, customer-supplier partnerships, global scale, continuous achievement, and team rather than individual accountability. This provides a balanced view of both financial and operational performance measures.

The balanced scorecard measures business performance from four perspectives as illustrated in Figure 6.2:

- Customer perspective.
- Internal perspective.
- Innovation and learning perspective.
- Financial perspective.

Balanced scorecard

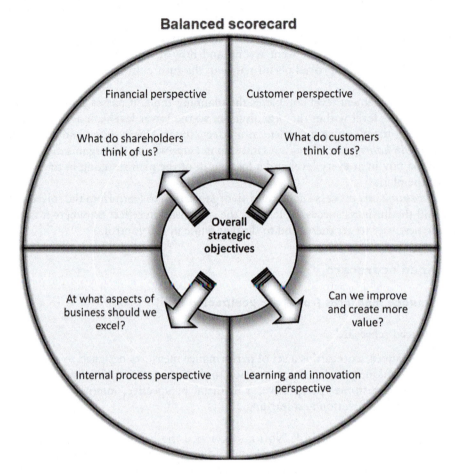

Figure 6.2 Balanced scorecard – Performance measures from four perspectives adapted from Kaplan, R. S., & Norton, D. P. (1992, Jan – Feb). The balanced scorecard – Measures that drive performance. *Harvard Business Review, 70*(1), 71–79.

Customer perspective

The customer perspective asks how customers see the organisation. Organisations may have a strategic objective to add value to customers, satisfy customer needs, listen to customer wants, allow customers to participate in process and product design, and to act and think from a customer's viewpoint. This needs measuring from a customer perspective by asking customers for their views.

Cost, quality, delivery, flexibility, and service form the basis of competitive capability. Customers share these concerns. A customer view of cost considers the total cost and not just the price. An organisation establishes prices for their products and services, and they receive these amounts for products produced and services delivered. The missing part is the extra that the customer must add to the price to arrive at the total cost to the customer. Additional cost could be taxes, freight, storage, inspection, quality assurance, quarantine, pilferage, deterioration, and obsolescence. This needs measuring from a customer perspective.

The organisation measures quality inside the organisation using quality control, quality assurance, and process capability. Customers only see external quality; they value the product in their own hands, and measure aspects such as delivery in full, on time, and in specification (DIFOTIS).

Delivery measurements often measure the time and date that products leave the supplier's premises and the actual delivery performance is up to the customer to negotiate. Customers do not see it this way. They want products delivered to their premises when and how they want them. Just because they have not contracted the service and are not paying for the service (such as transport, delivery, and storage) does not absolve suppliers of responsibility.

Organisations often demonstrate flexibility after they have stated the rules of engagement. Flexibility is often at the supplier's convenience, not when it suits the customer. The supplier makes deliveries at a supplier-determined schedule. They arrange passenger and freight transport at the transport operator's advertised schedule. Customers adjust their preferences according to the schedule even though those schedules may not be ideal. Suppliers rarely ask customers for comment on schedules, yet convenience is often a determining factor. Other service elements usually have customer feedback and require adjustment accordingly.

An excellent supplier can charge a premium for products and services and remain the lowest-cost supplier because it supplies defect-free products at exactly the right quantity, at exactly the right time, directly to the production process, and it minimises transaction costs by communicating electronically.

Internal perspective

The customer perspective looks at the organisation from the outside, whereas the internal perspective looks at the organisation from the inside and determines the aspects of business at which it should excel. Process design and process improvement all occur internally and the results of these initiatives affect customers.

Processes measured as part of the balanced scorecard have the most impact on customer satisfaction. Clearly, these affect lead time, throughput time, employee skills and attitudes, flexibility, availability, responsiveness, and information systems.

Organisations decide on competitive capability as a part of strategy, and they develop core competence to deliver that capability. They design and improve processes to enhance core competence from a customer perspective. These are all internal processes suitable for measuring from an internal perspective.

When the business identifies aspects adding value from a customer perspective, managers introduce measures that develop and reinforce those aspects. They can easily identify throughput time, quality, productivity, and cost as competitive capabilities for their organisation. Now they require processes that emphasise these attributes.

Information and communication technology play an important part in the internal perspective. When the balanced scorecard identifies problems, analysis of the relevant data is often a responsibility of information systems. As an example, if managers highlight delivery performance as a customer issue, they can analyse delivery data to determine the delivery status and possibly identify the root cause.

This is where flexible information systems dominate, as there was no need for the analysis prior to identifying the problem. This requires a speedy and thorough analysis as soon as the problem becomes apparent; the use of flexible systems is the only way to achieve this.

Innovation and learning perspective

The innovation and learning perspective asks whether the organisation can continue to improve and create value. Competitive activities constantly challenge every organisation's position. All other organisations challenge the organisation at the top of the league. Even organisations positioned somewhere in the middle must face constant challenges for their position. Customer expectations are constantly changing, and these force organisations to be very aware of the range and scope of those changes.

Each business must be able to create new products and services, and update the delivery of those products and services to customers. This requires innovation and learning.

Innovation provides new ideas, concepts, processes, approaches, and technologies. The business must update existing ideas, concepts, processes, approaches, and technologies – this requires learning. Businesses listen to their customers and learn from comments and reactions received – this requires understanding and judgement.

Financial perspective

The financial perspective asks for the shareholders' view of the organisation. Ultimately, the bottom line counts. Organisations can have any amount of customer satisfaction, close to perfection with internal processes, unlimited innovation and learning, and still fail on financial measures.

The trick is to capitalise on the other perspectives and translate gains into financial achievements. Financial measures are often short term. Quarterly and half-yearly reporting does not provide much opportunity for process improvement and capital spending to generate tangible figures. The improvements may be present, but reality determines financial outcomes.

Taking a quality view, organisations should concentrate on operational excellence and allow financial results to flow naturally. Traditional financial measures do not improve customer satisfaction, quality, throughput time, and employee motivation. In fact, some financial measures, such as a price increase, alienate customers and force them to go elsewhere.

Some customers regard price increases as inevitable and accept them without question. From 2002 to 2008, the spot price for oil was increasing and this received almost daily mention in news media. Airlines incorporated a fuel surcharge into their fares, and customers accepted this fare increase without questioning the validity of the actual numbers, without challenging the hedging policies of the airline companies, and without examining the root cause of the problem.

A well-researched and implemented strategy is not necessarily correct. Not every strategy has to be successful. Consider a sports team entering a competition with a winning strategy but failing to secure the winning trophy. The same applies to business. An organisation may have a winning strategy, or believe it has a winning strategy, only to find that another organisation has a better one.

There is no scale on strategy.

Linking strategy with operations

Ever since Kaplan and Norton published their balanced scorecard approach, various authors have attacked their premise by quoting examples claiming the balanced scorecard was difficult to implement and often only partially implemented. Widely acknowledged (even by its authors), the original balanced scorecard was not a perfect tool:

> In our original conception of the strategy map and the balanced scorecard, we encouraged companies to select initiatives independently for each objective. We came to realise, however, that by doing so, companies would fail to benefit from the integrated and cumulative impact of multiple, related strategic initiatives.[9]

Kaplan and Norton continued experimenting and researching, and they suggested that if businesses were having trouble using the balanced scorecard, they should try using strategy maps. They maintained that companies achieved a better implementation of the balanced scorecard by using strategy maps.[10] However, strategy maps can be difficult to implement. Organisations implementing the balanced scorecard using strategy maps can easily have core processes that do not support any competitive priority and, conversely, competitive priorities without any core process support. Another challenge for businesses is to ensure that the balanced scorecard effectively cascades down to lower levels of the organisation.

Sven Voelpel, Marios Leibold, and Robert Eckhoff generated a major challenge to the balanced scorecard theories by asking if the balanced scorecard had any value at all when applied in its current format and with traditional assumptions.[11] They proposed the balanced scorecard fails in five ways:

- It is a relatively rigid measure, forcing indicators into one of four categories.
- The level of focus on specific goals created in the use of the balanced scorecard aims the company directly at one goal, but under-utilises potential energy in other directions by focusing on this goal alone.
- The balanced scorecard is an internally focused document, and it largely ignores the needs of a networked innovation economy where competition is partly giving way to cooperation.
- The balanced scorecard uses an inflexible system to measure the value of innovation.
- The balanced scorecard takes a mechanistic approach to management and does not suit more organic business models.

Kaplan and Norton replied very directly to these criticisms by claiming that each of the points was inaccurate and/or available literature already addressed the criticism. In 2008, Kaplan and Norton outlined how to use the balanced scorecard as part of an organic strategy generation model. Their latest version of the balanced scorecard operates as a framework within a closed-loop management system implemented using strategy maps. Even when the company formulates the strategy using strategy maps and then implements and measures it using the balanced scorecard, it still requires constant revision based on feedback. Strategy formulation and execution is a fluid learning process with constant monitoring and updates.

Thus, the balanced scorecard returns to its original role as part of a larger solution, if perhaps not 'the' solution in and of itself. It is too early to say whether the closed-loop management system can react quickly enough to market changes to work as an organic strategy-generation model, and it still requires proof that the system can be simple enough to implement consistently. While the balanced scorecard is a tool for the implementation of strategy, by itself it does not ensure implementation of the best strategy. Successfully implementing a money-losing or disastrous strategy will result in successfully losing money or creating a disaster. The tool is not to blame.

Closed-loop management system

An organisation's underperformance results from a breakdown in the management system. This includes the integrated set of processes and tools an organisation uses to develop the strategy, translate it into operational actions, and monitor and improve the effectiveness of both. Organisations can avoid this by using a closed-loop management system comprising the following stages: Develop the strategy, translate the strategy, plan the operations, monitor and learn, and, finally, test and adapt the strategy.

Develop the strategy

Developing the strategy starts with defining the mission, vision, and values of the organisation. Essentially this identifies the business the organisation is in and why. A strategic analysis follows to isolate the key issues the organisation faces by looking at external as well as internal situations and challenges, before clearly stating how the organisation is going to achieve the vision.

Translate the strategy

The organisation translates the strategy into objectives and measurements. It communicates this clearly and succinctly to all employees using language they understand. The strategy map provides a powerful tool for visualising the strategy as a chain of cause-and-effect relationships between strategic objectives. Start with the organisation's long-term financial objectives and link these to objectives for customer loyalty and the value proposition. Continue to link to goals related to critical processes and eventually to the people, technology, and organisational climate and culture required for successful strategy execution.

Plan the operations

The organisation next develops an operational plan, laying out the actions that will accomplish the strategic objectives. This stage starts with setting priorities for process improvement projects, followed by preparing a detailed sales plan, a resource capacity plan, an operating budget, and a capital budget.

Monitor and learn

The execution of business processes takes place between the previous step and this step. The organisation reviews the performance of operating departments and business functions to address any problems that have arisen or remain. Strategy management convenes meetings that review balanced scorecard performance indicators to assess progress and identify barriers to strategy execution.

Test and adapt the strategy

In this step, the organisation assesses the performance of the strategy itself and changes it if necessary. From time to time, managers may discover that some of the assumptions underlying their strategy are flawed, or are no longer applicable or relevant. When that happens, managers need to rigorously re-examine their strategy and change it by deciding whether incremental improvements will be enough, or whether managers require a new, transformational strategy. This step closes the loop of the management system.

Driving performance metrics

Performance metrics are changing

Performance metrics are changing as organisations strive to improve performance and realise that traditional methods to evaluate performance are no longer appropriate. Amitabh S. Raturi and James R. Evans describe their view on the changing scope of operations management.[12]

Scope of operations management

The scope of operations management is shifting from a cost-centric to a balanced approach. With a cost view, organisations measure everything by cost and this is usually the initial price. Therefore, an organisation with a cost view purchases raw materials from a cheaper supplier because it does not cost as much. This is particularly attractive when operating with strict financial budgets, but not so attractive when management adds in other processing costs.

Customer-centric definitions of quality require an intimate knowledge of the customer and their behaviours. This new approach demands strategic capability based around quality, delivery, flexibility, and service.

Operations strategy

An organisation with a winning strategy will have competitors copying the strategy and trying to use it to their advantage. Raturi and Evans describe knowledge as syntactic, semantic, and pragmatic. Syntactic knowledge implies doing the right thing; semantic knowledge recognises the implications of social interactions; pragmatic knowledge implies recognising all contingencies to deliver results. Operations strategy, therefore, is changing from syntactic to pragmatic.

Organisations are looking to the environment for sustainability and renewable advantage. Modern organisations exhibit agility and are simultaneously competitive and cooperative.

Product design

Product design is showing marked shifts in emphasis. Organisations are bundling single products together or they bundle them with a complementary service package. Some organisations are bundling services together so they do not offer just one service – they may contract for the whole package.

A true understanding and response to customer needs requires speed of development, integration of hardware and software, and a learning environment built on knowledge management.

Process design

Process design is changing from an inside-out approach to an outside-in approach. This examines processes using a customer-centric definition, and re-engineers the processes that utilise the knowledge gained from customer feedback. Organisations design processes with process innovation rather than strict control.

Facility design

The global nature of business as well as the speed and ease of transporting products influence facility design. Commodity production may still use large facilities, but the emphasis now is on modular and flexible layouts.

Quality management

Most organisations have elevated the importance of quality systems. Quality is no longer a function of the quality department; quality is everyone's job. It is a prerequisite for playing the game. Six sigma is changing the perception of quality so it is a pervasive, formal, and systematic process. Results measure quality.

Supply chain management

Global supply chain and global sourcing requires an integrated approach rather than an uncoordinated one. Relationships with customers and suppliers are flexible with innovations in contracting, pricing, and other coordination mechanisms. Information and communications technology drives many of the changes in supply chain management.

The Internet, point of sale technology (POS), radio-frequency identification (RFI), electronic product codes (EPC), enterprise requirements planning (ERP), advanced planning systems (APS), artificial intelligence (AI), autonomous vehicles, automation, robotics, and omnichannel retailing are all changing the face of supply chain management.

Schedule management

Schedule management is changing from disciplined to flexible. Discipline is still present, especially when incorporating advanced information technology systems. The real difference is in the use of these systems to reflect actual situations rather than planned or theoretical situations.

Advanced planning systems use actual current queue times and schedule activities on a production floor using current demonstrated process rates. This provides flexibility coupled with accuracy.

Lean thinking

Lean thinking is also changing from disciplined to flexible, with a simultaneous focus on efficiency and flexibility. Lean six sigma, which is a marriage between the lean thinking philosophy and six sigma, drives quality and productivity improvements.

Benchmarking

Benchmarking

Benchmarking is the process of measuring a company's products, services, costs, and practices and comparing that measurement with the best in the industry, the best of class or world class. The aim is to use that measurement to improve performance.

Best practice

Best practice is the measurement or performance standard for evaluating similar items. Approaches that produce exceptional results are usually innovative in terms of the use of technology or human resources, and customers or industry experts recognised these.

A benchmark is a standard, or a point of reference, to measure or judge something, and competitive benchmarking involves analysing the performance and practices of best of class companies. The best of class demonstrates best practice, and their performance becomes a benchmark to which a business can compare its own performance. Once a business has made the comparison between the benchmark and its own performance, it can improve its own processes.

Figure 6.3 shows a schematic of the benchmark process that is a radar graph resembling a spider's web. Radials representing each benchmark criterion emanate from the centre of the web with the average value at the centre. The average value itself is in most cases arbitrary, but when comparing performances, it is not appropriate to be below average.

The chosen radials and the scale incorporated on each radial are at the discretion of the organisation using the benchmark. The best of class designation demonstrates best practice and we position it at the extremity of the radial. Somewhere just short of best of class is the category called world class. Again, that is an arbitrary position, but

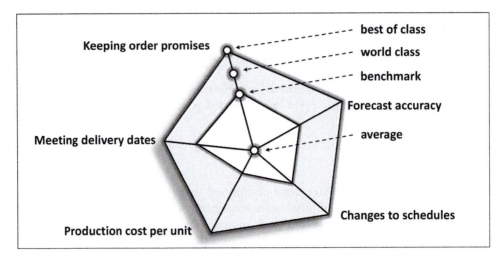

Figure 6.3 Schematic of benchmark process with sample benchmarks

it incorporates a group that we consider to be world-class performers for that chosen characteristic.

The schematic illustrates the benchmark process with five sample benchmark criteria. For the criterion 'keeping order promises', the best of class is at the extremity of the radial. Just inside the extremity is the nominated world-class position.

For the other four criteria, we have not labelled the best of class, but we may assume the radial limit is the value attributed to best of class. Also, not shown is the world-class value, but we may assume it to be just inside the best of class mark.

A lighter-shaded area lies juxtaposed in the centre. The organisation makes an estimate of the organisation's performance on each criterion and marks that estimate on the radial. When we have marked all radials, we construct a line joining the radial marks to enclose the inner area. This becomes the organisation's benchmark.

The shape of the inner area is a radar graph of the organisation's performance, and the organisation compares this with world class and best of class. In this example, 'keeping order promises' and 'meeting delivery dates' are pretty good and are approaching world class. However, the other three criteria need improvement.

Measurement determines behaviour

Self-interest

Individuals make their own choices to further their own personal aspirations while organisations do not.[13] Self-interest applies when measurement systems encourage behaviour contrary to the best interests of the organisations, such as:

- A production manager at a steel mill receives a production bonus based on tonnes produced. This encourages the production manager to produce fast, easy-to-make, heavy products that may not sell or will only sell at a discount.

- A salesperson encourages a customer to place an order for products that increases the salesperson's commission, but creates capacity problems during production.
- A finance manager may restrict the ability of a customer to place large orders because they are tardy with paying their invoices, when the real reason is that accounts receivables outstanding is a performance measure for the manager.
- A maintenance team carries a truckload of spare parts because their measurement is speedy repair.
- A call-centre operator terminates calls at three minutes because they must average 20 calls an hour. When this behaviour is evident, the customer rings back to complete the conversation and uses another three minutes.
- A real estate salesperson encourages a client to buy a particular property because they personally know the vendor, thus creating a conflict of interest.
- A contracts manager lets a contract to a service contractor because the manager expects a kickback in the future.

Individuals operate within sets of rules. Some of these are legal rules, the organisation imposes some of them, and individuals base some on personal beliefs and society norms. Just because a rule exists does not make it correct and does not necessarily create an optimum solution for all parties. Usually with any rule, one party benefits at the expense of the other.

Diversity

People operate at different rates, managers interact differently with staff, and different things motivate employees. The diversity issue applied to operations relates to the differing abilities of employees. An employee that excels in one area may not excel in another. Diversity is most evident when operating with a sequential assembly line. Teams compensate for diversity, and that explains why many organisations use a team approach to production rather than individual approaches.

Process documentation protects an organisation from diversity and provides increased flexibility. When the organisation has not documented processes, then long-serving employees hold all the production intricacies and nuances in their heads. When these individuals leave, or are absent from work, the lack of documented process causes chaos. With good process documentation, any cross-trained employee can perform any required task.

People have differing attitudes to life, and people want different things from their work environment as well as their home environment. Managers who thrive on power and control may divest some power and control to employees, believing the employees want more power and control. This may not be the case, however, as some people are quite happy just going with the flow.

Responsibility and authority

Responsibility without commensurate authority is demoralising and counterproductive. Management often recognises and rewards behaviour outside the control and authority of the individual.

W. Edwards Deming, the quality pioneer, used the 'red bead' experiment to illustrate this point. He mixed a handful of red beads into a large bowl of white beads.

He gave employees (volunteers from the audience) a wooden paddle with slots to accommodate exactly 50 beads, and told them that the aim was to get white beads only. The red beads contaminated the system, so the task was almost impossible to start with. However, the employee who obtained the lowest number of red beads received a promotion. The next day Deming repeated the experiment. Deming, who was a statistician, knew that the likelihood of the same employee repeating the performance and getting the lowest number again was very slim. Usually the promoted employee did not maintain the standard and Deming would chuckle, 'The raise went to his head'.

In this example, the system is wrong, and the employees are achieving the best possible result given the system parameters.

Chapter summary

There are many ways of measuring performance. Productivity is just one facet of performance. The essence of performance measurement is to understand why the measurement is taking place in the first place.

An improvement in performance measurement does not imply improved system performance. The red bead experiment (by W. Edwards Deming) illustrates this fallacy. We should not trust performance measures implicitly. A balanced view requires more than one performance measurement. Actual measurements should be revolutionary and not evolutionary, and they should have infrequent change.

Hoshin kanri is a systematic planning process that looks at the organisation and defines the long-range business objectives. The methodology provides for breakthrough objective focus to determine the most effective actions and the development of plans to support those actions. Organisations implement formal review processes to measure performance and to provide a framework for learning.

The balanced scorecard approach, advocated by Kaplan and Norton, includes a customer perspective, a financial perspective, an internal business-process perspective, and an innovation and learning perspective. The customer perspective identifies how customers view the organisation. The financial perspective asks how shareholders see the organisation. The internal perspective looks at the organisation from the inside and identifies the aspects of business at which the organisation should excel. The innovation and learning perspective establishes whether the organisation can continue to improve and create value. The implementation of the balanced scorecard improves when using a closed-loop management system comprising the following stages: Develop the strategy, translate the strategy, plan the operations, monitor and learn, and, finally, test and adapt the strategy.

Competitive activities are constantly challenging every organisation's position. All other organisations challenge the organisation at the top of the league. Even organisations positioned somewhere in the middle must face constant challenges for their position. Customer expectations are constantly changing, and these force organisations to be aware of the range and scope of those changes.

Benchmarking is a process of learning from others, and proposes the premise that there is a better performance somewhere in the world. Once a business has made the comparison between the benchmark and its own performance, it can improve its own processes.

Discussion questions

1 Explain how performance measurement may change individual and team behaviours.
2 Explain the balanced scorecard approach.
3 Evaluate *hoshin kanri* as a strategic planning system.
4 Evaluate *hoshin kanri* as a performance measuring system.
5 What are some financial measurements for an organisation?
6 What are some operational measurements for an organisation?
7 How should an organisation measure innovation and learning?
8 What is an appropriate measurement for internal processes?
9 Given a performance measurement 'delivery', explain what this means and how to devise a measurement system to measure it.
10 What performance measurements are suitable for a call centre, an airline, and a hospital?
11 Explain the prerequisites for using benchmarking as a measurement tool.
12 How does benchmarking benefit an organisation?
13 What should an organisation do to maintain 'best of class' performance when they believe they have that status?

Key terms

balanced scorecard, 199

benchmarking, 207

best practice, 207

hoshin kanri process, 197

performance measure, 191

Notes

1 Nokia. (n.d.). *Who we are: Our history*. Retrieved from www.nokia.com/about-us/who-we-are/our-history/
2 3310 was a bestseller, 5110 had interchangeable covers, 7650 was the first model with a camera, 8210 was very light.
3 iPhone is a trademark of Apple Inc. registered in the United States and other countries.
4 World Economic Forum. (2019, January 23). *Global agenda: 5G will redefine entire business models*. Here's how. Retrieved from www.weforum.org/agenda/2019/01/5g-will-redefine-entire-business-models-here-s-how/
5 Nokia. (2018). *Digital manufacturing: Reinventing factories, supply chains and logistics*. Retrieved from www.nokia.com/about-us/what-we-do/nokia-stories/digital-manufacturing/
6 Womack, J. P. (2003). *In search of the perfect process*. Retrieved from www.lean.org/Search/Documents/98.pdf
7 Hammer, M. (2001). *The agenda: What every business must do to dominate the decade*. New York, NY: Crown Business.
8 Kaplan, R. S., & Norton, D. P. (1992, January–February). The balanced scorecard: Measures that drive performance. *Harvard Business Review, 70*(1), 71–79.
9 Kaplan, R. S., & Norton, D. P. (2008, January–February). Mastering the management system. *Harvard Business Review, 86*(1), 68.
10 Kaplan, R. S., & Norton, D. P. (2000, September–October). Having trouble with your strategy? Then map it. *Harvard Business Review, 78*(5), 167–176.
11 Voelpel, S. C., Leibold, M., & Eckhoff, R. A. (2006). The tyranny of the balanced scorecard in the innovation economy. *Journal of Intellectual Capital, 7*(1), 43–60.
12 Raturi, A. S., & Evans, J. R. (2005). *Principles of operations management*. Mason, OH: Thomson and South-Western, pp. 318–340.
13 Hopp, W. J., & Spearman, M. L. (2008). *Factory physics* (3rd ed.). Long Grove, IL: Waveland Press, pp. 384–398.

Additional reading on achieving balanced results and measuring performance

Akao, Y. (1991). *Hoshin Kanri: Policy deployment for successful TQM* (G. H. Mazur, Trans.). New York, NY: Productivity Press.

Barad, M., & Dror, S. (2008, December). Strategy maps as improvement paths of enterprises. *International Journal of Production Research*, 46(23), 6627–6647.

Hopp, W. J., & Spearman, M. L. (2008). *Factory physics* (3rd ed.). Long Grove, IL: Waveland Press.

Kaplan, R. S., & Norton, D. P. (1992, January–February). The balanced scorecard: Measures that drive performance. *Harvard Business Review*, 70(1), 71–79.

Kaplan, R. S., & Norton, D. P. (1996). *The balanced scorecard*. Boston, MA: Harvard Business School Press.

Kaplan, R. S., & Norton, D. P. (1996, January–February). Using the balanced scorecard as a strategic management system. *Harvard Business Review*, 74(1), 75–85.

Kaplan, R. S., & Norton, D. P. (2000, September–October). Having trouble with your strategy? Then map it. *Harvard Business Review*, 78(5), 167–176.

Kaplan, R. S., & Norton, D. P. (2004). *Strategy maps: Converting intangible assets into tangible outcomes*. Boston, MA: Harvard Business School Press.

Kaplan, R. S., & Norton, D. P. (2008, January–February). Mastering the management system. Special issue on HBS Centennial. *Harvard Business Review*, 86(1), 62–77.

Liker, J. K., & Convis, G. (2012). *The Toyota way to lean leadership: Achieving and sustaining excellence through leadership development*. New York, NY: McGraw-Hill.

Pittman, P. H., & Atwater, J. B. (2016). *APICS dictionary* (15th ed.). Chicago, IL: APICS.

Voelpel, S. C., Leibold, M., & Eckhoff, R. A. (2006). The tyranny of the balanced scorecard in the innovation economy. *Journal of Intellectual Capital*, 7(1), 43–60.

Quality management and product design

Perspective – customer requirements in product design

Your mission, if you choose to accept it, is to design and bring to market a transportation device for a multinational organisation. You currently work for an international business consultancy as an adviser on technology products and you lead a small team of specialists who understand the need to satisfy customer requirements and who possess an unrivalled understanding of available technologies.

Where do you start? The assignment says 'transportation device' so you may assume it is a vehicle of some sort. What will power your new design – a combustion engine, an electric motor, a hydrogen fuel cell, some combination of combustion engine, electric motor, and hydrogen fuel cell, or something else?

The International Monetary Fund, in a working paper on the transition from oil, quotes various sources that predict that electric cars will occupy 25–30% of all vehicles by 2030 and about 50% by 2040. The paper compares the demise of the combustion engine in the automobile industry as like the Swiss watch industry in the 1970s and the 1980s. As a matter of interest, they remind us that at the start of the twentieth century about 30% of all vehicles in the United States were electric-powered.[1] Electric vehicles are not new!

Good designers recognise change, and they would not want to obtain notoriety by missing an opportunity:

- Eastman Kodak tried to protect its photographic film business and failed to recognise the potential of digital cameras. After all, an engineer at Eastman Kodak claimed credit for inventing the digital camera in 1975. It took 23 seconds to transfer the picture onto a tape cassette for viewing on a TV. Kodak management looked at the model with blank faces.[2]
- Nokia failed to recognise the shift from product-based competition to one based on platforms. For their phones, they developed an operating system that was unique to each model of phone. A single, simple answer cannot explain Nokia's decline in mobile phones: Nokia developed dysfunctional organisational structures, a growing bureaucracy, and deep internal rivalries that prevented them from seeing a major shift in their market – one that they had dominated for a decade, or more.[3]

Now, back to your assignment: If powered in full, or in part, by electricity, then how will the customer recharge the vehicle? Will they use electric vehicle power stations? Will the vehicle have on-board batteries? What are the supply statistics for the battery? What power systems will you utilise? How long will it take to recharge? What are the power requirements? Will the vehicle require a driver or will it be driverless? What performance characteristics does the customer want? What characteristics can your client supply? What is the vehicle configuration – will it be sedan, a sports utility vehicle, a two-wheeled cycle, or a truck?

Media reports may influence your design. Ford decided to have only one saloon car from 2019 – the Mustang. The rest are sports utility vehicles.[4] They are investing $11 billion in electric vehicles and expect to have 22 electric vehicles by 2022. Sixteen of these will be fully electric and the rest will be hybrid. Volkswagen AG plan to invest $40 billion in electric vehicles before 2022. General Motors and Toyota Motor Corporation have aggressive plans for their electric vehicle fleets. They are targeting customers who desire luxury, performance, and a sports utility style. Tesla has capitalised on their high profile to convince customers that electric vehicles are truly viable.[5]

If you decide to go electric, you should consider the flow-on effect involving the combustion engine supply and maintenance industry. This is not a direct function or responsibility of the design team but will be an economic and social consideration nevertheless.

Physical characteristics become the responsibility of the chassis design team whose design decisions are predominantly beyond the comprehension of most vehicle owners, but the customer is stuck with the outcome of each decision. Therefore, your design team must assume the role of the customer and interpret what the customer wants. Thus, you will determine the composition of the body shell, the engine or propulsion methodology, the transmission components including the clutch, the gearbox, the final drive, and the differential, the suspension system, the steering mechanism, the braking system, and the electrical equipment.

Most customers rely on consumer advocacy groups for detailed technical evaluation and advice in testing for reliability, acceleration, braking, safety systems, displays and controls, driving positions for various sizes and ages of drivers, fuel economy, emissions, fit and finish, power of headlights, autonomous safety and guidance systems, road noise, off-road capability (if applicable), handling, transmission, and the trunk and luggage space. The advocates assume the role of the customer as they conduct their evaluations and summarise their findings so that customers can match their needs with the findings.

Comfort and safety attributes influence customers who make subjective evaluations based on peripheral features such as:

- Comfortable seats for driver and passengers.
- Ease of ingress and egress, especially for people experiencing mobility issues.
- Height-adjustable lumbar support for driver's seat.
- Forward-collision warning to alert the driver to a potential crash.
- Automatic emergency braking to sense a potential collision.
- Reversing camera to provide visibility of objects at the rear of the vehicle.
- Blind-spot monitoring to recognise the presence of another car in the blind spot.
- Smart phone usability to the vehicle's dashboard.
- Bluetooth connectivity allowing the driver to answer a mobile phone call hands-free.
- Wi-Fi capability.
- Parking assistance to make manoeuvring in tight situations a breeze.
- Status displays such as current speed, navigation information, and audio selections on the windshield directly in front of the driver.
- USB port and external power supply.
- Multi-zone automatic climate control allowing users to fine-tune temperature settings.
- Automatic high beams to turn off the high beams for oncoming traffic, and then turning them back up once the cars have passed.
- Keyless entry and push-button start.
- Navigation on a big screen integrated with the car's controls.
- Lane-centring assist to nudge the steering wheel when needed.
- Adaptive cruise control.
- Traffic jams assist.
- Motorway autopilot and self-drive capability.

We have started this perspective with many questions – and we have not finished yet! The person next to you represents the customer. What does the customer want? We will define quality as whatever the customer wants it to be. Therefore, we are about to design a 'quality' vehicle. It does not have to be expensive – many people name expensive European vehicles as symbols of quality. Yes, they do represent quality products but you must not equate quality with cost; there is no correlation:

- What range can the vehicle travel?
- What speed and acceleration will it attain?
- What safety features will it have?
- What colours will it have? (Henry Ford reportedly offered any colour provided it was black!)

- What communications capabilities will it have?
- What artificial intelligence capability (for repairs and maintenance) will it have?
- How will this vehicle appeal to customers who possess strong feelings about preserving the environment and sustainability?
- How will you market this vehicle?
- How will you finance the development and lifetime costs?

We will stop the questions for a moment and let you get on with your assignment.

You have 24 months to bring the new design to market, and, by the way, just make sure that the quality you build into the product at least matches the quality your customers expect.

Introduction

New product and service design is a strategic decision for most organisations. The selection of products and services generated by an organisation is their offering to their customers. Get it right and the organisation has the potential to make a lot of money. Get it wrong and the organisation may quickly go out of business.

We examine several methods to understand what the customer wants and how designers build quality into the product or service. Whether it is a product or a service, the underlying criteria requires the product, or the service, to meet, or exceed, customer requirements. The process capability ratio and the process capability index help to understand how the process should be operating and how it is operating. This leads directly to a discussion on six sigma quality.

Design for the customer

Voice of the customer

Voice of the customer

Voice of the customer (VOC) is the actual customer description of the functions and features the customer desires.

Capturing the voice of the customer is of paramount importance when trying to establish true customer needs. Market research, customer interviews, focus groups, and Delphi interviews all provide an insight into customer requirements. Too often, though, the person providing the answers has a limited understanding of the discussion topic, or is incapable of expressing ideas coherently, or the question style limits the response.

Market researchers often telephone prospects (or suspects) during the evening and hope to gain an interview. The choice of responders is immediately limited to those who choose to stay on the line and answer the questions. The responses, if offered, have little preconceived thought and may even be the opposite of true feelings and attitudes. There is no way of telling if an individual is playing a game or is providing good, honest opinions.

Many excellent ideas come from ethnographic studies, or observations, in our own environment. Studies like this observe participants in various settings, and this reflects the needs and wants of the customer. As an example, imagine having a video camera watching what happens in a restaurant kitchen. By studying the footage, it may be possible to design a better layout and provide more process technology (and to see what happens).

Understanding the voice of the customer is the starting point for designing products and processes. It focuses on customer needs, it drives the design process, and it requires continual monitoring to ensure it is meeting customer needs.

All functional areas have a responsibility to understand the role the customer plays in this process. Each function orients itself towards providing additional value for the customer. It provides the basis for critical measurements on product and process design.

Customer requirements

The process of product or service design starts with an understanding of customer requirements. Customers suggest improving existing products and services. Required changes come from customers; they want more value. They want to receive more benefits compared to the price they pay.

When there is no existing product and the design team is starting with a concept, it is considerably harder to get customer inputs. The challenge for the design team is to get the product, or service, to market so that it creates excitement on the part of the customer and reaches the market first. Think back a few years and consider cell phones designed to take digital photographs. Who wanted one? Designers of cell phones that took digital photographs introduced a 'wow' factor that caught the imagination of millions of customers worldwide when first introduced. Now think back and put yourself on the design team of the early models. What are you going to do first?

Kano model

Professor Noriaki Kano developed the Kano model as a product development methodology to understand customer-defined quality. It starts by classifying customer preferences as basic needs, performance wants, and excitement. The process identifies which features create customer satisfaction and which cause dissatisfaction. With this knowledge, the designer prioritises development activities and decides where to spend resources improving these requirements.[6]

Kano model

The Kano model is a product development methodology to understand customer-defined quality. It starts by classifying customer preferences as basic needs, performance wants, and excitement. The process identifies which features create customer satisfaction and which cause dissatisfaction. With this knowledge, the designer prioritises development activities and decides where to spend resources improving these requirements.

Basic needs

Basic needs are characteristics of the product that must be present. In most cases, the customer does not even ask for them; they assume they are present. Basic needs do not lead to satisfaction. As an example, when buying a new house, a customer would expect to find at least one bathroom and one toilet. Basic characteristics form the price of entry into a market and must be present.

Customers may not even notice when basic needs are present, but when absent they complain. Customers usually complain first about basic needs. Customers do not ask for the basic needs; they assume they will be present without having to ask for them. When these needs are present, they often go completely unnoticed. For example, when a bus service operates on schedule, the customer learns to accept that, but when it operates erratically, or not at all, the customer complains.

In Figure 7.1, the basic needs, or must-have features, appear in the bottom right-hand corner, with function and performance attributes varying, and customer satisfaction measures remaining neutral and even extending to dissatisfaction at the bottom end of the satisfaction index.

Performance wants

Customer satisfaction is proportional to performance for some products. Increased performance of the product or service provides increased satisfaction. Conversely, decreased performance provides decreased satisfaction. Performance wants are very

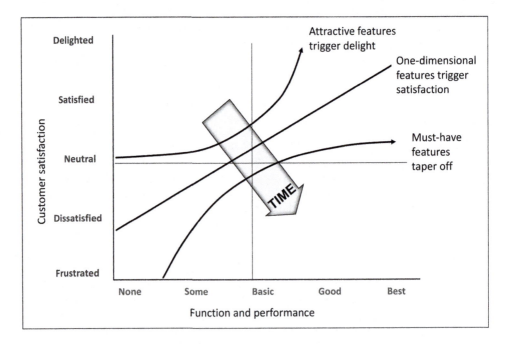

Figure 7.1 Kano model diagram, adapted from Walden, D. (1993, fall). Kano's method for understanding customer-defined quality. *Center for Quality of Management Journal*, 2(4), 4.

visible and appear at the top of the list when evaluating options. Customers want more satisfaction from these performance wants, which are one-dimensional attributes. Price, for example, is often a one-dimensional attribute.

Customers want these attributes, and these may well swing the deal. A customer may walk into a store with a checklist of requirements and tick each requirement off the list. If the customer can tick all the requirement boxes, the customer is happy; if the customer cannot tick all the requirement boxes, the customer may become dissatisfied.

A customer buying a new house may want a second bathroom and toilet, and an en suite bathroom. If these are present, the customer is satisfied. Performance wants arise when basic needs have previously been missing and customers have expectations derived from magazines, friends, or salespeople.

Figure 7.1 shows a Kano diagram with the customer satisfaction index on the vertical axis and function and performance attributes on the horizontal axis. The diagonal line is the one-dimensional line.

Excitement

Customers are prepared to pay a premium to get features offering excitement. They do not expect these features, and are delighted and excited when they are available. Customers may have difficulty explaining exactly what they really want, and the designer may have difficulty translating customer needs into design requirements. These needs are difficult to establish up front.

When buying the new house, the customer may be delighted with a home-security system that senses the homeowners and allows them access without having to press buttons. Alternatively, when buying a new car, the customer may prefer the brand with an automatic 'drive home safely' capability.

The essence of excitement is surprise, and the essence of surprise is the unexpected.

Customer expectations change and a feature that evokes excitement one day may turn into a performance want the next day, and maybe even a basic need the following week. Thus, there is a general trend for the attributes to start in the top left-hand corner and drift diagonally to the bottom right-hand quadrant, as indicated by the large arrow in Figure 7.1.

Questionnaire

The Kano model assumes it is feasible to establish customer requirements using a questionnaire that recognises that it is not what the customer is saying that is important, but what they are thinking. If the customer is indifferent, it simply says that the customer does not care whether that feature is present or not; they are completely neutral. On the other hand, reverse requirements cause dissatisfaction when present and satisfaction when absent. These are very rare, but do happen occasionally.

The questionnaire asks questions as a positive and a negative. The questions ask, 'What is your reaction if this feature is present?' and, 'What is your reaction if this feature is not present?'

Possible answers are, 'I like it that way', 'It must be that way', 'I am neutral', 'I can live with it that way', and 'I dislike it that way'.[7]

The questioner tabulates the answers to arrive at a ranked list of customer requirements.

Quality function deployment

Quality function deployment

Quality function deployment is a methodology to assure customer satisfaction and value with new and existing products by designing in, from different levels, and from different perspectives, the requirements that are most important to the customer.

Quality function deployment is a methodology to prioritise spoken and unspoken customer excitement, performance wants, and basic needs, then translate these needs into actions and designs such as technical characteristics and specifications, and build and deliver quality products and services by focusing business functions on a common goal of achieving customer satisfaction.[8] The literal definition says that the methodology deploys 'quality function' to all business functions that are charged with assuring quality and customer satisfaction. It assesses the true quality obtained from the customer, the quality characteristics of the product, and the process characteristics. Quality function deployment picks up the spoken and unspoken customer requirements and maximises positive excitement, such as ease of use, fun, and luxurious feel. This creates value in the customers' eyes.

Traditional design aims at minimising negative aspects, such as defects and poor service. The aim of traditional design in this sense is to obtain zero defects. What is the point of difference when all organisations have zero defects?

Quality function deployment is a quality system that implements elements of systems thinking and psychology. The systems view looks at the whole system, and the psychology part looks at the customer needs, how they evaluate value, and what makes a customer choose one product or service over another.

Performance wants and excitement characteristics provide opportunities for organisations to gain competitive advantage. Knowledge about market segments and changing customer requirements helps to hit the customer targets. Quality function deployment is knowledge-based and allows invisible customer requirements to become visible. The process aims to quantify the customer needs, the importance of the needs, and the magnitude of the expected benefits. The analysis concentrates on the needs, not the features. The analytic hierarchy process is a commonly used tool that uses a pairwise comparison on a nine-level scale. This method yields ratio-scaled priorities that are more accurate than ordinal-scale buckets that were popular in early implementations of quality function deployment.

The perspective at the beginning of this chapter provided a long list of desirable features for a new transportation device. Quality function deployment prioritises the potential benefit to the customer from having the customer problems solved, their opportunity enabled, or their image enhanced. It states the potential benefit to the customer positively, describes a single issue, and is independent of the product or the features. The collective voice of the customer may identify the need for a vehicle that is safe. The quality function deployment process may translate this into required technical features such as forward-collision warning to alert the driver to a potential crash, automatic emergency braking to sense a potential collision, reversing cameras to provide visibility of objects at the rear of the vehicle, and blind-spot monitoring to recognise the presence of another car in the blind spot. Now the design team can concentrate their activities on the requirements that maximises customer satisfaction.

The International Organization for Standardization (ISO) publishes ISO 16355 to demonstrate the dynamic nature of a customer-driven approach to product design. This standard provides guidelines for the implementation of quality function deployment.[9]

House of quality

House of quality

House of quality is a structured process that relates customer-demanded quality attributes to the technical features needed to support and generate these attributes. This technique forces designers to consider customer needs and the degree to which the proposed designs satisfy those needs.

The house of quality is an assembly of other deployment hierarchies and tables; these include the demanded quality hierarchy (rows), the quality characteristics hierarchy (columns), the causal relationships matrix, the quality planning table (right-side room), and the design planning table (bottom room). Figure 7.2 illustrates the house of quality.

Demanded quality hierarchy (rows)

The demanded quality hierarchy is the left-side room and arranges customer requirements coming from customer statements in rows. These state in customer terminology

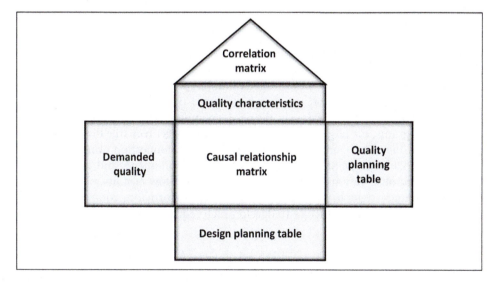

Figure 7.2 House of quality

exactly what the customer wants. For finished products, this analysis could derive from a Kano analysis.

As an example, the customer requirements for a cell phone might be:

- Light, collapsible, ergonomically designed yet strong enough to withstand dropping.
- Long-lasting battery for a quick recharge.
- Display with high contrast and a large colour gamut.
- Video camera suitable for business use.
- Call management features (call waiting, call forwarding, conference calling).
- Web-enabled with high-speed connection – 4G and 5G capability.
- Differentiating features such as a clock at the top cover of the phone which glows, or a flat membrane keypad giving a feel of etched metal.

Quality characteristics hierarchy (columns)

The quality characteristics hierarchy arranges the technical response to the demanded quality in columns. If the demanded quality is the voice of the customer, then quality characteristics are the voice of the engineer.

Relationships matrix

The relationships matrix relates the demanded quality hierarchy with the quality characteristics hierarchy. Design engineers have choices of materials, technologies, composition, and specifications at their disposal. This matrix quantifies the technical solution to the customer requirements.

Quality planning table

The quality planning table, or competitive assessment, is in the right-side room. This provides a qualitative benchmark comparison with other products, other solutions, and other methods.

Design planning table

The design planning table, or set of target values, appears in the bottom room. This provides the target values that the design team are trying to reach. Using the cell phone example mentioned previously, the design planning table might provide the target weight in grams, the target battery life in days, the target recharge time in minutes, the quality of the video camera, and the target internet connection in megabytes per second. It provides relevant, measurable, technical requirements and product characteristics, and observations from market surveys that show customers' perceptions. Design planning assigns benchmarks and measures performance compared to competitive products and the difficulty to develop each requirement.

Correlation

The correlation of technical requirements to support or impede product design appears in the roof.

Total quality management

What is quality?

Quality

Quality is exceeding or surpassing in excellence.

Quality is fitness for intended use as defined by the customer.

Quality is the customer perception of value.

Quality is the degree of customer satisfaction with the product's characteristics and features.

Total quality management

Total quality management is a management approach to long-term success through customer satisfaction.

Quality is exceeding, or surpassing, in excellence

Quality is exceeding, or surpassing, excellence. This is a very high-level view of quality. Taking this high-level view, quality is an ideal; it is transcendent. Excellence is being exceptionally good, having extreme merit, and superiority. That is excellence. Now quality is exceeding in excellence; exceeding this lofty standard.

Quality is fitness for intended use, as defined by the customer

Quality is fitness for intended use, or fitness for purpose, as defined by the customer with a need for a product or service; the customer may state or imply this need. A customer walks into a store hoping to satisfy a need and surveys a variety of excellent products. However, are they all suitable for the purpose the customer intends? As an example, consider purchasing a high-performance sports car with carbon fibre chassis, low-profile magnesium alloy wheels, ceramic disc brakes, and capable of accelerating to 100 kilometres per hour in three seconds. That is a perfectly fine choice, and there is a significant market for this type of vehicle. However, in this case the customer wants a vehicle to go off the main road and into the mountains for some recreational hunting and fishing. Clearly, the particular use the customer has in mind renders the high-performance sports car unsuitable.

Quality is the customer perception of value

Value is a measure of the benefits derived from a product or service compared to the price paid in return. A product may have both physical and functional requirements when assessed by the customer. However, the asking price exceeds expectation, or may seem overpriced, when compared to similar products on the market. The same product or service may be available from another supplier at a sale price indicating exceedingly good value for the money. Quality is not a price; it involves basic human reactions and psychology.

Quality is the degree of customer satisfaction with the product's characteristics and features

With this definition, quality is design. Customer expectations are constantly changing and are often extremely difficult to define. The ideal expectation is the best possible, and sometimes this may not be achievable given the price or the industry standard. A desirable expectation is the standard the customer wants to receive, while a deserved expectation is the level of performance the customer ought to receive given the perceived costs. As an example, a tourist staying in a backpackers' hostel should not expect the service and standards of a luxury hotel. The minimum tolerable expectation is the minimum standard the customer should receive. At the bottom of the list of expectations is the intolerable, which is a standard the customer should not receive.[10]

David A. Garvin proposed the dimensions of quality to help understand customer expectations. Additionally, they provide a language for describing quality:[11]

- Aesthetics includes sensory characteristics, such as sound, feel, look, smell, and taste.
- Conformance measures how well the product meets the documented design specifications.
- Durability determines the useful life of the product and defines how long it will last.
- Features are the little extras that come with the product, and often these are the exciters, such as whether a new car has a global positioning system installed.
- Perception is confidence based on past performance and intangibles such as brand name.
- Performance is the primary operating characteristics of the product, such as the colour and clarity of a television set.
- Reliability is the consistency of performance over time, such as its need for repair or corrective action.
- Serviceability defines the speed, courtesy, and competence of repairs, and the difficulty or cost of repair.

The product dimensions of Garvin do not apply directly to services, although some people have attempted to draw an analogy. Valarie A. Zeithaml, A. Parasuraman, and Leonard L. Berry published numerous qualitative studies on the dimensions of quality, and their list of dimensions has evolved into five dimensions for service:[12]

- Assurance is the knowledge and courtesy of employees and their ability to convey trust and confidence.
- Empathy is the degree of caring and individualised attention the business provides its customers, such as the scheduling of deliveries to fit in with customer requirements rather than keeping to a schedule and avoiding the use of technical jargon when explaining problems and solutions. This use of technical language is evident in the information and communications technology industry and in domestic solar power specifications and requirements.
- Reliability reflects the ability to perform the promised service dependably and accurately. It determines whether the service follows the exact specifications of

the client, whether the service performs right the first time, whether the service meets promised delivery dates, whether the level of service is always the same, and whether all members of staff deliver the same performance.

- Responsiveness is a willingness to help customers and provide prompt service. This dimension measures how willing service people are to answer customer questions, and whether the organisation responds quickly when needed.
- Tangibles describe the appearance of physical facilities, equipment, appearance of staff and communication materials. This measures whether the facilities are attractive, whether staff dress appropriately, whether written materials are easy to understand, and whether technology looks modern.

Quality is not perfection; it is not a standard; it is not a procedure; it is not a measure; and it is not even an adjective. Quality is everywhere. Quality evaluates how specific needs are satisfied.

Total quality management (TQM) is managing the entire organisation so it excels in all dimensions of products and services that are important to the customer. The key notions are that quality extends throughout the organisation in everything it does, and that the customer ultimately defines quality. Translating the customer quality demands into specifications requires marketing (or product development) to assess what the customer wants accurately, and then it requires product designers to develop a product (or service) that has the capability for consistent production and quality.

In today's competitive marketplace, the production and delivery of high-quality goods and services is a key element of any organisation's success. Quality can be a competitive or strategic weapon for an organisation. Many will argue that, if you are competing solely on quality, you have missed the boat. They say quality is a 'given'. This is a rather narrow view because if we examine the definition of quality, it is apparent we are striving to improve the product or service in the hands of the customer. Customer needs are changing, so our delivery of quality must also change.

Total quality management is a management philosophy based on the participation of everyone in the organisation with an aim of long-term success. Organisations achieve this through customer satisfaction and by providing benefits to all members of the organisation and to society. Thus, total quality management manages an organisation in a way that enables it to meet stakeholder needs and expectations efficiently and effectively, without compromising ethical values. Total quality management is a way of thinking about goals, organisations, processes, and people to ensure that the organisation does the right things right, first time, and every time. This thought process changes attitudes and behaviours and achieves better results.

Service definition of quality

Quantitative measures may not be appropriate for observing quality in a service environment. For example, how do you define and measure friendliness, courtesy, ambience, excitement, physical and mental well-being, health, and memories?

The travel industry provides transport and accommodation services for customers, and the actual services provided and the connections made are quantifiable. However, what about the experience? How do you value a week of relaxation on a tropical beach, or a tour through the vineyards of France, or the sense of accomplishment after ascending a high mountain in the Himalayas, or attending a Broadway concert, or sailing around the Caribbean, or listening to a very eloquent tour guide? What value does the customer place on the experience and the memories?

Health services provide a quantifiable service that diagnoses illnesses, prescribes medicines and drugs, performs surgical operations, assists with the delivery of babies, and provides long-term care for the terminally ill. Now the physical and mental well-being of the whole community comes to the fore. How do you measure wellness or just feeling good?

Therefore, service takes on a different meaning when attempting to describe quality. Service delivery is difficult to repeat reliably, especially as it usually involves the interaction and participation of the customer.

Horst Schulze, in an interview with Robert Green shortly after his company, The Ritz-Carlton Hotel Company, received the Baldridge Award for the second time, described his understanding of quality:

> Basic quality is understanding not just what the customer wants, but truly understanding the customer and then creating processes, with the involvement of the employees connected with each process, to deliver that and finally, quality means continuing to see how well you're doing and how to do it better and then doing that, eventually bringing the processes to zero defects.[13]

The Ritz-Carlton is a hotel company. Not really – they are in the experience business, for when a guest stays at a Ritz-Carlton it is not the softness of the bed, or the size of the room, they normally remember; they remember the exquisite service they encounter at every turn.

The Ritz-Carlton is a premium hotel chain (although that does not fully describe them) with 91 hotels worldwide and a staff contingent of over 40,000 'ladies and gentlemen'.[14] Their motto – 'We are Ladies and Gentlemen serving Ladies and Gentlemen' – exemplifies the anticipatory service provided by all staff members. The Ritz-Carlton philosophy says that an organisation should not be concerned just with its function, but driven by its philosophical beliefs as well. 'Ladies and Gentlemen' has two values; it shows that Ritz-Carlton values the employees and sets a level of expectation for them. Their jobs may be different, but they are equal. They are in service, but they are not servants.

At the Ritz-Carlton, people are their number one asset, but, unlike other companies that claim the same, they mean it. They pride themselves on a process for selecting warm and caring people. In fact, it would seem they have hit a nerve in modern society. Ritz-Carlton is a place where everyone is pleasant, helpful, and willing to go the extra step for the smallest thing to ensure the guest stay is the best it possibly could be. If only every service experience were the same.

The aim of Ritz-Carlton Hotels is to satisfy every customer. To do so, they have sought not only to understand the needs and wants of each customer, but also to deliver them. With that in mind, they have designed their processes with the involvement of the employees. The Ritz-Carlton runs a database profiling its customers, which is available to any branch, allowing them to know what the specific customer tends to like, whether it is more fruit, or a softer pillow, or extra blankets. This allows the Ritz to 'wow' its customers with apparent foresight.

Quality at Ritz-Carlton is of paramount importance and would not be possible were it not for the continuous improvement, structure, and underlying philosophy of the company. Their target goals are a blending of three components embodied in the Gold Standard of the Ritz, and they are summarised in their credo:

- The Ritz-Carlton Hotel is a place where the genuine care and comfort of our guests is our highest mission.
- We pledge to provide the finest personal service and facilities for our guests who will always enjoy a warm, relaxed, yet refined ambience.
- The Ritz-Carlton experience enlivens the senses, instils well-being, and fulfils even the unexpressed wishes and needs of our guests.

Their three steps of service follow:

- Provide a warm and sincere greeting. Use the guest's name.
- Anticipate and fulfil each guest's needs.
- End with a fond farewell. Give a warm good-bye and use the guest's name.

Their service values, 'I am proud to be Ritz-Carlton', follow:

- I build strong relationships and create Ritz-Carlton guests for life.
- I am always responsive to the expressed and unexpressed wishes and needs of our guests.
- I am empowered to create unique, memorable, and personal experiences for our guests.
- I understand my role in achieving the Key Success Factors, embracing Community Footprints, and creating The Ritz-Carlton Mystique.
- I continuously seek opportunities to innovate and improve The Ritz-Carlton experience.
- I own and immediately resolve guest problems.
- I create a work environment of teamwork and lateral service so that the needs of our guests and each other are met.
- I can continuously learn and grow.
- I am involved in the planning of the work that affects me.
- I am proud of my professional appearance, language, and behaviour.
- I protect the privacy and security of our guests, my fellow employees and the company's confidential information and assets.
- I am responsible for uncompromising levels of cleanliness and creating a safe and accident-free environment.

However, the philosophy is itself backed up by a bulletproof process of quality improvement. In fact, the Ritz has determined that there are over 1000 possible problems encountered by an overnight guest. They have documented each possible defect, devised a solution, and trained each team member on the defects they may encounter within their role.

To ensure that patrons enjoy the best possible experience, management sanction each staff member to spend up to $2000 to fix any problem encountered by a guest.

This includes the cleaning personnel, who consider themselves to be just like a professional service business of one. The solution does not have to be to fix a complaint; it could be to make the guest experience just that little bit more memorable.

So, when the Ritz-Carlton says their greatest asset is their 'Ladies and Gentlemen', they back it up with the trust and authority bestowed on them, empowering their staff to be the champions of quality within the company and adding to the mystique and emotional engagement which is the Ritz-Carlton.[15]

Traditional costs of quality

Costs of quality

Costs of quality are the overall costs associated with prevention activities, improvement activities, and recovering from cases in which the product fails to satisfy the customer completely. There are four categories of costs – external failure (incurred after the customer receives the product or service), internal failure (incurred before the customer receives the product or service), appraisal (incurred to determine the degree of conformance to quality requirements), and prevention (incurred in preventing errors).

External failure costs

External failure costs relate to problems found after the product reaches the customer, such as warranty expenses, product recalls, product returns, loss of orders, and loss of customers.

Internal failure costs

Internal failure costs relate to problems with the product before it reaches the customer, such as waste, scrap, rework, product downgrade, and process yield loss.

Appraisal costs

Appraisal costs are associated with the formal evaluation and audit of quality within the organisation, such as inspection, quality audits, equipment calibration, and measuring systems.

Prevention costs

Prevention costs are the investments made in improvement activities aimed at reducing internal and external failure, such as education, training, and supplier certification.

The basic assumptions when considering the traditional costs of quality are that failures do happen, prevention is cheaper than allowing the failure to incur in the first place, and performance is measurable. The purpose of introducing the notion of these costs was to highlight to management that there is significant cost incurred when the quality is not what the customer expects. Some of these costs are hard to quantify and some (such as losing customers) can be detrimental to the very existence of the organisation.

Figure 7.3 shows the total costs of quality made up from the costs of not meeting customer specification and the costs of compliance. External failure and internal failure costs represent the costs of not meeting customer expectations, while appraisal and prevention costs encompass the costs of compliance, or the costs of achieving standards. The little arrows shown in the diagram indicate the direction of initial investment. Organisations should not invest extra money in external failure, internal failure, or appraisal. Instead, they should invest in prevention.

External failure costs are the costs of defects that pass through the system and occur after the product or service has left the production system. They are the costs incurred to correct nonconforming work after delivery to the customer or to correct work that did not satisfy a customer's specified need. Examples include customer warranty replacements, product recalls, replacements, allowances, handling complaints, product repairs, returns, liability and legal judgements, payment of interest penalties, negative word-of-mouth, loss of customer or goodwill, and loss of future business.

Internal failure costs are those incurred within the system before the customer sees it or uses it. They are costs incurred to correct work before delivery to the customer. Examples include scrap, rework, retest, yield losses, machine downtime, and disposing of defective material.

Appraisal costs are the costs of inspection, testing, and other tasks to ensure the product or process is acceptable. They are the costs incurred to ascertain the condition of a product or service to determine whether it conforms to quality standards. Examples include inspection of incoming goods, inspection and testing of work-in-process, testing of new products before installation, maintaining accuracy of test equipment, process control procedures, checking process data, balancing process outputs, verifying process data, and the materials and services consumed during testing. Some would argue that these costs are necessary for production processes to operate properly.

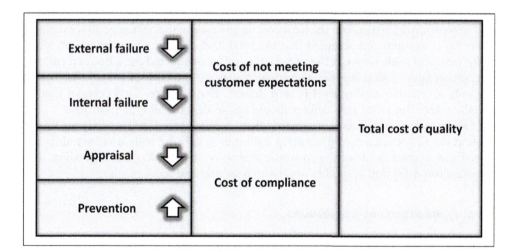

Figure 7.3 Total cost of quality made up of external failure, internal failure, appraisal, and prevention

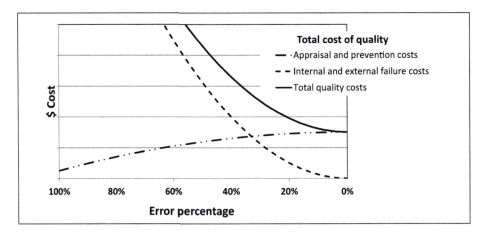

Figure 7.4 Total costs of quality should approach zero as an ideal

However, the firm should reduce spending on appraisal costs as this indirectly affects the customer. Preference should be on prevention.

Prevention costs are the costs of preventing defects, identifying the causes of defects, implementing corrective action to eliminate the cause, training personnel, redesigning the product or system, redesigning the process, and for the purchase of new equipment or modifications. They are the costs associated with operations or activities that keep failure from happening and minimise detection costs. Examples include product design and review, process design and review, recruitment, selection and education of staff, job design and job training, quality improvement projects, quality planning, and working with suppliers.

Figure 7.4 shows the internal and external failure costs decreasing to zero when there are zero errors remaining. While these costs are falling, the costs of appraisal and prevention are rising, and the total cost of quality equals the sum of all these costs. Years ago, organisations accepted that the total cost of quality was minimised when there were still some errors in the system. Organisations would use a five percent or a ten percent figure and accept this as normal. It was the acceptable quality level. Today, the only acceptable quality level is zero defects. Furthermore, total costs of quality equalling zero dollars at zero defects should be an ideal for all organisations.

Concentrating on defects is a negative view. A much better and positive view is to look at the opportunities of generating customer delight by truly understanding the stated and implied needs of the customer and delivering on that understanding. The Ritz-Carlton definition of quality applies to products and services alike.

Quality management frameworks

Excellence Model 2013 (EFQM)

EFQM, located in Brussels,[16] is the creator of the European Quality Awards, which recognise the very top companies each year and is the owner of the EFQM Excellence

Model 2013, which allows people to understand the cause-and-effect relationships between what the organisation does and the results that are achieved.

EFQM has developed its fundamental concepts of excellence. When organisations understand these principles and are comfortable with them, they can progress as a business. There is no significance intended in the order of the concepts. The foundation updated the fundamental concepts of excellence in 2013 and the concepts are as follows:[17]

- Adding value to customers. Excellent organisations consistently add value for customers by understanding, anticipating, and fulfilling needs, expectations, and opportunities.
- Creating a sustainable future. Excellent organisations have a positive impact on the world around them by enhancing their performance whilst simultaneously advancing the economic, environmental, and social conditions within the communities they touch.
- Developing organisational capability. Excellent organisations enhance their capabilities by effectively managing change within and beyond the organisational boundaries.
- Harnessing creativity and innovation. Excellent organisations generate increased value and levels of performance through continual improvement and systematic innovation by harnessing the creativity of their stakeholders.
- Leading with vision, inspiration, and integrity. Excellent organisations have leaders who shape the future and make it happen, acting as role models for its values and ethics.
- Managing with agility. People recognise excellent organisations for their ability to identify and respond effectively and efficiently to opportunities and threats.
- Succeeding through the talent of people. Excellent organisations value their people and create a culture of empowerment for the achievement of both organisational and personal goals.
- Sustaining outstanding results. Excellent organisations achieve sustained outstanding results that meet both the short- and long-term needs of all their stakeholders, within the context of their operating environment.

EFQM will publish an updated version of its fundamental concepts of excellence in 2020.

ISO 9000 – quality management

The International Organization for Standardization (ISO) publishes the ISO 9000 series based on seven quality management principles, which senior management can use as a framework to guide their organisations towards improved performance. The principles derive from the collective experience and knowledge of the international experts who participate in ISO Technical Committee ISO/TC 176, *Quality management and quality assurance*, which is responsible for developing and maintaining the ISO 9000 standards.[18]

- **Customer focus.** Organisations depend on their customers and therefore should understand current and future customer needs, should meet customer requirements, and strive to exceed customer expectations.
- **Leadership.** Leaders establish unity of purpose and direction of the organisation. They should create and maintain the internal environment in which people can become fully involved in achieving the organisation's objectives.

- **Engagement of people.** People at all levels of an organisation are essential to create and deliver value.
- **Process approach.** Organisations achieve desired results more effectively and efficiently when they manage activities and related resources as a coherent system.
- **Continual improvement.** Successful organisations have an ongoing focus on improvement.
- **Evidence-based decision making.** Base effective decisions on analysis of data and information.
- **Relationship management.** An organisation manages its relationships with interested parties such as suppliers.

Process capability and six sigma quality

Process cause and variation

Assignable cause

Assignable cause is a source of variation in a process that can be isolated, such as environmental conditions and changes in input parameters. The variation arises from external sources not inherent in the process. The variation appears sporadically and disrupts the random pattern of common causes. When assignable causes are isolated, the organisation can potentially remove them to allow the process to continue with just common or normal variation.

Assignable variation

Assignable variation is the result of one or more causes that the organisation can identify and remove.

Common cause

Common cause is a cause of variation that is inherent in the process over time. The cause is random and is the opposite of assignable cause.

Common cause variation

Common cause variation is the variability in product quality resulting from numerous uncontrollable everyday factors such as temperature and humidity.

All processes have variation. Variation occurs in input and output variables. Process transformation can have controlled and uncontrolled variables. Temperature and humidity, for example, are controlled variables when the process performs inside a building, and they are uncontrolled variables when performed outside in the open.

The customer may be satisfied when variation occurs within a satisfactory range of values – the tolerance range. As an example, consider a loaf of bread. It bakes in an oven for a fixed time at a temperature fluctuating inside a narrow range (the tolerance range of temperature variation). If the temperature is too low (below the acceptable lower limit), the customer shows dissatisfaction since the loaf may be undercooked. If the temperature is too high (above the acceptable upper limit), the customer shows dissatisfaction since the loaf may be overcooked and burnt. Using the same example, but this time considering just the time in the oven – the bread has a fixed baking time but will vary a little, either shorter or longer, for each batch of bread. If the time in the oven is too short (below the acceptable lower limit), the customer shows dissatisfaction since the loaf may be undercooked. If the time in the oven is too long (above the acceptable upper limit), the customer shows dissatisfaction since the loaf may be overcooked or burnt.

Figure 7.5 shows process variation. The horizontal line measures the variable, which can be any attribute with a continuous scale, such as temperature, time, weight, length, pressure, or condition. The target value in the middle is the ideal value for the process. The tolerable range of variables indicates a range from the lowest tolerable value to the highest tolerable value of the variable. The customer is satisfied if the variable falls somewhere inside this range. Beyond this range, the values of the variable cause customer dissatisfaction.

Figure 7.6 shows the standard Normal distribution. Basic statistics describe a normally distributed population as follows:

- 68.26% of the distribution lies within plus and minus one standard deviation of the mean – written as $\pm1\sigma$
- 95.44% of the distribution lies within plus and minus two standard deviations of the mean – written as $\pm2\sigma$
- 99.73% of the distribution lies within plus and minus three standard deviations of the mean – written as $\pm3\sigma$
- 99.9936% of the distribution lies within plus and minus four standard deviations of the mean – written as $\pm4\sigma$
- 99.999943% of the distribution lies within plus and minus five standard deviations of the mean – written as $\pm5\sigma$
- 99.9999998% of the distribution lies within plus and minus six standard deviations of the mean – written as $\pm6\sigma$
- 99.9999999997% of the distribution lies within plus and minus seven standard deviations of the mean – written as $\pm7\sigma$
- 99.9999999999999% of the distribution lies within plus and minus eight standard deviations of the mean – written as $\pm8\sigma$
- μ is the process mean.

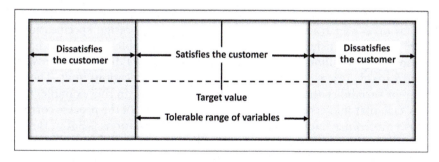

Figure 7.5 Process variation satisfies the customer when variation is within tolerance range

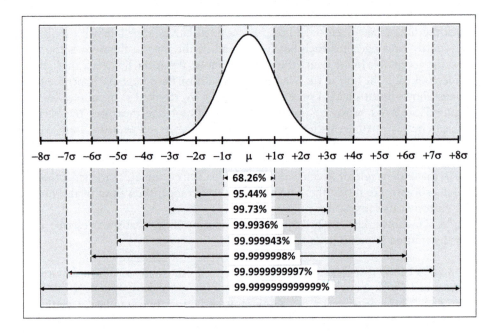

Figure 7.6 Standard Normal distribution

The starting point for measuring process capability requires 99.73% of the process variation to lie within the tolerance limits. This is the starting and minimum acceptable value.

Using the bread-baking example above, the standard Normal distribution could represent the variability of the oven temperature while the bread bakes and the probability that the oven maintains a specified temperature. The horizontal axis measures standard deviations of the process. The customer wants the upper tolerance (specification) limit to be greater than three standard deviations ($+3\sigma$ from the target value (further to the right)), and the lower tolerance (specification) to also have a value greater than three standard deviations (-3σ from the target value (but the direction is further to the left)).

Figure 7.7 shows a process operating with process specifications (-3σ from the process mean to $+3\sigma$ from the process mean) equal to design specifications. The customer shows dissatisfaction when the measured variable exceeds the upper tolerance (specification) limit. Similarly, the customer shows dissatisfaction when the measured variable is less than the lower tolerance (specification) limit. The process has inherent variability that is normally distributed, and (in this example) the variability is such that minus three standard deviations (-3σ) of the process corresponds to the lower tolerance limit, and plus three standard deviations ($+3\sigma$) of the process corresponds to the upper tolerance limit. The process specification from -3σ to $+3\sigma$ equals the design specification and provides a process range of six standard deviations.

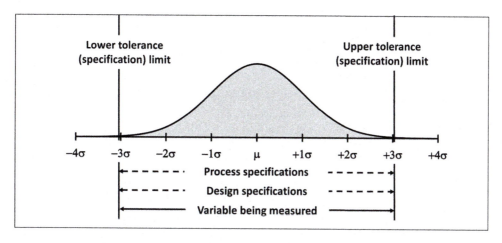

Figure 7.7 Process operating with process specifications equal to design specifications

Having demonstrated that only random causes of variation are present, the next task is to compare the precision of the process with the required specification tolerances by calculating the process capability ratio, C_p, and the process capability index, C_{pk}. C_p measures the spread (or variation) of the process, while C_{pk} measures the spread and positioning of the process. C_p measures the theoretical capability, while C_{pk} measures the actual capability. The next section discusses these terms.

Process capability measurements

Process capability

Process capability is the ability of a process to produce outputs that conform to customer-defined specifications. The base starting point for process capability is plus and minus three standard deviations ($\pm 3\sigma$) of the process. At this point, 99.73% of the process output is acceptable. A higher percentage is better; a lower percentage is not acceptable.

Process capability ratio, C_p

C_p is the process capability ratio and measures theoretical process capability. Calculate C_p by dividing the range from upper tolerance limit to lower tolerance limit by six times the standard deviation of the process.

Process capability index, C_{pk}

C_{pk} is the process capability index and measures actual process capability. Calculate C_{pk} by dividing the difference between the process mean and the nearest tolerance limit by three times the standard deviation of the process. Ideally, C_{pk} should equal C_p, and this occurs when the process mean is equidistant from the upper tolerance limit and the lower tolerance limit (i.e., centred).

Defect

Defect occurs when a product or a service does not meet intended requirements or reasonable expectation for use.

Defects per million opportunities

Defects per million opportunities (DPMO) is the quantity of defects per million opportunities. When a process operating at $\pm 6\sigma$ has drifted by 1.5σ the process has 3.4 defects per million opportunities (3.4 DPMO). That same process, when centred, has just two defects per billion opportunities.

Six sigma capability

Six sigma capability occurs when a process is operating inside the design specification with a range of at least 12 standard deviations, 12σ from -6σ to $+6\sigma$. Thus, the process is operating with process specifications equal to half of the design specifications. This is $\pm 6\sigma$ capability, or six sigma capability.

Measuring process variability and capability

Figure 7.8 shows a process operating with process specifications (-3σ from the process mean to $+3\sigma$ from the process mean) equal to half of the design specifications. Turning that around, the design specifications are twice the process specifications. The upper and lower tolerance limits are unchanged from the previous figure (Figure 7.7). The process has inherent variability that is normally distributed, and the variability is such that minus six standard deviations (-6σ) of the process corresponds to the lower tolerance limit and plus six standard deviations ($+6\sigma$) of the process corresponds to the upper tolerance limit.

Thus, the process is operating inside the design specification with a range of 12σ, from -6σ to $+6\sigma$. This is $\pm 6\sigma$ capability, or six-sigma capability.

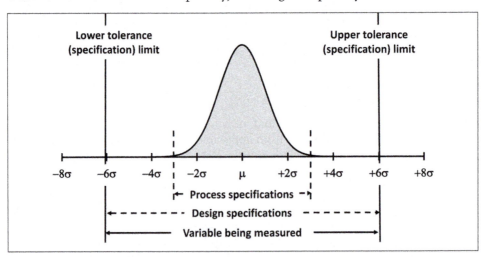

Figure 7.8 Process operating with process specifications equal to half the design specifications

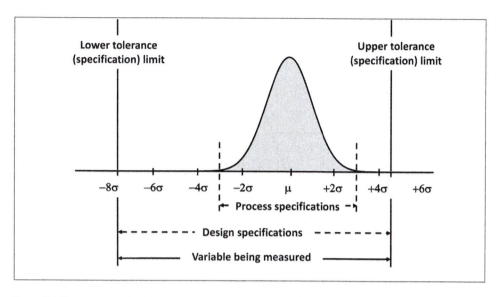

Figure 7.9 Process operating with a process drift of 1.5σ

Figure 7.9 shows a process drift of one and a half standard deviations (1.5σ) to the right. A process does not stay centred forever. Over time, it will drift. This may be because of wear and tear, or it may be because of special variation outside the control of the process itself. New brake pads installed in a car work well when new, but gradually deteriorate over several months of regular use. It does not happen suddenly, but gradually. In this figure, the process mean is at +1.5σ. At this point, the probability of process output falling outside the tolerance limit is 3.4 parts per million opportunities.

Process capability ratio, Cp

The process capability ratio, C_p, measures theoretical process capability. The formula for the process capability ratio is:

$$C_p = \frac{\text{Upper tolerance limit} - \text{Lower tolerance limit}}{6\sigma} \qquad (7.1)$$

Figure 7.10 is a schematic of the process capability ratio, C_p. The numerator of the equation uses the range from the lower to the upper tolerance limits while the denominator is six standard deviations (6σ). Process capability is relative to plus and minus three standard deviations (±3σ), so when the numerator is greater than six standard deviations (6σ) of the process, then the process capability ratio, C_p, is greater than 1.00. A value less than 1.00 indicates that less than 99.73% of the process output is within customer-defined tolerance. A value of 1.33 (sometimes referred to as an 'average value') indicates that 99.9936% of the process output is acceptable. This value (1.33) indicates that the process has a theoretical capability of four-sigma. The target for the process capability ratio, C_p, should be at least 2.0.

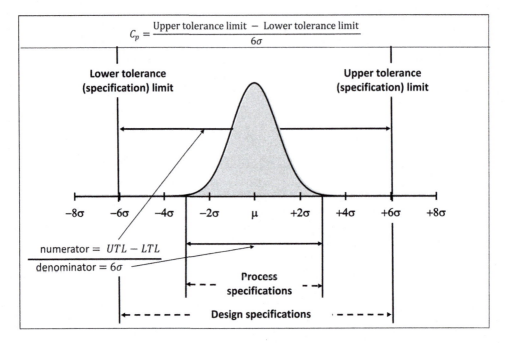

$$C_p = \frac{\text{Upper tolerance limit} - \text{Lower tolerance limit}}{6\sigma}$$

Figure 7.10 Process capability ratio, C_p, with the numerator equal to the range and the denominator equal to 6σ

Process capability index, C_{pk}

The process capability index, C_{pk}, measures theoretical process capability. The formula for the process capability index is:

$$C_{pk} = \min\left[\frac{\bar{\bar{x}} - LTL}{3\sigma}, \frac{UTL - \bar{\bar{x}}}{3\sigma}\right] \tag{7.2}$$

Figure 7.11 is a schematic of the process capability index, C_{pk}, derived by calculating two values and using the smaller of them. The first value is the distance from the upper tolerance limit to the process mean, divided by three times the standard deviation of the process. The second value is the distance from the lower tolerance limit to the process mean, divided by three times the standard deviation of the process. The process capability index, C_{pk}, is the smaller of these two values. Essentially, this is the distance from the process mean to the closest limit, divided by three times the process standard deviation.

Process capability is relative to plus and minus three standard deviations ($\pm 3\sigma$) so when the numerator is greater than three standard deviations of the process (3σ), the process capability index, C_{pk}, is greater than 1.00. A value less than 1.00 indicates less than 99.73% of the process output is within tolerance limits. The process capability

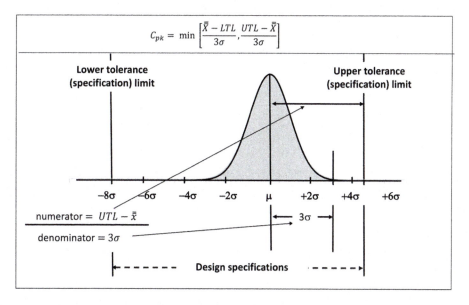

$$C_{pk} = \min\left[\frac{\bar{\bar{X}} - LTL}{3\sigma}, \frac{UTL - \bar{\bar{X}}}{3\sigma}\right]$$

Lower tolerance (specification) limit

Upper tolerance (specification) limit

-8σ -6σ -4σ -2σ μ $+2\sigma$ $+4\sigma$ $+6\sigma$

numerator $= UTL - \bar{x}$

3σ

denominator $= 3\sigma$

Design specifications

Figure 7.11 Process capability index, C_{pk}, with the numerator the distance from process mean to closest limit and the denominator 3σ

index, C_{pk}, should equal the process capability ratio, C_p, and this only occurs with a centred process.

The process variation may not fall within a range, and may need to be greater than a given value or less than a given value. For example, the delivery of a parcel should be less than three days. There is no lower limit – just an upper limit of three days.

Worked example 7.1

A drink processing plant is about to commission a new bottle filling line. The label on each bottle says that the volume is 1.25 litres. Customers show dissatisfaction if the fill volume falls below this level and the company monitors the process to minimise the number of bottles that are below this measurement. The maximum fill volume that is physically possible is 1.33 litres. Unacceptable spillage occurs when the machine attempts to over-fill the bottles. Analysts monitored the process during extensive testing and regular samples taken from the filling line gave a standard deviation based on a normal distribution of 0.01 litres. Calculate the process capability ratio, C_p.

Given: The maximum volume is 1.33 litres, the minimum volume is 1.25 litres, and the standard deviation is 0.01 litres. Using equation (7.1), the formula for the process capability ratio, C_p, is:

$$C_p = \frac{\text{Upper tolerance limit} - \text{Lower tolerance limit}}{6\sigma}$$

In this example, the upper tolerance limit is the maximum volume, and the lower tolerance limit is the minimum volume. Substituting values:

$$C_p = \frac{\text{maximum volume} - \text{minimum volume}}{6 \times \text{standard deviation}}$$

$$C_p = \left| \frac{1.33 - 1.25}{6 \times 0.01} \right|$$

$$C_p = 1.33$$

Therefore, the process capability ratio, C_p, is 1.33. Figure 7.12 illustrates the solution for worked example 7.1.

Worked example 7.2

Continuing from worked example 7.1: What is the required target volume setting to achieve four-sigma process capability?

Four-sigma process capability requires the distance between the lower tolerance limit and the process mean to be four standard deviations (four sigma). Therefore, we need the process mean to be the lower tolerance limit plus four standard deviations.

Process mean = 1.25 + (4 × 0.01) = 1.29 litres.

Thus, the process mean becomes the target volume setting of 1.29 litres being four standard deviations (four sigma) from the minimum value of 1.25 litres.

Therefore, the target volume setting to achieve four-sigma process capability is 1.29 litres.

Note: The target volume setting is also four standard deviations from the upper tolerance limit (maximum value).

Figure 7.13 illustrates the solution for worked example 7.2.

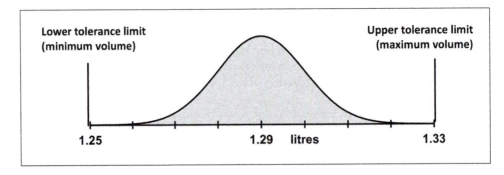

Figure 7.12 Illustration for worked example 7.1

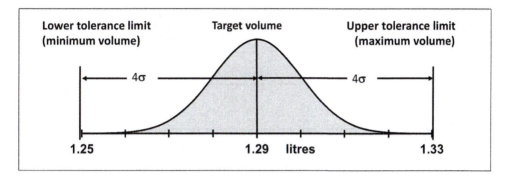

Figure 7.13 Illustration for worked example 7.2

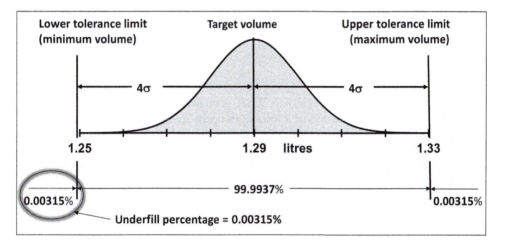

Figure 7.14 Illustration for worked example 7.3

Worked example 7.3

Continuing from worked example 7.2: What percentage of containers is under-filled (below 1.25 litres) with a four-sigma process centred at the target volume?

Referring to Figure 7.6, with a centred four-sigma process, 99.9937% of output lies within the tolerance limits (specification limits) and 0.0063% lies outside the tolerance limits. To be outside, the containers are either under-filled or over-filled.

Therefore, the under-filled is half of 0.0063%. (The other half is over-filled.)

Thus, the under-filled percentage is 0.0063% ÷ 2 = 0.00315%.

Therefore, the percentage of containers that is under-filled (below 1.25 litres) with a four-sigma process centred at the target volume is 0.00315%.

Figure 7.14 illustrates the solution for worked example 7.3.

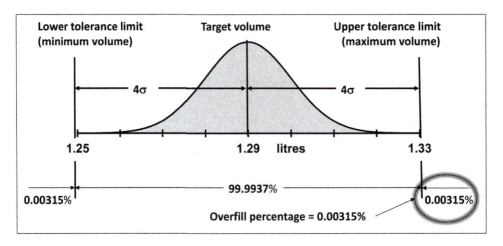

Figure 7.15 Illustration for worked example 7.4

Worked example 7.4

Continuing from worked example 7.3: What percentage of containers has unacceptable spillage (over 1.25 litres) with a four-sigma process centred at the target value?

As per the previous answer, the percentage of over-fill equals the percentage of under-fill (with a centred process). Therefore, the percentage of containers with unacceptable spillage (over 1.25 litres) with a four-sigma process centred at the target value is 0.00315%.

Figure 7.15 illustrates the solution for worked example 7.4.

Worked example 7.5

Continuing from worked example 7.4: Operators observed the process mean drifting to 1.275 litres. Calculate the process capability index, C_{pk}.

Using equation (7.2), the formula for process capability index, C_{pk}, is

$$C_{pk} = \min\left[\frac{\bar{\bar{x}} - LTL}{3\sigma}, \frac{UTL - \bar{\bar{x}}}{3\sigma}\right]$$

Interpreting and substituting in this equation gives:

$$C_{pk} = \min\left[\frac{\text{process mean} - \text{lower tolerance limit}}{3 \text{ standard deviations}}, \frac{\text{upper tolerance limit} - \text{process mean}}{3 \text{ standard deviations}}\right]$$

$$= \min\left[\frac{1.275 - 1.25}{3 \times 0.01}, \frac{1.33 - 1.275}{3 \times 0.01}\right]$$

$$= \min\left[\frac{0.025}{0.03}, \frac{0.055}{0.03}\right]$$

$$= \min[0.8333, 1.8333]$$

$$= 0.8333$$

Figure 7.16 illustrates the solution for worked example 7.5.

Worked example 7.6

Continuing from worked example 7.5: Calculate the required standard deviation (4 dp) of the filling process to achieve a six-sigma process capability.

In this example, the upper tolerance limit is the maximum volume, the lower tolerance limit is the minimum volume, and C_p equals 2.00. The process mean is equidistant from the upper and lower tolerance limits and the design limits (from -6σ to $+6\sigma$, lower tolerance limit to upper tolerance limit) are two times the process limits (from -3σ to $+3\sigma$). Thus, with the given formula for C_p, the missing value is standard deviation and this is what we want.

Using equation (7.1), the formula for the process capability ratio, C_p, is:

$$C_p = \frac{\text{Upper tolerance limit} - \text{Lower tolerance limit}}{6\sigma}$$

Substituting values:

$$C_p = \frac{\text{maximum volume} - \text{minimum volume}}{6 \times \text{standard deviation}}$$

$$C_p = \left[\frac{1.33 - 1.25}{6 \times \sigma}\right] = 2.00$$

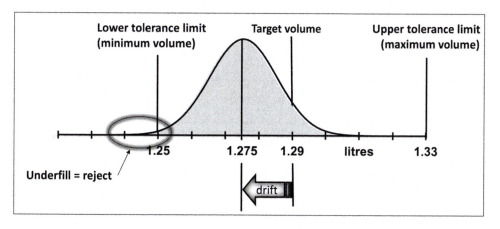

Figure 7.16 Illustration for worked example 7.5

Cross-multiplying:

$$12\sigma = 0.08$$
$$\sigma = 0.0067$$

Figure 7.17 illustrates the solution for worked example 7.6.

Therefore, the required standard deviation (4 dp) of the filling process to achieve a six-sigma process capability is 0.0067 litres. Putting this into perspective, when the process is centred and we have the standard deviation of the process equal to 0.0067 litres, the upper tolerance limit is six standard deviations ($+6\sigma$) above the process mean and the lower tolerance limit is six standard deviations (-6σ) below the process mean. Now, the process has a theoretical process capability of $\pm 6\sigma$ or has six-sigma process capability.

Six sigma quality

Six sigma quality

Six sigma quality is a business improvement approach that seeks to reduce process variation and product deficiencies in manufacturing and service processes by focusing on outputs critical to customers and with a clear financial return for the organisation. It is a business process allowing organisations to improve bottom-line performance, create and monitor business activities to reduce waste and resource requirements, and increase customer satisfaction.

Financial figures have provided the basis for business strategy for a long time. Companies base performance measurement almost entirely on financial figures in isolation. However, what is the point of having a financial profit target, or a revenue target, if that target is physically unattainable?

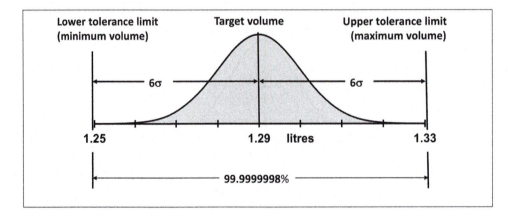

Figure 7.17 Illustration for worked example 7.6

Six sigma quality is a proven methodology for driving and achieving transformational change within an organisation. It is a business improvement process focusing on customer requirements, process alignment, analytical rigour, and timely execution.

In its original form it concentrated on manufacturing variables, both controlled and uncontrolled, such as temperature, pressure, flow rate, and time. It also improved the process output variables, such as yield, waste, capacity, downtime, and production rate. Organisations have extended it to include non-manufacturing variables, both controlled and uncontrolled, such as communication methods, completeness, accuracy, training, inventory levels, shipping methods, promise dates, days of the week, seasons of the year, and customer required date. It improves output variables, such as order correctness, delivery time, and package quality.

Six sigma quality aims to align executives to the right objectives and targets, to mobilise improvement teams, to accelerate results, and to govern sustained improvement. Motorola has practised this for over 40 years, and other large organisations have since unravelled the mysteries and applied the gains to their organisations. Implementation has been rather slow within smaller companies. However, the basic concepts are now more widespread within small to medium enterprises, despite the start-up costs and commitment required. In fact, service companies are now achieving some of the real benefits.

It has its foundations in statistics – well, that is where the name comes from. Motorola termed it plus and minus six sigma ($\pm$ six sigma) capability, and it measured the variation of each process. A qualifying process measures plus and minus six standard deviations ($\pm$ six sigma) of the process within the customer-defined process limits. Six sigma quality allows organisations to identify the customer requirements and to design, and subsequently modify, business processes to achieve nothing less than the minimum of customer requirements consistently. Keep the customer happy, supply them with exactly what they want, and when they want it, and they will come back for more.

A concentration on increased reliability by making processes more repeatable helps improve production, yield, and efficiency. Resources focus on the right products and the right projects.

Define-measure-analyse-improve-control

Define-measure-analyse-improve-control (DMAIC)

Define-measure-analyse-improve-control (DMAIC) are the five stages of process improvement. Determine the nature of the problem, measure existing performance, analyse the data to establish root cause, improve the process, and monitor the process until the solution becomes established.

Six sigma quality uses a define-measure-analyse-improve-control methodology to optimise the use of resources to reduce total supply chain costs. The focus is on establishing consistent processes, measurements, and an infrastructure for real-time visibility and exception management.

Define by studying customer requirements to determine what is acceptable and what is outside the tolerance range. Define the process improvement goals consistent with customer demands and overall strategy.

Measure and collect data on key internal processes identified as critical to quality. Make baseline measurements on the current process for future comparison. Map and measure the process and collect required process data.

Analyse and study the data, and determine reasons why mistakes occur. Determine the root causes of errors.

Improve and identify the problem statement, create the solution, and change the process to stay within tolerance.

Control and monitor the improvement process to stay within goals.

Lean six sigma

Lean six sigma

Lean six sigma is an approach that combines principles of lean thinking with six sigma quality initiatives to enhance operations performance.

Critical to quality

Critical to quality (CTQ) are characteristics of the product or service that the organisation must meet to satisfy the customer.

Design for six sigma (DFSS)

Design for six sigma (DFSS) is a product development process to ensure goods and services will meet customer needs and achieve performance objectives, and the processes used to make and deliver them achieve six sigma capabilities.

Lean six sigma analyses processes and eliminates the non-value-adding steps in the process. This translates to getting rid of all the waste in a process to produce a process that is as effective as possible. Every step in the process adds value to the product or service; simplify the process and improve quality further. Service organisations add more sensitivity and understanding towards customer needs.

Strategic product design

Design quality

Design quality is the inherent value of the product in the marketplace, and is thus a strategic decision for the business.

Design review

Design review is a process to help standardisation and reduce the costs associated with frequent design changes by evaluating proposed design to ensure the design is supported by adequate materials, will perform successfully when in use, can be manufactured at low cost, and is suitable for prompt field maintenance.

Product design is usually a significant part of the operations strategy. It establishes the detailed characteristics of each product and these directly affect the production

---

Strategic design

1960	Design to meet specifications
1970	Design so it is fit for use
1980	Design based on price
1990	Design for latent needs
2000	Design for the environment
2010	Design for individual needs
2020	Design for sustainability
2030	...

Figure 7.18 Strategic design drivers by decade

process, which determines the production system design. Additionally, product design directly affects product quality, production costs, and customer satisfaction.

Design is a strategic decision for any organisation. When an organisation launches a new product or service, it must live with that product for the entire product life cycle. For some products, this may be just a few weeks, whereas in others it may be many years. The approach that the organisation takes towards design determines the success or otherwise of the organisation. Looking back over the past several decades, the strategic design drivers have changed dramatically.

As shown in Figure 7.18 the design drivers in 1960 were to make sure products met specifications. In 1970, the main drivers were to make sure the product was fit for use. This is also about the time companies worldwide started to become aware of the need for quality in their products. By 1980, the emphasis was on price, as designers believed customers wanted cheaper products. By 1990, designers recognised that customers wanted to see potential without making it obvious. By 2000, the effects of irreparable damage to the environment allowed organisations to use organic ingredients and to obtain certification to show they were not polluting the rivers and the atmosphere (ISO 14000). By 2010, the stated and inferred needs of individuals became design criteria, and successful businesses were able to capitalise on the changing needs of changing markets using flexible production technologies. By 2020, customers still want their products but they are conscious of the need for long-term sustainability. What challenges lie ahead for the next 50 years?

Structured product development

The design concept initiates design activity. The first stage of a conventional design process starts with a recognition that a customer has a need for a product.

The second phase is a screening process and problem definition. This includes determining the physical and functional characteristics of the product and how it is going to work. The origins of a product idea should come from listening to the consumer needs and screening the alternatives to select the product.

Preliminary design or a synthesis of alternative designs follows. This is a very creative phase. Often this phase is crucial and is where the designer employs creativity. Preliminary or conceptual design, usually involves producing several design choices and the start of the product specification.

The design phase establishes 70% or more of the cost associated with product marketing and the way the product goes through the life cycle. The life-cycle issues can include design, process capability, production scheduling, purchasing of components from suppliers, assembly, inspection, use, repair, modernisation, and scrapping. Of these problems, perhaps the most difficult one is process capability, as discussed earlier in this chapter.

The design undergoes analysis, evaluation, and improvement. Analysis as part of the design phase includes compatibility (fitting together and proper articulation of parts during operation) and simplification (exclusion of features that raise production costs). Analysis also includes material selection, testing, structural design, and structural analysis. Techniques for structural design include finite element modelling (FEM) and finite element analysis (FEA). The need for prototypes has diminished with the development of additive manufacturing (3D printing), which allows designers to visualise products and test them on the computer.

The final stage is to implement the final design and launch the product.

Identifying the processes is much more than installing equipment. Sound management needs good information. High-quality management decisions require the aggregation of data from operations. Information integration is the core of business and management processes. It is the set of tools that structures data, as well as the process of turning concepts into products or services. Finally, information integration assists in the execution phase of the product or service.

Product development portfolios

Product development portfolio

The product development portfolio is the set of new product and service development projects for a business.

New product and service development requires a careful balance between uncertainty and risk. Craig Davis identifies uncertainty as a property of nature that resists quantification while risk is quantifiable and manageable. New product development discovers knowledge but the objectives are often unclear, measurements are ambiguous, and the process used to develop new products does not affect success or failure. The challenge with research is to overcome technology that may not work, while the challenge in development is to avoid products or services that may not be successful.

Product development portfolios traditionally divide into four categories:[19]

- New venture products and services are revolutionary and new to the world. Some recent electronic products fit into this category.

- New category products and services are new to the organisation and may be breakthrough products. They depart significantly from existing offerings and create one or more of the following: New markets, new customer experiences, new technologies, or new needs – but do not consist of taking a product or service into a new geographical location.
- New platform products and services serve as a launchpad, or a foundation, enabling the bundling of additional products or services. They may extend across a range of market segments and may be a new technology or process. Again, it does not consist of taking a product or service into a new geographical location.
- New variant products and services are incremental adjustments to an existing product or service and provide the customer with a perceptible difference. It is a derivative of an existing product and affects customer behaviour.

The marketing risk element is at its lowest with a new variant and increases for new platforms and new categories. It is at its greatest with new ventures. Davis developed a risk weighting to help assess market risk, technical risk, and user risk. Ideally there is a balance between high-risk and low-risk, short-term and long-term, genuinely new products and services versus improvements and extensions. A strategically aligned portfolio is one where all the projects are on strategy, and where the spending breakdown mirrors the strategic priorities of the business.

First, it is necessary to develop a product or service innovation and technology strategy defining the new product and service goals of the business, the arenas for strategic thrust, and the spending splits (priorities) across these arenas. Strategy begins when you start spending money. Next, build strategic criteria into your project selection so that all projects are consistent with strategy. Finally ensure that spending splits by arena and by project type mirror the desired splits and strategy.

Robust design

Quality loss function

Quality loss function is a parabolic approximation of the quality loss occurring when a quality characteristic deviates from the target value. The cost increase follows a quadratic function as the quality characteristic moves further from the target value. Genichi Taguchi introduced the quality loss function.

Taguchi methods

Product design uses Taguchi methods. They are a concept of considering system design, parameter design, and tolerance design as three phases of product design. The objective is to reduce quality loss by reducing the variability of the characteristics of the product.

Participative design

Participative design is a concept referring to the simultaneous participation of all functional areas of the business in product design activity. This includes suppliers and customers. The intent is to enhance the design with the input of all key stakeholders. It is synonymous with concurrent engineering and simultaneous engineering.

Participative design details the design while simultaneously developing the production capability, field-support capability, and quality. It consists of a methodology using multi-disciplined teams to carry this out concurrently. The tools used include algorithms, techniques, software, and the expertise and judgement of people who make up the complete design and production sequence. The essence is the integration of product design and process planning into one common activity. Participative design helps improve the quality of early design decisions and has a tremendous impact on the life-cycle cost of the product.

This design process achieves an optimum design using five interrelated elements:

- Careful analysis and understanding of the production and assembly processes.
- Strategic product design conceived to support a specific strategy for making and selling the product.
- Rationalised production system design coordinated into product design.
- Economic analysis of design and production alternatives to permit rational choices among design alternatives.
- Product and system designs characterised by robustness.

Design for operations

A set of guidelines called 'design for operations' outlines some basic ideas that should be incorporated into product and service design. Earlier versions of these guidelines were design for assembly, design for manufacturing, and design for manufacturing and assembly. These other terms have a strong manufacturing connotation, whereas the principles apply to services as well as production industries. The guidelines for the design for operations are:

- Link product and process designs to operational success factors.
- Design to target markets and target costs.
- Minimise the number of components and number of operations.
- Know customer requirements and design to those requirements.
- Ensure process capabilities are known (and this applies to supplier capabilities) and design to those capabilities.
- Use standard procedures, materials, and processes with already known and proven quality.
- Design multifunctional and multi-use components and service elements and modules.
- Design for ease of joining, separating, re-joining (goods), and ease of coupling and decoupling (services).
- Design for one-way assembly and one-way travel by avoiding backtracking and return visits.
- Avoid special fasteners and connectors (products) and off-line or misfit service elements.
- Avoid fragile designs requiring extraordinary effort, attentiveness, or processes that tempt substandard or unsafe performance.

Chapter summary

The Kano model and quality function deployment encourages a better understanding of customer requirements. These requirements translate into product specifications as part of a structured design process and eventually to the launch of a new product or service.

Quality is inherent in every product and process, but the measurement of quality relies on customers to determine. It is the customer view that prevails. The product design provides tolerances and specifications, but it requires a process to perform the transformation and produce the product or service. Process capability is a measure of the inherent variation of the process relative to the design specifications.

Total quality management and six sigma are quite different. Six sigma has executive ownership and is part of business strategy execution. It is truly cross-functional; it is not a quality initiative operating within one function. Six sigma uses focused training with verifiable return on investment. It is business results oriented and is not just statistics and quality oriented.

Discussion covered strategic product design, structured product development, product development portfolios, and robust design.

Discussion questions

1   How is the problem of technology choice related to process selection and product design?
2   How much detailed technical knowledge do managers require when selecting computer systems?
3   Suppose you need to select a computer to use in your office. What issues do you want resolved? What performance characteristics of the technology would you assess? How would you get the necessary information to make the decision?
4   What is the main obstacle to using a manufacturing approach to the delivery of services?
5   Explain how an organisation measures process capability.
6   Explain the difference between C_p and C_{pk}.
7   What is quality management?
8   Explain the difference between total quality management and six sigma quality.
9   Does quality management always lead to improvement?
10   What advantages would an organisation obtain by bringing a product to market early?

Key terms

appraisal costs, 228
assignable cause, 232
assignable variation, 232
common cause, 232
common cause variation, 232
costs of quality, 228
C_p. *See* process capability ratio
C_{pk}. *See* process capability index
critical to quality, 246

defect, 236
defects per million opportunities, 236
define-measure-analyse-improve-control, 245
design for six sigma, 246
design quality, 246
design review, 246
DMAIC. *See* define-measure-analyse-improve-control

external failure costs, 228
house of quality, 221
internal failure costs, 228
lean six sigma, 246
participative design, 249
prevention costs, 228
process capability, 232
process capability index, 235
process capability ratio, 235

product development portfolio, 248
quality, 223
quality function deployment, 220
quality loss function, 249
six sigma capability, 236
six sigma quality, 244
Taguchi methods, 249
total quality management, 223
voice of the customer, 216

Notes

1 Cherif, R., Hasanov, F., & Pande, A. (2017). Riding the energy transition: Oil beyond 2040. *International Monetary Fund*. Retrieved from www.imf.org/en/Publications/WP/Issues/2017/05/22/Riding-the-Energy-Transition-Oil-Beyond-2040-44932

2 Usborne, D. (2012, January 20). The moment it all went wrong for Kodak. *The Independent*. Retrieved from www.independent.co.uk/news/business/analysis-and-features/the-moment-it-all-went-wrong-for-kodak-6292212.html

3 Doz, Y. L. (2017). *The strategic decisions that caused Nokia's failure*. Retrieved from https://knowledge.insead.edu/strategy/the-strategic-decisions-that-caused-nokias-failure-7766 and this online source referenced Doz, Y. L., & Wilson, K. (2018). *Ringtone: Exploring the rise and fall of Nokia in mobile phones*. Oxford, England: Oxford University Press.

4 Ford Media Centre. (2018, March 15). *Ford readies North America's freshest lineup by 2020 with onslaught of connected new trucks, SUVs and hybrids* [Press release]. Retrieved from https://media.ford.com/content/fordmedia/fna/us/en/news/2018/03/15/ford-readies-north-americas-freshest-lineup-by-2020.html

5 Carey, N., & White, J. (2018, January 15). Ford plans $11 billion investment, 40 electrified vehicles by 2022. *Reuters*. Retrieved from www.reuters.com/article/us-autoshow-detroit-ford-motor/ford-plans-11-billion-investment-40-electrified-vehicles-by-2022-idUSKBN1F30YZ

6 Kano, N., Seraku, N., Takahashi, F., & Tsuji, S. (1984, April 15). Attractive quality and must-be quality. *Hinshitsu, the Journal of the Japanese Society for Quality Control*, 14(2), 147–156.

7 Walden, D. (1993, Fall). Kano's method for understanding customer-defined quality. *Center for Quality of Management Journal*, 2(4), 8.

8 QFD Institute. (n.d.). *Quality function deployment*. Retrieved from www.qfdi.org

9 International Organization for Standardization. (2015). ISO16355–1: 2015. Retrieved from www.iso.org/standard/62626.html

10 Zeithaml, V. A., Berry, L. L., & Parasuraman, A. (1993, January). The nature and determinants of customer expectations of service. *Journal of the Academy of Marketing Science*, 21(1), 1–12, cited in Johnston, R., & Clark, G. (2001). *Service operations management*. Harlow, England: Prentice Hall, p. 84.

11 Garvin, D. A. (1987, November–December). Competing on the eight dimensions of quality. *Harvard Business Review*, 65(6), 101–109.

12 Berry, L. L., Parasuraman, A., & Zeithaml, V. A. (1990, Summer). Five imperatives for improving service quality service. *MIT Sloan Management Review*, 30(4), 29.

13 Green, R. (2000, August). Baldrige award winner profile: An interview with Horst Schulze, president (at the time) and COO of The Ritz-Carlton Hotel Co. *LLC*. Retrieved from www.qualitydigest.com/aug00/html/baldrige.html

14 The Ritz-Carlton Hotel Company. (2018). *Fact sheet*. Retrieved from www.ritzcarlton.com/en/about/factsheet

15 The Ritz-Carlton Hotel Company. (n.d.). *Gold standards*. Retrieved from www.ritzcarlton

16 EFQM, 2 Avenue des Olympiades, 5th floor, 1140 Brussels, Belgium.

17 EFQM. (2013). *EFQM excellence model*. Brussels, Belgium: EFQM. This publication may be downloaded for free from www.EFQM.org

18 International Organization for Standardization. (2015). *Quality management principles*. Geneva, Switzerland: International Organization for Standardization.
19 Davis, C. R. (2002, Summer). Calculated risk: A framework for evaluating product development. *MIT Sloan Management Review*, 43(4), 73.

Additional reading on quality management and product design

Akao, Y. (1990). *Quality function deployment: Integrating customer requirements into product design* (G. H. Mazur, Trans.). Portland, OR: Productivity Press.

Chapman, J. (2017). *Routledge handbook of sustainable product design*. New York: Routledge and Taylor & Francis Group.

De Feo, J. A. (2017). *Juran's quality handbook: The complete guide to performance excellence* (7th ed.). New York, NY: McGraw Hill Education.

Deming, W. E. (1986). *Out of the crisis*. Cambridge, MA: Massachusetts Institute of Technology and Center for Advanced Engineering Study.

Deming, W. E., Orsini, J. N., & Cahil, D. D. (2013). *The essential Deming: Leadership principles from the father of quality*. New York, NY: McGraw Hill.

EFQM. (2013). *EFQM excellence model*. Brussels, Belgium: EFQM.

Garvin, D. A. (1987, November–December). Competing on the eight dimensions of quality. *Harvard Business Review*, 65(6), 101–109.

Oakland, J. S. (2014). *Total quality management and operational excellence: Text with cases* (4th ed.). Abingdon, England: Routledge.

Pittman, P. H., & Atwater, J. B. (2016). *APICS dictionary* (15th ed.). Chicago, IL: APICS.

Snee, R. D., & Hoerl, R. W. (2003). *Leading six sigma: A step-by-step guide*. Upper Saddle River, NJ: Prentice Hall.

Tague, N. R. (2005). *The quality toolbox* (2nd ed.). Milwaukee, WI: ASQ Quality Press.

Ulrich, K. T., & Eppinger, S. D. (2016). *Product design and development* (6th ed.). New York, NY: McGraw-Hill Education.

Zeithaml, V. A., Parasuraman, A., & Berry, L. L. (1990). *Delivering quality service: Balancing customer perceptions and expectations*. New York, NY: The Free Press.

Chapter 8

Inventory and resource planning

Learning objectives

At the end of this chapter, you should be able to:

- Explain the reason for having inventory.
- Describe the new approaches and considerations for inventory.
- Discuss the concept of strategic inventory positioning.
- Describe a fixed reorder quantity model.
- Explain why the economic order quantity (EOQ) is not appropriate for modern business.
- Describe a fixed reorder period model.
- Describe the newsvendor problem.
- Describe material requirements planning (MRP).
- Describe demand driven material requirements planning (DDMRP).
- Describe the process for sales and operations planning (S&OP).
- Describe the operations scheduling process.
- Discuss process industries and process flow scheduling.
- Discuss the theory of constraints.
- Discuss scheduling using the theory of constraints.

Perspective: Fonterra – too much milk then and not enough milk now[1]

Fonterra Co-operative Group, a New Zealand-based co-operative, is one of the world's largest producers of dairy nutrition for export, with products including milk powders, cheese, and butter. It ranks fourth in the world behind Nestlé (Switzerland), Danone (France), and Lactalis (France). Globally, Fonterra processes over 22 billion litres of milk annually and (in 2018) sold 4.12 million metric tonnes of product worth NZ$20.4 billion.[2] It has over 50 processing sites worldwide, with 30 in New Zealand and 7 in Australia. The co-operative collects over 16 billion litres of milk a year from New Zealand farms, and uses that to produce more than 2.32 million metric tonnes of product.

Fonterra operates in about 140 markets around the world – it is the only true multi-national in New Zealand. Export returns from these markets account for about 25% of New Zealand's total export earnings. Fonterra is a significant employer with over 22,000 permanent employees, of which more than 12,000 reside in New Zealand. Over 29,000 farmers and farm workers provide the milk from 4.7 million milking cows grazing on 1.8 million hectares of pastoral land, where rain, sunlight, and soil produce natural grass. Some additional inputs include fertiliser, irrigated water, and animal nutrition.[3]

Fonterra produces dairy commodities such as milk proteins, milk powders, butter, cheese, and dairy ingredients for food manufacturers. In addition, it produces branded dairy products such as milk, spreads, yoghurts, cheeses, dairy desserts, and ice cream. The brand portfolio includes Anchor, Mainland, Fresh'n Fruity, Fernleaf, Tip Top, and Kāpiti (and many more). The Anchor brand originated in 1886, and Tip Top celebrated its 60th anniversary in 2017. In May 2019, Fonterra announced the sale of Tip Top to Froneri, the third-largest ice-cream manufacturer in the world.[4] As part of the deal, Fonterra agreed to supply grass-fed milk to Froneri and licensed the Kāpiti brand to Froneri to use in ice cream.

In 2009, the co-operative commissioned a new milk powder manufacturing plant, capable of producing one metric tonne of whole milk powder every two minutes, at Edendale, in Southland. This is the cooperative's largest milk-powder processing site, with the capacity to process more than 15 million litres of milk per day.

In 2012, Fonterra opened a new site at Darfield, just west of Christchurch. The Darfield drier can process 6.6 million litres of milk per day and convert that to milk powder at the rate of 1000 metric tonnes per day. Apart from the plant technology, the main advantages to Fonterra are the reduced distances for milk tankers to travel and the proximity to the export port of Lyttleton.

In 2018, they revamped the Litchfield plant in the Waikato with improved milk powder production capability. Natural gas powers the plant, which processes 4.4 million litres of milk per day. The plant condenses steam from the heating and drying process and saves the water for irrigation. A new distribution centre can store 40,000 metric tonnes of whole milk powder ready for loading directly onto rail at an in-built siding, thus reducing the volume of truck transport.[5]

These investments in drier capability take the pressure off during the peak of the season and allow Fonterra to produce higher-yielding products at other times during the year. The investments allow the co-operative to strike a balance in their processing which means they can switch quickly between products to meet demand changes in global markets, push the pace on production when milk volumes dictate, and ultimately deliver the best product mix to generate returns.[6]

The processing site at Whareroa, in the heart of Taranaki, produces the largest volume of dairy ingredients from a single factory anywhere in the world. It has five powder plants, two cheese plants, and plants producing cream product, casein, and whey. It collects up to 14 million litres of milk a day, and every hour it can produce 20 metric tonnes of powders. This site processes a fifth of Fonterra's dairy production in New Zealand. On an annual basis, it produces 428,000 tonnes of milk powder, 200,000 tonnes of whole milk powder and skim milk powder, 95,000 tonnes of cheese products, 88,000 tonnes of cream products, 35,000 tonnes of protein products, and 10,000 tonnes of lactic casein.

Another large site at Clandeboye, just outside Temuka in the South Island, processes up to 13.2 million litres of milk per day. With new technology, they now produce enough mozzarella cheese per year to top half a billion pizzas.[7] Fonterra does not disclose the production figures claiming that the exact amount of mozzarella produced is commercially sensitive. Similarly, they do not disclose the mozzarella recipe, which, unlike traditional methods requiring months to produce, takes only hours at Clandeboye.

Around 10,000 New Zealand dairy farmer shareholders own the co-operative with NZ$18 billion in assets. Additionally, the Fonterra Shareholders' Fund provides opportunities for investors to receive dividends. Fonterra pays its operating surplus to shareholders as payment for milk and distributes its value added returns (essentially profit) as a component of that payment. They have a cooperative agreement with their dairy farmers to take the entire production of milk, providing a challenge for the production systems as they endeavour to coordinate production output with demand requirements. Demand is relatively flat for the entire year with relatively little seasonality and a small upward-trending global growth. Southern Hemisphere supply, on the other hand, peaks in the spring months of September and October and drops significantly in the winter months of May and June as illustrated in Figure 8.1.

The Fonterra business systems incorporate sales and operations planning processes. Clearly, the need is obvious. The supply surplus in spring and the supply shortfall in winter require careful management to guarantee product delivery to Fonterra's worldwide customers. This is not just a production problem. It involves all functions of the cooperative – marketing, sales, new product development, finance, purchasing, production, and supply chain.

The monthly sales and operations planning cycle uses a demand planning tool to develop an unconstrained baseline demand forecast extending for at least 18 months and capturing actual customer demand regardless of any influencing factors, and provides a continuous live view of demand to guide production quantities at Fonterra's sites.

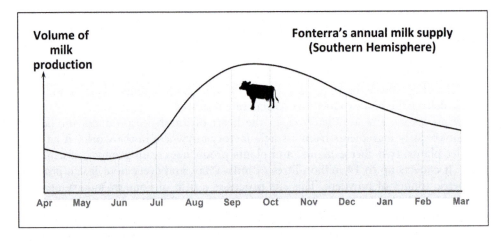

Figure 8.1 Fonterra's annual milk production (Southern Hemisphere) peaks in September and October

In parallel, they plan the aggregate supply of milk. Seasonal weather patterns, which may not be seasonal, heavily influence supply. Fonterra has no control over the timing and quantity of supply.

They confirm the sales and operations plan via meetings with senior executives representing cross-functional business units, including sales and marketing, operations (purchasing, inventory management, supply chain operations, and master production scheduling), and finance.

While this may sound straightforward (and boring), the reality is that all functions must deliver to that plan. Sales and marketing commit to sell the agreed level of sales, operations agree to supply the agreed volumes of product, and finance agrees to make sure it can all happen from a financial aspect.

Fonterra Co-operative Group is an excellent example of a global manufacturing and trading organisation that balances its demand with its supply. Assume the role of the sales director and make your customers ecstatically delighted. At the same time assume the role of the supply chain director and keep your suppliers ecstatically satisfied. That is relatively easy when everything goes to plan. However, what happens when a major customer changes their mind and increases or decreases their requirements, what happens when weather patterns change the expected harvest quantities, what happens when a supply facility is wiped out by a natural disaster, what happens when a transport operator is prevented from honouring commitments, what happens when . . . ?

Introduction

This is a chapter on inventory management and resource planning systems. Possibly, there have been more books and articles written on inventory management systems than any other topic in operations management. That is understandable given that inventory represents a significant investment for most organisations. All the goods on the shelves in a retail store are inventory items; all the products waiting in warehouses are inventory items; all the materials and products in the supply chain represent inventory investment. Therefore, it makes sense to have a good understanding of the strategic role inventory takes in organisations and some of the tools and techniques for managing inventory investments.

Larger organisations utilise planning systems, and the use of information technology influences the implementation of these planning systems. Many businesses invest thousands, if not millions, of dollars implementing planning systems, but few of these systems are successful. Why are they unsuccessful? It is a simplification, but the reason often comes back to a lack of understanding of the real business need for the planning system in the first place. It is not appropriate to implement one brand and type of system just because someone else has implemented it.

Many organisations have tried material requirements planning systems over the past 50 years, but the design breaks down when implementing them in a demand-pull environment. This chapter introduces demand driven material requirements planning as a forward-looking concept for managing supply chain inventories. Demand driven material requirements planning systems present a new perspective on the placement and quantities of inventories.

Chapter 3 introduced the sales and operations planning process. The current chapter describes the actual process for sales and operations planning and the hierarchical flow-on to master production scheduling, material requirements planning, and throughput planning.

The chapter closes by examining the theory of constraints, which throws a different light on inventory, inventory investment, and production scheduling.

Inventory and inventory management

Inventory

Inventory is the stock or items used to support production processes (raw material and work in process), customer service (finished goods and spare parts), and other activities such as maintenance and repairs.

Raw material

Raw material was originally the raw material extracted from the ground to start a production process. Now it is any purchased or extracted item used as input to the production process and converted into components and finished products.

Work in process (WIP)

Work in process (WIP) is the material and components in a production process between the first input (raw material) and the final output stage (finished goods).

Finished goods

Finished goods are the items that have had all production processes completed.

Inventory management

Inventory management is the process of planning and controlling inventories.

Nearly all organisations have inventory, although some service organisations may not call it inventory and may not visualise inventory as a problem. It is easy for production organisations to visualise inventory since they are purchasing raw materials in large quantities and transforming them into finished goods all the time. That is their role in life. They survive by being able to manage the inflow of raw materials, process them effectively through their production processes, and sell the outputs to their customers. Production inventory includes materials that contribute to, or become part of, an organisation's product output. The typical classifications are raw materials, finished goods, component parts, operating supplies, and work in process.

Service organisations hold inventory as well. Supermarkets hold inventory stocks on their shelves and constantly replenish empty spaces as customers remove items from the shelves and take them home. Restaurants have food items as inventory, and the kitchen staff estimate how much they require on a regular basis and purchase accordingly. Hospitals and medical centres purchase medicines, pharmaceuticals, instruments, dressings, food, blood, and cleaning materials. Banks and financial institutions have stocks of credit applications, stationery, information technology equipment, and food items. Property investment organisations manage their inventories of properties. Plumbers, builders, painters, and maintenance companies carry limited amounts of inventory with employees as they travel from one job to the next. Domestic households have a refrigerator and a pantry with food items waiting for the household to consume them.

Service inventory includes the tangible goods awaiting sale and sometimes the service delivery requires the inventory. Service inventory classifications include goods for sale or rent, physical space, number of workspaces, service personnel, production equipment, and supplies.

All of these are inventories and all have the same inventory problems to solve. What is the best place to store inventory? What is the best time to place an order? What is the order quantity? Inventory management is the process of planning and controlling physical inventory; each of these examples requires inventory management.

Inventory purpose

Inventory costs money, so when an organisation obtains more inventory it costs them more money. If they obtain a lot more inventory, it costs them a lot more money. The inventory investment ties up that money and it is unavailable for any other purpose. During storage, inventory may appreciate, but more than likely, it will depreciate. Appreciation arises in times of rising prices and currency fluctuations. Depreciation is more common as customers are not prepared to pay full price for something that is not brand-new.

As seen in Chapter 5, in the section on lean thinking, inventory compensates for poor delivery performance, high levels of scrap and rework, poorly maintained equipment, incorrect quantities used and supplied, and poor buying decisions. Inventory, in this sense, encourages ineffective behaviour and poor performance; it hides problems.

Inventory requires storage places such as warehouses, storage sheds, retail shelves, containers, and transport systems to hold and manage inventory. This is a real concern when the items held are large and bulky and carry little value. A foam upholstery block is an example of a product made almost entirely of air. It is relatively cheap to make but relatively expensive to store.

Inventory slows down the speed of production as batches of product move through the production systems. As inventories increase, their transport systems become bigger, slower, clumsier, and less able to cope with changing customer demands.

Inventory encourages obsolescence or it may even become obsolete. The use-by date pasted on supermarket items encourages households to buy in smaller quantities and hold smaller quantities inside their homes to prevent the goods expiring.

Some inventory requires special handling conditions and may be hazardous to store. Dangerous chemicals and flammable liquids need specially constructed storage areas, and staff need specialist training when handling and using these inventory items.

Inventory managers may initiate processes to count inventory, to administer it, to manage it, and they may insure it against loss. These actions take up time and money for the people involved.

Additionally, inventory provides a buffer to decouple different rates of demand. Customers demand products from a warehouse at a given rate, and the manufacturing unit supplies the warehouse at a given rate. Having some inventory available at the warehouse allows these two rates to be different. Likewise, the output rate from one process is unlikely to match exactly the input rate at the next process, especially if one of those processes involves transport. Inventory provides a buffer to decouple the different rates.

Fluctuation inventory provides a cushion against the variability of demand and supply.

Anticipation inventory occurs with highly seasonal products having short selling periods. Some organisations know they will have future demand that exceeds available capacity at the time, so they build up stock in anticipation of the future demand. Organisations hold inventory to prepare for future demand and to cope when expected demand exceeds their ability to replenish supply. Chapter 3 discussed this as a stock build using the level production strategy. Inventory held for this reason is a result of a strategic decision, as considerable investment in inventory and storage space can easily go unchecked.

Food-processing companies purchase an entire harvest during harvest time and partially process the food. It may be several months before the process continues. The companies obtain inventory during periods of abundance to compensate for periods of restricted supply, or even no supply. The processing companies may have signed contracts before the suppliers sow the seeds for crops such as tomatoes, green peas, and fruit. The contract might say that the company will take the entire harvest regardless of available quantity at harvest. This provides a guarantee of a sale to the grower and processing uncertainty to the processor. The Fonterra example in the perspective at the start of this chapter illustrates this provision.

Pipeline, or transportation, inventory relates to inventory in transit from one location to another. Sometimes this is difficult for supply chain systems to track, since it has left the supply location but has not arrived at the receiving location. Someone owns it and someone is carrying the cost of ownership. Pipeline inventory occurs when delivery distances are great and when delivery methods are slow. The inventory reduces when the supplier is near the customer and delivery methods are fast. Flow time through the pipeline has a major effect on the amount of inventory required in the pipeline.

Some businesses hedge inventory as an investment especially when they anticipate rising suppliers' prices, they expect transport problems, they foresee supply shortages looming, and they know that regulators are introducing new rules and conditions. Sometimes businesses hold inventory so it can appreciate. This may be an investment opportunity, but it is an investment in inventory and requires the same management decisions as regular purchases of depreciating inventory. Examples of appreciating inventory are fine art, stamps, and fine wines.

Some organisations obtain inventory in bulk to obtain a lower unit price. Referred to as lot-size inventory, this is a good practice when the quantity obtained matches a shipping quantity such as a pallet, or a container, and the organisation can consume the quantity in a reasonable timeframe. It is not good practice when storage costs, quality issues, obsolescence, pilferage, and other carrying costs are greater than the gain made with the initial purchase.

Why hold inventory?

Ask, 'Why hold inventory?' of a retailer or a manufacturer holding finished goods. Inevitably, they will respond by saying they hold inventory in anticipation of customer demand. Try turning that around and suggest that the only reason organisations hold inventory is that nobody wants to buy it right now. Customers may want to buy it tomorrow, but right now, nobody wants it.

We must resolve three questions when considering the role that inventory plays in the flexibility of the supply chain:

- How can an organisation maintain high service levels? If a retailer, or a manufacturer, has the required inventory available, they can satisfy customer requirements. Shortages or stock-outs disrupt production flow, have an adverse effect on customer satisfaction, and often result in additional freight costs, urgent orders, scheduling changes, and reduced service levels.
- How can organisations shorten lead times as much as possible? Organisations that have consistently short purchasing, production, and delivery lead times have distinct advantages over those that have inconsistent and long lead times. Customers want delivery certainty and having a quick response to demand enhances this requirement.
- How can organisations keep their inventory investment synchronised with demand? Most organisations strive to keep inventory investment as low as possible, but this may detract from maintaining a high service level. Therefore, it is essential to have a balance between inventory investment and demand.

Variability within the organisation and within the supply chain is the main reason for holding inventories. If an organisation knows tomorrow's demand, it could take immediate steps to ensure it had exactly that quantity ready for sale first thing tomorrow morning. By evening, it has sold all stock and the inventory balance would be zero. The problems start because organisations do not know exactly what demand will be tomorrow, or the following day, so they hold extra stock to maintain service levels just in case. The organisation may be able to control some variation within their organisation but may have difficulty controlling external supply chain variation.

Demand variability occurs when the demand pattern deviates from the expected pattern. Lack of visibility adds to the problem, and this amplifies as the demand travels along the supply chain towards the original supplier. The next chapter discusses this effect, known as the bullwhip effect, or demand amplification, in more detail.

Supply variability occurs with disrupted or unreliable supply chains. Natural disasters such as earthquakes, tsunamis, and floods may cause disruptions. Customers start with requested delivery dates, and suppliers respond with expected or promised delivery dates. The problems start when suppliers and customers cannot reconcile these dates, and the problems continue with subsequent changes. Supply chain reliability is essential and it does not take much change to dates and/or quantities to cause major disruptions.

Organisations hold inventories because of delivery uncertainty in both delivery lead times and quantities. If delivery was instantaneous and delivery quantities guaranteed there would be no need to store inventories. Electricity and water supplies for individual consumers replenish instantly, and the required quantities are always available (within reason). This example assumes an organisation, or a household, resides in a town or city in a developed country. It does not belittle the supply problems of the generation, distribution, and supply organisations, as they manage limited resources to maintain the instantaneous replenishment and flexible volume requirements demanded of their services.

Some organisations use lead-time-based pricing to increase revenue when demand is random and capacity fixed. Using this model, a make-to-order business, operating in its own best interests, can dynamically quote lead times and vary the associated prices when customers accept, or reject, a delay in delivery. The policies are both highly intuitive and provide delay guarantees for all served customers. Shorter delivery periods carry higher prices. Significant revenue benefits to the supplier can accrue by using these dynamic policies, and, likewise, cost benefits accrue to the customer when they adjust their expectation of delivery time.

New approaches and considerations

For want of a nail, the shoe was lost
For want of a shoe, the horse was lost
For want of a horse, the rider was lost
For want of a rider, the battle was lost
For want of a battle, the kingdom was lost
And all for the want of a horseshoe nail.[8]

The correct amount of inventory is the required quantity to satisfy customer demand. Firms balance the cost of having inventory and the cost of not having it. Receipts of purchased materials and completed production orders increase the quantity of inventory available, while deliveries to customers, usage at production processes, and scrap decrease the quantity available. Inventory management attempts to control the increases and the decreases.

Achieving a balance between the inputs and outputs requires skill. Inventory sitting in a warehouse is neither an input nor an output. An understanding and appreciation of the direct link between inputs and outputs enhances the required balancing skills. Inventory needed as inputs for transformation processes increases total inventory as it enters the organisation. Likewise, inventory required as outputs to satisfy customer requirements decreases total inventory as it leaves the organisation.

One of the drivers for most organisations is the effect inventories have on performance measurements. For financial reasons, inventory appears as an asset on the balance sheet, and finance managers try to manipulate the level of inventory investment to enhance the reporting figures in the balance sheet. Policies of delaying inventory purchases until new reporting periods (month, quarter, or year) have a direct effect on the balance sheet and income statement. Unfortunately, from an operations and supply chain viewpoint, some of these policies are detrimental to usage requirements and flow.

Carrying inventory is a requirement but it is waste when stored in the wrong place, or in the wrong quantity. Sales and marketing often ask for large quantities of products with all the product options to be available to satisfy whatever products and quantities their customers demand. This requires a rethink as to where they store product options and how quickly the business can assemble and deliver products to their customers.

Inventory turnover, or inventory turns, is a common measure for evaluating inventory. The aim is to increase the turnover number as much as possible. The metric measures inventory turnover but excludes service level. It is easy to increase the result by lowering the average inventory, but that encourages lower service levels when insufficient quantity was available to service customer requirements. Thus, inventory turnover on its own is not a good metric, especially when the overall objective is customer satisfaction.

Supply chain partners must think of the supply chain as a system and determine the best place to store inventory. Placing inventory everywhere is a waste since it is not necessary. Having no inventory is a waste and increases risk and viability.

Strategically positioning inventory ensures the organisation's ability to absorb expected variability with the least investment. Most educational materials emphasise the calculation of the order quantity and the timing of when the organisation should place the order, without considering where to store the inventory.

Critical positioning factors

The six critical positioning factors to determine the proper place for placing inventory are:[9]

- **Customer tolerance time** is the demand lead time and represents the time a typical customer is willing to wait.
- **Market potential lead time** is the lead time that would change the way the market operates. Shortening the lead time may allow an increase in price, and/or it may capture additional customers. Earlier, we mentioned the concept of lead-time-based pricing.
- **Variable rate of demand** is a calculation, and organisations should recognise that this stretches available resources and they should take mitigating steps.
- **Variable rate of supply,** sometimes called supply continuity variability, calculates the variance of promise dates to actual delivery dates.
- **Inventory leverage and flexibility** requires the organisation to explore where it can make the most leverage and provide the most flexibility. In manufacturing, this usually means having enough raw materials and sub-assemblies to allow the making of any combination of finished products. Likewise, in distribution, this allows the organisation to realign the distribution network to a hub-and-spoke model.
- **Critical operational areas** require protection from disruption to maintain the flow. In the theory of constraints, we refer to this as the drum; in lean thinking, we refer to this as the pacesetter.

These critical positioning factors apply across the entire supply chain.

Distribution inventory

The concept of strategic inventory positioning applies also to the design of distribution networks. Usually the distribution centre, which has visibility of retail demand, manages the distribution network. Orders from the distribution centre tend to be lumpy, and this defines the manufacturer's picture of demand; the manufacturer does not see retail demand. Inventory sent to distribution centres is available to that distribution centre and not available to other distribution centres without incurring additional transport expense. This invariably results in one or more distribution centres having too much inventory while others have too little.

Generic inventory management model

Lead time

Lead time is the time between recognition of the need for an order and receipt of that order.

Safety lead time

Safety lead time is an element of time added to the normal lead time to protect against fluctuations in demand and/or supply.

Supplier lead time

Supplier lead time is the elapsed time from when the supplier receives the order to when the supplier ships the order.

Service level

Service level is the probability that current inventory or planned production satisfies customer demand in time to meet customer-requested delivery dates and quantities.

Figure 8.2 illustrates the generic inventory management model. Demand and inventory enter the system, and customer demand exists for an indeterminate future period. Knowing customer demand allows the organisation to arrange for enough inventory to enter the system to meet the demand. Estimating customer demand allows the organisation to take a position on how much demand it will process in the future, and arranges for enough inventory to enter the system to meet anticipated demand. Ideally, the rate of demand should equal the rate of inventory entering the system.

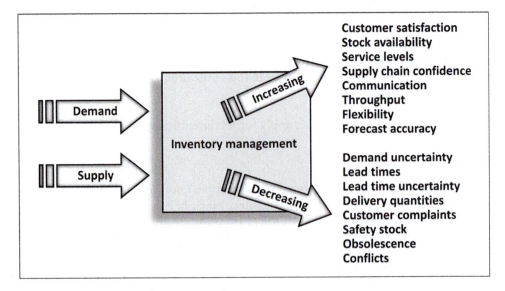

Figure 8.2 Generic inventory management model

When enough inventories are available to meet demand, the following measures **increase**:

- Customer satisfaction increases since customer demands are being satisfied with products meeting quality and quantity needs.
- Stock availability increases with the required quantity of required products available and fewer stock-outs.
- Service levels increase with stock availability and customer satisfaction.
- Supply chain confidence increases with end-customer demand communicated throughout the entire supply chain.
- Communication increases and this tends to be honest and true.
- Throughput increases by stocking and supplying demanded products. In this way, products are not sitting for extended periods waiting for a customer.
- Flexibility increases with known demand and production systems based on agility.
- Forecast accuracy increases with a better understanding of demand variation.

When enough inventories are available to meet demand, the following measures **decrease**:

- Demand uncertainty decreases with known end-customer demand and communication throughout the entire supply chain.
- Lead times decrease with better communication and advanced planning.
- Lead time uncertainty decreases with better communication on capacity and demand.
- Delivery quantities decrease with restored order confidence.
- Customer complaints decrease because customers have the required products in the required quantities, and the products meet the expected quality standards.
- Safety stocks decrease when demand uncertainty decreases and lead time uncertainty decreases.
- Obsolescence decreases as inventory flows through the system for consumption.
- Conflicts decrease as organisations satisfy all demands and do not need to trade off one customer demand against another.

Lead time is the time between recognition of the need for an order and receipt of that order. The longer the lead time, the longer the period of demand uncertainty and the greater the possibility of lead time variation; therefore, the need for safety stock is greater. Safety stock is an overhead cost, and it acts as an additional storage and cost burden for the organisation when not used on a regular basis. The need for safety stock diminishes as demand uncertainty and lead time decreases. There is no need for any safety stock when lead time is zero.

Safety lead time is a better mechanism to combat variations in demand and/or supply. Safety stock just sits there on average. Safety lead time in contrast allows the required inventory to arrive earlier than needed.

Supplier lead time is a subset of lead time and is the time required for the supplier to respond to an order request. For many organisations, this is a variable and the cause of considerable frustration when handling late orders. The concept of efficient consumer response, covered in Chapter 9, requires greater visibility of true customer demand at all points on the supply chain. With this visibility, the supplier can anticipate demand when it suits the supplier to respond, so when the actual order arrives the supplier is ready and prepared.

Capacity buying is a purchasing practice whereby a company commits to a supplier for a given amount of its capacity. Subsequently, the company schedules individual products or services. This usually happens with long lead times and when the company does not know actual production requirements until well inside the lead time.

Capable-to-promise is the process of committing orders against available capacity as well as inventory. It determines delivery details for new or unscheduled customer orders. The process uses a finite-scheduling model of the manufacturing system to determine the delivery date for each item. It includes any constraints that might restrict the production, such as availability of resources, lead times for raw materials or purchased parts, and requirements for lower-level components or sub-assemblies. The resulting delivery dates consider production capacity, the current manufacturing environment, and future order commitments. The objective is to reduce the time spent by production planners in expediting orders and adjusting plans because of inaccurate delivery-date promises.

Inventory management systems

Order point

Order point is a pre-determined inventory level to initiate replenishment action if the total stock on hand plus on order reaches this point or falls below it. Calculate the order point value using the demand during replenishment lead time plus safety stock.

Fixed order quantity

Fixed order quantity is a lot-sizing technique using a predetermined fixed quantity, or a multiple of a fixed quantity, as the reorder quantity.

The demand for inventory can be either independent or dependent. Independent items supply the demand that comes from outside the organisation. Fixed quantity, fixed period, minimum-maximum, and budget allocations manage independent demand items. Dependent demand items supply requirements from inside the organisation; they are components of other products, so their rate of use is dependent on the production schedule and the rate of use of the other items. We define independent and dependent demand in Chapter 2. Material requirements planning and lean thinking approaches manage dependent demand items by keeping inventories as low as possible.

Most inventory models use a reorder point. With inventory consumption, the quantity on hand diminishes until it reaches some arbitrary point called the order point. When reaching this point, a trigger of some sort initiates a replenishment order. Possibly the most common trigger signal is the light on a motor vehicle dashboard to indicate low fuel levels. When interpreted correctly, it signals that the vehicle requires additional fuel. Some drivers may estimate how long they have before they run out and this may be 50–100 kilometres. Depending on the driver, the conditions, the

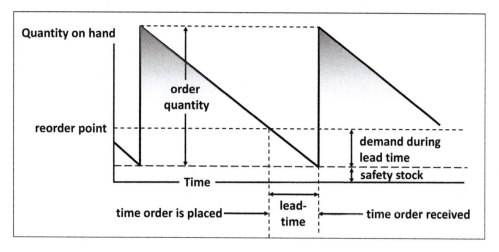

Figure 8.3 Fixed reorder quantity model

driver's risk tolerance, and the level of excitement required, this trigger might indicate two or three days of driving. Whichever way you look at it, it is a reorder point.

Inventory systems use either a fixed reorder quantity model or a fixed reorder cycle model.

Fixed reorder quantity model

Fixed reorder quantity model

The fixed reorder quantity model is an independent demand management model in which an order quantity is a predetermined fixed quantity. The interval between placing orders is variable.

In the fixed reorder quantity model, as illustrated in Figure 8.3, the firm orders a predetermined constant quantity whenever the number of units on hand reaches a specified order point. Thus, the order quantity is the same each time.

Calculate the reorder point using the demand during the lead time plus any safety stock requirements. The predicted demand during the lead time should be close to actual demand, and the safety stock should be enough to cover variations of demand. This model fails when actual demand exceeds predicted demand by more than the safety stock. Short lead times, reliable suppliers, and dynamic safety stock calculations alleviate the stock-out problem.

Economic order quantity model

Ordering cost

Ordering cost is the cost incurred by placing purchase orders with suppliers and organising the ordered items for production within a plant. It includes costs associated with preparing, releasing, monitoring, receiving and payment of orders, and the physical handling of inwards goods.

Carrying cost

Carrying cost is the cost of carrying or holding inventory. Carrying cost depends mainly on the cost of capital invested in the inventory, but also includes insurance, obsolescence, spoilage, and space occupied.

Set-up cost

Set-up cost is the fixed cost associated with production that includes paperwork, machine set-up, calibration, downtime, and start-up scrap that can be associated with the changeover from one product to the next.

Set-up time

Set-up time is the time spent to change from one product type to another. This time includes arranging tools, changing dies, setting machine speeds, cleaning equipment, and checking initial outputs. In most cases, the set-up time is variable and depends on the previous product ending and the current product starting.

Teardown time

Teardown time is the time required to remove a job from a machine prior to setting up for the next job. Usually, the next job incurs the time and cost of the teardown activity. However, teardown is a function of the previous job and the following job in combination. Thus, set-up time may vary because of the previous job. As an example, when printing and dyeing it is quicker to move from light through to dark colours rather than the other way around.

Economic order quantity (EOQ)

Economic order quantity is a fixed order quantity model attempting to find the optimum order quantity. Modern business dictates the use of the EOQ is no longer appropriate.

The inventory debate has traditionally been cost-based. Inventory analysts calculate the total cost of inventory and attempt to minimise it. Organisations try to cut inventory costs by optimising the total cost equation.

Ford W. Harris takes the credit for one of the earliest applications of mathematics to factory management.[10] In 1913, Harris developed the economic order quantity (EOQ) model, which calculates the annual set-up cost (cost of ordering) and the annual interest and depreciation on stock (cost of carrying). He differentiated the total variable cost using calculus; the minimum value (of the first differential) corresponds to a quantity called the economic order quantity. When ordering this quantity, the variable inventory costs for the year are minimised. The assumption that the annual cost of acquisition is constant regardless of order quantity eliminates the need to use it in the calculation.

This is a staple diet for nearly all books on inventory and most books on operations management, but it is not a foundation topic for this book. The economic order quantity model is not appropriate for modern business applications. Throughout this book, the concept of flow and the requirement to supply exactly what the customer wants when they want it is emphasised. Rather than calculating the financial impact of order size, it is far better to order the quantity required.

To calculate the economic order quantity requires the following assumptions to be true:

- The organisation knows future demand for the next year. This is a constant and deterministic value, which means there is certainty about quantity and timing of demand. Thus, the future demand curve is a straight horizontal line.
- Each production run incurs a fixed set-up cost, which is the same regardless of actual quantity made and regardless of the previous job.
- Ordering costs are variable when for most organisations they are a fixed value. The number of permanent employees involved with processing orders remains constant and does not vary directly as a function of order size and numbers of orders. Monthly salaries, for example, do not adjust as a function of ordering cost.
- Storage costs are variable when for most organisations they are a fixed value. The cost of running a warehouse when it is full is not much different from when it is just a quarter full. The materials handling costs, insurance costs, and cost of permanent staff fulfilling warehouse functions remains constant and does not vary directly as a function of order size and numbers of orders. Monthly salaries, for example, do not adjust as a function of storage costs.
- Production is instantaneous, suggesting there is no constraint on capacity.
- Delivery is immediate, indicating no delay between production and availability.
- The organisation analyses products individually, suggesting there is no sharing of resources. Organisations want to optimise all items collectively, and considering one item at a time does not achieve this.

Very rarely will these assumptions hold true. For most organisations, capacity is a constraint, at least for some of the time. Usually, demand is not deterministic and not constant over time. As for set-up, the time to perform a set-up varies according to the previous product, and the teardown is a function of the following product. Thus, set-up is a variable and not a constant.

When set-up and/or teardown times are large, organisations attempt to increase the quantity produced to amortise the cost of the set-up across more units and lower the set-up cost per unit produced. There is no attempt to minimise set-up with the economic order quantity, or even to reduce it. The concepts of lean thinking, in Chapter 5, suggest a batch quantity of one. Therefore, the application of the economic order quantity model to a lean environment requires a reduction in the set-up costs until the optimal quantity is one.

The basic economic order quantity model uses a constant value for set-up. In fact, Harris claimed that the set-up cost proper has general acceptance and in a large factory could exceed $1.00 per order.[11] The historical quote, attributed to Harris, highlights a real problem for organisations using the economic order quantity. They calculate the cost of ordering (set-up time multiplied by cost multiplied by number of orders per year) by some arbitrary means, and then set that figure in stone. To use it with a little more credence, it should be dynamically calculated and constantly updated.

The calculation uses future period values and this means the organisation knows future costs. The model uses future annual cost, monthly cost, or any other fixed period cost, provided the rates and percentages used are still applicable and the units of measure have been normalised.

The assumption of a one-product business limits the effectiveness of the basic economic order quantity model, and the formula does not allow for combining several different products in the same production (works) order. Further, it does not consider the cost of not having inventory. How often does an inexpensive component hold up production? How often is an order lost because an item is not available in stock?

None of this is sound business logic for an organisation striving for excellence.

Fixed reorder cycle model

Fixed reorder cycle model

Fixed reorder cycle model is an inventory management system that checks inventory at fixed intervals. The reorder quantity is variable and essentially replaces the items consumed during the current period.

Target inventory level

Target inventory level is the quantity set as the target, and equals the order point plus a variable order quantity.

Figure 8.4 illustrates the fixed reorder cycle model. Using this model, the organisation places an order at the end of a specified period and adjusts the quantity to bring

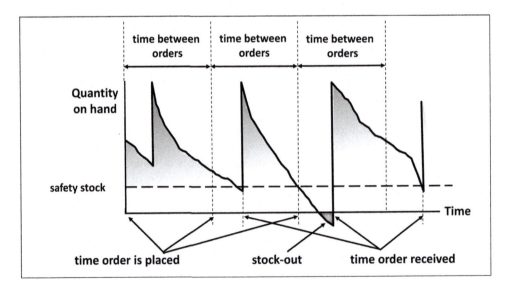

Figure 8.4 Fixed reorder cycle model

inventory up to a predetermined target level. This means that the same time interval elapses between orders. This type of ordering system operates when a sales representative calls regularly on a retail store, assesses current stock, and places a replenishment order to bring stock levels up to a predetermined target level. The order quantity is likely to be different with every order and depends on the demand pattern between orders.

The order quantity must be enough to last from the placing of one order until the receipt of the next order. The quantity ordered considers the demand during the review period plus the demand during the lead time.

Newsvendor problem

Newsvendor problem

The newsvendor problem is an extension of the fixed reorder cycle model and determines the order quantity that maximises the expected profit in a single period probabilistic demand framework.

Every morning, the owner of a newspaper stand at a busy transport terminal orders the newspapers for the day. However, how many newspapers should the owner order? If the owner orders too many, the owner throws unsold papers away or sells them as scrap. The salvage value is the money received for scrap. If the owner orders too few, some customers will be disappointed and sales and profits will suffer. The newsvendor problem is to find the best (optimal) number of newspapers to buy that will maximise the expected profit given known demand distribution and cost parameters.

It is an extension of the fixed reorder cycle model, except the order is a different product each time – there is a different newspaper each day. The newsvendor problem extends across many different business applications, such as:

- What is the best quantity of seasonal products, such as sunglasses, swimsuits, fashion items, and religious festival items to purchase once per season? A season in this context can be a day, a week, or a year. If the retailer buys too much, there is excess stock at the end of the season; if the retailer buys too little, customers are disappointed, reducing sales and profits.
- What is the right capacity to obtain? Manufacturers buy machines with a given capacity. If capacity is too high, capital costs are too high; if capacity is too low, stock-outs occur.
- How much blood should a hospital obtain? If the hospital secures too much blood, some blood goes beyond the use-by date and the hospital discards the excess; if the hospital secures too little blood, it has insufficient supplies when needed.
- What target inventory level should be set? Salespeople often carry a supply of inventory in their vehicles so they can deliver as they make sales calls. The target inventory level controls the inventory. If the target is too high, the salesperson returns to base with unsold products; if the target is too low, stock-outs occur.
- What cash reserves should a business establish? Organisations make financial arrangements with their bank to carry them through busy trading periods. If those arrangements are too generous, the organisation has high lending facility costs to

pay. If the arrangement is too frugal, the organisation may face an embarrassing shortfall of funds. This example may extend to people saving for retirement.

- How many employees does a project require? When resourcing a project, a key decision is the number of employees required. If the number obtained is too large, the project may finish early (which may be a good outcome) or some resource may be idle waiting for other activities to complete. If the number is too small, activities miss the due dates and delay project completion.
- How many customers should an airline overbook? In revenue management, if an airline overbooks too much, it may incur the cost of compensating inconvenienced passengers; if the airline does not allow enough for last minute rescheduling and cancellations, it may incur an opportunity cost of lost revenue by flying with empty seats.

Notation

The problem occurs when ordering a single product at the start of a period and this satisfies demand during that period only. All newsvendor problems share the following:

- C_o is the marginal cost of overstocking or overage cost. This is the cost of positive inventory remaining at the end of the selling season. In a retail example, the overage cost is the cost of one unit of inventory, c, less the salvage value, v. Thus, $c_o = c - v$. The salvage value is the money received for scrapped products (recovery value).
- C_u is the marginal benefit of one extra unit or underage cost. This is the cost per unit of unsatisfied demand; we call it the stock-out or shortage cost. In a retail example, the underage cost is the lost contribution to profit, which is the unit price, p, less the unit cost, c. Thus $c_u = p - c$.
- D is the demand that is a non-negative random variable defined by a demand distribution such as a Normal distribution, or a Poisson distribution, and estimates of the distribution parameters such as the mean and standard deviation. The demand pattern may be continuous or discrete (integer).
- Q is the quantity of units to purchase at the start of the season. The newsvendor problem endeavours to find the optimal order quantity, Q^*.

The newsvendor problem uses a single period so does not need discounted cash flows.

To determine the optimum quantity, it helps to examine the logic behind the development of the model. The newsvendor could order one copy of the paper and there is a very good chance of selling the paper for a profit. The expected gain equals the probability of selling the first unit times the gain from the first unit. There is, however, a slight chance of not selling the first unit, in which case the newsvendor incurs a loss equal to the overage cost. The probability of this happening is very small, so the expected loss is close to zero. In balance, the expected gain exceeds the expected loss, so the profit from ordering one unit is positive and represents a good deal.

One unit is a good deal so the newsvendor tries two units, then three units, and so on. As the quantity increases, the probability of selling the extra unit decreases and the probability of not selling the extra unit increases. Thus, the expected gain decreases and the expected loss increases. Eventually the newsvendor finds that the expected gain is less than the expected loss and it no longer represents a viable business proposition.

There is a trade-off between ordering too much (and left with unsold products) and ordering too little (and foregoing some extra demand). There is a cost of ordering too much and a cost of ordering too little. The newsvendor can maximise expected profit by minimising these costs. c_o is the marginal cost of overstocking or overage cost. c_u is the marginal benefit of one extra unit or underage cost.

The optimum quantity Q^* occurs when the expected gain equals the expected loss. The formula for calculating the optimal value of Q^* is as follows:

$$\text{Probability that demand does not exceed } Q = P(D \leq Q) = \frac{c_u}{c_o + c_u} \qquad (8.1)$$

where D is assumed to be normally distributed
  Q = the quantity purchased and available at the start of the season
  c_o = the marginal cost of overstocking or overage cost
  c_u = the marginal benefit of understocking or underage cost

$\dfrac{c_u}{c_o + c_u}$ = the critical ratio

The optimal $Q = Q^* = \sigma Z + \mu$ \qquad (8.2)

where σ = the standard deviation
  Z = the standard Normal variable and used to calculate probability
  μ = the mean

Alternatively, using Microsoft Excel®

Q^* = NORM.INV (probability_cr,mean_μ,standard_deviation_σ)

Continuous probability distributions describe the demand for worked examples 8.1 and 8.2. If the demand is discrete, the distribution function increases in jumps and it is unlikely that any of its values exactly equals the critical ratio. The critical ratio will generally fall between two values $P(D \leq Q)$. The optimal solution is to find the critical ratio between two values of $P(D \leq Q)$ and choose the Q corresponding to the higher value. In the two worked examples, the optimum Q was the closest value because the ordered units come in discrete amounts and demand is continuous.

Worked example 8.1

A retailer purchases new magazines weekly, and from experience the weekly demand exhibits approximately a Normal distribution with a mean, μ = 13.20 and standard deviation, σ = 3.75. The purchase cost price of each magazine is $7.51 and the publisher pays $2.55 (salvage price) for any unsold copies. The retail price is $14.95. Calculate the optimal quantity.

$$\mu = 13.20 \qquad\qquad \text{mean}$$

$$\sigma = 3.75 \qquad\qquad \text{standard deviation}$$

$$p = 14.95 \qquad\qquad \text{retail price}$$

$$c = 7.51 \qquad\qquad \text{cost price}$$

$$v = 2.55 \qquad\qquad \text{salvage price}$$

$$c_o = c - v = 7.51 - 2.55 = 4.96 \qquad\qquad \text{overage cost}$$

$$c_u = p - c = 14.95 - 7.51 = 7.44 \qquad\qquad \text{underage cost}$$

$$\frac{c_u}{c_o + c_u} = \frac{7.44}{4.96 + 7.44} = 0.6 \qquad\qquad \text{critical ratio}$$

Using equation (8.1),

probability that demand does not exceed $Q = P(D \le Q) = \dfrac{c_u}{c_o \mid c_u} = 0.6$

Using Figure 8.5 for the area under the Normal curve gives Z-score = 0.254 Thus using equation (8.2), the optimal $Q = Q^* = \sigma Z + \mu = 3.75 \times 0.254 + 13.20 = 14.15 \approx 14$

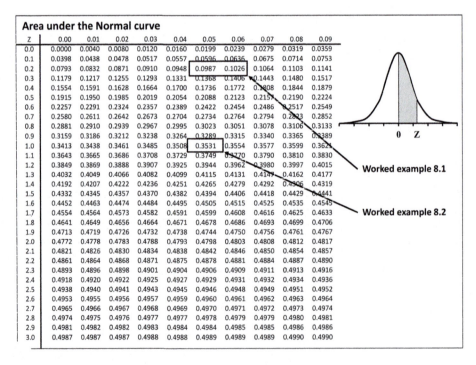

Area under the Normal curve

z	0.00	0.01	0.02	0.03	0.04	0.05	0.06	0.07	0.08	0.09
0.0	0.0000	0.0040	0.0080	0.0120	0.0160	0.0199	0.0239	0.0279	0.0319	0.0359
0.1	0.0398	0.0438	0.0478	0.0517	0.0557	0.0596	0.0636	0.0675	0.0714	0.0753
0.2	0.0793	0.0832	0.0871	0.0910	0.0948	0.0987	0.1026	0.1064	0.1103	0.1141
0.3	0.1179	0.1217	0.1255	0.1293	0.1331	0.1368	0.1406	0.1443	0.1480	0.1517
0.4	0.1554	0.1591	0.1628	0.1664	0.1700	0.1736	0.1772	0.1808	0.1844	0.1879
0.5	0.1915	0.1950	0.1985	0.2019	0.2054	0.2088	0.2123	0.2157	0.2190	0.2224
0.6	0.2257	0.2291	0.2324	0.2357	0.2389	0.2422	0.2454	0.2486	0.2517	0.2549
0.7	0.2580	0.2611	0.2642	0.2673	0.2704	0.2734	0.2764	0.2794	0.2823	0.2852
0.8	0.2881	0.2910	0.2939	0.2967	0.2995	0.3023	0.3051	0.3078	0.3106	0.3133
0.9	0.3159	0.3186	0.3212	0.3238	0.3264	0.3289	0.3315	0.3340	0.3365	0.3389
1.0	0.3413	0.3438	0.3461	0.3485	0.3508	0.3531	0.3554	0.3577	0.3599	0.3621
1.1	0.3643	0.3665	0.3686	0.3708	0.3729	0.3749	0.3770	0.3790	0.3810	0.3830
1.2	0.3849	0.3869	0.3888	0.3907	0.3925	0.3944	0.3962	0.3980	0.3997	0.4015
1.3	0.4032	0.4049	0.4066	0.4082	0.4099	0.4115	0.4131	0.4147	0.4162	0.4177
1.4	0.4192	0.4207	0.4222	0.4236	0.4251	0.4265	0.4279	0.4292	0.4306	0.4319
1.5	0.4332	0.4345	0.4357	0.4370	0.4382	0.4394	0.4406	0.4418	0.4429	0.4441
1.6	0.4452	0.4463	0.4474	0.4484	0.4495	0.4505	0.4515	0.4525	0.4535	0.4545
1.7	0.4554	0.4564	0.4573	0.4582	0.4591	0.4599	0.4608	0.4616	0.4625	0.4633
1.8	0.4641	0.4649	0.4656	0.4664	0.4671	0.4678	0.4686	0.4693	0.4699	0.4706
1.9	0.4713	0.4719	0.4726	0.4732	0.4738	0.4744	0.4750	0.4756	0.4761	0.4767
2.0	0.4772	0.4778	0.4783	0.4788	0.4793	0.4798	0.4803	0.4808	0.4812	0.4817
2.1	0.4821	0.4826	0.4830	0.4834	0.4838	0.4842	0.4846	0.4850	0.4854	0.4857
2.2	0.4861	0.4864	0.4868	0.4871	0.4875	0.4878	0.4881	0.4884	0.4887	0.4890
2.3	0.4893	0.4896	0.4898	0.4901	0.4904	0.4906	0.4909	0.4911	0.4913	0.4916
2.4	0.4918	0.4920	0.4922	0.4925	0.4927	0.4929	0.4931	0.4932	0.4934	0.4936
2.5	0.4938	0.4940	0.4941	0.4943	0.4945	0.4946	0.4948	0.4949	0.4951	0.4952
2.6	0.4953	0.4955	0.4956	0.4957	0.4959	0.4960	0.4961	0.4962	0.4963	0.4964
2.7	0.4965	0.4966	0.4967	0.4968	0.4969	0.4970	0.4971	0.4972	0.4973	0.4974
2.8	0.4974	0.4975	0.4976	0.4977	0.4977	0.4978	0.4979	0.4979	0.4980	0.4981
2.9	0.4981	0.4982	0.4982	0.4983	0.4984	0.4984	0.4985	0.4985	0.4986	0.4986
3.0	0.4987	0.4987	0.4987	0.4988	0.4988	0.4989	0.4989	0.4989	0.4990	0.4990

Worked example 8.1

Worked example 8.2

Figure 8.5 Area under the Normal curve

Alternatively, using Microsoft Excel®

$$Q^* = \text{NORM.INV}(0.6, 13.20, 3.75) = 14.15 \approx 14$$

Thus, the optimal number of magazines to purchase each week is 14.

The values in the body of Figure 8.5 represent the area between the mean and the value of Z. In worked example 8.1, the critical ratio is 0.6, so we need to find the value of Z that achieves 60% of the area under the Normal curve. Fifty per cent of the area is to the left of the mean and 50% is to the right. Thus, 60% includes the area to the left of the mean plus 0.1000 (10%) of the area to the right. Looking at the body of the Figure 8.5, Z = 0.25 has an area of 0.0987 and Z = 0.26 has an area of 0.1026.

A calculated guess makes Z = 0.254. The table highlights the two values (0.0987 and 0.1026).

Worked example 8.2

A retail store purchases their leather products once a year direct from the manufacturer in Italy. The unit cost of each product to the store is \$38.50 and the product sells for \$160.00. A discount store purchases any products not sold by the end of the season for \$17.60. A detailed analysis of past data suggests that sales demand exhibits approximately a Normal distribution with a mean, $\mu = 150$ and standard deviation, $\sigma = 20$. Calculate the optimal quantity of products to purchase.

$$\mu = 150 \qquad \text{mean}$$
$$\sigma = 20 \qquad \text{standard deviation}$$
$$p = 160 \qquad \text{retail price}$$
$$c = 38.5 \qquad \text{cost price}$$
$$v = 17.60 \qquad \text{salvage price}$$
$$c_o = c - v = 38.5 - 17.60 = 20.90 \qquad \text{overage cost}$$
$$c_u = p - c = 160 - 38.50 = 121.50 \qquad \text{underage cost}$$
$$\frac{c_u}{c_o + c_u} = \frac{121.50}{20.90 + 121.50} = 0.6 \qquad \text{critical ratio}$$

Using equation (8.1),
probability that demand does not exceed $Q = P(D \leq Q) = \dfrac{c_u}{c_o + c_u} = 0.8532$

Using Figure 8.5 for the area under the Normal curve gives Z-score = 1.05
Thus using equation (8.2), the optimal $Q = Q^* = \sigma Z + \mu = 20 \times 1.05 + 150 = 171$

Alternatively, using Microsoft Excel®,

$$Q^* = \text{NORM.INV}(0.8532, 150, 20) = 171$$

Thus, the optimal number of leather products to purchase each year is 171.

The values in the body of Figure 8.5 are the area between the mean and the value of Z. In worked example 8.2, the critical ratio is 0.8532, so we need to find the value of Z that achieves 85.32% of the area under the Normal curve. Fifty per cent of the area is to the left of the mean and 50% is to the right. Thus, 85.32% includes the area to the left of the mean plus 0.3532 (35.32%) of the area to the right. Looking at the body of Figure 8.5, Z = 1.05 has an area of 0.3531, which is close enough.

Material requirements planning (MRP)

Material requirements planning (MRP)

Material requirements planning (MRP) is a set of techniques using bills of material, inventory data, and the master production schedule to calculate the requirements of component materials. MRP starts with each specific item and quantity listed in the master production schedule, calculates the quantities of the components and materials making those items, and establishes the date those items must be available for use. MRP explodes the bill of material, adjusts for inventory quantities that are on hand or already on order, and calculates net requirements offset by the lead time.

Bill of material (BOM)

A bill of material (BOM) is a listing of the number and type of sub-assemblies, components, and raw materials needed to make an assembly. It is synonymous with formula, recipe, and ingredient list.

Bill of resources

A bill of resources is a listing of the required capacity and key resources needed to produce (or deliver) one unit of a selected item or family.

Gross requirement

The gross requirement is the total requirement of an item generated from the master production schedule and subsequent levels in the bill of material. Starting with the gross requirement, process the inventory on hand, scheduled receipts, and safety stock to calculate the net requirement.

Master production schedule (MPS)

Master production schedule is a line on the master schedule grid reflecting the anticipated build schedule for items assigned to the master scheduler. It represents what the company can build and will build, expressed in specific product configurations, quantities, and dates.

Net requirement

Net requirement is the result of applying a gross requirement against inventory on hand, allocations, scheduled receipts, and safety stock. The net requirement is then lot-sized and offset for lead time and becomes a planned order.

Planned order

A planned order is a suggested order quantity, release date, and due date created by the logic of a planning system when it encounters a net requirement in MRP. The computer creates planned orders – they exist only within the computer and subsequent computer processing may change or delete them if conditions change.

Planned order receipt

A planned order receipt is the receipt quantity planned for a future date because of a planned order release. Planned order receipts await release.

Planned order release

Derive a planned order release from a planned order receipt by taking the planned order receipt quantity and offsetting the due date by the appropriate lead time.

Push system

A push system is a system in which a pre-planned schedule of production dictates the sequence and timing of the production process.

Quantity per

Quantity per is the quantity of a component used in making one unit of the parent item.

Scheduled receipt

A scheduled receipt is an open order with an assigned due date.

Joseph Orlicky, George Plossl, and Oliver Wight developed materials requirements planning (MRP) in 1960.[12] Before this, manufacturing companies managed all inventories as if they exhibited independent demand. They relied on a reorder point to trigger the need, and fixed order quantities to satisfy that need. Manufacturers relied on excess stock and rough estimates, and hoped that they had enough materials.

Orlicky used computers to calculate the requirements of each component that made up the finished product. Starting with a statement of the specific quantity of each specific product for each specific required date – called the master production schedule – he exploded the bills of material to calculate the quantities of components. He considered the lead time for each item and offset the release of the replenishment order to compensate for the lead time. Progressively this built up gross requirements at the next level down the bill of material, so he subjected these to the same logic.

This development had profound implications for manufacturing systems. The driver to this method is the master production schedule, which must be realistic and achievable. At the finished goods level, it reflects the quantities of finished products that must be available for sale in each period. If this is true, the subsequent calculations may deliver meaningful results.

The bill of material reflects actual material requirements per item. It is like a recipe or a formula. In fact, some industries, such as pharmaceuticals and food processing, refer to their bills of material as recipes and formulas. Variation, scrap, wastage, shrinkage, loss, pilferage, and misplacement require the introduction of some compensation.

Lead times use fixed numbers and these offset the release of each replenishment order. Therefore, an organisation places an order for an item next week if it requires the item in four weeks and there is a three-week delivery. This calculates raw material supply and delivers it at the latest possible due date.

MRP systems require inventory accuracy of quantities on hand and on order. If the computer shows an item is in plentiful supply, the MRP system will not suggest replenishment. If the storage bin is empty, it remains empty until production requires the item, when it may be too late to obtain replacement. Software developers have developed MRP systems very well and the logic is quite straightforward.

To develop a very basic MRP, you need:

- A master production schedule with the forecast of products, quantities, and dates for the next few months.
- A bill of material, or a recipe, indicating the quantities of components required to make each product.
- The lead time required to obtain or manufacture all products and materials.
- The quantity to order or the batch size.
- The quantity on hand or the inventory balance.

The master production schedule translates into gross requirements for all materials by period. MRP calculates the net requirements by subtracting current stocks and current on order quantities from the overall gross requirement. The bills of materials control the explosion process. If net requirements are greater than zero, the system plans an order receipt. The system logic offsets the order release from the required order receipt date by the lead time.

Computerised systems are necessary because of the sheer volume of calculations involving materials, supplies, components, purchase orders, and production orders. MRP systems allow production planners to see the planned schedule before the actual release of orders. They can react to changing conditions by expediting, de-expediting, delaying, or cancelling orders, by changing order quantities, by advancing or delaying order due dates, by making changes in the master production schedule, and by changing available capacity.

MRP outputs include planned orders, order release notices, changes in open orders due to rescheduling, and inventory status data. The resulting planned order releases become the detailed production schedules after checking against resource availability for each period. If the capacity is inadequate to meet the schedule, a modified master production schedule drives the MRP program again. This procedure repeats until the master production schedule and available capacity have a reasonable match. This capability reduces inventory, reduces idle time, reduces set-up and teardown costs, increases sales, and provides better customer service and response to market demands.

The theory of MRP is right but the execution falls short. The variables are too great for many organisations to manage. When developed, MRP was a break-through solution, and it worked well with the manufacturing technology and thinking at the time.

However, when lean thinking ideas started to infiltrate manufacturing, the system designers had difficulty merging the longer-term planning push systems of MRP with the shorter-term pull systems of just-in-time (JIT – that eventually became lean thinking). Some users would say that an organisation can have one but not both. Other users would say that MRP solved the longer-term purchasing decisions and JIT facilitated the shorter-term production decisions. JIT provided a very narrow view and lacked the wider systems approach that MRP produced.

MRP depends on demand forecasts to drive the master production schedule, which is one of the prime inputs. MRP uses safety stock to protect against forecast deviation and variability of lead times. It is very easy to upset an MRP system and cause panic and chaos. One simple way is to increase all safety stocks by one unit. Another way is to add five days to all lead times. Final demand is unchanged but both actions create immediate urgent orders for all items affected by changed safety stock and lead time data.

Demand driven material requirements planning (DDMRP)

Demand driven material requirements planning (DDMRP)

Demand driven material requirements planning (DDMRP) is an innovative method to plan materials, enabling an organisation to build more closely to actual market requirements.[13]

DDMRP builds on the strengths of traditional MRP. It takes advantage of the vast technological improvements over the past 60 years, and recognises the consumer demand for shorter lead times and the competitive advantage achievable by delivering to customer demand. It is a blend of material requirements planning, distribution requirements planning, lean thinking, theory of constraints, and innovation[14] as illustrated in Figure 8.6.

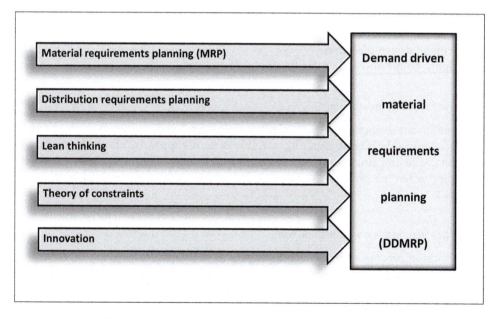

Figure 8.6 Elements leading to DDMRP, adapted from Ptak, C.A., & Smith, C.J. (2011). *Orlicky's material requirements planning* (3rd ed.). New York, NY: McGraw-Hill, p. 388.

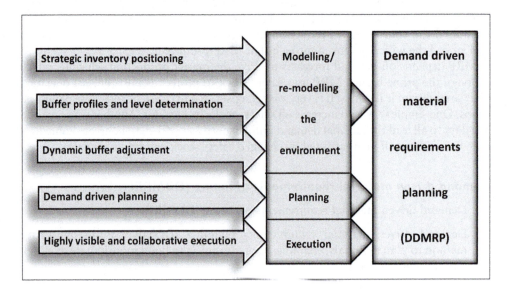

Figure 8.7 Components of DDMRP, adapted from Ptak, C. A., & Smith, C. J. (2011). *Orlicky's material requirements planning* (3rd ed.). New York, NY: McGraw-Hill, p. 390.

The five primary components of DDMRP as illustrated in Figure 8.7 are:

- Strategic inventory positioning.
- Buffer profiles and level determination.
- Dynamic buffer adjustment.
- Demand driven planning.
- Highly visible and collaborative execution.

Strategic inventory positioning

Strategic inventory positioning considers customer tolerance time, market potential lead time, variable rate of demand, variable rate of supply, inventory leverage and flexibility, and the protection of key operational areas. These considerations help determine where to position inventories physically to shorten the lead time to the customer.

Buffer profiles and level determination

With positioning considered, the next step is to determine how much inventory by defining buffer profiles, providing buffer zones, and calculating buffer levels. The buffer profile is a combination of the item type, demand variability, supply variability, lead time, and order policies. DDMRP uses colour codes for the buffer zones for easy visibility. Dark red is a stock-out, red is an alert, yellow identifies items with a reorder already placed, green means that the item is okay and requires no immediate action,

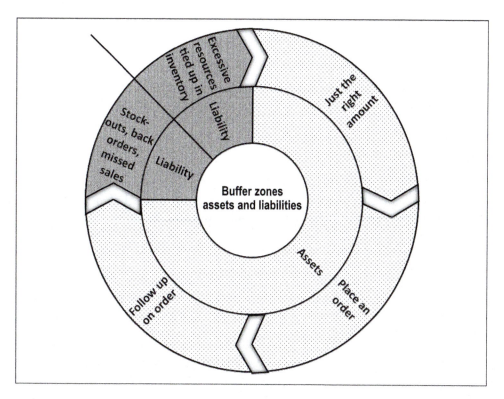

Figure 8.8 Buffer zones with inventory as an asset or a liability, adapted from Ptak, C.A., & Smith, C.J. (2011). *Orlicky's material requirements planning* (3rd ed.). New York, NY: McGraw-Hill, p. 413.

and light blue highlights an overstocked position.[15] Figure 8.8 illustrates these buffer zones.

Dynamic buffer adjustment

The system recalculates buffers based on changing circumstances, either planned or unplanned. Lead times may change when choosing a new supplier, demand variability may change when entering new markets, items and components subject to seasonality may require buffer adjustment, and stock levels may deliberately change. All these situations require buffer recalculation.

Demand driven planning

Demand driven planning processes utilise the power of modern computers to generate, coordinate, and prioritise actionable signals to the planner so that action takes place before it is too late. Planners use flags and alerts incorporating the new rules and calculations for available stock balances when demand and/or supply spikes occur.

This allows planners to see quickly where the signals are coming from and to take appropriate action.

Highly visible and collaborative execution

Traditional MRP suggests purchase orders and manufacturing orders, and hopes that when released they deliver as per their due dates. In most cases, that creates a problem. DDMRP identifies the orders that are placing the whole system at risk by highlighting the items that require attention.

What makes DDMRP different?

DDMRP uses supply chain modelling before generating material plans to determine the optimum places in the supply chain to hold inventory. Traditional MRP assumes that every level in the bill of material holds inventory. Lean thinking, on the other hand, is isolationist and just considers the inventory positioned at the next process in the assembly line.

Traditional MRP uses relatively fixed values for safety stock, and once established it is difficult to change or get rid of them. In many cases, safety stock is dead stock, since a well-running system will plan replenishment before using safety stock. Lean thinking, however, considers all inventories, especially work-in-process inventories, as waste and endeavours to eliminate that waste. DDMRP tries to find the right amount of inventory at the right place in the supply chain to encourage flow and reduce working capital – both are attributes of lean thinking. DDMRP uses critical positioning factors as discussed earlier in this chapter.

Traditional MRP uses two lead time calculations, namely order lead time and cumulative manufacturing lead time. The order lead time is the time required to source a component and assumes it is available. Find the cumulative manufacturing lead time by calculating all the lead times for each bill of material path below the end item and the longest is the cumulative lead time. The cumulative manufacturing lead time is the same (as cumulative lead time) but assumes the purchased items are in stock and none of the sub-assemblies are in stock. DDMRP uses actively synchronised replenishment (ASR) lead time which is a qualified cumulative lead time defined as the longest unprotected/unbuffered sequence in a bill of material where protection is a strategic stocking point.[16]

Actual customer orders with compressed lead times, provided by strategically placed inventories at the semi-finished level and component level, drive DDMRP. Traditional MRP requires an accurate forecast to drive the master production schedule.

DDMRP is both a planning tool and an execution tool. This is quite different from MRP, which is a planning tool, and from lean thinking in its narrowest sense, which is an execution tool.

Other planning and scheduling systems

Manufacturing resource planning (MRP II)

Manufacturing resource planning (MRP II) is a method for the effective planning of all resources of a manufacturing company. Ideally, it addresses operational planning in units, financial planning in dollars, and has a simulation capability to answer **what-if questions.**

Oliver Wight and George Plossl pioneered the concept of manufacturing resource planning (MRP II). This links to MRP but adds all the activities of a manufacturing company, including sales, purchasing, finance, maintenance, design, and engineering.

MRP II plans all the resources of a manufacturing company, including business planning, sales and operations planning, master production scheduling, material requirements planning, capacity requirements planning, and the execution support systems for capacity requirements planning and production. Output of these systems integrates with financial reports, such as the business plan, purchasing commitment plans, logistics budgets, and inventory projections. MRP II is a direct outgrowth and extension of MRP.

Enterprise resource planning (ERP)

Enterprise resource planning (ERP) is a planning and control system that includes all relevant enterprise functions beyond manufacturing, such as distribution, warehousing, and financial management.

Advanced planning and scheduling

Advanced planning and scheduling is a process to analyse and plan logistics and manufacturing over the short-, intermediate-, and long-term periods. It uses advanced mathematical algorithms, or logic, to perform optimisation, or simulation, on finite capacity scheduling, sourcing, capital planning, resource planning, forecasting, demand management, and other aspects of business. These techniques simultaneously consider a range of constraints and business rules to provide real-time planning and scheduling, decision support, and available-to-promise capabilities.

Distribution

Distribution is the activities associated with the movement of material, usually finished goods from the manufacturer to the customer. These activities encompass the functions of transportation, warehousing, inventory control, material handling, order administration, site and location analysis, industrial packaging, and the communications network necessary for effective management.

Flexibility

Flexibility is the ability of the production system to respond quickly in range, volume, and time so it can cope with various forms of uncertainty, such as mix, volume, and so on. The different categories of flexibility are mix, design changeover, modification, volume, re-routing, and material flexibility.

With inventory models, the key questions relate to order quantity, order time, lead time, and time of order receipt. Quantitative analysis becomes complicated and convoluted as analysts attempt to find the optimum time to place the optimum quantity to achieve optimum performance. The complication grows with demand uncertainty. With known demand, the calculations become easier. Lead time uncertainty is another difficulty. When lead time is known and reliable, the calculations become easier.

Set-up is associated with lead time, since for production models there is one set-up required for every production run. Internal and external components comprise set-up. Internal set-up occurs while the production process is stationary. External set-up occurs while the previous production run is still running, or the current run has started.

Flexibility allows a production system to respond to any demand. It does not matter how many set-ups occur when set-up time is zero. The timing of the order placement does not matter when lead time is zero. The order quantity does not matter when suppliers are reliable. When suppliers can supply anything and any quantity, customers demand anything and any quantity. This is flexibility.

Resource planning

Sales and operations planning

Executive sales and operations planning (Exec S&OP)

Executive sales and operations planning (Exec S&OP) is the executive portion of the sales and operations planning set of processes. It is a decision-making activity involving the leader of the organisation, their staff, middle managers, and specialists. Its mission is to balance supply and demand at the aggregate level, to align operational planning with financial planning, and to link strategic planning with day-to-day sales and operational activities.

Sales and operations planning (S&OP)

Sales and operations planning (S&OP) is a business process helping companies keep demand and supply in balance. It focuses on aggregate volumes (product families and groups) to handle mix issues (individual products and customer orders) more readily. It usually occurs on a monthly cycle and displays information in quantity and monetary units. The organisation's strategic plan links to its detailed processes. Used properly, it enables the organisation to view the business holistically and provide a window into the future.

At first sight, these two definitions look very similar. Sales and operations planning is the original term for the business process that helps organisations balance demand and supply. Originally, it did that by focusing on aggregate volumes (product families and groups), but through popular usage this has extended to include the more detailed calculations relating to mix issues (individual products and customer orders). The executive sales and operations planning processes just consider the executive portion.

Sales and operations planning executive leadership[17]

Executive leadership defines the strategic drivers for the whole set of processes. Business strategy, as discussed in Chapter 1, requires clear understanding.

An organisation following a cost leadership strategy emphasises supply elements and endeavours to match demand at the lowest cost. The focus is on volume and cost. To achieve this the organisation responds by improving forecasts, reducing demand variability, and securing long-term, low-cost supply arrangements. Supply chain and finance functions dominate the whole set of processes.

An organisation with a strong strategic marketing emphasis develops sales and operations planning processes around customer retention, market growth, product promotions, and channel development. Marketing, finance, and supply support sales executives as they develop their sales and operations plans. Executive decisions target increasing volumes and revenues, endeavouring to retain customers, and making existing customer accounts more profitable.

An organisation with a strategy based on new product development directs their sales and operations plans towards the timing and introduction of new products. As such, they invest heavily in research and development, and develop a strong marketing function to start trends and influence customer preferences. Executive decisions evaluate market opportunities, market share, and product risk. Supporting processes measure the time to introduce products to market and the proportion of new product revenues compared to total revenues.

Integrated reconciliation[18]

Integrated reconciliation is an iterative process conducted by senior cross-functional teams within the organisation. For many organisations, the team is composed of executives-in-training and the reconciliation process provides a training ground for their development by exposing them to all the decisions that senior executives need to make. The team evaluates the changes that have occurred within the past period and the likely effect those changes might have on the business. The team re-evaluates the basic assumptions for the previous plans and reconciles the differences each function brings to the process.

In traditional sales and operations planning, the integrated reconciliation was the pre-S&OP meeting. It largely focused on volume at the aggregate level and the impact that volume would have on resources. The demand scenario matched the supply response, and the pre-S&OP meeting tried to resolve any differences and prepare an agenda for senior executives to decide at the full sales and operations planning meeting. By its very nature, this process was operational and not strategic.

Integrated reconciliation is strategic rather than operational. It predicts the impact that supply, demand, and new activities might have on the organisation. It attempts to identify emerging issues, gaps, opportunities, and risks. In this process, the finance function plays an integral role by supporting the other functions and considering various scenarios with the desire to make better decisions in the future.

Managing the portfolio of new activities[19]

Early implementations of sales and operations planning considered the introduction of new products and the phasing out of existing products, and the effect these actions had on capacity and supply. Now the emphasis is on activities and processes, rather than on products. This step identifies activities that may have a significant impact on demand and/or supply (volume and value) and related support activities. These activities may originate in one part of the business but influence other parts in a positive or negative way. Executives need to understand and appreciate these seemingly unrelated activities. Management must view all the scenarios and possibilities, and this leads to better prioritisation, resource allocation, and decisions.

Sales and operations planning processes link the organisation's strategic plans and business plan to its detailed processes. Used properly, it enables the organisation's managers to view the business holistically and gives them a window into the future.[20]

Managing demand

The demand management process starts with an unconstrained baseline demand forecast. The sales team captures actual customer demand, regardless of any influencing factors (in other words, unconstrained). The demand capture process involves working collaboratively with end customers to understand the true demand drivers. The process presents demand at an aggregate (or family) level and extends from three months to three years. Typically, an organisation would have between 6 and 12 groups or families.

The sales and marketing functions adjust demand figures based on planned advertising and promotional activity and consider any new product launches, competitive activity, economic conditions, and industry dynamics. While sales and marketing are the functions driving this process, the determination of future demand is a cross-functional activity that considers volume and value. Finance and supply chain have an interest in the forecast. Strategic marketing, research and development, and new product development have a longer-range view.

The process of determining demand is a combination of strategic (long-range view) and tactical (short-range view). The brand and/or markets, not production capability, forms the basis of the product grouping.

Managing supply

The operations and supply chain functions use the demand data from sales and marketing and attempts to balance supply with demand. The mix combines key information, such as the business inventory strategy, production throughput capacity, production constraints, supply chain capacity, and all internal constraints, such as workforce, health and safety, shifts, and so on.

The supply function considers supply attributes on a rough-cut basis that does not consider inventory levels and production lead times. Accuracy, reliability, and consistency of all demand and supply data are critical. The organisation can and will deliver the agreed supply value. This analysis may identify demand exceeding delivery capability, or supply that exceeds demand. Data used to identify supply constraints must represent reality and provide some credibility to the decisions made in subsequent planning meetings. Demand, supply, financial, new product development, and performance measurement data must be consistent and accurate to maintain the integrity of the entire process.

Monthly integration

The integration of demand and supply chain functions is an iterative process with regularly scheduled formal meetings (monthly or more often if required) to develop the final operating plan for the following periods. This team meeting includes sales and marketing (demand management and forecasting), operations (purchasing, inventory management, supply chain, operations, master production scheduling, warehousing, and transport), new product development, and finance. It is a cross-functional team meeting.

Sales and operations planning sets the volume of production required to meet demand, and subsequent steps disseminate the volume figures into specific product, quantity, and date. Discussion on various scenarios continues until agreement on the final volume plan. When agreement is beyond reach, the planning meeting documents the issues, researches the options, and presents these for senior management to resolve.

Upon agreement, the operations, supply chain, and sales functions perform detailed planning on both demand and supply numbers. A mature planning process highlights potential issues and constraints and communicates collaboratively with customers and suppliers. This allows external parties full visibility of the confirmed plan so they can plan more accurately.

Final sign-off

A formal meeting signs off the plan, usually towards the end of the planning month. All functions attend and sign off on the plan for the next period. Moreover, the signing process is indicative that they are prepared to deliver precisely to that plan. Often this step carries the connotation 'signed with blood', and, because of this, senior executives should champion the whole process to ensure it maintains the correct focus.

Review and continuous improvement

The results and effectiveness of the sales and operations planning process needs performance measurement to allow all functions to better understand how the process is working and identify areas for improvement.

Measurements for the supply-planning teams include inventory on hand, obsolete inventory, inventory stock-outs, schedule changes, frequency of expediting, quality, and capacity utilisation. Measures vary between industry and product families. Sales measurements include sales growth, market share, and forecast accuracy, while finance measurements include market share, sales dollars, share price, and return on capital invested. The organisation derives internal and external benchmarks to measure progress.

Organisations often struggle to implement sales and operations planning processes due to the need to develop new business processes, the need to develop a new internal collaborative culture, and a breaking down of functional, isolating silos. When developed, the model needs continuous improvement to incorporate gradual changes in understanding the process and appreciating the requirements.

This framework moves from the silo-driven to event-driven collaboration, and the organisation moves from limited integration to a seamlessly integrated organisation that focuses on company profit optimisation rather than using a cost/profit-centre approach.

Scheduling

Scheduling

Scheduling is the assignment of priorities to customers and/or production orders, and the allocation of work to specific work centres and/or resources.

Rate-based scheduling

Rate-based scheduling is a method for scheduling and producing based on a rate per period. High-volume process industries use this method when basing schedules on, for example, tonnes per day.

The objective of operations scheduling is to meet customer delivery promise dates. Inherent in this objective is the need to minimise lead times, set-up time, work-in-process inventory, and use of resources.

Scheduling and controlling involves the dynamic interaction of a constantly changing variety of jobs that are usually competing for the same resources. Many random variables – such as differences in materials, skills, attitudes, and machine breakdowns – influence performance. Schedulers could use several criteria, and some are mutually conflicting.

A schedule is a timetable for performing activities, utilising resources, or allocating facilities. The purpose of scheduling is to disaggregate the general production plan into time-phased weekly, daily, or hourly activities. The schedule should efficiently perform functions such as establishing job priorities, initiating the scheduled work, following up, expediting orders, and revising the schedule to reflect changes in order status.

The variables of the scheduling problem to resolve are:

- Number and volumes of products to make.
- Number and variety of available processes.
- Number and skill level of available process workers.
- Production flow pattern.
- Priority rules for selecting which product to produce first.

The scheduling evaluation process considers the following criteria:

- Meeting promised customer due dates.
- Minimising throughput time (the time from the start of the first process until the end of the last process).
- Minimising work in process inventory.
- Effective use of processes.

The scheduling problem in service organisations concentrates on staffing levels and scheduling each work period.

Process industries

Process industry

Process industry produces products by mixing, separating, forming, and/or performing chemical processes. Dairy production, pulp and paper, refineries, and chemical plants are examples of process industries.

Process flow scheduling[21]

Process flow scheduling is a method for developing a production schedule using the process structure as a guide. This is suitable in process industries.

Process train

A process train is a representation of the flow of materials through production systems showing equipment and inventories. A process unit identifies a piece of equipment that performs a basic manufacturing function, such as mixing, blending, or packaging. Process units combine into stages, and stages combine into process trains. Inventories decouple the scheduling of sequential stages within a process train.

Material-dominated scheduling

Material-dominated scheduling is a technique that schedules materials before equipment or capacity. This aids the efficient use of materials.

Processor-dominated scheduling

Processor-dominated scheduling is a technique that schedules the process before the materials.

Forward-flow scheduling

Forward-flow scheduling builds process trains that start with scheduling the first stage and progress towards scheduling the last stage.

Mixed-flow scheduling

Mixed-flow scheduling is a procedure used in some process industries for building process train schedules that start at an initial stage and work towards the terminal process stage. This is effective for scheduling where several bottleneck stages may exist.

Reverse-flow scheduling

Reverse-flow scheduling is the procedure of building process trains that start with scheduling the last stage and progress against the flow to the first stage.

Campaign

A campaign is a series of batches of the same or similar products run as a sequence. The campaign cycle includes the full range of products.

Process flow scheduling is applicable in manufacturing units where:

- All products have similar routings, leading to a flow of material through a series of process stages.
- The scheduling of production often meets forecast demand rather than individual customer orders.
- Production is authorised by production schedules – not works orders.

The principles of process flow scheduling are:

- The process structure guides the scheduling calculations.
- Processor-dominated or material-dominated approaches schedule the stages/clusters.
- Forward-flow, mixed-flow, or reverse-flow scheduling methods schedule the process trains.

Theory of constraints

Theory of constraints

The theory of constraints is a philosophy of continuous improvement based on the premise that constraints determine the performance of any system. It has three interrelated parts:

- Performance measurement includes throughput, inventory, and operating expense, and the five focusing steps.
- Logical thinking process tools aim to identify the root problem (current reality tree), identify and expand solutions (evaporating clouds and future reality tree), and develop implementation plans (prerequisite tree, transition tree, and future reality tree).
- Logistics includes drum-buffer-rope scheduling.

Bottleneck

A bottleneck is an operation, resource, function, or facility having insufficient capacity to meet demand.

Constraint

A constraint is any resource lack preventing the system from achieving continuously higher levels of performance.

Capacity-constrained resource

A capacity-constrained resource is a resource that is not a constraint but can become a constraint unless scheduled carefully.

Throughput-based constraint

A throughput-based constraint is an internal physical constraint that directly affects the ability of an organisation to achieve its goals.

Behaviour-based constraint

A behaviour-based constraint is a non-physical constraint and includes the entire system of procedures, measurements, and even the mindset that governs the strategic, tactical, and operational (day-to-day) decisions of the organisation.

Eliyahu Goldratt and Jeff Cox introduced the theory of constraints in the 1984 book, *The Goal: Excellence in Manufacturing*. This textbook is a novel about creating and accepting improvements, making continuous progress, and changing for the better.[22]

Bottleneck processes hold up production and are usually easy to identify because a queue forms in front of them. Chapter 4 discussed the design of processes, and Chapter 5 discussed the improvement of processes. The concept of flow is the fundamental idea underlying these two chapters. When a process is flowing, it processes the inputs as they arrive, and it delivers the outputs to customers, as they demand them. It would be marvellous when this happens.

Every process has inherent variability, and any calculations based entirely on averages will be incorrect on average.[23] Organisations should consider process variation when contemplating process flow. One process step may operate slightly faster and another may operate slightly slower. That is within the bounds of expected normal variation. Eventually, a bottleneck develops as a process with insufficient capacity fails to cope with demand; it is slower than other processes. When other processes get behind, they can catch up because they are faster. However, the slowest process can never catch up because it is the slowest. The bottleneck becomes the constraint limiting system performance. Total output can never exceed the average output from the constraint over the long term.

A non-bottleneck is a resource whose capacity is greater than the demand placed upon it and contains idle time. A capacity-constrained resource is one whose utilisation is close to capacity and could become a bottleneck if not scheduled carefully. The theory of constraints emphasises the need to identify and manage constraints within the production system, the organisation itself, or the network of supply and distribution activities. A throughput-based constraint is an internal physical constraint that directly affects the ability of an organisation to achieve its goals. A behaviour-based constraint is a non-physical constraint and includes the entire system of procedures and measurements and even the mindset that governs the strategic, tactical, and operational (day-to-day) decisions of the organisation.

Both types of constraint could emerge in the marketplace, the engineering system, or inside the supplier's functions. The constraints limit output. Common constraints involve machines and people. Each machine can produce a volume of output (capacity) and people can deliver an amount of work (their capacity). When these capacities are insufficient to meet demand, they become either constraints or capacity-constrained resources.

Information and communications technology may create constraints if the order-entry process takes longer to process an order than the transformation system needs to produce the product or deliver the service.

Effective planning and management of capacity-constrained resources uses realistic production goals that consider capacity constraints. Production plans, master production schedules, and all other plans should focus on bottleneck activities since these limit system outputs. Unrealistic demands on bottleneck resources create unrealistic demands and expectations on the entire system. Operations managers should adapt workflows to encourage effective use of capacity-constrained resources.

Performance measurement

Throughput

Throughput is the rate at which the system generates goal units. Because throughput is a rate, organisations always express it for a given period (month, week, day, or even minute). If the goal units are money, throughput will be the amount of money per period. In that case, the calculation for throughput is revenues minus variable costs divided by the chosen period.

Inventory

Inventory is all the money currently tied up in the system. It includes the equipment, fixtures, and buildings the system owns – as well as inventory in the form of raw materials, work in process, and finished goods.

Operating expense

Operating expense is the money spent in converting inventory to throughput.

Goldratt and Cox explain that the goal of the firm is to make money by:

- Increasing throughput, which is the rate at which sales generates money.
- Reducing inventory, which is the money spent on buying items for subsequent sale.
- Reducing operating expense, which is the money spent to convert inventory into throughput.[24]

Traditionally, management emphasises reducing operating expense and reducing inventory. Organisations take pride in proclaiming they are on a 'cost-cutting drive'. They target opportunities to cut expenses and reduce inventory. Expenses are easy to cut when the organisation stops spending money. Likewise, inventory is easy to reduce when the organisation stops replenishing supplies.

What happens when the organisation reaches zero operating expenses and/or zero inventories? Managers argue that they will not actually reach zero and they will stop before they reach that limit. However, they do not know where, when, or how to stop. They just say, 'Reduce operating expenses and inventory!' The finite limit is zero. What kind of business exists when operating expenses are zero and/or inventories are zero?

There is no finite limit to increasing throughput, which is the rate at which sales generates money (goal units). Having raw materials sitting in the yard does not make the manufacturer successful. Having products sitting in a warehouse does not make a business profitable. Having products sitting on the shelf in a retail store does not make the retailer wealthy. The only way to get rich, according to Goldratt and Cox, is to make products, sell them, receive payment for them, and make sure the amount received exceeds the amount spent on inventory and operating expenses.

The theory of constraints requires the entire production process to work together to achieve the goals of the firm. Measurement systems should encourage the increase in net profits, return on investment, and cash flow. Organisations can achieve this when, at the operations level, they recognise and reward performance based on the amount of throughput, inventory, and operating expense created.

Logical thinking process

Five focusing steps

Five focusing steps is a process that evaluates a system and seeks to improve its performance by following these steps:

1   Identify the system's constraint(s).
2   Decide how to exploit the system's constraint(s).
3   Subordinate everything else to the decision made in step 2.
4   Elevate the system's constraint(s).
5   If a previous step breaks the constraint, return to step 1. Do not let inertia cause a system constraint.

Current reality tree

The current reality tree is a logic-based tool for using cause-and-effect relationships to determine the root cause of problems. It is a similar concept to root cause analysis.

Evaporating cloud

The evaporating cloud is a logic-based tool for isolating assumptions related to a conflict, or a problem. Once the assumptions are isolated, actions to break an assumption and solve (evaporate) the problem can be determined.

Future reality tree

The future reality tree is a logic-based tool for building and testing potential solutions before implementation.

Prerequisite tree

The prerequisite tree is a logic-based tool for determining the obstacles that might block the implementation of a problem solution or an idea.

Transition tree

The transition tree is a logic-based tool for identifying and sequencing actions to accomplish an objective. The transitions represent the stages in moving from the present situation to the desired objective.

Undesirable effect

An undesirable effect is the negative effects of a current system or of a planned change.

The five focusing steps form the basis for continuous improvement. Constraints are always present, and it is not feasible to imagine a system without any constraints since that would suggest infinite performance. The five focusing steps focus on the constraint.

The theory of constraints thinking process focuses on the factors currently preventing the system from achieving its goals. It starts by identifying the core problem (current reality tree) and endeavours to gain an understanding of the conflict that underlies the core problem (evaporating cloud). It tests the effectiveness of the proposed solution (future reality tree) and implements the solution (prerequisite tree and transition tree).

Logistics including drum-buffer-rope scheduling

Drum-buffer-rope

Drum-buffer-rope is a finite scheduling process that balances the flow of the system. The drum is a system constraint or other critical resource that sets the pace that drives the rest of the schedule. Buffers are work-in-process inventories maintained just in front of the resource. The ropes are schedules that tie the release of raw materials and customer promise dates to the production at the drum.

Constraint buffer

A constraint buffer is the amount of inventory placed in front of a constraint.

Time buffer

A time buffer is the time gap between material release and requirements.

A drum at the bottleneck controls production. This is a figurative term because the drum strikes the beat for the rest of the system. All parts of the process influenced by the drum respond to the drumbeat. If there is no bottleneck, then the drum is located at a capacity-constrained resource.

Two things happen at the drum:

- A scheduler places a buffer inventory (or time buffer) in front of the bottleneck or capacity-constrained resource to make sure it never runs out of work. If it does run out of work, it will never catch up, so it should always have something to work on.
- A scheduler establishes a rope (or communication link) upstream to the material release point to release new work to the system at the rate it is passing through the bottleneck or capacity-constrained resource. It releases work to the beat of the drum.

The buffer decouples, or eliminates, direct dependencies between resources. A time buffer creates a physical amount of stock that is enough to last for an order delivery period. A constraint buffer placed immediately before the constraint makes sure the constraint does not run out of work. An assembly buffer uses non-constraint parts before an assembly to make any required assembly. A shipping buffer placed immediately before shipping absorbs disruptions that could delay shipment.

Figure 8.9 is an example of drum-buffer-rope operating with a time buffer. As drawn, this buffer is also a shipping buffer placed just in front of distribution and would be enough to cope with demand variation and the lead time for replenishment. As product leaves the system and enters distribution, the rope sends the signal back to the start of the process to initiate replenishment.

Figure 8.10 is an example of drum-buffer-rope operating with a constraint buffer. The buffer, placed just in front of the bottleneck (or a capacity-constrained resource), is enough to keep the bottleneck operating during any possible delay in the supplying processes. A rope connects the bottleneck resource to the start of the production process. This prevents inventory building up. The rope can be formal, such as a schedule,

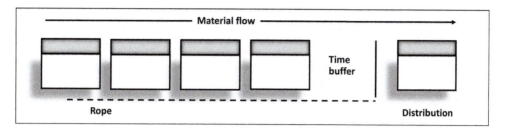

Figure 8.9 Drum-buffer-rope using a time buffer

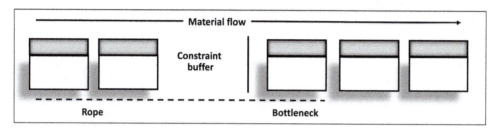

Figure 8.10 Drum-buffer-rope using a constraint buffer

or informal, such as a daily discussion. The scheduler looks at past performances and calculates statistically the required buffer size.

Sometimes the drum is the capacity-constrained resource and this requires two buffers. The capacity-constrained resource has one buffer placed in front of it and finished goods receive the other. The finished goods inventory protects the market and the time buffer in front of the capacity-constrained resource protects throughput. Figure 8.11 illustrates this use of buffers. The two buffers need two ropes. One communicates from finished goods inventory back to the drum to increase or decrease output. The other travels from the drum back to the start of the process, specifying the material requirement.

Larger batch sizes require fewer set-ups and therefore can generate more processing time and more output. For bottleneck resources, larger batch sizes are desirable. For non-bottleneck resources, smaller batch sizes are possible (by using up the existing idle time), thereby reducing work-in-process inventory.

The transfer batch is the quantity of material moved from one process to the next process. This might be a pallet, a carton, or a truckload. A process batch is the production lot size and is the total quantity produced. This quantity is determined by customer requirements, the size of the machine, the size of input or output containers, or the quantity that one shift can produce. Transfer batches refer to the movement of a part of the process batch. Rather than wait for the entire process batch to finish, work that has completed an operation can move to the next downstream work station so it can begin working. The use of transfer batches reduces lead time and work-in-process inventory.

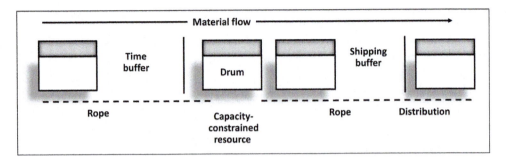

Figure 8.11 Drum-buffer-rope using a constraint and a time buffer

Scheduling using theory of constraints

Activation

Activation is the use of unconstrained resources to make parts or products above the level needed to support the system constraint(s), resulting in excessive work-in-process inventories, or finished goods inventories, or both.

Utilisation

Utilisation, in the theory of constraints, is the ratio of the required time to support the constraint to the time available for the resource, expressed as a percentage.

Decouple

Decouple is to create independence between supply and use of material. Usually it means providing inventory between two process steps so they can each operate at slightly different, or fluctuating, rates without causing disruption to flow.

Safety capacity

Safety capacity is the planned amount by which the available capacity exceeds current productive capacity.

The theory of constraints differentiates utilisation of a resource from mere activation. Activating a resource allows it to produce outputs just to keep it busy. Activation occurs when production runs are longer than necessary and when idle machines start and produce outputs not actually required.

In contrast, utilising uses a resource to produce outputs required to support bottlenecks or are the result of a bottleneck process. These outputs contribute to throughput (generating goal units or money from sales) and corporate performance.

Utilisation is a strange term for many organisations that use a cost-based mentality to manage and measure production. Executives of these organisations set utilisation targets and provide bonuses to employees to recognise achievement of these targets. The utilisation may, for example, be 90%, which means they expect the machine to run for 90% of the available time. Employees wanting to receive the bonus adjust their behaviour to make sure the machine is working and producing outputs. Night-shift operators are notorious for following these guidelines. When employees reach their production quantities and the end of their shift approaches, it is a much easier option to just keep going and get the morning shift to stop and set up for the next product. This is activation, not utilisation.

Executives may place volume targets on employees and production processes because they believe the capital investment is most efficient when it is being utilised. Using the theory of constraints, output that exceeds actual requirements activates the process and does not utilise it.

To use capacity-constrained resources effectively, operations managers should rethink how they determine lot sizes and production schedules. They should run the largest possible process batch at the bottleneck resource to reduce non-productive set-up. In contrast, they should run small batches at non-bottleneck resources to meet their primary roles of feeding steady flows of inputs to support continuous operations at bottlenecks. Small batches with frequent set-ups consume significant capacity, but this lost capacity should not affect overall system output (throughput) because non-bottlenecks have excess capacity. The bottleneck resource determines overall system performance.

Operating guidelines

Some operating guidelines that develop from the theory of constraints include:

- Balance the material flow through the factory, rather than the capacity. Processes are subject to disruption, such as machine breakdown, operator absence, accidents, and defects. Variables can accumulate and lead to increased delays. Concentrate on developing a flow of material rather than trying to keep every process busy.
- An hour lost at a bottleneck is an hour lost forever. An hour lost at a bottleneck is an hour lost to the entire system since it can never catch up. An hour lost at a non-bottleneck can catch up since the non-bottleneck is faster than the bottleneck.
- Time at a bottleneck resource has a negligible marginal value.
- Utilisation at a non-bottleneck depends on some other constraint(s) within the system.
- Bottlenecks govern throughput, inventory, and quality.
- Utilise resources and do not simply activate them. Utilisation occurs when a production unit contributes to throughput; activation does not contribute to throughput.
- Allow processing batch sizes to vary along an order's route and over time. Lot sizes should be variable and not fixed. Lot sizes are a function of the schedule, and thus should vary over time and from one operation to the next. When different machines manufacture different components, the lot size should vary to achieve a smooth and timely flow of products to the customer.
- Production schedules should accommodate all constraints simultaneously.
- Lead times result from scheduled sequences, so planners cannot determine them in advance. Lead times are usually determined before making the product and communicated to the customer in advance. Organisations establish lead times as fixed periods and customers accept them as fixed periods. Material requirements planning makes plans based on predetermined fixed lead times. The theory of

constraints requires established schedules with known system constraints, and this suggests that perhaps, by adjusting the schedule, organisations can improve client lead times in the supply chain.

Chapter summary

The correct amount of inventory is enough to satisfy customer demand. The cost of having inventory needs to balance against the cost of not having it.

Inventory costs money, so when an organisation obtains more inventory it costs them more money. If they obtain a lot more inventory, it costs them a lot more money. That inventory investment is unavailable for any other purpose.

Inventory hides problems, requires storage places to hold it, slows down the speed of production, encourages obsolescence, may require special handling conditions, and may be hazardous to store. Inventory managers may initiate processes to count inventory, to administer it, to manage it, and they may insure it against loss. These actions take up time and money for the people involved.

Demand uncertainty is the main reason for holding inventory. Safety stocks provide some level of protection against stock-outs. The service level allows stock on hand (including safety stock) to meet a specified percentage of total demand.

The fixed reorder quantity model suggests a predetermined constant order quantity whenever the number of units on hand reaches a specified order point. The fixed reorder cycle model suggests an order quantity to bring the inventory up to a predetermined level at the end of a specified period.

Sales and operations planning is a business process helping organisations keep demand and supply in balance by focusing on aggregate volumes (product families and groups).

Material requirements planning is a set of techniques using bills of material, inventory data, and the master production schedule to calculate the requirements of component materials. DDMRP builds on the strengths of traditional MRP, taking advantage of the vast technology improvements over the past 60 years, and recognising the consumer demand for shorter lead times and the competitive advantage achievable by delivering to customer demand. It is a blend of material requirements planning, distribution requirements planning, lean thinking, theory of constraints, and innovation.

The theory of constraints is a philosophy of continuous improvement based on the premise that constraints determine the performance of any system. It has three interrelated parts: Performance measurement, logical thinking process tools, and logistics.

Drum-buffer-rope is a finite scheduling process that balances the flow of the system. The drum is a system constraint or other critical resource that sets the pace that drives the rest of the schedule. Buffers are work-in-process inventories maintained just in front of the resource. The ropes are schedules that tie the release of raw materials and customer promise dates to the production at the drum.

Discussion questions

1 Explain the difference between MRP and MRP II.
2 Explain the sales and operations planning process.
3 Discuss the mathematics involved with the newsvendor model.

4 Explain the difference between a fixed-order quantity and a periodic review system.
5 Explain why the economic order quantity is no longer appropriate.
6 What makes DDMRP different from traditional MRP?
7 Explain the concept of strategic inventory positioning.
8 Explain the difference between executive sales and operations planning and sales and operations planning.
9 Explain the theory of constraints focusing system.
10 Explain how drum-buffer-rope works.
11 Explain the difference between a capacity-constrained resource and a bottleneck.
12 Explain why an organisation might carry safety stock.
13 Explain throughput, inventory, and operating expense in the context of the theory of constraints.
14 Performance measurement in the theory of constraints (throughput, inventory, and operating expense) conflicts with traditional accounting systems. Explain those conflicts.
15 Explain why process industries require process flow scheduling.

Key terms

activation, 296
advanced planning and scheduling, 283
behaviour-based constraint, 290
bill of material, 276
bill of resources, 276
BOM. *See* bill of material
bottleneck, 290
campaign, 289
capacity-constrained resource, 290
carrying cost, 268
constraint, 290
constraint buffer, 294
current reality tree, 293
DDMRP. *See* demand driven material requirements planning
decouple, 296
demand driven material requirements planning, 279
distribution, 283
drum-buffer-rope, 294
economic order quantity (EOQ), 268
enterprise resource planning, 283
EOQ. *See* economic order quantity
ERP. *See* enterprise resource planning
evaporating cloud, 293
Exec S&OP. *See* executive sales and operations planning

executive sales and operations planning, 284
finished goods, 258
five focusing steps, 292
fixed order quantity, 266
fixed reorder cycle model, 270
fixed reorder quantity model, 267
flexibility, 283
forward-flow scheduling, 289
future reality tree, 293
gross requirement, 276
inventory, 258, 292
inventory management, 258
lead time, 264
manufacturing resource planning, 282
master production schedule, 276
material requirements planning, 276
material-dominated scheduling, 289
mixed-flow scheduling, 289
MPS. *See* master production schedule
MRP. *See* material requirements planning
MRP II. *See* manufacturing resource planning
net requirement, 276
newsvendor problem, 271
operating expense, 292

order point, 266
ordering cost, 267
planned order, 277
planned order receipt, 277
planned order release, 277
prerequisite tree, 293
process flow scheduling, 289
process industry, 288
process train, 289
processor-dominated scheduling, 289
push system, 277
quantity per, 277
rate-based scheduling, 288
raw material, 258
reverse-flow scheduling, 289
S&OP. *See* sales and operations planning
safety capacity, 296
safety lead time, 264

sales and operations planning, 284
scheduled receipt, 277
scheduling, 288
service level, 264
set-up cost, 268
set-up time, 268
supplier lead time, 264
target inventory level, 270
teardown time, 268
theory of constraints, 290
throughput, 291
throughput-based constraint, 290
time buffer, 294
transition tree, 293
undesirable effects, 293
utilisation, 296
WIP. *See* work-in-process
work-in-process, 258

Notes

1 Perspective written with material available on Fonterra Co-Operative Group website and valuable inputs from Fonterra Communications. Fonterra Co-operative Group (n.d.). Retrieved from www.fonterra.com/

2 Fonterra Co-Operative Group. (2018). *Fonterra annual report 2018*, p. 50. Retrieved from https://view.publitas.com/fonterra/https-view-publitas-com-fonterra-fonterra-annual-review-2018/page/54-55

3 Fonterra Co-Operative Group. (2018, July 31). *Fonterra sustainability report 2018*, p. 16. Retrieved from https://view.publitas.com/fonterra/sustainability-report-2018/page/18-19

4 Tip Top to join Froneri global family. (2019, May 13). [Press release]. Retrieved from www.fonterra.com/nz/en/our-stories/media/tip-top-to-join-froneri-global-family.html

5 Fonterra Co-Operative Group. (2018). *Litchfield: Investing in new technologies*. Retrieved from www.fonterra.com/nz/en/what-we-stand-for/innovation.html

6 Fonterra Co-Operative Group. (2016, December 2). Fonterra officially opens world's joint largest milk powder dryer at Lichfield [Press release]. Retrieved from www.fonterra.com/nz/en/our-stories/media/fonterra-officially-opens-worlds-joint-largest-milk-powder-dryer-at-lichfield.html

7 Fonterra Co-Operative Group. (2014, September 4). A little piece of Clandeboye in half a billion pizzas [Press release]. Retrieved from www.fonterra.com/nz/en/our-stories/media/a-little-piece-of-clandeboye-in-half-a-billion-pizzas.html

8 Attributed to Benjamin Franklin. (1758, June). *The complete poor Richard's almanacks*. Philadelphia, PA: Benjamin Franklin.

9 Ptak, C. A., & Smith, C. J. (2011). *Material requirements planning* (3rd ed.). New York, NY: McGraw-Hill, p. 61.

10 Harris, F. W. (1913). How many parts to make at once. *Factory: The Magazine of Management*, 10(2), 135–136, 152, cited inHopp, W. J., & Spearman, M. L. (2008). *Factory physics* (3rd ed.). New York, NY: McGraw-Hill Irwin, p. 50.

11 Hopp, W. J., & Spearman, M. L. (2008). *Factory physics* (3rd ed.). New York, NY: McGraw-Hill Irwin, p. 54.

12 Orlicky, J. (1975). *Material requirements planning: The new way of life in production and inventory management*. New York, NY: McGraw-Hill, p. ix.

13 Ptak, C. A., & Smith, C. J. (2011). *Op. cit.*, p. 502.

14 *Ibid.*, p. 388.
15 *Ibid.*, p. 412.
16 *Ibid.*, p. 501.
17 *Ibid.*, p. 347.
18 *Ibid.*, p. 336.
19 *Ibid.*, p. 337.
20 Wallace, T. F. (2008). *Sales and operations planning: The how-to handbook*. Cincinnati, OH: T. F. Wallace & Company, p. 7.
21 Taylor, S. G., & Bolander, S. F. (1994). *Process flow scheduling: A scheduling systems framework for flow manufacturing*. Falls Church, VA: APICS.
22 Goldratt, E. M., & Cox, J. (1984). *The goal: Excellence in manufacturing*. Croton-on-Hudson, NY: North River Press is the original publication. A more recent edition is Goldratt, E. M., & Cox, J. (2004). *The goal: A process of ongoing improvement* (3rd ed.). Great Barrington, MA: North River Press.
23 In Chapter 4 we discussed Sam Savage's book (2009). *The flaw of averages: Why we underestimate risk in the face of uncertainty*. Hoboken, NJ: John Wiley & Sons.
24 Goldratt, E. M., & Cox, J. (1984). *Op. cit.*

Additional reading on inventory and resource planning

Goldratt, E. M., & Cox, J. (2004). *The goal: A process of ongoing improvement* (3rd ed.). Great Barrington, MA: North River Press.

Hopp, W. J., & Spearman, M. L. (2008). *Factory physics* (3rd ed.). New York, NY: McGraw-Hill Irwin.

Orlicky, J. (1975). *Material requirements planning: The new way of life in production and inventory management*. New York, NY: McGraw-Hill.

Pittman, P. H., & Atwater, J. B. (2016). *APICS dictionary* (15th ed.). Chicago, IL: APICS.

Ptak, C. A., & Smith, C. J. (2011). *Material requirements planning* (3rd ed.). New York, NY: McGraw-Hill.

Ptak, C. A., & Smith, C. J. (2016). *Demand driven material requirements planning (DDMRP)*. South Norwalk, CT: Industrial Press, Inc.

Wallace, T. F. (2008). *Sales and operations planning: The how-to handbook*. Cincinnati, OH: T. F. Wallace & Company.

Wallace, T. F. (2011). *Sales and operations planning: Beyond the basics*. Cincinnati, OH: T. F. Wallace & Company.

Wallace, T. F., & Stahl, R. A. (2006). *Sales and operations planning: The executive guide*. Cincinnati, OH: T. F. Wallace & Company.

Chapter 9

Collaborative supply chains

Learning objectives

At the end of this chapter, you should be able to:

- Define supply chain management from a strategic view.
- Discuss the bullwhip effect or demand amplification.
- Define collaborative supply chains.
- Discuss the strategic role of inventory in supply chains.
- Explain the triple-A approach to supply chains.
- Discuss the concept of demand chains.
- Discuss efficient consumer response.
- Identify the role of information technology in supply chains.
- Discuss vendor-managed inventory and joint replenishment.
- Argue the case for multiple suppliers and single suppliers.
- Discuss the criteria for supplier selection.
- Discuss supply chain system metrics and inventory system metrics.

Perspective: Weta Group – the creative art of motion pictures

A common observation from people who work in service-oriented companies suggests that supply chain management does not apply to them. Manufacturing companies embrace supply chain management and service companies are different. By way of contrast, we present an example of concepts, ideas, and digital animation in the movie industry to illustrate that service companies do have supply chains to manage.

The British Academy of Film and Television Arts have presented eight BAFTA awards and the Academy of Motion Picture Arts and Sciences have presented ten Academy Awards®[1] to staff from the Weta Group of Companies since 2002. Twelve of those awards were for visual effects.

The Weta Group of Companies incorporates Weta Workshop, Weta Digital, Park Road Post, and Stone Street Studios, all located conveniently within a few minutes of each other in a central suburb of Wellington, the capital city of New Zealand. The group provides ground-breaking conceptual ideas and design for the entertainment and creative industries with a focus on film, television, gaming, digital assets, and themed environments.

This collective community, a heart of filmmaking and creativity, works together to provide a comprehensive range of design studio services including scene illustrations and environments, design, fantasy armour and costumes, weapons, character and creature design, special make-up effects, miniatures, specialty costumes, props, and prosthetics. Additionally, they have the capability to manufacture any genre of armour and costume from a single outfit to equipping entire armies using traditional handcraft skills and innovative hi-tech 3D milling, printing, and laser-cutting technologies.[2]

Weta Digital specialises in digital animation, motion capture, and crowd generation. The early Academy Awards® and BAFTA Awards recognised the birth of motion-capture, a digital technique allowing an actor to dance, move, and exert physical energy while the computer technology captures every physical gesture and detail (such as an eye flutter, or a wry smile) and presents each and every movement as a digital animation of the character being portrayed. For instance, in *The Lord of the Rings* trilogy, Andy Serkis, an English actor and film director, played Gollum, a creature deformed and twisted in body and mind and with a disgusting gurgling choking cough. When the filming of the trilogy had finished, Andy Serkis played Kong, a giant movie monster resembling a gorilla, in the 2005 movie *King Kong*. What a contrast of characters – all made feasible with digital animation.[3]

In this chapter, we will define supply chain management as the design, planning, execution, control, and monitoring of supply chain activities, with the objective of creating net value, building a competitive infrastructure, leveraging worldwide logistics, synchronising supply and demand, and measuring performance globally. This definition is easy to visualise for a global manufacturing company and much harder to envisage for a service company. However, this definition encompasses, in a unique manner, the creative activities of motion pictures.

The *Lord of the Rings* trilogy (Director – Peter Jackson, 2001–2003) project lasted seven years and featured design, armour, weapons, creatures, special make-up effects, and miniatures created at Weta Workshop. *Avatar* (Director – James Cameron, 2009) combined design, weapons, specialty costumes, and props. *The Hobbit* trilogy (Director – Peter Jackson, 2012–2014) employed design, creatures, costumes, armour, weapons, special make-up effects, and prosthetics. More recently, Weta Workshop created about 5000 pieces of artwork and practical effects, ranging from intricate prosthetics and animatronics through to props, miniatures, and specialty costumes to simulate the cybernetic world for *Ghost in the Shell* (Director – Rupert Sanders, 2017). Weta Workshop integrated practical miniatures, selected cinematography, and concept design work for *Blade Runner 2049* (Director – Denis Villeneuve, 2017). The Workshop's 3D, costume, and props departments collaborated to manufacture a series of armour suits and costumes for *Thor: Ragnarok* (Director – Taika Waititi, 2017). *Pacific Rim Uprising* (Director – Steven S. DeKnight, 2018) features creature design and sci-fi suits produced by the crew of Weta Workshop.

Now, review the definition for supply chain management against the backdrop of the Weta Group of Companies. They design, plan, execute, control, and monitor activities with the objective of creating net value, building a competitive infrastructure, leveraging worldwide logistics, synchronising supply and demand, and measuring performance globally. All departments – 3D modelling, costume and leatherworking, digital animation, electronics and animatronics, engineering and metal shop, hair, imaging, make-up, prosthetics and creatures, smithy, sculpting, weapons, miniatures, model-making and props, moulding, and paint shop – every one of them is contributing to the overall success of the product – the finished movie.

This example clearly demonstrates how creative arts play an important role in the supply chain for major international movie productions. Manufacturing and service components of the supply chain need to work in harmony to achieve the desired outputs and create a sustainable business model. The following achievements exemplify this sentiment:

In 2002, *The Lord of the Rings: The Fellowship of the Ring* received two BAFTA Awards – Achievement for Special Visual Effects and Best Makeup and Hair[4] as well as three Academy Award® – Best Visual Effects, Best Costume Design, and Best Makeup.[5]

In 2003, *The Lord of the Rings: The Two Towers* received two BAFTA Awards – Achievement for Special Visual Effects and Best Costume Design[6] and the Academy Award® – Best Visual Effects.[7]

In 2004, *The Lord of the Rings: The Return of the King* received the BAFTA Achievement for Special Visual Effects[8] and three Academy Awards® – Best Visual Effects, Best Costume Design, and Best Makeup.[9]

In 2006, *King Kong* received the BAFTA Achievement for Special Visual Effects[10] and the Academy Award® – Best Visual Effects.[11]

In 2010, *Avatar* received the BAFTA Achievement for Special Visual Effects[12] and the Academy Award® – Best Visual Effects.[13]

In 2017, *The Jungle Book* received the BAFTA Special Visual Effects[14] and the Academy Award® – Best Visual Effects.[15]

Introduction

Supply chain management has changed significantly in recent years and several noticeable changes are evident. Underlying these changes is the role played by the customer. All customers, and not just end customers, want more for less; they are more demanding, and want their products and services in shorter lead times and at lower prices. A growing trend in supply chain design is the flow of information throughout the chain using information technology and communication.

This chapter examines the role of supply chains as they get products to customers. It discusses the dynamics of the supply chain and the responsibility and placement of inventory. The real essence of this chapter is to view the supply chain as consisting of all the interactions that exist from original supplier to end customer. Too often organisations try to optimise their own position in the supply chain to the detriment of the entire supply chain.

This is not a chapter on production industries alone. Service industries play a very important role in supply chain management by facilitating the flow of goods and information. Additionally, service providers use products during the execution of their services. End consumers measure service performance in conjunction with the performance of the supply chain itself.

The chapter discusses the bullwhip effect, discusses the triple-A approach to supply chains, and includes a section on choosing suppliers.

Supply chain management

Supplier

A supplier is an entity that provides inputs to a process.

Supply chain

The supply chain is a network that describes the flow of raw materials from suppliers through plants that transform them into useful products, and finally to distribution centres that deliver those products to end customers.

Supply chain management

Supply chain management is the design, planning, execution, control, and monitoring of supply chain activities with the objective of creating net value, building a competitive infrastructure, leveraging worldwide logistics, synchronising supply and demand, and measuring performance globally.

Echelon

An echelon is a node in a supply chain network. Each echelon adds operating expense, holds inventory, adds to the cycle time, and expects to make a profit. As an example, a manufacturer that supplies distribution warehouses that supply retail stores has two echelons between the factory and the end customer.

Materials management

Materials management is a set of business processes that includes the purchase of raw materials and components, the planning and material movements in production, and the warehousing and distribution of the finished product.

Logistics

Logistics, in an industrial context, is the art and science of obtaining, producing, and distributing material and product in the proper place and in proper quantities.

Supply chain overview

Supply chain management includes all the interactions that occur from original supply through to the end customer or consumer. Generally, the supply chain involves the flow of materials from suppliers to customers until the product reaches the end consumer. These linkages constitute the supply chain. Coupled with the material flow, each supplier sends ideas and design suggestions to satisfy customers, and provides credit facilities to the customers. Clearly, the strength of the entire chain depends on its weakest link, and the end customer's satisfaction depends on how well all linkages in the supply chain work.

However, the supply chain involves more than just the flow of materials. It involves market research data, customer requirements, the flow of orders, and the flow of cash in a reverse direction – from customer back to supplier. Thus, information and cash flows from the end customer back up the supply chain to the original supplier.

The flow of materials, ideas, and credit moves from left to right, while the flow of requirements, orders, and cash flows from right to left, as illustrated in Figure 9.1. When implementing any information technology-based business system involving a supply chain, it is extremely important to recognise these opposing flows. Thus, supply chains involve all suppliers, manufacturers, distributors, retailers, and customers.

Service companies often see themselves as different and separate from supply chain companies. However, they are usually an integral part of the supply chain. Transport companies supply transport services over land, sea, and air. Banks and finance companies provide credit and other facilities at every interaction in the supply chain. Insurance companies, import/export companies, advertising companies, and promotion companies ease the material and data flows of supply chains. Manufacturers, distributors, and retailers provide services to ensure service suppliers have the goods to provide to their customers. Hotels and restaurants rely on inwards goods arriving at the end of a supply chain. Health services need inwards goods such as pharmaceuticals, food, uniforms, pens, papers, and operating supplies before they can even start providing care and attention to patients. Figure 9.2 illustrates the role of a service provider in the supply chain.

This sequence of supplier/customer linkages continues upstream as far as the original supplier and downstream as far as the end customer, as illustrated in Figure 9.3. Each organisation has a set of suppliers and a set of customers; these are first echelon suppliers and first echelon customers. The word 'echelon' derives from the French *échelon* meaning a rung in a ladder. They represent the first tier of contact along the supply chain for that organisation. Additionally, each first echelon supplier may have their own set of suppliers that supply goods and services to them. Relative to the first organisation, these are now the second echelon suppliers. Similarly, organisations

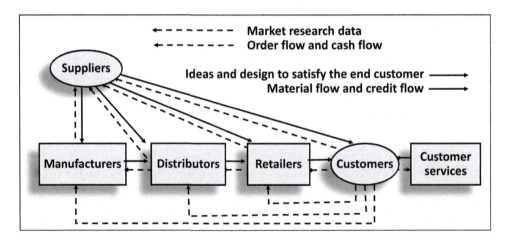

Figure 9.1 Supply chain management involving manufacturers, distributors, and retailers

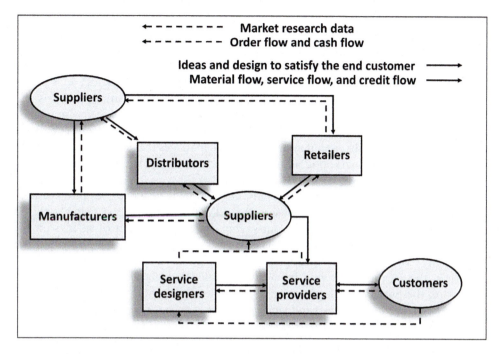

Figure 9.2 Supply chain management for service providers

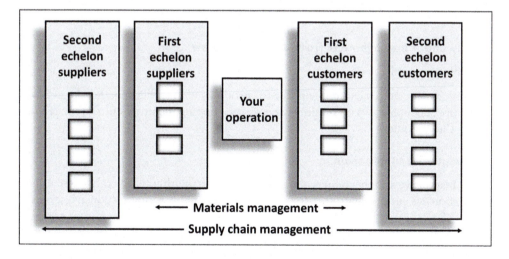

Figure 9.3 Echelons of supply chain management

may have second echelon customers. These echelons continue to span all the interactions from original supplier to final customer. Essentially each echelon is a supplier-customer linkage. When designing supply chains and thinking about the dynamics of supply chains, all these interactions require consideration.

Materials management, a subset of supply chain management, is the set of business processes that includes the purchase of raw materials and components, the planning and movement of materials in production, and the warehousing and distribution of the finished product. Generally, materials management occurs inside each organisation and extends to the immediate supplier and immediate customer.

There is a difference between 'materials management' and 'logistics'. In production, logistics refers to the art and science of obtaining and distributing materials and product. In a military sense (where it has greater usage), its meaning can also include the movement of personnel. The purchasing department controls the front end of the materials flow system, the manufacturing function manages the flow within the manufacturing system, and marketing administers the flow of finished goods into storage and distribution.

The average manufacturer purchases about two-thirds of what goes into the final product – two-thirds of the cost of goods sold. This percentage is rising with the increasing use of technology and labour-saving devices. The effect of savings on the bought-in materials bill of most organisations has a disproportionate effect on their profitability. The greater the proportion of their total costs devoted to bought-in materials, the greater the saving for a given reduction in bought-in material costs. Therefore, the purchasing department, through its philosophies, knowledge of processes, knowledge of materials, and vendor selection, has more opportunities to affect quality than the production department.

The basic objective of logistics and materials management is to ensure the right item is at the right place, at the right time, at a reasonable cost. Purchased materials and supplies constitute the major cost elements in most manufacturing businesses and, indeed, a sizeable working-capital investment in many service organisations.

Supply chain management from a strategic view

Efficient supply chain

An efficient supply chain is suitable for products with stable demand. An efficient supply chain focuses on minimising costs of shipping the product from the factory to the customer.

Responsive supply chain

A responsive supply chain is suitable for products with unpredictable demand. A responsive supply chain focuses on customer availability and responsive service.

A customer walking into a retail store and purchasing an item is, by default, acknowledging all interactions of the entire supply chain that delivered the product to the retail store. The entire supply chain should benefit from each retail transaction. A successful retailer demands more goods and services of wholesalers and distributors. Successful wholesalers and distributors demand more goods and services from manufacturers. Successful manufacturers demand more goods and services from processors (or fabricators or component manufacturers). Successful processors demand more goods and services from raw material suppliers.

The supply chain designed to get products to market can be efficient or responsive. An efficient supply chain is one designed for products with stable demand and with a focus on minimising costs of shipping the product from the factory to the customer. A responsive supply chain is one designed for products with unpredictable demand and with a focus on customer availability and responsive service.

Bullwhip effect – demand amplification

Bullwhip effect

The bullwhip effect creates large oscillations of inventory in the supply chain network. Small changes in downstream demand create large changes in upstream supply. Synchronising the supply chain eliminates the effect.

Traditionally, when a retailer needed more supplies to fill up shelves, they would place an order with their wholesaler or distributor. They, in turn, would place an order with their manufacturer when their warehouse levels reached a reorder point. When the stock on hand of raw materials and components at the manufacturer reached a level that necessitated additional supplies, they would contact the raw material supplier and place an order. Generally, the order size increases as the demand progresses upstream. This all takes time and is subject to quantity consolidation, tending to amplify the true demand. The bullwhip effect or demand amplification characterises this phenomenon.

The bullwhip effect, described by Hau Lee, V. Padmanabhan, and Seungjin Whang in their *MIT Sloan Management Review* article[16] in 1997, creates large oscillations of inventory in the supply chain network. Small changes in downstream demand create large changes upstream. Synchronising the supply chain eliminates (or minimises) this effect.

When each link in the supply does not fully understand the dynamics of the consumer sales pattern, the pattern distorts and amplifies as demand transmits up the supply chain. The effect can occur with any range of products and at any level in the supply chain, but is most noticeable with consumer commodity products. If demand for an item is relatively constant at final retail points, then the available inventory in the retail store gradually diminishes until it is time for the retailer to place a replenishment order with the wholesaler.

The supply chain expects the wholesaler to hold relatively large quantities of products to meet supply demands from multiple retailers. The wholesaler wants favourable pricing arrangements, and this encourages the wholesaler to order large quantities from the manufacturer. The wholesaler may even delay ordering from the manufacturer until they have a very large order and thus can secure even better payment and delivery terms.

Thus, the manufacturer does not see actual demand at consumer level and just receives a large order from the wholesaler. This may indicate that the demanded product is experiencing an increase in popularity, and, to compensate for that popularity, the manufacturer schedules larger production runs. However, to be able to make the larger production runs, the manufacturer must secure raw materials from their supplier. Original suppliers supply in bulk and often have large minimum and large multiple orders. Therefore, the manufacturer orders even larger quantities of raw material.

Figure 9.4 shows the demand information flow amplified as it travels from the customer back to the original supplier. The reactions of retailers, distributors, wholesalers, and manufacturers all contribute to this amplification. The diagram clearly shows a relatively stable environment at the customer end but a very dynamic environment at supplier level. Similarly, the reverse is true; the supply flow amplifies from supplier forwards to the customer. Any variation in supply in the early stages of a supply chain becomes a major issue by the time the information reaches the customer.

The bullwhip effect is a direct result of individuals making rational decisions within the supply chain infrastructure. Organisations can mitigate the effects by examining the infrastructure of the supply chain, rather than attempting to change the rational behaviour patterns.

Lee et al. identified the following four major causes of the bullwhip effect:

- Demand forecast updating.
- Order batching.
- Price fluctuation.
- Rationing and shortage gaming.

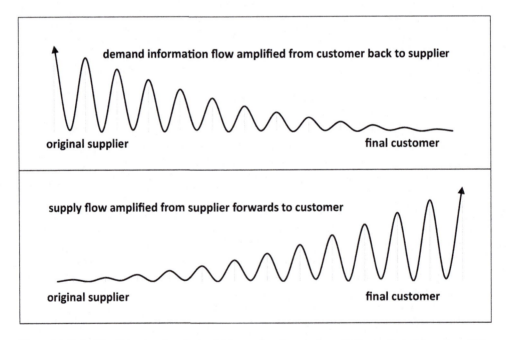

Figure 9.4 Bullwhip effect showing demand information flow and supply flow, adapted from Lee, H. L., Padmanabhan, V., & Whang, S. (1997, spring). The bullwhip effect in supply chains. *MIT Sloan Management Review, 38*(3), p. 94.

Demand forecast updating

Every supply chain organisation needs to replace the products it sells. They study their current and historical demand patterns, and somehow, they forecast demand. The quantity they order from their supplier considers the supplier lead time and anticipated demand during that lead time. The organisation usually carries safety stock in case demand exceeds expectation or delivery lead times are longer than expected.

The supplier at the next echelon up the supply chain studies the demand pattern presented and somehow forecasts demand. Again, they usually carry safety stock in case demand exceeds expectation or delivery lead times are longer than expected.

Safety stocks increase when delivery lead times increase. Likewise, safety stocks increase when demand uncertainty increases. As we move up the supply chain, we usually find safety stocks increasing to cover demand uncertainty and lead time fluctuations. This just adds to the bullwhip effect.

Order batching

In a supply chain, most organisations use inventory management techniques to calculate order sizes. Organisations base these calculations on price breaks for higher volumes, minimum order sizes introduced by suppliers, transport lot sizes such as full container-loads, or may be orders placed at regular but infrequent intervals. Suppliers offering payment terms based on 'twentieth of the month following' experience few orders at the end of the month and significant increases at the start of the month. Often the cost of placing and receiving orders forces organisations to change behaviour and place larger orders, less frequently. This is the opposite effect to that encouraged by lean thinking.

All this encourages a highly erratic stream of orders, with spikes appearing usually at the beginning of the month. This method of periodic ordering and batching of orders to reach minimums amplifies variability and contributes to the bullwhip effect. The effect reduces when suppliers receive payment before delivery, or they offer payment terms of a fixed number of days, regardless of order date.

Price fluctuation

Transactions between manufacturers and distributors are usually on a forward buy arrangement whereby the customer obtains the goods in advance of requirements. The supplier often introduces inducements to encourage buying more than required in the short term and buying sooner than required. The supplier offers incentives such as quantity discounts, end-of-year specials, clearance sales, stock-take specials, rebates and – although they may not admit it – sometimes offers personal kickbacks to the purchaser. Thus, the customer buys in quantities greater than needed and before the customer needs them. Putting it another way, the rate of buying is different from the rate of consumption, and this means the variation in demand is different from the variation in supply.

This is the opposite effect to that encouraged by lean thinking.

Rationing and shortage gaming

During times of supply shortage, the supplier may choose to ration supply. For example, they may limit supply to 50% of each order. As soon as the customer realises this behaviour is present, they order twice as much as they need and receive just 50% of that quantity, which is what they wanted anyway. Taking it to an extreme, the customer may order four times what they need and receive 50% of that quantity, resulting in a delivery of twice their needs. This means they can stockpile the shortage goods without fear of running out.

During the 1980s, some computer companies, marketing large mainframe computers, operated a 'first-day-window' of about 12 weeks for newly announced architectures. During that time, customers could place one order for the new computer and qualify for order delivery as if the order signing occurred on the day of announcement (the first day). Then the computer company would ballot all the orders to create a delivery sequence. This created an equal opportunity for organisations to place orders without having to rush an order in on the first day and, subsequently, realise the configuration was not suitable. However, corporate customers placed single orders from several business entities (divisions, subsidiaries, and so on) and effectively generated multiple orders. They still followed the rules of the game by placing only one order per customer, but they created extra customers with individual orders coming from each division of the organisation. After the announcement of the order delivery allocation, the corporate customers would assess how well they had fared in the process and cancelled orders that were unsatisfactory and retained orders that suited their purpose and plans.

How to counteract the bullwhip effect

Demand forecast updating is minimised when every organisation in the supply chain understands the system dynamics. Making downstream demand data available to upstream organisations benefits all participants. In this way, all organisations use the same demand data. The alternative requires each organisation to base demand forecasts on just those parts of the supply chain that they can see. Clearly, accurate point-of-sale data and electronic data interchange would facilitate the better flow of information. Other methods include making retail sales data available to the entire supply chain using secure websites.

Order batching is minimised by encouraging organisations to order regular, smaller batches within a long-term pricing/volume arrangement. The purchasing organisation prepares long-term forecasts of consumption and agrees to purchase a certain quantity over either a fixed or a rolling period. When quantity discounts are available over extended periods, the size of each order does not matter. The extended period could be a rolling 12 months. If suppliers fixed the extended period at 12 months, the same order-batching problem would occur at the end and beginning of the extended period. Another issue with smaller batches is the added costs for ordering, distribution, and payment. Third-party logistics (3PL) should be able to provide distribution solutions and that just leaves ordering and payment. Computer-based ordering, continuous replenishment programs, and electronic payments can address most of these concerns.

Stable prices avoid forward buying and diversions. Two terms used now are everyday low prices (EDLP) and everyday low costs (EDLC). When organisations have payment terms of 'twentieth of the month following', they are in effect offering two prices. Order at the end of a month and pay full price in 20 days, or order at the start of the month and pay full price in 50 days. The extra days of credit effectively generate a lower price. These practices are contrary to the ideas behind lean thinking and collaboration. Counteract this behaviour by offering a constant number of days' credit or even zero days of credit.

Eliminate the gaming activities that exist at times of shortage. Organisations should allocate orders based on past orders. Regular customers can continue to receive regular deliveries. If an organisation offers no penalty for returning unsold products, then retailers buy quantities that exceed their requirements and simply return the goods back to the manufacturer/wholesaler/distributor at the end of the season without penalty. This is encouraging the retailers to buy up large and upstream companies carry the risk. Sharing that risk by allowing upstream companies to allocate resources to facilitate the retail sales helps alleviate the gaming effects.

Net effect of variation on supply chains

Small changes in demand downstream cause an extreme change in supply position upstream. Quick response is a system for linking final retail sales back through the entire supply chain. It relies on point-of-sale analysis of actual sales and the ability to communicate that data to all linkages on the entire supply chain. The benefits include a faster response to resupply.

Quick response shortens the total elapsed time from the need for goods to the time they are available for sale in the store. This has the effect of significantly reducing the time to place an order and the time to deliver that order. This, in turn, significantly reduces the amount of inventory in transit in the system, through the production facilities, and through the distribution networks.

Computer-based technology identifies products and communicates product requirements up the supply chain. Advanced implementations allow the electronic creation of orders into the supplier's system. Furthermore, retailers and manufacturers form strategic partnerships to find methods to achieve performance goals that are mutually rewarding.

Collaborative supply chains

Collaborative supply chain

A collaborative supply chain is a supply chain based on collaborative planning, forecasting, and replenishment.

Collaborative planning, forecasting, and replenishment (CPFR)

Collaborative planning, forecasting, and replenishment (CPFR) is a collaborative process that allows supply chain partners to jointly plan key supply chain activities from production and delivery of raw materials to production and delivery of final products to end customers. This encompasses business planning, sales forecasting, and the operations required to replenish raw materials and finished goods.

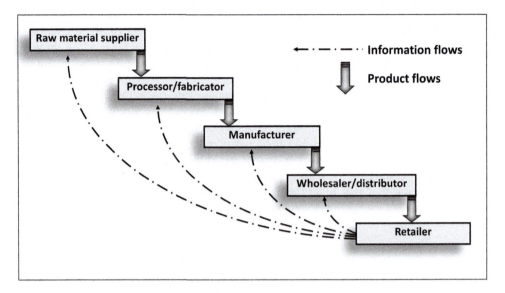

Figure 9.5 Collaborative supply chain in action

The supply chain is a partnership between organisations involved in delivering a product or service to the customer. This usually involves organisations at many levels within the supply chain. The raw materials provider, manufacturer, and retailer are but a few of the many entities involved in processing and handling a product before it gets to the end customer. A collaborative supply chain indicates that members of the supply chain have coordinated their effort in some manner to achieve their goal, which is the satisfactory supply to the end user. This is the very essence of a collaborative supply chain.

Figure 9.5 illustrates a collaborative supply chain in action, with the information flowing upstream from the final retail sales, ensuring every participant in the supply chain is fully aware of the actual demand pattern of the end customer. Each participant adjusts their volumes to replace products at the rate they are leaving the system and delivered to the end customer. In the past, a single entity would have sourced the raw material, manufactured the product, distributed the product, provided the sales and marketing, and controlled these activities from within one enterprise. Today, most supply chains are decentralised and often involve many companies with each one playing a different role within the demand/supply cycle. Collaboration is the only way to provide visibility.

Characteristics of a collaborative supply chain

There are eight defining characteristics of a collaborative supply chain.[17] These are:

- Base relationships on collaborative win-win situations rather than arm's length scenarios, which are always win-lose situations.
- Recognise the stakeholder status of those involved and therefore the need for each stakeholder to create value in the chain.

- Operate a pull strategy (rather than a push), since the focus is on the end customer, and everything must be based on the end customer and true demand.
- Strive to deliver value to the end customer, and, as with any strategy, the aim is to create as much value as possible for the benefit of the end customer.
- Eliminate waste by mitigating the bullwhip effect.
- Create lean logistics processes to ensure maximum effectiveness in delivery and output.
- Segment suppliers and customers since each subset of suppliers and customers may have differing requirements and need separate treatment.
- Develop a supplier network to share experiences and learning.

Toyota is an excellent example of a lean manufacturer that turned the automotive industry on its head with its demand driven strategies. Implementation of a collaborative supply chain is not easy, and it is not quick since there are several enabling and impeding factors at work. It requires trust and equality with all the supply chain stakeholders. This requires:

- Open and honest communication between all parties to ensure accurate non-biased information feeds through the chain.
- All stakeholders to have stakes in the supply chain, to be willing to sort out issues, and to address opportunities.
- Each partner requiring clearly documented expectations and creating a sense of cooperation in the attainment of goals.
- A clear statement of leadership activities to aid the definition of goals and targets.
- All supply chain partners benefiting from the collaboration. It is not a winner-takes-all attitude. Rather, it is an attitude that everyone is a winner, with the spoils shared amicably and fairly.
- Accurate and timely transfer of information. Technology underlines this transfer, and partners must agree on the level and type of technology.

Each organisation varies the implementation of these factors. Clearly, they incorporate their own circumstances into the mix and create opportunities for differentiation.

Two quite different examples illustrate this point. Dell Inc. (computers) uses demand management effectively to enable a responsive build-to-order capability. They hold no finished goods inventory. In fact, they do not own their manufacturing facilities. This lack of inventory in their direct system gives them an advantage over their competitors. IKEA, a furniture manufacturer, distributor, and retailer, on the other hand, operates a build-to-stock system. As a product sells, the factory makes a unit replacement, so stocks held throughout the system are constant. The furniture industry typically uses a batch production process.

Advantages of collaboration

There are several key advantages to a collaborative supply chain when compared to a stand-alone business built on the old adversarial model. They are:

- Greater flow of information from the end customer.
- Reduced inventory at all linkages in the supply chain.

- Effective use of resources and the subsequent reduction in costs.
- Reduced lead times driven mainly by accurate demand data.
- Increased 'speed to market' and responsiveness to market changes.
- More focus on each organisation's capabilities and competences.
- Availability of demand driven or pull strategies.
- Service-level gains – such as delivery in full, on time, and in specification (DIFOTIS).
- Business process cost reduction.
- Product cost reduction influenced by total cost reduction.

Inclusion and cooperation are at the very heart of collaboration within the supply chain. The combined effort of the supply chain partners realises that true advantage. The timely and accurate information from the end customer drives the supply chain and ultimately determines its success or failure. With accurate information and a pull-based strategy, market mediation becomes a reality. The supply chain produces and supplies real demand, and the need for extra inventory and extra resources reduces to everyone's benefit.

Moreover, the cooperation amongst the partners ensures that there are significant reductions in costs, lead times, and process blockages. Typically, without such a partnership, organisations rely on bullying tactics to ensure speedy delivery of goods or services. They might threaten to take their business elsewhere or try to obtain a discount to pressure the supplier to meet their demands. However, when companies work in partnership and have open and honest communication, even about pricing, the opportunity to decrease actual and transactional costs is staggering.

Other noticeable advantages include reduced inventory safety stocks (and inventory holding costs), fewer markdowns of obsolescent goods, less price protection, and a reduction in lost sales.

The logic of supply chain collaboration makes a lot of sense. However, as with anything that seems too good to be true, the path to successful implementation does present some problems. Companies wishing to embark on the road towards supply chain collaboration must realise that the hurdles are high and hard to overcome. Here are some of these hurdles:

- The older mindsets based on confrontation require considerable effort to change, and this change to collaboration is sometimes too great a change in basic assumptions to achieve.
- Accounting practices and tax laws are often so antiquated that they do not recognise such structures and, therefore, make some seemingly profitable ventures seem less appealing.
- Policies, practices, and procedures based on logic that is the antithesis of collaboration. Policies, such as payment terms '20th of the month following', distort the true demand and supply of products by forcing customers to buy at the start of a month so that they benefit from the extended credit terms.
- Practices, such as using accounts payable (creditors) to finance the operations, delay payment flows throughout the entire supply chain. Individual businesses

believe they are benefiting from such actions when in fact they are inflating the costs and reducing the competitiveness of the entire supply chain.

- Organisations provide opportunities for individuals to operate inside silos. Employees endeavour to promote their own activities, or their own goals, rather than the goals of the organisation.
- Organisations negotiate contracts aimed at getting the best deal for the organisation rather than striving for win-win results for the entire supply chain. Organisations should negotiate on conformance quality, process capability, availability of supply, continuity of demand, and mutual resolution of demand/supply issues, rather than just on price.
- Supply chains require time and effort to run smoothly. Ineffective allocation of resources, poorly designed processes, and unrealistic time limits waste time, and these create time constraints that require too much effort to manage. This becomes a heavy burden on smaller organisations and reinforces the need to choose partners carefully.
- Poor communication or non-standardised formats play a huge part in the poor performance of supply chains, mainly because supply chains need a free flow of accurate, timely information.
- Misleading and inaccurate information means organisations are working towards the wrong goals. They are attempting to meet unnecessary deadlines and quantities exceeding immediate requirements. The adversarial nature of business means that companies might inflate figures, or present a rosier view, just to push their case and keep the other party happy.

As shown in Figure 9.6, the aim of the collaboration exercise is to achieve a better ratio of benefits to price than the competition. If an organisation can manage to construct a collaborative supply chain, then it must be conscious of the enabling and impeding factors at play. The identification of these factors allows the organisation to move on with implementing its strategy.

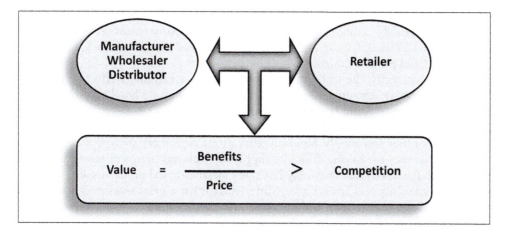

Figure 9.6 The aim of collaboration is to achieve better benefits-to-price ratio than the competition

Competitive advantage

Supply chain collaboration should provide competitive advantage. However, this is a narrow and fault-ridden argument. Networks form the basis for today's business world, with very few degrees of separation between rivals. It is critical for the business to ensure that the chosen partners are reliable and not involved in similar relationships with competitors.

Small-to-medium enterprises might have difficulty initiating discussion on collaboration with larger organisations that may initiate negotiation by requesting a price reduction as the guarantee for continued business. Trust in the partnership relationship is essential, as is an acceptance that the proposed initiatives require commercial confidence, at least in the short term.

When a company is not the dominant force in a market and does not worry about the release of ideas to the general marketplace, then the collaborative supply chain is a good option to maximise competitive advantage. Companies can maximise their competitive advantage by focusing on one or more of six key areas:

- Organisations can seek to gain competitive advantage with a low-cost strategy by reducing transaction costs, including production activities, safety stocks, payment terms, and transport consolidation. They minimise the need for incurring cost by challenging the very existence of cost and using process improvement to seek minimisation.
- A key success factor of a supply chain is the ability to have products available for sale when needed. For example, a manufacturer might minimise customer downtime by providing delivery guarantees based on availability.
- Service is a key differentiator. For example, Dell Inc. (computers) collaborates with express carriers to decrease its customer delivery times. Walmart (department stores) is so good at extracting service-level gains that they emulate a logistics company impersonating as a mass merchandiser.
- Product design incorporates supply chain collaboration. HP (computers and printers) has been very successful with their postponement policies. They postpone the configuration or differentiation of a product for a specific customer until the latest possible point in the supply network. Companies must think through all the processes used to make and deliver products, and integrate these ideas into the product and process design.[18]
- Applied correctly, the order management system is extremely effective in creating competitive advantage. Airline reservation systems and hotel accommodation systems provide examples of order management.
- Dell Inc. uses pricing strategies to direct customers to order computer configurations that they can supply. Similarly, they direct customers away from configurations that they are having difficulty supplying. This has been a relatively easy feat for Dell Inc. given that they only have one Internet-based point of sale.
- A unique solution is always a key differentiator for a mass-marketed product. A supply chain that is agile and adaptive can create untold competitive advantage using batches of one for individual customers.

Although risky, collaboration through a partnered supply chain can have resounding benefits for the organisation.

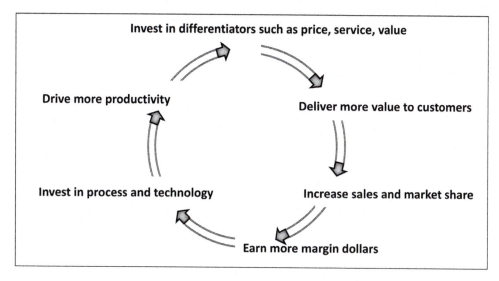

Figure 9.7 Value creation cycle using supply chain collaboration

However, the primary driver should not be just competitive advantage. Collaboration is a mechanism by which an organisation can expand on its core competences and competitive capabilities as illustrated in Figure 9.7.

Start by investing in process and technology to minimise variability, accentuate flexibility, reduce process waste, meet delivery times, and satisfy customer requirements. These attributes drive productivity improvements that allow the organisation to exploit the advantage gained and invest in product and service differentiators, such as price, service, and value. Customers see these differentiators as offering more value, so they in turn increase sales and market share. These naturally flow on to increased profits, which are available to invest back into process and technology.

Traditional business entities such as manufacturing, distributing, and retailing are ideal candidates for a collaborative supply chain approach. This may be difficult to manage and offers considerable risk; however, the potential payback makes the effort worthwhile.

By trusting supply chain partners to complete their part of the chain efficiently and effectively, a company can eliminate wasted time and effort. Customer satisfaction and throughput increases when the gain in time and resource channels back into the productive activities of the organisation.

Service chain management

Service chain management

Service chain management is the collection of resources provided by external service providers that have the capability to deliver specific services to their customers.

Supply chain management is primarily concerned with the movement of goods from suppliers to customers. To facilitate this movement, supply chain organisations obtain specialised services from service organisations. There are an increasing number of service organisations with expanding areas of expertise. They provide specialised skills in areas such as information and communication technology, project management, business consulting, call centres, data centres, transport and distribution, marketing, advertising, media communications, accommodation, finance, investment, cleaning, and health services.

Organisations are occasionally very quick to take on these services and have learned how to obtain them, but they can struggle to manage them effectively. The management of services needs to be part of the business strategy and needs to be a core competence of the hiring organisation.

Service chain management requires very different skills when compared to supply chain management skills. The difference lies in the services themselves. Supply chain management deals with products, while service chain management deals with services.

The primary differences between supply companies and service companies are:

- The service is an ongoing process and the customer participates in the service. For example, an organisation providing information technology services works closely with the client organisation on a day-to-day basis as well as guiding the client towards a long-term strategic position.
- Services have an intangible nature to them especially when based on ideas and concepts. For example, a business-consulting organisation provides ideas for improvement, and an architect designs a building concept.
- Services are perishable and are not suitable for storage. This affects the timing, availability, and quantity of service delivery. The same issues arise in supply chains, but warehouses can store goods in anticipation of future demand and if anticipated volumes are less than forecast. Services possessing this perishable nature include transport, distribution, cleaning, and health services.
- Production and consumption of services occurs simultaneously. The accommodation industry, including hotels, motels, and hostels, provide accommodation facilities at the same time as guests use them. Providers need to anticipate the demand and have the facilities in place prior to actual demand, but the delivery of the service is simultaneous with the consumption.
- Services involve people in both delivery and consumption. The requirements of the customer are often difficult to define in human terms, and the delivery of the service is often difficult to define in human terms. This is simply because organisations base the requirements and the performance on human capabilities, and these vary from person to person and from time to time.
- Management ensures that they deliver on service performance. It is relatively easy to obtain the service, but the customer is buying the capability to deliver. It requires careful management to ensure the capability transforms into reality.

Primary value components of service chain management

The primary value components of service chain management start with strategy. The customer builds the need for the outsourcing of specific services into their strategy, and the provider of the services develops core competences that deliver the required services at the required level of performance.

The relationships that develop in the service chain require clear definition. These relationships go beyond the normal day-to-day contact relationships. They extend to risk evaluation, initiating change, providing innovation, responsibility for performance and non-performance, and ownership of the output.

Business processes included in the service chain need clear definition, especially at the linkages with those business processes undertaken by the customer. Process definitions need to resolve ownership and responsibility clearly. As an example, with transport and distribution, ownership may change at the point of physical delivery to an address and a delivery receipt exchanged. However, what happens when an organisation receives a demand request outside the original specifications? One might argue that the customer should have anticipated the request. Likewise, one might argue that the supplier should have anticipated the need for such a request. Furthermore, it should be the responsibility of the supplier to provide services.

Most service organisations appear to be proficient at obtaining services but deficient at managing services. Testament to that is the number of failed information technology projects and the number of business and construction projects that run over budget and over time.

The criteria for performance measurement and performance improvement need to be clear and achievable. Current industry benchmarks may be a good starting point on which to base performance measurement. There is a need to identify where performance failure is likely to occur and where to concentrate improvement activities.

As the relationship develops and matures, there is a learning process with all parties involved. The entire service chain benefits by leveraging this learning process.

Strategic view of supply chains

Agility

Agility is the ability to produce a variety of products economically in any quantity with rapid changeovers. It merges the four competitive capabilities – cost, quality, delivery, and flexibility.

Adaptability

Adaptability is a measure of how well a supply chain adjusts its design to meet structural shifts in markets and modifies the supply network to changing strategies, products, and technologies.

Alignment

Alignment creates incentives for better performance of the supply chain by exchanging information and knowledge freely with suppliers and customers, discussing and documenting roles, tasks, and responsibilities clearly for suppliers and customers, and sharing risks, costs, and improvement gains equitably.

Triple-A supply chain

The triple-A supply chain is a collaborative supply chain approach based on agility, adaptability, and alignment.

Postponement

Postponement shifts product differentiation closer to the consumer by postponing identity changes, such as assembly or packaging, to the last possible supply chain location.

Speed and cost reduction provide the basis for collaboration. Unfortunately, not all participants realise the real benefits. Supply chains work well when the rewards have a fair distribution throughout the chain. Organisations should not endeavour to optimise their own position; rather, they should encourage other participants in the supply chain to improve everyone's performance and benefits. In other words, each organisation should strive to do what is best for the supply chain, rather than what they believe is best for them in isolation. Hau L. Lee proposed that supply chains needed the triple-A approach based on agility, adaptability, and alignment.

The concept of agility defines how easily the supply chain can respond to short-term fluctuations in the market, supply disruptions, and environmental changes. Changes in end-user demand and disruptions to the source of certain materials are examples. Adaptability epitomises how well the supply chain can adjust to market changes over time, to changes in retail channel strategies to support new products, or the commoditisation of products that leads to changes in sourcing strategies. Finally, the concept of alignment defines how well the participants in the supply chain operate and support the overall objective, which is to deliver value to the end customer, as opposed to extracting maximum value for individual participants.

Agility

The objective of agility is to respond to short-term changes in demand or supply quickly and handle external disruptions smoothly. Demand and supply patterns often change rapidly, and organisations struggle to get a balance between demand and supply. For commodity products with established demand patterns, it should be relatively easy to maintain supply. For new product introductions, it is virtually impossible to establish in advance the true level of demand and thus the required level of supply.

Organisations typically focus on costs, or speed of delivery, and lose track of the need to be agile. Demand shocks are exogenous events that cause havoc to supply chains. They seem to happen more often and with greater effect. Who would have anticipated the effects on demand because of the terrorist attacks in New York in 2001? Or the demand patterns following natural disasters such as the tsunami in South East Asia at the end of 2004, Hurricane Katrina that struck the southeastern United States in late August 2005, the earthquake that occurred in Haiti in 2010, the earthquakes that struck New Zealand in 2010 and 2011, or the earthquake and tsunami that hit Japan in 2011. Demand patterns further disrupt when fear infiltrates our news systems and changes consumer behaviour. Examples include the SARS (severe acute respiratory syndrome) epidemic of 2001–2003. United Kingdom voted in 2016 to leave the European Union and created supply chain uncertainty as companies endeavoured to prepare for whatever outcome evolved.

The reality is that demand patterns change and organisations require agility to respond to those changes. The following methods provide agility:

- Promote the flow of information with suppliers and customers so they can all respond quickly.
- Develop collaborative relationships with suppliers and customers so they can work together to design and redesign products and processes quickly.
- Design products for postponement by using common parts and components, and delay the final configuration until after receipt of the customer order. For many years, HP (computers and printers) has practised this concept of delaying final configurations.[19]
- Maintain a stockpile of inexpensive but key components so production can continue even when component delivery experiences delays or components become unavailable from suppliers. Clothing manufacturers provide an excellent opportunity to have stocks of buttons, zips, tapes, labels, and other findings. Organisations often have elaborate methods to calculate the optimum quantity to purchase and the optimum time to place an order for items that are of little or no actual monetary value, but have very significant value during a stock-out.
- Have a dependable logistics system that works well with other transport providers.
- Draw up contingency plans to identify and mitigate risk.

Adaptability

The objective of adaptability is to adjust the design of the supply chain to meet structural shifts in markets, and to modify the supply network to changing strategies, products, and technologies. Markets do not stand still and the needs of customers are not static. Therefore, it makes sense to have a supply chain that can adapt to changes in market structure, the economy, demand patterns, political and social environments, and advances in technology.

Once an organisation has identified the competitive priorities that it wants to emphasise, it translates these priorities into patterns of decisions. These strategic decisions are of three types – structural, infrastructural, and integration. The categories of structural decisions include capacity, facilities, process technology, vertical integration, and supplier relationships. Categories of infrastructural decisions include human resources, quality, production planning/inventory control, new product and service development, performance measurement and reward, and organisation/systems. Integration decisions relate to communication, alignment, and linkage.

Adaptability may require changes in structural decisions as well as infrastructural decisions. The following methods provide adaptability:

- Track new trends, especially in developing markets. As products become established and markets develop, new players enter the market both in competition and in support of the development. These new entrants provide opportunities for consolidation and outsourcing.

- Develop fresh suppliers and build on the logistics infrastructure. This is particularly true with a growing market handling increasing volumes. The decision points with low volumes are considerably different from those with high volumes.
- Evaluate the needs of the ultimate consumers – not just immediate customers.
- Create flexible product designs to make it relatively easy to adapt to changing demand patterns.
- Determine where products stand in terms of technology cycles and product life cycles.

Alignment

The objective of alignment is to create incentives for better performance. The following methods help alignment:

- Exchange information and knowledge freely with suppliers and customers.
- Discuss and document roles, tasks, and responsibilities clearly for suppliers and customers.
- Share the risks, the costs, and the improvement gains equitably.

V. G. Narayanan and Ananth Raman in their *Harvard Business Review* article[20] identified the need for alignment in the supply chain. Indeed, they observed that operational efficiency is at stake when supply chain partners do not align incentives. By aligning incentives, it was possible to obtain a bigger share of the profits, since this reduced the costs of the entire supply chain, creating a situation that benefits all participants.

Hidden actions by partner organisations, hidden information, and poorly designed incentives cause incentive problems in supply chains. When manufacturers deliver a product into a retail store, they realise they have little influence over the presentation of their product to customers. They may offer a price incentive, or operate a rebate system, to encourage the retail organisation to stock their products; however, they have little influence over the interaction between the salesperson and the customer. Manufacturers are unaware of the actions of salespeople.

Alignment is difficult when only one organisation has access to relevant information. This information might include cost data, profit margins, capacity cushions, or potential disruptions. Small and medium enterprises are reluctant to disclose their cost structures for fear larger companies will squeeze their profit margins. Thus, they hold back on releasing data and protect their rights to it. They hide and retain data or knowledge from some of the organisations in the supply chain.

Poorly designed incentive schemes often result in the opposite effect to the intended outcome. A steelmaker might offer production managers a bonus based on tonnes of output. Any self-interested manager would arrange for the production schedule to include extra tonnes of the fastest and heaviest product to make. With reinforcing steel bars, this product is a 50 mm round; it is one of the easiest to make in a steel rolling mill and generates more tonnes of output a day than any other product. The managers receive their bonus for lifting production volumes. However, the extra tonnes of output may need a discount, resulting in lower profit margins. The company loses because of poorly designed incentives.

Implementing alignment

Managers can resolve incentive problems by firstly acknowledging they exist. Managers should analyse their incentive and bonus schemes, and they should check their pricing and discount structures for anomalies. Finally, they should realign their incentives to encourage the wanted behaviour patterns.

If supply chain partners can acknowledge that such problems exist, they can lay the issues on the table and discuss them. By hiding problems or covering them up by deceit, or even deliberately setting them in place, one or two organisations optimise their own position to the detriment of the entire chain.

By diagnosing the cause and creating incentives that induce partners to behave in ways that maximise the profits of the entire supply chain, organisations move from self-optimisation to supply chain optimisation.

The redesign and realignment of incentives is usually quite difficult for individual managers to perform, since they may not have influence over parts of the supply chain beyond their first echelon suppliers and first echelon customers. The redesign should reward partners for acting in the best interests of the supply chain.

Referring to the steelmaker mentioned previously, the production managers should receive an incentive bonus for steel production volumes sold at full price. This would discourage end-of-period discounting and scrapping excess production.

In addition, during the redesign phase, organisations need to gather or share previously hidden information and develop trust with supply chain partners. They can prevent incentive problems by conducting incentive audits, educating managers about processes and incentives, and make contract negotiations less personal.

Timing is also important. If one linkage in the supply chain has realigned its incentives, this may cause disruption, or poor alignment, to other links in the chain. Thus, it is necessary to perform the realignment across the entire supply chain at the same time.

Strategic role of inventory in supply chains

Pull system

Pull system, in distribution, is one in which upstream entities respond to the demand signals from downstream entities in the supply chain.

Push system

Push system, in distribution, is one in which factory production is based on a forecast (as opposed to real demand), and the factory pushes products downstream to distributors and retailers.

A pull distribution system is one in which upstream entities respond to the demand signals from downstream entities in the supply chain. Pull system processes happen only in response to a signal from an immediate, downstream user.

In contrast, a push distribution system is one in which factory production is based on a forecast (as opposed to real demand), and the factory pushes products downstream to distributors and retailers. Thus, in a push system, a pre-planned schedule of production dictates the sequence and timing of the production process.

Regardless of whether organisations operate within a push system or a pull system, the placement and quantity of inventory has a significant impact on how the supply chain operates.

With a pull system operating, the end customer demands products and services, and the upstream organisations respond accordingly. To be in a position where they can deliver in full and on time, the upstream organisation needs to have enough inventory available to promise, or a production facility capable of delivering inside the customer-requested delivery lead time. This task becomes easier if demand patterns are stable. However, if demand patterns are uncertain or dynamic, the supply chain needs inventory placed in strategic points along the supply chain.

The performance of the supply chain in a pull system depends on how well the supply chain can manage demand, and how well the supply chain can manage supply. Pull systems incorporate the philosophies of lean thinking.

With a push system operating, it is the function of an upstream organisation to determine demand, and the upstream organisation produces a quantity of product that is available for downstream organisations to purchase. This system should work well if the upstream organisation has an intimate knowledge of true demand, but this is not the usual case. Often the upstream organisation determines demand based on historical data and organisations base this data on sales and not demand, since sales represent the ability of organisations to deliver. Only in rare cases does the sales pattern truly reflect demand patterns.

A push system tends to build an imbalance of inventory, with manufacturers and distributors endeavouring to off-load their stocks and push it into the retail stores. Many retailers source their products from suppliers that require them to import enough quantities at the start of a season to last the entire season with the decision based on price and shipping convenience.

By ordering in large quantities, the purchaser can negotiate the unit price on better terms. As an example, try going into a home improvement store during the spring season, or the start of summer, and count the number of outdoor furniture units on display. More than likely, you will find that the imported product the store has received from the importer/wholesaler/distributor occupies most of the floor space. The volumes are such that the importer/wholesaler/distributor cannot possibly store all the stock, and so they offload it onto their retail outlets.

Demand chain management

Demand chain management

Demand chain management views a supply chain from the customer's perspective, focusing on a demand-pull mode of operation.

Demand chain management views a supply chain from the customer's perspective, focusing on a demand-pull mode of operation. There must be a good understanding of the nature of the demand for a supply chain to work effectively and deliver value to the end customer. This relies on a certain level of trust as end customer suppliers reveal true independent consumer demand information to the rest of the supply chain. Independent demand data is crucial to the supplier's ability to understand the nature of the market that they are ultimately serving.

The bullwhip effect illustrates how consumer-demand data amplifies as it travels up a traditional disjointed supply chain, leading to upstream waste and inefficiency. Supply chains require good forecasting and forecast measurement processes, with the results of forecasts communicated amongst the members. High-performing supply chains operate a regular, frequent forecasting cycle and formally communicate results up the chain.

Good demand management does not just mean disciplined forecasting processes and a good understanding of the nature of demand; it also encompasses the ability to modify and influence demand through pricing and availability mechanisms in response to actual supply levels. This is a particularly important attribute of a supply chain when dealing effectively with unforeseen and external supply issues, such as natural disasters or industrial strikes.

Effective and responsive data exchange

Collaborative supply chains exchange various types of proprietary data or data that an individual member of the chain owns simply because they have collected or generated it. The types of data vary from static design and process capability to dynamic demand and inventory data. Collaborative supply chains rely on the fast exchange of data to understand the dynamics of the market in which they operate. Timely data on demand and inventory levels is essential for a supplier to make effective operational decisions regarding customer replenishment, internal production, and supplier signalling. Conversely, the exchange of supply data is important for producers so they can make timely contingency and demand-management decisions in response to delays and disruptions before the impact hits their customers and, ultimately, the consumer.

Exchange of process and design information

To bring new products to market effectively, supply chain members must understand the production capabilities and limitations of the other members. They must give each other the opportunity to take part in the design process. By sharing design decisions as they take place, suppliers obtain the opportunity to work on processes that support the design in parallel to the design phase. This provides overlap of what would otherwise be sequential steps in the introduction of new products, which in turn reduces the overall time to market. Collaborative relationships encourage the designing company to call upon the skill sets of a supplier to assist with all aspects of the design to ensure manufacturing and distributing capability.

Pull-based supply methodology

A collaborative supply chain uses the data exchanged between members to facilitate a pull-based replenishment system. A pull-based replenishment system aims to respond to consumer demand as the supply chain becomes aware of it. This requires timely data exchange between end-customer delivery and the upstream suppliers. One of the benefits of a pull-based replenishment system is that only the product quantity currently demanded attracts supply chain resources. However, pull-based replenishment requires a good understanding of the nature of the probable consumer demand levels and variations to prepare the supply chain for the actual demand.

With a lean-thinking philosophy, stock production without actual demand is waste. Firms need stock to buffer the uncertainty of demand, but one method to reduce potential excess and obsolete stock is postponement of the final product configuration to a point as close to the demand as possible. The Spanish-based clothing manufacturer Zara, as an example, purchases more than 50% of its fabric un-dyed, which gives it the ability to react to mid-season colour changes.[21]

Rhythmic planning cycles

Effective supply chains require rhythmic planning and operating. The cycle of forecasting, planning, ordering, and replenishing perform with clockwork precision. The entire supply chain from top to bottom shares the results of this cycle. The emphasis is on continual supply and avoidance of jerky, unforeseen spikes or troughs. This rhythmic pace allows managers to stay in tune with the current demands and to pay due attention to each step in the demand replenishment cycle.

Efficient consumer response

Efficient consumer response

Efficient consumer response is a demand-driven replenishment system linking suppliers with point-of-sale data for retail products, allowing all organisations on the supply chain to anticipate demand.

Organisations forming part of a supply chain that eventually supplies supermarkets, or large retail chains, should be fully aware of efficient consumer response. In its simplest form, efficient consumer response eliminates internal barriers that result in costs and time that add little or no value to end consumers.

Proctor & Gamble (household and personal care) and Walmart Stores (department stores) in the United States provide the best examples of efficient consumer response. However, most of the recent developments are occurring in Europe with a true focus on the consumer. Traditionally, the retailer generates replenishment orders from the wholesaler or manufacturer. With efficient consumer response, the suppliers determine the replenishment quantities based on information on stock and sales received from the retailer.

With a refined application of this process, all suppliers participating in the supply chain have access to current details of consumer demand at the retail level. This information travels electronically to them, or they can access it themselves from the retailers' websites. Thus, all suppliers know the true demand and they can initiate replenishment before the actual request filters through the supply chain to them. This allows the suppliers throughout the entire supply chain, not just the first echelon suppliers, to prepare goods for dispatch, confident that replenishment orders will arrive.

Figure 9.5 illustrates products flowing downstream from the raw material supplier all the way to the retailer and the information flowing upstream from the retailer to all participants in the supply chain. The supply side of efficient consumer response addresses the need for rapid and efficient replenishment of products in the overall supply chain. The delivery process speeds up and the suppliers have a better understanding of true consumer demand. The process electronically integrates information about product movement (as recorded at the point of sale), outside factors that affect demand (such as seasonal changes), actual inventory levels, product receipts, and an acceptable agreed safety stock level.

The demand side of efficient consumer response focuses on the effectiveness of the demand creation process. Trading partners agree to develop a market-specific plan that fundamentally describes what quantity is available for sale, the promotion activities, in what marketplace, and during what period. The focus is on delivering consumer value. Organisations introduce new products and services based on changing consumer demand.

The four main strategies on the demand side are:

- Efficient store assortment determines what products and quantities each store carries, how many items each store holds in each category, what quantities each store has available, and what sizes, varieties, and packaging sizes each store offers.
- Efficient replenishment starts with accurate point-of-sale data and tries to shorten the order cycle and the inefficiencies that exist in the order cycle. The replenishment methods use technology-based processes, such as continuous replenishment programs, computer-assisted ordering, and cross-docking:
- Efficient promotion allows the supplier to work with the retailer to promote products. This means they work together and share the risk on quantities and timing.
- Efficient new product introduction improves the introduction of new products and the phasing out of old products. Again, the supplier works with the retailer to share the risk on quantities and timing.

Promotion strategies that affect all aspects of the supply chain include consumer advertising, consumer promotion, and trade promotion. Consumer advertising can be a joint effort between the manufacturer and the retailer. Consumer promotion may use electronic consumer cards to track consumer behaviour. Trade promotion affects transactions between companies and does not affect the end consumer.

Collaboration and cooperation with all parts of the supply chain are important when exploiting the benefits of efficient consumer response. This approach is different from other initiatives in this area because it has a true customer focus. It aims at providing end-customer value and removing all the inefficiencies and added costs that do not add value to the end customer. Supply chain partners critically examine the entire supply chain and endeavour to maximise end-customer value and minimise inefficiencies throughout the entire supply chain.

Trading partners often attempt to optimise their own trading position. This makes sense on the surface and in the short term. Every organisation wants to make a profit at the end of the day. Therefore, an opportunity to off-load a volume of product onto an unsuspecting customer seems like good business. Likewise, given an opportunity to screw a bargain out of a supplier seems, on the surface, to be good business.

The real issue with supply chain collaboration is establishing the order quantity. A supplier-customer relationship works well during the buying season of a single product with a short life cycle. However, at the end of the season, the customer sells the residual items at a discounted sales price to avoid the costs associated with carrying the excess items in stock. In addition, the supplier offers quantity discounts as incentive policies. With collaboration, the manufacturer (supplier) uses discount policies to induce the retailer (customer) to order the agreed quantity such that the expected profit of the supply chain tends to be optimal.

With efficient consumer response, it is the responsibility of the trading partners in the supply chain to work together, collaboratively, for the benefit of the entire supply chain. If the supply chain is successful, then all partners benefit from the increased end-consumer satisfaction.

The supply chain bases business processes going upstream from the point-of sale on true end-customer demand. With this information passing upstream, all partners can base order policies on actual demand and not inflated or distorted demand. Essentially, the supply chain removes risk from the downstream flow of goods. The supply chain does not require inventories based on uncertainty.

Purchasing

Purchasing function

Purchasing is the business function responsible for acquiring materials, supplies, and services.

Purchasing is possibly the most under-rated function in supply chain organisations, which often bury it inside a larger function such as logistics, or handle it by a first line manager or supervisor.

Elevating the importance of purchasing within the organisation allows the function to sense the competitive priorities necessary for each major product or service. Purchasing activities should reinforce the overall strategies of the organisation and aim to lower production costs, achieve fast, accurate, and on-time deliveries, produce high-quality products and services, and demonstrate flexibility in volume and timing.

The purchasing function should achieve the following aims:

- Develop purchasing plans that are consistent with operations strategies for each major product and service obtained externally.
- Develop, evaluate, and determine the best supplier, price, and delivery for these products and services.

When organisations view purchasing as a low-level function, the main activities relate to producing purchase orders and following up on deliveries. However, when elevated in importance, the major responsibilities include:

- Selecting suitable suppliers that can form meaningful and long-lasting supply arrangements.
- Educating suppliers, if necessary, so that they fully appreciate how they can add value to their customer (the purchaser).

- Negotiating the terms and conditions of purchases.
- Scheduling supplier deliveries that fit in with customer requirements.
- Providing evaluation and feedback on supply performance.
- Assisting the supplier with certification if required.
- Developing the supplier financially if required.

Supplier selection

In a collaborative supply chain, the choice of supplier assumes an extremely important position. It is unfortunate that many small and medium organisations still pick suppliers based on price. One of the first questions asked in negotiation is, 'What's your price?'

The modern approach to collaboration suggests purchasing should evaluate each supplier on the following criteria:

- Potential to develop a close long-term relationship.
- Financial strength and capability.
- Process capability and ability to conform to agreed specification.
- Research, technical ability, and new product development strategy.
- Ability to deliver frequently, quickly, and reliably.
- Management structures and attitudes to collaboration.
- Pricing structures and dependencies.
- Trustworthiness and ability to have timely communications on problems.

Multiple suppliers

Single sourcing

Single sourcing is a method whereby only one supplier supplies a purchased item even though more suppliers are available.

Sole sourcing

Sole sourcing occurs when the supply of a product or a service is available from only one organisation.

Multi-sourcing

Multi-sourcing occurs when more than one independent supplier supplies a good or a service.

An organisation requires high-quality suppliers with acceptable costs and timely delivery. Historically, a common objective of purchasing and materials management has been to have two or more suppliers. Organisations believed that competition would drive prices down and reduce the supply risk. Lean thinking and collaborative supply chains with a critical need for quality and timely delivery and the new worldwide emphasis on quality products is changing buyer/supplier relationships.

Single sourcing

The advantages of single sourcing are:

- Potentially better quality as the supplier can concentrate on production processes.
- Stronger more durable relationships.
- Greater dependency, encouraging more commitment and effort.
- Better and more open communication.
- Easier to cooperate and share ideas on new product development.
- Possibility of economies of scale or, more importantly, the opportunity for the supplier to choose the production quantity that may be different from the order quantity.
- Higher confidentiality and trust.

The disadvantages of single sourcing are:

- The purchaser is more vulnerable to disruption should a failure occur.
- Volume fluctuations may affect individual suppliers more.
- The supplier might exert upward pressure on prices if no alternative supplier is available.

This is quite different from sole sourcing, which occurs when there is only one supplier available.

Multi-sourcing

The advantages of multi-sourcing are:

- The purchaser can drive the price down by competitive tendering.
- The purchaser can switch sources in case of supply shortage or failure.
- The purchaser has access to a wider source of knowledge and expertise.

The disadvantages of multi-sourcing are:

- It is difficult to encourage commitment to supply.
- It is less easy to develop effective quality assurance.
- Suppliers and customers need more effort to communicate effectively.
- Suppliers are less likely to invest in new processes.
- It is more difficult to obtain economies of scale.

An example to illustrate the disadvantages of multi-sourcing relates to a chemical processor in Auckland. They were the only New Zealand user of a specialist chemical imported from Germany. There were two suppliers based in Auckland and neither of them would commit to import and stock supplies of the chemical compound. The purchasing organisation could not understand why neither organisation would stock their requirements. They failed to realise that it would suit their own objectives if they committed to buy from one, or both, of the suppliers. To evaluate this scenario properly, try putting yourself in the position of the supplier. What chances have you of selling your imported chemical without a guarantee of a buyer?

Replenishment

Continuous replenishment

Continuous replenishment is a process in which the supplier receives daily notification of actual sales and commits to replenish these sales without stock-outs and without receiving a replenishment order. This results in a lowering of total inventory in the system and a subsequent lowering of associated costs.

Joint replenishment

Joint replenishment is a replenishment process for a family or a group of items obtained from one supplier. The agreed pricing structure dictates that each item in the group has an ordering cost, and the supplier produces an invoice for each order. The price is independent of the specific order quantity. Additionally, the supplier makes one fixed charge that is independent of the variety of purchased items each time the order includes any item in the family. The family ordering cost covers fixed transport costs and other activities performed with each order.

Usually considered a purchasing process, joint replenishment applies equally to internal production activities requiring a major set-up at the start, followed by minor set-ups between the various items in the family.

Vendor-managed inventory

Vendor-managed inventory is a process in which a supplier monitors and manages inventory for the customer. The supplier has access to the customer inventory data and assumes responsibility for maintaining the inventory level as required by the customer.

Cross-docking

Cross-docking is the concept of sending products from a supplier to a distribution warehouse with the products packaged and labelled ready for their destination. They arrive at the distribution warehouse on one vehicle, 'cross the dock', and leave the warehouse as consolidated loads for delivery to their destinations.

Outsourcing

Outsourcing is the process of contracting outside suppliers to provide goods and services previously provided internally. This process replaces internal capacity and production with that of the supplier.

Outpartnering

Outpartnering is the process of involving the supplier in a close partnership with the organisation and its operations management system. Outpartnering is characterised by close working relationships between buyers and suppliers, high levels of trust, mutual respect, and emphasis on joint problem solving and cooperation.

With outpartnering, the buyer views the supplier as a source of knowledge, expertise, and complementary core competences, rather than as an alternative source of goods and services (as found in outsourcing).

Outsourcing is the process of buying inputs from suppliers without much involvement beyond ordering and receiving procedures, while outpartnering is the practice of buying inputs from suppliers as part of a deep and continuing relationship between two organisations.

Organisations freely attempt to outsource production and support capability, but what they should endeavour to achieve is outpartnering. The benefits of outpartnering include:

- Freed resources as the organisation allocates tasks to another supplier.
- Reduced operating costs, often offset by increased purchase costs.
- Easier cost control by consolidating costs into just one regular bill.
- Superior design, assuming the partner can add value to the design process.
- Increased market perception of sound design based on the reputation of the supplier.
- Increased access to capacity provided by the supplier.
- More up-to-date technology, assuming the supplier can keep up to date.
- Increased access to world-class capabilities, again assuming the supplier is ahead of the market.
- Increased focus on own core tasks, and this is important if you need to concentrate on your own core competencies.

The disadvantages of outpartnering include:

- The purchasing organisation may lose control of important capabilities and this is vital when, for example, organisations outsource their information technology capabilities.
- The purchasing organisation may find it difficult, or even impossible, to reverse the decision.
- Managing an external supplier is different to managing an internal function.

Vertical integration

There are several value-adding steps to transform raw material into the final product for the consumer. Vertical integration is a measure of the degree or extent of these activities undertaken by the organisation. When an organisation chooses to acquire ownership of some of the supply activities it is backward integrating its business. When they choose to acquire ownership of some of the customer activities (such as distribution and, ultimately, sale to the consumer) they are forward integrating the business.

Forward integration

Forward integration is a part of vertical integration in which the organisation expands by buying or owning the parts of the production and distribution channel forward towards the final consumer.

Backward integration

Backward integration is a part of vertical integration in which the organisation expands by buying or owning the parts of the supply channel backward towards the original supplier.

Vertical integration involves backward and/or forward integration. Backward integration represents movement upstream towards the source of raw materials, such as a supermarket having its own plant to produce house brands. Forward integration occurs when an organisation acquires more channels of distribution, such as its own distribution centre and retail outlets.

Vertical integration is the degree to which an organisation decides to produce multiple value-adding stages directly – from raw materials to the sale of the product to the ultimate customer. The more steps in that sequence, the greater the vertical integration. A manufacturer that decides to begin producing parts, components, and materials that it normally purchases is using backward integration. Likewise, a manufacturer that decides to take over distribution and perhaps sale to the ultimate consumer is using forward integration.

The advantages of increased vertical integration are disadvantages of more outsourcing. Similarly, the advantages of more outsourcing are disadvantages of more vertical integration. Outsourcing is the process of contracting outside suppliers to provide goods and services previously provided internally.

Supply chain system metrics

A collaborative supply chain should exhibit elements of the three key qualities of agility, adaptability, and alignment, and, to achieve that, some of the following attributes should be present:

- The supply chain should show high stock turns throughout the entire chain and not just at specific points such as the retail level.
- There should be low product obsolescence because of the ability to manage product life cycles, consumer demand, and product exchange data. This implies that supply chain partners apply universally understood standard measures of obsolescence.
- The supply chain should exhibit rapid product introduction and short time to market by sharing product design and production capability information, and collaborating on new product introduction across the entire chain. In fact, it should have a rapid time to value, which measures the time it takes from development to payback of the development costs.
- For organisations to collaborate effectively there must be a high degree of trust requiring them to reveal aspects of their operations that might be confidential. This could include design, product, and costing data, process constraint information, and supplier data.
- Collaboration requires clearly understood performance measures that show how well each organisation is supporting the entire value chain and not just their individual enterprise. The objective of this metric is to promote alignment of the organisation's goals with that of the supply chain.

- The supply chain needs aligned objectives since any misalignment might lead to non-optimal financial performance.
- A collaborative supply chain must show a propensity towards elimination of waste. This means a desire to deliver value to the customer and requires the continuous elimination of waste in all processes used.

Chapter summary

The supply chain is a network that describes the flow of raw materials from suppliers through plants that transform them into useful products and finally to distribution centres that deliver those products to end customers.

The supply chain is a partnership existing between organisations involved in delivering a product or service to the customer. This partnership usually involves organisations at many levels within the supply chain. The raw materials provider, the manufacturer, and the retailer are but a few of the many entities involved in the processing of a product before it gets to the end customer.

The bullwhip effect occurs when the supply chain transmits, distorts, and amplifies consumer sales data up the supply chain. It happens when each link in the supply chain does not fully understand the dynamics of the consumer sales pattern. The triple-A approach based on agility, adaptability, and alignment suggests that all supply chain partners tune into the same music.

Efficient customer response is a demand driven replenishment system linking suppliers with point-of-sale data for retail products. This allows all organisations on the supply chain to anticipate future demand.

The purchasing role is of paramount importance for most production and service organisations. They have the choice of obtaining products and services from single suppliers or from multiple suppliers.

Supply chain partners have several purchasing options available, including vendor-managed inventory, continuous replenishment programs, joint replenishment, outsourcing, outpartnering, and vertical integration.

Discussion questions

1 Discuss the bullwhip effect – how it happens and what a supply chain can do to minimise any adverse effects.
2 Discuss the criteria for selecting a supplier.
3 Discuss the triple-A supply chain approach.
4 Describe the concepts of efficient consumer response.
5 Present the argument for outsourcing and outpartnering.
6 Explain the difference between outsourcing and outpartnering.
7 Discuss replenishment systems such as vendor-managed inventory and joint replenishment.
8 Why do organisations use vertical integration?
9 What is service chain management?
10 Discuss collaborative planning, forecasting, and replenishment.
11 Describe a triple-A supply chain.
12 How does vendor-managed inventory help the customer-supplier relationship?

Key terms

adaptability, 321
agility, 321
alignment, 321
backward integration, 335
bullwhip effect, 309
collaborative planning, forecasting,
and replenishment, 313
collaborative supply chain, 313
continuous replenishment, 333
cross-docking, 333
demand amplification. *See* bullwhip
effect
demand chain management, 326
echelon, 305
efficient consumer response, 328
efficient supply chain, 308
forward integration, 334
joint replenishment, 333
logistics, 305

materials management, 305
multi-sourcing, 331
outpartnering, 333
outsourcing, 333
postponement, 322
pull system, 325
purchasing function, 330
push system, 325
responsive supply chain, 308
service chain management, 319
single sourcing, 331
sole sourcing, 331
supplier, 305
supply chain, 305
supply chain management, 305
triple-A supply chain, 322
vendor-managed inventory, 333
vertical integration, 334

Notes

1 Academy Award®, Academy Awards® and Oscar® are trademarks and service marks of the
   Academy of Motion Picture Arts and Sciences.
2 Weta Workshop. (n.d.). *Manufacturing services.* Retrieved from https://wetaworkshop.
   com/services/manufacturing-services/
3 Weta Digital. (n.d.). *Awards.* Retrieved from www.wetafx.co.nz/awards/
4 2002 BAFTA: Achievement in Special Visual Effects. *The Lord of the Rings: The Fellowship
   of the Ring.* Jim Rygiel, Richard Taylor, Alex Funke, Randall William Cook, Mark Stetson.
   Makeup and Hair Winner. *The Lord of the Rings: The Fellowship of the Ring.* Peter Owen,
   Peter King and Richard Taylor. Retrieved from http://awards.bafta.org/award/2002/film/
5 The 74th Academy Awards 2002: Visual Effects Winner. *The Lord of the Rings: The Fellowship of the Ring.* Jim Rygiel, Richard Taylor, Alex Funke, Randall William Cook, Mark
   Stetson. Retrieved from https://oscars.org/oscars/ceremonies/2002
6 2003 BAFTA: Achievement in Special Visual Effects. *The Lord of the Rings: The Two Towers.* Jim Rygiel, Joe Letteri, Randall William Cook, Alex Funke. Costume Design Winner.
   The Lord of the Rings: The Fellowship of the Ring. Ngila Dickson and Richard Taylor.
   Retrieved from http://awards.bafta.org/award/2003/film/
7 The 75th Academy Awards 2003: Visual Effects Winner. *The Lord of the Rings: The Two
   Towers.* Jim Rygiel, Joe Letteri, Randall William Cook, Alex Funke. Retrieved from https://
   oscars.org/oscars/ceremonies/2003
8 2004 BAFTA: Achievement in Special Visual Effects. *The Lord of the Rings: The Return of
   the King.* Joe Letteri, Jim Rygiel, Randall William Cook, Alex Funke. Retrieved from http://
   awards.bafta.org/award/2004/film/
9 The 76th Academy Awards 2004: Visual Effects Winner. *The Lord of the Rings: The Return
   of the King.* Jim Rygiel, Joe Letteri, Randall William Cook, Alex Funke. Costume Design
   Winner. *The Lord of the Rings: The Return of the King.* Ngila Dickson and Richard Taylor.
   Retrieved from https://oscars.org/oscars/ceremonies/2004
10 2006 BAFTA: Achievement in Special Visual Effects. *King Kong.* Joe Letteri, Christian Rivers,
   Brian Van't Hul, Richard Taylor. Retrieved from http://awards.bafta.org/award/2006/film/

11 The 78th Academy Awards 2006: Visual Effects Winner. *King Kong*. Joe Letteri, Brian Van't Hul, Christian Rivers, Richard Taylor. Retrieved from https://oscars.org/oscars/ceremonies/2006

12 2010 BAFTA: Special Visual Effects. *Avatar*. Joe Letteri, Stephen Rosenbaum, Richard Baneham, Andrew R Jones. Retrieved from http://awards.bafta.org/award/2010/film/

13 The 82nd Academy Awards 2010: Visual Effects Winner. *Avatar*. Joe Letteri, Stephen Rosenbaum, Richard Baneham, Andrew R. Jones. Retrieved from https://oscars.org/oscars/ceremonies/2010

14 2017 BAFTA: Achievement in Special Visual Effects. *The Jungle Book*. Robert Legato, Dan Lemmon, Andrew R. Jones, Adam Valdez. Retrieved from http://awards.bafta.org/award/2017/film/

15 The 89th Academy Awards 2017: Visual Effects Winner. *The Jungle Book*. Robert Legato, Adam Valdez, Andrew R. Jones, Dan Lemmon. Retrieved from https://oscars.org/oscars/ceremonies/2017

16 Lee, H. L., Padmanabhan, V., & Whang, S. (1997, Spring). The bullwhip effect in supply chains. *MIT Sloan Management Review*, 38(3), 93–102.

17 Cox, A. (1999). Power, value and supply chain management. *Supply Chain Management: An International Journal*, 4(4), 167–175.

18 Feitzinger, E., & Lee, H. L. (1997, January–February). Mass customization at Hewlett-Packard: The power of postponement. *Harvard Business Review*, 75(1), 116.

19 *Ibid.*

20 Narayanan, V. G., & Raman, A. (2004, November). Aligning incentives in supply chains. *Harvard Business Review*, 82(11), 94–102.

21 Ferdows, K. M., Lewis, A., & Machuca, J. A. (2004, November). Rapid-fire fulfilment. *Harvard Business Review*, 82(11), 104–110.

Additional reading on collaborative supply chains

Baker, P., Croucher, P., & Rushton, A. (2017). *The handbook of logistics and distribution management: Understanding the supply chain* (6th ed.). London, England: Kogan Page Publishers.

Christopher, M. (2016). *Logistics and supply chain management* (5th ed.). Harlow, England: Pearson Education.

Ferdows, K. M., Lewis, A., & Machuca, J. A. (2004, November). Rapid-fire fulfilment. *Harvard Business Review*, 82(11), 104–110.

Jacobs, F. R., Berry, W. L., Whybark, D. C., & Vollmann, V. E. (2018). *Manufacturing planning and control for supply chain management: The CPIM reference*. New York, NY: McGraw-Hill Education.

Kopczak, L. R., & Johnson, M. E. (2003, Spring). The supply chain management effect. *MIT Sloan Management Review*, 44(3), 27–34.

Lee, H. L. (2004, October). The triple-A supply chain. *Harvard Business Review*, 82(10), 102–112.

Lee, H. L., Padmanabhan, V., & Whang, S. (1997, Spring). The bullwhip effect in supply chains. *MIT Sloan Management Review*, 38(3), 93–102.

Love, S. F. (1979). *Inventory control*. New York, NY: McGraw Hill.

Narayanan, V. G., & Raman, A. (2004, November). Aligning incentives in supply chains. *Harvard Business Review*, 82(11), 94–102.

Pittman, P. H., & Atwater, J. B. (2016). *APICS dictionary* (15th ed.). Chicago, IL: APICS.

Chapter 10

Advanced supply chain concepts
Technology and sustainability

Learning objectives

At the end of this chapter, you should be able to:

- Be aware and respond to trends and developments in supply chains.
- Discuss the impact of new technologies on operations, logistics, and the supply chain.
- Discuss the potential of autonomous vehicles in supply chain management.
- Illustrate the application of autonomous vehicles across various parts of the supply chain.
- Explain the rationale for automation and robotics across the supply chain.
- Discuss the practical application of automation and robotics and their potential.
- Explain the characteristics of omnichannel retailing.
- Evaluate the differences of an omnichannel strategy in comparison to multichannel.
- Discuss the importance of returns management considering customer expectations.
- Explain strategic and operational steps of returns management processes.
- Illustrate different strategies to returns management based on product characteristics.
- Explain the sustainability concept and how it applies to supply chain management.
- Discuss how to integrate sustainability into operations practically.
- Assess trade-offs between the sustainability dimensions.

Perspective: Warehouse of the future

We live in a world of change and part of that change is that large parts of the population have more disposable income and higher expectations in terms of lifestyle. What impact will this have on the design of future supply chains? It is fair to assume that products will need to move closer to consumers to increase shopping convenience and shorten waiting times. The supply chain will also need to support customised production and provide same-day delivery through multiple retail channels. This puts increasing pressure on storage locations, and this in turn poses the following question: What does the warehouse of the future look like? We base this perspective on the white paper, *Future Perspectives: Planning for the Warehouse of the Future*,[1] which examines trends in society and resulting trends in supply chain management and furthermore discusses the role of emerging technologies in the future design of supply chains.

Undeniably, social trends are influencing supply chain requirements. Most developed countries have an aging population and globally more people are living in urban areas, which continue to develop into mega-cities (over ten million inhabitants). The middle class is increasing, especially in developing countries, and these people thus enjoy more purchasing power, greater mobility, and increased access to information. In developing countries, the population is growing while the population is aging in developed countries. As a result, the working-age population should see an explosive growth in developing countries while the opposite is true for most advanced economies, with a future decline of the workforce. These factors change consumption and spending patterns, which have dramatic consequences for shopping behaviour and in turn supply chain considerations such as production, network design, warehousing, and retailing.

The sharing economy will continue to grow with companies like Uber, Airbnb, and TaskRabbit. Globalisation, the movement of goods, capital, and workers across national boundaries, is increasing. However, in contrast, we also see an increase in de-globalisation and re-shoring which is the desire to source products, particularly food, on a local basis.

Other trends, fuelled by broader changes in society and technology, affect the supply chain. The growth of e-commerce is already creating significant disruption in current supply chains. Not too long ago, we were content to wait a week or more for deliveries. Now, we want same-day delivery, or at the very least, next-day delivery. Consumers use multiple channels for their shopping; they start and end their buying journey at different points and expect lots of information along the way, fast and reliable delivery, and personalised experiences. As e-commerce expands to new categories such as food, e-tailers are compressing delivery times and exploring multiple options to achieve next-day or same-day delivery consistently. Online retailers, such as supermarkets, predict orders before they have occurred, based on previous consumption patterns. They use this information to move goods closer to the potential customer to enable faster delivery. This anticipation of demand will extend across the value chain. The customer advantages of multiple retail channels include flexible delivery times, alternative delivery destinations or pick-up locations, as well as the price and speed of delivery. A bonus for customers who live some distance from a supermarket is that frozen grocery items arrive frozen – no partially thawed products and no need for a chiller bag.

Production technology can customise products by accepting a customer order, manufacture a batch size of one, and ship the finished product direct to the customer for same-day delivery. As an example, Adidas uses completely automated machinery at factories called Speedfactories (one in Germany and the other in Atlanta, Georgia) to manufacture sneakers designed to accommodate the specific demands of the customer's city, based on its terrain, weather, and various running surfaces like asphalt, cobblestones, concrete, or grass. The impact on warehousing and the supply chain is significant – these customised shoes never see a warehouse – Adidas ships them directly from the factory to the customer, reducing the need for warehouse space. This concept extends to various other industries and applications including, for example, spare-part logistics and the on-demand manufacture of slow-moving products.

Several emerging technologies are likely to play a significant role in shaping the warehouse of the future and supporting faster delivery. The major technology developments on the horizon include drones, 3D printing, and autonomous vehicles:

- Drones could deliver parcels in congested cities and allow consumers in rural areas to get the same high-speed delivery found in cities. Larger drones may play a role in connecting cities and even doing long-haul cargo flights. Inside the warehouse, drones already facilitate stock counting and thus help to check and control physical inventory.
- 3D printing will significantly change the way many products get to market. The most common 3D-printing application today is small plastic parts. However, additive manufacturing is likely to extend towards new applications and on-demand production in the warehouse.
- Warehouses have used autonomous guided vehicles (AGVs) for 30 years or more. In the next ten years, the use of AGVs in warehouses will grow further. Increasing demand for flexibility in warehousing is driving this trend. AGVs provide the required flexibility demanded by changes in processes, product ranges, and distribution channels. Traditional, bolted-down automated conveyor systems are not able to adapt to these changes. Additionally, the cost for AGVs is decreasing whilst their performance is increasing.

Key capabilities of the supply chain of the future will include the storing of products closer to consumers, customised production, and omnichannel retailing. These developments drive the operational response – more people living in cities and ordering products online, which will increase the need to support same-day delivery. At the same time, cities will battle increased congestion and air pollution.

Customised production minimises the requirement for storage space. However, it requires fast transport and sortation networks, and potentially some storage to synchronise product flows with consumer schedules. In the short term, luxury items, spare parts, and fashion items will be candidates for customised production. Factories will still produce essentials to stock – probably in smaller batches than today, but certainly enough to require some form of warehousing.

Omnichannel retailing provides consumers with options that extend beyond traditional delivery, such as in-store collection or convenient pickup points. Self-learning, predictive analytics will forecast what consumers will be ordering and minimise inventory holding. Technology advances, such as self-driving trucks and robotic loading and unloading systems, will minimise the costs of those movements.

Supply chain managers need to be in tune with current and future technological developments and exploit the associated opportunities. The changes occurring in society are creating pressures, making the adoption of technological solutions in the warehouse and across the supply chain necessary. However, selecting the most appropriate technologies, investing into the right opportunities and upskill requirements remain problematic choices. It is frequently mentioned that nowadays 'companies don't compete, supply chains compete' and within the supply chain a well-managed warehouse will continue to be a source for competitive advantage.

Introduction

Supply chain management is a dynamic field. Terms such as digitalisation, robotics, automation, and supply chain 4.0 (as the supply chain equivalent of Industry 4.0) have dominated and driven this topic forward over recent years. These new approaches and technologies hold the potential to transform our current ways of operating supply chains. Some organisations have already applied some of these concepts, while other ideas are still in development and the level of impact is uncertain. Regardless of the future success of a single technology, in combination these advanced concepts continue to transform operations and entire supply chains. This leads to higher levels of technology integration and hence dependence on said technology, but it will be the main driver for increasing efficiencies across supply chains. On one side, this offers opportunities for businesses but it also presents multiple challenges in terms of, for example, social acceptance, sustainability, and investment requirements. Furthermore, companies need to evaluate themselves and pose questions, such as 'Do we need to be an early adopter?', 'What is our competition up to?', or 'How much longer can we sustain our current operating model?'

In this dynamic time, this chapter introduces the reader to several new developments across the field of supply chain management. It presents a selection of topics and discusses key concepts. We place this chapter at the end of this book because the aspects mentioned here have the power to transform the operational concepts introduced in earlier chapters. We advise the reader to make connections to earlier chapters and not to read this chapter in isolation. The discussion questions at the end of this chapter emphasise the linkages to earlier chapters.

Autonomous vehicles

Autonomous vehicle

An autonomous vehicle can guide itself without a human driver. Also known as a driverless vehicle, a robot car, or a self-driving car, they use various kinds of technologies such as global positioning systems to assist navigation and may use sensors and other equipment to avoid collisions. They also incorporate augmented reality to display information to drivers and passengers in new and innovative ways.

Fully autonomous, or driverless vehicles, are the next major step in the evolution of transport and, whilst still a vision for the future in many areas of public life, they hold significant promise to revolutionise transportation. The reasons are manifold, including the reduction of labour costs, fewer driving-time restrictions, improved vehicles utilisation, and increased safety. Not surprisingly, major players in the automotive and logistics industry are investing in this area to reap associated benefits.

This section introduces key characteristics of autonomous vehicles and then continues with a more focused look at their adoption in various areas of logistics and the supply chain.

Categories and benefits of autonomous vehicles

Categories of autonomous vehicles[2]

When defining autonomous vehicles, it is important to distinguish between different categories, or levels, of autonomous driving. All the levels outlined already exist today, albeit with different degrees of practical adoption. Automobiles have employed onboard computers and driver assistance systems for over 40 years with early applications being anti-lock braking and camera systems. Current production vehicles can follow and switch lanes automatically or park on command.

Based on the level of automation offered, the Society of Automotive Engineers (SAE) defines the following six levels of driving automation:[3]

- Level 0 – No automation. The human driver performs all driving tasks and the vehicle issues warnings and may intervene.
- Level 1 – Driver assist. The system fulfils either steering or acceleration/braking using environmental information.
- Level 2 – Partial automation. The vehicle performs steering, acceleration, and braking without driver interaction.
- Level 3 – Conditional automation. The vehicle can handle all driving situations but requires human intervention within a limited time when requested.
- Level 4 – High automation. The car fulfils the same processes as in Level 3 but without requiring driver attention.
- Level 5 – Full automation. The system performs all aspects of dynamic driving tasks under all roadway and environmental conditions.

Key benefits

Autonomous vehicles hold the potential to provide cost savings and operational improvements to its users with the following advantages envisioned:

- Road safety increases since autonomous vehicles have faster reaction times than human drivers do.
- Accident avoidance based on enhanced sensor technology and constant information exchange with other vehicles on the road regarding, for example, speed, brake distances, routing direction, etc.
- Efficiency increases by reducing road congestion and having fewer accidents and traffic incidents.
- Highway lane capacity increases because adaptive cruise control improves the average speed.
- Real-time traffic information improves route optimisation.
- More operational hours due to fewer break times.
- The productivity of drivers increases because the driver can concentrate on other productive tasks while driving and regulators will extend allowable driving times.

Public acceptance

At least initially, public acceptance may be a major hurdle for the success of autonomous driving. Autonomous vehicles are not yet able to react like human beings when, for example, an approaching vehicle is out of control and the need for corrective action arises. In their report on self-driving vehicles in logistics,[4] DHL has used the following illustrative situation to show the ethical dilemma that a driver may face and the related considerations for driverless vehicles:

> You are driving downhill on a narrow mountain road between two big trucks. Suddenly, the brakes on the truck behind you fail, and it rapidly gains speed. If you stay in your lane, you will be crushed between the trucks. If you veer to the right, you will fall off a cliff. If you veer to the left, you will strike a motorcyclist.

The crucial question in this regard is whether a difference between a driver's decision and the autonomous decision making of a vehicle is acceptable. Ethical dilemmas arise if a vehicle for example favours protecting its driver over other road users. The likely impacts of decisions on the traffic situation overall need consideration. Autonomous vehicles may in fact eventually surpass human decision making in most situations, which would positively influence public acceptance.

Autonomous vehicles in logistics

Discourse on autonomous vehicles is frequently focused on the effects for individual mobility and personal car transport on public roads, neglecting the impact of driverless technology on the field of logistics and the supply chain overall. With the anticipated advances in this technology and the likely market increases, autonomous vehicles have the potential to disrupt the logistics industry. We already witness the use of driverless technologies in many parts of the supply chain including warehouses, factories, airports, seaports, and in freight marshalling yards. These vehicles use advanced sensors and geo-guidance technologies to recognise and analyse their environment and to establish and evaluate their position in relation to other traffic. Warehouses and ports are ideally suited for autonomous vehicles. Such closed logistics systems allow for observing and controlling all traffic flows. Additionally, organisations can train all staff on how to interact with the vehicles since all access is authorised in a closed (controlled) logistics system.

Warehousing operations

For many years, warehouses have deployed autonomous vehicles that handle products of all shapes and sizes and can move around a warehouse as directed. Vision guidance technology employs depth cameras and lasers on the vehicle, and these devices constantly scan and capture the environment to identify the vehicle's position and any obstacles. Larger vehicles can transport loads such as pallets, roll cages, reels, and casks. Smaller vehicles may transport individual items, cartons, packages, and tote bins between different warehouse locations.

Apart from driving vehicles, warehouse operations can use autonomous flying drones for automatic stock counts. Counting pallets across the many racks and floor areas of large warehouses is a time-consuming activity. Drones promise faster counting times on a continuous basis to ensure accurate stock-holding information, in addition to reducing manual labour requirements.

Autonomous loading and transport

Self-driving vehicles in warehouses can transport goods and combine other steps, such as loading and unloading, to increase the overall efficiency of an entire process. They can provide efficiency gains and significantly increase the safety of transport and loading processes. Computer-controlled vehicles remember where they have placed items and any vehicle in the warehouse can find stored items and update stored volumes accordingly.

It is possible to have a swarm of self-driving forklifts handling small loads and pallets in a warehouse. The forklifts may firstly create a map of the warehouse, following a human-guided introductory tour. They communicate and coordinate tasks among themselves and adapt capacity to seasonal and daily fluctuations and to changing orders, customer preferences, and product structures. They adapt to specific operational locations including underneath shelves, on packing floors, and in picking spaces, receiving bays, and shipping areas making them ideal for picking a designated load from one level and moving it to another.

Assisted order picking

With order picking, carts can become very heavy and difficult to manage and transporting them to and from drop-off locations is usually a time-consuming and unproductive task. In fact, in a purely manual picking operation, most of the time is spent travelling to and from picking locations. Assisted picking carts can autonomously follow pickers as they move through the warehouse aisles. As the cart approaches full capacity, the warehouse system directs it to a drop-off location or packing area. Meanwhile, and immediately, another replacement cart joins the picker, ready for loading additional items. With the assistance of autonomous vehicles, order picking becomes more efficient and ergonomic whilst also reducing order-picking times.

Outdoor logistics operations

Utilising autonomous technology in outdoor logistics operations and open environments introduces less predictable conditions and traffic situations. The combination of material handling equipment, trucks, and pedestrians makes manoeuvring more difficult and potentially dangerous or inefficient. Logistics decision-makers are hence looking for ways to reduce congestion and improve safety in marshalling yards. Self-driving vehicles can already execute most standard marshalling yard movements including manoeuvring, reshuffling, and repositioning of containers and pallets.

One pioneering example is that of the HHLA Container Terminal in Hamburg, Germany, which many consider one of the most modern container handling facilities in the world. To get an idea of the scale of the logistics operations, the port provides the following information:

Around 9,000 ship calls per year, almost 300 berths, 43 kilometres of quay for seagoing vessels, more than 2,300 freight trains per week, 8.8 million standard containers (TEU) containing 136.5 million tons of cargo per year, four state-of-the-art container terminals, three cruise terminals, around 50 specialised bulk handling facilities, and about 7,300 logistics companies within the city limits – these are just a few of the factors making the Port of Hamburg one of the world's most flexible, high-performance universal ports.[5]

The port authority has almost completely automated container handling. Driverless vehicles transport containers between the wharf and the storage areas via the fastest possible routes. This greatly increases the speed and efficiency of container handling in comparison to traditional transport methods using trucks and cranes.

Line haul transport

Trucks typically form the basis for most line haul transport and general long-distance intercity freight transportation. When operating in public environments, there is always a risk of road traffic accidents, even for the most experienced truck drivers. No one can control all factors such as road user errors of judgment or the onset of adverse weather conditions. The analysis of accident scenarios often illustrates the difficulty of performing sudden manoeuvres with a large truck – these vehicles are heavy and may be transporting substantial amounts of cargo. Autonomous technology helps drivers to react faster to oncoming dangers and to calculate the safest manoeuvre, considering the truck's status and the driving conditions at hand.

Convoy systems

Truck convoys provide another opportunity for autonomous driving in line haul transportation. In this application, the driver of the first truck retains control of all steering functions and regulates the speed for the overall convoy. Drivers in the following trucks and other vehicles do not provide any steering, acceleration, or braking intervention. Technically, these vehicles can manage without any assistance by the drivers once underway in the convoy. The convoy can then move from one road service area to another, picking up and decoupling trucks as required at each location.

Assisted truck transport

A truck equipped with driver assist systems stays in its lane automatically, keeps a safe distance from the vehicle in front, and obeys the truck's maximum speed and/ or prescribed speed limit along the road. The driver performs tasks such as merging into traffic, overtaking, and leaving the road, although it is feasible to automate these functions in the future. The driver must be available and prepared to resume manual control at any time and at short notice.

Looking to the future, standard line haul transportation would have trucks travelling most of the journey without the intervention of a driver, or even completing the entire distance with no onboard driver. This frees the driver to rest and work on other tasks during the journey. When the truck nears its destination in an inner-city area, the driver retakes manual control for the final part of the trip. For line haul trips on the motorway the driver may not have to accompany the truck at all but could just guide the truck to the entrance of a motorway. The truck would then drive autonomously and non-stop until it approached its destination where another driver would be waiting to assist the truck further to a depot or inner-city destination.

As a practical example, the mining industry requires the transportation of materials in tough and dangerous terrain, putting strain on truck drivers. The multinational mining company Rio Tinto uses driverless automation to transport iron ore at its mining sites in Western Australia. They currently transport over 20 million tonnes of iron ore per month. Controllers in Perth, a city over 1200 kilometres away, oversee the operation of these vehicles.[6]

Last-mile delivery

Last-mile deliveries are the least predictable part of moving items as it usually takes place in congested urban areas that are full of trucks, cars, cyclists, pedestrians, and domestic animals. This complex and dynamic environment creates challenges for self-driving vehicles, particularly road users moving in different directions, at different times, and for different purposes. However, the last mile presents an advantage for self-driving vehicles since in cities, traffic normally moves according to lower speed limits. These conditions may eventually allow driverless vehicles to identify, monitor, and navigate their environment accurately and react in an appropriate timeframe to any emergencies and unexpected events.

The combination of a self-driving vehicle with deliveries to the door by a human operator is also a likely scenario. This utilises the ability of humans to reach hard to get to spaces with the navigation of autonomous vehicles, promising to make home deliveries more efficient.

Parcel station loading

Machine-to-person handover of parcels and letters may be beyond the current capability of autonomous technologies – there are many variables, and the delivery environment is typically complex. However, machine-to-parcel station handover is an achievable scenario. For example, in Germany, Deutsche Post DHL has established around 3,000 deposit locations, or so-called packstations, in central locations to serve multiple customers. Customers specify a packstation as their delivery address when ordering parcels or receiving letters. They receive a message when their order has arrived and they retrieve it from the packstation at their convenience. Currently, a delivery agent loads the right letters and parcels into the standardised delivery points. Soon, autonomous vehicles equipped with a specific attachment for parcel loading and unloading could make the process faster and provide greater flexibility regarding delivery times.[7]

Self-driving repositories

The self-driving repository is an interesting solution for the future of last-mile delivery. While today, the customer must go to a central location, in the future the repository could autonomously come (closer) to them – all without a driver. Self-driving repositories could thus become a model for mobile delivery of the future.

Smaller self-driving repositories are another futuristic solution for fully automated delivery of individual orders. These maintain the correct temperature, apply appropriate handling throughout the journey, and find the way directly to the recipients. Autonomous trucks offload several parcel-sized autonomous vehicles close to their final destinations. They would interact with each other and intelligently determine their last-mile delivery routes.

Robotics and automation

Robotics

Robotics is a branch of engineering incorporating multiple disciplines to design, build, program, and use robotic machines. Robotics and automation overlap each other because a robot usually has automated components.

Automation

Automation uses computer software, machines, and/or other technology to carry out tasks otherwise performed by a human worker.

Flexible manufacturing system

A flexible manufacturing system is a manufacturing process that responds quickly and easily to predicted and unpredicted changes. Machine flexibility produces different products and changes the order of operations. Routing flexibility allows multiple machines to perform the same operation on a product and directs production to one of several machines.[8]

Manufacturing facilities have used robotics and automation solutions since the 1960s; this is especially true in the automotive industry. Logistics and supply chain operations are more complex and subject to less constant conditions, which may have influenced the slower implementation of automation technology in logistics and supply chains. However, better cameras, sensors, and faster and more flexible automation solutions are making significant changes in logistics. The increased demand for sensor techniques and technological solutions in general is reducing prices.

Flexibility is a differentiating factor in automation and robotics. Automation uses inflexible automated machines whereas robotic systems incorporate automation that is more flexible and stationary, or implemented in a subordinated system. Automation is shaping society as artificial systems gradually support and may eventually completely eradicate the need for manual human labour.[9] Flexible manufacturing systems are most suitable in small-batch and high-variety production lines in order to be able to change the order of operations executed on a component as well as being able to absorb large-scale changes with regard to, for example, volume, capacity, or capability.

The continuing growth of e-commerce continues to push robotics and automation into various supply chain operations. Generally, online retailers cannot pick and ship individual products in large quantities but rather private purchasers determine the quantities. As a result, online retail operations can be more labour intensive as they frequently require picking and shipping in single units. The size and weight of each parcel may also be highly variable. In addition, the trend to same-day delivery demands accelerated picking rates and faster warehouse processes.

Technical basics of robotic systems

Industrial robots obtain their names by the spaces they occupy, for example, there is the Cartesian robot, the cylindrical robot, and the spherical robot. A robotic system consists of subordinated units and devices – the controlling unit, the executing unit, the working unit, and the peripheral devices:

- The controlling unit combines robotic control, the adaption interface, and the programming device. This control unit is the interface between the human beings and the machine.
- The executing unit comprises a robotic arm, a motion unit, and a hinge.
- The working unit includes mainly the gripping equipment.
- The peripheral devices are, for example, the rotary table and the workplace.

Stakeholders and risks of robotics and automation

Switching to more automation and robotics in logistics creates change that will affect supply chain stakeholders on numerous levels. Most directly, this includes internal corporate aspects, internal social stakeholders, external social stakeholders, and external economic stakeholders. These categories subdivide into the stakeholder groups as shown in Figure 10.1.

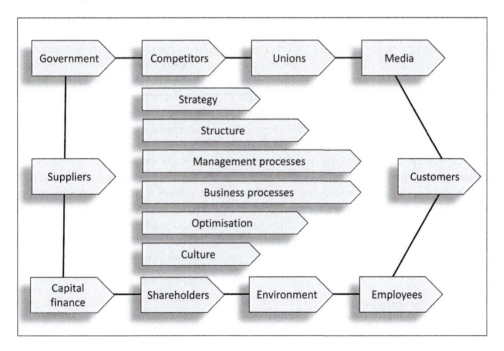

Figure 10.1 Stakeholders of robotics and automation in logistics adapted from Vahs, D., & Schäfer-Kunz, J. (2012). Einführung in die Betriebswirtschafslehre. Stuttgart: Schäffer Poeschel Verlag

Internal corporate aspects

The implementation of automation is a strategic decision and affects the overall organisational approach to production. Replacing a small part of the process with a new machine with some automated capability is entirely different from automating an entire production line and creating a 'lights out factory'.

Being aware of the company culture when approaching an automation and robotics project is essential for successful implementation. If the company culture is sympathetic to automation and robotics in general, then the implementation can proceed with internal support. For example, what are the human resource processes for handling displaced workers? Will parts of the workforce become redundant? Alternatively, will the organisation retrain them in preparation for other roles?

Structure is the next internal aspect to consider which relates to company and process structure. The company structure includes the hierarchical management reporting structure. Is the company organised as a functional organisation or does it use another format, such as a matrix organisation? The issue comes down to defining who is holding which responsibilities. The approach to implementing automation and robotics must adapt to the current company structure with its hierarchical and organisational structures and responsibilities.

We discussed process structures in Chapter 4. When changing to more automation and robotics the organisation must recognise the current process structure operating within the company. The process structure includes the process or work flow inside the company. It describes the value adding or primary processes, the supporting or secondary processes, and the management processes. This issue comes down to defining the implementation sequence and the interfacing of automation and robotics with current processes.[10]

The company strategy is the fourth internal aspect. Does automation and robotics form an integral part of the business strategy? Would an initiative to increase automation and robotics in logistics support the company strategy? Alternatively, is the strategic expectation to outsource logistics and not to alter internal logistic capabilities?

Eventually the organisation needs to assess all processes using these internal corporate aspects. This assessment includes the process risks from implementing automation or robotic systems. Another consideration is the management process that would need to adapt to any significant operational changes. The organisation may need to adjust the leadership and controlling activities as there is new information generated by the automated systems and highly skilled maintenance workers may necessitate a different leadership style. Increased automation improves traceability and exploiting robot and value stream data allows for advanced data analysis, which can ultimately reduce operational considerations such a throughput times and lead times. An organisation implementing automation and robotics in logistics must thus alter and align supporting information processes, internal services, and continuous improvement initiatives.

Internal social stakeholders

The performance and capability improvement of the robotics and automation equipment will, over time, decrease required investment to perform given tasks and the return on investment will increase due to higher efficiency of the equipment. In theory, this should ultimately lead to shorter amortisation times. Therefore, the demand for robotics and automation increases again and amortisation times reduce even more – a reinforcing cycle.

In the short term, the human labour required to support the steady rise of global logistics volumes will increase since robotics and automation are currently not sophisticated enough to fully compensate for human labour. However, as the technological sophistication and the availability of robotics increases and the costs decrease, employment in the logistics sector is likely to reduce in favour of robotics and automation – especially in areas with high labour costs.

External social stakeholders

Government agencies can create barriers to automation by introducing laws and regulations in order to alleviate security and safety concerns. Increased complexity of logistic networks and more diversity in technological solutions nourish such concerns. Moreover, increased software usage in logistics increases the probability of software errors or machine failures that may harm human workers. Regulations for human beings' safety are, for example, important when collaborative robots are going to operate in a common work area without safety barriers. Government agencies are addressing these evolving threats and current measures include safety regulations for protective gear and automated safety mechanisms.

Organisations should expect the power and influence of unions to have a considerable effect on automation implementation, and they should address this before implementation. The influence that unions possess varies from one industry to another, from one country to another, and potentially even from one branch to another within a country. Likely effects range from minimal disruptions to strike action preventing any production or transport activities.

Further, organisations should not underestimate the power of the media. This is a rather unique concern since the media could report about more automation and robotics in logistics in a company as a role model for the future, or they could demonise it as a job killer. Obviously, the first case is preferable in order to generate an innovative image. However, the second case risks extensive damage to the public opinion of a company. Thus, the organisation must handle the media carefully by selecting the right information to present in all media releases and with all media interactions. This could mean postponing a decision for more automation if the society in general and the media, in particular, oppose such a change. Most importantly, companies should of course adhere to social standards and plan a transition towards automation and robotics with appropriate change-management approaches.

With the increasing usage of robotics and automation solutions, the demands for metal raw materials and rare earths for batteries and electronics are rising. For example, each KIVA robot currently utilised by Amazon needs a replacement lead acid battery every year.[11] Whilst there will be improvements to battery technology over time, mining of raw materials is likely going to be associated with detrimental environmental impacts, as well as adverse working conditions in the places of origin, which are frequently developing countries.

Another point to consider is the carbon footprint of a robot or automated solution in comparison to a human workforce. For example, Figure 10.2 compares a human

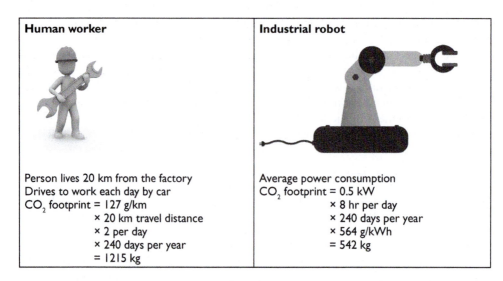

Human worker	Industrial robot

Person lives 20 km from the factory
Drives to work each day by car
CO_2 footprint = 127 g/km
   × 20 km travel distance
   × 2 per day
   × 240 days per year
   = 1215 kg
	Average power consumption
	CO_2 footprint = 0.5 kW
	   × 8 hr per day
	   × 240 days per year
	   × 564 g/kWh
	   = 542 kg

Figure 10.2 Comparing the carbon footprint of a human worker and an industrial robot. Picture credits pixabay.com

Figure 10.2 Comparing carbon footprint of a human worker and an industrial robot adapted from Robots, reality, and revolution. (2014, November 19). London, UK: Raconteur Media Ltd. Retrieved from www.raconteur.net/business/robots-reality-and-revolution

https://pixabay.com/illustrations/craftsmen-mechanic-helm-workers-1020156/

https://pixabay.com/illustrations/industrial-robot-automation-robot-3605115/

worker living 20 kilometres from the factory and driving a car to work to an industrial robot of Mitsubishi Electric Factory Automation. The CO_2 footprint of the robot amounts to less than half that of the human equivalent.[12]

The carbon footprint of the human worker consists only of the CO_2 emissions of the car journeys between the places of residence and work (using a typical emission level of 127 gram of CO_2 per kilometre). To estimate the average CO_2 emission of the robot, multiply the average power consumption by eight working hours, 240 days per year, and the average emission of 564 grams of CO_2 per kilowatt-hour of electricity. This calculation does not consider the potentially higher productivity of the robot. In addition, warehouse environments without human workers save energy due to reduced heating and lighting requirements.

External economic stakeholders

External and economic stakeholders include competitors, customers, capital providers, suppliers, and shareholders. Shareholders do generally not have a direct influence on management decisions or on decisions about automation or robotics in logistics. However, what are the interests of company shareholders? They generally expect an increase in shareholder value, which includes the dividend, the share price, and the earnings per share. One way to achieve this goal is to make an organisation more productive through automated or robotic systems. Furthermore, shareholders expect the company to become more cost competitive over time and provide increased service levels to keep ahead of the competition. Again, companies are likely to turn to automation solutions within the logistics function.

As discussed in Chapter 8, suppliers are the most crucial partners for a successful business. A supplier unable to deliver an increased volume prevents the customer company from making and selling more products. In turn, a company that manages to increase its potential volume through automation and robotics will only reap a reduced benefit from this development if its suppliers cannot handle increases in numbers. Thus, an organisation must check the scalability and ability of its supply base to provide for future demand before taking the final decision on investments into automated or robotic systems. Furthermore, the organisation obviously needs to choose their automation and robotic systems supplier carefully based on their technical capabilities and pricing, long-term support and maintenance, and even potential offerings and help regarding change management.

Wanting to create or maintain a competitive advantage, for example by reducing operational costs and increasing processing speed, motivates organisations to implement automated solutions. The organisation should anticipate the competitive reaction and the likely activities that competitors might take when they receive information regarding pending automation and robotics implementations. On the flipside, monitoring competitors and their automation strategies allows to plan for appropriate responses. This may prove especially relevant since investments into automation and robotics are usually high whilst implementation can be a lengthy undertaking.

Finally, yet importantly, the organisation should consider the customer. What does the customer expect? Customers want accurate and consistent delivery times. This means a delivery that is not too late, not too early, and simply dependable. Furthermore, customers want shorter delivery times regardless of how the supplier achieves them. They are generally not too concerned if the supplier installs automation and robotics. However, any implementation of automation and robotics must consider customer requirements. They will not tolerate an accompanying price increase due to cost-intensive automation or robotic equipment unless there are considerable advantages involved. Any implementing organisation should consider production or procurement lot sizes and customer order sizes when contemplating a decision regarding robotics and automation. For example, is it necessary to alter lot sizes of any kind and are these requirements compatible with customer expectations? The organisation should consider the increase of customer bargaining power when differentiation takes place. There could be different automated and robotic systems for different customer or market segments. Furthermore, the organisation should recognise ethical concerns and any aspects that could lead to a potential loss of customer support. This could be the case if certain decisions about automated and robotic systems lead to worker redundancies or similar social impacts. Ultimately, the customer pays for the services or products provided and organisational decision-makers must ask whether it is worth to implement more automation and robotic systems. Organisation should strive for the most appropriate amount of automation and robotics to achieve customer satisfaction. That is, meeting the expectations of the customers with least possible expenditure and avoiding unnecessary complexity.[13]

Omnichannel logistics

Omnichannel retailing

Omnichannel retailing is an integrated multichannel sales approach that provides the customer with a unified experience across online and offline channels. The customer can be shopping online from a desktop or a mobile device, or by telephone, or in a bricks and mortar store, and the experience would be seamless.

The share of online sales in retail is increasing globally. The convergence of physical stores and online retailing has led to the emergence of omnichannel retailing, an approach offering a unified shopping experience across all retail channel formats. This omnichannel retailing strategy requires management of the numerous channels and customer touchpoints that are available to optimise the customer experience and the performance over sales channels.

Operating multiple sales channels is standard practice for many retailers these days. Such multichannel operations involve selling products or services to customers using more than one channel and coordinating different channels to increase the customer value during relationship acquisition, retention, and development. Customers have the possibility to order items from different channels, but they cannot mix the returns process as the channels are not interrelated. Multichannel retailers treat each channel independently from the others with its own plans and objectives and without, or only limited, information sharing.

Differently, omnichannel management does not focus on each channel individually, representing a more progressive development of the multichannel concept. Omnichannel relates to the synergetic management of the numerous available channels and customer touchpoints. Goals are the optimisation of the customer experience and performance across channels with the possibility of switching between channels during the product research and purchase phases. In this enhanced experience, customers can thus choose the most preferred channel during their contact with the company, switching from one channel to another without interrupting the progress of their transactions, and with a consistent retail experience. In addition, information sharing across the business increases due to new data sources provided by social and mobile channels. Through channel integration, a significant amount of useful data can be gathered, analysed, and used for further enhancing customers' perceived shopping experiences, for example regarding brand or product preferences and shopping habits. Table 10.1 provides a comparison between multichannel and omnichannel retailing.[14]

Supply chain management and logistics usually mainly focuses on forward distribution (from retailer to customer). However, it is the reverse distribution or returns management, which also requires attention from retailers as they strive for customer satisfaction. Omnichannel retailing presents new challenges for product returns management. Consumers have multiple ways in which to initiate product returns; the process is no longer a linear, single channel phenomenon.

Table 10.1 Omnichannel and multichannel characteristics adapted from Verhoef, P. C., Kannan, P. K. & Inman, J. J., 2015. From multi-channel retailing to omni-channel retailing: Introduction to the special issue on multi-channel retailing. *Journal of Retailing*, 91(1), pp. 174–181

Characteristics	Multichannel	Omnichannel
Channel focus	Interactive channels	Interactive and mass-communication channels
Channel scope	Stores, online websites, direct marketing	Stores, online websites, direct marketing, mobile, social media touchpoints
Customer relationship	Retail channel focus	Retail channel and brand focus
Data	Data not shared across channels	Data sharing across all channels
Goals	Separate by channel	Across all channels and touchpoints
Interaction	Two-way	Various formats
Management	By individual channel	Across channels
Product/service/ information delivery	Via a single channel	Across channels and touchpoints
Separation	Channels without overlap and no switching between channels	Integrated seamless retail experience that allows for switching between channels

Reverse logistics and returns management

Reverse logistics

Reverse logistics is planning, implementing, and controlling the flow of materials, finished goods, and information from the consumer to the producer to recapture value or proper disposal.

Returns management

Returns management combines both strategic and operational decisions to effectively manage returns and reverse logistics processes, gatekeeping, and avoidance of returns.

In most retails supply chains, there is a requirement to take inventory back to the source. Such product returns are a reverse flow in the supply chain. Examples include companies that are honouring warranty claims or remanufacturers that are returning components for reconditioning. Recycling of paper, plastic, and other materials plays a role in driving the growth in reverse logistics, and legislators require companies to collect and sometimes recycle the goods they have sold. Lastly, there is an increasing amount of customer returns confronting companies. Reasons for customer returns include defects, poor quality, buying the wrong item, buyer's remorse, better price elsewhere, unwanted gifts, and wrong specification or size of items.

The growth of online sales and omnichannel retailing has changed the way consumers utilise return options. Liberal customer service policies encourage customers to return purchased products, and the online sales channel encourages higher return rates. Customer dissatisfaction increases if return processes are time-consuming, inconvenient, or unreliable. Hence, retailers need to view the effects of product returns as part of their logistics strategies and should place importance on the effective management of reverse logistics. For example, to lower transportation costs logistics may coordinate inbound freight with outbound freight operations. Furthermore, consolidation points help to combine materials and transport them as a consolidated load.

The strategic returns management process

The returns management process plays a critical role in the effectiveness of managing inventory levels, operational costs, and product recovery values. The goal of the strategic returns management process is to construct a formalised structure that determines and guides the execution of the operational processes using the following steps:

- **Determine returns management goals and strategy.** Retailers need to determine the role of returns management to recapture value and recover assets, review environmental and legal compliance issues, and understand the constraints and capabilities of their reverse supply chain. Returns policies can enhance customer loyalty, increase profitability, and improve the retailer's reputation. When a retailer has liberal product returns policies, customers perceive a lower risk when procuring items, and they are also more likely to commit to additional purchases, thus increasing the retailer's sales.
- **Develop guidelines for returns avoidance, gatekeeping, and disposition.** Avoiding the need for returns in the first place is the best approach to reduce the volume and cost of reverse logistics. Retailers achieve this by improving consistency in product quality, by providing guidelines to consumers about sizes and formats of products, and by instructing customers on how to use the product properly. Gatekeeping refers to the retailers' decisions about which products to allow into the reverse flow. Gatekeeping aims to eliminate the costs relating to products that customers should not have returned, or the cost of customers' returns to an inappropriate destination. The first point of entry into the reverse flow is usually the best point to eliminate unnecessary cost by screening unwarranted product returns. Disposition guidelines facilitate quick routing of returned products to the most appropriate destination with revenue maximisation as the guiding principle.
- **Develop returns network and flow options.** A retailer has a set of options available for dispositioning a returned item, such as sell as new, deploy to a different store, mark down and sell in store, send to an outlet location, repackage, refurbish, remanufacture, sell to a broker, donate to charity, recycle, or final disposal as scrap. Retailers must develop the returns network and determine the product flow options accordingly. Here, retailers develop the transportation modes and methodologies (e.g. milk runs, on demand, and full truckload solutions) and evaluate if it is appropriate to outsource any of the returns management activities to third-party logistics (3PL) providers.
- **Develop credit rules.** Retailers must develop rules on how to credit their customers for the returned product and hence need to decide on credit authorisation guidelines and policies. It is generally advisable for retailers to offer quick or

even instant refunds unless constrained by legislations, security, or uncertainty issues. Retailers enhance customer loyalty by updating the progress of product processing and the likely timing of the refund. However, retailers need to protect themselves from providing refunds for unwarranted returns claims.

- **Determine secondary markets.** Developing an effective return management strategy requires a solid understanding of secondary markets. It needs to support the timely disposition of products, ensure high recovery values, and protect brand equity. In addition to value recovery, secondary markets help to keep returned products from ending up in a landfill or incineration. Returning items back to the original supplier for credit is a favourable disposition option but is often not realistic. Hence, salvage brokers that buy in bulk and on-sell to smaller brokers or other players are a common solution. Eventually, products will become available to private consumers for purchase through alternative outlets but retailers need to ensure that they protect their own market position. Common alternative sales outlets include auctions, international dispositions, discount retailers, and charities.
- **Develop metrics framework.** The business impacts of returns and the performance of returns management requires assessment to analyse product return rates and identify their root causes. Common metrics include disposition cycle times, amount of product reclaimed and resold, percentage of material recycled and waste, percentage of cost recovered, per item handling cost, distance travelled, energy used in handling returns, and total cost of ownership.

Figure 10.3 illustrates the steps of both, the strategic returns management process and the operational returns management process.

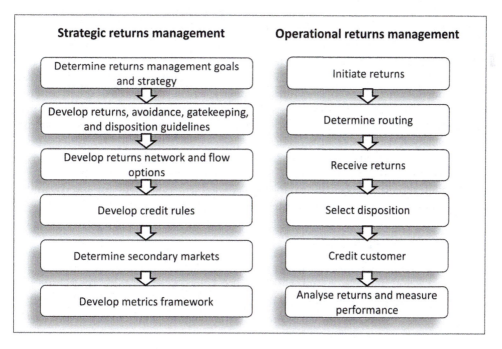

Figure 10.3 The strategic and the operational returns management processes.

The operational returns management process

The operational returns management process puts the decisions set out in the strategic returns management process into action. From an operational point of view, companies are primarily interested in developing cost-effective and flexible or scalable processes, whilst customers are interested in fast and transparent solutions. Separate the decisions to consider into several interconnected steps:

- **Initiate returns.** The operational returns management process starts when a customer returns a product. Depending on the type of product, companies may issue a returns merchandise authorisation before allowing returning items. This helps retailers to manage the reverse flow of products and assist in the process of screening and disposition.
- **Determine routing.** Once the retailer approves a return request, the mode of transport and destination are determined. The main options are return to a physical store, return to a collection and drop-off point, pick up at the customer location, and return via parcel carrier.
- **Receive returns.** Receiving returns involves verification, inspection, and processing of returned products with a focus on the most appropriate disposition option. Retailers should capture return reasons to develop more insightful performance metrics and obtain more information regarding purchasing habits. Ultimately, retailers want to avoid any returns, making information capture regarding customer behaviour and return reasons essential.
- **Select disposition.** Generally, disposition leads to one of three outcomes for the returned product. Retailers can deem the returned product fit for resale, fit for resale after repacking or refurbishing, or not fit for resale. When deemed not fit for resale, the retailer discards the product, recycles it, or disposes of it in the secondary market. A short disposition cycle time is desirable and the retailer should thus measure the disposition cycle times accordingly.
- **Credit customer.** The retailer needs to credit the customer after deciding credit authorisation and potential claim settlements, which requires clear credit authorisation guidelines. This step is obviously of critical importance to the customer, and hence to the retailer, since providing credit quickly leads to higher customer satisfaction with the returns process.
- **Analyse returns and measure performance.** The retailer should analyse returns in the ongoing strategic returns process to help develop avoidance guidelines. The retailer should analyse the performance, establish objectives for improvement, and communicate these within the firm and the supply chain.

Retail returns network design

An effective return network optimises transportation, reduces inventory holding and processing times, helps to avoid returns related warehousing costs, and should. It also affects customer satisfaction and retention. Thus, a retailer can consider effective returns management a strategic asset, and this is likely to grow in importance alongside the growth of omnichannel retail.

The retailer needs to make several decisions regarding returns network design, including the aspects presented on strategic and operational returns management processes. Regarding the actual returns network, retailers may want to base location and allocation decisions for the initial collection points and centralised return centres based on the trade-offs between discounted freight rate and reduced inventory costs. Additional parameters that influence decisions regarding the location of returns centres and the reverse flow of products include transportation, inspection, disassembly, and inventory costs. Furthermore, there may be benefits associated with outsourcing of returns operations to third-party logistics (3PL) providers to realise efficiencies through economies of scale. This may help to quickly attain returns-management knowledge, capacity for return processing, and access to specialist capabilities, such as information technology to support returns performance evaluations and customer-facing communication.

The time value of product returns

Typically, retailers have developed returns networks to minimise costs with less focus on fast processing operations. Slow returns processing can in turn lead to time delays regarding disposition decisions, customer crediting, and lower product recovery values respectively. Recovery values will typically drop over time due to delays in transportation, sortation, processing, and disposition. At the same time, delays are reducing the likelihood for an economically attractive reuse option. Retailers must be sensitive to the time value of returned products and use it as a tool to design or redesign their returns network in support of asset recovery. The time value of products varies between return product categories. For example, time-sensitive products such as computers and fashion items can lose values at rates exceeding one percent per week. The requirements regarding the speed of return handling may vary between high- and low-speed industries. The life cycle of products is hence a determinant factor for the design of the reverse network.

Returns network design

Differences in the marginal value of time drive the design decisions regarding the returns network. Two main models can be distinguished – centralised and decentralised handling of returns as illustrated in Figure 10.4. For products with a high marginal value of time such as computers and fashion items, a responsive returns network is ideal to minimise time delays in processing returns. For products characterised by a low marginal value of time, delays are less costly, and retailers can prioritise cost efficiency by, for example, centralising evaluation activities.[15]

Cost-efficient returns network: The centralised model

In a typical centralised cost-efficient returns network, all returned products are collected and then forwarded (often in bulk) to a central return centre to determine their condition and issue credit to the customers. Afterwards, the process channels returned products to the appropriate area or facility for final disposition as illustrated in the left-hand side of Figure 10.4. Benefits of a centralised returns network include economies of scale, the use of best assessment practices, as well as compliance with environmental legislation. Retailers can also offer salvage brokers larger volumes at

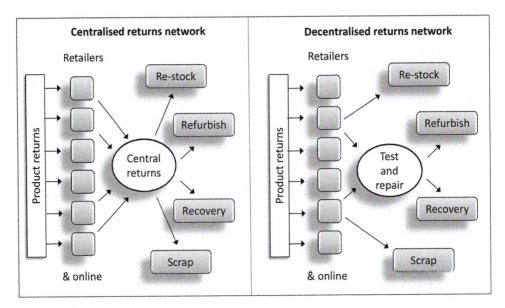

Figure 10.4 Centralised and decentralised returns network designs adapted from Blackburn, J.D., Guide, V.D.R., Souza, G.C. and Van Wassenhove, L.N. (2004), Reverse supply chains for commercial returns, *California Management Review*, 46(2), p 14

a time, which may be preferable to the salvage broker and result in higher recovery values for the retailer.

Responsive returns network: The decentralised model

Decentralised returns networks emphasise speed of response by handling returns at the drop-off point, such as the retail locations, and the concept of preponement applies to returns. Decentralisation of returns assessment can lead to several advantages:

- Reducing the time requirements for processing and disposition.
- Allowing for higher recovery values due to less product value loss.
- Preponement speeds up the processing of other products that require specialist handling for repair or refurbishment.

In a decentralised network, additional work is required at retail stores and store personnel will need respective training. The right-hand side of Figure 10.4 illustrates the decentralised returns network.

Returns management in omnichannel businesses

Omnichannel retailing attempts to offer a unified shopping experience across all retail channel formats. A key element is the retailer's capability to offer a unified, easy, and seamless customer returns-management process. Figure 10.5 illustrates the

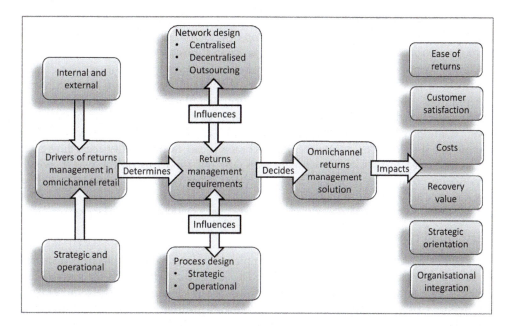

Figure 10.5 Model for returns management in omnichannel businesses

considerations for effective returns management in omnichannel environments based on the characteristics of omnichannel businesses, along with their dependencies and decision-making areas.

For retailers, effective management of returns in an omnichannel context starts with an understanding of the key drivers of returns management. These enable retailers to manage returns in a holistic way, which positively relates to the effectiveness of returns management. As omnichannel retailing aims to offer a seamless experience, ensuring the ease of returns across all retail channel formats is mandatory. Hence, retailers need to ensure easy consumers access to return entry points that align well with the existing network. Both the returns management process and the returns network design should reflect the ease of product returns across retail formats.

Sustainable supply chain management

Sustainable supply chain management

Sustainable supply chain management is the creation of coordinated supply chains through the voluntary integration of economic, environmental, and social considerations with key inter-organizational business systems designed to efficiently and effectively manage the material, information, and capital flows associated with the procurement, production, and distribution of products or services in order to meet stakeholder requirements and improve the profitability, competitiveness, and resilience of the organization over the short- and long-term.[16]

In the report 'Our Common Future', published in 1987 by the World Commission on Environment and Development, also commonly known as the Brundtland report, the term sustainability is defined as, *'development that meets the needs of the present without compromising the ability of future generations to meet their own needs'.*[17] Adding a corporate focus, John Elkington coined the term 'triple bottom line'.[18] The idea behind this approach is that companies should put emphasis on three different bottom lines (profit, people, and planet) in order to place the sustainability concept at the centre of their business decisions. The first bottom line is the corporate profit level, relating to the traditional company goals. Besides this financial profitability, companies should focus on people, i.e. embrace social responsibility regarding their own employees and society as whole. Lastly, there is the focus on the planet, which encourages companies to measure and account for environmental impacts of their operations and wider supply chain.

Sustainability stakeholders

Companies and their supply chains face complex sustainability demands from a variety of stakeholders as depicted in Figure 10.6. Decisions must align with the sustainability corporate strategy to create a positive company image and meet the requirements of investors or shareholders in terms of financial returns and risk avoidance. It is essential for companies to raise the awareness of employees regarding sustainability to create a focus on resource efficiency and on fostering sustainable operations across the supply chain. Competitors put pressure on other companies by improving their image and by introducing innovative but sustainable products to the market. Customers expect superior products offered at low prices and ideally produced with sustainable technologies under ethical work conditions. Finally, governmental guidelines,

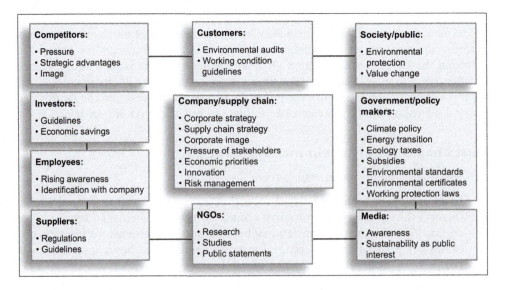

Figure 10.6 Sustainability stakeholders

restrictions, and policies are highly influential as they enforce, for example, emission targets and environmental protection along with potential taxes, fines, and incentive mechanisms to drive governmental sustainability targets.

Sustainable supply chain operations

Developing a sustainable supply chain remains a challenging goal and true sustainability may be difficult or even impossible to achieve in many cases. However, there are multiple tools and operational decisions that contribute to the development of sustainable operations and a more sustainable supply chain overall. Ultimately, sustainability considerations may be implemented across all supply chain partners and their operations and several examples are presented here.

Modal choices and advances in vehicle technology

Modal choice refers to the distribution of goods via different transportation modes, for example road transport, sea shipping, inland waterways, railway, and air. These transportation modes have distinguishing features and characteristics such as freight volume, speed, network-forming capability, safety, eco-friendliness, and costs. A broad comparison of the characteristics of these common transportation modes (road transport or truck, airfreight, rail, and water-based transport) is provided in Figure 10.7. Every transportation mode has its advantages and disadvantages and companies can select the most suitable option accordingly. More environmentally friendly options, such as rail transport, can help companies to become more sustainable by cutting emissions and reducing traffic congestion as well as road noise. However, most companies focus primarily on costs alongside ease of use and flexibility. Additionally, the available infrastructure represents a limiting factor. These reasons contribute to the fact that road transport by truck remains the standard distribution option especially for national and local deliveries.

Advances in vehicles technology may help in the endeavour for sustainable transport. Examples include the use of electric and hybrid cars which may have lower emissions but generally only present a more sustainable option if renewable means are used to produce the electricity. Regarding the use of electric vehicles currently, major

	HIGHEST	⟵⟶		LOWEST
Relative Cost	Air	Truck	Rail	Water
Transit Time	Water	Rail	Truck	Air
Capability and Access	Truck	Rail	Air	Water
Traceability	Air	Truck	Rail	Water
Emissions	Air	Truck	Rail	Water

Figure 10.7 Characteristics of transportation modes

problems that have to be overcome are the relatively low range, long charging times, lack of a charging infrastructure, and high purchase prices.

Companies can introduce training for their employees to change their driving behaviour. For example, professional truck, van, or bus drivers can be trained towards a more defensive driving style that also reduces fuel consumption. Companies can give incentives for their employees to use alternative transport means, for example rail transport instead of flying. A major problem is that comfort, functionality, and business priorities frequently outweigh and hence supersede sustainability considerations.

Packaging options

Packaging has a variety of functions. Packaging protects the product, thereby ensuring quality and hygiene. Furthermore, packaging is needed for product-handling operations throughout the supply chain and facilitates storage, transportation, tracking, transition, and separation activities. Additionally, packaging carries aspects such as bar codes, product information, labels, and prices. Sustainable packaging should be designed according to the 'cradle-to-cradle' principle meaning that used packaging or used components of packaging should be utilised in other processes or products rather than wasted. Companies using sustainable packaging must thus assess the impacts throughout the whole life cycle. This includes areas such as raw material extraction, production processes, usage of the packaging, and waste or reuse. Packaging and its production should use as little material and energy as possible and, in some cases, be avoided completely. In addition, by reducing the material being used for packaging, companies save costs. Reducing the size of packaging also contributes to reduced transport volumes, which cut down logistics costs.

De-speeding and co-loading

The demand for next-day deliveries and the increasing number of transported goods globally are factors that increase energy usage and emissions. One solution to reduce emissions is the de-speeding of supply chain operations. On the one hand, it means to slow down the transportation speed of, for example, container ships. On the other hand, customers can postpone the delivery dates for goods in order to combine multiple shipments and achieve significant load fill improvements. The main challenges when combining shipments are complexities regarding capacity planning and the acceptance of longer delivery times by the costumer.

To elaborate on the example of de-speeding a container ship: The fuel consumption mostly depends on the size of the ship and its cruising speed. A container ship with a capacity of over 10,000 standard containers requires over 350 tons of fuel per day for a cruise speed of 25 knots (maximum speed). By reducing the speed to 20–21 knots the consumption figures can be halved. A speed of 18–20 knots is known as 'slow steaming' and reduces the fuel consumption to levels of around 150 tons per day. This figure decreases further by employing 'extra slow steaming' at 17 knots and a consumption of 100 tons per day. Due to the obvious reductions in fuel consumption, and associated costs as well as emissions, slow steaming has become standard practice in sea container shipping.

In many instances, part of the truck fleet drive empty or only partially loaded. Co-loading is the consolidation of shipments across multiple companies on the same transportation vehicles. With co-loading it is easier to follow a full truck policy. For example, companies that do not use the full loading space of their transportation vehicles could share the unused loading space with other companies, thereby increasing capacity utilisation. This achieves significant reductions of transportation costs alongside a cut of emissions and total amount of vehicles on the road.

Supplier assessment

Stakeholders, customers, and regulative entities increasingly force or encourage companies to follow social, economic, and environmental standards that often require commitments and actions by not only the company but also its suppliers. To achieve needed transparency, companies make use of sustainability focused supplier assessments. Questionnaires can be utilised in order to assess topics like corruption, human rights, child labour, environment protection activities, work ethics, and adopted sustainability standards. Companies may motivate their suppliers to take part in the supplier assessment program by offering incentives and also by applying pressures, for example that any future contracts are dependent on successful sustainability assessments.

Through such evaluations, companies gain a better understanding of the sustainability related impacts in their supply chain. This knowledge helps the company and the suppliers to find starting points for improvement. Furthermore, sustainability responsibilities are transferred from an individual company to the wider supply chain.

A major challenge of supplier assessment programs is that only few suppliers may take part voluntarily. Thus, appropriate incentives must be established and expenses for the suppliers need to be minimised. Moreover, the answers of suppliers are dependent on local regulations and cultural views. For example, there may be a difference in how suppliers located in some developing countries view child labour as a sustainability issue in comparison to suppliers in countries with strict child protection laws.

Chapter summary

This chapter offers an introduction to a range of selected trends and developments in logistics and supply chain management. This selection is not intended to be a comprehensive list of all future trends in supply chains, but offers insights into several developments that are already highly influential and will continue to grow in importance going forward.

Organisations are already using autonomous vehicles in various formats, applications, and across different industries. Especially in logistics, autonomous vehicles promise various benefits, and these apply across warehousing operations, long-distance transport, and last-mile deliveries. Advantages include increased safety due to fewer human errors and superior sensor technology. Furthermore, organisations attain greater efficiency due to less downtime, reduced traffic congestion, platooning, fewer accidents, and real-time route optimisation.

Cost and competitive pressures as well as companies striving for more flexibility, dependability, quicker lead times, and a reduction of the human workforce drive the continuing adoption of robotics and automation in supply chains. In addition to these aspects, there are also potential disadvantages associated with the implementation of robotics and automation. Factors that may prevent companies from implementing automated solutions include social implications such as workforce reductions, the complexity of strategic and operational decisions required along with their long-term nature and, in many cases, their irreversibility.

Retailers continue to transform towards on omnichannel sales model that combines brick-and-mortar sales locations, online, and mobile sales channels. Especially for online channels, product returns are an increasing cost and operational issue. Liberal return policies are a component of customer service, but can also lead to high product return rates, for example more than 25% for many online retailers. Returns management requires sophisticated reverse logistics, which are especially challenging to design in omnichannel environments. The models for returns management presented in this chapter offer guidelines for effective returns management in omnichannel environments by identifying dependencies and decision-making areas.

Sustainability has become a guiding principle for many businesses and influences operational decisions accordingly. Sustainable business conduct is based on balancing economic requirements with environmental and social goals. Sustainable supply chain management extends the principles of sustainability from internal business operations towards the wider network of suppliers and customers. A long-term view towards business development, coupled with considered trade-off decisions, inevitably requires a true sustainability focus.

Discussion questions

1 Considering the trends and developments illustrated in this chapter, how likely is it that companies will adopt these going forward?
2 Are autonomous vehicles likely to revolutionise logistics? If so, what are the likely benefits and drawbacks?
3 What advantages and disadvantages have automated solutions in terms of scalability and throughput?
4 Describe potential examples of upcoming cutting-edge technologies in robotics and automation for logistics. How likely are they to impact operations and the supply chain as a whole?
5 Which internal and external stakeholders would you consider when implementing robotics and automation in logistics?
6 What are likely impacts of implementing autonomous vehicles, robotics, or automation with regard to social, environmental, and economic concerns?
7 How will omnichannel retailing continue to transform the retail environment for the internal and external supply chain stakeholders?
8 What are the likely challenges of implementing an omnichannel strategy? Consider for example the supply chain functions of procurement, inventory management, warehousing, distribution, and customer service.
9 Describe how the importance of returns management is likely to evolve over time. How will returns-management strategies need to adapt to changing requirements?
10 How can organisations manage the multiple trade-offs between the dimensions of sustainability (economic, environmental, and social)?

11 Should the sustainability dimensions (economic, environmental, and social) be treated as equally important or should goals in some dimensions be prioritised over others?

12 What sustainability impacts are robotics and automation going to have on supply chains? Consider impacts on economic, environmental, and social dimensions.

13 What are likely sustainability impacts of omnichannel retailing with its increased volumes of home deliveries and customer returns?

Key terms

automation, 348
autonomous vehicle, 342
flexible manufacturing system, 348
omnichannel retailing, 354

returns management, 355
reverse logistics, 355
robotics, 348
sustainable supply chain management, 361

Notes

1 Veenman, M., & Tagscherer, U. (2018). *Future perspectives: Planning for the warehouse of the future*. Retrieved from http://info.swisslog.com/rs/350-HXH-19/images/024496_WarehouseOfTheFuturewhitePaper_FIN_singles.pdf

2 Heutger, M. (2014). *Self-driving vehicles in logistics*. Troisdorf, Germany: DHL Customer Solutions & Innovation. Retrieved from https://discover.dhl.com/content/dam/dhl/downloads/interim/full/dhl-self-driving-vehicles.pdf

3 SAE International Releases Updated Visual Chart for Its "Levels of Driving Automation" Standard for Self-Driving Vehicles. (2018, December 11). Retrieved from www.sae.org/news/press-room/2018/12/sae-international-releases-updated-visual-chart-for-its-%E2%80%9Clevels-of-driving-automation%E2%80%9D-standard-for-self-driving-vehicles

4 Heutger, M. (2014). *Op Cit.*

5 *Port of Hamburg: Facts and figures*. (2016). Retrieved from www.hafen-hamburg.de/en/press/media/brochure/facts-and-figures-flyer-37891

6 Rio Tinto: Rolling out the world's first fully driverless mines. (2016, March 9). *Mining Technology*. Retrieved from www.mining-technology.com/features/featurerio-tinto-rolling-out-the-worlds-first-fully-driverless-mines-4831021/

7 Deutsche Post DHL annual report 2017. (2017). Bonn, Germany: Deutsche Post DHL.

8 Castle, D., & Jacobs, F. R. (2011). *APICS operations management body of knowledge framework*. Chicago IL: APICS.

9 Hesse, S., & Malissa, V. (Eds.). (2016). *Taschenbuch Robotik: Montage: Handhabung*. München: Carl Hanser Verlag.

10 Vahs, D., & Schäfer-Kunz, J. (2012). *Einführung in die Betriebswirtschafslehre*. Stuttgart: Schäffer Poeschel Verlag.

11 Spiller, G. (2015). Battery *assault: The innovation of batteries "powering" automotive manufacturing & manufacturing industries*. Retrieved from http://cerasis.com/2015/06/08/battery-assault/

12 Robots, reality, and revolution. (2014, November 19). London, UK: Raconteur Media Ltd. Retrieved from www.raconteur.net/business/robots-reality-and-revolution

13 Porter, M. E. (2004). *Competitive strategy: Techniques for analyzing industries and competitors*. New York, NY: Free Press.

14 Verhoef, P. C., Kannan, P. K., & Inman, J. J. (2015). From multi-channel retailing to omnichannel retailing: Introduction to the special issue on multi-channel retailing. *Journal of Retailing, 91*(1), 174–181.

15 Blackburn, J. D., Guide, V. D. R., Souza, G. C., & Van Wassenhove, L. N. (2004). Reverse supply chains for commercial returns. *California Management Review, 46*(2), 6–22.

16 Ahi, P., & Searcy, C. (2013). A comparative literature analysis of definitions for green and sustainable supply chain management. *Journal of Cleaner Production, 52*, 329–341.

17 WCED. (1987). *Our common future: The World Commission on Environment and Development (WCED)*. New York, NY: Oxford University Press.

18 Elkington, J. (1998). *Cannibals with forks: The triple bottom line of 21st century business*. Gabriola Island, BC and Stony Creek, CT: New Society Publishers.

Additional reading on advanced supply chain concepts

Baker, P., Croucher, P., & Rushton, A. (2017). *The handbook of logistics and distribution management: Understanding the supply chain* (6th ed.). London, England: Kogan Page Publishers.

Beitzen-Heineke, E. F., Balta-Ozkan, N., & Reefke, H. (2017). The prospects of zero-packaging grocery stores to improve the social and environmental impacts of the food supply chain. *Journal of Cleaner Production, 140*, 1528–1541.

Christopher, M. (2016). *Logistics and supply chain management* (5th ed.). Harlow, England: Pearson Education.

DHL Trend Research. (2014). *Self-driving vehicles in logistics*. Troisdorf, Germany: DHL Customer Solutions & Innovation.

DHL Trend Research. (2016). *Robotics in logistics: A DPDHL perspective on implications and use cases for the logistics industry*. Troisdorf, Germany: DHL Customer Solutions & Innovation.

DHL Trend Research. (2018). *Logistics trend radar: Delivering insight today, creating value tomorrow*. Troisdorf, Germany: DHL Customer Solutions & Innovation.

Frazelle, E. (2016). *World-class warehousing and material handling* (2nd ed.). New York, NY: McGraw-Hill Education.

Pittman, P. H., & Atwater, J. B. (2016). *APICS dictionary* (15th ed.). Chicago, IL: APICS.

Reefke, H., & Sundaram, D. (2017). Key themes and research opportunities in sustainable supply chain management: Identification and evaluation. *Omega, 66*, 195–211.

Reefke, H., & Sundaram, D. (2018). Sustainable supply chain management: Decision models for transformation and maturity. *Decision Support Systems, 113*, 56–72.

Richards, G. (2017). *Warehouse management: A complete guide to improving efficiency and minimizing costs in the modern warehouse* (3rd ed.). London, England: Kogan Page Publishers.

Case study summaries

Case 1: Three crises for Toyota

This case study primarily discusses lean thinking and how Toyota reacted to three crises that affected their production and sales. Links are made to product safety and quality as well as to company strengths, weaknesses, and leadership.

Case 2: Tube Forgings of America, Inc.

This case study primarily discusses demand driven material requirements planning and how the case company reacted to significant variations in sales volume. It illustrates the dangers of relying on forecasted demand and illustrates a company basing its business strategy on flexibility and versatility.

Case 3: Jarden Fresh Preserving

This case study discusses executive sales and operations planning and challenges executives to evaluate opportunity and risk when deciding how much to produce.

Case 4: Airbus and the A380

This case study discusses the strategy of distributed manufacturing in the context of the Airbus A380. It covers the early development issues, the political drivers, the intense competition with Boeing, and the eventual closing of the order book on A380.

Case 5: PUMA Sportlifestyle

This case study discusses the sustainability strategy of Puma Sportlifestyle and the sustainability of its entire supply chain.

Case 6: Ottoman Co.

This case study introduces the furniture producer Ottoman Co. and discusses aspects such as strategy, production capacity, process design, production scheduling, and the theory of constraints.

Case 7: SteelCom

This case study discusses the operational challenges of increasing production and building an inventory stockpile. The discussion considers international sourcing and pricing and links to international logistics.

Case 8: Tait Communications

This case study discusses how a very small company competes in a global market and how their overall strategy, inventory policies, automation, and lean-thinking implementation contribute to their success.

Case 9: Nat-pak and Tastie-food

This case study primarily discusses supply chain collaboration and compares two companies who have a radically different approach – cooperative and competitive.

Case 10: Waikato District Health Board

This case study examines the supply of elective surgery consumables for the operating theatres at Waikato Hospital in New Zealand. It charts a dramatic change in the internal processes for supplying consumables including the reasons for the change and the wide-ranging benefits gained.

Case 11: Implementing circular economy at HP

This case study discusses how HP has applied circular economy principles in order to support their sustainability/viability/profit. The discussion covers their sustainability strategy and their implementation of the circular economy.

Case 12: Fischer fixing systems

This case study is based on the implementation of automation technology in the distribution centre owned by fischer fixing systems in Germany. This provides an excellent study of change management.

Case 13: Bridging design prototypes

This case study uses three examples to illustrate bridging design prototype principles that endeavour to implement a prototype for early adoption enabling the user community to participate, contribute, and improve the product design process.

Three crises for Toyota

Jeffrey K. Liker

Jeffrey K. Liker, PhD, is professor of industrial and operations engineering at the University of Michigan. He is the author of the international bestseller, *The Toyota Way: 14 Management Principles from the World's Greatest Manufacturer*[1], and numerous other books about Toyota, including *Toyota Under Fire*[2], that provides more detail about the crises described here.

This description of the three crises for Toyota appeared as part of the Prologue to *The Toyota Way to lean leadership – Achieving and sustaining excellence through leadership development* by Jeffrey K. Liker and Gary L. Convis.[3] Reprinted with special permission Copyright © 2012 Jeffrey K. Liker.

The Great Recession

The recession hit the automobile industry earlier than most other industries. Leading up to 2008, raw material prices, particularly steel, were skyrocketing. Then, early in the summer of 2008, oil prices shot up, reaching the highest levels they had ever been. It was enough of a shock to send sales of popular pickup trucks and large sport utility vehicles (SUVs) that consume a lot of suddenly very expensive fuel into a nosedive. Losing 40% or more of sales was common in the industry, and Toyota was no exception.

Dealing with a crisis caused by broad economic forces was not new to Toyota. In fact, the Toyota Production System (TPS) became famous in Japan during the 1973 oil crisis, when Japanese internal sales and exports plummeted, yet Toyota recovered to profitability much faster than other Japanese companies. Why? Toyota's efforts to eliminate overproduction and inventory via just-in-time production throughout the supply chain meant that it could quickly adapt as demand for fuel-efficient Toyotas increased in the United States. This dramatic success led to a movement to teach TPS throughout Japanese industry and eventually throughout the world.

The 2008 recession was different. For several years, Toyota had been selling more large trucks and SUVs than they could produce. The company had allowed inventories of these vehicles to creep up to meet the strong demand; it had added significant new capacity for building trucks in the form of a new plant in San Antonio, Texas, dedicated to building Tundras. When the oil spike caused demand to plummet, the problems of excess inventory and overcapacity became frighteningly apparent. Toyota made the difficult decision to stop all United States production of the Tundra and Sequoia SUVs for three months to allow inventory levels to adjust.

While overproduction leading to this shutdown revealed some weaknesses in following the Toyota Way, in the response to the recession, the company showed that it had not abandoned Toyota Way principles. Even though Toyota shut the plants down for three months, team members were not laid off from Toyota factories during the downtime. Rather, the company invested in developing its people via training and *kaizen* activities. The great need for this training revealed that during the years of breakneck growth, the company had not been investing enough in developing team members. The training and kaizen in Toyota continued for many more months throughout the world as the global recession kicked in and demand plummeted for all vehicles.

Toyota's ability to invest in team members rather than laying off massive numbers of workers, as every other global automotive firm did during the recession, was based on another Toyota Way principle – self-reliance. Anticipating a phase of rapid growth after World War II, Toyota found itself deeply indebted to finance investments. When growth was not as fast as planned, the company nearly went bankrupt. As a result, the founder, Kiichiro Toyoda, was forced by the lenders to lay off workers, and then he resigned. The danger of relying on others for financing could not have been clearer. Since that time, the company has hoarded cash by being frugal even in the best of times so it can be independent in the worst of times. That is what happened during the Great Recession. The company had huge cash reserves and very little debt, as well as high debt quality ratings, allowing for very low interest rates for borrowing. As a result, it could invest in team members and absorb large short-term losses. It could continue to build for the future while most other companies focused simply on surviving the present. That does not mean that there was no cost cutting. However, the cost cutting was distinctly different from the common stories during the recession. Executives cut their own compensation first – salary as well as bonuses – and reduced their own perks before asking workers to share the pain. Ultimately, there were no involuntary layoffs in wholly owned Toyota Engineering and Manufacturing, though overtime, bonuses, and temporary labour were eliminated.

As a result of these forward-looking actions, the company survived the recession exceedingly well, returning to profitability quickly, with plants operating at even higher levels of quality, productivity, and safety than before the recession started. Then the recall crisis hit.

The recall crisis

The natural place to begin the story is with the horrific crash of a Lexus driven by an off-duty police officer in San Diego in August 2009. Unlike the vast majority of crashes, what happened during this tragic accident, which cost four people their lives, was recorded via a telephone call to a 911 operator.[4] The car in question was a loaner from a Lexus dealer (the family had dropped off its car for routine maintenance). While driving down a suburban highway, the driver lost control of the speed of the vehicle. The car would not slow down, no matter what the driver tried to do, but instead accelerated until it topped 175 kilometres per hour (110 miles per hour). A passenger in the car called 911 seeking help as the car sped along out of control. Before a solution that would stop the vehicle could be found, it collided with a sports utility vehicle, shot over an embankment, and crashed, killing all four passengers, and catching fire. Rampart speculation then began in the media that this was caused by electromagnetic interference that made the car's computer controls go haywire and accelerate the car out of control.

This set off investigations by newspapers, the National Traffic Safety Administration (NHTSA, the United States government body that regulates highway safety), the United States Congress, and eventually NASA, which was contracted by NHTSA. The *Los Angeles Times* set up a special investigative team (presumably aiming for a Pulitzer Prize) to focus on Toyota and expose serious electronic problems leading to sudden unintended acceleration (SUA) by Toyota vehicles, problems that Toyota was purportedly covering up. The situation illustrates how facts can be confused, leading to snowballing rumours and even vicious attacks to satisfy the interests of individuals and organisations.

By now at least a few people have read the San Diego police report, or summaries of the report, which was completed in October 2009 and posted on the Internet, two months after the accident and three months before the crisis reached its most fevered pitch, but which did not get a great deal of media attention until much later. The thorough police investigation demonstrated beyond doubt that the real cause was human error in the dealership that loaned out the car. The dealership put the wrong all-weather floor mat, a too large one from an SUV that barely fit into the driver compartment of the loaner passenger car, and failed to secure it to the clips designed to hold the mat in place – completely violating documented standard operating procedures. The result, predictably, was an entrapped accelerator pedal. There was no defect in the original vehicle; instead, the dealer who prepared the car created a defect. NHTSA, Toyota, and Toyota contractor Exponent ultimately investigated case after case of purported SUA, and none had been the result of electronics problems; in almost all cases, the cause was human error – the driver pushing down on the accelerator pedal when they thought that it was the brake pedal. To prove to a doubting Congress that this was true, NHTSA even contracted NASA to do an independent investigation, the results of which were reported one year after the most heated period of the crisis. In February 2011, one year after the frenzy, Secretary of Transportation Ray LaHood summarised the results of the investigation in a press conference, 'The verdict is in. There is no electronic-based cause for unintended high-speed acceleration on Toyotas. Period'.

So, everyone can walk away, go home, and forget that this misinformed attack on Toyota ever happened, right? Certainly, Toyota could not do that. Errors made by Toyota were revealed; for example, a sticky pedal that was slow to return on a small number of cars (12 confirmed cases in the United States, out of more than two million sold); Prius brakes with software adjusted so that the ABS system kicked in at unusual times, creating a strange sensation and possibly leading the driver to apply too little pressure; and a Lexus SUV's traction control not being sensitive enough for a *Consumer Reports* test of driving into a sharp turn at 96 kilometres per hour (60 miles per hour) and suddenly taking your foot off the accelerator without applying the brakes. Fortunately, none of these issues caused any known accidents, but they were errors nonetheless.

Recall after recall made Toyota appear to be suffering from sudden quality and safety issues galore. Most of this was caused by Toyota's reaction. After it became clear how deep the crisis was, Toyota began recalling anything and everything, often before it had the time to investigate. For example, the Lexus that was criticised by *Consumer Reports* was recalled the same day the *Consumer Reports* article came out. A closer look showed that this epidemic of recalls occurred only in the United States, and that all other car companies caught the disease in 2010, when 600 separate recalls and service campaigns were reported by NHTSA, the most since 2004.[5] Toyota was a small percentage of those in terms of the number of different recalls, although it was a large percentage in terms of the number of vehicles recalled, mainly because of the 2.3 million vehicles using the particular accelerator pedal that in rare circumstances could get sticky.

Arguably, Toyota did not have an unusual number of actual technical problems leading to these massive recalls, but got caught in a political tsunami caused by a multiplicity of interests: congressional representatives pursuing re-election, the media desperate to reverse shrinking revenue during the Great Recession, trial lawyers whose American targets were at or near bankruptcy, and 'expert' witnesses paid by trial lawyers. Yet, with all these speculations about rising quality problems because of focusing too much on growth and profitability over the decade from 2000 to 2010, in the autumn of 2009, Toyota had won more quality and safety awards than any other carmaker. The quality surveys dipped significantly in the spring of 2010, when Toyota was in the news nonstop for recalls, then suddenly, by the autumn of 2010, when the media had calmed down, Toyota had the leading vehicles in 10 out of 17 *Consumer Reports* categories and led all carmakers in J.D. Power awards for three-year durability and for vehicles lasting more than 200,000 miles (320,000 kilometres). Toyota topped all carmakers in awards. By halfway through 2010, it had regained its lead as number one in the United States in retail sales, with the Camry once again being the bestselling passenger car. Obviously, if its cars got diseased, the recovery was remarkable – a matter of months. This success was somewhat short-lived when the worst earthquake in Japanese history, followed by a tsunami, virtually halted parts of shipments from the hard-hit north of Japan, stopping or slowing most of Toyota production for months.

The great East Japan earthquake and tsunami

Just as Toyota's sales and profitability were returning and the company was again on the road to regaining its elite position, the Japanese earthquake and tsunami of 2011 struck. It was the worst disaster in the recorded history of Japan.

Toyota and its direct just-in-time suppliers were relatively unaffected, since the bulk of its operations are near Nagoya, inland in central Japan. They did have one plant up north producing Yaris, a compact vehicle sold around the world, but the damage was minor and the plant was back on line quickly. Another northern plant producing batteries for hybrid vehicles was also affected, but it came back quickly. Toyota engineers make quick work of realigning and revalidating equipment; production of hybrids resumed within two weeks of the disaster.

Yes, as Toyota quickly found, many of the basic raw materials its suppliers depended on came from the northeast of Japan, near the epicentre of the disaster. Most disturbing for Toyota, it discovered they knew little about the affected companies that were suppliers to suppliers and thus not directly managed by Toyota. Toyota worked with its suppliers, made some direct visits, and put together a map of all the suppliers affected by the disaster. It found there were 500 parts that it was not able to procure just after the March 11 quake.

Toyota immediately sent teams of engineers, along with equipment vendors, to the north to solve the problems of suppliers one by one. This meant removing debris, realigning machines, repairing them – whatever it took. By April, the list of unavailable parts had been cut to 150. By early May, it was down to 30 parts that Toyota could not procure. To make matters even worse, just as Toyota had all parts flowing in Japan, the worst earthquake in the history of Thailand stopped parts production and Toyota plants leading to the loss of several hundred thousand vehicles sold. In 2011, Toyota lost its crown as the global sales leader of automobiles.

After the recession, the recall crisis, and now this natural disaster, one might think Toyota's coffers were empty and it would need to turn to the old Western recipe of layoffs. But with Toyota's deep pockets, it continued to bring regular team members to work, even at plants that did not have the parts to make any cars, and continued the intensive kaizen and training, all awhile investing in one of the biggest overhauls of its product line-up ever through intensive research and development.

With the disciplined and heroic efforts of Toyota and its dedicated suppliers, the company was able to get most cars back to full production by early June, and full production was back by September – in about half the time of the original forecasts. With a spate of new models (about 80% of all models would be renewed in the next few years), it was preparing to roll again. The renewed financial crisis in August 2011 did not help the cause, but it seemed inevitable that in the next few years, the economy would recover enough to support a sales level sufficient to return Toyota to significant profitability and refill the coffers. In fact, by the first half of 2012, Toyota's global sales were at record numbers putting it back to number one in global sales; it was again dominating quality awards, and it was on track to healthy profits again.

While Toyota could have written this whole mess off as problems outside company control, while arguing quality and safety were as good as, or better than, ever through this period, the company chose a different path. They refused to point the finger at anyone but themselves, and took each opportunity to reflect on what they did wrong and what countermeasures would make the company stronger. They should not have allowed inventory to pile up in the period leading to the Great Recession, which led to a renewed focus on production and inventory control. They should have taken stronger public relations actions before allowing the recall crisis to become so severe and should have done a better job of listening to customer's subjective concerns. This was the result of centralised control of recall decisions and public relations in Japan and they decided to intensify efforts to make each region of the world more self-reliant. Listening to the customer ultimately led to designing vehicles that were more exciting and visually appealing. They should have known more about suppliers in Japan and mitigated the risk, even though they were suppliers to suppliers. Toyota literally turned the company upside down finding problems and putting in countless countermeasures. Perhaps the crises were a blessing in disguise.

Discussion questions

1 What lean thinking ideas do these crises demonstrate?
2 Did the three crises Toyota encountered result from serious problems in Toyota's culture or management system? If so, what were they?

3   Did the recall crisis indicate serious problems in the actual safety and quality of Toyota vehicles? If so, what were they? How can you reconcile the high number of recalled vehicles with the high marks Toyota received for the quality of those same cars from sources like *Consumer Reports* and J.D. Power?

4   What does the recall crisis suggest about American society and the way the country handles customer safety?

5   Overall, what company strengths were evident as Toyota worked its way through these three crises? What weaknesses?

6   What can we learn about lean leadership from these crises?

Notes

1 Liker, J. K. (2004). *The Toyota Way: 14 Management principles from the world's greatest manufacturer*. New York, NY: McGraw-Hill.

2 Liker, J. K. (2011). *Toyota under fire*. New York, NY: McGraw-Hill.

3 Liker, J. K., & Convis, G. (2012). *The Toyota Way to lean leadership: Achieving and sustaining excellence through leadership development*. New York, NY: McGraw-Hill.

4 911 is the emergency services number to call when in the United States and Canada. In the UK the number is 999, in the EU the number is 112, in Australia the number is triple zero 000, and in New Zealand 111.

5 Tse, A. (2010, June 28). Big auto recalls. *The Street*. Retrieved from www.thestreet.com/story/10792520/1/2010-us-auto-recalls-photo-gallery.html

Tube Forgings of America, Inc.

Surviving and thriving during the downturn

Carol A. Ptak and Chad Smith

Carol A. Ptak is a partner with the Demand Driven Institute, and was most recently at Pacific Lutheran University as Visiting Professor and Distinguished Executive in Residence. Previously, she was vice president and global industry executive for manufacturing and distribution industries at PeopleSoft where she developed the concept of demand driven manufacturing. She is the co-author of *Orlicky's Material Requirements Planning* (3rd ed.).[1]

Chad Smith is a partner with the Demand Driven Institute and is the co-author of *Orlicky's Material Requirements Planning* (3rd ed.). He is also co-founder and managing partner of Constraints Management Group, a services company specialising in demand driven manufacturing and supply chain management systems for mid-range and large manufacturers.

Company overview

Tube Forgings of America, Inc. is a family-owned business manufacturing welding fittings such as long radius elbows, short radius elbows, reducing elbows, caps, reducers, crosses, bends, tees, and 3R elbows. The company serves customers in oil refining, chemical, petro-chemical processing, gas transmission, power generation, shipbuilding, and commercial construction industries. Located in Portland, Oregon, it has been operating since 1955 and is part of the Zidell Group of Companies.

Early days

The 1980s and 1990s were very volatile business years and the market was very unpredictable. Customers' needs and their expectations began to change rapidly. The driving mindset was the sales forecast. The planned production volumes included whatever quantities the salespeople asked for and these were usually optimistic. Production concentrated on making each machine more efficient by increasing batch volumes. The common catch cry, 'The bigger the batch size, the cheaper the product'. The emphasis on cost was widespread throughout the plant and one of the main worries was the cost of being short of components. Having component shortages lead to an inability to deliver on time, so to compensate, production would always produce more. 'More is better. At least we won't run out' was a common expression.

Competition for market share was increasing with other companies producing similar products and the volume of cheaper imports increasing. So, something had to happen. To remain competitive the company had to make a change. In fact, to survive, the company had to make a change.

The task ahead

It was obvious that Tube Forgings had to break away from the old forecasting styles and traditional material planning systems. The company started to analyse their customers' past demand and used that to project their customers' needs. Somehow, they had to deal with rapid volume changes and plan for a greater versatility of the product line. The very core of the business was being challenged. They had to compete in an increasingly competitive world for their 'standard commodity business'.

In the fourth quarter of 1997, Tube Forgings made plans to discard the old material requirements planning (MRP) system. They had heard about 'throughput' logic and started to design production schedules on a spreadsheet using their early understanding of the theory of constraints. They established new inventory levels and control methods and activated the plan at the start of 1998.

Challenges to the system

Tube Forgings' annual sales continued to grow at an unpredictable rate. They expanded their product offerings into a 'specialty line' of 'make to order' products. This 'specialty line' targeted a market that was growing at a rapid pace. Tube Forgings' entrance into this market with an expanded product line was well received by their customers. Sales in this new line continued to expand rapidly over the next several years and began consuming more and more capacity, beyond what their current planning methods could handle.

Management believed that they had the right strategy in place. The 'future vision' based on flexibility and versatility was the necessary approach to keep up with the observed market change. However, even though the spreadsheet planning methods were improved, they could not keep up with the changing elements of the company. The tools in place were not capable of dealing with the higher volumes of made-to-order products.

Figure Case 2.1 illustrates the rapid growth from 2006 until the third quarter of 2008 followed by the sales crash in 2009 and recovery in 2010.

Solution

After spending almost ten years using the in-house developed 'worksheets' to implement constraint theory into their production processes, in 2007, Tube Forgings restarted their journey to upgrade their theory of constraint processes into what would become their current demand driven material requirements planning (DDMRP) process by acquiring the services of Constraint Management Group. The initial upgrade emphasis was inventory management and resource management. The rapid growth from 2006 until the third quarter of 2008 justified the investment in planning and

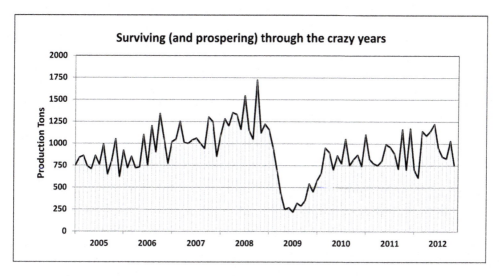

Figure Case 2.1 Production volumes for 2005–2012

scheduling systems. Even though the growth was rapid, they were still very volatile years. Then in 2009, it all came crashing down. The bottom fell from the market and only the strong could survive such turmoil.

Despite losing 34% of their sales volume, the demand driven system acted as a shock absorber. Tube Forgings remained profitable *and* flexible. While competitors wrestled with 'cost', Tube Forgings used their demand driven system to focus on service and flexibility. Customers began to lean out their inventory positions trusting in Tube Forgings' ability to supply when they said they would supply. Tube Forgings established itself as the most reliable and flexible supplier in their industry. Customers that bought exclusively from their competitors began to reward them with business citing the lack of reliability from competitors. Customers that bought from both Tube Forgings and competitors moved more and more business to Tube Forgings.

This fuelled a rapid recovery in 2010 restoring nearly 75% of the lost business volume of 2009. Growth returned in 2011 and accelerated through 2012. At the time of this writing Tube Forgings was on pace for the largest sales and profit year in the history of their company. Figure Case 2.2 illustrates the sales growth from 2002–2012 using 2002 as the base.

However, the volume volatility returned as well and the product mix was constantly changing. The period from 2010 through to 2012 was very volatile. However, Tube Forgings survived the crash (of 2009) and prospered through those crazy years. On reflection, they wonder how they managed to control the perfect storm. They had positioned themselves for ongoing growth and had developed planning, scheduling, and production systems to allow for any product to be made in any volume. They also realised that they had to do more to handle the production variations and respond to customer-demanded deadlines.

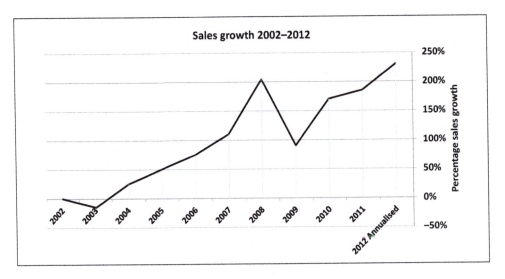

Figure Case 2.2 Sales growth 2002–2012 using 2002 as the base

Dynamic buffer calculations

The upgrade to their planning systems continued with an emphasis on inventory positions using the concepts of DDMRP. They use a four-month AMU (floating average monthly usage) for manufactured stock which can be adjusted if they see a trend that is not related to seasonal adjustments. This translates to changes in the calculated stock buffers, based upon real demand smoothed over an appropriate period. They are also able to phase in and out through seasonal adjustments.

They have learnt how to capitalise on change and their methods allow them to be proactive rather than reactive. They act in anticipation of future problems, needs, or changes. They have learnt that with DDMRP they can have disciplines in place to be 'diligent' and minimise the need to be 'urgent'. They use the planning methods to be diligent in the schedule review and the subsequent actions that are planned. The system generates signals to analyse potential problems and determine possible solutions. They use DDMRP for all future planning and this minimises the need for expediting. They realise that production cannot avoid expediting but it can be minimised if planning is performed properly. DDMRP has dynamic adjustments built into the system. Tube Forgings use them wisely.

Commentary

Here is an update from Wally Browning, Materials Manager, Tube Forgings of America:[2]

> We currently use DDMRP methods. Steel mills around the world supply our materials. Our supplier lead times run upwards of four–six months. We are a manufacturer that makes 60% of our items from stock. Our customers expect

shipment of product in one–three days with shipment of any backorders that might remain within two–three weeks.

DDMRP is more effective than trying to use forecast 'guesses' on what we think our customers might buy in the future. By continuously and automatically adjusting for changing actual market trends, DDMRP is constantly adjusting our stocking level signals to ensure we are stocking what our customers expect us to have, and ordering what we are going to need in raw materials in the future.

Using this method, we have reduced inventory and decreased work in process, while increasing serviceability to customers. Inventory planning adjusts quickly and smoothly, with very visible and easy to understand signals. As a result, we have been very successful during the recent economic crisis.

Our customers have learnt to rely on our delivery promises, therefore allowing them to change their buying habits, switching to order less more often. This change in their purchasing approach passes on the increased inventory turn benefits to them and gives us a very large marketable advantage. It also allows us to get away from the 'snake swallowing a rabbit' syndrome that traditionally affects a manufacturing facility when dealing with historically large monthly purchases placed by master distributors.

Summary

The strength of the DDMRP process has allowed the company to grow quickly and expeditiously during the good times, and enabled them to ramp down through the 'bad times' with a minimum of pain, thus positioning them as a strong viable company for the future.

Discussion questions

1 What makes DDMRP different? What aspects of DDMRP make it able to cope with the volume variations as experienced by Tube Forgings?
2 Explain the dangers for businesses relying entirely on forecast demand figures.
3 Tube Forgings base the current business strategy on flexibility and versatility. Is this the correct strategy? Explain.

Notes

1 Ptak, C. A., & Smith, C. J. (2011). *Orlicky's material requirements planning* (3rd ed.). New York, NY: McGraw-Hill.
2 Ptak, C. A., & Smith, C. J. (2012). *The state of demand driven MRP*. Retrieved from www.demanddriveninstitute.com

Jarden Fresh Preserving

Thomas F. Wallace

Tom Wallace is an author and teacher specialising in sales and operations planning, and is a Distinguished Fellow of the Ohio State University's Center for Operational Excellence. He has taught well over 10,000 business people in Australia, Belgium, Canada, China, France, Great Britain, Mexico, New Zealand, and the United States. Tom has written 12 books, including *Sales and Operations Planning: The How-to Handbook* (3rd ed),[1] *Sales and Operations Planning: The Executive* Guide,[2] and *Sales and Operations Planning: The Self-Audit Workbook*.[3] His books have been translated into Chinese, French, Italian, Mongolian, Portuguese (Brazil), Russian, and Thai.

This case study was first published in *Sales and Operations Planning: Beyond the Basics*.[4]

Copyright © 2011. T. F. Wallace & Company. Reproduced with permission from T. F. Wallace & Company.

Author's comments

Many years ago, when I was young, preserving food at home was a big thing; my mom did it every year and I 'helped' her. We called it canning, although we used glass jars not cans.

As you might imagine, the companies making the glass jars for canning have seasonal demand – high in summer and low in winter. Seasonal businesses can be difficult to manage and, of course, the more seasonal it is, the tougher it is. Some years ago, I worked with the Scotts Company, the folks who make lawn fertiliser and related products. Some of their product families sold over 90% of their annual volume in less than 90 days. It's intense.

We hear a lot about risk these days, much of it being supply chain risk, for example, when an earthquake and tsunami hit Japan in 2011. Another type of risk, which we will explore here, is market risk: What happens when the marketplace routinely wants substantially more than you are able to provide – or much less than you're geared up to provide?

Management of market risk

Fresh Preserving is a business unit within Jarden Corporation based in Daleville, Indiana. They sell glass preserving jars and associated lids to customers such as Walmart, Kmart, Target, and others. Demand is highly seasonal during mid-to-late summer, with a large percentage of annual volume shipping just before that period.

Why sales and operations planning (S&OP) became a priority

One of the key players at Fresh Preserving is Brad McCollum, Manager, Sales, and Operations Planning. Brad gives the background:

> This business has been around for a long time. As the company headed into the 2008 season, our models based on that lengthy history suggested we would see a relatively fat if not slightly declining season. As had been done for many seasons prior, supply plans were almost entirely level-loaded around these volume level demand assumptions – building up inventories in the off-season to accommodate the high demand that outstrips capacity during the season, with overtime serving as the primary buffer beyond these assumptions.

Towards the latter half of the 2008 season, Fresh Preserving began to see consumption (sales through retailers) increase significantly. They began to utilise overtime to supply the increased demand, but as the growth increased even more above the prior year, they quickly saw shortages in their longer lead time raw materials, primarily glass and steel.

In hindsight, Fresh Preserving could see the demand was different from any prior year because, first, they were entering into the recession of 2008; people were looking for lower cost sources of food, one of which was to grow or buy fresh food and then preserve it. Second, consumer trends were towards healthy eating, gardening, and natural foods. Since the company had never before experienced either of these, they were unforeseeable using the backward-looking historical demand models.

Here is Brad McCollum again:

> Ultimately, 2008 was a phenomenal growth year for the fresh preserving category and, unfortunately, a very painful year not only for the Jarden Fresh Preserving business but also for our customers and our end consumers.

Fresh Preserving S&OP design

After the experience in 2008, Fresh Preserving management elected to implement Executive S&OP and, further, to acquire an S&OP process with a demand model and supply model that allowed them to identify potential risks given different demand scenarios. With this, they reasoned, they could proactively plan mitigations where feasible, balancing customer service risks (fill rate, on-time delivery) with financial risks (working capital, EBIDTA[5]) and do so without passing those risks on to their labour force and/or vendors. More from Brad:

> Nothing in our historical data could have enabled us to predict the 2008 season, so it was critical that our S&OP demand model have forward-looking inputs based on extrinsic factors that we believed to be the drivers of the business. Key to this modelling process was to develop our ability to quantify those impacts, thereby:
>
> - Reaching consensus each month about the forecast based on each of those factors and thus producing not only a consensus demand number, but also . . .
> - Developing a range of demand scenarios that were data driven, not opinion driven.

The result was a model that helped take the decades of experience the company has in this area and translate it into quantifiable impacts to demand. It allows them each cycle to discuss the factors that drive the business and debate the assumptions around these factors.

Their demand model and process ultimately required debate and eventually alignment around not only factors such as distribution and promotion, but also the impacts of those key factors out of their control (such as weather and macroeconomic conditions). As a result, demand teams are able to offer supply teams not only a better forward-looking consensus demand plan, but also demand scenarios that represent where the forecast might likely be wrong and by how much.

Modelling supply flexibility

Fresh Preserving design their supply model around the constraints inherent within its supply capability, recognising not only the normal variation that may occur within production, but also recognising and modelling the flexibility that exists within the supply chain. Two important points:

1   Seasonal businesses usually have excess capacity in the off-season, so understating the details of the excess is important when determining how much capacity to utilise. One way to mitigate volume risk is just to build a bunch of products early and trim back as the season comes in. Sometimes that is exactly the bet that one must make.

    However, by understanding the flexibilities that do exist within the supply chain, one can better optimise the mitigation and possibly choose to make investments or make commitments to add flexibility where there would be benefit (such as labour flexibility, commitments with vendors to reserve material, capital equipment, and so forth).

2   Modelling constraints and flexibilities are necessary not only within the company itself, but also within that of its vendors.

    Within Fresh Preserving, if they see scenarios that call for 'x' percent increase in demand for lids, they will need more capacity to produce them but they will also need more steel and other raw materials, and in some cases, potentially more storage or even distribution capacity.

    If they do not exercise the scenario all the way through the supply chain, the Fresh Preserving people feel they really are not mitigating anything; as the saying goes, 'the chain is only as strong as its weakest link'. This deeper consideration within supply flexibility is based on the simple fact that capacity is useless without the raw materials and/or labour to utilise it.

Bridging demand to supply

Fresh Preserving's Executive S&OP process operates with market-facing product families, the preferred method. Their supply models are grouped around supply chain constraints, so the process requires a translation from demand family to supply

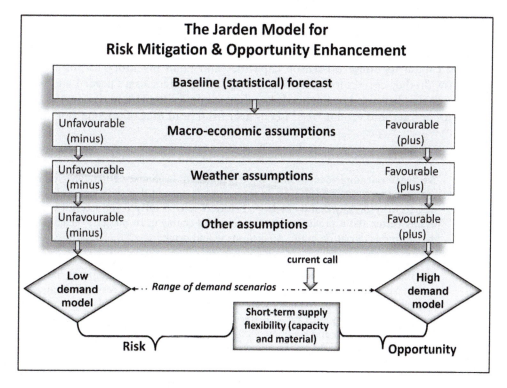

Figure Case 3.1 The Jarden model for risk mitigation and opportunity enhancement, adapted from T. F. Wallace (2011). *Sales and operations planning: Beyond the basics*. Cincinnati, OH: T. F. Wallace & Company, p 63.

Source: Copyright © 2011. T. F. Wallace & Company. Reproduced with permission from T. F. Wallace & Company.

constraint. This translation is based on mix assumptions that need to be monitored each cycle as well. Using run charts, the process monitors actual variation against the mix assumptions and the model is adjusted when appropriate. See Figure Case 3.1.

Scenario planning and mitigation

With these models established and routinely verified and updated, Fresh Preserving can model various demand scenarios and apply them to a corresponding set of supply scenarios. Because they have stayed at a high level (market-facing families on the demand side and key constraint groupings on the supply side), this scenario planning takes minutes instead of days. They can quickly run a matrix of scenarios around the consensus demand and identify risk areas created by the potential deviation within the demand models.

Once this matrix has been populated, the supply management and demand management teams are able to discuss the probability of various risks, and then develop and propose plans to mitigate those risks. If they have downside demand risk, what can be done to ensure that extra promotional activities or other business stimulators are ready to be activated?

If high demand is projected and hence there will be insufficient supply, where can Fresh Preserving find additional capacities during key times, or do they have the working capital to utilise off-season capacities and build inventory to buffer than risk? How do they correct for those decisions if those buffers aren't needed and what impact will that have on key financials (working capital, EBITDA, and so on) as well as the labour force and vendor base? Let us hear from Brad McCollum one more time:

Results

> We began our implementation of Executive S&OP in January 2009. That year we continued to see increased demand for our products and that year, as we all know, was again unlike any that we had seen before. While S&OP did not necessarily make us any better about predicting the future, it did enable us to mitigate the risks that the inevitable deviation in our predictions would bring.

> The year 2008 was again a great season for the fresh preserving marketplace, but this time we were able to service our growing business with significant improvements. Measures of on-time and complete shipments increased between six and ten percent. And our improvements were not lop-sided because we also saw an 11% increase in inventory turn rates. Better service with fewer inventories – ultimately, we delivered on time and complete 98% of the time in a year that was very different from the years prior and we continue to do so across the business.

The moral of the story

Simulation refers to the process of testing multiple scenarios to obtain a superior solution. The basics of S&OP would say to do this when there is a capacity constraint: You can't make enough to meet the demand – or when you don't have enough demand to meet the supply and thus need to know which production plan would be the least disruptive, cause the fewest layoffs, and so on.

This is an excellent example of a company doing simulation as a normal part of their S&OP process. It is an inherent, routine part of their process, rather than the more typical S&OP approach of something that has been done to address a specific problem. Simulations become a way of life.

Discussion questions

1 During 2008, sales were significantly higher than previous seasons but this year was described as 'very painful'. Why was it painful and what steps could/should have been taken?

2 S&OP has often been described as 'a supply chain thing'. Using this case study as an example, explain the fallacy of that description.

3 S&OP requires a good forecasting process. Using this case study as an example, explain the effect that S&OP might have on the forecasting process and how that might aid/hinder the organisation. Does S&OP actually require a good forecasting system as a prerequisite?

4 This case study was about risk mitigation. What risks does the S&OP process attempt to mitigate and how does Fresh Preserving use the S&OP process to mitigate them?
5 Figure Case 3.1 shows the Jarden model for risk mitigation and opportunity enhancement. How could this model be improved, and what effects might that improvement deliver?

Notes

1 Wallace, T. F. (2008). *Sales and operations planning: The how-to handbook* (3rd ed.). Cincinnati, OH: T. F. Wallace & Company.
2 Wallace, T. F., & Stahl, R. A. (2006). *Sales and operations planning: The executive guide.* Cincinnati, OH: T. F. Wallace & Company.
3 Wallace, T. F., & Stahl, R. A. (2009). *Sales and operations planning: The self-audit workbook* (2nd ed.). Cincinnati, OH: T. F. Wallace & Company.
4 Wallace, T. F. (2011). *Sales and operations planning: Beyond the basics.* Cincinnati, OH: T. F. Wallace & Company.
5 EBIDTA: Earnings Before Interest, Depreciation, Taxes, Amortisation.

Airbus and the A380

Lincoln C. Wood and Linh N. K. Duong

Dr Lincoln C. Wood is Senior Lecturer in operations and supply chain management in the Department of Management, the University of Otago (Dunedin, New Zealand) and Adjunct Research Fellow at the School of Management, Curtin University (Perth, Australia).

Dr Linh N. K. Duong is Lecturer in supply chain and operations management in the National Centre of Food Manufacturing, the University of Lincoln (United Kingdom).

The global airline industry consists of competitors of various sizes that tend to adopt either of two broad models of serving passengers. The traditionally adopted 'hub-and-spoke' model uses a major central airport as the hub with customers travelling from point A to B often being flown to the hub before being passed into a different flight to their destination. The short-haul flights from the hub tend to use smaller aircraft with longer, hub-to-hub flights dominated by larger aircraft with greater capacity. Lower-cost competitors, such as Southwest Airlines in the United States and Ryanair in Europe, championed the 'point-to-point' model. This model avoids the high charges at major airports that act as hubs and, instead, creates a web of routes often from smaller regional or secondary airports. The long-distance flights from hub-to-hub use larger planes with smaller planes shuttling passengers on the spokes; the point-to-point model tends to use smaller planes over shorter distances.

Most major airlines purchase aircraft from Airbus (Europe) and/or Boeing Corporation (United States). Established in 1970, Airbus is a consortium between the governments of the United Kingdom, France, Germany, and Spain.[1] Most design, production, and assembly processes occur at distributed locations around Europe, following the original vision for a European consortium. Airbus manufactures components throughout Europe before transporting them to Toulouse, France, for final assembly. With design and manufacturing work spread over European countries, Airbus must carefully manage the flow of information and materials.

The competitive advantage of Europe is debatable. According to common opinion, labourers in Europe are costly, highly regulated, unionised, and inflexible. The World Economic Forum warns that competitors from other parts of the world will soon pass European companies because the European Union is falling behind other countries in higher education, innovation, and training systems.[2] Despite these difficulties, Europe is still leading the field in many areas. Nine of the top 20 competitive countries are in Western Europe and the European Union has comparative advantages in about two-thirds of the manufacturing sector in the world, especially in highly sophisticated products. Airbus is one example of the success of the European model.

Airbus's achievement is based on its political foundation. While each government recognised that consolidating national strengths is the only way to create Airbus's competitiveness, the negotiation for the consolidation requires political sensitivity. The location of the manufacturing plants was the most sensitive decision. The easiest solution to resolve tensions was to site different parts of the plane in different partner countries. Another reason to spread this supply chain amongst original partners was to minimise arguments about where to put the final assembly line. Though the decision was to put the final assembly line in Toulouse, each country does as much work as possible in its own manufacturing plant. Thus, the time to assemble at the final assembly line is minimised.

Airbus believes that its spread supply chain enables the development of specialisation at each manufacturing site. It leads to innovation and lowers the production costs of its planes. For example, Airbus has developed and commissioned laser-beam welding technologies to reduce weight and corrosion. With its spread supply chain, Airbus also develops innovative means of collaboration. The 3D digital mock-up within Airbus has been developed and used for discussions between engineers at different countries where they can see every part of the plane. Airbus is one example of a company that is competitive because of the collaboration between countries. If each country follows its own national objectives, its domestic industries would not be able to compete with global competitors.

While the spread supply chain brings many advantages to Airbus, there is always the risk of limited supply due to disruptions (such as unforeseen technical issues and natural disasters). Stirring memories of cabling and quality problems at a Hamburg plant caused a shortage of engines, which in turn delayed aircraft deliveries. While production has ramped up due to increasing demand, a shortage of skilled workers is also a risk in its supply chain. Recent concerns relating to Brexit has made Airbus reconsider its investment in the United Kingdom.

Airbus has a vast and significant number of suppliers around the world; thus, it relies heavily on a global supply chain. In 2006, insufficient coordination between engineering departments and suppliers caused issues with Airbus A380 harnesses. Because of its development characteristics and strategies, Airbus has always advocated fair and balanced trade in which government support is an integral part. However, critics have accused Airbus of receiving low-interest loans from European countries. Airbus will continue to defend its position robustly and resolve the disputes.

As Asian countries become increasingly important customers, Airbus established a plant in Tianjin, China, in 2009, another in Harbin, China, in 2011, and in Mobile, Alabama, in 2013. The reasons for moving production to those locations are not that it is easier or cheaper to produce out of Europe, but because it is difficult to lure government support and break into those markets. Having a Chinese joint venture helps to increase sales in China. However, there is a long-term threat for this internationalisation strategy as those countries could develop their own aircraft manufacturing industries. In 2011, the first Chinese-built passenger jet flew more than 1300 kilometres from Shanghai to Xi'an, and officials hope the plane will become a rival of the Airbus A320 and the Boeing B737.

The success of Airbus A380 also puts Boeing into a race to gain back its market share. While Boeing focuses on the 'point-to-point' strategy, they need to do something to compete with Airbus on the long-haul flights market. Boeing has developed B777X to compete with Airbus A380. While Boeing B777X has 414 seats on board, Airbus A380 has over 500 seats. However, with more room for cargo, Boeing B777X will be a rival for Airbus A380.

In the 1990s, Airbus and Boeing collaborated on a very large commercial transport (VLCT) aircraft project. The joint feasibility study ended in 1993. In the following year, Airbus began development of the A3XX VLCT, and from 1997–2000 it targeted a 15–20% reduction in operating costs over the Boeing B747. In 2000, the Airbus supervisory board voted to launch an €8.8b development programme for the VLCT, dubbed the A380. Six key customers placed firm orders for 50 aircraft, providing confidence to progress. Manufacturing commenced in 2002 with aircraft expected to be worth US$330m each. A single flight can transport over 800 passengers with the correct configuration, providing a large capacity for long-distance movements from hub-to-hub.

The project was not easy or simple. The original Airbus approach included freighting components in specially enlarged jets; however, several A380 components were too large for this. French facilities make the control systems, cockpit, and the lower-centre section of the fuselage (length 28.26 metres, width 8 metres, height 10.07 metres, and weight 55.5 tonnes). A German facility makes the rest of the fuselage and a part of the centre section (length 23.17 metres, width 8 metres, height 10.3 metres, and weight 60 tonnes). A United Kingdom factory makes the wings (length 45.38 metres, wide 7.2 metres, height 11.9 metres, and weight 135 tonnes). The flags, the spoilers, and the moving parts of the wing are made in Holland. A Spanish facility makes the horizontal tail planes (length 27.35 metres, width 7.68 metres, height 11.68 metres, and weight 49.5 tonnes). Now, components are shipped on special ferries, then by boat and barge to a port near Toulouse, and then transported in convoys of six articulated lorries in the middle of the night to the assembly plant using a specially widened road. After assembly, the aircraft fly to Germany for painting. The supply chain is capable of producing four A380s per month.

Airbus cited the complexities associated with wiring as being the cause for delays in June 2005. Each aircraft contains 530 kilometres of wiring. A cause of the design problems was that British and French facilities changed to a new computer-aided design platform, while the German and Spanish facilities did not. With two different platforms, there were problems with sharing and distributing work between facilities. Further problems emerged as components were manufactured using materials that did not meet the original specification, requiring alternate design rules that were not easily transferred between the software versions being used by the different partners.

In June 2006, Airbus announced another delay, causing a 26% drop in the share price of Airbus's parent company, EADS, and forcing the departure of the CEOs at EADS and Airbus. In October 2006, Airbus announced a third delay and declared that full production of 45 aircraft would commence in 2010. At this point, the delay meant that there was a projected shortfall in earnings of €4.8b. To try to bring the project back on track, managers re-prioritised workloads and resources by pulling them from other projects and allocating them to the A380 passenger plane development.[3] One related project that suffered because of this resource allocation was the A380F, designed as a freighter. As a result, FedEx and UPS cancelled orders for the freighter version. Airbus does not have any orders for freighters and has not delivered any. In 2009, Airbus delivered ten passenger A380s; by the end of 2012, they had delivered 86; by the end of 2018, they had delivered 234 against an order book of 321.[4]

The sheer size of the new aircraft creates additional challenges in the use and scheduling of the aircraft. Airport facilities frequently require upgrades, with runways and the boarding facilities and procedures all requiring attention. With significantly more passengers on an A380, it becomes necessary to board passengers from two points, which few airports have been traditionally equipped to do. Introducing the plane on flights, therefore, requires airports to adapt and change.

The early delays in the A380 project, changes in the business environment, and costs associated with operating VLCT aircraft changed business decisions relating to these aircraft. Qantas (Australia) decided to delay their acquisition of further A380s for up to five years as part of their measure to reduce capital expenditure and invest in other, smaller, aircraft. As of January 2019, Qantas had 12 of 20 ordered[5] (the second largest order, globally). Qantas operates a mixture of jet- and turbo-propelled aircraft built by Airbus and Boeing.

One of the largest A380 customers has been Emirates; however, the lack of orders in late 2017 from this key customer led to perceived weakness.[6] In 2018, two A380s were even broken up and sold for parts, after being unable to sell. One challenge has been that manufacturers have updated and modified designs for smaller aircraft to enable them to fly longer distances. Over the life of Southwest Airlines, the single-aisle Boeing B737 has almost doubled the distance it can fly. By late 2018, none of the three major US airlines (American, Delta, and United) had purchased an A380 as they focused on the older B777 that can carry almost 400 passengers. While the big three US airlines own other Airbus planes, the two-engine nature of the B777 represents significant cost savings over a four-engine A380.

Emirates reduced its A380 orderbook by 39 aircraft in 2019 leaving 14 A380s remaining in the backlog yet to be delivered. Because of that decision and given the lack of order backlog with other airlines, Airbus announced in 2019 that deliveries of the A380 would cease in 2021.[7]

As the operating environment changes, Airbus continues to monitor developments. With two significantly sized players competing globally, there is little room for a strategic stumbling, with new competitors appearing as emerging economies continue to experience strong growth. The duration, size, and value of projects and significant penalties associated with failure to deliver on time and to specification means that aircraft manufacturers need to judge the market direction carefully. While Airbus has a focus on VLCT that enable airline companies to offer fewer flights, Boeing has turned its attention to improving the fuel efficiency of existing fleets and supporting mid-sized flights with the increasingly fuel-efficient B787 aircraft. However, Airbus believes that the emergence of megacities (they expect 95 by 2036) will drive more reliance on high-volume transport between these points, creating economies of scale and reducing the congestion at major airports by handling more passengers per plane. A final source of uncertainty has been the 2016 Brexit vote and the ongoing uncertainty about Britain's place in the European Union. Airbus employs 14,000 staff in Britain. Airbus labelled the scenario of a British withdrawal without an agreement as 'catastrophic'. If the United Kingdom leaves the European Union, Airbus would reconsider investments in Britain. The withdrawal would also disrupt supply chains and flow of goods over the borders with the European Union states.

Discussion questions

1 How does Airbus compete?
2 What are the challenges and benefits of Airbus's distributed manufacturing?
3 How would political issues affect competition between Airbus and Boeing?
4 How would you expect Airbus to engage with their suppliers and customers during the A380 development project?
5 What changes would you expect to see in the Airbus supply chain in the future?
6 Considering Qantas's experience, how might changing fuel prices and global financial shocks change the success of the A380?
7 What factors led to the (2019) decision by Airbus to cease production of A380 (in 2021)? How would that decision affect companies that already have the aircraft in their fleet?

Notes

1 Input relating to the Airbus company and their products retrieved from <www.airbus.com>
2 Gordon, S. (2014, May 23). Airbus: The European model. *Financial Times*. Retrieved from www.ft.com/content/c9a9a77c-db07-11e3-8273-00144feabdc0
3 Gumbel, P. (2006, October 8). Trying to untangle wires. *Time*. Retrieved from www.time.com/time/magazine/article/0,9171,1543879,00.html
4 Airbus. (2018, December 31). *Orders and deliveries*. Retrieved January, 2019, from www.airbus.com/aircraft/market/orders-deliveries.html
5 Qantas. (n. d.). *Qantas A380*. Retrieved from www.qantas.com/au/en/about-us/our-company/fleet/qantas-a380.html
6 Halsey III, A. (2018, August 19). Is the Airbus 380 the future of air travel or a relic of the past? *Washington Post*. Retrieved from www.washingtonpost.com/local/trafficandcommuting/is-the-airbus-380-the-future-of-air-travel-or-a-relic-of-the-past/2018/08/19/d98bae82–539f-11e8-9c91-7dab596e8252_story.html
7 Airbus reports strong full-year 2018 results, delivers on guidance. (2019, February 14). [Press release]. Retrieved from www.airbus.com/newsroom/press-releases/en/2019/02/airbus-reports-strong-fullyear-2018-results-delivers-on-guidance.html

PUMA Sportlifestyle

Journey towards sustainable supply chain management

Hendrik Reefke

Dr Hendrik Reefke is a Lecturer in Supply Chain Management at Cranfield School of Management, Cranfield University, UK. Hendrik is an active researcher, focusing primarily on sustainable supply chain management, service supply chains, performance measurement, and warehousing. He is a co-author of *Operations Management for Business Excellence: Building Sustainable Supply Chains 4e*.

Company overview

PUMA SE (Societas Europaea) is a multinational company headquartered in the small town of Herzogenaurach, Germany. PUMA is one of the world's largest producers of sports lifestyle footwear, apparel, and accessories behind its main competitors, Adidas and Nike. It has a long tradition in sportswear manufacturing, and, while initially mainly focused on athletic footwear, its product portfolio nowadays includes a large variety of sports and lifestyle clothing. PUMA's history reaches back to the 1920s when founder Rudolph Dassler first started to produce sport shoes with his brother, Adi Dassler. The two brothers started their own company in 1924, but parted ways after World War II. While his brother went on to start Adidas, Rudolph Dassler founded PUMA in 1948.[1] Throughout the years there has been a fierce rivalry between the two companies, which drove PUMA to introduce many innovative technologies and to engage in partnerships with other stakeholders in the industry. Over the years, PUMA also had to adjust its strategic orientation in order to match changing market requirements. In 1986, PUMA listed on the German stock exchange and has since undergone several transitions with regard to ownership and management control. Until recently, PUMA's main shareholder was the French luxury group Kering, which reduced its shareholding in 2018. This has significantly increased the availability of PUMA shares on the German MDAX stock exchange.[2] Today, PUMA is an independent company with close to 15,000 employees.

Criticism and controversies

Just as many other competitors in the clothing and sportswear industry, PUMA received its share of criticism over the years regarding managerial decisions and operational practices. PUMA has several hundred suppliers that are predominately located in countries characterised by relatively low labour costs. About 90% of production is located in Asia. Criticisms relating to unsustainable employment practices include inadequate wages, not allowing workers to maintain a minimum standard of living, and forcing workers to skip breaks and constantly work overtime. Furthermore, critics have accused PUMA of actively preventing the formation of unions at their suppliers through the lack of adequate policies, the use of short-term contracts, and questionable decisions regarding supplier selection. Environmentalists have also raised concerns. Critics have accused some of PUMA's suppliers of neglecting their responsibilities through the pollution of rivers and the surrounding environment as well as the unprotected use of hazardous materials. Working conditions inside production facilities have also been criticised for the maltreatment of the workforce, insufficient air quality, and malnourishment, as well as poor health of workers.

Reviewing the criticisms and controversies that PUMA is involved with, it becomes apparent that PUMA's network of suppliers plays a key role if the company wants to increase its sustainability performance. PUMA has understood this connection and started to invest into sustainable supply chain management.

Sustainable supply chain management

Globalisation trends have reshaped the environment that businesses operate in nowadays, and present new challenges as well as opportunities. The reduction of trade barriers and the potential cost advantages offered by offshore production foster the growing complexities in global supply chains. Increasingly, supply chain efforts are creating products and services. As a result, competition is nowadays predominantly between supply chains instead of between single companies. Companies of all sizes and locations rely on global supply chains. Managerial decisions and operational practices might therefore have far larger environmental and social impacts in addition to the ones visible locally. Supply chains operate in social systems governed by different cultures, values, beliefs, and perceptions of appropriate behaviour. Unsustainable supply chain practices can be an outcome of these values, and supply chains are at a crucial position to reshape business operations and reduce adverse supply chain impacts. Globalisation trends coupled with market pressures pushing for cost efficiencies, tighter regulations regarding sustainable business conduct, and increasing customer awareness, put pressure on supply chains to integrate sustainability principles into their strategic priorities and daily operations.

Sustainable supply chain management refers to a collaborative environment that facilitates these requirements. It broadens sustainability integration through a holistic focus on all supply chain processes compared to a localised view on single companies.[3] Many companies embrace the idea of applying the concept of sustainability to the supply chain, but implementation remains difficult. Reasons extend from a lack of understanding regarding necessary capabilities and strategies to incomplete knowledge or visibility in supply chains, to unknown supply chain impacts, and uncertainty regarding potential benefits. Supply chain leaders, especially the more influential ones, are in a position to reshape their supply chains since they may enforce strategic priorities beyond their company boundaries. PUMA, themselves the centre of responsibility within their supply chain, is a prime example of a company attempting to take advantage of sustainable supply chain management.

PUMA's sustainable supply chain

PUMA has set itself the goals to become the most desirable and sustainable sports life-style company in the world. In line with sustainability principles, PUMA has extended its planning horizon and it seeks a robust business model through a long-term strategy. As early as 1999, the company established their PUMA.Safe programme focusing on environmental and social issues.[4] Over time this programme evolved into a company department which is now responsible for humanity and ecology issues within PUMA's operations and its wider supply chain. Its mission is to address issues of non-compliance among PUMA's supply base and to build sustainability expertise at key points in the supply chain. One significant step the company took, with support of PricewaterhouseCoopers LLP and Trucost PLC, was the establishment of an environmental profit and loss account.[5] This allows PUMA to place monetary values on the environmental impacts related to the sourcing, production, marketing, and distribution of their products. It thereby illustrates product impacts to customers, facilitates comparisons, and supports strategic alignment, risk management, and transparency. PUMA published the first iteration of their environmental profit and loss account in 2010, and it is noteworthy that Kering, the majority shareholder at the time, later adopted this approach also. PUMA estimated its environmental impact at €145 million, which they attributed to greenhouse gas emissions, water and land use, air pollution, and waste production. These findings are summarised in Table Case 5.1.

Table Case 5.1 PUMA's environmental profit and loss account 2010[6]

	Water use	GHGs	Land use	Air pollution	Waste	Total	% of total
	€ million	€ million	€ million	€ million	€ million	€ million	
	33%	32%	26%	7%	2%	100%	
TOTAL	47	47	37	11	3	145	100%
PUMA operations	<1	7	<1	1	<1	8	6%
Tier 1 – manufacturers	1	9	<1	1	2	13	9%
Tier 2 – processors	4	7	<1	2	1	14	10%
Tier 3 – raw material processors	17	7	<1	3	<1	27	19%
Tier 4 – raw material producers	25	17	37	4	<1	83	57%
Geographic analysis							
EMEA	4	8	1	1	<1	14	10%
Americas	2	10	20	3	<1	35	24%
Asia/Pacific	41	29	16	7	3	96	66%
Segmental analysis							
Footwear	25	28	34	7	2	96	66%
Apparel	18	14	3	3	1	39	27%
Accessories	4	5	<1	1	<1	10	7%

During this unprecedented exercise, PUMA realised that their in-house operations caused only a small percentage of all impacts while its supply chain accounted for 94%. One astonishing discovery was that the production, usage, and final disposal of 100,000 pairs of conventional sneakers created 31 full truckloads of waste.

Based on these findings, the investigation of impacts and challenges within the supply chain became paramount for PUMA's sustainability strategy. Given that the bulk of impacts occur far removed from PUMA's core operations, with suppliers in tiers two to four, intensifies the complexity of such an endeavour. These suppliers usually serve many different customers with diverse wants and requirements, while PUMA's visibility of, and control over, them is limited. Collaboration with the various stakeholders in the supply chain is therefore essential to advance PUMA's strategy and to tackle shared impacts and responsibilities. PUMA has followed a stepwise approach to establish sustainable supply chain management, starting with its own operations and tier one suppliers. The company set targets accordingly, ranging from the introduction of 100% sustainable packaging to reductions of energy and water usage, as well as emission and pollution levels. In 2018, PUMA achieved a compliance monitoring of nearly all tier one suppliers with 94% passing all audits and PUMA is extending these efforts to their core tier-two suppliers.[2]

Puma bases current sustainability targets on the United Nations Sustainable Development Goals. Environmental goals include responsible sourcing of materials, reducing chemical use, and climate change, as well as sustainable product design, plastics, and packaging. PUMA also continues its work on reducing the environmental impacts caused by raw materials production and processing at tier-three and tier-four suppliers. The long-term strategy calls for an extension of such sustainability plans, initiatives, and activities towards lower-tier suppliers. Another important goal is the introduction of further advanced accounting practices, such as social and economic sustainability accounting, that complement the environmental goals.

PUMA markets its strategy well and shares its findings with customers, suppliers, governments, global initiatives, and other industry players through their marketing, annual reports, and targeted sustainability reporting. Supported by steady strategic advances, sustainability success stories, and extended coverage by governmental agencies and the media, PUMA may well be able to translate sustainable supply chain management into sustainable business success.

Discussion questions

1. What are the potential internal or external effects of the criticism and controversies that PUMA faces?
2. What potential advantages do you see for PUMA from its engagement in sustainable supply chain management?
3. What are particular challenges that PUMA has to overcome in order to push their sustainability agenda?
4. How would you evaluate PUMA's environmental profit-and-loss account in terms of its usability, effectiveness, and coverage of impacts?
5. Consider that Kering, a major French luxury goods company and shareholder of PUMA, adopted the concept of the environmental profit and loss account. What characteristics make this concept appealing to other companies?

6 How can smaller companies – potentially without the necessary resources in terms of workforce or knowledge – engage in sustainable supply chain management?

7 If all companies were more interested in the sustainability of their supply chains, how would this change the face of business?

Notes

1 PUMA SE. (n.d.). *History*. Retrieved from http://about.puma.com/category/company/history/
2 PUMA SE. (n.d.). *Annual report 2018*. Retrieved from https://annual-report-2018.puma.com/en/annual-report/additional-information/the-puma-share/
3 European Business and Biodiversity Campaign. (n.d.). Retrieved from www.business-biodiversity.eu
4 PUMA SE, Annual and sustainability report 2011. (n.d.). Retrieved from http://safe.puma.com/us/en/
5 McGill, A. (2011). PUMA's reporting highlights global business challenges. *PwC World Watch*, *2011*(3), 10–11. Retrieved from www.pwc.com/gx/en/ifrsreporting/assets/world-watch-issue-3-2011.pdf
6 *Ibid.*

Ottoman Co.

Laleh Haerian Ardekani

Laleh Haerian Ardekani completed her PhD in the Operations Management Department in University of Auckland Business School in 2011. She titled her PhD thesis, 'New insights on the multistage insertion formulation of the traveling salesman problem: Polytopes, algorithms, and experiments'. Laleh is currently a business systems analyst at Mackenzie Investments in Toronto, Canada.

Business model

Ottoman Co., a small family business, has been manufacturing furniture for almost four decades. Ottoman Co. is the only major producer of furniture in their small town with a population of around 70,000. They design and manufacture various pieces of furniture, ranging from elaborately designed and crafted heavy pieces of furniture, to the more contemporary and trendy simple modern products. Over the last five years, around 80% of their revenue derived from selling the simpler and more minimalistic works in their catalogue, which attracts younger clients.

Ottoman Co. has a well-equipped workshop with eight full-time employees, six of whom work on the shop floor, handling all the processes including design, assembly, carving, and painting. The company is proud to have always employed highly experienced artisans in charge of carving and designing their unique furniture. Some operations in the production process, such as assembly and sowing cushions, require medium-level expertise, and other operations such as cutting and sawing wood require staff with minimum skills.

Process design

Ottoman Co. faces complex production planning decisions because they are a small-sized workshop that manufactures a high variety of products. Each product manufactured in the workshop requires a specific sequence of processes and steps that uses a subset of resources (equipment, machines, and labour). Resources-sharing applies across different on-hand orders, based on priority of orders. Delivery dates promised to customers and the order sizes dictate the priority of orders and hence task schedules on the shop floor.

The current practice is that when an order is due, or when there is a rush order, they 'borrow' the required resources for that order from other orders, until they finish the high-priority order and hand it to the customer. This sometimes results in a bit of chaos on the shop floor, as they constantly switch resources back and forth between tasks when a rush order arrives. The business owners suspect that this constant reallocation of resources in the middle of operations and the constant breaking of machine set-ups partially cause the large piles of work in process inventory.

Challenges and current problems

There are rumours of an IKEA branch opening soon in their neighbouring town that is less than an hour's drive away. Although Ottoman Co. has been enjoying a niche market with their loyal customers and no major competitor up until now, chances are that it cannot compete with the new rising giant store. Ottoman Co. business owners worry that most of their customers will turn over to IKEA, for the simple fact of better service levels and shorter lead times, despite their non-customised and simpler designs.

Ottoman Co. believes that a practice like IKEA benefits from large finished goods inventories that enable them to offer high levels of service that also protects them against demand uncertainties. On the other hand, Ottoman Co. makes their furniture to order with significant lead times and frequent tardy deliveries. Long lead times and unreliable due dates by Ottoman Co. seem to be caused in part by the way operations are managed in the workshop. Workshop staff is constantly working; however, it seems that the overwhelming stack of overdue orders will never decrease.

With a significant shift in customer expectations and behaviour on the horizon, Ottoman Co. feels the need to modify their business process significantly to be able to stay in the market. They are looking to improve their business in various aspects. They wonder how they can increase their chances of survival and success, by coming up with methods that help decreasing their work in progress inventory, and their list of long-overdue orders.

Solutions for facing challenges ahead

Ottoman Co. is interested in investigating methods enabling them to improve competitiveness and to quote more accurate delivery times to their customers:

* **Improve the scheduling system.** Ottoman Co. processes orders based on proximity of their deadlines and order size. The expected order production times and the current production schedule are two major factors missing from this practice. In other words, when quoting delivery times to customers no one consults the production schedule. They may promise deliveries to customers that the shop floor is not able to fulfil. They also accept rush orders without evaluating its impact on production and other in-process orders. Ottoman Co. recognises they should investigate better methods for estimating order delivery times. An important component of this is being able to spot and then schedule the bottleneck in the system.
* **Locate the bottleneck.** Producing various products that each requires a different sequence of activities, machine settings, and resources results in different bottlenecks from one working day to the next. For example, the bottleneck when manufacturing a dining table with carvings is the carving step, however when producing a chair, it is the assembly step. Given the production plan of each

working day, when they produce various products at the same time, Ottoman Co. needs to perform capacity management and other analytical tools to find the bottleneck and make sure it is utilised as effectively as possible.

- **Decouple the bottleneck.** After locating the bottleneck, Ottoman Co. needs to make sure the bottleneck is not starved by its previous activities that are running late in supplying material to the bottleneck, or it is not blocked by processes after the bottleneck, that are not able to receive the bottleneck's output. By providing more independence for the bottlenecks from their predecessor or successor activities (through having inventory buffers), the bottleneck can work more efficiently.
- **Synchronise production schedule with the bottleneck's schedule.** Ottoman Co. needs to make sure that production and resource schedules are synchronised in a way that the bottleneck's time is not wasted. Currently the bottleneck remains idle as it waits for other resources to become available (such as when a staff member dedicated to a bottleneck is busy attending another non-bottleneck activity).
- **Provide more flexibility in the workforce.** Cross-training more staff will provide more flexibility on the shop floor and they will lose less time and capacity. Staff will be able to switch more easily between tasks, and they can assign staff to activities that need immediate attention.
- **Hold enough fast-moving raw materials in inventory.** Estimating future demand would help Ottoman Co. figure out what and how much raw material items to stock. By doing so, the manufacturing of some rush orders can commence earlier than before.

Ottoman Co. is hopeful that by putting these changes in place, they can provide higher service levels for their customers and have better insight into their operations, enabling them to meet deadlines better than before.

Discussion questions

1   Discuss the advantages and disadvantages of the current process design.
2   How would the furniture market change if an IKEA branch opens soon in their neighbouring town and how should Ottoman Co. respond?
3   Comment on each of the solutions for facing the challenges ahead.
4   Prepare an implementation schedule for process improvement. It may be difficult to put a timeframe for improvement activities. However, the question wants the sequence of activities that would provide the most benefits to Ottoman Co.
5   Consider the case where Ottoman Co. is about to start painting a dozen simple dining chairs, when two rush orders from two different customers come in; one is a custom-designed dining table with carvings, and the other is a set of eight simple dining chairs. Table Case 6.1 shows the production steps, required staff, and expected times for producing one unit of each of these products. Table Case 6.2 shows the available workforce in the workshop with their skill levels. Assume the following:

- There are eight hours in a working day.
- Each workstation can process only one unit of product at a time.
- Producing the dining table has a higher priority than the chairs.

- You can schedule transfer batches to move from a step to the next. A transfer batch (in the theory of constraints) is the quantity that transfers from a step to the next. It is (usually) smaller than the total production quantity. The sum of the transfer batches equals the process batch.

(a) Suggest a production plan for Ottoman Co. that enables them to deliver these two products as fast as possible.

(b) What is the earliest delivery date they can promise their customers?

(c) How would their production plan change if dining chairs have the higher priority?

Table Case 6.1 Product routing showing resource requirement and type by workstation

Order		Design*	Cutting	Assembly	Carving	Painting**	Making cushions
Dining Table	Human resource	A	D	One C or two D	B	one C or two D	–
	Expected time (hours)	4	4	5	10	2	–
Dining Chair	Human resource	A	D	C	–	one C or two D	C
	Expected time (hours)	I	2	1.5	–	I	1.5

*The design step is only performed once for each order.

** Painted products should remain in the panting workstation for a minimum of one working day, before they can be moved from the painting station.

Table Case 6.2 Workforce type, skill level, and number of workers available

Workforce Type Code	Skill level	Number of workers available
A	High (Product Design)	I
B	High (Carving)	I
C	Medium	2
D	Low	2

SteelCom

Lincoln C. Wood

Dr Lincoln C. Wood is a Senior Lecturer in operations and supply chain management in the Department of Management, the University of Otago (Dunedin, New Zealand) and an Adjunct Research Fellow at the School of Management, Curtin University (Perth, Australia).

Company and products

Based in Sydney, SteelCom (a fictitious firm) is a large supplier of structural steel components for the construction and infrastructure industries based in and around Australia. They employ about 200 staff on their industrial site.

Two significant products are steel mesh and structural steel. SteelCom creates **Mesh products** from iron wire that is supplied in spools, straightened, cut into the same length, collected in bundles, transferred to a separate machine that creates a grid pattern, and automatically welded together into the sheets of mesh. Materials-handling machines collate the sheets in a pile and transfer them into finished goods inventory. **Structural steel products** provide additional strength and structural support for the concrete used in buildings and other structures in the construction industry. Machines bend the steel rods into specific shapes and sizes. Thin components are made from large spools of wire. Machines straighten them and feed them through other machines that measure and then manipulate the steel rod through a sequence of turning and bending operations to create a specific shape, before cutting the wire. An operator removes the component and bundles it. Similar machines process long, thick, straight rods into the relatively thicker, heavier components. This process increases the amount of waste (relative to the spooled wire) as the operator discards the remainder of the rod after the final component is formed.

SteelCom also recently started an adjunct galvanising plant involving very labour-intensive operations. All the different steel components must be hung on special racks (looking like a washing line) using metal hooks. There is no algorithm or computer software available to help plan and manage this process. SteelCom relies on the ingenuity and experience of their workers to ensure that this process operates smoothly. The racks are brought to a series of pits. The first pits 'clean' the products, and the final pit, containing molten zinc, completes the galvanising process. The process sometimes leaves barbs or sharp corners. Workers must manually inspect all products and remove barbs by filing.

Inventory management

SteelCom's supply chain manager focuses on four main types of inventories: work in process, finished goods, consignment stocks, and raw materials.

Management of work in process and finished goods stock is relatively simple; much of SteelCom's business is make to order rather than make to stock. However, SteelCom sometimes manufactures certain components for customers, particularly when they know that a customer is going to be placing large orders soon. They require significant space to store these finished goods inventories. The materials are relatively low-value, and space is now at a premium at SteelCom's site after five years of strong growth.

Consignment stocks for key customers are important. A recent arrangement to secure a large new account for an infrastructure company has resulted in an agreement to own and operate consignment stocks at the customer's locations. The requirement to boost inventory led to a SteelCom project to increase production by 45% for three months before reducing production down to a level representing an increase of 25% over the previous production. The production increase ensured that they could produce the consignment inventory required for each location. SteelCom owns the inventory at the consignment locations; the customer takes ownership of the inventory when they withdraw it and begin to use it. SteelCom must monitor and manage their inventory carefully to meet agreed service levels.

The management of raw materials and the procurement/sourcing process remains challenging. All inputs are commodity products and are available globally. Steel prices vary over different geographic locations. In Australasia, the prices are quite high because of the high costs of labour, and the considerable cost of occupational health and safety regulations. In contrast, material from steel mills in Southeast Asia is cheaper, partly due to the economies of scale experienced by those steel mills. SteelCom can source from a local distributor with a relatively high unit cost and a lead time of several days and extremely consistent delivery schedules. Alternatively, they can source from a Southeast Asian supplier with a very low unit cost and average lead times of nine weeks with a standard deviation of 12 days. SteelCom receives notification when the products arrive in their local port. While investigating these options, the supply chain manager discovered that with the required volumes they could now negotiate very good prices with the Southeast Asian suppliers. An added challenge is that SteelCom manages the inventory from the local port, transports it to their facility, and stores it as raw materials. The supply chain manager has noted increased pressure on storage facilities at SteelCom's site, and it has become increasingly difficult to accommodate large increases in raw materials.

Recent projects have ensured that all the materials are traceable and SteelCom now sources only from steel mills accredited by the Australian Certification Authority of Reinforcing Steels (ACRS). In parallel, inventory accuracy has improved. The supply chain manager realises that SteelCom should have undertaken this project before taking on the new client with multiple consignment stock locations. It is now challenging to improve the inventory accuracy further in readiness for an enterprise resource planning (ERP) system deployment in six months.

Discussion questions

1 What would some of the operational challenges be when they increased production significantly to build up inventory for the consignment locations?

2 Compare local Australasian versus Asian sourcing. What are the implications for raw materials, work in process, and finished goods types of inventories?

3 Investigate price differences between Asian steel mills and those in Australasia. (You may use North American steel prices as a proxy for Australasian steel prices.) What are the inventory implications of the different sourcing strategies?

4 What are the operational consequences of the business decision to establish consignment stocks?

5 What alternative international logistics arrangements may SteelCom pursue with suppliers?

6 Given that commonly used barcode may be difficult to apply in this operational environment, what options are there to track and monitor inventory in SteelCom's operational environment?

Tait Communications

David Gardiner

David Gardiner has a lifetime of practical experience as a business consultant in operations management and supply chain management. He was a contract lecturer at the University of Auckland Business School for 25 years and currently teaches under contract at Massey University (New Zealand). He is a co-author of *Operations Management for Business Excellence: Building Sustainable Supply Chains 4e.*

Knighted in 1999 for his contribution to electronics, Sir Angus Tait lived and breathed radio communications all his working life. He started by designing and building mobile radios that operated from the boot of his car and formed Tait Electronics Limited in 1969 in Christchurch, New Zealand.[1]

During the 1970s the company concentrated on lightweight mobile radios, securing a majority share of the New Zealand market within a few years, and exporting a quarter of its production. The company established subsidiaries in the United Kingdom, the United States, and Singapore.

In the 1980s, the company moved to a larger production facility, which is part of their current location, and opened a subsidiary in Brisbane, Australia. In the days before cell phones became ubiquitous, their mobile radios were very popular in taxis and with transport operators and all businesses that needed to manage mobile workforces. In 2010, Tait opened facilities in Vienna, Austria and in 2011, in Melbourne, Australia. In December 2018, Tait announced the sale of a minority shareholding to JVCKENWOOD of Japan with some of the sale proceeds enhancing the development of cloud-based critical communications solutions.[2] Today, Tait employs about 650 people around the world, has offices in six countries, and maintains a network of distributors and dealers in another 150 countries. Tait exports about 95% of products from New Zealand.

The website describes the business as 'a global leader in designing, delivering, and managing innovative communication solutions that help utilities and public safety organisations to keep the lights on and communities safe'. The company is a small player with just two percent of the world market. Motorola Solutions dominates the world market with about 70% market share. Tait has about 40% of the New Zealand market and about 25% of the Australian market.

Tait's mobile radio equipment and software solutions suit any aspect of public safety, law enforcement and police, fire and emergency response, emergency medical services, utilities, transport, mining, oil and gas, and anywhere that requires highly reliable, private, and secure communications. As examples:

- About 9000 firefighters and volunteers, who make up Victoria's Country Fire Authority in Australia, use a P25 radio network[3] supplied and supported by Tait.

- London Bus – one of the largest and most comprehensive public transport systems in the world – uses Tait technology to deliver high-quality voice and data applications.
- São Paulo Military Police – the largest police force in Brazil, and one of the largest in the world – uses Tait P25 radios for visible street policing, anti-rioting, and the preservation of public order.
- Dublin Bus provides bus services throughout Dublin City and County Dublin (570 miles) with some services extending into the neighbouring counties of Meath, Kildare, and Wicklow. Their Tait system offers patrons up-to-date, real-time scheduling before they even leave home, as well as at bus stops and on-board buses.
- The New Zealand All Blacks rugby team uses Tait radio equipment for team communication at home and during overseas test matches.

The strategic product drivers are continued innovation with technology to develop and deliver high-quality products and services to satisfy customers' demands and fulfil their expectations. Tait employs designers and engineers who speak their customers' languages. Thus, clients can be more involved with product development that specifically meets their needs. From a common base, Tait can customise products to create unique solution offerings – all within a short time frame. Tait is small and agile enough to provide good customer service, but also experienced enough to have strong technological research and innovation.

Future solutions, integrating traditional private mobile radio with other carrier options such as broadband cellular, might allow public safety workers to stream live footage of accidents, fire, or earthquake scenes directly to a central command room, and to access large files and documents far more routinely and quickly than is possible today. Clients such as fire, police, and other emergency services utilising body cameras and remote camera technology need live-streaming capability to assist in providing safety for their staff and for monitoring various situations.

Advances in digital communication technology and the employment of differing rules governing these communication methods requires Tait to invest in research and development continually. Tait must be diligent in how it addresses intellectual property rights that may accompany these technologies and ensure it is able to meet licence conditions. It must keep up with what new solutions other players in the market are offering clients. Keeping ahead of competitors and understanding client needs is important to keep competitors at bay and offer future-proof solutions to clients.

The manufacturing base is in Christchurch, but this does not limit the company's ability to provide global communications solutions to its international customers. The Christchurch production facility can operate 24 hours per day, seven days per week, if demand dictates. Strategically placed within a couple of kilometres of Christchurch International Airport, Tait arranges for about half of all freight movements to be air freighted.

Most inventories are vendor-managed, whereby Tait is responsible for maintaining inventory levels but not obligated to pay for goods until consumed. Six-month rolling forecasts help control a demand-pull system for inventory, with inventory levels managed based on actual orders rather than historical data. Inventory supplies come from several countries around the world – Australia, Malaysia, Singapore, and Japan – as well as from within New Zealand.

Lean thinking is a way of life at Tait. It embarked on a lean manufacturing programme in late 2006 to ensure that its production environment could continue to deliver competitively-priced communications solutions, systems, and products to a global customer base. The lean journey has allowed the production line to increase unit production by 144%, with no increase in employee numbers and half the manufacturing space.

Tait makes products to order. By engaging with the client early in the development phase, Tait can anticipate orders several months in advance. The real value add is the relationship with the client that starts early in the order process. The design process identifies component requirements early on and the assembly process is located adjacent to design. Tait produces products in perfect quality and eliminates waste and customer hassle.

Currently Tait produces a wide range of digital encrypted radio technology products. In the critical communications industry (public safety, transport, and utilities), digital mobile radio is replacing analogue radio networks all over the world, and these replacement projects are providing a steady stream of work for Tait and other manufacturers to the sector. The market is now seeking increasingly complex product solutions, including the provision of broadband for data-heavy applications and services.

The global scale of Tait's operations provides a few challenges, including communications, language and cultural barriers, varying regulations, and political issues. Tait's size, market share, and product range affects its buying power. This, coupled with the distance from customers, and customer and country restrictions, creates a harder path to market when compared to some competitors. Each geographic environment presents its own challenges with country-specific rules and legislation for wireless communications. Tait must be fully aware of these potential issues. The company must develop its products to ensure all are effective and compliant in each of the markets and market verticals it targets. Tait must have clear and accurate communication with clients to build loyalty and goodwill. The focus on a consultative approach, as well as the flexibility and willingness to incorporate custom solutions, sets Tait apart.

Tait's majority owner is a charitable trust, a body whose founding principles include supporting the electronics industry and associated education in New Zealand. Tait uses profits flowing to the trust from the commercial enterprise, Tait Communications, to further these founding goals. The ongoing commitment to New Zealand as its manufacturing base and headquarters has necessitated a focus on delivering custom solutions. Thus, Tait can capture high-end customers and distinguish itself from high-volume manufacturing companies. As part of its strategy, Tait focuses on delivering managed services and taking responsibility for monitoring and operating a system or solution on behalf of a customer, rather than just supplying products. Customers turn to Tait for the complete communications system – sourced, deployed, supported, and managed in a fully integrated way.

Discussion questions

1   What is the target market for Tait Communications? Discuss the product range, the geographic markets, and customers' expectation for the products and services.
2   What is the current strategy for Tait Communications? What changes would you suggest and why would you support those changes?

3   Discuss the advantages and disadvantages of relocating design and/or manufacturing capability in another country.

4   What makes Tait Communications successful?

Notes

1 Case study written with reference to Tait Communications website Retrieved from www.taitradio.com, interviews with Chris Patient, Manager Hardware Engineering, Tait Communications, and editing assistance from Bryn Somerville, Head of Communications, Tait Communications.

2 Tait Communications to partner with JVCKENWOOD. (2018, December 10). [Press release]. Retrieved from www.taitradio.com/about-us/news/2018-news/tait-communications-to-partner-with-jvckenwood

3 P25 is a suite of standards for digital mobile radios in public sector environments in United States.

Nat-pak and Tastie-food

Anson K. T. Li

Anson K. T. Li, PhD, is a lecturer in operations management and supply chain management at the University of Auckland Business School.

Introduction

Nat-pak and Tastie-food are international food-packaging companies that produce and package food products including jams, sauces, and bottled drinks. Both companies have excellent performance records in customer satisfaction (their customers include retailers such as supermarkets, premium food stores, and restaurant chains), which is mainly attributed to their outstanding supply chain management innovations, strategies, and practices. Both companies aim to maximise customer value and satisfaction through effective and efficient management of supply chain relationships.

There are certain commonalities and differences between the two companies' supply chain philosophies. To start with, both companies aim to collaborate with its suppliers, and thus limit the number of suppliers. They also share extensive information with their own suppliers in order to reduce costs along the supply chain. Being in the same industry, however, both companies have strict confidentiality arrangements with their suppliers to ensure that they do not disclose any information to the other food-packaging company.

The difference between the two companies' supply chain relationship philosophies lies upon their approach towards collaboration. While Nat-pak collaborates with their suppliers with a cooperative approach through mutual support, Tastie-food pursues a competitive approach where most suppliers are responsible for their own performance in order to meet requirements imposed by Tastie-food.

Nat-pak

Nat-pak's key to success is the careful management of relationships along the supply chain, where customer value and the stability of its supply chain go hand-in-hand.

Supplier collaboration initiatives at Nat-pak typically begins at 6 to 12 months prior to the launch of new products, focusing on identifying and solving potential problems to the mutual benefit of both parties. Nat-pak usually relates key issues at this stage to product design and specifications. These include even minor details such as the packaging of new parts. Collaborative packaging design that caters to both the buyer's and the supplier's operations enables significant future cost savings along the supply chain. For example, the agreement on a certain-sized pallet for glass jar delivery ensures that the supplier performs the loading of pallets onto trucks easily, while Nat-pak feeds these smaller pallets immediately onto the automatic 'depalletising' machine at the food-packaging factory, which automatically transfers glass jars from the pallets onto the conveyor belt. Such positive results encouraged both parties to further offer visibility about their operations. With higher visibility and clearer information such as Nat-pak's annual volume goals, both parties have a better idea about whether plans and targets are feasible, and both parties can make adjustments accordingly.

Nat-pak and its suppliers face a different lot of issues once Nat-pak launches the product. The focus at this stage is on the suppliers' capability to effectively maintain and even improve its low defect rate. Suppliers maintain quality issues such as the consistency of glass jars and caps' specifications, freshness of ingredients, and the reliability of delivery schedules. They believed that 'there's more value to be gained by collaborating with a supplier than by merely harassing them on cost'.

Bearing such an important role in Nat-pak's operations, they choose their suppliers carefully with long-term concerns considered. The food packager meets chosen suppliers with active support and other collaborative efforts. For instance, Nat-pak keeps a limited number of suppliers for raw material and creates long-term partnerships by nurturing existing suppliers to expand and grow together, rather than to grow the number of suppliers in order to induce competitive price bidding. Supplier evaluation criteria include assessment of management attitudes, production facilities, and product quality. During the selection process, it is common for Nat-pak to visit the candidates' sites, observe, and comment on improvements. A supplier must meet extremely tough conditions to qualify. While the stringent requirements imposed by Nat-pak drives some of the prospective suppliers away, others consider that the requirements are to their advantage and believe that the advice on improving quality and competitive factors save them the cost of employing operations consultants.

Nat-pak offers suppliers stable order commitments. In managing some of the more important suppliers, Nat-pak would absorb a part of the business risks or even invest in equity positions. In return, Nat-pak expects the suppliers to improve and deliver superior quality products.

Given Nat-pak's dedication to nurturing its suppliers to develop long-term relationships, there comes times when the luxury of time is not readily available and 'short-cuts' have to be taken. Over the past five years while Nat-pak started rapid expansion to other foreign markets, it became increasingly dependent on suppliers abroad with whom it did not have decades of working experience (as with the other suppliers). Yet Nat-pak not only continued to trust in its sole-sourcing approach, it went even further, gaining unprecedented economies of scale by using single suppliers for entire ranges of its products across multiple markets. This is perceived as one of the main causes of quality problems which resulted in major recalls that took place over certain foreign markets in the previous year, as the trusted suppliers do not have the time to build up their capabilities in order to meet Nat-pak's quality standards. Neither do they have sufficient support from Nat-pak due to Nat-pak's limited resources to facilitate a fast-growing base of suppliers abroad. Nat-pak became ill-supported. Such failure resulted in a 'wake-up-call' for Nat-pak to review their supply chain strategies.

Overall, Nat-pak's supplier management approach features mutual support, long-term perspectives, and the sustainability of results. Yet such approach is not a one-size-fits-all solution as circumstances evolve through time.

Tastie-food

Tastie-food excels by following its fundamental strategy, leveraging its scale to create operational efficiencies that drive significant competitive advantage, through best execution and supply chain investments. The company has always focused its operating philosophy on customer satisfaction. It understands that its operations can be more customer-centric with better supply chain management. With higher level of customer loyalty, the chances of losing customers to competitors can be minimised.

The key to Tastie-food's supply chain collaboration is information visibility. The company shares with its suppliers some information such as point-of-sale consumption and future customer demand to facilitate effective reductions in inventory and other forms of wasted activities for both parties. Costs can thus be minimised, with savings passed along to customers.

For major suppliers of Tastie-food, the extent of information sharing went as far as both parties' investment of proprietary knowledge and processes into each other to improve quality and drive costs out of the business.

Given the advancements and novelty in Tastie-food's supply chain management philosophies, some of its tactics, however, have met major criticisms, especially on supplier relationship management.

In order to improve its performance and to gain customer satisfaction, Tastie-food aims to drive down its own operation's costs. Tastie-food achieves this partly by simply reducing its suppliers' prices. Due to the large scale of Tastie-food's operations, they can often impose reductions in their suppliers' prices with 'threats' to switch suppliers. The bargaining power of Tastie-food allows them also to impose other stringent policies upon its suppliers. It may quite straightforwardly tell suppliers to redesign everything from their packaging to their computer systems, in order to be compatible with Tastie-food's operations. When particular suppliers fail to perform to the required standards, Tastie-food will simply switch suppliers. The sheer size of Tastie-food's operations and business volume gives it tremendous power in negotiations. In some regions, suppliers of the food-packaging company consider Tastie-food's guidelines and requirements to be more important than the regulations of the local governments.

Through such stringent collaboration approaches, Tastie-food is successful in maintaining their own efficiency and costs, while keeping close to suppliers who are up to the challenge. Tastie-food handles supply chain relationships in a strict manner, while treating its suppliers in a fair and honest way. Its suppliers must also be as relentless and as microscopic at managing their own costs and efficiency. Some of the suppliers managed to make significant improvements in their own operations in order to keep up with Tastie-food's stringent requirements, while clinging on to life with a thin profit margin. However, the pressure to perform and to cut costs drove most suppliers out of business, especially under the difficult times with the recent financial crisis. Tastie-food is starting to realise that while it is important to leverage its performance with support from its supplier, it is also necessary to support key suppliers so that their performance may be maintained in the long run, resulting in better stability in their relationships. Tastie-food is now considering initiatives that are more cooperative with key suppliers in terms of mutually supportive arrangements such as collaborative developments and technology support for suppliers.

Discussion questions

1 Identify the pros and cons of each supply chain collaboration approach (cooperative and competitive).
2 Comment on both approaches in terms of their short- and long-term implications.
3 How may supply chain collaboration approaches evolve through time for sustainable performance and relationships?

Waikato District Health Board

Consumables supply for elective surgery

Crystal Beavis

Crystal Beavis, MA (Hons), PGDip (MgtSt), APR, is an award-winning marketing and communications professional with more than 25 years' experience in developing strategic communications programmes for organisations across a range of sectors in New Zealand including research, education, health, and local government. She moved into this field of work after an early career as a business journalist for the New Zealand Herald and National Business Review. Crystal has a special interest in health and currently serves as an elected board member of the Waikato District Health Board, which is the subject of this case study.

Introduction

This case study examines the supply of elective surgery consumables for the operating theatres at Waikato Hospital, a tertiary hospital managed by the Waikato District Health Board (Waikato DHB), in Hamilton, New Zealand.

It charts a dramatic change in the internal processes for supplying consumables that occurred over the final five years of a ten-year redevelopment programme of the hospital and its theatres. It also outlines the reasons for the change and the wide-ranging benefits gained.

While dramatic in nature, the change in process was staged gradually and further refinements were still under consideration when the processes identified in this case study were mapped.

Elective surgery refers to operations that are planned in advance for patients upon specialist medical advice. The surgeon schedules the procedure and a booking clerk enters it into the Waikato DHB patient management system. This case study excludes consumables supplies for acute (urgent) surgical operations which, while following a similar process, contains variations arising from differences in planning time and other factors.

The drivers of change in the process for supplying surgical consumables were threefold:

1 To meet requirements imposed by the Waikato DHB's own rebuilding programme, which included modernising and expanding the number of its operating theatres within the footprint of an existing building. The consumables supply process had to be redesigned to meet increased surgical demand and modern best-practice

standards within the layout constraints of the architectural design. The rebuilding programme was, in turn, driven by the need to:

- Meet the demands of a growing patient population.
- Reduce expensive outsourcing of private hospital theatres for surgical lists.
- Meet modern best-practice theatre standards by means of sterile 'shell' theatres with equipment and consumables which are able to be mobilised to adapt to different operational needs. Within the physical constraints of the Waikato DHB design a best-practice, fixed consumables-storage option was not possible and so consumables storage had to be removed from the operating theatres instead.

2   To gain control of the consumables inventory system.
3   To free up clinical staff time from administrative tasks, such as inventory stocking, and to move those tasks onto administrative personnel and IT systems.

The rebuilding programme

From 2005 until mid-2014, Waikato DHB undertook a $500 million service and facility redevelopment programme. The largest projects were at its Waikato Hospital campus in Hamilton. Among them – as part of the $130 million Meade Clinical Centre project – was the refurbishment and/or rebuilding of the hospital's 12 operating theatres and the construction of another 12 to provide 24 best-practice theatres, 22 of which were made operational immediately following the rebuild. The rebuild ensured theatres and suites for patient interventions were all co-located, providing all the facilities for the Waikato DHB's 13 surgical specialties – cardiac, vascular, orthopaedic, plastics, urology, gynaecology, maxillofacial, paediatrics, acute, ear-nose-and-throat, ophthalmology, neurosurgery, and general surgery.

The theatre rebuilding project was required not only to reduce surgical outsourcing, but also to bring Waikato DHB into line with modern best practice. The old-style theatres, dedicated to single specialties, allowed surgical supplies to be stored in-situ in wooden joinery around the room. The replacement modern 'shell' theatres, without storage, provided a sterile and more flexible environment. The new architecture underpins the best-practice principle that only the equipment and consumables required for the current procedure should be in the operating theatre. It also allows for more flexibility in the use of theatres by different surgical disciplines – particularly to allow for flexible rostering of acute surgery.

The extra consumables requirements for 22 modern theatres, four cardiac catheterisation laboratories (cathlabs), an angiography suite and four endoscopy suites, the adoption of best-practice principles in theatre design, and storage and space constraints within the theatre complex, together demanded a new internal supply system.

The need to gain control of the consumables inventory system

Under the old consumables supply system, the charge nurse for each surgical specialty (known as the clinical nurse coordinator or CNC), ensured the consumables for each operation in their theatre were picked from supplies on hand in the theatre and/or from four supply rooms situated on the two theatre floors. They laid these items out ready for use for operations the following morning or afternoon using their personal knowledge of the procedures and of the individual preferences of the operating surgeons, but without any particular understanding of the variability of costs between alternative line items. In this labour-intensive system, they picked, collated, and laid out individual items on a trolley outside the theatre ready for each operation. Their knowledge of the consumables required to ensure smooth operating procedures was variously passed on via personal documentation and/or supervised delegation. There was no standard contingency planning, and often issues to overcome, if the appropriate CNC was not available. Furthermore, fallback procedural options, such as flash sterilisation, were due to be phased out to meet best-practice principles.

Stores staff restocked the supply rooms daily on the principle of maintaining 'full shelves'. There was minimal dialogue between the stores staff and the clinical staff. The system made no allowance for frequency of use of items, or ensuring older stock was used first before it expired, and there was no clear policy about how or where to re-store unused sterile items for future use. Theatre staff maintained 'private stores' of particular items in the theatres, or elsewhere, to ensure they had the items they needed. Further illustration of the lack of inventory control was that when hospital wards ran short of consumables, ward nurses were often dispatched to restock ward supplies from the theatre stores as these represented a 'guaranteed' sure supply.

Map of the original process

The process map for the original theatre consumables supply process for elective surgery follows:

Process 1

- Step 1: Theatre list for elective surgery generated at 12:05 p.m.
- Step 2: Theatre list printed in hard copy and posted on each theatre noticeboard.
- Step 3: Clinical nurse coordinator (CNC) briefs/delegates clinical staff to collect consumables.
- Step 4: Clinical staff copy the list, or commit it to memory, or keep returning to it.
- Step 5: 3:00 p.m. Shift change: Allows time for clinical staff to pick the consumables for the first operation on the next morning's list, either from theatre storage or supply rooms.
- Step 6: Consumables for the first operation in the morning are supplemented from alternate supply source – general theatre supply rooms or in-theatre storage.
- Step 7: Consumables placed on separate trolley for each operation. Trolleys are loaded and placed in the corridor outside the theatre.
- Step 8: Clinical staff hand over to new shift and brief them on progress of consumables pick for next day's operations.
- Step 9: New shift clinical staff complete set-up for operation 1 and 2 with consumables, linen, and instruments.
- Step 10: Clinical nurse coordinator or delegate checks set-up for morning operations 1 and 2.

- Step 11: 'Pick' continues until set-ups are complete for all operations or until trolley supply runs out. Pick continues when first trolley is free.
- Step 12: After the operation is finished, unused sterile consumables are stored in theatre or wherever space available. Trolley freed for next pick.

Process 2

- Step 13: Stores staff walk from the distribution centre to the theatre floor in the morning to check theatre supply rooms.
- Step 14: They check gaps on marked shelves and record gaps on store supply sheet.
- Step 15: Walk back to the distribution centre to order consumables from external supply warehouse (3PL) for the next delivery (often multiple daily deliveries) to replenish shelves in supply rooms on each theatre floor.
- Step 16: Take consumables delivered from external supply warehouse to theatre floor to replenish shelves in supply rooms.
- Step 17–20: Repeat previous four steps at least once more per day.

Process improvements

Of more than 24,000 coded items in the Waikato Hospital inventory catalogue at that time there were 2,575 lines of surgical consumables in day-to-day use including items such as swabs, dressings, surgical blades, preparation fluids, catheters, suction tubing, bottles, specimen containers, masks, gloves, and so on.

Clinical staff could physically identify what they needed for operating procedures, but did not know how the inventory system coded them. Stores staff did not know what consumables were used for each operation, but needed to work with codings in order to gain control of the hospital inventory, including ordering, replenishment, and stock management.

To begin to address these issues, an interim process change was instituted while the rebuilding programme was underway. The four theatre supply rooms were removed and replaced with a single Theatre Store room on the theatre floor, and a dedicated theatre inventory team, the Theatre Services Team (TST), was formed to staff it. The clinical staff were asked to come directly to the Theatre Store with a daily 'shopping list' to replenish the individual theatre supplies. Over an 18-month period this allowed TST stores staff to work with clinical staff to identify the standard consumables used for every 'generic' or 'primary' operation, and the variables required for 'alternate' or 'surgeon specific' operations for different procedures and/or different surgeons. The new dedicated team of stores staff built knowledge of the clinical products and their application (generic, surgeon-specific, or specialty-related), while nursing staff undertook a project to get all of their procedures for each specialty into a standard format. Stores and clinical staff then worked together to code and validate the clinical consumables for each procedure and surgeon preference.

This led the way to a physical move of the Theatre Store room from the theatre floor to the basement and to a secondary change in process. TST stores staff now prepared packs or 'bills of materials' (BOMs) for every type of operation, each one of which was individually bar-coded and tracked in the enterprise resource planning

(ERP) computer system. Stores staff transacted all items within these packs to maintain control over the inventory for both the BOM packing and returns processes. When an operating procedure was cancelled, the whole BOM could be returned to the store intact and the components transacted back into inventory. If a BOM was partially used for any reason, consumables within the BOM that were still contained within unopened sterile packaging could also be returned to inventory.

This secondary change in process relieved the clinical staff of hours of physical inventory handling. The clinical staff now identified which BOMs were required for every operation scheduled the following day (depending on the operation, the surgeon, and procedures expected), while the physical task of 'picking and packing' the consumables for each operation was handed over to stores staff in the dedicated Theatres Services Team.

TST staff in the Theatre Store now maintained the contents lists for just under 1000 'primary' BOMs and 1500 'alternate' BOMs to match each surgeon's needs. For example, there were 15 variations in the standardised lists of consumables for a hip operation, depending on the surgeon and the procedures being followed.

TST staff routinely prepared 60–100 BOMs each day to support the next day's theatre schedules. This took about four–six hours every afternoon – relieving clinical nursing staff for the patient care for which they were primarily trained.

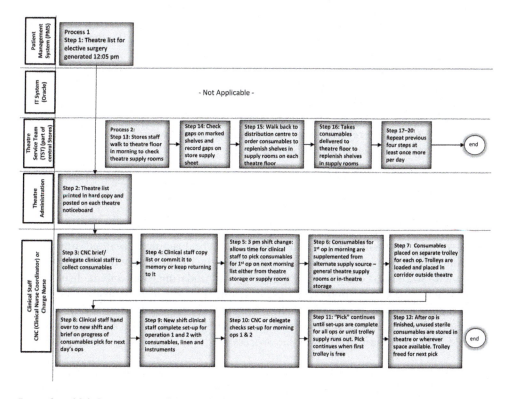

Figure Case 10.1 Process map of the original process at Waikato DHB

Map of the new 'BOM' process for supplying consumables for elective surgery

Process I

- Auto Step 1: Theatre list for elective surgery generated automatically at 12:05 p.m.
- Auto Step 2: Electronic theatre list stored on server.
- Step 1: Electronic theatre list is emailed to Theatre Administration by 12:15 p.m. daily.
- Step 2: Electronic theatre list received from Theatre Services Team in the Theatre Store.
- Step 3: Hard copy theatre list is printed for each operating theatre and delivered to clinical nurse coordinator for BOM coding.
- Step 4: Hard copy coded theatre lists received from each operating theatre's clinical nurse coordinator by 1:30 p.m.
- Step 5: Enter BOM codes to update the electronic theatre lists.
- Step 6: Email coded theatre lists to Theatre Services Team in the Theatre Store.
- Step 7: Coded theatre lists saved on server by 2:00 p.m.
- Auto Step 8: Import and run picking process.
- Auto Step 9: Work-in-process (WIP) job created.
- Auto Step 10: Consumables 'pick slip' generated.
- Step 11: Pick the required consumables from Theatre Store.
- Step 12: WIP transaction completed.
- Step 13: Take completed physical BOM to delivery point on the theatre floor. Is the operating procedure going ahead? Yes, go to Step 14. No, go to Step 17.
- Step 14: Complete the physical set-up of consumables, linen, and instruments.
- Step 15: Procedure completed.
- Auto Step 16: Complete/close WIP job.
- Step 17: Place unopened bundle in 'returns' area.
- Step 18: Complete returns transaction and put stock away.
- Auto Step 19: Expense WIP job to specialty.

Evaluation

Process weaknesses

There were two weaknesses in the new process where it required 'manual' input from the clinical nurse coordinators (CNCs). Accordingly, the process worked best for the CNCs who were most diligent in establishing, and updating, the contents lists for the BOMs they needed to support the operations in their theatres. It also worked best when the nurses correctly specified which BOMs were required for each days' theatre lists. In both these actions there was room for human error, however, there were two reliable fallback options to the regular process used:

1   A trolley of consumables considered most likely for 'extra' or 'emergency' needs for each surgical discipline was kept outside the theatres used by that discipline. TST staff check the trolleys and replenish as required on a regular basis.

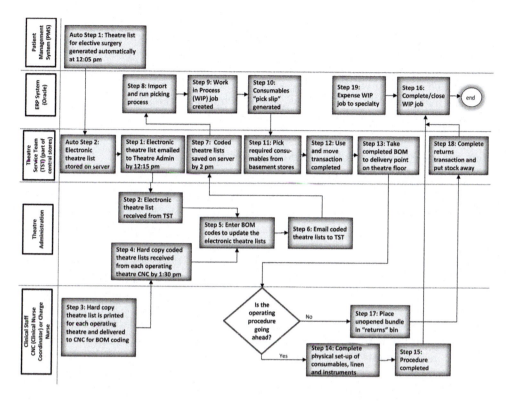

Figure Case 10.2 Process map of the improved process at Waikato DHB as of October 2014

2 If the first option failed to suffice, a clinical staff member walked, or took the lift, to the Theatre Store in the basement below the theatres and requested the Theatre Services Team to immediately issue them the extra consumables required for a specified procedure/patient/surgeon so the inventory could be adjusted in a controlled fashion. This took a minimum of ten minutes depending on the consumables required.

Both these areas were subjects for further improvement at the time the processes identified in this case study were mapped.

Process strengths

The new process for consumables supply for elective surgery at Waikato Hospital is still regarded as 'leading the way' for New Zealand. It has:

1 Met the need for a system that can reliably supply a large complex of 22 theatres and nine other co-located facilities designed to undertake patient procedures following the latest best-practice principles, including sterile procedures.
2 Established control over the inventory where previously there was no control.

3   Optimised the physical space available by moving all consumables to a single Theatre Store in the basement below the theatre floors.
4   Allowed for the development of trust between clinical and stores staff and relieved clinical nursing staff of many hours of daily physical stock work, enabling them to perform the patient care for which they trained.
5   Created a system which no longer relies upon individual experience and knowledge that can 'walk out the door', and which incorporates fallback procedures in case of human error/emergency.

How the new process helped enhance and strengthen the value chain in other ways

By reliably supporting a modernised theatre complex that is double the size of the old complex, the new consumables supply system helped support the means for realising a wide range of benefits – from operational cost benefits to enhanced safety and convenience for patients.

The new theatre complex and supply system was designed to accommodate the surgical demands of a growing population, changes in clinical approach in some disciplines (for example, spinal treatment) that had resulted in earlier and more frequent recourse to surgery for best outcomes, and the increasing breadth of the surgical specialties the Waikato DHB provided. Neurosurgery, for example, had been established at Waikato in 2006 to bring this specialty 'closer to home' for patients and their families, and to enable Waikato DHB to replace Auckland DHB as the provider of this tertiary service for the whole Midlands health region including four other DHBs – Taranaki, Lakes (based in Rotorua), Bay of Plenty, and Tairawhiti (based in Gisborne).

Projected savings at the time were a net $3.1 million per year (after offsetting the increased costs of internal theatre staffing against the costs of outsourcing private hospital facilities for some of Waikato DHB's surgical lists).

The new consumables supply system also supported best-practice sterile procedures in theatre and freed senior nurses from administrative tasks.

Excess inventory was stripped from the system. The old theatres, cathlabs, and storerooms were cleared of expired stock worth thousands of dollars ($87,000 worth from one specialty alone), and stock holdings for the original 12 theatres were reduced by about $500,000 to $1.2 million. As the new facilities were completed, and the new consumables supply system established, stock holdings settled back to $1.7 million – but with a significant difference in mix and volumes – to cope with the needs of all 22 theatres and another nine labs and suites in the new theatre complex.

In effect, the value of inventory once held for the original 12 operating theatres was pegged at the same level ($1.7 million) for a complex that was more than doubled in size with the co-location of cathlabs, angiography, and endoscopy suites. New system controls also ensured that stock no longer exceeded its expiry date.

The information systems developed to support the new consumables supply process now supplied better information for other hospital processes. For example, accurate invoicing of patient operations to external agencies such as the Accident Compensation Commission and insurance companies.

This information also provided the hospital and clinical staff with a better understanding of the different costs of each operation, depending on procedures and techniques used. For example, a hip replacement varied in cost by as much as $800 depending on surgeon preference and the techniques used. Reports at the time indicated clinical staff started to make changes to consumables used when it became apparent that cost-savings were available with no reduction to the quality of the procedure.

In summary, the new consumables supply process has contributed to enhanced patient care by theatre clinical staff freed of administrative responsibilities, enhanced understanding and communications between clinical and administrative staff, and cost-efficiencies and savings that could be re-invested into Waikato DHB's wider operations, thereby – overall – enhancing the organisation's value chain for the benefit of the community it serves.

Discussion questions

1 Discuss the lean thinking ideas used in this case study.
2 The number of process steps has only changed slightly, yet this case study is described as process improvement. Discuss the ramifications of process improvement by increasing the number of process steps using this case study as an example.
3 From a business perspective summarise the process improvement.

Note

The contents of this case study are based on a supply chain initiative directed by the Executive Group of the Waikato DHB and sponsored by the Chief of Staff Neville Hablous and Executive Director of Corporate Services Maureen Chrystall. The programme manager through the entire five-year process and person who made it all possible was Programme Manager Corporate Services Angela Morley, ably supported by a team of Oracle and supply chain specialists including Kerry Oldfield, Dean McLeod, and Dave White, and project managed by Renae Smart. Neville Hablous provided final approval for publication and use of this case study.

This case study was prepared for the purpose of class discussion, and not designed to provide a definitive review of the Waikato DHB's theatre complex and supply system.

References

Interviews with DHB staff including the executive director of corporate services, the former chief operating officer, and staff from logistics, supplies, and procurement.
Smart, R. (2014, October 21). BOM procedure picking process. Hamilton, New Zealand: Waikato District Health Board.

Implementing circular economy at HP

Carl Kühl and Hendrik Reefke

Carl Kühl is a PhD researcher at the Centre for Logistics, Procurement, and Supply Chain Management at Cranfield School of Management, Cranfield University, UK. His research interests focus around circular economy and servitisation. He is a Marie Skłodowska Curie Fellow and part of CircEuit, the Circular European Economy Innovative Training Network. It is an action funded by the European Commission under the Horizon 2020 Marie Skłodowska Curie Action 2016.

Dr Hendrik Reefke is a Lecturer in Supply Chain Management at Cranfield School of Management, Cranfield University, UK. Hendrik is an active researcher, focusing primarily on sustainable supply chain management, service supply chains, performance measurement, and warehousing. He is a co-author of *Operations Management for Business Excellence: Building Sustainable Supply Chains 4e*.

Company overview

HP Inc. is a multinational information technology company with headquarters in Palo Alto, California. It is a leading global provider of PCs, printers, printing supplies, and 3D printing solutions. Bill Hewlett and David Packard famously founded the company in a small garage in 1939. Now a Fortune 100 company, it generated $52.1 billion net revenues in 2017. As of 2017, they employed approximately 49,000 people worldwide. They have a global reach and deliver their products and services to individual customers, small- and medium-sized enterprises, large businesses, and organisations in government, healthcare, and education.

HP strives to reduce the environmental impact of its supply chain and its operations through the products and solutions they offer to their customers. As a result, they have committed to several environmental sustainability goals. For example, they plan to reduce greenhouse gas emissions from their global operations by 25% by 2025, compared to 2015.[1] The company understands that in light of increasing resource constraints due to global population growth, a growing middle class, and urbanisation, companies that are able to meet demand with lower resources will have significant advantages. As a result, they strive to recycle 1.2 million tonnes of hardware and supplies by 2025.[2]

HP and circular economy

Circular economy

Circular economy is 'a regenerative system in which resource input and waste, emission, and energy leakage are minimised by slowing, closing, and narrowing material and energy loops. This can be achieved through long-lasting design, maintenance, repair, reuse, remanufacturing, refurbishing, and recycling'.[3]

Circular economy is one of the main pillars through which HP strives to attain these goals. It is an emerging concept that acknowledges the limitations of our current 'linear' economic system in which raw materials are manufactured into goods, which are sold, used, and then become waste. This model is becoming increasingly untenable due to rising resource prices and supply risks. The circular economy aims to address these issues.

In addition, the CE concept advocates a transition towards business models around leasing, renting, and sharing. Companies that retain ownership over products have an incentive to reuse, repair, remanufacture, or recycle products, components, and materials. CE is gaining traction among policy-makers and businesses because it unifies different environmental priorities and provides clear guidance on actions that they need to take.

Implementing CE at HP

The company is committed to transforming its supply chains, business models, and product design for a more resource-efficient, low-carbon, and circular economy. The company is an industry leader in closed-loop recycling. Its recycling efforts date back to 1995, when the company introduced a take-back scheme for used ink cartridges. In 2005, HP started using recovered polyethylene terephthalate (PET) from returned cartridges, plastic apparel hangers, and plastic bottles. In this closed-loop system, cartridges are returned, separated, re-formulated, re-pelletised, and put directly into the company's manufacturing process. This reduced the environmental footprint of their cartridges by 33%. Today, more than 80% of HP ink cartridges contain 45–70% recycled plastics, while 100% of HP toner cartridges contain 10–33%. In 2016, the company expanded an initiative to source plastic bottles from Haiti for the closed-loop recycling process of cartridges. Through March 2018, the company sourced more than 170 tonnes of likely ocean-bound plastic. Through 2017, HP manufactured over 3.8 billion HP ink and toner cartridges, using more than 99,000 tonnes of recycled plastic. This has kept 784 million HP cartridges, 86 million apparel hangers, and four billion postconsumer plastic bottles from landfills.[4]

Based on the success of this recycling program, the company started recycling its hardware in 2016. In the United States, customers can return used printers at over 1500 locations and receive a 15% discount on new printers. This program increased recycling rates, supported increased printer sales, and reduced supply chain costs. HP's recycling services are available in 64 countries worldwide. The company offers repair, reuse, and refurbishment services to help extend the lifespan of its products and reduce environmental impacts from product disposal through a global network of vendors and sub-vendors. In 2017, the company repaired 4.6 million units of hardware and remarketed/reused another 1.27 million units.

The company's product design and business model supports its efforts to implement closed-loop supply chains. By switching to thinner and lighter notebooks, for example, the company was able to reduce the material intensity (tonnes/$ millions of net revenue) of its personal systems by eight percent and from its printers by six percent from 2016 to 2017. HP works to incorporate recycled and renewable materials in its products to help accelerate the development of secondary markets around the world. In addition to its ink and toner cartridges, the company now uses recovered materials in their larger products. In 2017, the company launched the production of the HP ENVY Photo Printers, which they make from more than ten percent in weight of recycled plastic. In addition, HP designs its products for durability and repairability. In 2016 and 2017, for example, several HP products scored very highly on the iFixit[5] product repair site.

HP is accelerating the transition to a circular economy by innovating its business models. HP offers leasing, renting, and other types of service contracts for ink, print, and PC services. In the product-as-a-service offerings, customers have access to the latest and most efficient HP products every two to three years, thus avoiding up-front purchasing costs. HP manages hardware, software, including refurbishing, parts reuse, and responsible recycling. This business model allows HP to build closer customer relationships, and get more insights on customer needs and behaviour. In addition, they increase utilisation rates and efficiency by optimising product fleets and regular maintenance extends the product life. In addition, HP recovers value at end-of-life through implementing repair, reuse, and recycling. For example, HP Managed Print Services (MPS) combines hardware and software with consulting services to manage, optimise, and improve customer's printer fleets. They service and maintain printers and refurbish them, if possible, to keep them in use longer.

HP is working to enable CE across other industries. In 2016, it developed the first production-ready commercial 3D printer. Additive manufacturing, or 3D printing, describes a number of computerised processes where materials are joined together to create three-dimensional objects. Leading innovation in this domain is critical for HP as it strives to retain its role as a leader in printing technology. Three-dimensional printing is a key technology of the Fourth Industrial Revolution and allows companies to design, make, and distribute products with lower costs and environmental impacts. HP was able to incorporate 3D-printed parts into their own products successfully. In one of the Latex printer models, for example, the company replaced an aluminium component with a 3D-printed nylon component, which resulted in a 95% reduction in greenhouse gas emissions, a 93% reduction in weight, and 50% lower costs.

In the pursuit of its sustainability goals, HP has committed itself to implementing CE principles along its supply chain. This is influencing the way it conducts its business along the entire value chain: from materials sourcing to product recovery. In a world that is growing increasingly uncertain, this strategy allows them to meet and exceed customers' environmental expectations, prepare for future macro trends, anticipate stricter regulations, and find disruptive and innovative solutions.

Discussion questions

1   What are the underlying principles of a CE?
2   What impact does CE have on supply chains?
3   What are some possible sustainability trade-offs?
4   How is CE contributing to HP's competitive advantage?
5   How could HP increase the circularity of its supply chains?

Notes

1 HP. (2017). *HP policy position: Climate action.* Retrieved from http://h20195.www2. hp.com/V2/getpdf. aspx/c05320887.pdf

2 HP. (2017). *HP sustainable impact goals: 2017 sustainable impact report*, p. 25. Retrieved from http://www8.hp.com/h20195/v2/GetPDF.aspx/c05968415.pdf

3 Geissdoerfer, M., Savaget, P., Bocken, N., & Hultink, E. (2017). The circular economy: A new sustainability paradigm. *Journal of Cleaner Production.* Elsevier Ltd, 143, 757–768. doi:10.1016/j.jclepro.2016.12.048

4 Strandberg, C. (2017). *HP and the circular economy*. HP Development Company L. P., p. 4. Retrieved from http://www8.hp.com/h20195/v2/getpdf.aspx/c05364027.pdf

5 iFixit is a global community of people helping each other repair stuff located at www.ifixit. com

Fischer fixing systems

Moving forward with the workforce – change communication at the Global Distribution Centre[1]

Klaus Möller, Julian Gabel, and Frank Bertagnolli

Dr.-Ing. Klaus Möller is professor for distribution logistics and **Dr.-Ing. Frank Bertagnolli** is professor for lean production and resource efficiency, both at the Business School at Pforzheim University. **Julian Gabel** received a BSc in business administration – purchasing and logistics and an MSc in information systems, also at the Business School at Pforzheim University.

The case is an amended version of the full text published in *Journal of Information Technology Education: Discussion Cases, Volume 5, Case Number 1, 2016*. Permission to reprint is granted by *Informing Science Institute*.

Introduction

The investment decision was made last year, and after a time-consuming selection process and intensive negotiations, the contract with the general contractor was signed. The business segment fixing systems of the fischer group of companies faced a significant investment in its logistics – the development of automation technology in the Global Distribution Centre (GDC). According to the project schedule, the transition to the automated small-parts storage with shuttle technology would take place in December of this year. It was mid-April, and therefore the right time for the Head of Logistics Matthias Wehle, of the business segment fischer fixing systems to describe the current status: Were all the important milestones achieved and would the subsequent steps ensure a smooth transition? The employees in logistics were accustomed to changes over the years. The company had successfully implemented structural changes such as the introduction of SAP R/3 in early 2000 and the establishment of the automated high-bay warehouse in 2008. It was the same with the continuous improvement process with the fischerProzessSystem (fPS). The introduction of pick-by-light technology for the picking of small-sized products with high demand had worked well, too. However, the last staff meeting about the launch of the shuttle system had left him with a feeling of uncertainty. He could already feel the spirit of optimism from some of the employees triggered by the upcoming introduction of the new system. The majority, however, listened patiently and Matthias Wehle sensed insecurity among the employees: How does this change affect me? Up until now, management had used multiple channels to communicate information to the employees. However, feedback from the workforce to those in charge was rather rare. Moreover, the logistics manager remembered that the use of pick-by-voice for picking had been stopped for a number of reasons. Now, because of the largest investment in recent years, the GDC faced a drastic operational change. With this in mind, Matthias Wehle pondered over the issue of employee communication again and again. And they had eight more months in order to take action until December . . .

The fischer group of companies

From a Swabian workshop to an international medium-sized company – this was the development of the fischer group of companies in a nutshell since its establishment in 1948. Distinctive for the company was its strong drive for innovation, which triggered not only releasing new products, but also forming new business divisions. Based on the number of patent applications, the fischer group was one of Germany's most innovative companies. The workforce generated 13.2 patent applications per 1000 employees annually, which was 20 times more patents per employee than the average in Germany. Thus, the fischer group from Waldachtal-Tumlingen in the Black Forest ranked third among the major patent applicants in Germany. The company introduced the well-known expansion plug to the market in 1958, fischertechnik followed seven years later, and with the introduction of the fischer CBOX in 1982, the company stepped into the automotive supplier industry. With fischer greenline, the company became the first to offer an assortment of bio-based fixing systems in 2014. In the following year, fischer introduced the universally usable DUOPOWER plug to the market.

As of 2014, the fischer group of companies divided itself into four main business divisions – fischer fixing systems, fischer automotive systems, fischertechnik, and fischer Consulting. At the core and the focus of fischer was the fixing systems division. This was the distinctive competence of the company. With more than 14,000 articles, fischer offered a solution for every fixing problem. The strength of this division was the ability to offer the right product in technical perfection for a wide range of customers, from the DIYer and the artisan all the way to a key account partner.

Fischer was active in over 100 countries worldwide. The business abroad ran through either a subsidiary or an importer. In 2014, the 43 subsidiaries handled the major share of foreign sales. In addition to the subsidiaries, there were roughly the same number of importers, which allowed fischer to have market presence around the globe. The unit of length used in a country was a key factor for the market development. The United States were one of the last industrialised countries not using the metric system officially. This resulted in specific issues for fischer when developing the US market.

Logistics processing via the Global Distribution Centre

The basis for the success of a product on the market is not only its quality, but also its availability and on-time delivery to the consumer. For this reason, the fischer group decided to build a central warehouse at the production site in Waldachtal-Tumlingen at the end of the 1970s. Already equipped with possible expansion areas, the fischer group established the Global Distribution Centre (GDC) in 1981. Simultaneously with the centralisation of logistics processes, the divisional management relied on the centralisation of information processes – divisional management introduced the ERP system SAP R/3 in the GDC in 2000. This introduction presented staff and management in the GDC with a major challenge, since the data processes practiced to date changed fundamentally from one day to the other – a first important experience with changes for management. Since then, SAP also controlled the conveyor technology. Immediately after the introduction of SAP, the GDC switched to paperless picking via radio data transmission.

With the standardisation of the core processes in the GDC, the fischer group could now carry out further steps of integration in terms of a clearly-oriented distribution strategy. The warehouse manager, Eckhard Hagen explained, 'The aim was to maximise centralisation in order to react to market demand with an expansion of the article range while keeping a low stock and appropriate delivery service at minimal costs'. Hence, the fischer group incorporated several regional distribution centres (RDC) in Germany into the GDC during 2013. The integration steps required enhancements of the technical facilities in the existing building. Thus, they extended the modular shelving system, from 2001 to 2005, to handle small-sized articles with low demand efficiently. At the same time, the fischer group targeted the use of new picking technologies. For this reason, they installed a pick-by-light system for small-sized products with high demand, especially the do-it-yourself (DIY) goods, in 2002. Because of the characteristics of DIY products with a large product diversity and a high product density per unit area, this technology was particularly useful; its use there resulted in a significantly higher productivity.

In anticipation of the extension of products by adding a product range of screws with another 2700 SKUs, they built a fully automated high-bay warehouse in 2008. Since this was an extension on existing premises, the basic processes in the GDC substantially remained the same. This investment was an important milestone for the warehouse manager, Eckhard Hagen, 'At that time we made the first significant step towards the automation of the order picking processes in the GDC'.

After they commissioned the automated high-bay warehouse, the opportunity presented itself for the use of pick-by-voice technology in the picking processes. The advantage was that the order pickers had both hands free for the actual picking process and the technology could handle the entire flow of information through a headset. The picker received the task through the headphone, walked to the storage location, grabbed the article, and gave confirmation through the microphone. An SAP consulting company helped the transition to this new technology. At the beginning, there were weaknesses with the technology; it became apparent that the workforce had only a rudimentarily preparation for this technology and the corresponding changes in the process flow. They gradually overcame the technical difficulties and picking quality increased steadily; however, the productivity declined. The employees expressed their dissatisfaction with the system; particularly the long response times in dialog mode were upsetting them. It became clear that large parts of the workforce no longer accepted the technology and, therefore, the logistics management decided to discontinue its use in 2013. The workers received this decision well. From this resulted an important experience for management concerning the support of future changes in the processes, particularly the use of new technologies.

Further investment in automation for productivity growth

The overall analysis confirmed the fundamental decision to set up a central distribution centre, the GDC in Waldachtal, as well as the decision in gradual investments in automation technology and process improvement. It became apparent that the continuous increase in output led to almost 2.4 million order lines in 2014 starting from 2.0 million order lines in 2008 by generating overall logistics cost that were significantly lower in 2014 compared to 2008. Especially because of the integration of the German RDCs during 2013, the parcel volume increased significantly. Simultaneously, they reached the maximum capacity of the GDC with its expansion and technology status.

In light of the analysis of the status quo, the logistics management drew an unambiguous conclusion. Investing in a further automation of processes was inevitable to secure the future viability of the GDC – the idea of a shuttle system was born. With the present order structure, the new system already offered the potential for an increase in productivity, and further integration steps such as the acquisition of a European distribution warehouse would be possible.

Within the shuttle storage and retrieval system, they positioned several load carriers such as tote bins behind one another in each channel. They used independent shuttles on each level to operate the channels. The advantages of the shuttle system were maximum floor and space utilisation along with high volume throughput. In the case of fischer, they would use the shuttle system in the picking processes of about 6000 small-sized products. This step, however, would entail a change in the workflow for about 90 employees. In particular, the picking principle would change. So far, many of the pickers had been driving to the storage bins with an order picking truck and collected the items systematically. They replaced this picker-to-goods principle by the goods-to-picker principle, in which a roller conveyor carried the tote bins to a picking station, where the pickers would unload the amount needed to fulfil the order.

For an order-related demand, the system would extract individual and unmixed tote bins from the shuttle system and transport them via a roller conveyor to the new picking area. This process design would avoid previous movements by the pickers in the warehouse. The project manager for the launch of the shuttle system, Hendrik Schote, reported on the results of a computer simulation, according to which the net energy requirement of the system would remain constant – with a simultaneous increase of the output by about 20%. Furthermore, the planning assumed that the shuttle system could process around 75% of the order lines.

They designed the shuttle system to make the processes as efficient as possible. This meant to choose the best combination of source containers and shipping boxes to work on as many order lines as possible in a short period of time. Another important advantage of the shuttle system would be in better ergonomics. The system automatically raised the containers to the optimum working height, and a height-adjustable floor, in combination with a rubberised floor surface, would be a physical relief for the pickers. They designed the picking workstation for the pallets to the same ergonomic principles. Nevertheless, the management team was asking whether working at those stations would be too repetitive and offer less variety in comparison with the previous process.

Employee communication

In Germany, employees in small and medium-sized companies usually enjoyed a long employment with the company. Between employers and employees, there is generally a cultural understanding for a respectful cooperation with the aim of positive corporate earnings. Typically, this also included a mutual intention to ensure long-term cooperation, which reflected in the statutory longer notice periods depending on the length of employment.

The regional proximity as well as the identification with the company and its products reduced fluctuation of staff and retained skilled workers at the company. Mission statements with a focus on the employees had a further positive effect and could result in press awards as outstanding employers. This in turn had a positive impact on employee satisfaction and hence their motivation. Because of this culture and its public image, new talented employees could be attracted.

A positive, functional working culture can be especially relevant when dealing with upcoming changes in structures and processes of a company. Based on the experience with previous changes, it was obvious to the GDC's management team that the communication with the employees was an important factor in order to make the shuttle system a success. In order to clearly associate all means of communication with this project, the project manager, Hendrik Schote, decided to develop a dedicated project logo. The logo represented the key objectives of the project, improving ergonomics and increasing productivity. In addition to this visualisation, the slogan 'fit for future', as well as a reference to the GDC and the fischer group were added. This uniform logo could be found on all means of communication, as well as on slides and textiles.

Essential elements of communication towards the employees were information events in which the management team informed on the main elements of the shuttle and the changes. The first event took place in December 2014. It focused on changes in the layout of the GDC, the operation of the shuttle system, its workstations, and upcoming milestones. During this event, every single employee received a personalised project t-shirt with the employee's name and project logo printed onto it. In a second meeting in March 2015, the information was deepened. They paid particular attention to the ergonomic benefits of the new workstations. At this event, the management team also presented the results of a computer simulation for a peak day in the GDC using the shuttle system, which clearly demonstrated the capabilities of the new system.

To strengthen the team spirit, the management team commissioned a picture of all the GDC's employees in front of a fischer truck and they printed a large-scale picture. After everyone had signed this poster and confirmed their commitment, the management team hung it visibly in the entrance area. Each and every employee walked past it at least twice a day.

Challenges in the change management

After talks with the general contractor, the logistics manager, Matthias Wehle, did not see any issues on the technical side of the implementation of the shuttle system. The information events from the logistics management team had presented the new situation in detail, and the team answered the employee's questions conclusively. Employees saw the large investment in the shuttle system as a commitment from the management board to the GDC and its jobs. Nevertheless, a feeling that a number of employees still were uncertain about the situation after the introduction of the shuttle remained present for Matthias Wehle. The employees believed in the necessity of the change as the previous system had reached the capacity limit.

However, the system would set the pace and hence a fear arose of having to work based on piece rates in the future. On the other hand, the employees expected that the setting of the pace by the shuttle would make for a fair distribution of work, since everyone would have to deliver the same performance. However, such a large change could lead to major difficulties in the beginning. With this said, Matthias Wehle could still remember pick-by-voice. It was necessary to learn from these experiences. Initial discussions about these topics with the project manager, Hendrik Schote, and the warehouse manager, Eckhard Hagen, showed that he was not the only one with this opinion. The performance data of the new system were impressive, but management based them on a workforce that is committed to fulfilling their tasks. According to a guiding principle of the owner and chairman of the fischer group of companies, Klaus Fischer, the employees were the greatest asset and most important success factor in the company, not the facilities and buildings. Therefore, after consulting with his management team, the head of logistics decided to take action.

Decision making

In order to introduce the new logistics system with a goods-to-picker principle, a good change management team had to put several things on the right track. During the change, the Head of Logistics Matthias Wehle had to make decisions in order to achieve his goal and be able to use the new system successfully.

He needed to answer the following questions in preparation for the implementation of the system:

- What is the target state of the new logistics processes and which strategy can accomplish it?
- What lessons can be learned from the implementation process of the pick-by-voice system? What experiences can be used for the current project?
- What are the advantages and disadvantages of the new shuttle system? What are the main advantages of the new technology from the perspective of the employees?
- What must the implementation schedule look like? Which actions must the project take?
- How can management prepare employees optimally for the introduction of the new system? What must management communicate, at which point of time, by whom, and using which means of communication? What messages should management proclaim and when should they do that?
- What is the role of the employees and works council in the project? What should they clarify in advance? Where could the works council support and where might it get critical?
- Could the works council expect resistance? If so, which stakeholder would resist? How should management deal with this potential resistance?

Note

1 Company specific information on fischer retrieved January 27, 2016, from www.fischer.de/en/Company

Additional readings

Kotter, J. P. (2012). *Leading change, with a new preface by the author*. Boston, MA: Harvard Business Review Press.

ten Hompel, M., & Schmidt, T. (2007). *Warehouse management: Automation and organisation of warehouse and order picking systems*. Berlin: Springer-Verlag.

Bridging design prototypes

*Gloria Gomez, Maigen Wilki Thygesen, Andreas Melson,
Mathias Halkjær Petersen, Casper Harlev, Enikö Rozsnyói,
and Thomas A. Rubaek*

Dr Gloria Gomez is co-founder, design strategist, and researcher at OceanBrowser Ltd., and an honorary senior lecturer at the University of Sydney. Dr Gomez undertakes applied design research in educational product development with bridging design prototypes (BDP). She currently supervises postgraduate students in the areas of visual design, inclusive design, social design, and online medical education. In Colombia, Denmark, New Zealand, and the United States, she has lectured and supervised graduate students of engineering and design backgrounds on projects using human-centred design methods including the BDP approach.

Understanding user needs for feature design

The bridging design prototype (BDP) approach aims to strengthen the activity of design in new product development undertaken by small enterprises. Design is the weak link in the fuzzy front-end process of new product development in small and medium-sized enterprises. Often, these enterprises cannot afford to bring a human-centred design perspective early into the research and development (R&D) process of innovative services or products. During the fuzzy front-end, the BDP approach provides a rapid and organised way to research and sort design opportunities into those that deserve more effort and those that the designer should defer.

A BDP is a rapid functional prototype built with features familiar to a user community and with novel features that a designer incorporates after careful analysis of relevant data. It capitalises on a user community's prior knowledge (i.e. the knowledge a user already has about a situation or an activity) and recognises their context realities. These characteristics bring users into the development process early: Users incorporate the prototype into their real activities, while a designer or R&D team employ it for learning about the users' context and their practice. Early adoption of a concept idea in the form of a rapid functional prototype may lead to socially inclusive products, active community participation, or help in raising early capital for a small enterprise. A user community will only be prepared to incorporate a new product in their context, when through personal experience they qualify such a product as being useful, usable, and desirable.

As part of research in interaction design, the first BDP was developed for gaining entry to real educational settings to work with difficult-to-access and technologically disinclined user communities. For its experiential qualities, BDPs can be experience prototypes or provotypes.[1] The main difference with the latter rapid prototypes is that

BDPs must be fully functional rapid prototypes. Experimentation should not require the presence of designers. By functional, it means that users must be able to implement them into real activities. But, BDPs are not necessarily minimum viable products, as the digital or tangible materials with which they are built could have a limited lifespan.

The BDP approach is comprised of six principles, underpinned by theoretical concepts drawn from user-centred design, inclusive design, participatory design, and the theory of meaningful learning. Designers apply the following principles to the development of BDPs:

- Develop a human-centred design study that brings a multidisciplinary thinking team approach to research the user community and the market.
- Become more empathic through the designer, R&D team, and the user community achieving similar mental models.
- Deeply understand the prior knowledge and familiar technological, behavioural, and social interactions of the user community.
- Develop features that make activities simpler.
- Develop features that broaden participation.
- Implement a prototype for early adoption enabling the user community to participate, contribute, and improve features in the design process.

The following cases, drawn from master's student reports on projects undertaken in collaboration with a start-up or a small or medium-sized enterprise, illustrate the effective use of BDPs in an early product development process. In particular, they report on how BDPs:

- Captured the voice of the customer and influenced the development of customer requirements.
- Obtained customer inputs and helped designers develop concepts of products that do not exist.

These product designers, who at the time were studying to become product managers and entrepreneurs, experienced first-hand how users interpret and incorporate BDPs into their real activities.

Case A: Evaluating digital games for dementia with the bridging design prototype principles

Maigen Wilki Thygesen and Andreas Melson

Maigen Wilki Thygesen works as a packaging and graphic designer at Smurfit Kappa Global Experience Center and the head office in Amsterdam.

Andreas Melson is a partner at Applikator and interested on user interfaces for people with cognitive disabilities.

Maigen used the BDP principles to evaluate an existing product called Touch & Play. Back in 2014, Applikator, a newly founded Danish company, was developing this product. Touch & Play is placed at nursing homes in Denmark. It uses games to offer fun cognitive and slightly physical training for people with dementia. The interactive screen is made of a large screen in regular hard wood, a projector, and a touch technology. The product content is software implemented as a set of different apps with various games, videos, and images. Touch & Play includes ten games (in Danish): Quick finger, memory, duel games, find colours, calculate, puzzle, match image and sound, match images, songs and videos, and images.

At the request of the CEO, Maigen undertook a product design evaluation in the spring of 2014. The time investment in the project was 60 hours, as required by the experience design class she was undertaking. At the stage when Maigen entered, the company had been heavily focusing on technology and business development. Maigen's task was to investigate Touch & Play in relation to dementia, engage with the user community, and learn about their context and practice. Ultimately, she sought to evaluate how well the product was representing their voice as customers, in particular, the voices of the elderly people with dementia and their caretakers i.e. the direct beneficiaries of the product.

The BDP principles were used to organise and make sense of findings to inform feature requirements. For example, they helped evaluate if the product included familiar features to the user community, and if the novel features chosen by the developers made sense. Maigen found that the technology was not capitalising enough on the users' prior knowledge of living with dementia at a nursing home. Therefore, the elderly and caretakers were not incorporating Touch & Play often enough into their routines.

Through empirical research activities at the nursing home, Maigen learned how dementia was affecting residents' human abilities. She had informal conversations with caretakers, observed how they were using the product with different residents, and embodied being a caretaker playing with a person with dementia. Luckily, Maigen already had experiential knowledge on how cognitive difficulties affect a person, since her father experienced severe internal bleedings in his brain in 2012, and was living with massive brain damage at the time. Such a difficult situation provided her with two years of personal experience in helping with cognitive training at different levels. Since then, her father has gradually become far better. Additionally, it gave her a personal motivation to create great products for cognitive training.

Data fragments drawn from personal experience, the embodiment, conversations, and relevant literature reviews were carefully analysed using empathic inferences. A finding was that Touch & Play's games were originally developed for cognitive training, and not for people with dementia. But, they could become suitable for use by people with dementia with a small amount of customization. The requirements for these changes were established in cooperation with a centre for autism located in one of Denmark's regions. Another finding was that the BDP principle 'similar mental models' had not been met; the conceptual model of the games' user interface did not match the mental model that the users had for them. In other words, the users could not play the games on the screen in the way that the designers intended. The elderly people had difficulty in understanding well-known games such as solving a puzzle, tic-tac-toe, or four in a row. Maigen identified that there were:

- Gaps in relation, as the games did not have a traditional visual appearance that the elderly users could relate to. The visual design chosen for the games did not make the activity of playing simpler (BDP principle).

- Gaps in age, as the elderly users did not have prior knowledge with a touch-screen technology (BDP principle).
- Gaps in knowledge about dementia diseases on the part of the R&D team. These diseases have a direct effect on the brain's visual system, creating difficulty with depth of perception, spatial orientation, and judging colour contrast.

Understanding of these knowledge gaps should improve the future development of user interface requirements. Colours for games should be chosen with care, for example, black should be avoided as it is not seen as a colour, and images should be made with clear contrast.

Maigen reflected upon the value of the product and its relevance in the environment. An essential part here is how the company views usefulness in contrast to how the users view it. For the company, the value of the product appears to be cognitive training, since this is what the municipalities and government push for. But, for the people with dementia, the value of the product lies in facilitating the joy of the moment. These two contradicting sets of values slow down product adoption. Additionally, there is a challenge in the environment that the product is placed in, since elderly people with dementia are not used to playing games presented in digital form and in large touch-screen technologies. The difficulties in usability slowed down adoption, since they made it harder for the product to fit the world of a nursing home, and thus be truly desirable for the people with dementia. For the designers' vision to be fully realised a deep understanding of the user community is paramount.

Case B: Bridging design prototype of a plant sensor

Mathias Halkjær Petersen and Casper Harlev

Mathias Halkjær Petersen, MSc product development and innovation, is an innate number-cruncher obsessed with intangible conundrums in innovation, design, and management.

Casper Harlev, BSc product development and innovation, is co-founder and CEO at Sensohive, which sells IoT sensors for food and construction applications globally.

Mathias conceptualised a new product for Danish company Sensohive back in 2016. This company develops Internet of Things (IoT) and smart systems. With a time investment of 60 hours, as required by the experience design class he was taking, he developed a BDP for a plant system. The BDP development had to have great emphasis in systems thinking, largely because of the product's technical nature in terms of form and usage. The product was to be sold B2B with two distinct customers and users.

At the stage when Mathias became involved in the project, a lot of well thought out decisions, in terms of scope and focus had been taken around the infrastructure of the processes in which the product was to be inserted. In terms of applying the BDP approach, there was not much flexibility on product ideation, but it worked very well in actual fitting with the B2B customer's (end-)user and using the principle of 'the smoothest interaction is the one that does not happen'. Carrying out this project with the BDP approach enabled Mathias to practice activities to develop the human aspect of system thinking, which he was new to and found difficult at first.

The BDP principle 'multidisciplinary thinking team approach to research the user community and the market' involved data gathering through primary sources (guided tours of facility, and customer and expert interviews) and secondary sources (selected scientific papers and online videos for overall understanding of greenhouses, plants, and plant treatment). Mathias developed a framework for analysing selected data fragments. With the involvement of the company's electronic engineers, he used the findings to develop recommendations, guidelines, and requirements, which in turn were used to implement a provotype and a BDP of an in-plant sensor. These were socialised with the company's employees and a B2B customer for obtaining feedback.

Mathias found that the in-plant sensor made activities simpler (BDP principle). He noticed that it could enable a desired process change or improve interactions at the intersection of two systems, each of which had its own various processes. Furthermore, it created opportunities for having conversations with stakeholders that could lead to improvements in product specifications.

To discover the main areas of human interaction with the product, Mathias undertook a complete mapping of activities. The most important area of human interaction was between the production manager and the gardener, which occurred very distantly through various process steps. Additionally, the production manager used the data gathered by the in-plant sensor (placed in the soil by the gardener) to configure watering and heating systems that in turn help the plants grow.

Mathias created a theoretically-informed model 'multidisciplinary B2B offerings' to organise the multidisciplinary thinking perspectives and outcomes that an individual designer has gathered over a project period, and to avoid neglecting findings from different sources and points of view for lack of a way to structure them. This model considered value for the company's users, market, business, and technology. The BDP principle 'similar mental models' could be met.

The BDP principle 'broadening participation' was applied by ensuring that requirements were inclusive of every member of the user community. Extreme user embodiment was undertaken to improve usage for average users. Two examples illustrate:

- If an employee (a user/gardener) with attention deficit hyperactivity disorder (ADHD) undertook the activity, simple intuitive workflows would be required, therefore workflows were improved by cutting down on procedures through automation.
- Imagining he was a person with Parkinson's by handling the BDP with big gloves, resulted in a requirement to create a handle with a hole for better grip and more control over the sensor.

This principle also led to considering practical non-human related issues (e.g. interactions between systems or inanimate objects such as machines) that raised questions such as: What machines will the plants have to go through at the customer's greenhouses? Or what would happen if the in-plant sensor might not fit inside plants because they are too small? Mathias found that the 'broadening participation' principle was applicable and valuable even in a project that was technical in nature, already defined in scope, and full of constraints. He found that using a creative process like extreme user embodiment could add real benefits for the average user in the form of function and feature design.

When critically reflecting about the project, Mathias concluded that undertaking a BDP process 'has been an exciting, anxiety-filled, frustrating, but learning-full journey'. The resulting product was well received due to how the user interviews were used in the development of customer requirements, and 'the clear strategic choices regarding features concluded from these'. He also thinks that it was humbling having to put on these many hats to make sure all-important multidisciplinary thinking perspectives were covered. And as a consequence, it was empowering to develop his own mapping model for dissecting and sorting the information gained into various categories, based on this multidisciplinary thinking. He concluded that while the aesthetic part of the design skill-set is not his strongest part, he now has a toolbox with the most basic and swift tools to validate concepts from a design-thinking perspective. Such skill set enables him to refine and design product systems on a more macro-level.

Case C: Bridging design prototype of a user research framework for a robotics start-up

Enikő Rozsnyói and Thomas A. Rubaek

Enikő Rozsnyói, MSc product development and innovation, is currently a product manager for digital products and experienced in new product development projects.

Thomas A. Rubaek is vice-president of product development at Blue Ocean Robotics.
Enikő undertook her master's thesis in partnership with Blue Ocean Robotics in 2016. The project lasted one semester with a time investment of approximately 1000 hours. In agreement with her company supervisor, she investigated how the BDP approach could be used within the existing product development model (or methodology) of this robotics company. The fuzzy front-end phase of early product development is structured through a process model called 'RoBi-Design' that is similar to the stage-gate model. The activities performed during this conceptualization phase are opportunity screening, product definition, market analysis, creating business case, forming of product concepts, preparing for product development, and creating the business plan. After all stages are completed, the decision is made if a product goes forward for product development. The 'RoBi-Design' phase yields a qualified product concept, but not functional prototypes.

Phase one of the project involved an evaluation of the 'RoBi-Design' process to understand how the BDP principles could be used to decrease fuzziness at the front end of innovation. Enikő was assigned to a hospital project and carried out activities in the stages of 'product definition' and 'product concept'. She developed a human-centred design study (BDP principle) that involved observations, personal discussions, and review of secondary sources (e.g. literature review of other product development models), and participated in important internal meetings. The meetings facilitated understanding of the roles and activities that team members had to undertake as part of a 'RoBi-Design' process. Data fragments selected using empathic inferencing were organised, analysed, and used to develop feature requirements. For use and feedback, four rapid functional prototypes (including a BDP) were created and shared with team members and their supervisor, who was also VP of Product Development:

- Rapid prototype 1 was a template to help to structure recommendations, guidelines, and requirements, resulting from the human-centred design study.

- Rapid prototype 2 was a BDP canvas – a mental checklist of the six BDP principles to assure that a human-centred perspective was followed during data gathering, conceptualisation, and prototyping.
- Rapid prototype 3 was a visualisation tool for evaluating the hospital product's concept with the six BDP principles.
- The BDP of the user research framework.

Rapid prototype 1 was regarded as the one that could solve issues that the R&D team struggled with. The project manager said, 'I like it; this is where we struggle'. Prototypes 2 and 3 were found confusing and too theoretical to use in a rapid product development process; the learning curve for implementation would have been too long. The project manager said, 'I don't see how it will make our process faster and our products better'. Furthermore, these BDP principles were somewhat represented in activities of the 'RoBi-Design' process. This company practices user-centred design with rapid ethnographic methods, as well as participatory design by involving users as much as possible through meetings, workshops, sharing, and giving feedback on outcomes.

Enikő reflected that perhaps rapid prototype 1 was rapidly adopted because it addressed specific issues in product definition, and it was a novel idea presented within a familiar framework that they could all understand (BDP principle). For rapid prototypes 2 and 3 to be rapidly adopted, a similar process should have been followed to develop the theoretical concepts into a more practical format by incorporating the company's language for product development.

Rapid prototype 1 was chosen for further development. Phase two of the project involved the development of the user research framework for better organising user research findings so the R&D team could effectively use them in the development of guidelines and requirements, that later would inform feature design. The user research framework design is inspired by the BDP principle 'develop a human-centred design study that brings a multidisciplinary thinking approach to research the user community and the market'. In a spreadsheet format, the user research framework has six features to organise and keep track of data analysed, and offers a process for making conclusions. The features are README, job-to-be-done, data collection and analysis, the current scenario of workflow analysis, design guidelines, and business case parameters. The user research framework:

- Facilitates the identification of latent user and customer's needs.
- Increases efficiency in knowledge transfer during the product definition stage and between the product definition and product concept stages.
- Facilitates process descriptions for the activities in each stage of 'RoBi-Design', which improves communication within the company.

With the view of becoming part of the 'RoBi-Design' template collection, the user research framework was implemented in Google DriveTM[2] with tools familiar to the team (BDP principle). While Enikő was working on her thesis, the company's staff created the folder structure for the whole 'RoBi-Design' process. She took part in creation of the templates, and her BDP became part of one of the templates. Whenever a project is started locally or in one of the company's joint ventures around the world, the templates are copied to a new location and used to guide projects through the 'RoBi-Design' activities. All the process templates serve as a standardised format that is understood by the team members who have to work with them and is used to check a project's status.

Five employees provided feedback on the user research framework's usefulness – an intern, a student assistant, a robot developer, a project manager, and a human-robot interaction expert. Experienced employees liked the tool more than the intern and assistant. The process of working with the user research framework was useful but needed time and prior experience to understand it. Since students and interns would be the ones interacting with it the most, changes around visual design and more detailed explanation should be implemented so both novice and expert employees can use it with little stress and confusion (BDP principle 'broadening participation'). Overall, the user research framework improves inter-functional knowledge transfer by guiding its users (e.g. team, stakeholders, customers) from data fragments representing users' thoughts, etc. to design guidelines and requirements.

Discussion questions

1   What customer requirements did the BDP help discover or reconsider?
2   Using the BDP, what activities helped to capture the voice of the customer?
3   How did the BDP features help or hinder to identify customer satisfaction?
4   How did the BDP help designers to recognise change and identify a good design opportunity?
5   How did the BDP help to make correct interpretations of customers' wants?

Notes

1 In the spirit of Preben Mogensen's work, the term 'provotypes' is used when artifacts (e.g. off-the-shelf ware, prototypes, and mock-ups) are used to provoke experiential reactions in current practice, instead of focusing on how artifacts, or the use of them, could be improved.
2 ©2018 Google LLC All rights reserved. Google Drive is a trademark of Google LLC.

References of student cases

Halkjær Petersen, M. (2016). *Reflective essay on Sensohive*. Exam essay. Unpublished manuscript. Department of Technology and Innovation, University of Southern Denmark, Odense, Denmark.

Rozsnyói, E. (2016). *Creating a user research framework within the existing product design model of Blue Ocean Robotics*. Product Development and Innovation. Master in Science. Department of Technology and Innovation, University of Southern Denmark, Odense, Denmark.

Wilki Thygesen, M. (2014). *Experience based designing 2: How I found a purpose with my education through the XbD courses*. Exam essay. Unpublished manuscript. Department of Technology and Innovation, University of Southern Denmark, Odense, Denmark.

Index

Note: Page numbers in *italics* indicate case studies. Page numbers in **bold** indicate key term definitions.

3.4 defects per million opportunities 237
3D printing 341, *424*

Academy Awards® 303–4
Academy of Motion Picture Arts and Sciences 302
activation **296**
adaptability **321**; objective 323; performance metrics 335
adding value to customers 125, 231
adding value to forecasting 58, 192
additive manufacturing *see* 3D printing
adequate process 136
Adidas 340
advanced planning and scheduling **283**
advantage: autonomous vehicles 343; collaboration 315; competitive (*see* competitive advantage); decentralised returns 360; distinctive 32; first-mover 30; flexibility 31; last-mile delivery 347; multi sourcing 332; product levelling 167; sales and operations planning 86; single sourcing 332; strategic 25; transportation modes 363
agility **321**; managing with 231; methods to achieve 323; objective 322; performance metrics 335
AGV *see* autonomous guided vehicle
Airbnb 22, 340
Airbus 2
Airline of the Year 2
AirlineRatings.com 2
Air New Zealand 2, 20
Akst, David 118
alignment **321**; automation process 350; decisions 35; demand and supply model *384*; implementing 325; performance metrics 335; process 245; strategic *395*; triple-A 324

ally customer type 120
Amazon 30, 351
American Airlines 110
analytical rigour in six sigma quality 245
anarchist customer type 121
andon problem display board 152
Angwin, Duncan 21
Apple HQ Cupertino, CA 79
Apple Inc. 40
appraisal costs **228**; examples 229
Armstrong, J. Scott 50
artificial intelligence 117
assembly line process *see* repetitive process
assignable cause 174, **232**
assignable variation **232**
assurance dimension of service 224
automation **348**; external considerations 351–3; flexibility a differentiating factor 348; with a human touch 152, internal considerations and strategy 350; introduction 348; levels of automation 343; stakeholders and risk 349; substitution for labour 117; autonomous guided vehicle 341
autonomous vehicle **342**; assisted order picking 345; categories 343; ethical dilemma example 344; key benefits 343; last-mile delivery 347; line haul and convoy systems 346; loading and transport 345; outdoor logistics operations 345; parcel station loading 347; public acceptance 344; self-driving repositories 347; warehousing operations 344
Autor, David 117
available process 136
available-to-promise date 43
average of ranges formula 181
average of sample means formula 180

Babbage, Charles 5
backward integration **335**
BAFTA Awards 303, 304
Baines, Tim 16
balanced scorecard **199**; balanced view
    199; challenge to theory 203; customer
    perspective 200; financial perspective
    202; *versus hoshin kanri* 198; innovation
    and learning perspective 202; internal
    perspective 201; linking strategy
    with operations 203; part of a larger
    solution 204
Baldridge Award 226
baristas 179
basic seven tools of quality **168**
batch process **131–2**
BDP *see* bridging design prototype
behaviour, revenue management buyer 113
behaviour-based constraint **290**
benchmarking **207**; average, best, and world-
    class values 207
best operating level **100**
best practice **207**
bias **52**; causes 53; formula 54; performance
    measurement 192; reports past
    performance 58; worked example 55
bill of material **276–7**
bill of resources **276**
BMW: business strategy 27; competing on
    quality 30
Boeing 2
BOM *see* bill of material
booking limit **107**, 111
bottleneck **290**
bread-baking example 232–4
bridging design prototype *433–40*
British Academy of Film and Television
    Arts 302
British Airways 109
Brundtland report 362
Brynjolfsson, Erik 117
buffer: constraint and time 294; dynamic
    adjustment 281; dynamic calculations *380*;
    inventory decouples different rates 259;
    profiles, zones, and levels 280; queues and
    waiting lines 113
bullwhip effect **309–13**; demand and supply
    flow 310; demand chain management 327;
    demand variability 261; how to counteract
    312; major causes 310
Burr, Donald 110

Cameron, James 303
campaign **289**
capability: competitive 28, 127, 200; process
    (*see* process capability); six sigma (*see* six
    sigma capability)

capable process 136
capacity **81**; buying **101**; contrasting choices
    83; creating adjustable 109; demonstrated
    101; design 100; difficult to alter, revenue
    management 104; effective 101; flexibility
    101–2; links to long-range forecasts 46;
    links to medium-range forecasts 47; links
    to short-range forecasts 48; long-range 81;
    maximum demonstrated 101; medium-
    range 81; revenue management 109,
    111–12; safety 296; service 113; short-range
    81; strategic 81; structural decisions 32
capacity constrained resource **290**
capacity management **81**; hierarchy 82;
    performance measurement 193
capacity planning **81–2**; available options
    89; balancing act 87; learning curve 102;
    process 85; strategic decisions 83; timing is
    critical 87
carbon footprint 352
carrying cost **268**
Caterpillar 17
causal data 59
cause, assignable and common 232
cause-and-effect diagram **168**
CDV *see* coefficient of demand variation
cellular production **128**, 130
champion customer type 121
chart: $\bar{x}$ or mean control 177; control 174;
    flow 170; hierarchical organisation 119;
    histogram 171; Pareto 172; R or range
    control 177; scatter 173
chase production method 89, 91; worked
    example 96
Chase, Richard 17
check sheet **169**
Chelsea Sugar 148
Cho, Fujio 155
circular economy *422*
Clark, Graham 120
closed loop management system 204
coefficient of demand variation **75**
collaboration, customer 74
collaborative planning, forecasting, and
    replenishment **313**
collaborative supply chain **313**; characteristics
    314; competitive advantage 318; effective
    and responsive data exchange 327;
    hurdles to overcome 316; implementation
    315; key advantages 315; performance
    measurement 197; performance metrics
    335; supplier selection 331; triple-A supply
    chain 322
co-loading 364
common cause **232**
common cause variation **232**
communication decisions 35

competence: core 23; differentiating 24
competition, revenue management 112
competitive advantage 23; automation
    353; based on competencies 28; based
    on flexibility 31; how to maximise 318;
    links to corporate strategy 28; low-cost
    producer 29; mass customisation 134;
    performance wants and excitement
    characteristics 220; product design 195;
    sales and operations planning 86; supply
    chain collaboration 318; time-based
    competition 31
competitive capability 28, 127, 200
components of demand 61
conscious factory, Nokia 190
constraint 290; behaviour-based and
    throughput-based 290; buffer 294
continual improvement 232
continuous improvement 163–4, 186; three
    building blocks 155
continuous process 131–2
continuous replenishment 333
control chart 174–5, 177–85; establishing
    179; explanation 177; interpreting with
    examples 184–5
control limit 177–83; establishing 179;
    factors for determining 180
core competence 23
corporate strategy 24
correlation, house of quality 222
cost: appraisal 228–9; carrying 268;
    competing on 29; external failure 228–9;
    high marginal capacity 106; internal
    failure 228–9; low marginal sales 106;
    ordering 267; prevention 228, 230; of
    quality 228; set-up 268; total quality 230
cost adding 124
cost advantage 29; McDonald's Corporation
    32; offshore production 394
cost leadership 137
Cox, Jeff 290, 292
C_p see process capability ratio
C_{pk} see process capability index
creating adjustable capacity 109
creativity and innovation 231
critical operational areas 263
critical ratio 282
critical to quality 246
cross-docking 333
cross-training employees 109
CTQ see critical to quality
current reality tree 293
customer 8; centricity 118; classify by type
    119–20; collaboration 74; experience
    paradigm 17; focus 231; identify and specify
    value 154; increasing participation 109;
    intimacy 20; loyalty in service-profit chain
    140–1; the next process 8; requirements
    for a cell phone 222; requirements in
    perspective 213; requirements in six sigma
    quality 245; requirements Kano model
    217; revenue management 112; satisfaction
    hard to measure 8; satisfaction in service-
    profit chain 141; tolerance time 263; value
    three core processes 125; where the work
    goes next 8
customer perspective, balanced scorecard 200
cyclical component 61

Danone S. A. 254
data exchange, demand change management
    327
Davis, Craig 248
DDMRP see demand driven material
    requirements planning
decision making evidence-based 232
decisions: infrastructural 34; integration 35;
    revenue management 112; structural 32
decomposition 67
decouple 296
defect 236
defects per million opportunities 236
define-measure-analyse-improve-control 245
definitions 224
DeKnight, Steven S. 303
delivery in full, on time, and in specification
    7, 201, 316
delivery, basis for competition 30
Dell EMC 22
Dell Inc. 31, 315, 318
Delphi method 73, 216
demand 42; amplification (see bullwhip
    effect); chain management 326;
    components of 63; dependent 75;
    deseasonalised 67; expected and
    unexpected patterns 51; forecast with
    accuracy revenue management 105;
    forecasting 42; highly variable, revenue
    management 105; independent 75;
    management 42–3; revenue management
    109; segment by market, revenue
    management 104; smoothing 74;
    variability 261; variable rate of 263
demand driven material requirements
    planning 279, 378; what makes it
    different? 282
demand forecasting, revenue management 111
demand forecast updating, bullwhip effect 311
demand management 43; available-to-
    promise date 43; effective 44; performance
    measurement 192; process 89, 91–2
demanded quality hierarchy, house of
    quality 221
Deming, W. Edwards 209

demonstrated capacity **101**
dependent demand **75**
deseasonalised demand: formula 67; worked
    example 67
design: capacity **100**; drivers 247; for
    operations 250; planning table, house of
    quality 222; process, interrelated steps
    250; quality **246**; review **246**; for six sigma
    246; specifications 236
de-speeding 364
Deutsche Post DHL 347
developing reservation systems 109
deviation: bias 53; forecast 52; mean
    absolute 53–4; mean absolute percentage
    53, 55; random 53
DFSS *see* design, for six sigma
DHL 344
differentiation 137
DIFOTIS *see* delivery in full, on time, and in
    specification
digital ubiquity 6–7, 116–17
diseconomy of scale **100**
distinctive advantage 32
distribution **283**
diversity 209
DMAIC *see* define-measure-analyse-improve-
    control
DPMO *see* defects per million opportunities
drone 341
drum-buffer-rope **294**
Dublin Bus *406*
dynamic buffer adjustment 281

Eastman Kodak, missed opportunity 214
easy to do business with 123, 194
echelon **305–6**
Eckhoff, Robert 203
e-commerce 340, 348
economic order quantity (EOQ) **268**; basic
    assumptions 269; inventory waste 158
economies of volume, capacity and
    technology 101
economy of scale **100**
economy of scope **100**
ECR *see* efficient consumer response
EDLC *see* everyday low costs and prices
EDLP *see* everyday low costs and prices
effective capacity **101**
efficient consumer response **328–30**
efficient supply chain **308**
EFQM *see* Excellence Model 2013
electric vehicles: Ford, General Motors,
    Volkswagen, Toyota 214; International
    Monetary Fund prediction 79; market
    penetration 213
electricity generation 79

Elkington, John 362
empathy dimension of service 224
employee retention and satisfaction, service-
    profit chain 142
employing part-time staff 109
enterprise resource planning **283**, *403*, *417*
EOQ *see* economic order quantity
ERP *see* enterprise resource planning
ETDBW *see* easy to do business with
European Quality Awards 230
Evans, James R. 205
Evans, Oliver 133
evaporating cloud **293**
everyday low costs and prices 313
Excellence Model 2013 230
Exec S&OP *see* executive sales and
    operations planning
execution, highly visible and collaborative 282
executive sales and operations planning 84,
    86, **284**
experience curve *see* learning curve
experience paradigm 17–18
external failure costs **228–9**

facility decisions 33
facility design, performance metric
    changing 206
finance and accounting function 26
financial perspective, balanced scorecard 202
finished goods **258**
fishbone diagram *see* cause-and-effect
    diagram
Fitzsimmons, James and Mona 136, 138
five dimensions for service 224
five focusing steps **292**
five forces model 19
fixed order quantity **266**
fixed reorder cycle model **270**
fixed reorder quantity model **267**
flaw of averages 135
flexibility **283**; automation 348; autonomous
    guided vehicles 341; basis for competition
    31; capacity 101–2; hospital theatre usage
    414; job shop, batch, repetitive 132;
    process focused 130; supplier convenience
    201; supply *384*; supply chain 74, 261, *384*
flexible manufacturing system **348**
flexible process 136
flowchart **170**
focus 137
focus groups 216
Fonterra Co-operative Group 254–5
Ford, Henry 116, 153; any colour provided
    it is black 215
Ford Motor Company: plans for electric
    vehicles 214; Toyota study trips 153

forecast 44; accuracy 70; deviation 52–3; management 44; optimistic or pessimistic 51
forecasting 44; aggregate demand 50; alternative approaches 74; causal data 59; characteristics of 48; collaborative planning and replenishment 313; constrained or unconstrained 40; demand 42; demand driven techniques 49; effect of price changes 44; functional manipulation 59; long-range 46; medium-range 47; model to determine spending 45; operations and supply chain view 50; process 59; qualitative 73; quantitative 60, 63; range of values 51; short-range 48; strategic nature of 46, 49; sudden and gradual demand changes 51; three horizons 46; value of data 45
forecast value added 58–9; performance measurement 192; process 59– 60
formula: average of ranges 181; average of sample means 180; bias 54; deseasonalised demand 67; mean absolute deviation 54; mean absolute percentage deviation 56; mean absolute percentage variation 56; newsvendor problem 273; process capability index 238; process capability ratio 237; regression analysis 64; seasonal index 67; upper and lower control limits 181
forward flow scheduling 289
forward integration 334
four-sigma process capability, worked example 240
Fourth Industrial Revolution 424
Froneri International 255
Fukushima accident 79
functional responsibilities of the organisation 7
future reality tree 293
FVA see forecast value added

gaming at times of shortage 313
Garvin, David A. 224
genchi genbutsu 155
General Electric 117
General Motors: plans for electric vehicles 214; Toyota study trips 153
Gilliland, Michael 59
globalisation 340
Goldratt, Eliyahu 290, 292
Google 22
Green, Robert 226
greenhouse gas emissions 79, 422
gross requirement 276
group reservations, revenue management 111

Hamad International Airport in Doha 109
Hamel, Gary 24

Hammer, Michael 123, 194
Harris, Ford W. 268
Hartley's constant 180
Hawthorne plant 5
Hayes, Robert H. 26, 133
heijunka 166
Heskett, James 139, 144
HHLA Container Terminal 345
hierarchical organisation 119
histogram 171
historical analogy 74
history of operations management 4
hoshin kanri process 197–8
hostage customer type 120
house of quality 221
Hout, Thomas 30
HP 318
human relations movement 5
human resources, decisions 34

Iansiti, Marco 117
IATA see International Air Transport Association
IBM Corporation 16
IKEA 315, 399
illumination experiment 5
improvement: continuous 163–4, 186; process 163–4
incompetent customer type 121
independent demand 75
Inditex strategy 27
Industrial Revolution 4
Industry 4.0 342
information and communication technology 201
information technology, revenue management 112
infrastructural decisions 34
innovation and learning perspective 202
integration: backward 335; balanced scorecard 199; channel 354; decisions 35, 323; forward 334; information 248; lean thinking 150; product design and process planning 250; technology 342; vertical 33, 334
internal failure costs 228–9
internal perspective, balanced scorecard 201
internal quality, service-profit chain 143
International Air Transport Association 1
International Humanitarian City 22
International Monetary Fund 79, 213
International Organization for Standardization 221, 231
Internet: airline data analytics 2; customer order example 135; customer perceived control 139; Dell point of sale example 318; house of quality example 222;

Nokia product capability 189; provides opportunities 123; recent developments 5; revenue management reservations 111; software download 15; supply chain management 206

intolerant customer type 121

inventory **258**, **292**; accuracy 278; anticipation 260; approaches and considerations 262; carrying 262; characteristics and types 259–60; control decisions 34; distribution 263; finished goods 258; fluctuation 260; lead-time-based pricing 262; leverage 263; lot-size 260; performance measurement 196, 262; perishable nature, revenue management 105; pipeline or transportation 260; purpose 259–60; raw material 258; reasons for holding 261; service organisations 258; strategic positioning 263, 280; supply chain flexibility 261; target level 270; turnover or turns 262; vendor-managed 333; work in process 258

inventory management **258**, 264, *398*, *403*, *405*

inventory management systems: economic order quantity model 267; fixed reorder cycle model 270; fixed reorder quantity model 267

Ishikawa diagram *see* cause-and-effect diagram

Ishikawa, Kaoru 168

ISO *see* International Organization for Standardization

ISO 16355 221

ISO 9000 231

ISO Technical Committee 231

Jackson, Peter 303

jidoka **151**, 152

JIT *see* just-in-time

job shop process **131**–2

Johnson, Gerry 21

Johnston, Robert 120

joint replenishment **333**

Jones, Daniel 154, 156

Jones, Thomas 139, 144

just-in-time (JIT) **152**, 278–9

kaizen 155, **163**–4; three principles 164

kanban **166**; supermarket 152

Kano, Noriaki 217

Kano model 217–20; diagram 218; questionnaire 219

Kaplan, Robert S. 199, 203

knowledge syntactic, semantic and pragmatic 205

Lactalis International 254

Lakhani, Karim R. 117

Lapide, Larry 59

lead time **264**, 278; market potential 263; safety 264; supplier 264

leadership 231

lean consumption 9, 151

lean enterprise 167

lean production **165**, 167; history of operations 5

lean six sigma **246**

lean thinking **150**; batch size of one 153; case example *371*, *407*; examples of lean 153, 159; five principles 154, 156; fundamental ideas 151; history of lean 151; implementation 175; introduction 150; material requirements planning 278; performance measurement 195, 207; prerequisites 176; service environments 176; understanding and implementing 153

learning curve **102**

Lee, Hau L. 309, 322

Leibold, Marios 203

level determination 280

level production method 89–90; worked example 94

Lewis, Mike 26

Lightfoot, Howard 16

Liker, Jeffrey K. 155–6, 175

linkage decisions 35

logical thinking process 292

logistics **305**; basic objective 308; compared to materials management 308; reverse 355

London Bus *406*

London Heathrow 109

London Mayor's Transport Strategy 27

Loveman, Gary 139, 144

loyal customer 122, 140–1, 144, *399*

MAD *see* mean absolute deviation

manage fixed supply capacity 109

management: accounting view 25; capacity (*see* capacity management); channels and customer touchpoints 354; closed loop system 204; demand (*see* demand management); demand chain 326; effective 6; effective demand 44; inventory (*see* inventory management); materials 305; omnichannel 354; process for automation 350; production view 25; relationship 232; returns (*see* returns management); revenue (*see* revenue management); sales view 25; scientific 5; service chain (*see* service chain management); structure for automation 350; supply chain (*see* supply chain management); sustainable supply

chain 361; Taylor's four principles 5; total
  quality (*see* total quality management);
  yield (*see* revenue management)
MAN Truck and Bus UK 17
manufacturing cell *see* cellular production
manufacturing resource planning **282**
MAPD *see* mean absolute percentage
  deviation
MAPV *see* mean absolute percentage
  variation
marketing function 25; influencing demand 44
market potential lead time 263
market research 216
master production schedule **276**, 278–9
material-dominated scheduling **289**
material requirements planning **276**, *378*;
  basic systems needs 278; depends on
  demand forecasts 279; lean thinking 278;
  precursor to manufacturing resource
  planning 283
materials management **305**; basic objective
  308; compared to logistics 308
maximum demonstrated capacity **101**
Mayo, Elton 5
McAfee, Andrew 117
McDonald's Corporation: cost advantage 32;
  strategy 27
McKay Sugar Limited 150
mean absolute deviation **53**–4; formula 54;
  performance measurement 192; reports
  past performance 58; worked example 54
mean absolute percentage deviation **53**, 55,
  73; formula 56; how to use it 58; reports
  past performance 58; worked example 56
mean absolute percentage variation **53**, 56,
  73; formula 56; main purpose 58; worked
  example 56
Microsoft Excel® 65, 70, 273, 275
Mintzberg, Henry 19, 21
Mitsubishi Electric Factory Automation 352
mixed-flow scheduling **289**
mixed-model production **166**
MPS *see* master production schedule
MRP *see* material requirements planning
MRP II *see* manufacturing resource planning
multi-sourcing **331**–2

Narayanan, V. G. 324
natural disaster examples 322, *374*
Nest 117
Nestlé S. A. 254
net requirement **276**
new product and service development 26,
  34, 248
New Zealand All Blacks *406*
Newcomen, Thomas 4

newsvendor problem **271**; formula 273;
  notation 272; worked example 273, 275
Nokia Corporation 189; 5G communications
  technology 190; missed opportunity 214
non-value adding **157**
Normal distribution, basic statistics 233
Norton, David P. 199, 203

objectives: business 87–8; closed-loop
  management 204; financial 192; *hoshin
  kanri* process 197; lean enterprise
  167; new product development 248;
  omnichannel retailing 354; operations
  management 8; performance 85, 119;
  production 103; revenue management
  conflicts 112; six sigma quality 245;
  strategic 18; supply chain participants 197
offering off-peak incentives 109
Ohno, Taiichi 152–3, 158
omnichannel retailing 341, **354**; compared
  to multichannel 354; customers
  choose preferred channel 354; returns
  management challenges 354
operating expense **292**
operational excellence 20
operations filters 86
operations management **6**; career
  opportunities 6; customer viewpoint 8;
  forecasting essential 42; forecasting view
  50; functional role 26; general objective 7;
  history of 4; performance measurement
  192; shifting scope 205; strategic role 4
operations research 5
operations strategy **26**; competitive capability
  28; customer-driven 28; performance
  metric changing 205; strategic service
  vision 137
order batching 312
order batching, bullwhip effect 311
ordering cost **267**
order planned, receipt and release 277
order point **266**
organisational capability 231
organisation systems, structural decisions 35
Orlicky, Joseph 277
outpartnering **333**; benefits and
  disadvantages 334
outside tolerance limits, worked example
  241–2
outsourcing **333**

pacemaker process 167
packaging functions 364
Packstations 347
Padmanabhan, V. 309
Parasuraman, A. 224

Pareto, Vilfredo 172
Pareto analysis **172**
Pareto chart **172**
participative design **249**
partitioning demand 109
patient customer type 121
Pavagada solar park 79
PDCA *see* plan-do-check-adjust
people 156; engagement 232; succeeding
  through talent 231
People Express 110
perfect espresso 179
perfection lean principle 155
perfect process 136, 194
performance measure **191**
performance measurement: balanced
  scorecard 199; capacity 193; determines
  behaviour 208; forecast accuracy 70;
  forecasting 192; *hoshin kanri* 198;
  infrastructural decisions 34; inventory
  262; mangerial process 126; Nokia
  perspective 189; operations management
  192; process design and improvement 194;
  product design and quality 195; sales and
  operations planning 286–7; supply chain
  197; theory of constraints 290–1
performance metrics 205
perspective balanced scorecard: customer
  200; financial 202; innovation and
  learning 202; internal 201
plan-do-check-adjust 163–4; illustration 164
planned order **277**; receipt **277**; release 277–8
planning: advanced and scheduling 283;
  aggregate level 88; capacity (*see* capacity
  planning); chase production method 89;
  collaborative 313; demand driven 281;
  demand driven material requirements
  (*see* demand driven material requirements
  planning); demand management process
  89; enterprise resource (*see* enterprise
  resource planning); executive sales and
  operations (*see* executive sales and
  operations planning); level production
  method 89; manufacturing resource
  (*see* manufacturing resource planning);
  material requirements (*see* material
  requirements planning); production
  (*see* production planning); resource
  (*see* resource planning); rhythmic cycles
  328; sales and operations (*see* sales and
  operations planning); strategic 19, 197;
  strategic capacity 83–4
Plossl, George 277, 283
Porter, Michael 19, 137
postponement 318, **322**, 328
pragmatic knowledge 205

Prahalad, C. K. 24
Premier Packers 148
prerequisite tree **293**
prevention costs **228**, 230
price fluctuation, bullwhip effect 311
primary process **124**, 126
proactive collaboration 75
process **122**; adequate 136; approach 232;
  available 136; batch 131–2; capable
  136; cause and variation 232; cellular
  production 128, 130; classifications
  and types 127; continuous 131–2; cost
  adding 124; extraction 179; flexible 136;
  flexible manufacturing system 348; flow
  scheduling **289**; focused **128–9**; *hoshin
  kanri* 197–8; improvement **163–4**, 194;
  industry **288**; inherent variability 236;
  internal 126; job shop 131–2; managerial
  126; operational returns management
  357; organisational 126; pacemaker 167;
  parcel station loading 347; participative
  design 249; perfect 136, 194; plan-do-
  check-adjust 163; primary 124, 126;
  product design 217; product focused 130;
  project 131; quality improvement 227;
  repetitive 131–2; returns management 355;
  returns network 359; reverse logistics 355;
  secondary 124, 126; service design 217;
  specifications 236; statistical control 177;
  strategic returns management 356, 357;
  supporting 126; technology decisions 33;
  thinking **122**; train **289**; transformation
  (*see* transformation process); valuable
  136; value adding 124; value-adding 126;
  variability 134–6; variation 233
process capability **232**, 235; 4-sigma 240;
  6-sigma 243; actual 235, 238; bread-
  baking example 232, 234; measuring 236;
  performance measurement 196; process
  drift 237; starting point for measuring
  234; theoretical 235–8
process capability index **235**; C_{pk} 238;
  formula 238; schematic 238; smaller of
  two values 238; worked example 242
process capability ratio **235**; C_p 237; formula
  237; schematic 237; worked example 239
process design: adds value or cost 145;
  concentrates on customer 120; creates
  value 125; customer-centred 126; drivers
  125; internal perspective 201; performance
  measurement 194; performance metric
  changing 206; waste of overprocessing 161
processor-dominated scheduling **289**
Proctor & Gamble 328
product **13**, 167; advance purchase, revenue
  management 105; centricity 119; design

in perspective 213; design performance
measurement 195, 206; development
portfolio 248; focused 128, 130; focused
examples 130; leadership 20; levelling or
heijunka 167; structured development 247
production: cellular 128; customised 340–1;
environment 8, 133, 176, *407*; lean 165;
mixed-model 166
production plan 84; worked example 96
production planning 84, 87, *398*; approaches
89; chase method 89; decisions 34;
demand management process 89; level
method 89; model 92; process 87, 92;
worked example 94
production rate 88
product-process matrix 133
products and services 13; comparison 14;
distinction between 15; similarities 15
profitability and growth, service profit
chain 140
project 131
project process 131
promoting off-peak demand 109
protection level 107, 111
pull system 154, 167, 325–6
purchasing function 330; aims and
responsibilities 330
push system 277, 325–6

Qatar Airlines 109
QFD *see* quality function deployment
qualitative forecasting 73; methods 73
quality 223; basis for competition 30; costs
of 228; customer defined 8; decisions 34;
definitions 223; design 246; dimensions
of 224; health services industry 226;
performance measurement 196; price is
not a factor revenue management 106;
Ritz-Carlton view 226; service definition
225; six sigma 244; statistical control 177;
total costs 230; total quality management
228; traditional costs 228; travel industry
experience 225
quality characteristics hierarchy, house of
quality 222
quality control limits, worked example 181
quality function deployment 195, 220
quality loss function 249
quality management: frameworks 230; ISO
16355 221; ISO 9000 231; performance
metric changing 206
quality planning table, house of quality 222
quantitative forecasting 60; methods 63
quantity: defects per million opportunities
236; economic order (*see* economic order
quantity); fixed order 266; fixed order

model 267; kanban 166; supply 87; supply
and demand 13; volume flexibility 31
quantity per 277
queues 113
quick response 313

Raman, Ananth 324
random component 61
random variation 52
rate-based scheduling 288
rationing and shortage gaming, bullwhip
effect 312
Raturi, Amitabh S. 205
raw material 258
R chart 177
red bead experiment 209–10
Regnér, Patrick 21
regression analysis 63; formula 64; worked
example 64
relationship management 232
relationships matrix, house of quality 222
reliability dimension of service 224
repetitive process 130–2
replenishment 313; continuous 333; joint 333
requirements: customer 9; customer in
perspective 213; customer Kano model
217; electricity 46; electricity supply 80;
forecasting data 48; gross 276; gross to net
material planning 278; Kano model 219;
net 276; resource 47
resource planning 284; enterprise
(*see* enterprise resource planning);
manufacturing (*see* manufacturing
resource planning)
resources: inadequate 22; threshold 23;
unique 23
respect for people, two building blocks 156
responsibility and authority 209
responsiveness dimension of service 225
responsive supply chain 308
retailing: omnichannel 354; unified shopping
experience 354
returns management 355; omnichannel
businesses 360; operational returns
management 358; strategic returns process
356–7
returns network: centralised cost-efficient
model 359; decentralised responsive model
360; design 358–9; time value of product
returns 359
revenue management 103; balancing demand
with supply 106–7, 110; benefits and
ability to compete 110–11; booking limit
107; complications and extensions 111–13;
factors when most effective 104–6; options
to influence demand 109; options to

influence supply 109–10; overview and objective 103; People Express example 110; protection level 107
reverse flow scheduling 289
reverse logistics 355
Rio Tinto 347
Ritz-Carlton Hotel Company: competing on service 31; definition of basic quality 226; employee empowerment 36; operations strategy 27; philosophy and values 226–7
robotics 348; technical basics 349
Rolls-Royce 17
Roth, Aleda 17

S&OP see sales and operations planning
SAE see Society of Automotive Engineers
safety capacity 296
safety lead time 264
sales and operations planning 84, 284, 383; execution process 284–7; strategic planning 86
Sanders, Rupert 303
São Paulo Military Police 406
Sasser, Earl Jr. 139, 144
Savage, Sam 135
scatter chart 173
scheduled receipt 277
schedule management, performance metric changing 207
scheduling 288; drum-buffer-rope 294; master production 276; process flow 289; rate-based 288
Schlesinger, Leonard 139, 144
Scholes, Kevan 21
Schulze, Horst 226
scientific management 5
scope of activities 21
seasonal component 61
seasonal index 67; formula 67
secondary process 124, 126
self-interest 208
semantic knowledge 205
Serkis, Andy 303
service 13; base, intermediate, and advanced 16; basis for competition 31; capacity 113; characteristics 13–14, 320; customer experience 17–18; encounter 138; environment 9; level 264; operations 137; package 15–16; value, service-profit chain 142
service chain management 319–21
service-profit chain 139; draws on three theories 144; in perspective 144; linkages 140–3; underlying philosophy 140
servitisation 16, 20
set-up cost 268

set-up examples 102
set-up time 268
seven tools of quality see basic seven tools of quality
seven wastes 157
sharing capacity with another supplier 109
sharing economy 340
Shulver, Michael 120
single sourcing 331–2
six sigma capability 236, 245
six sigma quality 232, 244
Slack, Nigel 26
Society of Automotive Engineers 343
solar power generation 79
sole sourcing 331
Southwest Airlines strategy 27
SPC see statistical process control
Speedfactory 340
SQC see statistical quality control
Stalk, George Jr. 30
standard deviation worked example 243
statistical process control 177–85; worked example 181
statistical quality control 177
strategic: capability 22–3, 205; capacity planning 81, 83–4; inventory positioning 280; mission 25; plan 19; planning 19; service vision 136
strategy 18; a pattern of actions 20; analogy, running a race 21; closed-loop management system 204–5; company examples 27; corporate 24; customer intimacy 20; decisions without knowing outcomes 21; demand management 43; linking with operations 203; long-term direction 21; Mintzberg's five p's 19; operational excellence 20; operations 26, 205; origins in military 19; performance measurement 192; product leadership 20
structural decisions 32
supplier 305; assessment 365; lead time 264; relations 33; selection 331
supply 87; variable rate of 263
supply chain 305; achieving cost advantage 29; capabilities of the future 341; collaborative (see collaborative supply chain); efficient 308; influence of social trends 340; net effect of variation 313; partnership 314; performance metrics 335; push and pull system 326; responsive 308; restricted view of demand 309; source for competitive advantage 341; strategic role of inventory 325; sustainable 361; triple-A 322
supply chain 4.0 342

supply chain collaboration: competitive advantage 318; establishing order quantity 329; hurdles to overcome 316
supply chain engineering 74
supply chain management 305; career opportunities 6; creative arts 302–4; customer viewpoint 8; echelons 308; forecasting essential 42; forecasting view 50; functional role 26; overview 305; performance measurement 196; performance metric changing 206; service providers 306; strategic role 4; strategic view 308; uses service providers 320
supply variability 261
Suri, Rajeev 190
sustainability 362–5
sustainable future creation 231
sustainable supply chain management 361, 363–5, 393–4
sustaining outstanding results 231
syntactic knowledge 205
system: closed-loop management 203; demand driven material requirement planning 281; flexible manufacturing 348; inventory management 266; lean production 5; lean thinking 151; material and resource planning 257; material requirements planning 278; measurement 193; push and pull 325–7; quality 220; revenue management reservation 109; theory of constraints 290–2; Toyota Production 136, 152, 156, 176

Taguchi methods 249
Taguchi quality loss function see quality loss function
Taguchi, Genichi 249
takt time 162, 167
tangibles dimension of service 225
target inventory level 270
TaskRabbit 340
Taylor, Frederick W. 5
teardown time 268
Ted 22
terrorist customer type 121
theory of constraints 290, 399; drum-buffer-rope 294; Eliyahu Goldratt and Jeff Cox 290; logical thinking process 292; operating guidelines 297; performance measurement 291; scheduling 296; utilisation 291
Thinking Production System 153
throughput 291
throughput-based constraint 290
tier see echelon
time, set-up and teardown 268

time-based competition 30
time buffer 294
timely execution in six sigma quality 245
time series decomposition 67
TOC see theory of constraints
tolerant customer type 121
total quality management 223, 225
Toyoda, Eiji 152
Toyoda, Kiichiro 152, 372
Toyoda, Sakichi 152
Toyoda Automatic Loom Works 152
Toyota Motor Corporation 175; birthplace of lean thinking 152, 165; business strategy 28; competing on quality 30; developed just-in-time 5; example of lean manufacturer 315; plans for electric vehicles 214; production control methods 153; respect for people 155; the Toyota Way 155; True North vision 175
Toyota Production System 371; developed by Taiichi Ohno 152; Jeffrey Liker 14 Principles 156; links to Ford and General Motors 153; original seven wastes 158; perfect process 136
Toyota Way: 14 principles 156; five core values 155; lean leadership style 175; self-reliance principle 372
TPS see Toyota Production System
TQM see total quality management
Trader Joe's 22
transformation process 6, 10, 128; extension to show variables 134; production industries 11; service industries 12
transition tree 293
transportation modes 363
Treacy, Michael 20
trend component 61
triple-A supply chain 322
triple bottom line 362
True North vision 175

Uber 10, 22, 117, 340
U-cell see cellular production
undesirable effects 293
unified shopping experience 354
Upton, David 26
utilisation 296; demonstrated capacity 101; impacts service quality 113; not a performance measure 194; theory of constraints 291, 296–7

valuable process 136
value 24, 124, 157; adding 157; and waste 157; creation cycle 319; customer-defined 125; is a perception 125; proposition 120
value adding 124

value-adding process 126
value stream 154, **162**
value stream mapping **162**
variability of demand and supply 261, 263
variation: assignable 232; coefficient of
    demand 75; common cause 232; controlled
    134; mean absolute percentage 53; mean
    adsolute absolute percentage 56; random
    52; uncontrolled 134
vehicle, autonomous 342
vendor-managed inventory 333, *406*
vertical integration 33, **334**
very large commercial transport *390*
victim customer type 121
Victoria's Country Fire Authority *405*
Villeneuve, Denis 303
Virgin Atlantic 22; competing on service 31
vision: for the future 22; guidance technology
    344; *hoshin kanri* 197; inspiration, and
    integrity 231; long-term 155; managerial
    process 126; operations strategy 28;
    overall strategic 153; strategic service
    136; strategy statement 192; Toyota
    management model 176; value stream
    mapping future state 162
VOC *see* voice of the customer
Voelpel, Sven 203
voice of the customer **216–17**
Volkswagen AG, plans for electric vehicles 214
Voss, Chris 17
VSM *see* value stream mapping

waiting lines 113
Waititi, Taika 303
Walmart Stores 318, 328
Warby Parker 22
warehouse of the future 339
waste **157**; defects, scrap, or rework 161;
    elimination 150, 154, 157, 161; original
    seven categories 158; overprocessing
    161; overproduction 158; reduction
    149; six sigma quality 244; time-based

competition 30; transporting 160;
    unnecessary inventory 160; unnecessary
    motion 160; waiting 159
Watt, James 4
Western Electric 5
Weta Group of Companies 302–3
Whang, Seungjin 309
Wheelwright, Steven C. 133
Whitney, Eli 5
Whittington, Richard 21
Wiersema, Fred 20
Wight, Oliver 277, 283
Wilmar International 150
wind power generation 79
WIP *see* work in process
Womack, James 136, 154, 156, 194
worked example: bias 55; chase production
    method 96; deseasonalised demand 67;
    four-month plan 98; four-sigma process
    capability 240; level production method 94;
    mean absolute deviation 54; mean absolute
    percentage deviation 56; mixed strategy
    96; newsvendor problem 273, 275; outside
    tolerance limits 241–2; process capability
    index 242; process capability ratio 239;
    production plan 96; production planning
    94; quality control limits 181; regression
    analysis 64; standard deviation 243
work in process **258**; case study example
    381, 399, 403, 418; inventory component
    292; scheduling evaluation 288; theory of
    constraints 295
World Commission on Environment and
    Development 362
World Economic Forum 190

$\bar{x}$ chart **177**

yield management *see* revenue management

Zara 22, 27, 328
Zeithaml, Valarie A. 224